Enaction

Toward a New Paradigm for Cognitive Science

Edited by John Stewart, Olivier Gapenne, and Ezequiel A. Di Paolo

A Bradford Book
The MIT Press
Cambridge, Massachusetts
London, England

First MIT Press paperback edition, 2014
© 2010 Massachusetts Institute of Technology

For information about special quantity discounts, please email special_sales@ mitpress.mit.edu

This book was set in Stone Sans and Stone Serif by Toppan Best-set Premedia Limited. Printed and bound in the United States of America.

Library of Congress Cataloging-in-Publication Data

Enaction : toward a new paradigm for cognitive science / edited by John Stewart, Olivier Gapenne, and Ezequiel A. Di Paolo.
    p. cm.
"A Bradford book."
"Based on an International CNRS Summer School organized by the Association pour la Recherche Cognitive (ARC), held from 29 May to 03 June 2006, Ile d'Oléron, France"—Text.
Includes bibliographical references and index.
ISBN 978-0-262-01460-1 (hc : alk. paper)—978-0-262-52601-2 (pb.) 1. Cognition—Philosophy. 2. Philosophy and cognitive science. 3. Cognitive science.
I. Stewart, John Robert, 1941– II. Gapenne, Olivier. III. Di Paolo, Ezequiel A.
IV. Association pour la recherche cognitive (France) V. Ecole d'été du CNRS sur les sciences cognitives (2006 : Ile d'Oléron, France)
BF311E495 2011
153—dc22

                                                                2010006930

10 9 8 7 6 5 4 3 2

Contents

Introduction

John Stewart, Olivier Gapenne, and Ezequiel A. Di Paolo

The aim of this book is to present the paradigm of enaction as a framework for a far-reaching renewal of cognitive science as a whole.[1] There have been many critiques of classical, first-generation cognitivism based on the Computational Theory of Mind. A distinctive feature of this book is a deliberate choice not to go over that old ground yet again, but to reserve the energy for positive exploration of new paths.

Enaction, initially articulated as a program for understanding cognition by Varela, Thompson, and Rosch (1991), has seen an explosion of activity in recent years, including a follow-up book investigating the deeper connections between life and mind (Thompson 2007), related special journal issues (Barandiaran and Ruiz-Mirazo 2008; Di Paolo 2009; Rohde and Ikegami 2009; Torrance 2005, 2007), many articles reporting on theoretical and empirical advances and several regular meetings, summer schools, and funded projects. This program makes a radical break with the formalisms of information-processing and symbolic representations prevalent in cognitive science. In their stead, as explained in the first text, by John Stewart, cognition is grounded in the sensorimotor dynamics of the interactions between a living organism and its environment. In the classical scheme, perception is relegated to a preliminary "module" based on sensory input alone, to be followed in a linear sequence by "cognitive" planning and representations of goals, and culminating in a decision to act. In this scheme, "cognition" is thus sandwiched between two layers—sensory input and motor output—which are not themselves considered as properly cognitive. The perspective of enaction overturns this scheme quite radically. A living organism *enacts* the world it lives in; its effective, embodied action in the world actually constitutes its perception and thereby grounds its cognition. The text by Renaud Barbaras takes as its springboard the observation that "to live" *is* to have intentional conscious experience of living, and engages a profound phenomenological analysis of the implications, including the relation between life and metabolism.

In fact, there is a growing realization and acceptance in cognitive science that perception is not just a subsidiary module, and that embodied action is at the root of cognition as a whole. Nevertheless, there lingers a persistent impression in the community that this may be all very well for "low-level" cognition, but that when it comes to "high-level" cognition—thought, reasoning, planning, problem-solving (which after all is what "real cognition" is about)—then computational cognitivism remains the only viable option. A major aim of this book is to show that this impression is quite false, and to substantiate the claim, not just in abstract principle but in terms of actual research, that the paradigm of enaction has its own and highly distinctive approach to higher-level cognition. Thus, the themes of consciousness (Benny Shanon), socially shared abstract concepts (Ed Hutchins), mathematics (Rafael Nuñez), language (Didier Bottineau), the human brain (Andreas Engel)—particularly its relation to lived experience (Michel Le Van Quyen), and emotion (Giovanna Colombetti)—all form important chapters in the book.

Indeed, if there is a problem, it is not so much *engaging* with "high-level" cognition, which, as we have seen, the paradigm of enaction does in richly varied ways; it may be, rather, in ensuring an adequate *articulation* between "low-level" embodiment and high-level human cognition. A significant and relatively original contribution of this book is that it does not seek to evade this issue, but addresses it quite squarely. Thus, the opening chapter by Stewart proposes a methodological principle—that of studying cognitive phenomena by way of their historical *genesis* through phylogeny and ontogeny—which aims precisely at overcoming any such hiatus. Chapter 2, by Ezequiel Di Paolo, Marieke Rohde, and Hanne De Jaegher specifically seeks to characterize enaction as a paradigm, with its core ideas and its horizons. They provide enactive accounts of value-generation and social interaction, which they compare favorably to computational approaches. They adopt a bottom-up approach, including but not restricted to evolutionary robotics as a method for grounding complex ideas in simple models. And, exploring an enactive route to higher level forms of cognition, they show how *play*, an activity that allows the development of meaning-manipulation skills as well as a further level of autonomous cognitive self characteristic of human beings, can emerge as a value-generating process from the basis of embodied sense-making.

More generally, we invite our readers to pay particular attention to the ways in which, *within* each chapter, the question of the relations between different levels of organization are addressed. Chapter 3, by Renaud Barbaras, does this in the most striking manner, by positing straight off that the lowest level of all—the basic processes of metabolism and movement—should be studied in such a way that it can be understood as containing already the germ of the highest level of all: reflexive consciousness as investigated by phenomenology. The next four chapters, devoted to questions of embodiment, each do so in a way that highlights developmental aspects. Chapter 4, by Adam Sheya and Linda B. Smith, is explicitly developmental, and suggests that Piaget's notion of a certain pattern of activity—an accidental action that leads to an interesting and arousing outcome and thus more activity and the re-experience of the outcome—sets up an autonomous dynamic that may be foundational to development itself. Giovanna Colombetti (chapter 5) considers that much of current emotion research suffers a form of "Cartesian anxiety," stemming from the false assumption that cognitive evaluations are necessary to trigger behavioral responses appropriate to the situation. She proposes an "enactivist therapy" in order to recover the intimate unity of mind and body that Descartes himself recognized as being the core of emotions. Maxine Sheets-Johnstone (chapter 6) evokes research studies of infant understandings of *in*, *insideness*, and so on, which are highly revealing for what they say and do not say about kinesthesia and thinking in movement. Careful reflection on these studies from an experiential perspective shows that we put the world together in a spatial sense through movement and do so from the very beginning of our lives. Spatial concepts are born in kinesthesia and in our correlative capacity to think in movement. Accordingly, the constitution of space begins not with adult thoughts about space but in infant experience. Finally, in this group of chapters, Olivier Gapenne (chapter 7) considers that the constitution of a "kinesthetic function," itself rooted in proprioception, is foundational for the emergence of the prereflective experience of spatiality and distal objects. His main point is to suggest that the distally perceived (tangibility and form) object is nothing else than the experience of body motion. In line with this, the spatial extension of the perceived object results from a multiscale bodily deployment constrained through a multisensory flow which defines an enactive dynamics.

With the next two chapters, we turn from embodiment to the nervous system and the brain. This is, however, anything but a break. Andreas K. Engel (chapter 8) recalls that in current cognitive science there is a "pragmatic turn" away from the traditional representation-centered framework toward a paradigm based on the notions of "situatedness" and "embodiment" that focuses on understanding the relevance of cognition for action, and the real-world interactions of the brain. Such an "action-oriented" paradigm has earliest and most explicitly been developed in robotics, and has only recently begun to have an increasing impact on cognitive psychology and neurobiology. The basic concept is that cognition should not be understood as a capacity of deriving world-models, which then might provide a "database" for thinking, planning, and problem solving. Rather, it is emphasized that cognitive systems are always engaged in contexts of action that require fast selection of relevant information and constant sensorimotor exchange. In the context of such an action-oriented conceptual framework, investigation of the intrinsic dynamics of neural circuits becomes increasingly important. There is ample evidence that the processing of stimuli is controlled by top-down influences that strongly shape the dynamics of thalamocortical networks and constantly create predictions about forthcoming sensory events. Therefore, perceptual processing is increasingly considered as being active and highly selective in nature. Engel discusses recent neurobiological evidence supporting this "pragmatic turn" and the implications of this view for future research strategies in cognitive neuroscience.

Michel Le Van Quyen (chapter 9) presents the original approach, initially proposed by Francisco Varela, which is termed "neurophenomenology." The idea is to articulate rigorously controlled accounts of first-person lived experience with sophisticated third-person data concerning brain activity. We find here a leitmotif that is quite general in the paradigm of enaction, and that is manifested in several of the contributions to this book. When seeking to articulate two apparently distinct domains, it is not a question of hierarchically reducing one domain to the other; rather, the aim is to create the conditions for a fruitful circulation between the domains, each of which retains its autonomy, in a way that is mutually beneficial. We may call this leitmotif, to which we shall return, the way of *hermeneutical circulation*. This is not a mere abstract idea: in the precise case study presented by Le Van Quyen, he recounts how this approach provides valuable clues for identifying what is really relevant in the complex mass of neurobiological data, and conversely, how it enables epileptic patients to gain a new degree of control over their lives.

The first set of chapters we have presented, up to chapter 9, share the feature that the "point of entry" is a relatively low level of organization grounded in embodiment and neuronal processes; these chapters focus on the emergence of higher-level phenomena. With the next two chapters, concerned with language, we pass a watershed (which is, however, anything but a discontinuous break) toward a "point of entry" at a relatively high level of organization, the focus now being on the articulation with underlying lower-level processes. Chapter 10 by Didier Bottineau is bold and original; it plunges straight into the question of lived experience as it is brought about by "languaging" (an appropriate revival of a neologism initially due to Maturana). Enaction is about the instant and eternity, the organ and the being, the individual and the environment, the self and the kin, the ego and the tribe, the species and life. So is language, spanning from the instant one-syllable order *Go!* to the questions of the origin and evolution of language and languages through all the manifestations and categories—conversations, texts, styles, genres, jargons, dialects, languages, lexicons, grammars. In accordance with the anchoring of enaction in experience, this chapter focuses mainly on the immediate experience of languaging, and occasionally broaches more general subjects like acquisition and evolution. Particularly interesting and challenging is the renewal of perspective on the questions of lexicons and grammars: far from being pregiven as in traditional (notably Chomskian) approaches, we see here how such structures can emerge in the actual practice of languaging.

Chapter 11, by Rafael E. Núñez, takes up the gauntlet of examining what happens with the enaction paradigm when addressing an area of cognition that, by definition, lacks a physical reality available for empirical observation. What happens with this paradigm when dealing with rigorous and precise cognitive entities that are entirely *imaginary*? In this chapter, he argues that such a case is provided by one of the most abstract and precise conceptual systems human beings have ever created: mathematics. In particular, he argues that mathematical infinity, as an object of cognition that by definition is not directly available to experience due to the finite nature of living systems, is an excellent candidate for fully exploring the power of enaction as a paradigm for cognitive science. His argument rests on the observation that language is a medium for the expression of *bodily* metaphors, and that this relation to embodiment, far from dissolving, is more relevant than ever in the case of the extension to purely abstract thought.

The last four chapters deal with questions that are usually considered as the exclusive reserve of the human and social sciences. A framework is provided by Véronique Havelange (chapter 12), who starts by examining how the phenomenology of Husserl, starting from a position of transcendental idealism, is lead by the *internal* logic of the phenomenological investigation to take into account elements such as time, the living body, the Other, worldly objects and culture; these elements are thus not merely constitut*ed*, they are irreducibly constitut*ive* of the

subjective, intersubjective and sociohistorical life of intentional consciousness. This leads to recognizing a "dual and mutual presupposition between
science and the pre-donation of the world," giving rise to a hermeneutical circularity between phenomenology and cognitive science. And again,
this is not merely an abstract petition of principle: Havelange illustrates
this approach by referring to cutting-edge empirical research on perceptual
supplementation.

In chapter 13, Diego Cosmelli and Evan Thompson address the topic of
phenomenal selfhood and prereflective, intransitive self-consciousness,
which is closely related to awareness of the body as subject. They raise the
question of the minimal biological requirements for this type of phenomenal selfhood. Re-evaluating the notorious thought experiment of a "brain
in a vat," they argue that (1) brain activity is largely endogenously and
spontaneously generated, (2) this activity requires massive resources and
regulatory processes from the rest of the body, and (3) this activity plays
a crucial role in the life-regulation processes of the whole organism. They
conclude that the "vat" would have to be in effect a surrogate body, so
that the minimal biological substrate of phenomenal selfhood is not particular brain regions or areas, or even the brain alone, but some crucial
subset of autonomous and interactive brain-body systems.

Chapter 14, by Benny Shanon, seeks to rehabilitate psychology as a
full-fledged human science in its own right, liberated from an inferiority
complex with respect to third-person natural science. To this end, Shanon
proposes a reconsideration of the status of seven factors—the *context* of
cognitive activity, the *medium* in which it is expressed, the *body,* the external physical *world,* the *social other,* the noncognitive faculties of *affect and
motivation,* and *time*—which classical cognitivism typically regards as
merely secondary. When the primary import of these factors is appreciated,
one reaches the conclusion that rather than being the basis for cognition,
representations are the products of cognitive activity, and that the basic
capability of mind is not information processing and symbol manipulation
but rather being and acting in the world. The locus of cognitive activity is
not exclusively internal and mental, but rather external, taking place in
the interface where organism and world meet. With this, the focus of
psychological science shifts from the domain of the unconscious to that
of the conscious. Shanon presents several lines of inquiry into the phenomenology of human consciousness: thought sequences, the systematic
typology of experience, and a novel approach for the study of nonordinary
states of consciousness. Together, these lead to the conceptualization of a
general theory of consciousness.

In his previous work, Edwin Hutchins (1995) pointed out that first-generation cognitive science considered that human culture was a secondary phenomenon; and, in a spirit analogous to that of Shanon, proposed to turn this around and to consider that "culture" is a central feature of human cognition. He put particular emphasis on the importance of technical devices and *external* representations such as maps. In chapter 15, Hutchins takes up these themes and relates them explicitly to embodiment and the enaction framework, showing how these imply a new approach to the analysis of ongoing activity. He then uses this approach to sketch a speculative experimental analysis of an example of real-world problem solving that includes a moment of Aha! insight. Finally, he points out that external representations must be "enacted" in order to make sense, and discusses how this may help us explain how high-level cognitive processes can arise from low-level perceptual and motor abilities. It is to be noted that this case study well illustrates the "hermeneutical circulation" between enactive cognitive science and the human and social sciences (in this case, cultural anthropology) called for by Havelange.

To conclude this brief introduction, we would like to say a few words in order to situate the paradigm of enaction with respect to the numerous currents and schools of thought, past and present, with which it has natural relations of affinity. The references at the end of each chapter give an indication of these related currents; they are however so numerous that an attempt at a commented list would be both incomplete and inevitably superficial. Instead, we shall rather proceed thematically, by identifying three salient characteristics that mark the originality and the specificity of enaction as a paradigm.

The first of these three themes is the relation between first-person lived experience and third-person natural science. The proposal that cognitive science should seriously take into account the dimension of lived experience from a first-person point of view was one of Francisco Varela's most audacious and original contributions (Varela, Thompson, and Rosch 1991; see also chapter 9, this volume). This feature distinguishes the perspective of enaction from other related schools of thought, notably Gibsonian ecological psychology (Gibson 1979), which (in certain interpretations at least) is more than compatible with enaction but which explicitly eschews the first-person dimension. Even the sensorimotor contingency theory (O'Regan and Noë 2001), which does explicitly aim at explaining the "qualia" of lived experience, eschews first-person accounts (and hence phenomenology) as such. Conversely, phenomenology itself (which is of course grounded in first-person experience) is typically (although not necessarily, as argued by Havelange in chapter 12) ill at ease in taking fully into account the perspective of third-person natural science. One possible approach, among others, is to ask the question: "How does an experiencing subject *appear* to an external observer?" The French philosopher Raymond Ruyer (1937) has made a bold and original proposal: on his account, the brain *is* neither more nor less than the appearance of consciousness for an external observer. In its original form, this proposal is not entirely satisfactory (Barbaras 2007), but it does open up new perspectives for a way of doing research in neuroscience that would fully live up to its role in cognitive science.

To conclude on this theme, a modest disclaimer is in order here. None of this amounts to claiming that enaction has found a definitive "final solution" to the problem of connecting first-person and third-person accounts, but we do consider that this very difficult question most definitely is on the agenda of cognitive science.

The second theme is the ambition of enaction as a paradigm to provide an encompassing framework for articulating the many domains and levels of organization that are involved in cognitive science. This is perhaps most clearly expressed in the opening text by Stewart, which runs the whole gamut from physicochemical dissipative structures, basic biological metabolism, and autopoiesis through to specifically human culture and historical consciousness. An aspect that has been gaining increasing attention over the last two or three years is the question of *social cognition*. An issue that is currently the object of lively debate is the articulation between "micro-level" processes—typically dyadic or triadic interactions between individuals—and the "macro-level" phenomena of social structures and human society as a whole. At this macro level, we may especially note the key role accorded to a thematization of technical artifacts and systems, and the modes of their appropriation and actual use by human agents (Havelange 2005). This is indeed the hallmark of the "Compiegne School," according to which "Technology is Anthropologically Constitutive." Integrated into the paradigm of enaction, this marks an important difference from purely biological approaches on one hand, but also from much work in the more traditional human and social sciences, in which the *material* dimension is rarely taken fully into account.

Coming back to the macro/micro debate, it may be useful to note that an analogous debate has already occurred in the realm of the social sciences. Durkheim, widely recognized as the "founding father" of modern sociology, laid emphasis on the importance (and reality!) of global social norms and institutions. Garfinkel (1967), who introduced the notion of "ethnomethodology," focused attention on much smaller-scale processes involving the short-term dynamics of interactions at the individual level. Perhaps the most fruitful resolution of this debate lies in the proposal by Giddens (1976) that micro-level and macro-level approaches should be seen as complementary rather than antagonistic. Macro-level social structures are continuously "enacted" by individual actions and interactions; it is in this way that they (slowly) evolve over historical time. On the other hand, for each new generation of individuals, social structures are "always already there," and fundamentally condition the processes of individual development and "socialization."

To conclude on this second theme, another important disclaimer is in order. The fact that enaction has the ambition of providing an "encompassing framework" does *not* mean that if this paradigm develops to its fullest potential, it would thereby render other, more focused approaches redundant. Reductionist eliminativism does exist—in cognitive science, most notably with respect to the view that a full development of cerebral neuroscience would supersede all other approaches to cognition. But the spirit of the paradigm of enaction is quite the opposite of this; rather, the aim is to organize a *hermeneutical circulation* between diverse approaches, in which each retain their autonomy and their validity.

The third theme is that of reflexivity. The activities of a community of cognitive scientists are, *themselves*, a form of cognition. It follows that if a paradigm in cognitive science is thoroughgoing (and enaction certainly aims at this), it cannot avoid being reflexive and applying to itself. This complexity is not without appeal, and may indeed be considered fascinating, but it is salutary to recognize that it is not without its own difficulties. Russell's paradox[2] is there to remind us that reflexivity has its dangers, as it can so easily introduce fatal contradictions. Husserl, evoking the "paradox of anthropology," was well aware of these formidable difficulties. One way of illustrating the difficulty is based on Maturana's fable of the "man in the submarine." His friends on the shore admire the skill with which he avoids reefs and shoals and brings the submarine safely into port during a storm; they congratulate him. But he retorts: "'Shoals'? 'Reefs'? 'Storm'? I don't know what you're talking about. All *I* know are the readings on dials, and the levers I must push and pull so as to maintain invariant certain relations between the meter-readings." This is the point of the difficult notion of "operational closure" (chapter 2, this volume): it is vital to maintain a clear distinction between what can be perceived by an external observer, and what can be perceived by the organism itself. The problem is that when we ambition to apply the whole scheme of enaction *to ourselves as cognitive scientists*, it would seem that we are disobeying this injunction and hence running the risk of introducing a fatal contradiction;

of trying to do precisely what the principle of operational closure deems to be impossible.

There are, let it be said, several possible lines of attack on this difficult problem. In *The Tree of Knowledge*, Maturana and Varela quite deliberately adopt a form of presentation, which comes full circle back to its own starting point. A social-constructivist approach to scientific activity (Latour and Woolgar 1979) is itself a scientific study, and therefore necessarily applies to itself. The conception of establishing a "hermeneutical circle," notably between static phenomenology and genetic phenomenology (chapter 12, this volume) also shares this reflexive character. Finally, the concluding remarks in the chapter by Stewart (see section 1.3) quite explicitly evoke this reflexive feature: we may start out with elementary forms of life; going through all the increasingly complex forms of life that have arisen on Earth, we end up with . . . the biologist studying elementary forms of life. In other words, the enactive topology is rather like that of a Möbius strip: by going full circle, we end up at the starting point—but with the *object* of scientific study having changed sides on the subject-object relation, becoming itself the *subject* of scientific enquiry.

We shall close this introduction, then, with another modest disclaimer: the paradigm of enaction, at least in its present state, cannot pretend to have already a satisfactory solution to these problems. It does, however, at least *admit* the issue of reflexivity as an interesting and valid question; it also presents a promising attempt at providing an encompassing account of cognition from cell to society, and it adopts as a methodological pillar, despite many unresolved issues, the need for circulation between first-person experience and third-personal scientific methods. These features are sufficient to characterize it distinctively compared to other trends and approaches in cognitive science.

Notes

1. The book is based on an International CNRS Summer School organized by the Association pour la Recherche Cognitive (ARCo), held from May 29 to June 3, 2006, in Ile d'Oléron, France, and attended by sixty participants. The climate of vigorous discussion during that meeting provided the momentum for this book. Several chapters are the outcome of those interactions and it was only natural to extend the conversation to a wider community. A number of additional contributions address topics and points of view that could not be fully covered in the summer school.

2. This paradox is both simple and amusing. A barber proposes to shave all the men in town who do not shave themselves. The reflexive conundrum is then: does the barber shave himself? If he does not, he should—but if he does, he should not!

References

Barandiaran, X., and Ruiz-Mirazo, K. (guest editors). (2008). Modelling autonomy. Special issue of *BioSystems* 91 (2).

Barbaras, R. (2007). Vie et extériorité. Le problème de la perception chez Ruyer. *Les études philosophiques* 80:15–37.

Di Paolo, E. (guest editor). (2009). The social and enactive mind. Special issue of *Phenomenology and the Cognitive Sciences* 8 (4): 409–415.

Garfinkel, H. (1967). *Studies in ethnomethodology.* Englewood Cliffs, NJ: Prentice-Hall.

Gibson, J. J. (1979). *The ecological approach to visual perception.* Boston: Houghton Mifflin.

Giddens, A. (1976). *New rules of sociological method.* London: Hutchinson.

Havelange, V. (2005). De l'outil à la médiation constitutive: Pour une réévaluation phénoménologique, biologique et anthropologique de la technique. In *Suppléances perceptives et interfaces*, ed. O. Gapenne and P. Gaussier, vol. 1, 8–45. http://www.univ-rouen.fr/Arobase.

Hutchins, E. (1995). *Cognition in the wild.* Cambridge, MA: MIT Press.

Latour, B., and Woolgar, S. (1979). *Laboratory life: The social construction of scientific facts.* Beverly Hills, CA: Sage.

Maturana, H., and Varela, F. J. (1987). *The tree of knowledge.* Boston: Shambhala.

O'Regan, J. K., and Noë, A. (2001). A sensorimotor account of vision and visual consciousness. *Behavioral and Brain Sciences* 24 (5): 939–1031.

Rohde, M., and Ikegami, T. (guest editors). (2009). Agency in natural and artificial systems. Special issue of *Adaptive Behavior* 17 (5).

Ruyer, R. (1937). *La conscience et le corps.* Paris: Alcan.

Thompson, E. (2007). *Mind in life: Biology, phenomenology, and the sciences of mind.* Cambridge, MA: Harvard University Press.

Torrance, S. (guest editor). (2005). Enactive experience. Special issue of *Phenomenology and the Cognitive Sciences* 4 (4).

Torrance, S. (guest editor). (2007). Enactive experience. Special issue of *Phenomenology and the Cognitive Sciences* 6 (4).

Varela, F., Thompson, E., and Rosch, E. (1991). *The embodied mind.* Cambridge, MA: MIT Press.

1 Foundational Issues in Enaction as a Paradigm for Cognitive Science: From the Origin of Life to Consciousness and Writing

John Stewart

1.1 Introduction

1.1.1 Requirements for a Paradigm

There are two basic requirements for any paradigm in cognitive science: it must provide a genuine resolution of the mind-body problem, and it must provide for a genuine core articulation between a multiplicity of disciplines—at the very least between psychology, linguistics and neuroscience. Cognitive science owes its very existence to the fact the Computational Theory of Mind (CTM), whatever its defects and limitations, does fulfill these two requirements. In order even to get off the ground, any candidate for the role of an "alternative paradigm" must do at least as well as CTM in both these respects. The aim of this text is to explain how the proto-paradigm of enaction does just this.

1.1.2 The Mind-Matter Problem

How can a material state *be* a mental state? Hoary it may be, yet the problem is anything but solved. The most common attitude consists of drifting evasively between Cartesian dualism, idealistic monism, and materialistic monism, none of which is tenable when examined fairly and squarely.

The paradigm of enaction solves this problem by grounding all cognition as an essential feature of living organisms. For Descartes, there was no problem in considering that all animals are mere machines, so the ontological split came between animals and humans. For Maturana and Varela (1980) and Jonas (1963), by contrast, the great divide comes between matter and living organisms. Of course, this does not in itself solve the problem, for we now have to ask how a material process can *be* a living process. Vitalism reminds us that an ontological dualism is conceivable

here also. Schematically, the root of the answer lies in the theory of
autopoiesis:

An autopoietic system is organized (defined as a unity) as a network of processes of
production (transformation and destruction) of components that produces the components that

a) through their interactions and transformations continuously regenerate and
   realize the network of processes (relations) that produce them and
b) constitute it (the machine) as a concrete unity in the space in which they
   exist by specifying the topological domain of its realization as such a network.
   (Varela 1979)

Thus, a living organism is not so much a "thing," but rather a process with
the particular property of *engendering itself* indefinitely. However, although
autopoiesis is clearly a necessary condition for life, it is not sure that
minimal autopoiesis (such as Varela's tesselation automaton) is a sufficient
condition.

The question has been rephrased in an interesting fashion by the French
philosopher Simondon (1989). One of Simondon's basic concepts is that
of *individuation*: in the Heraclitean tradition, entities are not reified "things,"
but rather pure processes of becoming. Examples are a whirlpool; the
growing faces of a crystal (the mass that is left behind is already "dead,"
like the wood in the center of a tree trunk); a candle flame; or a cyclone.
In contemporary scientific terms, these are thermodynamically open
systems, far-from-equilibrium "dissipative structures" that presuppose a
flux of matter and energy. Prior to the emergence of a dissipative structure,
there is just an undifferentiated "medium"; Simondon (like Whitehead
1926) emphasizes the "vague" nature of this "pre-individual" state, which
is the ground for everything that can emerge, but about which it is very
difficult to say anything precise. The emergence of a dissipative structure
brings about the differentiation between two inseparable entities: the
"organism" on one hand, its "ecological niche" on the other. In Simondon's terms, niche and organism are "transductive"; that is, they exist, as
such, only in their relation to each other.

With these concepts in place, we see that purely physicochemical individuation is quite possible, as illustrated by the previous examples, but
Simondon makes the point that such entities are *intrinsically ephemeral*.
They last only as long as certain external boundary conditions, *over which
they exert no control*, just happen to be maintained. In other words, their
existence is contingent. This sets the stage for a definition of *biological*
individuation: a process of individuation is biological (i.e., living) if its own
functioning exerts a control over the relation between the organism and

its ecological niche *such that* the process of individuation can continue indefinitely. Coming back to autopoiesis and cognitive science, this introduces the notion of a *sensorimotor loop*. As discussed in Bourgine and Stewart 2004, we may define a system as "cognitive" if and only if it generates its actions, and the feedback sensations serve to guide actions, in a very specific way so as to maintain its autopoiesis and hence its very existence. With these definitions, "cognition" and "life" are fundamentally the *same* phenomena; and, in principle, the mind-matter problem is solved.[1]

This is satisfactory, of course, only if it can be made plausible that a sensorimotor loop is minimally "cognitive." There are two parts to the answer (see figure 1.1).

First, the sensory inputs, S, must be used to guide the actions, A, *in a particular way* so as to maintain autopoiesis. This is a form of knowledge: not indeed propositional "knowing that" (which as we shall see comes much later in evolution), but a form of "knowing how" expressed directly in action. For the paradigm of enaction, this form of knowledge is indeed much more basic and much more generic than symbolic knowledge.

The second part of the answer stems from the fact that the actions A modify the environment and/or the relation of the organism to its environment, and hence modify in return the sensory input. Together with the first part, this closes the loop and sets up a dynamic system. Now the key point is this: what the world "is" *for* the organism amounts to neither more nor less than the consequences of its actions for its sensory inputs; this in turn clearly depends on the repertoire of possible actions. Without action, there is no "world" and no perception. This is the heart of the concept of enaction: every living organism *enacts*, or as Maturana (1987) liked to say *brings forth* the world in which it exists. This has important ontological consequences, as it means that "reality" is not pregiven but co-constructed by the organism.

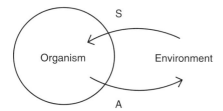

Figure 1.1

The sensorimotor coupling between and organism and its environment. The sensory inputs, S, guide the actions, A; the actions A modify the sensory returns.

The basic scheme of figure 1.1 applies already to animals: in the 1920s, the German ethologist von Uexküll (1909, 1966) characterized "animal worlds" (e.g., "the world of the tick") on the basis of sensorimotor contingencies as they function in ecological context. In fact, it applies already to the simplest living organisms of all, bacteria: there is a nice example, by now a classic, of the precise mechanism by which bacteria are able to progressively approach a source of nutrition.

1.1.3   Articulating Levels of Cognition

I have dealt in summary fashion with autopoiesis and minimal cognition, because it is vital to realize that although this does provides a grounding, a principled solution to the mind-matter problem, it is only a starting point. In cognitive science, there is an increasing—if still somewhat grudging—recognition of the importance of sensorimotor dynamics: dynamic systems theory (Thelen and Smith 1994; van Gelder 1998), sensorimotor contingency theory (O'Regan and Noë 2001); and a strong revival of a neo-Gibsonian ecological approach to perception (Stoffregen and Bardy 2001). There is, however, a strong tendency to confine this renewal to "lower-level" cognition; the dominant view remains that when it comes to "higher-level" cognition, the computational paradigm is still without a serious rival. I most emphatically contest this view; in my opinion, the paradigm of enaction has its own and highly distinctive approach to higher-level cognition. On the one hand, enaction takes first-person lived experience, and in particular the phenomena of consciousness, far more seriously than the computational paradigm;[2] this is notably the case with Varela's "neurophenomenology" (Varela 1996). On the other hand, as I will explain in somewhat more detail later, the paradigm of enaction is very naturally able to take into account the bulk of the social and human sciences, notably anthropology, by examining the processes of hominization that made the link between animal worlds and human worlds.

The way in which enaction meets the second requirement for a paradigm in cognitive science, that of a core articulation between the various areas and disciplines involved in cognitive science, is to follow the natural process of the genesis[3] of living forms. In other words, the interdisciplinary articulation can be achieved by mobilizing all the relevant disciplines around this common project of studying how "cognition" has evolved and developed over time. It follows indeed from the equation "cognition = life" that the historical evolution in forms of life, ever since its origin, *is* an evolution in forms of cognition. This enriches von Uexküll's original inspiration by showing how "animal worlds" are linked and related to our "human world." In section 1.2, which constitutes the main body of this text, I therefore propose to sketch out the succession of major phylogenetic events that have occurred, first in biological evolution, then in the process of hominization, and finally in the course of human history. My approach will be thematic rather than strictly chronological, because from the point of view of cognition, there are a number of major phenomena, each with its own history that is inextricably intertwined with that of the others.

"Follow the natural process of their genesis through history" may sound simple, and in its principle it is indeed a simple idea, but there are difficult methodological issues involved, as we cannot go back and observe historical genesis directly. Life-forms of the past do leave traces—fossils for biological evolution, archeological remains for prehistory, written documents and inscriptions for human history—and these are invaluable in providing a "backbone" to historical reconstructions. However, even apart from gaps in the record, because cognition and life are *processes* and not "things," reified traces alone are insufficient. A second string to the bow of reconstructing the past is the comparison of contemporary life-forms. This approach is based on the idea that certain contemporary life-forms are relatively "primitive" and may thus reasonably be taken as representative of past life-forms. For example, the sequence "jawless fishes –> cartilaginous fishes –> bony fishes –> amphibians –> reptiles –> mammals" can be taken as representing vertebrate evolution. In its simplistic version, this idea is simply wrong: all contemporary life-forms have exactly the same chronological age (going back to their common ancestors at the origin of life) and are thus all equally "evolved." If phylogeny were a continuous, gradual process that occurred everywhere at the same rate, this objection would be decisive. However, as Eldredge and Gould (1972) have pointed out, phylogeny is not regular and continuous; rather, it occurs by "punctuated equilibria" with long periods of stability punctuated by relatively rare events when major, rapid evolution occurs. Thus, although due care must be taken in interpretation, comparative studies do give information on the succession of ancestral forms. A third string to the bow is provided by ontogeny, as will be explained in section 1.2.2.3. None of these approaches taken alone is sufficient, but if they are combined and articulated, within a serious theoretical framework, a reasonably coherent picture can be constructed.

1.2   Cognition = Life: Implications for Higher-Level Cognition

1.2.1   The Origin of Life
When exactly did life arise on the planet Earth? The planet was formed about 4.5 Gyr ago;[4] it is generally agreed that life was not possible before 3.9 Gyr, because the planet had to cool down, and there was also a heavy meteoric bombardment that ceased around that time. Life had certainly started by 2.7 Gyr: this is the date of the earliest incontrovertible fossils with molecular remains, and it fits with the date of the most recent common ancestor of the three major lineages of living organisms, archeobacteria, eubacteria, and eukaryotes as calculated by a "molecular clock." But life must have started well before this—organisms with a DNA-protein system, as we know them today, cannot themselves have arisen by spontaneous generation, and so must have derived from simpler ancestors. Vesicle-like structures have been observed in rocks as old as 3,8 Gyr, but their interpretation is uncertain and controversial. Nevertheless, it is clear that life arose on Earth remarkably soon after the physical conditions made it possible. Stephen Jay Gould, the foremost evolutionary biologist of our time, remarked that life on Earth has been strongly affected by a number of "accidents" (e.g., large meteoric explosions, an episode of "snowball Earth," the half-dozen mass extinctions, and so on), but he did not count the origin of life itself as one of these "accidents," because coming so soon after it was possible at all, scenarios for this event must explain it as statistically normal and likely. There is, however, a missing link between the very first forms of life, which by definition must be capable of spontaneous generation, and the simplest living organisms existing today, which all have a DNA-protein system. Fascinating though these questions are, I shall not say more here.

1.2.2   Multicellular Organisms and Ontogenesis
About 600 Myr ago,[5] there occurred what is arguably the most momentous event in the whole of biological evolution after the origin of life itself; this event is known as the "Cambrian explosion" (Gould 1989). Until that time, all living organisms were unicellular and macroscopic—bacteria, amoebae, and the like. Then, within a mere geological instant,[6] a whole range of macroscopic multicellular animals made their appearance. All present-day animals belong to one of seven major orders, each characterized by a specific Bauplan or bodily architecture (with either radial or bilateral symmetry). These orders are sponges, corals, coelentera (jellyfish and so on), mollusks, echinoderms, arthropods (crustaceans, insects, and so on), and

chordates (notably vertebrates). One might have thought that sponges and jellyfish are "primitive," and vertebrates (including ourselves) are "advanced," but the fact is that these seven orders *all* appeared at the time of the Cambrian explosion. Not only that, but there were also an equal number of other Bauplans, some of which appear to us touchingly bizarre, that then disappeared without leaving any evolutionary descendants. It is to be noted that no new Bauplans have been invented since that time. This striking configuration—all the creativity in terms of the Bauplans of multicellular animals being crammed into a tiny period, with nothing either before or since—clearly calls for explanation, but again I have not space to enter the discussion.

Beyond the drama of the historical event—the Cambrian explosion—the origin of multicellular animals raises some fundamental theoretical questions. Here, I will briefly address three: the mechanisms underlying ontogenesis, learning, and the relation between ontogenesis and phylogenesis.

1.2.2.1 The Mechanisms of Ontogenesis Ontogenesis is the process leading from a fertilized egg cell via embryogenesis to birth, and which continues through maturation to an adult, and then through senescence to death at the term of a life span characteristic of the species (if not before by accident[7]). The process of ontogenesis is awe-inspiring in its complexity, and indeed quite simply in its aesthetics; given that complexity, it is also awe-inspiring in its regularity. This regularity arises, robustly, from principles of dynamic self-organization. A striking example is that of identical twins: if an embryo is separated in two, even at quite a late stage, the result is not one left-half and one right-half individual, but two complete, perfectly formed individuals.

The process of ontogenesis has been very well described, in particular from an anatomical and morphological point of view. In the first part of the twentieth century, a start was made in trying to understand the mechanisms at work. D'Arcy Wentworth Thompson (1917) remarked that morphogenesis in living organisms is necessarily based on the same physical principles as morphogenesis in natural nonliving systems—he was particularly impressed by landscapes and coastlines. Spemann (1938), and others, started a program of experimental embryology, investigating the consequences of perturbing the process in various ways. Waddington (1956, 1957), with the concepts of "epigenetic landscape" and "chreode," made a step toward a possible mathematical formulation such as the "catastrophe theory" of Thom (1972). However, at the present time, a real

understanding of ontogenesis as a self-organized system is severely handi-
capped by the unfortunate notion of a "genetic program," which has lead
biologists to look at DNA sequences as though these could contain the key
to the secret. For a critique, and the modest beginnings of a more adequate
approach, see Oyama 1985 and Stewart 2004.

Interestingly enough, the best conceptual approach to the fundamental
enigmas of ontogenesis remains that of Piaget. This is, of course, of particular interest for cognitive science. It is not often recognized that Piaget
was, basically, a neo-Kantian: he sought to understand how the apparently
canonical and timeless principles of logic and mathematics—the "synthetic a priori categories" of Kant—could be regularly and reliably *constructed* in the course of an empirical, material process. His answer, as is
well known, consisted of analyzing the cognitive development of children
in terms of a succession of historical *stages*, each of which resulted from
previous stages, and in turn set the scene for the emergence of subsequent
stages. Of particular interest for paradigm of enaction, we may note that
Piaget took sensorimotor dynamics as the very first stage in the ontogeny
of cognition.

1.2.2.2 Learning Learning is a property of multicellular organisms. An
individual unicellular organism such as a single bacterium cannot learn.
Superficially, it looks as though unicellular organisms such as bacteria can
"learn"; for example, following the widespread use of antibiotics, resistant
strains of bacteria have become prevalent. However, careful analysis shows
that the mechanism involved is not individual learning, but natural selection at the level of the population. A few antibiotic-resistant bacteria
existed already *prior* to the advent of antibiotics; in the presence of antibiotics, the "normal" (i.e., sensitive) bacteria were unable to reproduce and
to compete for resources, so the resistant bacteria flourished and came to
dominate the population. We may also note that when a unicellular organism grows and divides, the two "daughter" cells are generally identical to
the previous "parent" cell. Thus, if unicellular individuals were able to
learn, the benefits would be passed on to their progeny, and we would
have an example of the inheritance of acquired characteristics. According
to conventional neo-Darwinian theory, this is precisely what does not
happen.

Thus, "learning" is a phenomenon which takes place in the context of
a developing multicellular organism, at a particular point in its life-history.
It follows that "learning" can only be a modification of the developmental
process; this means that what *can* be "learned" is both *enabled* and *con-*

strained by the epigenetic landscape. Development, and therefore learning, is essentially an endogenously self-generating process; it is therefore unnecessary—and impossible—to "instruct" it from the outside. This runs directly counter to the widespread notion that "learning" is a process of "instruction," by which is meant a process of information transfer from teacher to pupil. This is not the place to enter into a wholesale critique of the notion of "information." Suffice it to say that "information," in the strict Shannonian sense of the term, can and does specify which of a number of predefined possibilities will be realized; however, it does not *and cannot* specify what those possibilities are in the first place. This means that *instruction*, in the strict sense of the term, is radically impossible. The limitations—and possibilities—concerning what can be learned do not stem from the fact that there are certain bits of information that are "in the genes" and not in the environment. They stem from the fact that at any particular stage in the dynamical process of development, only a very restricted set of "next steps" are possible.

If "instruction" is impossible, then the only things that can be "learned" are things that were *already possible* at that stage of development. This is reminiscent of Vygotsky's notion of "region of proximal development" (Vygotsky 1962). Human parents often have the intuitive gift of attributing a capacity to their infant *just before* they are actually capable of the performance in question: they attribute to a one-year-old baby the capacity to walk *just before* she is actually able to take her first steps; they attribute to a two-year-old the capacity to understand what is said, and interpret his response as an intelligent, meaningful expression, *just before* this is spontaneously the case. What is fascinating is that by doing so, the parents actually trigger the emergence of the capacity in question.

1.2.2.3 Ontogeny and Phylogeny According to Darwinian theory, evolution results from the combination of variation and selection. It follows, logically, that selection can only operate on the variation that is there in the first place to be selected, and hence that the course of evolution will depend, crucially, on the variation that can arise. In the currently orthodox neo-Darwinian version of the theory, the variation is supposed to be "random," so that the course of evolution is determined by natural selection. However, the concept of "randomness" is tricky; events cannot be "random" in any absolute sense, only relative to the background of a given set of possibilities. In the case of biological evolution, the variation that arises, and that selection can act upon, can only be considered "random" from a narrowly gene-centered point of view. Mutations in the nucleotide sequence of DNA are, indeed, quasi-random. But from an organism-centered point of view, the variation that *can* arise is anything but random: it is completely conditioned by the initial form and dynamic organization of the organism itself.

The evolutionary significance of multicellular organisms with an ontogeny is that they can vary not just in terms of cell physiology, but in terms of the developmental process. As a graphic illustration of the fantastic variation that can be produced in this way, consider the incredible variety of life-forms and life-strategies of multicellular animals, plants and fungi that exist today—from mice to oak trees, elephants to crabs to daffodils, bats and whales and eagles and sparrows to bees and spiders, from snails and worms and squids and sea urchins to corals and toadstools. Correlatively, of course, the richness and variety of "worlds" that can be enacted expands also. Compared to this, unicellular organisms are inevitably monotonous. Basically, the only thing they do is to feed themselves so as to maintain their own metabolism and cellular autopoiesis. This is, of course, already a tremendous achievement, and we are still far from understanding scientifically how it is possible, but the hard fact remains that there are not so many different ways of doing it, and so variation in the life-forms and life-strategies of single-celled organisms is inevitably very restricted. With the advent of multicellular organisms, the rate and indeed the very nature of biological evolution changed dramatically because of an explosion in the variety of organisms that could arise.

There is thus an intimate and reciprocal relation between ontogeny and phylogeny. Phylogeny is both constrained and enabled by ontogeny: natural selection can only operate on variation that is engendered by variations in the developmental process, but this is also enabling, because this variation is sometimes original and surprising (the developmental geneticist Goldschmidt [1940] spoke of "hopeful monsters"). In fact, it is important to remember that what is "inherited" from generation to generation is *not* the adult organism (and even less any particular "character" of that organism), but rather the *developmental system* (Oyama 1985). Conversely, ontogeny in turn is both constrained and enabled by phylogeny: developmental systems have to make do with piecemeal step-by-step tinkering and cannot be redesigned from scratch,[8] but this is also enabling, because the tinkering can be effected cumulatively, and on occasion benefits from unforseen "pre-adaptations."

The intimate relation between phylogeny and ontogeny is primarily important for the effects it has on both, but, secondarily, it also has a methodological significance. In the nineteenth century, Haeckel proposed a "law" of recapitulation, according to which the course of ontogeny is a sort of accelerated version of the phylogenetic history of the species in question. Strictly speaking, this is wrong: it could be correct only if phylogeny rigorously conserved the ontogeny of the previous evolutionary stage, and just added an additional stage at the end. This is not systematically the case at all; evolution often occurs by "neoteny" (the evolutionary later form resembles the *early* developmental stages of the ancestor), and sometimes the later developmental stages are discarded altogether. But because of the intimate reciprocal relations we have outlined thus far, Haeckel's idea is less wrong than one might have thought; with due care in interpretation, it can be included as a third strand in the endeavor to reconstruct evolutionary history.

1.2.3   The Nervous System
Almost everyone today, whatever their theoretical tendencies, takes it for granted that cognition is something that happens in the brain. I happen to conclude that if there is a consensus so apparently absolute, there must be something wrong with it. I won't labor the point that Aristotle—a very respectable intellectual with a serious interest in natural science—thought that the brain was an organ whose most important function was to cool the body. I will even admit that, other things being sufficiently equal, a *difference* in brain state can be the cause of a *difference* in cognitive/behavioral/conscious functioning. But I remain adamant in maintaining that this does not show that cognition happens "in" the brain, nor does it show, in a properly scientific fashion, what it is that the brain really does.

I will start by applying the methodology I announced earlier: "Follow the natural process of their genesis through history." Before we even get to brains and central networks of neurons, this leads us to identify the biological role of the very first individual neurons. It seems that these arose in jellyfish-like creatures, linking a stimulus (a relatively nonspecific irritation) to an action (contraction of all the muscles which produces fleeing behavior). The situation is not so different in the giant axons of the squid that were put to such good use by Hodgkin and Huxley. Thus, right from the start, neurons were involved in establishing sensorimotor dynamics. Studies with robots show that artificial neuronal networks of even a modest size can participate in the generation of complex behaviors.

The other strand in "enactive" neuroscience has to do with the development of central nervous systems. In phylogenetic terms, admittedly focusing on vertebrates, there was first the emergence of a spinal column, present even in lampreys and hagfish, and then, very progressively, the development of a brain (reptile brain, limbic brain, cortical brain). The functional definition of a central nervous system is that the number of "interneurons" having synaptic connections only to only other neurons is large compared to sensory and motor interface neurons. Varela, Thompson, and Rosch (1991, 94) remark that if part A of a brain has connections to part B, then empirically B has reciprocal connections going back to A. The result of this is that a brain can exhibit self-engendered activity even in the absence of any sensorimotor connexion with the world. Because of this, Maturana and Varela (1980) insisted on the "operational closure" of the nervous system; as a dynamic system, the nervous system defines its *own* set of "attractors," and interaction with the environment will not define what these attractors *are*, but rather "trigger" the switch from one dynamic attractor to another. Varela used to say, on this basis, that the brain does not have "feature *detectors*"—the classical view according to which "reality" is predefined, and the role of the brain is to detect preexisting features. Rather, the brain—or should we say the brain in a living body in an ecological niche?—is a "feature *specifier*," because the central theme of enaction is that organisms *bring forth* their own world, and the function of the brain is to be understood in this sense.

There is room for debate on the correct way to articulate these two strands, which can appear as contradictory: on the one hand, we have the radical dependence of the nervous system on its insertion in the context of sensorimotor dynamics; on the other, there is the apparent "autonomy" and operational closure of the central nervous system.

1.2.4 Communication

In this section, I shall follow a procedure that I think is quite general when applying the maxim "Follow the natural process of their genesis through history." It is first necessary to give a theoretical definition of the phenomenon under consideration—one can examine the evolutionary origin and subsequent development of a phenomenon only if one knows sufficiently what it is. Then, in a second phase, one can examine the deployment of the phenomenon by referring to a synthetic reconstruction of evolutionary history based on comparative studies and developmental studies.

Maturana and Varela define "communication" as follows (see figure 1.2). In the context of sensorimotor coupling between an organism and its world, the range of actions can be enlarged to include *the emission of signals* that will affect the actions of other organisms (usually, but not necessarily, of the same species); conversely, the *reception of signals* emitted by other organisms will modulate the actions of the organism in question.

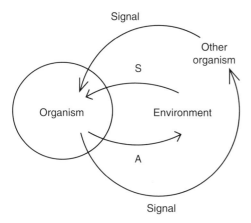

Figure 1.2
The basic scheme of figure 1.1 extended to include the emission of signals, and the modulation of actions by the reception of signals, thus giving rise to a coordination of actions and communication.

We can say that there is "communication" if and only if the signal-mediated interactions between the organisms result in a *coordination of actions* that contributes to satisfying the viability constraint of maintaining their autopoiesis.

Thus defined, the first really important instantiation of "communication" is the intercellular interactions involved in the coherent ontogenesis of multicellular organisms that we have examined in 1.2.2. In the animal kingdom, communication seems to be of rather sporadic importance, with no clear evolutionary trend. It is absolutely crucial in the case of the so-called social insects—ants, termites, bees, wasps. In this area, there are a number of beautiful case studies that combine observations in the field, laboratory experiments (identifying explicitly the mechanisms that trigger the emission of a signal, and the effect that perception of a signal has on behavior), and mathematical modeling (showing that the mechanisms identified are indeed sufficient to generate the observed natural coordination of actions); classical examples include the formation of food trails and the construction of nests (Bonabeau, Dorigo, and Theraulaz 1999). At the other extreme, there are animals who are essentially solitary (e.g., lynxes who meet only for copulation).

In the light of these examples, there are several points to note about the proposed definition. The first is that the material nature of the signal is quite irrelevant—all that counts is the dynamics that are engendered.

Thus, in the case of social insects, a massive role is played by pheromones, which are actually quite specific biochemical molecules, but any other molecules, *on condition* that they had the same conditions for emission and the same effects on behavior, would do just as well. Linguists make a big point about the "arbitrary" nature of semiotic signs; that is, there is no necessary relation between the phonetic form of a word and its semantic meaning. As we shall see, there are major qualitative differences between animal communication and human language—but the arbitrary nature of the sign is not among them.

The second point is that biological organisms "know" what to do, and they have the "know-how" to do it—but they do not know *that* they know. There is an important sense in which they do not *understand* what it is that they are doing; they do not have "intentions" in the ordinary commonsense meaning of the word. This comes as no surprise at all in the case of the cells that "communicate" to form a multicellular animal. It is not too surprising in the case of insects, where perception-action loops function without the necessity for high-level cognitive understanding of the results.[9] But it is somewhat surprising to find that the same applies to situations of "animal communication" even among relatively evolved species. A classic case is that of the alarm calls emitted by vervet monkeys. There are three distinctive calls: the emission of Call_1 is triggered, in a natural situation, by the perception of an eagle; Call_2 by the perception of a snake; and Call_3 by the perception of a feline predator. And upon hearing these calls, other animals respond to Call_1 by crouching on the ground under cover of leaves; to Call_2, on the contrary, by climbing up into the trees; and to Call_3 by taking horizontal cover and peering anxiously into the distance. These reactions make so much sense—they are adequate reactions to the threats posed by each of these three predators—that it is difficult for us to imagine that the monkeys do *not* "understand what they are doing." But experiments in the laboratory show that this is not actually the case. The emission of Call_1 will be triggered even if the animal is safe in its cage and no eagle could possibly reach it, merely by a cardboard shape with the right angular size and velocity being drawn across the top of the cage. It will be triggered also even if there are no other monkeys anywhere around (so there would be no point in calling "look out, there's an eagle around!"). And the perception of Call_1 will trigger the crouching behavior, even if the monkey is safe in its cage and can *see* that there are no eagles anywhere around.

The general conclusion is that "animal communication," both the emission of signals and the behavior triggered by perception of them, are stereotyped reactions that are typical for all normal members of the species.[10] As such, they can perfectly well be explained by natural selection, and do not necessarily imply "understanding."

1.2.5 Language

Here again, I shall start with a theoretical definition, before looking at empirical evidence and attempting a reconstruction of the evolutionary history. I have deliberately characterized "animal communication" as (1) stereotyped and (2) not involving an intention to communicate, because these are precisely the points of contrast with human language. Human language is dramatically *not* stereotyped. First, because of the combinatorial mechanisms at work (phonemes or letters into words, words into sentences), the number of different "signals" is stupendous. The number of different semantic *meanings* is even greater. Considering the word as a unit, the meaning of a word can vary according to its linguistic context (the neighboring words with which it is combined) and even more according to its pragmatic context. Taking this into due account, one could seriously put forward the hypothesis that *no* word has ever been used twice to mean *exactly* the same thing.

This, however, immediately raises a problem. Animal communication functions (without understanding) *because* it is stereotyped. If human language is not stereotyped, how do human beings ever communicate correctly by talking? A part of the answer is that in general we probably understand each other far less than we fondly imagine. Garfinkel (1967), in his foundational work in ethnomethodology, impishly pointed out that in the course of normal conversation, the socially acceptable thing to do is to *accept* to have only a very vague and imperfect understanding of what is actually being said, and riding the wave of good faith that things will become "sufficiently clear" as we go along. Arguably, some of the most significant moments of communication occur when speakers identify a *misunderstanding*; paradoxical though it may seems, what happens is that they then *realize* that up until that point, they had been misinterpreting each other (with the best of intentions, of course). My point here is not nihilistic; I am not saying that we do not understand each other *at all*, only that our understanding is not, and cannot be, "100% perfect" as the "information-transfer" model would suggest is possible.

If we accept that a verbal utterance *radically underdetermines* the meaning to be communicated, how can some degree of communication nevertheless occur? This is where the *intention to communicate* comes in. First, the hearer puts great creativity into *inventing, imagining,* and *guessing* what the speaker might be trying to say. Of course, this is (at best) a hypothesis; the communication can be consolidated only if there is some feedback. This is why such phrases as: "Do you mean that . . ." (followed by a paraphrase) or "I don't understand what you mean at all, please say it again" or (sometimes) "Yes, yes, I see, go on" are so common in ordinary conversation. It is to be noted that these metalinguistic messages—absolutely vital for linguistic intercomprehension, on this account—are often replaced by facial gestures and mimics: a frown, a deliberate silence, a nod of the head, winking the eyes, and so on. Such gestures are not usually counted as "linguistic" (they are not words), but if this theory is right, such metalinguistic signals are actually at the core of what is characteristically linguistic. Thus, linguistic communication is governed by a (mutual) *intention* to communicate. It is thus, theoretically, a *second-order* communication about the status of the first-level intercomprehension.

This discursive elaboration is meant to put some flesh on Maturana and Varela's rather dry formulation of the "linguistic domain": language is a second-order metacommunication, a *coordination of coordination of actions.* Something to note here is that language, characteristically, has an effect of *taking a distance* from the action itself. To put it crudely, as long as two people are hurling verbal insults at each other, they have not actually come to blows.

With this attempted theoretical characterization of what language is, we may now take a look at some empirical studies. I shall start with the comparative studies: taking our nearest biological relatives (chimpanzees, gorillas and orangutans) as "representative" of our most recent common ancestors some 5 Myr ago, what can be said of their linguistic capabilities?

To tell it properly, this is a long and polemical story, and I shall be abrupt and superficial. To my mind, by far the best work in this area remains the pioneering studies carried out by Alex and Beatrice Gardner. It was they who recognized that vocal signals were inappropriate: not just because chimpanzees have difficulty in producing them, but more profoundly because in their natural ecology vocalizations are expressive of extreme emotional states (fear, anger, and so on) that are antithetical to the "distancing" register characteristic of language. They had the brilliant idea of employing the "sign languages" developed for and by deaf humans— the status of these "sign languages" as full human languages, a polemical issue, is now increasingly recognized.[11] but at the time it was a bold step. The Gardners therefore made the dual commitment, first of seriously learning sign language themselves, and second of raising several baby chimpanzees in their home as their own children.[12]

I will restrict myself to two anecdotes that to my mind are extremely telling. The first concerns Washoe, the eldest of their "children." Washoe loved to play with Roger, the young man who kept her during the day, and one of her favorite games was to ask Roger to tickle her. The corresponding sign sequences were carefully recorded on video, and Roger was quite proud of them. One morning, apparent disaster struck: Washoe, in a skittish mood, did not make the usual sign sequence "Roger-tickle-Washoe," but signed "Washoe-tickle-Roger." Poor Roger was dismayed, and hoped that the tell-tale cameras were not functioning: what ammunition it would be for the critics who were only too ready to accuse Washoe of just fooling around without really understanding anything. Roger tried to rescue the situation; he signed "No, Washoe, you've got it wrong: Roger-tickle-Washoe," and he tried to tickle her as usual. But this did not suit Washoe, who stuck to her idea; she signed in reply "No; *Washoe-tickle-Roger*," and to show what she meant actually started to tickle Roger! We have here a fine example of second-order "communication about communication" at work (and incidentally, an understanding of grammatical relationships); by this standard, then, far from being a failure it is precisely this sequence that is illustrative of a genuinely linguistic capability.

The second example concerns another baby chimpanzee raised by the Gardners, Lucy. Like many human children, Lucy was distressed when her (adoptive) parents left her at home in the morning to go to work at the university. She developed a routine of "acting out," expressing her distress by behaving badly, throwing the cushions and furniture around and so on—much to the discomfort of the young man who was her babysitter. One morning, however, there was a change in the pattern: when Lucy espied the Gardners escaping down the garden path, *instead* of acting out her scene, she signed: "Lucy-cry." Notably, this linguistic expression *replaced* the action: we have here a striking illustration of the effect of language in creating a distance from first-degree action. It is not difficult to imagine the transformation of the situation: instead of having to control his irritation at the scene, the babysitter was able to take Lucy in his arms and comfort her.

It seems legitimate to conclude, therefore, that chimpanzees (and probably the other great apes) have the capacity to acquire linguistic communication of a type qualitatively different from animal communication in general. There are, however, two qualifications to be made. The first is that in spite of deliberate trials in this direction, when returned to a situation of semicaptivity removed from human interference, chimpanzees do not seem motivated to develop or even maintain their linguistic skills in spontaneous communication among themselves.

The second qualification is that their linguistic communication is never far removed from what is actually going on in the present. They are not totally unable to understand "tomorrow" and "yesterday," but the very notion of a *fictional story* seems to be beyond their ken. They can well invent little fibs, but they do not really tell stories, and when it comes to "Once upon a time, there was a beautiful princess who lived in a tower on an island . . . " they are lost. In other words, their linguistic capacities seem to stop at the stage of *narration.* It is interesting to compare this with child development (Stern 1990). Newborn human infants do not speak; they reach a first stage of capability at around two years of age, and this seems to be (roughly) the stage achievable by chimpanzees: we may call this "Language_1." For human children, there is a second stage, which they achieve around four years of age, when the narrative register (both telling and understanding stories) reaches a threshold of maturity: we may call this "Language_2."

With these concepts and empirical references in place, we can turn (briefly) to a reconstruction of the origin and development of language in human pre-history. Having long been banned by the International Society of Linguistics, in recent years, a fruitful return has been made to the question, fueled both by the sort of evidence presented thus far but also, of course, by reconstruction on the basis of hominid fossils (Bickerton 1990). Interestingly, a major current in recent studies is to suggest that here, too, the processes occurred in two stages: a "Language_1" in early homo species as much as 2 Myr ago; "Language_2" considerably later, with homo sapiens sapiens around 150 Kyr (the pace of historical change accelerates, so that for human prehistory the time scale becomes thousands of years, or Kyr).

1.2.6 Tools and Technology

It is not particularly original—but not necessarily wrong because of that— to consider that hominization, and the difference between humans and other animals, resides in two features. We have just dealt with the first, that is, language; the second is the use and fabrication of tools. According to the general methodology I propose, I shall start with a theoretical discussion before going on to look at some of the historical evidence.

In figure 1.3, we see the basic scheme for considering tools; comparing with figure 1.1, we see that what tools do is increase the range of possible actions, and increase the range of possible sensory returns. Thus, human beings live in a world that they themselves have constructed—not just in

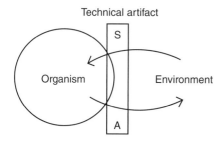

Figure 1.3
The basic scheme of figure 1.1 extended to include the mediation of sensorimotor coupling by technical artifacts.

the sense that they modify their environment (buildings, streets, towns, etc.), important though this is, but because to the extent that their sensorimotor coupling with the environment is mediated by tools, what the "world" *is* for human beings is largely constituted by these tools. This is, of course, more than ever true today.

In order to grasp the full import of the invention of tools, it is important to note that a tool (unlike a sensory or motor organ) exists in two distinct modes, that we can call "in-hand" and "put-down." When it is being used, a tool as such typically disappears from consciousness; attention is quite naturally focused on the particular sort of "world" that is brought about by the successful mediation of the tool.[13] This is the "in-hand" mode. But tools, typically, can also be detached from the body and "put down." It is in this second mode that they become themselves the focus of attention, and can be repaired, or made, or invented. The dual nature of tools comes from the fact that there is a constant back-and-forth between these two modes.

The first human tools for which there is solid evidence are the well-known flint tools.[14] There is a very nice sequence, running from the first "choppers," crudely made just by banging two pebbles against each other, through the increasingly sophisticated and finely-chiseled bi-face tools, to the exquisite polished arrowheads of the Neolithic period. Leroi-Gourhan (1964) proposed a quantitative measure, the length of useful cutting edge per kilogram of raw material (the brute flints were a relatively rare and precious resource). This measure, which we may denote by LCE/W, increased gradually and continuously over several million years, from the very first stone tools (ca. 3 Myr) until about 100 Kyr. The pace of historical change was thus very slow, in tune with the pace of anatomical change and in particular the increase in brain size. Leroi-Gourhan remarked that during all this time, "man secreted his tools almost as though they were nails or teeth." Thus, the inaugural event was not (as we fondly like to think) a sudden and dramatic increase in the size of the brain. After the shock of Darwin's suggestion that human beings had common ancestors with apes, the question arose as to the nature of the intermediate stages. The expectation was that the "missing link" would be a creature with a human head on an ape-like body.[15] As Leroi-Gourhan said, "We were ready for anything but this: mankind began by the feet." Thus Lucy, like other early Australopithecus fossil specimens, had a *small* head; what was distinctive were the legs and feet, adapted for standing upright with a biped means of locomotion. Not only is such locomotion remarkably efficient from a mechanical and energetic point of view; it also frees the hands, and creates an "anterior field" between head and hand, which is the prerequisite for making and using tools.

If there is a "break" between biological evolution and human prehistory, it comes *after* this period, which was largely continuous with biological evolution. Around 50 Kyr ago, there seems to have occurred an "event" that we can characterize by the superposition of several apparently unrelated indications. One of these, noted by Leroi-Gourhan, is a radical change in the *slope* of the curve of LCE/W against time: suddenly, the values were multiplied by tens and hundreds. Looking more closely at the tools themselves, the reason for this change becomes apparent: whereas before, the useful part of the tool was what was left behind by the chiseling process, now what was used were the *chips*. Now in order to produce useable chips, a long and elaborate process of preparing the flint is necessary, *before* the final blow knocks off the chip. From a cognitive point of view, this requires a strongly developed capacity for *anticipation*. From a technical point of view, this innovation was followed quite rapidly by a whole series—weaving, the use of fire and pottery, then agriculture and the creation of towns. From a symbolical point of view, this is also the period of the first cave art; symbolically, also, it is marked by the disappearance of Neanderthal man, the last surviving species of our numerous biological cousins. Can we find any explanation for this apparent "event"?

First, we may note that our own species, homo sapiens sapiens, arose in Africa around 150 Kyr. The "event" at 50 Kyr marks an acceleration in the rate of cultural evolution that relegates further biological evolution to relative insignificance. Guille-Escuret (1994) has put forward an intriguing hypothesis. By 50 Kyr, the making and using of tools was already established with its own history (and ethologists have claimed that all sorts of animals, not only apes but also crows and others, make and use tools); on the other hand, language was also developed, with its own history. But there is no evidence of any *connection* between language and tool-use. As modern stone-nappers have found, talking is neither necessary nor sufficient when one is trying to make a primitive bi-face. It is plausible to suppose that language was used first of all in the context of personal social relations; as is still true today, this leads to a runaway effect. As our social life becomes more complex, we need linguistic communication to cope with it, but ironically, one of the main effects of talking about our social life is . . . to make it even more complex! This sets the stage for Guille-Escuret's hypothesis: the "event" at 50 Kyr could have been the meeting of these two strains, of *using language to talk about technical artifacts* (making, using, and especially inventing them). Etymologically, this corresponds exactly to the birth of "techno-logos," that is, technology.

Just a reminder, to keep contact with the theme of cognition: on the view put forward here, all these events and processes *are* key stages in the historical genesis of cognition.

1.2.7 Consciousness

Here again I will start with some indispensable elements of theoretical definition, and then put the phenomenon in the context of its historical genesis. The word "conscious," as it is used in ordinary language, is remarkably polysemic; it is important to distinguish between different forms of consciousness, at the very least between what Edelman has called "Consciousness_1" and "Consciousness_2." Consciousness_1 corresponds to "animal consciousness," states of self-awareness and emotional feelings, the fact of having some sort of lived experience; it seems, to a first approximation, to have developed gradually over a long period—in the vertebrate lineage, from fishes to reptiles to mammals. "Consciousness_2" or "reflexive consciousness" is a much more sharply delineated phenomenon; it is specifically human, and inseparably related to language. Jaynes (1976) gives a most interesting definition: reflexive consciousness is "an analogue metaphrand based on visual perception of spatial relations." I cannot even begin to explain this theory properly; the idea, in a nutshell, is that consciousness is a process which occurs in an *imaginary* metaphorical "space."

With a theoretical definition in place, the major part of Jaynes's remarkable book is devoted to putting forth a highly imaginative scenario for the origin of consciousness. His main idea is that between animal consciousness and our current form of consciousness there is a "missing link" that he calls the "Bicameral mind"; "Consciousness_2" first arose in the form of visions and voices of gods—what today we would call hallucinations, but that at the time of the first great urban civilizations (Mesopotamian, Egyptian, Aztec, Incas) were not only normal but were absolutely necessary to social life.[16] Modern consciousness was born in suffering, at a time of crisis with the *breakdown* of the "bicameral mind." To support this astonishing hypothesis, Jaynes appeals very effectively to written texts—specifically, to the contrast between the *Iliad* and the *Odyssey* of Homer, and to the contrast between Old Testament prophets such as Amos, and the "modern" mentality of Ecclesiastes. These texts, in the form that we now have them, are of course later transcriptions of what was originally an oral tradition—the bards of what was to become the Homeric epic and the oral tradition of the Jews. Thus, the birth of modern consciousness can be given a quasi-historical date: around 5000 BC. The point I really want to insist on is not this or that fine detail of Jaynes imaginative (although deeply researched) account; it is, rather, the *principle* that consciousness results from process of historical genesis, and this process is open to scientific investigation.

1.2.8 Writing: The Domestication of the Savage Mind

If we look at cognition in general and human cognition in particular from a historical point of view, there is a feature of overriding importance that we cannot ignore. In one of its guises, it is known as the "Greek miracle": in the space of a few hundred years, the Greeks of antiquity invented philosophy, history, mathematics, logic, "modern" sculpture and dramatic art, democracy, a formal legal system, and . . . coined money. Many of these accomplishments lapsed during the "Dark Ages" and were revived only at the end of the Middle Ages in the historical movement explicitly known as the "Renaissance." The self-styled "modern" way of being human, which is still basically ours today, had its origin in ancient Greece. Goody (1977) quotes Lévi-Strauss and notes the following list of dichotomies that distinguish "domesticated" from "savage" forms of social life:

Domesticated	Savage
Modern	Neolithic
Science of the abstract	Science of the concrete
Scientific knowledge	Magical thought
Engineering	Tinkering
Abstract thought	Intuition/imagination/perception
Using concepts	Using signs
History	Atemporality; myths and rites

Goody's proposal is to examine to what extent these *cognitive* oppositions can be understood as deriving from the *technical* innovation of writing. Writing was invented not by the Greeks, but around 3000 BC in Mesopotamia. In its earliest form, in Uruk, it consisted of clay tablets that were attached to objects in order to identify their owners; later, the objects were represented by signs, which made it possible to detach the tablets from the objects. This system owes its origin to administrative and economic needs. The gains in productivity resulting from state-controlled systems of irrigation gave rise to an agricultural surplus. This surplus had to be stocked in warehouses in town, and redistributed; hence the need for a system of accounting. Two things are worthy of note here. First, writing was right from the start inseparable from a system of social relations themselves structured by technology: this system was both the reason for the invention of writing, and in return writing aided its development. Second (and quite contrary to what many contemporary linguists assume), writing is not a simple derivative transcription of spoken language; right from the start, writing is an integral part of cognitive operations that would be simply impossible on the sole basis of spoken language.

The earliest form of written language is thus the *list*—catalogs and inventories of persons, objects, and events. One can distinguish three types of list: retrospective, prospective, and lexical. Retrospective lists of events can be organized either by reference to episodes (chronicles) or by reference to the calendar (annals); together, they constitute the documentary archives that are indispensable for the emergence of "history" in the modern sense of Thucydides and Herodotus. Prospective lists are a key tool for an important form of cognition: programming and planning action. One of the important functions of reflexive consciousness is that it creates the possibility of imagining several possible future scenarios, and to choose one after envisaging their probable consequences; the practical development of programmed action is multiplied by use of the written list, as is illustrated by the contemporary examples of shopping lists and cookery recipes. In Mesopotamia and Egypt, there were annals of astronomical observations combined with the height of the rivers, which aided the development of irrigation—yet another example of the synergy between writing and technological development.

Lexical lists were initially less frequent than administrative lists, but later they became very important, notably in Sumer and in Egypt. This third type of list is particularly interesting, because it illustrates the endogenous dynamics set in motion by the development of writing. These lists typically appear in educational institutions, for teaching purposes; in other words, there is an effect of decontextualization with respect to immediate practical needs. It is to be noted that the simple fact of writing a list of words induces cognitive effects, in particular categorization.

How can the words in a list be grouped? The grouping can be thematic, related to the properties of the objects. Thus, in the temple school of Nippur, there are many such lists of trees (84), stones (12), gods (9), officials (8), farm animals (8), reeds (8), and so on. Landsberger (1937) considers that the large number of these lists results is a consequence of the nature of the Sumerian language, which has a transparent and nonambiguous structure particularly suitable for classifying the world. Goody (1977) suggests that the relation is at least as much the reverse: it is the practice of constituting lists that influenced the language by forcing it to become less ambiguous.

Alternatively, the grouping can be organized on the basis of the *form* (and not the semantic content) of the words themselves. This principle is clearly at work in the Mesopotamian and Egyptian lists. The first systems of writing were pictographic or hieroglyphic, but in this case, it is difficult to order the signs on the basis of their graphical form. In the archeological record, it is found that the signs were ordered according to the similarity of the *sound* (in particular, the initial sound). The key point is that this manner of ordering induces an evolution in the system of writing itself: from pictographic to syllabic, then consonantic, and finally alphabetical. In other words, alphabetic writing is not the simple result of phonetic transcription; it is the result of a systemic evolution internal to the process of writing itself. Thus the invention of alphabetic writing—generally attributed to the Greeks—is not a sudden "miracle" mysteriously fallen from the heavens; rather, it can be understood as the logical result of a process spanning thousands of years.

At the same time, without being miraculous, the invention of alphabetic writing had in turn some very important effects. Because it is, indeed, a phonetical coding, it brings spoken and written language much closer together; because of this, writing extends beyond the rather narrow and specific limits of its origins to cover virtually all the domains of language. This extension was helped by the relative simplicity of alphabetic writing. Pictographic, hieroglyphic, or ideographic systems contain thousands of different signs that must be memorized; because of this, the access to these systems is inevitably restricted to a small caste of scribes, whereas alphabetic writing can (in principle at least) be made accessible to all members of a society. Thus, it is with the advent of the alphabet that writing fully invests the *genres* of narration and sto-rytelling (fictional or otherwise), of poetry, of dialog and monologue (including the interior monologue/dialog that we call "thought"). Now however paradoxical it may seem, it is at the very moment when written language comes the closest to spoken language that the originality and the specificity of its contribution to cognition becomes most apparent. Without attempting to be exhaustive, I will examine this contribution in three domains of enormous cognitive import: history, philosophy and mathematics.

The contrast between "myth" and "history" is one of the major head-ings in the series of oppositions between "savage" and "domesticated" thought. Goody argues that this opposition is in large part due to the contribution of writing. We have already remarked that the accumulation of documentary archives—that are only possible because of writing, obvi-ously—is the basic condition that makes the work of an historian (in the modern sense of the word) possible. We have already noted that the nar-rative dimension is made possible in written form by the invention of the alphabet; it is then possible to juxtapose different versions of the "same" story, and to compare them in detail to identify on one hand the conver-gences and confirmations, and on the other the divergences and contradic-tions. In the heat of the moment, in the real time of the chanting of a ballad by a gifted orator, all sorts of collective emotional effects are pos-sible. By contrast, writing is structurally individual and private, both during reading and the writing itself; it is thus an instrument that induces a criti-cal distance, which dissipates collective emotion and promotes what is called "objectivity." It is not a question of *reducing* the difference between "myth" and "history" to one simple cause; it is not writing as such, con-sidered in isolation, that mechanically and inevitably produces all these effects. The causal relations are not linear, but circular and complex: the introduction of writing, limited in the first instance, produces certain results which are also limited, but these results have feedback effects on the practice of writing, and lead to its extension. At the culmination of this process, writing appears as an integral and essential part of a major cultural mutation.

These multiple cognitive effects of writing are not limited to the passage from "myth" to "history"; they also illuminate what has been called the "invention of philosophy." Goody notes that writing has the instrumental effect of *spatializing* language and, thus, of rendering linguistic statements visible. This change in modality produces a qualitative effect. When one observes a written inscription, one can look at it in all directions, for as long as one desires; this is not at all the case with a phonetic statement whose trace is intrinsically transitory. It is thus writing which gives the force of apodictic conviction to a syllogism: it is, indeed, the fact that one can continue a skeptical examination of each step in the argument for just as long one likes, and come back to the argument to reexamine it at will, which in the end overcomes all resistance and conveys a *free* adhesion to the argument. There is a strong affinity between Greek philosophy and mathematics: the motto "None enter here who are not geometers" is well known. It was by reflecting on the constitution of mathematical entities *as pure ideals* that Husserl recognized the essential role of writing. We may note that this role functions both at the individual level, but also at the collective, social level: the fact that alphabetic writing can be reliably and controllably copied independently of its interpretation, contributes decisively to the formation of a common conviction that is freely shared.

The heart of Greek philosophy resides in the nexus where questions of Truth and Idealities meet; it is from this base that ethical, moral and existential questions are addressed. In all these areas, the hallmark of alphabetic writing—its capacity to follow all the meanders of thought processes—is decisive. Western philosophy is *par excellence* an exercise in the clarification of thought, where the identification of ambiguities and contradictions is structurally essential. This style of thought is, quite literally, inconceivable without the contribution of writing.

This is a key point in the paradigm of enaction as a whole. The question that is posed here is whether material technologies, which are classically considered as empirical and therefore as only constituted, can reach back "upstream" of the transcendental conditions of possibility and thus attain the status of contributing to the very constitution of reality. Now it must be noted that writing is a material technology; the thesis presented here is that writing is indeed the condition of possibility for the constitution of mathematical and logical idealities. Derrida (1978) has built on the germ of this idea in the writings of Husserl, extending it to the much larger domain of what he calls "archi-écriture"; and Stiegler (1998), in turn, has extended this theme to technical artifacts that form a "tertiary retention," in other words, a form of memory that constitutes human society by providing that which is "always already there" for human beings.

I cannot end without remarking on the affinity between the emergence of reflexive consciousness in section 1.2.7, and the question of philosophy as evoked here. In the terms of Jaynes's theory, a metaphorical process of spatialization and visualization appears to be at the heart of the constitution of "reflexive consciousness." According to Goody, it is again a process of spatialization and visualization—this time materialized by the technique of alphabetic writing—which is at the heart of Western philosophy. The two processes—the one metaphorical, the other material and technical—are not strictly identical. Nevertheless, their affinity is evident; their complementarity, their convergence, and their synergy are such that their proximity in space and time (both occurred in ancient Greece, at an interval of several centuries) cannot be considered a simple coincidence.

1.3 Concluding Remarks

To conclude, it is important to note that cognitive science is a reflexive enterprise: doing cognitive science is itself a cognitive activity, and so cognitive science applies to itself. It is not the least of the merits of the paradigm of enaction that this reflexive dimension falls very neatly into place.

First, there is the question of epistemology (the processes by which knowledge comes about) and its relation to ontology (the nature of that which exists in order to *be* known). An epistemology always presupposes an ontology, but this is often masked by the fact that an "objectivist" ontology—according to which that which exists (and can therefore be an object of knowledge) preexists quite independently of the process of knowing—is implicitly presupposed as being so obvious that it would be non-sensical to question it. Thus in spite of their energetic disagreements, the majority of epistemological positions—empiricism, idealism, nominalism, hypothetico-deduction, relativism, and so on—actually share a commitment to objectivism.

It should be clear, but I state it here explicitly, that the paradigm of enaction is ontologically nonobjectivist—or to put it more positively, radically constructivist. "The world," as it can be diversely known by living organisms from bacteria to contemporary humans, is actually brought about, "enacted," by the cognitive organism itself. This is an unusual point of view, and it may be considered exciting, or depressing and even a source of *Angst*, depending on one's mood. But the fact of the matter is this: what the knowable world is, for each of us, is *not* independent of who we are, and how we go about our daily business of living. This is not meant to be an "individualistic" credo, on the contrary; as humans we are profoundly social beings, and therefore the world that exists for us is highly dependent on our forms of social existence.

If sections 1.2.1–1.2.8 had been prolonged one step further, we would have come full cycle and included ourselves as a part of the scheme. In other words, this text can be understood as a narration; the fact that it is written down means that we can look at it critically—whatever resists will be something significant we have in common. I would just like to leave you with this reminder: when we adopt a paradigm in cognitive science, we enact a shared world—and enact ourselves into the bargain.

Notes

1. Needless to say, there remains a host of unsolved problems; I will give here just an indicative sample. There is the problem of a proper mathematical formulation of the theory of autopoiesis, and its relation to the concept of "closure under efficient cause" proposed by Rosen (1991); there is the problem of the origin of life, and there is the problem of the origin of a genetic system (*all* contemporary living organisms possess a DNA-protein system, but such a system cannot possibly have arisen spontaneously from scratch).

2. After all, computers are not conscious! And consciousness is arguably indeed the "highest" level of cognition.

3. Namely, the genesis of the *objects* of the disciplines, rather than the much more recent historical development of the disciplines themselves—although this latter possibility becomes relevant when we address the questions of the intrinsic reflexivity of cognitive science. See section 1.3.

4. Gyr = one gigayear, or a thousand million years. This is the natural time scale for cosmological events; note that the "Big Bang" itself occurred "only" 13.7 Gyr ago.

5. A megayear (Myr) is one million years. This is the "natural" time scale for biological evolution.

6. The process must have taken the order of one or several Myr (see previous note), but in terms of fossils, the space of time was so short that it there is no trace in the geological record of intermediate stages: in one strata of rocks, there is nothing (i.e., only microscopic protozoa); in the next, the whole range of the Cambrian fauna.

7. This remark is less trivial than it appears. Medawar (1957) has argued that "senescence" only occurs in animals kept in protected captivity, but practically never in the wild. In his view, nothing is less natural than so-called "natural death from old age"; indeed, it is because of this that the process of senescence exists, rather than being eliminated by natural selection.

8. As a human engineer is just itching to do, confronted for example by the mechanical disaster of the human vertebral column in a vertical gravitational field.

9. An example: a certain species of wasp builds an L-shaped nest. An experimenter cuts a small hole at the bend of the L. If the wasp had the least idea of the overall situation, nothing would be easier than to mend the hole. But no: the new situation triggers a sequence of action-perception loops, with the result that the wasp builds *another* L on top of the old one, starting from the hole.

10. It is usual to call such reactions "instinctive" or "innate," but I prefer to avoid this term, with its connotations of the disastrous "nature versus nurture" debate.

11. A delightful anecdote: at an international conference (including both hearing and nonhearing participants), a speaker said something like: "Sign language cannot be a true language, because it is irredeemably iconic; therefore, it cannot express metaphoric meanings and even less abstract ideas." The joke is that the interpreter, who was translating in real time, had little difficulty in expressing this pretty abstract idea in sign language, and could not help raising her eyebrows at the end. The deaf participants were rolling in the aisles.

12. In the polemical atmosphere, they were heavily criticized for this. Their retort was that if a *human* infant were raised in accordance with the "double-blind" methodologies that are the standard in a certain sort of experimental psychology, this would be a pretty good recipe for producing an autistic child.

13. One of my favorite examples is that of skis: a snow-covered mountain *becomes* an entirely different place if you have skis on your feet (and if you know how to ski!).

14. It is overwhelmingly likely that there is a methodological bias here: the flint tools lasted until archeologists found them, whereas tools made of bone, wood, and other less durable materials crumbled away.

15. It was because it pandered to this expectation that the "Piltdown man" was not immediately exposed as a hoax.

16. Today the situation has changed and they are socially unacceptable, so that those who hear or see such visions are put in mental asylums, or treated with psychoactive drugs to make the symptoms disappear.

References

Bickerton, D. (1990). *Language and species*. Chicago: University of Chicago Press.

Bonabeau, E., Dorigo, M., and Theraulaz, G. (1999). *Swarm intelligence: From natural to artificial systems*. Oxford: Oxford University Press.

Bourgine, P., and Stewart, J. (2004). Autopoiesis and cognition. *Artificial Life* 10:327–345.

Derrida, J. (1978). *Edmund Husserl's origin of geometry*. Stony Brook, NY: Nicolas Hays.

Eldredge, N., and Gould, S. J. (1972). Punctuated equilibria: An alternative to phyletic gradualism. In *Models in paleobiology*, ed. T. J. M. Schopf, 82–115. San Francisco: Freeman Cooper.

Garfinkel, H. (1967). *Studies in ethnomethodology*. Englewood Cliffs, NJ: Prentice-Hall.

Goldschmidt, R. (1940). *The material basis of evolution*. New Haven: Yale University Press.

Goody, J. R. (1977). *The domestication of the savage mind*. Cambridge: Cambridge University Press.

Gould, S. J. (1989). *Wonderful life: The Burgess Shale and the nature of history*. New York: W. W. Norton.

Guille-Escuret, G. (1994). *Le décalage humain. Le fait social dans l'évolution*. Paris: Kimé.

Jaynes, J. (1976). *The origin of consciousness in the breakdown of the bicameral mind*. Boston: Houghton Mifflin.

Jonas, H. (1963). *The phenomenon of life: Toward a philosophical biology*. New York: Harper and Row.

Landsberger, B. (1937). *Materialen zum sumerischen Lexikon*. Rome: Sumptibus Pontificii Instituti Biblici.

Leroi-Gourhan, A. (1964). *Le geste et la parole. I. Technique et langage. II. La mémoire et les rythmes*. Paris: Albin Michel.

Maturana, H. (1987). Everything is said by an observer. In *Gaia: A way of knowing. Political implications of the new biology*, ed. W. I. Thompson, 65–82. New York: Lindisfarne Press.

Maturana, H., and Varela, F. J. (1980). *Autopoiesis and cognition: The realization of the living*. Boston: Reidel.

Medawar, P. B. (1957). *The uniqueness of the individual*. London: Methuen.

O'Regan, J. K., and Noë, A. (2001). A sensorimotor account of vision and visual consciousness. *Behavioral and Brain Sciences* 24 (5): 939–1031.

Oyama, S. (1985). *The ontogeny of information: Developmental systems and evolution*. Cambridge: Cambridge University Press.

Rosen, R. (1991). *Life itself: A comprehensive enquiry into the nature, origin and fabrication of life*. New York: Columbia University Press.

Simondon, G. (1989). *L'individuation psychique et collective*. Paris: Aubier.

Spemann, H. (1938). *Embryonic development and induction*. New Haven: Yale University Press.

Stern, D. N. (1990). *Diary of a baby*. New York: Basic Books.

Stewart, J. (2004). *La vie existe-t-elle? Réconcilier la génétique et la biologie*. Paris: Vuibert.

Stiegler, B. (1998). *Technics and time, 1: The fault of Epimetheus*. Stanford: Stanford University Press.

Stoffregen, T., and Bardy, B. G. (2001). On specification and the senses. *Behavioral and Brain Sciences* 24:195–261.

Thelen, E., and Smith, L. B. (1994). *A dynamic systems approach to the development of cognition and action*. Cambridge, MA: MIT Press.

Thom, R. (1972). *Stabilité structurelle et morphogénèse. Essai d'une théorie génétique des modèles*. Paris: *Ediscience*.

Thompson, D. W. (1917). *On growth and form*. Cambridge: Cambridge University Press. Republished 1942, 1961.

van Gelder, T. J. (1998). The dynamical hypothesis in cognitive science. *Behavioral and Brain Sciences* 21:1–14.

Varela, F. J. (1979). *Principles of biological autonomy*. New York: Elsevier North Holland.

Varela, F. (1996). Neurophenomenology: A methodological remedy to the hard problem. *Journal of Consciousness Studies* 3:330–350.

Varela, F., Thompson, E., and Rosch, E. (1991). *The embodied mind*. Cambridge, MA: MIT Press.

von Uexküll, J. (1909). *Umwelt und Innenwelt der Tiere*. Berlin: J. Springer.

von Uexküll, J. (1966). *Mondes animaux et monde humain*. Paris: Gonthier.

Vygotsky, L. S. (1962). *Thought and language*. Trans. E. Hanfmann and G. Vakar. Cambridge, MA: MIT Press.

Waddington, C. H. (1956). *Principles of embryology*. London: George Allen & Unwin.

Waddington, C. H. (1957). *The strategy of the genes*. London: George Allen & Unwin.

Whitehead, A. N. (1926). *Science and the modern world*. Cambridge: Cambridge University Press.

2 Horizons for the Enactive Mind: Values, Social Interaction, and Play

Ezequiel A. Di Paolo, Marieke Rohde, and Hanne De Jaegher

2.1 Introduction

Almost two decades since the publication of *The Embodied Mind* (Varela, Thompson, and Rosch 1991), the term *enactive* has moved out of relative obscurity to become a fashionable banner in many regions of cognitive science. It has found its way into diverse areas, from education and human-computer interaction, to autonomous robotics and consciousness studies. On the surface, this acceptance indicates the success of the ideas articulated by Varela and his colleagues, and their view of the mind with its emphasis on the role of embodied experience, autonomy and the relation of co-determination between cognitive agents and their world. Theirs was not only an achieved synthesis of existing criticisms to a predominantly computationalist paradigm, but also the articulation of a set of postulates to move these ideas forward. Indeed, the increasing use of enactive terminology serves as an indication that the time is ripe for a new era in cognitive science. To a great extent, we believe this to be so.

However, on closer inspection, a significant variety of meaning is revealed in the use of the word "enactive" (as happens with closely associated terms such as *autonomous, embodied, situated,* and *dynamical*). The label sometimes indicates only the partial adoption of enactive views, vaguely connected to the ideas in *The Embodied Mind*. In the worst cases, we see the raising of implausible hybrids risking self-contradiction in their mixture of the new and the old. There seems to be a lack of consensus about what constitutes enactivism or embodied cognitive science in general (Wilson 2002). Enactive has often been taken simply as synonymous of active, embodied as synonymous of physical, dynamical as synonymous of changing, and situated as synonymous of exchanging information with the environment, all properties that could be claimed by practically every robot, cognitive model or theory proposed since symbolic artificial intelligence (AI) first made its debut as the theoretical core of cognitive science about fifty years ago. This situation can lead to confusion and eventually to the loss of meaning attached to these terms— indeed, a perceived ambiguity between revolution and reform was already noticed by early commentators (Dennett, 1993).

We find at least two reasons for this situation, both indicating pressing problems that must be addressed if enactive cognitive science is to get off the ground. The first one is a watering down of the original ideas of enactivism by their partial adoption or sublimation into other frameworks. The second, related reason is a genuine lack of enactive proposals to advance open questions in cognitive science that motivate more traditional frameworks, such as the problems of higher-level cognition. These reasons lead to the misappropriation of the previously mentioned keywords through the acceptance of the lessons of enactivism, but only for a restricted range of influence. In the opinion of many, the usefulness of enactive ideas is confined to the "lower levels" of human cognition. This is the "reform-not-revolution" interpretation. For instance, embodied and situated engagement with the environment may be sufficient to describe insect navigation, but it will not tell us how we can plan a trip from Brighton to La Rochelle. Or enactive-like ideas could well account for complex skills such as mastering sensorimotor contingencies in visual perception (O'Regan and Noë 2001), or becoming an expert car driver (Dreyfus 2002), but— important though these skills are—they remain cognitively marginal (Clark and Toribio 1994) and fall short of explaining performances such as preparing for a mathematics final or designing a house. For some researchers, enactive ideas are useful but confined to the understanding of sensorimotor engagements. As soon as anything more complex is needed, we must somehow recover newly clothed versions of representationalism and computationalism (Clark and Toribio 1994; Clark 1997; Clark and Grush 1999; Grush 2004).

We would do wrong in ignoring such positions. They are good indicators of what is at the core of the struggle between traditional and unorthodox temperaments in cognitive science today. Indeed, the current situation serves as a reminder of the dangerous fate that fresh and radical ideas may suffer: that of dilution into a background essentially indistinguishable from that which they initially intended to reject. We believe that it is mistaken to conclude that what enactivism cannot yet account for must necessarily be explained using an updated version of old ideas with a debatable success record. But it will remain tempting to do so *as long as the principal tenets and implications of enactivism remain insufficiently clear.* It would also be wrong to ignore arguments that show the limitations of enactivism. These challenges reveal how much is left to be done. *Enactivism is a framework that must be coherently developed and extended.*

For this reason, in trying to answer the question "What is enactivism?" it is important not to straightjacket concepts that may still be partly in development. Some gaps may not yet be satisfactorily closed; some contradictions may or may not be only apparent. We should resist the temptation to decree solutions to these problems simply because we are dealing with definitional matters. The usefulness of a research program also lies with its capability to grow and improve itself. It can do so only if problems and contradictions are brought to the center and we let them do their work. For this, it is important to be engendering rather than conclusive, to indicate horizons rather than boundaries.

There are still many important areas in enactive cognitive science that demand serious development. These remain the stronghold of traditional conceptions. Most of the underdeveloped areas within the enactive approach involve higher levels of cognitive performance: thinking, imagining, interpreting the behavior of others, and so on. For as long as enactive ideas are taken as filling in details or as playing a contextual role in the explanation of such phenomena, the situation will not change.

We dedicate this chapter to clarifying the central tenets of enactivism and exploring some of the themes currently under development. In this exercise, following the logic of the central ideas of enactivism can sometimes lead to unexpected hypotheses and implications. We must not underestimate the value of a new framework in allowing us to *formulate questions in a different vocabulary*, even if satisfactory answers are not yet forthcoming. Implicitly, the exploration of these questions and possible answers is at the same time a demonstration of the variety of methods available to enactivism, from phenomenology, to theory/experiment cycles, and to the synthesis of minimal models and validation by construction—an additional thread that runs through this chapter and that we will pick up again in the discussion.

In particular, after introducing the five core ideas of enactivism, we focus on value generation and question the coherence of the idea of a *value system* in cognitive architectures (both computationalist and embodied) and similar modular structures whose function is to generate or judge the *meaning* of a situation. This question allows us to highlight right from the start one of the main differences between enactive and traditional views: a grounding of notions such as values and meaning. Many influential theories in cognitive science make use of the idea that value or meaning is some information appraised by an internal module within an agent's cognitive architecture, whereas in an enactive perspective, meaning is inseparable from the whole of context-dependent, life-motivated, embodied activity, without being at all a hazy concept beyond the reach of scientific understanding. We also explore, continuing on the issue of the origins of meaning, the field of social cognition, the focus of many recent phenomenologically inspired criticisms (Thompson 2001; Gallagher 2001, 2005). Our exploration leads us toward a middle way between individualistic and holistic views of social interaction and to highlighting the central role played by the temporality of social engagements in generating and transforming social understanding at different time scales through joint participation. In the final part, we take a speculative look at the embodied capability to manipulate the meaning of concrete situations by exploring the role of play in the development of human cognition. These explorations do not attempt to be complete, nor do they put the whole of human cognition within the reach of enactivism and forever banish representational/computational explanations. But they do extend the conceptual horizon and allow us to formulate the problem of higher cognitive performance in an alternative, enactive way.

2.2   The Core of Enactivism

It would be misleading to think of the enactive approach as a set of all radically novel ideas. It is much rather a synthesis of some new but also several old themes that mutually support each other. Overall, enactivism may be construed as a kind of nonreductive, nonfunctionalist naturalism. It sees the properties of life and mind as forming part of a continuum and consequently advocates a scientific program that explores several phases along this dimension.

Among the predecessors to enactivism we find, for example, Piaget's theory of cognitive development through sensorimotor equilibration (Piaget 1936, 1967), Poincaré's theory of the active role of movement in the construction of spatial perception (Poincaré 1907), Goldstein's theory of the self-actualizing organism (Goldstein [1934] 1995), and others. The very term "enactive" has been similarly used before, for example by Bruner in the 1960s, to describe knowledge that is acquired and manifested through action (Bruner 1966). Equally, we find philosophical affinities with existential phenomenology (Heidegger 1962; Merleau-Ponty 1962), with Eastern mindfulness traditions, with Hans Jonas's biophilosophy (Jonas 1966), and with pragmatic thinkers such as Dewey (1929). Current compatibilities can be also found with many embodied and dynamical systems ideas in contemporary cognitive science (Beer 2000; Chiel and Beer 1997; Thelen and Smith 1994; Hutchins 1995a; Juarrero 1999; Kelso 1995), neuroscience (Bach-y-Rita et al. 1969; Damasio 1994; Skarda and Freeman 1987; Engel, Fries, and Singer 2001), evolutionary biology (Lewontin 1983; Oyama 2000), and AI/robotics (Beer 2003; Brooks 1991; Harvey et al. 1997; Nolfi and Floreano 2000; Winograd and Flores 1986). Some of these connections are made explicit in *The Embodied Mind*, others have been elaborated later in the literature, and still others remain to be better established.

What is the core of the enactive approach? Views that take cognition as embodied and situated, or take experience seriously, or explore the purchase of dynamical systems ideas, will all share something with enactivism. But to call them enactive just because there is some conceptual overlap may only contribute to a meaningless proliferation of the term. This is unless we can show both that (1) such views share or are developed from a basic core of enactive ideas, and (2) extensions to these ideas do not result in irresolvable contradictions with this basic core. We can identify five highly intertwined ideas that constitute the basic enactive approach (Varela, Thompson, and Rosch 1991; Thompson 2005): *autonomy, sensemaking, emergence, embodiment,* and *experience.* Partially implying each other, these ideas sit on the blind spots of traditional views. We will not attempt to disentangle all of their connections in order to obtain a set of perfectly independent postulates. Indeed, the internal relations between these concepts speak for the strength of their association under a single banner.

2.2.1 Autonomy

Living organisms are autonomous—they follow laws set up by their own activity. Fundamentally, they can be autonomous only by virtue of their self-generated identity as distinct entities. A system whose identity is fully specified by a designer and cannot, by means of its own actions, regenerate its own constitution, can only follow the laws contained in its design, no matter how plastic, adaptive, or lifelike its performance. In order for a system to generate its own laws, it must be able to build itself *at some level of identity.* If a system "has no say" in defining its own organization, then it is condemned to follow an externally given design like a railroad track. As such, it may be endowed with ways of changing its behavior depending on history, but at some level it will encounter an externally imposed functional (as opposed to physical) limitation to the extent to which it can change itself. This can be avoided only if the system's limitations result partly from its own processes.

The autonomy (or freedom) of a self-constituted system is by no means unconstrained (being able to influence one's own limitations does not imply being able to fully remove them; on the contrary, it means being able to set up new ways of constraining one's own actions). Hans Jonas (1966) speaks of life as sustaining a relation of *needful freedom* with respect to its environment. Matter and energy are needed to fuel metabolism. In turn, by its constant material turnover, metabolism sustains its form (its identity) by dynamically disassociating itself from specific material configurations.

It should be clear that by expressions like "self-constitution" and "generating its own laws" no mysterious vitalism is intended. However, the acceptance of an operational concept of emergence (discussed shortly) is implied. By saying that a system is self-constituted, we mean that its dynamics generate and sustain an identity. An *identity* is generated whenever a precarious network of dynamical processes becomes operationally closed. A system is operationally closed if, for any given process P that forms part of the system (1) we can find among its enabling conditions other processes that make up the system, and (2) we can find other processes in the system that depend on P. This means that at some level of description, the conditions that sustain any given process in such a network always include those conditions provided by the operation of the other processes in the network, and that the result of their global activity is an identifiable unity in the same domain or level of description (it does not, of course, mean that the system is isolated from interactions with the environment). Autonomy as operational closure is intended to describe self-generated identities at many possible levels (Varela 1979, 1997; Di Paolo 2009).

Cognitive systems are also autonomous in an interactive sense in terms of their engagement with their environment as agents and not simply as systems coupled to other systems (Moreno and Etxeberria 2005; Di Paolo 2005). As such, they not only respond to external perturbations in the traditional sense of producing the appropriate action for a given situation, they do in fact actively and asymmetrically *regulate* the conditions of their exchange with the environment, and in doing so, enact a world or cognitive domain.

To view cognitive systems as autonomous is therefore to reject the traditional poles of seeing mind as responding to environmental stimuli on the one hand, or as satisfying internal demands on the other—both of which subordinate the agent to a role of obedience to external or internal factors. It is also to recognize the "ongoingness" of sensorimotor couplings that lead to patterns of perception and action twinned to the point that the distinction is often dissolved. Autonomous agency goes even further than the recognition of ongoing sensorimotor couplings as dynamical and emphasizes the role of the agent in constructing, organizing, maintaining, and regulating those closed sensorimotor loops. In doing so, the cognitive agent plays a role in determining the norms that it will follow, the "game" that is being played.

2.2.2 Sense-Making

Already implied in the notion of interactive autonomy is the realization that organisms cast a web of significance on their world. Regulation of structural coupling with the environment entails a direction that this process is aiming toward: that of the continuity of the self-generated identity or identities that initiate the regulation. This establishes a *perspective on the world* with its own normativity, which is the counterpart of the agent being a center of *activity in the world* (Varela 1997; Weber and Varela 2002; Di Paolo 2005; Thompson 2007). Exchanges with the world are thus inherently significant for the agent, and this is the definitional property of a cognitive system: the creation and appreciation of meaning or *sense-making*, in short.

It will be important to notice already— this issue is treated more extensively in the following section—that sense-making is an inherently active idea. Organisms do not passively receive information from their environments, which they then translate into internal representations. Natural cognitive systems are simply not in the business of accessing their world in order to build accurate pictures of it. They participate in the generation of meaning through their bodies and action often engaging in transformational and not merely informational interactions; *they enact a world.* Enactivism thus differs from other nonrepresentational views such as Gibsonian ecological psychology on this point (Varela, Thompson, and Rosch 1991, 203–204). For the enactivist, sense is not an invariant present in the environment that must be retrieved by direct (or indirect) means. Invariants are instead the outcome of the dialog between the active principle of organisms in action and the dynamics of the environment. The "finding" of meaning must be enacted in a concrete and specific reduction of the dimensions that the organism-environment system affords along the axis of relevance for autonomy; it is always an activity with a *formative* trace, never merely about the innocent extraction of information as if this was already present to a fully realized (and thus inert) agent. This is another idea that sets the enactive framework apart from more traditional views in cognitive science: a dynamical, biologically grounded, theory of sense-making. Like few notions in the past, this concept strikes at the heart of what is to be cognitive. We will elaborate this point in the next section and show how elusive this way of thinking can be even among researchers who have taken embodiment and situatedness very seriously.

2.2.3   Emergence

The overarching question in cognitive science is: How does it work? For the enactive approach, the connected concepts of autonomy and sense-making already invoke some notion of emergence in addressing this question. Autonomy is not a property of a collection of components, but the consequence of a new identity that arises out of dynamical processes in precarious operational closure. Meaning is not to be found in elements belonging to the environment or in the internal dynamics of the agent, but belongs to the relational domain established between the two.

The idea of emergence has been much debated in various domains from metaphysics to epistemology and has had a furious revival over the last three decades with the advent of the sciences of complexity. Beyond the debates about the possibility of ontological emergence (Kim 1999; Silberstein and McGeever 1999), there is a pragmatic application of the term that stems from the well-understood phenomenon of self-organization. This has served to remove the air of mystery around emergence in order to bring it back in line with a naturalistic project. There is also a demand for emergentist explanations in biology, in which hierarchical organization is all too evident (e.g., genetic regulation, cells, extracellular matrices, tissues, organs, organism, dyads, groups, institutions, societies).

Emergence is used to describe the formation of a novel property or process out of the interaction of different existing processes or events (Thompson 2007; Thompson and Varela 2001). In order to distinguish an emergent process from simply an aggregate of dynamical elements, two things must hold (1) the emergent process must have its own autonomous identity, and (2) the sustaining of this identity and the interaction between the emergent process and its context must lead to constraints and modulation to the operation of the underlying levels.[1] The first property indicates the identifiability of the emergent process whose characteristics are enabled but not fully determined by the properties of the component processes. The second property refers to the mutual constraining between emerging and enabling levels (sometimes described as circular or downward causation).

We find the clearest example of emergence in life itself. The property of continuous self-production, renewal, and regeneration of a physically bounded network of molecular transformations (autopoiesis) is not to be found at any level below that of the living cell itself. Being a self-sustaining bounded network of chemical transformations is not (it cannot be) the property or the responsibility of single components in this network. The new level is not only autonomous in terms of exhibiting its own identity and laws of transformation; it also introduces, through interaction with its codefined context, modulations to the boundary conditions of the lower-level processes that give rise to it.

This phenomenon repeats itself at various levels in multicellular organisms and in particular animals and humans. Variations on this theme have been used to describe the emergence of the self/nonself distinction in immune networks (Stewart and Coutinho 2004); the generation, maintenance, and eventual dissolution of coherent modes of synchronous activity in the brain (Engel, Fries, and Singer 2001; Thompson and Varela 2001); and also between these coherent modes and action/perception cycles (Rodriguez et al. 2001; Le Van Quyen and Petitmengin 2002). Emergent phenomena, as indicated in the previous examples, can be fleeting. Single acts can bear a relation of emergence with respect to their sensorimotor component phases.

Taking emergence seriously makes the enactive approach very skeptical about the localization of function corresponding to one level in specific components at a lower level (homuncularity) and consequently leads to the rejection of "boxology" as a valid method to address the "how does it work" question. Any labeling of subsystemic components and variables with names belonging naturally to properties of emergent levels (e.g., value systems, cognitive maps, emotional modules, mirror neurons) should be treated with extreme caution.

Having said all this, emergence remains problematic, due often to its opaqueness and the ease with which the term can be misused. The weight of explaining how a given phenomenon constitutes a proper case of emergence remains with the supporters of this view. The very blurring of distinctions between levels that the enactive approach criticizes of cognitivism has allowed the latter paradigm to connect personal and subpersonal levels with indiscriminate ease. The properties of higher levels are thus explained in terms of lower-level ones, because they are already magically present there. For the emergentist, instead, the connection and the interaction between levels becomes a problem to be addressed case by case, often by recourse to complex concepts and tools derived from dynamical systems theory. It is clear that much work is still needed for clarifying and operationalizing the concept of emergence. In this context, synthetic models can prove very valuable as tools for grasping emergent phenomena.

2.2.4 Embodiment

In a concrete and practical sense, a cognitive system is embodied to the extent to which its activity depends nontrivially on the body. However, the widespread use of the term has led in some cases to the loss of the original contrast with computationalism and even to the serious consideration of trivial senses of embodiment as mere physical presence—in this view, a word processor running on a computer would be embodied, (cf. Chrisley 2003). It is easy to miss a fundamental motivation behind embodiment. Nontrivial dependence on the body can easily be construed in functionalist term, and this falls short of the more radical implications of enactivism. It is not only a question of moving the mind from a highly sheltered realm of computational modules in the head into messy bodily structures. So-called embodied approaches that do not move beyond this first step remain largely functionalist and see the body as yet another information processing device; a convenient way to offload computations that would be too hard to handle by the neural tissue (Clark 1997). This is a Cartesian view of embodiment in its separation between mind as function on the one hand and body as implementation on the other. A similar adopted view is that of the mind as controller and the body as controlled. Despite their tension, these views often go together. By contrast, for the enactivist the body is the ultimate source of significance; embodiment means that mind is inherent in the precarious, active, normative, and worldful process of animation, that the body is not a puppet controlled by the brain but a whole animate system with many autonomous layers of self-constitution, self-coordination, and self-organization and varying degrees of openness to the world that create its sense-making activity.

Indeed, to say that cognition is embodied is to express a tautology—it simply cannot *but* be embodied if we understand the core of cognition as sense-making. The latter goes hand in hand with the conservation of emergent identities (autonomy) ultimately constituted by material processes in precarious conditions (i.e., unable to sustain a 'function' independently of each other or indefinitely). In other words, mind is possible because a body is always a decaying body (a fact that cannot be captured in functionalist terms).

For enactivism, therefore, cognition is embodied in a fundamental, non-functionalist sense although it may still nurture itself by the fascinating examples of how bodily structures and dynamics may be cleverly exploited to resolved complex problems both in human performance (Lenay 2003) and in robots (Pfeifer and Scheier 1999; Salomon 1998). The relevance of the body is not restricted to concrete sensorimotor activities. There is much evidence that higher-level cognitive skills, such as reasoning and problem solving, mental image manipulation, and language use depend crucially on bodily structures (Wilson 2002; Lakoff 1987).

There are enactive accounts of the potential layering of several identities into a more or less integrated body-in-interaction (Varela 1997; Di Paolo 2005, 2009). These can serve to make sense of a further twist to the role played by the body in the case of human cognition—one that could explain the resilience of Cartesian modes of thinking. Even though our bodies are not puppets, to say that we control our bodies is, in a sense, not entirely wrong. We certainly do. But we do so in subtle ways that relate to the emergence of forms of reflexive autonomy, this time of a sociolinguistic nature. Like an alien presence, I set new aims for my body (I decide to embrace the pain of a yoga class, I decide to go on a diet). Being able to support and transform new identities is one way in which the body creates the experience of a self not quite the same as (and sometimes at odds with) the metabolic self. Taken in isolation, this is an experience that nurtures Cartesianism. In fact, the body, by further manipulating its sense-making activity, is capable of putting itself in a novel situation that is partly its own creation. In doing so, it is playing a highly skillful dual role. This is afforded by the plasticity of the human body, but it would not be possible without immersion within a symbolic order and the social mediation that makes our bodies fit to a scheme of control and observation of behavioral and cultural norms thus giving rise to sociolinguistic and narrative selves.

2.2.5 Experience

For enactivism, experience is central both methodologically and thematically. Far from being an epiphenomenon or a puzzle as it is for cognitivism, experience in the enactive approach is intertwined with being alive and immersed in a world of significance. As part of the enactive method, experience goes beyond being data to be explained. It becomes a guiding force in a dialog between phenomenology and science, resulting in an ongoing pragmatic circulation and mutual illumination between the two (Gallagher 1997; van Gelder 1999; Varela 1996, 1999).

Many modern accounts of cognitive activity already take experience seriously. For instance, Dreyfus's defense of nonrepresentational skill acquisition (2002) is based on paying careful attention to the experience of undergoing a process of task improvement. As we make the journey from beginners to experts through practice, not only is skillful performance improved, but experience is also transformed. This is to be expected if embodiment in the enactive sense is taken seriously. If experience and the body-in-interaction were to relate to each other as two mutually external systems, we would expect either an unchangeable or a fleeting relation between our bodies and our experience. Instead we find a lawful relation of bodily and experience transformations. Becoming a wine connoisseur is certainly an achievable goal but expertise in this field (as in any other) is not obtained through gaining the right kind of *information* but through the right kind of *transformation*—one that can only be brought about by appropriate time-extended training (experimenting, making mistakes, and so on). Experience is altered in a lawful manner through the process. It is itself a skillful aspect of embodied activity.

An embodied perspective results in serious attention being paid to iso-morphisms between mechanisms and experience. Varela (1999) and van Gelder (1999) provide different, but related, dynamical systems accounts of mechanisms that might underlie the protentive and retentive structure of time consciousness as described by Husserl. Kelly (2000) considers neural models of pointing and grasping that run parallel to Merleau-Ponty's con-cepts of the intentional arc and maximal grip. Wheeler (2005) explores isomorphic relationships between embodied/embedded accounts of situ-ated action and Heideggerian categories such as the ready-to-hand, break-downs, and present-at-hand. What is interesting in many of these accounts is that the process of circulation is not one of assimilating scientific hypoth-eses into phenomenology, but may itself inform phenomenology. This is as it should be in a proper dialog, and such is the methodology advocated by first-person methods in the joint study of experience and brain-body activity (Varela 1996; Lutz 2002).

Experience may also serve the role of clarifying our commitments. Hans Jonas (1966) looks into the world of living beings and sees that life is a process with interiority. Metabolism has all the existential credentials of concernful being. It is precarious, it separates itself from nonbeing, it struggles to keep itself going and preserve its identity, and it relates to the world in value-laden terms. However, the inward aspect of life cannot be demonstrated using our current scientific tools. This does not make it any less factual for Jonas. He knows that all life is connected along evolutionary chains, and he knows that we ourselves are embodied living creatures with an inner life. This is how we can then know that living beings are forms of existence and that they also have an inner life.

This example is telling, because it already contains a difficult-to-swallow consequence of the dialog between science and experience, which is, at the same time, perhaps its most revolutionary implication. Phenomenologically informed science goes beyond black marks on paper or experimental procedures for measuring data, and dives straight into the realm of personal experience. No amount of rational argument will convince a reader of Jonas's claim that, as an embodied organism, he is concerned with his own existence if the reader cannot see this for himself. Jonas appeals to the performance of a gesture that goes beyond comprehending a scientific text. The implication is that in order to work as a source of knowledge, enactivism will contain an element of personal practice. It is necessary to come back to the phenomenology and confirm that our theories make sense, but this means that sometimes we must become skillful in our phenomenology as well—personally so.

2.3 Values and the Limits of Evolutionary Explanations

The previous section shows that there are certain ideas in cognitive science that the enactive approach clearly rejects, such as homuncularity, boxology, separability between action and perception, and representationalism. In this section, we will revisit some of these themes in a more focused manner.

In everyday life, we experience the world in value-laden terms. This fact is hard to avoid and has been the subject of much philosophical debate. For enactivism, value is simply an aspect of all sense-making, as sense-making is, at its root, the evaluation of the consequences of interaction for the conservation of an identity. Perhaps as a reaction to the subjective overtones of this issue, traditional cognitive science has not dwelled much on the explicit mechanisms involved in value judgment as an inherent aspect of cognitive activity. In general, questions about value or natural purposes have been dealt with separately, preferably with reference to evolutionary history (Millikan 1984): everything living organisms do is ultimately reduced to survival strategies in situations like those encountered by their ancestors, or to the urge to spread their genes as widely as possible. In a more traditional cognitive modeling framework, this idea translates to values being "built-in" by evolution—phylogenetically invariant yardsticks against which actual lifetime encounters are measured and structured, and from which cognitive mechanisms that are themselves independent of these values deduce the meaning of situations, actions, and perceptions.

Explanations of this kind are in tension with the principles of enactivism, in particular with the concept of sense-making. In this section, we juxtapose such traditional views, in which ultimate ends come in evolutionarily sealed boxes, with an alternative, more enactive view that explains values and meanings as consequences of the kind of dynamical system a living organism is. We discuss an enactive theory of value in its rudimentary form, which is based on the theory of autopoiesis. A number of open questions, such as the explanation of nonmetabolic values or transitions in value-generating mechanisms are raised and implications for computational models of cognition are discussed.

2.3.1   Values: Built-in or Constructed?

Weber and Varela (2002) were the first to suggest a derivation of intrinsic teleology, natural purposes, and the capacity of sense-making from autopoiesis, drawing on Kant's *Critique of Judgment* and Hans Jonas's philosophy of biology (Jonas 1966), and the position argued for here commits to this general idea. In this kind of reasoning, the struggle for continuing autopoiesis—in other words, survival—is at the core of intrinsic teleology and the capacity of sense-making. Even though survival plays a central role in both autopoietic and evolutionary explanations of value (one must first survive in order to reproduce), there are essential differences between the claim that what affects an organism's autopoietic organization is of value and the claim that values are built-in because they benefit survival and hence have been selected for.

If values are built-in, they need to have some form of priority over the living, acting creature, either temporally or logically. Typically, claims about biological traits being built-in are about them being part of the genetic package. "Value" is a term that describes the meaning of organismic behavior, not one of its physiological or mechanistic properties, like, for instance, the blood type. Therefore, the idea of built-in values relies on some kind of a priori *semantics*: parts of the genetic code are thought to execute according to preprogrammed rules and, thereby, generate values. This automated "sense lookup" is not the same as sense-making. Similarly, we are dealing with *pre-factum* evolutionary teleonomy, not with autonomy. Instead of emergence, we find a direct reduction of evaluative function to physical structures. Instead of embodiment, we find abstract principles that are presumed independent of embodied interaction. Finally, lived experience is subdued as secondary to historical selection pressure—whether value is manifested experientially seems irrelevant. The idea of built-in values and the enactive approach diverge along all those lines.

This may sound like a very black-and-white picture. Maybe not all that living organisms do can be explained through built-in values, but there are surely some basic properties and behaviors that will always benefit survival, such as that oxygen, food, water, and light will always be good for most animals, so what is wrong with claiming that there are some built-in basic values like "water is good," "light is good," "this food is good"? The point is not to argue that such norms do not exist across individuals of a species, but rather that they should be searched for on the emergent level of autonomous interaction, not on the level of mechanism. If we imagine that a mechanistic structure inside a living organism were solely responsible for the generation of values, does that mean that the remainder of the organism is value-agnostic, that the values generated by this mechanism are arbitrary? Would that not imply that a mutation of the genetic code that tells the organism that "food is good" could result in the generation of the value "poison is good"? For the mutant system, poison would then be of positive value, just as food was for its ancestor, even if this mutation would eventually kill it, which seems a strange idea. The facts that food and water and light are good and that poison is bad are a result of the kind of system that an organism is here and now and that they are of consequence for its conservation. In this sense, no mutation can create the value "poison is good" without changing the organization of the system so that it thrives on "poison." The value for this organism would again be "food is good," not "poison is good." In other words, "good to eat" in enactive terms is equivalent to "stuff I can turn into more of me." The organism is an ontological center that imbues interactions with the environment with significance they do not have in its absence, and this significance is not arbitrary. It is dynamically constructed, and that is the essence of the idea of sense-making.

The thrust behind the idea of precoded values, in contrast, is the assumption of an isomorphism between what is genuinely good or bad for the organism and what the executed genetic value programs say is good. Precoded values are thought to predict the effect of lifetime encounters for metabolism, on the basis of phylogenetic history. Therefore, they rely on phylogenetic constancies. However, cases in which we can observe a change of relation between a value and an organism demonstrate the ontological priority of biological autonomy. The most striking examples of such value changes—which can shatter the functionality of established relations—include illness, perceptual supplementation, and other perturbations to the body (distortions or impairments). Bach-y-Rita et al. (1969) have demonstrated the amazing human capacity to perceive visually, despite a loss of sight, by relaying pixeled images, recorded with a head-mounted camera, to arrays of tactile stimulators. What kind of preexistent, evolutionarily shaped, built-in value mechanism could be responsible for assigning the meaning sighted people make of light patterns to tickling stimuli on the skin when the situation does not correspond to any history of selective pressures?

Or consider a patient who, during the course of a disease, is subjected to increasing dosages of a pharmaceutical agent, with the result that he not only survives dosages of the drug that would be fatal to the average human being, but also that his metabolism relies on the medicine in a way that deprivation would cause his death. The value of this substance for the metabolism is inverted as a consequence of the changes undergone by the organism. But the transformation is not arbitrary. On the contrary, the kind of system that the organism becomes will determine the drug's altered value, and this determination cannot be attributed to a local module, evolutionarily dedicated to the task of assigning meaning, but to the system as a whole. If constancies break down, we observe that local mechanisms gradually undergo a change in how their function relates to meaning such that local processes are not anymore about the same thing they once were when they were selected for. We call this phenomenon *semantic drift*; it comes up again in section 2.3.3.

Even if it is true that specific internal structures play a fundamental role in the value-appraisal process, reducing the latter to the former is a category mistake; it confounds the domains of mechanism and of behavior. To localize the correlated function in these structures is like saying that the speed of a car is in the gas pedal.

2.3.2   Kinds of Values

We propose to define value as *the extent to which a situation affects the viability of a self-sustaining and precarious network of processes that generates an identity*. The most widely discussed and most intensely analyzed such process is autopoiesis, the continuous material regeneration of a self-bounded, self-constructing network of molecular transformations in a far-from-equilibrium situation. Encounters will be good or bad depending on their effect on autopoiesis. Up to this point, our discussion has exclusively argued the case of this basic "metabolic value," as it seems the least controversial. It now remains to be established what kinds of other processes might be self-sustaining, precarious, and generate an identity, that is, what other processes might generate values?

Logically, there are two possibilities for value generation by processes other than metabolism itself: value generation alongside autopoiesis and value generation independent of autopoiesis. Both scenarios immediately lead to further questions. If there are self-sustaining precarious processes that generate an identity, but are fully independent of living organisms, where does teleology come from? Can we really say that such processes generate value, and if yes, value for whom or for what? By contrast, if such processes "parasite" on the process of living, how do the values they generate relate to the basic metabolic value? What happens in case of a conflict? The enactive paradigm leaves space for a multitude of possible positions on these matters; these questions are far from settled and this section cannot but present a few existing positions and our own thoughts in progress.

Varela's own perspective on the organism as a "meshwork of selfless selves" (1991, 1997) can be seen as an exploration into value-generating mechanisms, mainly of the first kind—that is, based on autopoiesis as the most basic form of autonomy and identity generation. Identity generation, for him, entails that an invariant quality is maintained coherently by an operationally closed process whose primary effect is its own sustained production. Varela studied three mechanisms to bring about such processes: autopoiesis (cellular identity), the immune system (multicellular biochemical identity) and the nervous system (neurocognitive identity). He acknowledges the existence or possibility of other levels of identity, reaching from precellular identity (e.g., identity of self-replicating molecules) to sociolinguistic identity and superorganismic identity. Similar ideas are elaborated by Jonas (1966); see also Di Paolo 2009. In a similar spirit, Barandiaran, Di Paolo, and Rohde (2009) have studied the mutual constraints between autonomy (such as a living organism's metabolic self-production) and agency (embodied sensorimotor behavior).

We want to touch on some examples from a nonexhaustive listing of transitions in value-generating mechanisms (figure 2.1) that we consider particularly important or interesting, drawing on some of Varela's and Jonas's ideas. The first three stages of this scale are frequently not treated as distinct. However, it has recently been argued (Di Paolo 2005) that mere autopoiesis, according to the original definition, even though it is sufficient to generate natural teleology and metabolic value, does not entail active appraisal of the corresponding metabolic norms: an autopoietic entity can be robust to perturbations without the logical necessity to

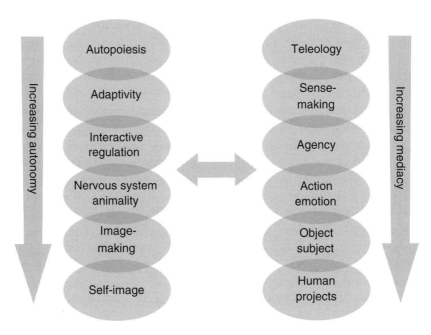

Figure 2.1
Life-mind continuity and the scale of increasing autonomy and mediacy.

actively monitor its own state and act to improve the conditions for continued autopoiesis. Only *adaptive* autopoietic entities that improve the
conditions for continued autopoiesis, by actively monitoring their own
state, identifying at least some tendencies that bring them closer to the
boundary of viability and counteracting these tendencies can be actual
"sense-makers." A similarly subtle distinction is the one between adaptive
organisms and interactive regulators (Moreno and Etxeberria 2005):
although the former act to counter hostile tendencies by changing their
internal organization, the latter act on the environment and thereby
exhibit the most fundamental form of agency (cf. Barandiaran, Di Paolo,
and Rohde 2009). An example of a just-adaptive organism is the sulfur
bacterium that survives anaerobically in marine sediments, whereas bacteria swimming up a sugar gradient would, by virtue of their motion, qualify
for minimal agency.

The further stages on the scale (figure 2.1) are largely adopted from
Jonas's work. Animals, through their motility, exhibit the capacity to act
and perceive as well as fear or desire for something distal. And humans,
through socially mediated capacities such as image-making and ultimately
for constructing a self-image, gain the ability to regard situations objec-

tively and define themselves as subjects, to distinguish truth from false-hood, and to experience happiness and frustration (Jonas 1966; Di Paolo 2005). This ladder follows the "gradient of autonomy and mediacy." It connects increasing degrees of mediation between an urge and its satisfaction to higher degrees of precariousness, and to the consequent liberation of ways to generate values. For instance, only a sense-making organism is capable of mistakes by virtue of the mediacy of urge and satisfaction. A bacterium that swims up the 'saccharine' gradient, as it would in a sugar gradient, can be properly said to have assigned significance to a sign that is not immediately related to its metabolism, even though it is still bound to generate meanings solely based on the consequences for its metabolism. With increasing mediacy, the possibilities to create meaning for signs become less and less constrained by the instantaneous metabolic needs of the organism. Such hierarchies of processes bringing about different kinds of identities and values relate to the study of the major transitions in evolution like the evolution of the eukaryote cell, of sex, or of multicellularity (Maynard Smith and Szathmáry 1995). However, even though different organizations of living creatures enable new and more complex kinds of value-generating processes, transitions in structure cannot immediately be equated with transitions in value, the evolution of value-generating processes proceeds in a more gradual and continuous fashion. The exact relation between complication of material organization through processes of reproduction and selection and the evolution of values is largely unexplored territory that certainly deserves future attention.

One of the riddles in this picture is how different kinds of values are tied together to form a unitary self (and whether they always do). By calling the organism a "meshwork of selfless selves," Varela avoids the answer to this question: "Organism as self, then, cannot be broached as a single process. We are forced to discover "regions" that interweave in complex manners, and, in the case of humans, that extend beyond the strict confines of the body into the socio-linguistic register" (1991, 102). It is certainly true that levels of value generation can be in conflict: how can it be that your body will fight for its life despite the deliberate attempt to end autopoiesis through an overdose of sleeping pills? Or, the other way around, how can the body attack itself in an autoimmune disease, to the dismay of the self that is able to express itself linguistically? Here, we disagree with Weber (2003), who seems to imply that value is always primordial and one-dimensional, that is, that everything that is of value to an organism can be ultimately derived from metabolic value (he calls it "existential value"). Such reductions may provide adequate description for forms of life that do not involve high degrees of mediacy, but not if several levels of value generation coexist and come into conflict. For a smoker, the mechanisms of addiction may be explained with reference to metabolism, but it does not follow that smoking is in any way *about* survival in the way that breathing is.

How do different—sometimes competing, self-sustaining, and precarious—processes, spanning various levels of identity generation, often exceeding the boundaries of the autopoietic individual, relate to the cognizing subject? Could there be genuine values without autopoiesis? These are big questions that remain to be solved. But it seems clear that drawing a box labeled "value" is an unsatisfactory answer to these complex questions.

2.3.3 Modeling Values
In this section, we want to discuss how to model values following the enactive view. We see a large potential for advancing the enactive approach through the adequate use of synthetic models. However, it is very difficult to avoid remnants of Cartesian ways of thinking that are concealed in apparently innocent modeling assumptions. Partially rehearsing previous arguments by Rutkowska (1997), we want to uncover such "lurking homunculi" in "value-system architectures," a class of architectures that feature a local mechanism to assign values.

The term "value system" is taken from the theory of neuronal group selection (TNGS), mainly proposed by Edelman and others (e.g., Edelman 1989). For instance, Sporns and Edelman define value systems as neural modules that are "already specified during embryogenesis as the result of evolutionary selection upon the phenotype" (Sporns and Edelman 1993, 968) and that internally generate reinforcement signals to direct future ontogenetic adaptation. A value system for reaching would become active if the hand comes close to the target. However, the point made here is not limited to neuronal group selection but instead extends to any model that features a strict functional and structural division between behavior-generating mechanisms and mechanisms of value-based adaptation, which we refer to as "value system architectures" in the following.

In order to point out the difficulties that result from such a separation of value judgment (built-in, figure 2.2a) from value execution (ongoing, figure 2.2b), we present two examples of our own research in simulated agent modeling. The deliberately simple first set of simulation experiments is described in more detail in Rohde 2010 and illustrates the difficulties of embedding functional modules into an otherwise dynamic and embodied

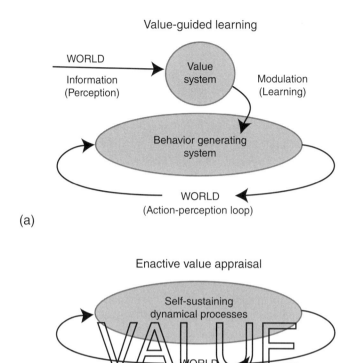

Figure 2.2
An illustration of the value systems (a) and the enactive approach (b) to conceptualizing values.

system. A mobile, two-wheeled agent is controlled by a neural network, which is generated automatically, using an evolutionary algorithm, such that the agent's behavior optimizes a performance measure. This "evolutionary robotics" technique mimics the principles of Darwinian natural selection in a simplified manner and is useful to the enactivist for several reasons. Because the performance criterion rates the *behavior* of an agent in a given environment, not its input/output mappings, this method provides a natural account of the situatedness, embodiment, and dynamics of behavior. Also, although the experimenter determines function by specifying the performance criterion, he or she underspecifies the mechanism that brings it about—this is shaped by automated search. Thereby, prior assumptions about the relation between function and mechanism are minimized, which can lead to behavior emerging from mechanism in ways that the experimenter could not have foreseen, be it due to implicit prior assumptions, or due to cognitive limitations in dealing with complex dynamical systems (Harvey et al. 2005).

Value system architectures are inspired by findings on neural assemblies whose activity corresponds to salient events in the agent/environment interaction that are interpreted as internally generated reinforcement signals. In order to explore just how such a "value signal" could be generated, without caring yet about its function, an agent moving on a plane is evolved to perform light seeking behavior for a set of light sources presented sequentially and, at the same time, to generate a signal that corresponds to how well its approach to the light is being performed. Therefore, this value signal should go up only when the agent is progressing in its task.

The network controller evolved to control the two-wheeled simulated agent is extremely simple, but strikingly good at estimating how close the agent is to a light source, despite the poor sensory endowment (two light sensors generating only on/off signals) and the consequent massive ambiguity in the sensory space. The encircled group of three neurons is the part of the structure that generates the value signal (figure 2.3a). When investigating what this "value system" does, we find that it responds positively to activity on the left light sensor, but negatively to activity on the right light sensor, which, intuitively, does not make sense. The successful judgment can be understood only by taking the sensorimotor context into consideration, that is, the agent's light seeking strategy (figure 2.3b). If the agent does not see the light, it turns to the right, until it senses the light with both sensors. It then approaches the light from the right, constantly bringing the light source in and out of range of the right sensor. In the end, the agent circles around the light source, perceiving the light with the left sensor only. Knowing this sensorimotor context, it is much easier to understand how the "value system" achieves a correct estimation of the distance to the light. The approach behavior starts only when the light is in range of the left light sensor, and this sensor remains activated from then on, which explains the positive response to left sensor activation. The right sensor, however, is activated only during the approach trajectory, and for increasingly short intervals, but not once the light source has been reached, and therefore is negatively correlated to progress in performance.

This simple example demonstrates an important theoretical possibility: a value signal that correlates to behavioral success, even if it is generated by a neural structure that is disconnected from the motor system, can rely

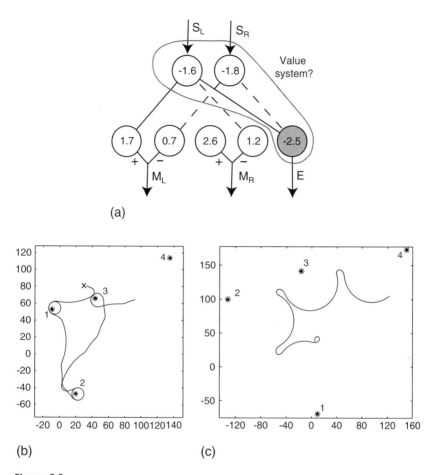

(a)

(b)   (c)

Figure 2.3
(a) The value-judging and light-seeking agent controller. (b) The successful light-seeking behavior. (c) The deterioration of light seeking through applications of the principles of neural Darwinism.

on an existing sensorimotor context. Why is this possibility important? Because it undermines the very idea of top-down behavioral adaptation on the basis of value system judgment: by identifying a correlation between activity in a separate cell assembly and behavioral success, we infer that this module is a value system (figure 2.2a) that informs the organism if a performed behavior is successful. But what if this module relies itself, in a circular fashion, on sensorimotor invariants in order to perform its judgment?

We explore this question in a second experiment. We allow the synaptic weights between sensors and motors (behavior generating subsystem) to change in order to maximize the output of the value system from the previous experiment. Such "neural Darwinism" is proposed as the source of adaptation in TNGS. We literally search for parameters of the behavior generating subsystem that make the agent behave so as to optimize the value signal. According to TNGS, this should result in an improved performance by the agent. In fact, figure 2.3c illustrates how, on the contrary, for this embodied value system, this type of parametrical modulation quickly results in a *deterioration* of performance. In a system that exploits sensorimotor couplings to generate a value signal, if these couplings are modified, their semantic contribution to the generation of meaningful judgment is gradually withdrawn, and we observe a semantic drift of the value signal: activity in the value system causes a change in behavior, which in turn causes a change of "meaning" of the activity of the value system, which causes a change in behavior, and so on. The system described previously, in isolation, rewards activity of the left sensor and punishes activity of the right. So if the semantic contribution of the sensorimotor couplings is gradually modified, the agent ends up avoiding the light source in a large circle, because this is the behavior that optimizes value system output, but not phototaxis.

This deterioration of performance is hardly surprising, given the structure of the value system and the way it works. But it demonstrates that value system architectures as outlined are not guaranteed to work without taking on board further premises. It has to be ensured that a value system estimates performance independently of the presence of reciprocal causal links, feedback loops, and semantic drift of local structures. If a value system is implemented in a rigid context, as it has been done in some robots with a limited behavioral domain (Verschure et al. 1995), the meaning of the signal can be preserved as independent of the modulation of behavior, such that the proposed circuits of adaptation do indeed work. However, in order to be convincing as a biological theory, it is necessary to specify how such a rigid wiring and "disembodiment" of value systems is realized in a living organism that is in constant material flux and embedded in multiple reciprocal loops with the environment. This is exactly the kind of problem that classical computationalist approaches have failed to answer satisfactorily. Indeed, we see value systems, because of their disembodied nature and top-down supervision of adaptation, as leftovers from a Cartesian mode of thinking. Such leftovers are not surprising; decades of exercising a computationalist methodology persist in the very language used to formulate questions.

An enactive approach, however, is based on the idea that values self-organize and emerge from a constantly varying material substrate. They are not reduced to local physical structures, such as a value system, and therefore there are no problems of explaining the semantic rigidity of material subunits.

We now discuss an evolutionary robotics experiment that we conceive of as a first step toward a model of sense-making (Di Paolo 2000b). The task and agent are similar to the experiment described earlier, that is, seeking a sequence of different light sources (see figure 2.4a for a sketch of the agent). The controller consists of a network of homeostatic units, that is, neurons that regulate their connections to other neurons so that their own activity is maintained within a target range. This regulation is achieved by inducing local changes in the weighted connections, a design that is inspired by Ashby's homeostat (1960). These networks were set up to achieve both phototaxis and internal homeostasis by artificial evolution.

Every displacement of the light source (peaks in distance) is followed by a quick approaching behavior (figure 2.4b). The interesting fact about this agent is that it adapts against left/right swapping of its sensors, a situation that it has not been explicitly evolved to cope with (figure 2.4c): even though initially, the agent moves away from the light source—as we would expect if the visual field is inverted—over time it changes its behavior back to approaching the light; that is, the agent *reinterprets* its sensory channels according to the alterations of sensorimotor coupling it experiences, even though it had never been subjected to such alterations during evolution.

To what extent can these experiments be seen as more enactive than value system architectures? First, we ask: why does adaptation to visual inversion occur at all? Like in Bach-y-Rita's tactile vision system, there is no previous evolutionary history to explain how appropriate sense is made of a novel situation. Internal homeostasis acts as a dynamical organization trying to conserve itself, a minimal case of a self-sustained identity. The changes thus introduced can be said to conserve the *autonomy* of the neural process (see also Di Paolo and Iizuka 2008). This conservation has been linked through evolution to behavioral performance, that is, phototaxis.

Ezequiel A. Di Paolo, Marieke Rohde, and Hanne De Jaegher

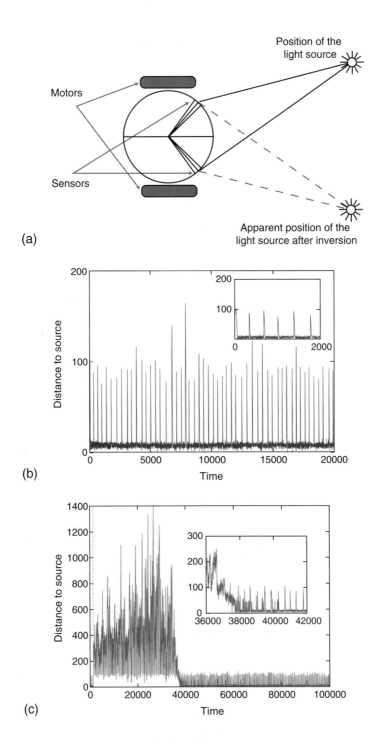

(a)

(b)

(c)

Hence light is of positive value for this agent. When the body is disrupted, performance is disrupted as well, which can only be "interpreted" by the autonomous dynamics as a challenge to its conservation. The recovery of homeostasis results also in the reinterpretation of the sensorimotor coupling (and eventually in the regaining of phototaxis). However, the positive value of light demonstrated by the adaptive process cannot be reduced to the local plastic dynamics; it *emerges* through the ongoing internal and interactive dynamics of the agent in its environment. The meaning of light sensor activity and its functional role for phototaxis is dynamically constructed during the interaction. This minimal dynamic *sense-making* is very different from the a priori semantics of value systems we illustrated in our first model, which have to be protected from semantic drift. We find stability of neural dynamics, even if the system is not explicitly designed to serve as adaptation mechanism for a particular class of predicted problems, and this emergent meaningful adaptation can be explained through the study of mechanism and the parallel study of the behavior it brings about.

This example also demonstrates the usefulness of simulation modeling as a method for the enactive framework by showing how problems of functional reduction can be avoided, and even some degree of dynamical autonomy can be achieved that brings about adaptation through emergent value generation.

2.4 Enacting Social Meaning: Participatory Sense-Making

In this section, we explore what an enactive approach to social understanding would look like. Some authors have suggested ways of conceptualizing social understanding that touch upon some of the enactive ideas outlined in section 2.2. For Gallagher (2001), for instance, the basis of social understanding lies in the abilities of primary intersubjectivity (see also Trevarthen 1979). These include intentionality detection, the detection of eye direction, imitation, the perception of emotion, and meaning in postures

◀ **Figure 2.4**
Experiments in homeostatic adaptation using a two-wheeled light seeking agent (a). The agent's distance to a long series of light sources is plotted as a function of time both for the case of normal (b) and inverted (c) visual fields. In (b), the agent approaches each new source of light that replaces the old one; in (c), immediately after sensors are inverted, the agent moves away from new light sources in its vicinity until adaptation ensues and light seeking behavior is recovered.

and movements. Thompson (2001) has suggested that we understand each other as part of an ongoing "self-other codetermination" that takes place when we are in interaction. But these approaches can be elaborated further. As with the case of values, the one important question that needs an answer before we can say that we grasp social understanding is: *where does meaning come from?* Current mainstream representational approaches do not give an answer to this question, nor do many embodied alternatives. The enactive approach, as we have seen, offers the concept of sense-making to address this issue. This section explains the kind of specific answer we can expect from an enactive approach to social cognition. One thing is clear: *interaction dynamics* as well as a specific notion of *autonomy* will play a crucial role in it.

2.4.1 Toward Enactive Social Understanding

Before laying out our proposal for an enactive approach to social understanding, let us examine the gaps in traditional takes on social cognition. The underlying assumption of central paradigms such as Theory of Mind theory (ToM) and simulation theory is that minds are enclosed and opaque, and hence others are puzzles for us to solve. The proposal of ToM is that we cognitively figure out others: we understand others by applying a capacity to draw logical inferences to sets of knowledge and perceptions. Simulation theory was proposed in reaction to what is thought of as the "cold reasoning" of ToM. We find out about what another is thinking or doing through an internal simulation of their behavior. Simulation comes in roughly two guises. There is Gordon's radical simulationism, in which we act out the other's stance (Gordon 1996), that is, we "become the other" for a short while in order to understand her. On the less radical version of simulation, we imagine ourselves in the shoes of the person we are trying to understand. The different versions of ToM and of simulation theory all presuppose a thorough disconnection between subjects and an internalist (thus hidden) view of intentions. In a social situation, we are confronted with an impenetrable other and so we find ourselves again and again thrown upon our own resources of reasoning and/or imagination.

Apart from suffering from internal contradictions, in this kind of approach the body plays no role of any significance. Issues of autonomy, emergence, and self-organization also remain untouched. As regards sense-making, meaning is supposedly derived from good old-fashioned information processing. Experience could be said to come into simulation approaches, but we would have to wax very lyrical about it—too much so—for the kind of experience implicated here to be anything like what it is understood to mean in an enactive approach.

Alternatives to both mind-reading and simulation approaches have been suggested. Gallagher, for instance, has criticized both because of their assumption that minds are private. Instead, he says, what we think, intend, desire, and so on is practiced, expressed and recognized in our body (Gallagher 2001, 2005). According to Gallagher, "in most intersubjective situations we have a direct understanding of another person's intentions because their intentions are explicitly expressed in their embodied actions, and mirrored in our own capabilities for action" (2005, 224). Basically, we know others because of our own embodied experience—not so much because their bodies look like ours, but because we experience them as other persons through our own bodies. We are not confronted with an object to dismantle, but with someone that we already relate to at a very basic, bodily level. But proposals of embodied social cognition like these have a drawback: they often presuppose coupling between persons. Because of this, *how people interact* does not in itself become an explicit topic for investigation.[2]

But if we are to investigate social understanding along enactive lines, we need to pay special attention to the process of social interaction (De Jaegher 2006). Therefore, we suggest that, in order to understand social cognition, the embodied aspects investigated by several researchers need to be supplemented by an investigation of social interaction, in analogy with the interaction between agent and world described in section 2.2. In order to fully understand how meaning comes about in social understanding, we need not only to focus on the embodiment of interactors, but also on the interaction process that takes place between them.

There have been suggestions along these lines. Hobson (2002), for example, discusses "interpersonal engagement" or the intersubjective sharing of experiences that forms the fertile ground for the development of our capacity for thinking. There is also a large amount of research on dialog and interaction (see e.g., Sacks, Schegloff, and Jefferson 1974; Goffman 1983; Kendon 1990). This work has generated interesting results, but the research in these fields has often been geared toward notes on empirical findings, more than toward generating theoretical principles of communication or interaction. In order to start providing the latter, we need to look more concretely at the mechanism of social interaction as such.

2.4.2 Interaction and Coordination

An enactive approach to social understanding starts from the study of interaction and coordination. *Interaction* is here understood as the coupling between an agent and a specific aspect of its world: another agent.

Interaction is the mutual interdependence (or bidirectional, co-regulated coupling) of the behaviors of two social agents. Precisely which behaviors of the agents are implicated in this process will depend on the specific interaction and the situation in which it takes place (and on what its observer is interested in). What is of most interest right now, however, is what kinds of interdependence can exist.

In dynamical terms, systems can be *correlated*; that is, we may find similarities or coherences of behavior above and beyond what would be expected from what is known about their normal functioning. Of all the correlated behaviors, some are *accidentally correlated*, and some are *nonaccidentally correlated*. We are most interested here in the latter form of interdependence, which we call *coordination*. In social situations, coordination thus refers to the nonaccidental correlation of behaviors of two or more social agents. It is brought about by one or more common and/or connecting factors.

Imagine two people walking down the street. Suddenly, both of them turn their heads. Suppose we notice that their head-turning behavior has been prompted by someone screaming behind them. Their behaviors are thus *externally coordinated*, because there is a common external triggering factor. In the absence of such a factor, their behaviors might have been in a fortuitous correlation or the result of *precoordination*. When two people turn their heads at the same time because they are both—say, for some strange neurological reason—set to turn their heads every hour on the hour, the observed coherence is brought about by a preestablished coordination: their shared predisposition for hourly head turning. Again, there is a common factor: an internal "head-turning clock." Common factors in precoordination can be of diverse origin, but often they involve a similar internal mechanism or shared histories.

Some precoordination is present in almost all social encounters, even if only by the existence of a common cultural background. But hardly any encounter, even with some precoordination, can unfold on the basis of it alone. Interactors need to coordinate their actions there and then. Such on-the-spot coordination is mostly achieved *interactionally*. We therefore call it *interactional coordination*, to refer to the fact that the interaction process itself plays a generative and facilitative role in the coordination. To illustrate, ways of greeting vary greatly between cultures, but even people with a common background may have to coordinate their hello's and goodbye's on their first rendezvous.

Moreover, coordination can also make interaction more likely to happen and continue. An example of this is making an appointment in order to meet. Coordination thus can have an interactional function. This we call *functional coordination*. A beautiful example of this is the case of wolf circling (Moran, Fentress, and Golani 1981). Sometimes, as a wolf walks past another one that is seated, the sitting one gets up and starts to move in the opposite direction. However, rather than pass each other and walk away, they start to move in a circle together, head to tail. This behavior makes it possible for the wolves to size each other up, as it were, and to decide upon fighting or not, which can be said to be the function of this bodily coordination. Such coordination often serves an interactional function, namely that of facilitating or continuing the interaction, whatever it may lead to or change into.

Interactional coordination and functional coordination are not easy to separate; they are two sides of the same coin and describe the reciprocal influence between coordinated behavior and interaction as a process. As an extreme case of coordination through interaction we find the phenomenon of *one-sided coordination*. This happens when an individual coordinates *to* rather than *with* another. This distinction is further illustrated in the models described shortly.

In the following section, we discuss two examples of how to investigate these phenomena. We describe two evolutionary robotics models, one of which is based on an empirical study of "perceptual crossing." Following this, we connect to the issue of meaning generation in social interaction via the introduction of the notions of *interaction rhythm* and *participatory sense-making*.

2.4.3 Modeling Embodied Coordination

One approach to the question of how coordination between social interactors may be established is illustrated by some evolutionary robotics work on social interaction. More than half a century ago, W. Grey Walter explored simple forms of social robot coordination with his "tortoises" (Walter 1950). Such experiments demonstrated how a couple of very simple individual behaviors (such as wandering around and approaching a source of light) could result in complex, dance-like coordination when two such robots were put in mutual interaction. Recent studies using evolutionary methods also demonstrate this. For instance, in a simple simulation model, mobile agents must interact through an acoustic medium (Di Paolo 2000a). This work shows how different kinds of coordination are a direct result of the embodied interaction between agents over time.

The model again is deliberately simple. Two mobile agents are placed in an unbounded two-dimensional arena. Their bodies are circular and can move by differential steering of two opposing wheels, which are controlled by a small continuous-time neural network. These agents are also provided with a loudspeaker that they use to regulate continuously the volume of the sound they emit. As sensors they have two microphones located symmetrically in their bodies, which are used to pick up any sound in the environment, including the sound they produce themselves. There is an inherent problem of distinguishing a signal produced by an external source and by the agent itself, because all sound signals are added up. A sound signal that travels through the body of an agent decays in intensity, so there is a significant difference to the sensor activity if the sound impinges directly on it or must go through the listener's body first; this self-shadowing property is indeed used by many mammals to detect sound source location.

With this setup, the task set for the agents is to locate and remain close to each other. There are no other restrictions to the agent's activity: they are allowed to evolve any kind of continuous sound signal or move in any way. The problem is nontrivial, because of the lack of other sensors and the single sound channel. Shouting at the top of their voices will not work, because the self-produced signal will overwhelm the sensors, but remaining quiet will not give any clue as to the agent's position that can be used to achieve the task. Consequently, sound must be used strategically. Because of their random initial positions, coordination between the agents must be achieved in order to facilitate a continuing interaction.

Successful agent pairs acquire a coordinated pattern of signaling in which individuals take turns in emitting sound so that each may hear the other. They solve the "self/nonself" distinction problem by making use of the self-shadowing property. If an agent constantly rotates, an external source of sound produces a regularly rhythmic pattern in the agent's sensors, while the sensing of its own signal is unaffected. A simple embodied strategy simplifies what would otherwise be a complex pattern recognition problem. This regular pattern affects their own sound production so that they also signal rhythmically, and finally through a process of mutual modulation the production of sound is coordinated in an anti-phase entrainment of signals. Further coordination is observed during interaction in proximity when patterns of regularly alternate movements are produced that resemble a dance (figure 2.5). Both the sound and movement coordination patterns are achieved through a process of coadaptation—tests on individual agents show that they are not capable of producing any of these behaviors in the presence of a noncontingent recording of a partner from

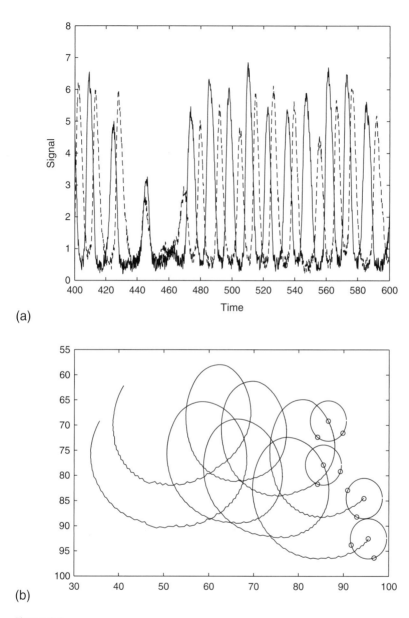

(a)

(b)

Figure 2.5
Sound patterns of agents in coordination: showing turn-taking activity (a), and trajectories of agents in coordination (b).

a previous interaction; that is, they are capable of interactional coordination but not of one-sided coordination (the same result has been found in models of detection of social contingencies; see Di Paolo, Rohde, and Iizuka 2008).

This and similar models demonstrate that the achievement of coordination *through* the interaction process is indeed something that can be expected to happen (as opposed to something that demands purpose-built mechanisms) in a broad range of dynamical systems in interaction. The agents in this example use their bodies and the time structure of their own movement to generate coordination. The generated patterns themselves help maintain the continuous coordination, and periods of breakdown followed by recovery of coordination are observed.

Experiments like these are sometimes disregarded because they seem so simple and "low-level" that it seems hard to see how they relate to human cognition. An alternative challenge for synthetic modeling is to try to account for empirical research conducted on human subjects that is driven by a similar aspiration for minimalism.

Auvray, Lenay, and Stewart (2009) have investigated the phenomenon of "perceptual crossing" in a similarly minimalistic manner. Blindfolded human participants interacting in a shared minimal virtual environment are asked to recognize the presence of each other. The only possibility to act is to move the cursor left and right along a virtual "tape" that wraps around using a computer mouse. Subjects sense the presence of an object or the other player only through a touch sensor whenever their own cursor "steps" on them. To make the task nontrivial, there is also a static object of the same size as the other subject on the tape (fixed lure), as well as a mobile object that shadows the motion of the other subject at a constant distance (attached lure). The problem is therefore not only distinguishing moving from nonmoving entities along the tape using the touch feedback, but distinguishing between two entities that move exactly the same, only one of which represents the "sensing" position of the other subject. Moment-to-moment sensory patterns therefore do not suffice to distinguish the three entities that may be encountered. Even so, recognition still results from the mutual search for each other.

Successful recognition relies on the global pattern of sensorimotor coordination between the participants, rather than on an individual's capacity to express a confident judgment on whether a stimulus is caused by the partner. When subjects encounter a stimulus, they tend to oscillate around it, and these scanning movements only remain stable in the case that both players are in contact with each other. A subject could be fooled by the other player's attached lure, but only to the point that the other player remains largely on the spot (one-way coordination). This situation is unstable, as the other player will eventually move away to continue the search. Only when the two-way interaction condition is established does the situation remain globally stable. Hence the solution is truly interactional, because it is established by both partners searching for each other but does not rely on individuals performing the right kind of perceptual recognition between responsive and nonresponsive objects.

We have applied the technique of evolutionary robotics to gain further insight into this task (Di Paolo, Rohde, and Iizuka 2008). The virtual environment and task are the same and the agents are controlled by a neural network. The resulting global strategy is similar,[3] but it raises an interesting further possibility regarding the role of interactional coordination. The empirical study shows that humans do not confuse a static lure with another subject. At first sight, it seems obvious that telling a mobile stimulus from a static one is the easiest task to solve in this experiment. Humans could, for instance, rapidly learn to discount changes to stimuli generated by their own movement using proprioception. The agents evolved in our model have another solution to the problem. If we take a closer look, we find a striking similarity between sensorimotor patterns for perceptual crossing involving the other player and for scanning a fixed lure (figure 2.6a, b). Encountering any stimulus makes the agent revert its direction of movement, which leads to another encounter followed by another inversion of velocity, and so forth. When we inspect the duration of the stimulus upon crossing a fixed object, we realize that it lasts longer than when crossing a moving partner. This is because the fixed object does not move itself. Therefore the *perceived size* differs for the two cases: longer in the case of a fixed object and shorter in the case of a moving object. The agent seems simply to rely on integrating sensory stimulation over time to make the distinction. This can be confirmed from the fact that the agent is quite easily tricked into making the wrong decision if the size of the fixed lure is varied.

What is interesting is that the smaller perceived size in the case of perceptual crossing depends on encounters remaining in an antiphase pattern (figure 2.6a). In other words, it depends on interactional coordination. Hence a systematic distinction in individually perceived size (between objects having the same objective size) is *co-constructed* during coordinated interaction, and in turn, individuals respond to the apparently smaller object by remaining in coordinated interaction. Looking more closely at the empirical data, Auvray, Lenay, and Stewart (2009) found that human participants may indeed use this strategy unconsciously to decide when to click. Here we see the importance of simple models as generators of ideas.

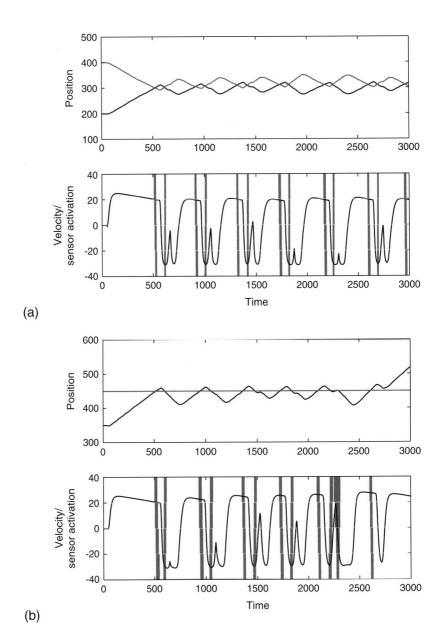

(a)

(b)

Figure 2.6
Perceptual crossing model. Top plots show the trajectories of agents over time; plots
at the bottom show the motor commands (dark line) and sensor input (gray line).
Stabilized social perceptual crossing (a); scanning of a fixed object (b).

These examples demonstrate the potential of an enactive modeling approach for the study of social interaction; instead of limiting the view to what happens inside one individual, the interaction process can be taken seriously, operationalized and studied in dynamical terms. Thereby these models have the possibility to capture the rich dynamics of reciprocity that are left outside of traditional individualistic approaches. The models demonstrate the importance of *timing* in interaction and suggest how it can affect sensorimotor processes at the individual level to the point that recognizing an interaction partner is possible thanks to the interplay and mutual modulation between the interaction and individual cognitive properties.

2.4.4   Social Perception as a Social Skill

How do we get from here to meaning generation in social encounters between humans? How do interactors understand each other? We believe that meaning generation and transformation can take place in the processes of interaction and coordination, as has also been suggested by the experiments discussed. Interactional coordination and functional coordination can be seen as the processes by which social encounters self-organize. In social situations in the human world, meaning is generated continuously in the interaction out of this self-organization, in combination with the histories, backgrounds, expectations, thoughts, and moods of the interactors. But how?

Our proposal is that enacting the social world relates to the precise timing of the functional and interactional coordination processes taking place in social situations. We call this timing *interaction rhythm*. Interaction rhythm refers to the diverse aspects of the temporality of the interaction—a necessary, though not sufficient, aspect of establishing, maintaining, and closing social interactions. Timing coordination in interaction is done at many different levels of movement, including utterances, posture maintenance, and so on. Rhythm as a term is preferred over the more general "temporality," because it captures the *active* role that these elements play in the generation and organization of social interactions. As used here, the term "rhythm" does not refer to a continual strict temporal regularity or periodicity (the everyday meaning of the term), but rather to the *possible and actual temporal variability of timing in interaction*, including, at times and at certain levels of behavior, regular timing.

Interaction rhythm, moreover, refers to the self-organization in time of several elements and processes that *span* the individuals, that is, the organization of elements across and *between* individuals. This process can take on a strong role and momentum of its own; it can itself become an autonomous phenomenon. In order to illustrate the potential autonomy of the social interaction, imagine the situation of two people walking in opposite directions in a narrow corridor, each on their way to their respective office. When they get close, they attempt to pass by each other. Each of them steps out of the way, but to the same side, so that they end up in front of each other and unable to walk on. And then they step to the other side, at the same time. And again. And again. They remain in front of each other for a brief time, meanwhile unable to continue on their way. Here, an unintended coordination takes place, and the interaction emerges and subsists—even if only briefly—outside of the intentions and goals of each of the two people.

If the interaction process is like this – sometimes autonomous and overriding or even working against individual intentions – it can alter and have an effect on the behaviors of the individuals involved. Another example is the perception of object size in the perceptual crossing model. In human interactions, the individuals involved are autonomous themselves, and this makes for the complexity of social interaction. If we are to understand meaning generation or sense-making in social interaction, we need to grasp what goes on in this interplay between the different states of the interaction process itself and those of the individuals engaged in it. We operationalize this interplay in our definition of social interaction: *Social interaction is the regulated coupling between at least two autonomous agents, where the regulation concerns aspects of the coupling itself and constitutes an emergent autonomous organization in the domain of relational dynamics, without destroying in the process the autonomy of the agents involved (though the latter's scope can be augmented or reduced)* (adapted from De Jaegher and Di Paolo 2007, 493).

How can we conceptualize social aptitude in this framework? We propose that social skill depends on a "rhythmic capacity." This is not a capacity strictly of an individual, but one that comes about in interaction and is changed by both the interactional process and the individuals involved. We define this central capacity of social cognition as *the ability to coordinate through the interaction with another person.* Through such plastic coordination, the rhythm of an interaction can be adapted to varying circumstances, changes in goals, moods, and so on. This capacity is crucially dependent both on the individual interactors and on the process of engagement that ensues between them in every interaction.

In this view, social perception is not about finding hidden intentions in the other but is based on the mastery of self-other contingencies

(McGann and De Jaegher 2009). These contingencies tend to be mostly in the domain of values, intentions, and affects. They are negotiated during the encounter itself. They arise from interlocking bodily, interactive, and cultural processes, and unlike most cases of object perception they are protean in character. The social skills that must be mastered for social perception are the skills of coping interactively with regularities that can, and often will, change unexpectedly. According to McGann and De Jaegher, social skill is a mastery of negotiation.

We cannot say who is in charge of the process of the interaction. Therefore, here again, interactions need to be studied as wholes, plus their histories. Social meaning generation relies on the coordination of individual sense-making. It relies on *coordination as a process*, not an outcome. That is, precise mutual attunement of sense-makings is not necessarily the goal of interacting. Rather, it is the process of coordination between actions involved in sense-making that contributes to people understanding each other.

2.4.5 Participatory Sense-Making

To conclude, we propose the notion of *participatory sense-making* for social understanding in an enactive framework. Participatory sense-making is the extension of the enactive notion of sense-making into the realm of social cognition once we have taken into account the aforegoing discussion about the importance of interaction (De Jaegher and Di Paolo 2007, 2008; De Jaegher 2009). In sense-making, active coupling with the world brings forth a realm of significance. In a social situation, the active coupling is with another social agent. Social agents can be engaged in individual sense-making, but when they start interacting, their sense-making is modified in accordance with the specific aspect of the world they are now interacting with—another social agent—according to the specifications laid out previously. Generation of social meaning relies on the process of coordination of individual sense-making, achieved in the interaction rhythm and by the rhythmic capacity.

Not only this, but participatory sense-making also opens up domains of sense-making that are not open to the individual on his own. Participatory sense-making constitutes a continuum from less participatory to highly participatory sense-making. At the former end of the spectrum, we find for instance *orientation*, in which individual A orients B to aspects of B's cognitive domain. This is not very participatory, because there is not much mutuality to the sense-making. As we move away from this end of the range, the sense-making activities of the individuals involved are increasingly mutually changed by their coordinated sense-making, and also change it. At the most participatory end of the spectrum, individuals truly intertwine their sense-making activities, with consequences for each in the process, in the form of the interactional generation of new meanings and the transformation of existing meanings. Academic collaborations are a good example of this. Sometimes, when the partnership is especially fruitful, a completely new vantage point on a problem arises, or a fresh interpretation of a result occurs. Sometimes it is impossible to attribute this development to one of the participants only.

It can seem as if the account we propose here is only applicable to live interactions. But what about observational social understanding—for instance, when watching a film? Or even understanding someone in a letter exchange or in an email conversation? How does social understanding happen when there is no live interaction and coordination? The point of our proposal is not that social understanding only happens in situations where the participants are physically present to each other. It is rather that social understanding has its developmental and logical origins in social interaction. Without experience of interacting in development, we would not reach the sophisticated forms of intersubjectivity we have. And without studying interactional coordination, scientists cannot get to the bottom of how it is that we understand others.

In conclusion, using the notions of sense-making, interaction rhythm, the rhythmic capacity, and our definition of social interaction enables us to conceptualize social understanding as something that is enacted—co-constructed—in the interaction. We do not need to posit a specialized module in the brain, but propose to explain social understanding as always based on and supported by the dynamics of interaction between the cognitive agent and the environment. Because an enactive approach places great importance on the autonomy of the individuals involved, this approach to social cognition, while focusing on the interaction process, paradoxically also gives social agents an autonomy and role that has not been thematized before: that of participation in contrast to mere observation.

2.5   Play: Enactive Re-creation

We come back to some of the problems raised in the introduction. This section will draw on what has been learned so far about the horizons of enactivism to approach the general question of human cognition (the umbrella term under which cognitive scientists gather conceptual thinking, planning, language, social competences, and so on).

We have already mentioned that the impact of the enactive approach in cognitive science, and that of embodied and dynamical views in general, has been acknowledged by many sectors, but not yet as a proper replacement for representationalism in what concerns higher level cognition. Some arguments have been advanced regarding the very possibility of a nonrepresentational framework for this task. Clark and Toribio (1994) question how the very situatedness of action-oriented and richly dynamical couplings between agent and environment is not at the same time responsible for "tying down" cognition to the present situation. Internal representations, the argument concludes, will have to reenter the picture to account for activities that seem decoupled from the current situation, such as picturing the house of your childhood.

The argument is right in that, from an enactive perspective, such high-level skills are indeed still unexplained. But the argument simply assumes that they are also unexplainable in enactive terms. Importantly, the argument relies on a misunderstanding of the idea of situatedness. To say that we are present in a situation with our bodies does not mean that the situation boils down to the physical couplings that we encounter, that is, that we are shackled to our present physical circumstances. This is why the concept of sense-making is so interesting. It is all too easy to interpret this idea in a one-sided manner—events in the world are given meaning by the agent—and ignore the crucial possibility that the cognitive agent may also be an *active creator of meaning* and that such creation can be subject to change and eventual control by emergent levels of cognitive identity.

Could this point be a way of making progress in an enactive account of human cognition? Let us try to formulate the essence of the problem first. What is essential to human cognition as opposed to other forms of animal cognition? Margaret Donaldson (1992) formulates the issue in a very useful way. She puzzles about the amazing human capability of constantly inventing new goals so that we invest them with value and submit passionately to them (sports, hobbies, record breaking). An explanation of human intelligence should perhaps not concentrate so much on issues such as, say, how we manage to do math. It should bring to the center the question of *why* we do those things at all—when did they become valuable for us?

Donaldson describes different ways to be a human mind. As a developmental psychologist, she concentrates on how transitions between these different modes occur throughout a lifetime. The question parallels how Jonas and others have treated the history of life and mind as transitions in scales of mediacy. Donaldson distinguishes four modes in which we function as minds depending on the focus of concern. This is amenable to the whole of our previous discussion. To have different foci of concern is no more or less than to have different modes of value generation. The *point mode* deals with here-and-now coping (most animal activity, skillful practices in humans). The *line mode* expands the focus of concern to the immediate past and the possible future as well as to other spatial localities (understanding of immediate causes and consequences of events). The *construct mode* produces a decentering of cognitive activity; concern focuses on events that have happened or may happen at some point in time or somewhere, and not necessarily involving the cognitive agent (induction, generalization). Finally, the *transcendent mode* has no locus; it deals with nowhere, no-time (abstract thought, metaphysics).

These modes are manifested to different degrees in different circumstances and with respect to different mental "components" such as perception, action, emotion, and thought. The modes are transversed developmentally, building upon previous stages. The generation of different kinds of intention and the manipulation of our own consciousness are the central factors in this development. This backdrop can help us describe our problem as that of formulating an enactive account of how to move beyond the point mode and into the line and construct modes.

This transition indicates the development of a capacity to "unstick" meanings from a given situation and "stick" novel ones onto it (to put it graphically), or, generally, the capacity to influence meaning generation. This has confusingly been described as offline intelligence (Clark 1997; Wheeler 2005), whereas "decentering" or "meaning manipulation" may be better labels. Such a capability is indeed a challenge for dynamical accounts of cognition that emphasize coupling with the environment. It would seem that cognitive activity is "glued" to the here and now in such accounts, that is, always in the point mode. By contrast, cognitivism sees no challenge in this. Manipulation of representations to deal with the here and now is not fundamentally different from manipulation of representations to deal with the there and then, or with nowhere, no-time. This is hardly surprising. Cognitivism starts at the high end of the spectrum. It is based on nontemporal, nonspatial, unsituated mechanisms (and consequently, its own challenge is how to move in the opposite direction, toward ongoing coping).

If we look historically or developmentally for an activity that could play a part in this transition we must conclude that (1) it should be an embodied activity, accountable for by means of the many skills that we can already explain in enactive terms, and (2) it should allow for ambiguity of meaning as well as the generation of novel kinds of value. The worst possible candidates are concrete goal-directed activities in which meaning is well defined by situational constraints. The best candidates are those goal-generating activities where meaning is fluid. Jonas points to image-making, which is indeed an excellent example. But it is already too sophisticated and immediately invites representational thinking. More parsimonious possibilities include dance, music, ritual, and play. Here we briefly explore the last of these possibilities.

Can we sketch an enactive account of play? There is a significant literature on play in animals as well as different forms of play in human children and how play relates to socialization, self-regulation, attachment, use of language, and the development of cognitive capabilities.[4] The interesting fact for our present discussion is that elements of the meaning manipulation that this activity can afford are already present in all forms of play. We have already mentioned the possibility of sense-making leading to increasingly removed manipulation of meaning. Might not the presumed bacterium swimming up a saccharine (not sugar) gradient and the young baboon accepting to be chased around by the smaller playful infant share something in common? Are not both deceived to different degrees in their sense-making activities, the one unknowingly, the other willingly?

The first thing to note about play is that it is hard to define and easy to recognize. Miller (1973) lists some properties of play, such as the repetition of motor patterns, lack of economy, exaggeration, lack of a direct practical end, production of novel sequences of behavior, combinatorial flexibility, egalitarianism, and others. Play occurs only in the absence of more urgent motivations related to survival; hence it is the privilege of species where individuals have enough spare energy, time, and protection. Not all animals do it, and in those species that play, mainly infants and juveniles do it—exceptions are humans and species that are given safety through their adulthood such as cats, dogs, and domesticated monkeys and apes. Evolutionary explanations of play abound. They typically refer to beneficial by-products such as the training of motor skills. The merits of such explanations must be assessed in each individual case, but in general terms understanding even quite "unsophisticated" bodily play (rough and tumble, simulated pursuit-evasion, etc.) cannot be fully achieved without an experiential approach. Much is missed if we cannot understand why animals are *interested* in play. Maxine Sheets-Johnstone (2003) answers this question by indicating the dimension of kinesthetic feeling that animals explore in play: the dimension of corporeal powers, the *I-can* and *I-cannot*.

The experiential dimension of value explored in this way is opened up by the element of social interaction and the forms of participatory sense-making that it affords. It is here that kinaesthetic pleasure turns into make-believe. Running may be fun, running from or after someone even more. The excitement of aggressive or sexual encounters can be safely explored if distinguished from real ones by appropriate signals and conventions. It is this novel way of socially exploring the meaning of fake situations using real and concrete interactions that is taken to its pinnacle by humans in the form of pretend play. Here we are already at the other side of the transition, because if the arrangement of wooden cubes can be a house and the pen a spaceship, the root capacity of meaning creation and manipulation is already going strong.

Cognitivist accounts of pretence in play, such as Leslie (1987), go very much in line with similar accounts of social understanding already examined, and their criticisms, such as Hobson (1990), complete the parallel. Piaget's views on pretend play are closer to the enactive approach (1951). For him, the beginnings of play are rooted in the assimilative function, whereby new situations are coped with using existing sensorimotor schemas. A fifteen-month-old infant deals with a pillow using certain actions (touching, laying his or her head on it, going to sleep). As soon as another object (a blanket) is assimilated into the same structures, it becomes a make-believe pillow. The infant finds pleasure in the assimilative function and smiles. Donaldson (1992) criticizes this view (see also Sutton-Smith 1966). If only assimilation were taking place, the blanket and the pillow would be indistinguishable. There would be no reason to smile unless there was a simultaneous awareness of the difference between the two cases and the sense of "getting away with something." Make-believe relies crucially on the *combined similarity and difference* between two situations: one concrete, tied to physical events, and the other in terms of manipulated meaning (the tension of this combination reappears in other creative activities such as making images).

The view of play as predominant assimilation misses out on the active element of construction of new environmentally and bodily mediated meaning. Play breaks from the constraints of self-equilibrating cognition. It does not have the structure of a cognitive confrontation with an environment that places demands on the agent. Play is precisely *not* a problem requiring a solution. In fact, play is the breaking of this pattern, or rather its redeployment into an active construction of meaningful action where no such sense-making is directly demanded from the environment or from definite internal needs. The urge to play (at least during the creative phases of play) is indeed present but remains undefined until the activity of play itself helps the child make this urge clearer.

How is this possible within an accommodation/assimilation/equilibration dynamic? It seems impossible if we resist acknowledging the active participation of the child in transforming his or her world. Vygotsky (1966) gives us a glimpse of how such manipulation of sense-making could happen. In play, the child begins to detach meaning from a situation and to regulate such meanings first with respect to objects and later to his or her own actions. This is motivated by the inability to satisfy immediate needs. Play becomes a way of substitution for real satisfaction and a way of dealing with an insurmountable mediacy. Soon the value-generating properties of play become evident and the activity is done for its own sake. "Detachment" is an embodied activity. It begins by relying on concrete similarities—a doll resembles a person—but soon these similarities are mostly given by the child's own use of gestural schemas and not the objects themselves (Watson and Jackowitz 1984). If something is treated as a horse, if it is made to move and sound like a horse, then the child accepts it as a horse (without forgetting that it is not one). This is the ambiguity that, according to Donaldson (1992), can produce laughter and exhilaration, the bringing into presence of what is not there, a cheating of "reality."

Once objects in the environment are imbued with meaning by actions that in turn demand from the child an (adaptive) interpretation, these objects become toys—would-be cars, houses, and creatures. The child is now acting at the pinnacle of his or her enactive capabilities, because he or she is bringing forth an alienated meaning through gestural schemas and then—and here lies the equally radical trick—submitting to the reality thus created through adaptive equilibration (the absence of which would make play unchallenging and "unreal").

The combination of a concrete embodied situation with alienated virtual meaning is the freedom-engendering paradox of play. But it would not be a paradox if all there was to pretence was the manipulation of internal representations. This would result in no sense of ambiguity. Cognitivism cannot explain fun. When the child becomes the regulator of play, the activity takes off as a proper form of life. The child explores the new freedom by following pleasurable activities, but at the same time, learns to generate new rules—new constraints that structure and reevaluate reality and that must be followed strictly (otherwise play becomes random and boring). The child is unhappy if he or she cannot bounce the ball more than the nine times managed so far. The norm is arbitrary, invented by the child, but in allowing his or her body to submit to it, it becomes as serious as other social or biological norms. The player is the lawgiver and the rule-follower, the question maker and the responder. Play is thereby autonomous in the strict sense advocated by enactivism because it engenders a self-sustaining network of activities.

Pretending is only possible if a novel way of generating norms and values arises in conjunction with exploratory play. The best players are those that create new rules in a contextual manner so that they can continue to play and fun does not run down by exhausting the possibilities of the game. Rules are made up in play; they are solidified versions of norms. Fun is the exploration of the limits thus imposed on bodily activity and social interaction. But when the possibilities are extinguished, the game becomes boring. Fun is also the change and revision of norms that reopen play. Over time, play is a self-structuring process governed by the dialectics of expansion and exhaustion of possibilities. Its freedom lies in the capability that players acquire of creating new meaningful (not arbitrary) constraints. The playful body is a new form of autonomous being—a novel mode of the cognitive self. It can now steer its sense-making activity and set new laws for itself and others to follow. This might help to answer the question we raised at the end of our discussion about embodiment in section 2.2.4.

We find that play is an area particularly rich for the exploration of enactive themes from emergence of identities and levels of social coordination, to manipulation of sense-making through experientially guided bodily action. Perhaps no other framework is better placed to explain play and its paradoxes, and this may be why there is such a paucity of references to play in cognitive science. When a child skillfully supplements the perceptual lack of similarity between a spoon and a car by making the spoon move and sound like a car, he or she has grasped in an embodied manner the extent to which perception can be action-mediated. With his or her body, the child can now alter sense-making activity, both on external objects, as well as his or her own actions and those of others. The child has become a practitioner of enactive *re-creation*.

2.6   Conclusion

A proper extension of the enactive approach into a solid and mainstream framework for understanding cognition in all its manifestations will be a job of many and lasting for many years. This chapter has attempted only to point to specific directions and show that enactivism can be made into a coherent set of ideas, distinguishable from other alternatives, and that it can provide the language to formulate problems and the tools to advance on issues that are sometimes out of the focal range of traditional perspectives (if not in their blind spot). The strength of any scientific proposal will eventually be in how it advances our understanding, whether in the form of predictability and control, or in the form of synthetic constructions, models, and technologies for coping and interacting with complex systems such as education policies, methods for diagnosis, novel therapies, and so on. For this, it is crucial for ideas to be intelligible and promising.

In this respect, we would like to draw attention to the valuable role played by minimal models and experiments. Their function goes beyond the study of a given phenomenon. Minimal modeling provides crucial conceptual training that would be hard to obtain otherwise (Beer 2003; Harvey et al. 2005; Rohde 2010). Analytical thinking is at home with linear causality, well-defined and unchanging systems, and reduction. The alternatives of emergent, many-layered, causally spread, nonlinear systems in constant constitutive and interactive flux are very hard to manage conceptually. This is an important focus of resistance to many enactive ideas. It is here that synthetic modeling techniques may have their major impact: in producing novel ways of thinking and generating proofs of concept to show that some proposals may not be as coherent as they sound (as in our critical study on value system architectures) or to demonstrate that apparently hazy concepts find clear instantiations even in simple systems (as in the case of emergent coordination through social interaction processes). Methodological minimalism is, therefore, a key element contributing to the acceptability of enactive ideas.

Models that attempt to illuminate the enactive framework must take into account the core ideas of enactivism. A serious take on embodiment will depend on the extent to which a system's behavior relies nontrivially on its body and its sensorimotor coupling with the environment as opposed to input/output information processing. Emergent properties and functionality will contrast with misplaced localization in subagential modules. Autonomy, to the extent that it can be captured in simulation or robotic models, will depend on how the model instantiates the dynamics of self-constituted precarious processes that generate an identity and how such processes create a normativity at the interactive level that leads to sense-making. Enactive modeling must also relate to experience. As a scientific tool, it belongs to the realm of third person methods, so the relation will have to find its place in the process of mutual constraining that has been proposed for the empirical sciences and first person methods already mentioned.

Alongside the explorations presented in this work and the horizons of questions, methods, and explanations that they open, there will be many other areas where enactive views could make a contribution. We repeat that we have not aspired to be exhaustive in neither breadth nor depth. But we do think that we have moved in the direction in which enactivism could grow the strongest: toward higher forms of cognition. Some of the ideas we have explored raise more questions than definitive answers. And this is as it should be in the current context. Focusing on the core concepts of enactivism has been a way of changing perspectives on well-known problems. This will inevitably lead to novel questions, which we have raised throughout the chapter. How do different modes of value-generation coexist in a human subject? How does sense-making get socially coordinated through different kinds of participation? How is the creation of novel meaning achieved in transitional activities such as play? Each of these areas indicates a direction in which much further work is needed and that might possibly lead to newer horizons.

Notes

1. Emergence in this view is close to the notion proposed in Thompson and Varela (2001) and Thompson (2007) with the exception that our second requirement is there presented only as a possibility. We favor a stronger definition, because we want to emphasize the role of mutual causation in order to introduce a sharper contrast between enactivism and reductionism.

2. This is a problem shared by other sensorimotor theories of social cognition such as those built upon the role of "mirror neurons" (Gallese 2001); additionally, such neural correlations themselves should be treated as suspect of the meaning reduction criticized in section 2.3.

3. Interestingly, the agent's behavior resembles the human behavior only if we include a delay between an agent's encounter of an object and input to the neuro-controller. If such a delay is not present, the agent's position eventually converges to a fixed point and stands still. This result raises an interesting question: why do participants keep oscillating around each other, rather than to just "stand on top of each other" after recognition? Our model predicts that sensory delays play a role in this phenomenon and that the amplitude of the scanning oscillations around a target is positively correlated with the amount of delay.

4. Although there is a paucity of research on play strictly from within cognitive science, important relevant works on the subject can be found in the fields of cultural anthropology (Schwartzman 1978), developmental psychology (Sutton-Smith 1997), phenomenology (Fink 1968), animal behavior (Fagen 1981), psychoanalysis (Winnicott 1971), and social science (Goffman 1961; Huizinga 1949).

References

Ashby, W. R. (1960). *Design for a brain: The origin of adaptive behaviour.* 2nd edition. London: Chapman and Hall.

Auvray, M., Lenay, C., and Stewart, J. (2009). Perceptual interactions in a minimalist virtual environment. *New Ideas in Psychology* 27 (1): 32–47.

Bach-y-Rita, P., Collins, C. C., Sauders, F., White, B., and Scadden, L. (1969). Vision substitution by tactile image projection. *Nature* 221:963–964.

Barandiaran, X., Di Paolo, E., and Rohde, M. (2009). Defining agency individuality, normativity, asymmetry and spatio-temporality in action. *Adaptive Behavior* 17 (5): 367–386.

Beer, R. (2003). The dynamics of active categorical perception in an evolved model agent. *Adaptive Behavior* 11:209–243.

Beer, R. (2000). Dynamical approaches to cognitive science. *Trends in Cognitive Sciences* 4:91–99.

Brooks, R. A. (1991). Intelligence without representation. *Artificial Intelligence* 47:139–159.

Bruner, J. (1966). *Toward a theory of instruction.* Cambridge, MA: Harvard University Press.

Chiel, H. J., and Beer, R. (1997). The brain has a body: Adaptive behavior emerges from interactions of nervous system, body and environment. *Trends in Neurosciences* 20:553–557.

Chrisley, R. (2003). Embodied artificial intelligence. *Artificial Intelligence* 149:131–150.

Clark, A., and Toribio, J. (1994). Doing without representing? *Synthese* 101:401–431.

Clark, A. (1997). *Being there: Putting brain, body, and world together again.* Cambridge, MA: MIT Press.

Clark, A., and Grush, R. (1999). Towards a cognitive robotics. *Adaptive Behavior* 7:5–16.

Damasio, A. (1994). *Descartes' error: Emotion, reason, and the human brain.* New York: Putnam.

De Jaegher, H. (2006). Social interaction rhythm and participatory sense-making. An embodied, interactional approach to social understanding, with implications for autism. Unpublished DPhil thesis, University of Sussex.

De Jaegher, H. (2009). Social understanding through direct perception? Yes, by interacting. *Consciousness and Cognition* 18 (2): 535–542.

De Jaegher, H., and Di Paolo, E. (2007). Participatory sense-making: An enactive approach to social cognition. *Phenomenology and the Cognitive Sciences* 6 (4): 485–507.

De Jaegher, H., and Di Paolo, E. (2008). Making sense in participation. An enactive approach to social cognition. In *Enacting intersubjectivity: A cognitive and social perspective to the study of interactions*, ed. F. Morganti, A. Carassa, and G. Riva, 33–47. Amsterdam: IOS Press.

Dennett, D. C. (1993). Review of F. Varela, E. Thompson, and E. Rosch, *The Embodied Mind*. *American Journal of Psychology* 106:121–126.

Dewey, J. [1929] (1958). *Experience and nature*. 2nd edition. New York: Dover.

Di Paolo, E. A. (2000a). Behavioral coordination, structural congruence and entrainment in acoustically coupled agents. *Adaptive Behavior* 8:27–47.

Di Paolo, E. A. (2000b). Homeostatic adaptation to inversion of the visual field and other sensorimotor disruptions. In *From Animals to Animats 6: Proceedings of the Sixth International Conference on the Simulation of Adaptive Behavior*, ed. J.-A. Meyer, A. Berthoz, D. Floreano, H. Roitblat, and S. Wilson, 440–449. Cambridge, MA: MIT Press.

Di Paolo, E. A. (2005). Autopoiesis, adaptivity, teleology, agency. *Phenomenology and the Cognitive Sciences* 4:429–452.

Di Paolo, E. A. (2009). Extended life. *Topoi* 28:9–21.

Di Paolo, E. A., and Iizuka, H. (2008). How (not) to model autonomous behaviour. *BioSystems* 91:409–423.

Di Paolo, E., Rohde, M., and Iizuka, H. (2008). Sensitivity to social contingency or stability of interaction? Modelling the dynamics of perceptual crossing. *New Ideas in Psychology* 26 (2): 278–294.

Donaldson, M. (1992). *Human minds: An exploration*. London: Penguin Books.

Dreyfus, H. L. (2002). Intelligence without representation—Merleau-Ponty's critique of mental representation. The relevance of phenomenology to scientific explanation. *Phenomenology and the Cognitive Sciences* 1:67–383.

Edelman, G. M. (1989). *The remembered present: A biological theory of consciousness*. Oxford: Oxford University Press.

Engel, A. K., Fries, P., and Singer, W. (2001). Dynamic predictions: Oscillations and synchrony in top-down processing. *Nature Reviews Neuroscience* 2:704–716.

Fagen, R. (1981). *Animal play behavior*. Oxford: Oxford University Press.

Fink, E. (1968). The oasis of happiness: Toward an ontology of play. *Yale French Studies* 41:19–30.

Gallagher, S. (1997). Mutual enlightenment: Recent phenomenology in cognitive science. *Journal of Consciousness Studies* 4:195–215.

Gallagher, S. (2001). The practice of mind: Theory, simulation or interaction? In *Between ourselves: Second-person issues in the study of consciousness*, ed. E. Thompson, 83–107. Exeter, UK: Imprint Academic.

Gallagher, S. (2005). *How the body shapes the mind*. New York: Basic Books.

Gallese, V. (2001). The "Shared Manifold" hypothesis: From mirror neurons to empathy. In *Between ourselves: Second-person issues in the study of consciousness*, ed. E. Thompson, 33–50. Exeter, UK: Imprint Academic.

Goffman, E. (1961). *Encounters*. Indianapolis: Bobbs-Merrill.

Goffman, E. (1983). The interaction order. *American Sociological Review* 48:1–17.

Goldstein, K. [1934] (1995). *The organism*. New York: Zone Books.

Gordon, R. M. (1996). "Radical" simulationism. In *Theories of theories of mind*, ed. P. Carruthers and P. K. Smith, 11–21. Cambridge: Cambridge University Press.

Grush, R. (2004). The emulation theory of representation: Motor control, imagery and perception. *Behavioral and Brain Sciences* 27 (3): 377–396.

Harvey, I., Di Paolo, E. A., Wood, R., Quinn, M., and Tuci, E. (2005). Evolutionary robotics: A new scientific tool for studying cognition. *Artificial Life* 11:79–98.

Harvey, I., Husbands, P., Cliff, D., Thompson, A., and Jakobi, N. (1997). Evolutionary robotics: The Sussex approach. *Robotics and Autonomous Systems* 20:207–224.

Heidegger, M. (1962). *Being and time*. Trans. J. Macquarrie and E. Robinson. Oxford: Blackwell.

Hobson, P. (1990). On acquiring knowledge about people and the capacity to pretend: Response to Leslie (1987). *Psychological Review* 97:114–121.

Hobson, P. (2002). *The cradle of thought*. London: Macmillan.

Huizinga, J. (1949). *Homo Ludens*. London: Routledge.

Husserl, E. (1973). *The phenomenology of internal time-consciousness*. Ed. M. Heidegger, trans. James S. Churchill. Bloomington: Indiana University Press.

Hutchins, E. (1995a). *Cognition in the wild*. Cambridge, MA: MIT Press.

Jonas, H. (1966). *The phenomenon of life: Towards a philosophical biology*. Evanston, IL: Northwestern University Press.

Juarrero, A. (1999). *Dynamics in action: Intentional behavior as a complex system*. Cambridge, MA: MIT Press.

Kant, I. (1998). *The critique of judgement.* Trans. James C. Meredith. Oxford: Clarendon Press.

Kelly, S. (2000). Grasping at straws: Motor intentionality and the cognitive science of skillful action. In *Heidegger, coping, and cognitive science: Essays in honor of Hubert L. Dreyfus,* vol. II, ed. M. Wrathall and J. Malpas, 161–177. Cambridge, MA: MIT Press.

Kelso, J. A. S. (1995). *Dynamic patterns: The self-organization of brain and behavior.* Cambridge, MA: MIT Press.

Kendon, A. (1990). *Conducting interaction: Patterns of behavior in focused encounters.* Cambridge: Cambridge University Press.

Kim, J. (1999). Making sense of emergence. *Philosophical Studies* 95:3–36.

Lakoff, G. (1987). *Women, fire, and dangerous things: What categories reveal about the mind.* Chicago: University of Chicago Press.

Le Van Quyen, M., and Petitmengin, C. (2002). Neuronal dynamics and conscious experience: An example of reciprocal causation before epileptic seizures. *Phenomenology and the Cognitive Sciences* 1:169–180.

Lenay, C. (2003). Ignorance et suppléance: La question de l'espace (Ignorance and augmentation: The question of space). HDR 2002, Université de Technologie de Compiègne.

Leslie, A. (1987). Pretence and representations: The origins of "Theory of Mind." *Psychological Review* 94:412–426.

Lewontin, R. C. (1983). The organism as the subject and object of evolution. *Scientia* 118:63–82.

Lutz, A. (2002). Toward a neurophenomenology as an account of generative passages: A first empirical case study. *Phenomenology and the Cognitive Sciences* 1: 133–167.

Maynard Smith, J., and Szathmáry, E. (1995). *The major transitions in evolution.* Oxford: W. H. Freeman.

McGann, M., and De Jaegher, H. (2009). Self-other contingencies: Enacting social perception. *Phenomenology and the Cognitive Sciences* 8 (4): 417–437.

Merleau-Ponty, M. (1962). *Phenomenology of perception.* London: Routledge.

Miller, S. (1973). Ends, means, and galumphing: Some leitmotifs of play. *American Anthropologist* 75:87–98.

Millikan, R. G. (1984). *Language, thought and other biological categories: New foundations for realism.* Cambridge, MA: MIT Press.

Moran, G., Fentress, J. C., and Golani, I. (1981). A description of relational patterns during "ritualized fighting" in wolves. *Animal Behaviour* 29:1146–1165.

Moreno, A., and Etxeberria, A. (2005). Agency in natural and artificial systems. *Artificial Life* 11:161–176.

Nolfi, S., and Floreano, D. (2000). *Evolutionary robotics. The biology, intelligence, and technology of self-organizing machines.* Cambridge, MA: MIT Press.

O'Regan, J. K., and Noë, A. (2001). A sensorimotor account of vision and visual consciousness. *Behavioral and Brain Sciences* 24 (5): 883–917.

Oyama, S. (2000). *The ontogeny of information: Developmental systems and evolution.* 2nd edition. Durham, NC: Duke University Press.

Pfeifer, R., and Scheier, C. (1999). *Understanding Intelligence.* Cambridge, MA: MIT Press.

Piaget, J. (1936). *La naissance de l'intelligence chez l'enfant.* Neuchâtel-Paris: Delachaux et Niestlé.

Piaget, J. (1951). *Play, dreams and imitation in childhood.* London: Routledge.

Piaget, J. (1967). *Biologie et connaissance: Essai sur les relations entre les régulations organiques et les processus cognitifs.* Paris: Gallimard.

Poincaré, H. (1907). *La science et l'hypothèse.* Paris: Flammarion.

Rodriguez, E., George, N., Lachaux, J.-P., Matinerie, J., Reanault, B., and Varela, F. J. (2001). Perception's shadow: long-distance synchronization of human brain activity. *Nature* 397:430–433.

Rohde, M. (2010). *Enaction, embodiment, evolutionary robotics. Simulation models for a post-cognitivist science of mind.* Thinking Machines book series. Amsterdam and Paris: Atlantis Press.

Rutkowska, J. C. (1997). What's value worth? Constraining unsupervised behaviour acquisition. In *Fourth European Conference on Artificial Life,* ed. P. Husbands and I. Harvey, 290–298. Cambridge, MA: MIT Press.

Sacks, H., Schegloff, E. A., and Jefferson, G. (1974). A simplest systematics for the organization of turn-taking for conversation. *Language* 50 (4): 696–735.

Salomon, R. (1998). Achieving robust behavior by using proprioceptive activity patterns. *BioSystems* 47:193–206.

Schiffrin, D. (1994). *Approaches to discourse.* Oxford: Blackwell.

Schwartzman, H. B. (1978). *Transformations: The anthropology of children's of play.* New York: Plenum.

Sheets-Johnstone, M. (2003). Child's play: A multidisciplinary perspective. *Human Studies* 26:409–430.

Silberstein, M., and McGeever, J. (1999). The search for ontological emergence. *Philosophical Quarterly* 49:182–200.

Skarda, C. A., and Freeman, W. J. (1987). How brains make chaos in order to make sense of the world. *Behavioral and Brain Sciences* 10:161–195.

Sporns, O., and Edelman, G. M. (1993). Solving Bernstein's problem: A proposal for the development of coordinated movement by selection. *Child Development* 64:960–981.

Stewart, J., and Coutinho, A. (2004). The affirmation of self: A new perspective on the immune system. *Artificial Life* 10:261–267.

Sutton-Smith, B. (1966). Piaget on play: a critique. *Psychological Review* 73:104–110.

Sutton-Smith, B. (1997). *The ambiguity of play*. Cambridge, MA: Harvard University Press.

Thelen, E., and Smith, L. B. (1994). *A dynamic systems approach to the development of cognition and action*. Cambridge, MA: MIT Press.

Thompson, E. (2001). Empathy and consciousness. In *Between ourselves: Second-person issues in the study of consciousness*, ed. E. Thompson, 1–32. Exeter, UK: Imprint Academic.

Thompson, E. (2005). Sensorimotor subjectivity and the enactive approach to experience. *Phenomenology and the Cognitive Sciences* 4:407–427.

Thompson, E. (2007). *Mind in life: Biology, phenomenology, and the sciences of mind*. Cambridge, MA: Harvard University Press.

Thompson, E., and Varela, F. (2001). Radical embodiment: Neural dynamics and consciousness. *Trends in Cognitive Sciences* 5:418–425.

Trevarthen, C. (1979). Communication and cooperation in early infancy: A description of primary intersubjectivity. In *Before speech*, ed. M. Bullowa, 39–52. Cambridge: Cambridge University Press.

van Gelder, T. (1999). Wooden iron? Husserlian phenomenology meets cognitive science. In *Naturalizing phenomenology: Issues in contemporary phenomenology and cognitive science*, ed. J. Petitot, F. J. Varela, B. Pachoud, and J.-M. Roy, 245–265. Stanford, CA: Stanford University Press.

Varela, F. J. (1979). *Principles of biological autonomy*. New York: Elsevier North Holland.

Varela, F. J. (1991). Organism: A meshwork of selfless selves. In *Organism and the origin of the self*, ed. A. I. Tauber, 79–107. Netherlands: Kluwer Academic.

Varela, F. J. (1996). Neurophenomenology: A methodological remedy for the hard problem. *Journal of Consciousness Studies* 3:330–350.

Varela, F. J. (1997). Patterns of life: Intertwining identity and cognition. *Brain and Cognition* 34:72–87.

Varela, F. J. (1999). The specious present: A neurophenomenology of time consciousness. In *Naturalizing phenomenology: Issues in contemporary phenomenology and cognitive science*, ed. J. Petitot, F. J. Varela, B. Pachoud, and J.-M. Roy, 266–314. Stanford, CA: Stanford University Press.

Varela, F. J., Lachaux, J.-P., Rodriguez, E., and Matinerie, J. (2001). The brainweb: Phase synchronization and large-scale integration. *Nature Reviews Neuroscience* 2:229–230.

Varela, F. J., Thompson, E., and Rosch, E. (1991). *The embodied mind: Cognitive science and human experience*. Cambridge, MA: MIT Press.

Verschure, P. J., Wray, J., Sporns, O., Tononi, G., and Edelman, G. M. (1995). Multilevel analysis of classical conditioning in a behaving real world artifact. *Robotics and Autonomous Systems* 16:247–265.

Vygotsky, L. S. (1966). Play and its role in the mental development of the child. *Social Psychology* 12:62–76.

Walter, W. G. (1950). An imitation of life. *Scientific American* 182 (5): 42–45.

Watson, M. W., and Jackowitz, E. R. (1984). Agents and recipient objects in the development of early symbolic play. *Child Development* 55:1091–1097.

Weber, A. (2003). *Natur als Bedeutung. Versuch einer Semiotischen Theorie des Lebendigen*. Würzburg: Königshausen and Neumann.

Weber, A., and Varela, F. J. (2002). Life after Kant: Natural purposes and the autopoietic foundations of biological individuality. *Phenomenology and the Cognitive Sciences* 1:97–125.

Wheeler, M. (2005). *Reconstructing the cognitive world: The next step*. Cambridge, MA: MIT Press.

Wilson, M. (2002). Six views of embodied cognition. *Psychonomic Bulletin & Review* 9:625–636.

Winnicott, D. (1971). *Playing and reality*. London: Routledge.

Winograd, T., and Flores, F. (1986). *Understanding computers and cognition*. Norwood, NJ: Ablex.

3 Life and Exteriority: The Problem of Metabolism

Renaud Barbaras

In the French language, the verb *vivre* means both "to be alive" (*Leben*) and "to have an experience, to feel something" (*Erleben*): it is neutral with respect to the distinction between the transitive life that we call consciousness, and the intransitive life of organisms that merely keep themselves alive. In this text, we put forward the hypothesis that this neutrality, far from being a simple accident of language, is highly revealing as to the primordial status of life; it thus indicates the direction that a phenomenology of life should take. The question that a phenomenology of life has to confront is thus the following: what is the primordial meaning of life such that it precedes the distinction between intransitive and transitive life, and thereby makes this distinction possible? In other words: what is life such that the possibility of consciousness is grounded therein? From the moment we consider that consciousness is basically characterized by intentionality, primordial life must already contain the germ of a fundamental transitivity where intentionality can be grounded; it follows from this that the question of the Being of intentionality, and that of the mode of Being of life, are one and the same question.

The philosophy of life presented by Hans Jonas seems to indicate the route to follow. His book *The Phenomenon of Life* opens with the following declaration: "Contemporary existentialism, obsessed with man alone, is in the habit of claiming as his unique privilege and predicament much of what is rooted in organic existence as such: in so doing, it withholds from the organic world the insights to be learned from awareness of self" (Jonas 1966, ix). In other words, in Jonas's view, the "insights" that derive from consciousness should properly be attributed to organic existence as such; the task that Jonas sets himself is to conceive of life in such a way that intentional consciousness can find a true grounding therein. Jonas considers that the concept of *metabolism*, by which he characterizes living organisms, meets this requirement. A phenomenology that is concerned with the conceiving of life on the horizon of intentionality must thus examine closely the concept of metabolism in order to evaluate whether it is indeed sufficient to fully account for life, and in particular for that opening toward exteriority that characterizes living experience. If it should turn out that the concept of metabolism, as developed by Jonas's philosophy, does not succeed in giving a fully adequate account of life, then the identification of its limitations will represent a positive step toward defining the conditions for a true phenomenology of life.

Jonas defines life on the basis of metabolism, but this requires, of course, that we are clear about what the term "metabolism" actually means. It turns out that the function of metabolism, as employed by Jonas, is not actually to define life itself, because other physical realities are characterized by identical processes; it is, rather, to give a key to the essence of living organisms precisely to the extent that they escape from strictly material processes. The term metabolism designates the process by which a "whole" maintains itself as such by means of the incessant renewal of the material components of which it is made up. And it is indeed in the very nature of living organisms that their form is maintained in spite of (and in fact because of) an incessant exchange of matter with the environment. Thus, although at any given moment the form does coincide with its matter, over the course of time the form transcends matter, because it remains the same whereas the matter changes. Always different concerning its material constitution, a living organism is always identical concerning its formal identity; namely, it remains the living organism that it is. A signal characteristic of life is that at two moments in time that are sufficiently far apart, its matter cannot be the same; this means that conversely, if the material content is indeed identical at two different moments in time, then we are dealing with an organism that has stopped living and is dead. This is the description that we can give of life as a process, if we restrict ourselves to matter and the laws that govern configurations of matter. In a striking image, Jonas says that if "God were a mathematician" endowed with complete and perfect knowledge of the laws of the physical universe, this is the vision of life that He would have. The question now is whether such a God would really have knowledge of *life*; in other words, whether metabolism is adequate to characterize life itself. Put the other way round, the question is whether it is possible to attain the essence of living organisms strictly in the domain of material processes, which is the domain of metabolism. Now it must be admitted that other physical realities come under this definition, so that God the mathematician would be quite unable to distinguish them from living organisms. A wave, for example, is a dynamic whole that over time is distinct from its material components, that is, the water particles over which the wave passes but which do not themselves move: "the oscillating units of which it successively consists in its progress perform their movements singly, each participating only momentarily in the constitution of the individual 'wave'; yet this as the comprehensive form of the propagated disturbance has its own distinct unity, its own history, and its own laws" (Jonas 1966, 77). This means that in spite of the temporal difference between the wave and its material components, the wave has no reality other than that of the events that compose it; it follows that the wave can be entirely explained on the basis of these events. The wave maintains its form only by means of the incessant renewal of its material parts; it is only temporally distinct from these local processes. This amounts to saying that the permanence of a configuration via renewal of its parts is a mere abstraction, because it has no reality other than that of its parts. Now on the face of it, at least from the point of view of a mathematician-God, living organisms seem to fit this description exactly. There is no reason to invoke anything other than the laws which govern the movements of the parts that, through their renewal, give rise to a permanent configuration.

However, the fact remains that a wave is not a living organism. Jonas concludes that what actually characterizes life itself must be revealed to me in a different domain, namely the experience that I have of my own life. His description of life is situated at the point of convergence between a physicobiological approach to living organisms, which identifies them as forms of metabolism, and an anthropocentric approach, which we might also describe as a phenomenological approach, which makes it possible to specify the metabolism of living organisms by adding a dimension to which we have access only through our own first-person experience. This is the dimension of true individuality, of internal identity through self-constitution or self-realization, and in truth it is here that the real definition of life resides. As Jonas says, "On the strength of the immediate testimony of our bodies *we* are able to say what no disembodied onlooker would have a cause for saying: that the mathematical God in his homogeneous analytical view misses the decisive point—the point of life itself: its being self-centered individuality, being for itself and in contraposition to all the rest of the world, with an essential boundary dividing 'inside' and 'outside'" (Jonas 1966, 79). Thus, being ourselves living organisms, we experience something that a mathematician-God, by His very essence, does not and cannot know: to wit, life as active interiority. Contrary to what a mathematician-God might think, it is not at all the case that a living organism is a consequence of metabolism; it is just the opposite, a vital metabolism is itself a production of an organic unity: "Here whole-ness is self-integrating in active performance, and form for once is the cause rather than the result of the material collections in which it succes-sively subsists. Unity here is self-unifying, by means of changing multiplic-ity. Sameness, while it lasts (and it does not last inertially, in the manner of static identity or of on-moving continuity), is perpetual self-renewal through process, borne on the shift of otherness" (Jonas 1966, 79; see also Jonas 2000, 39). The essence of a living organism resides in the feature that the form is not the consequence but the *cause* of the renewal of matter. The persistence of a form, the metabolic continuity, is the result of an *act*: the unity of a living organism is a uni*fying* unity and not a uni*fied* unity.

This initial analysis of life calls for a number of remarks. First of all, the dimension of self—the internal identity to which we have access in our own experience—can be reinvested in the external description of living organisms only on the condition that it is considered as an *act*. It is not the interiority of an intellectual substance, or even the interiority of a lived experience, and this is what distinguishes Jonas from the spiritualist tradi-tion that he criticizes. According to that tradition, life proceeds by adding a sphere of interiority to a certain sort of physical processes. However, when interiority is understood as an act, it can be integrated with exterior-ity; it can take its place in a physical process precisely as that which gives an impulse to the process. Life thus appears as the cause that was missing for a full explanation of living metabolism. In other words, it is because the internal identity is straight away identified as a vital *activity* that it can be invested in exteriority, and profitably employed for the requisite clari-fication of what "metabolism" actually means.

Second, this theory of life refers to a theory of *individuation*. The funda-mental presupposition here is that a living organism is an individual, and that a living individuality is the only authentic form of individuality. And indeed, the mere unification of diversity, whether by virtue of a synthetic perception or by the play of forces that unite material particles to consti-tute a form that lasts over time, never gives rise to an authentic individu-ation. In that case, it is a mere external or abstract unity, that is only the result of an act of synthesis or a play of forces: such individuality has no reality in itself, but is only the product of the multiplicity that is unified. Jonas concludes that the only true form of individuality is internal, as an essentially active unity that engages in the process of unifying its elements; the only true individuality is that of an act of individuation. This is why there is a reciprocity in the definition of living organisms and individuality: "Only those entities are individuals whose being is their own doing (and thus, in a sense, their task): entities, in other words, that are delivered up to their being for their being, so that their being is committed to them, and they are committed to keeping up this being by ever renewed acts of it. Entities, therefore, which in their being are exposed to the alternative of not-being as potentially imminent, and achieve being in answer to this constant imminence" (Jonas 1968, 233; see also Jonas 2000, 30, 43). This definition of individuality as act, which is just as much a definition of life, situates life in an essential relation with exteriority. Because the only individuality is that which proceeds from a movement or an act of individuation, to be rigorously accurate it must be concluded that the *relation*—in other words, the tense polarity between interior and exterior—is primordial with respect to the terms of the relation. The individuality that characterizes a living organism is the realization of self by "self-isolation" from the rest of reality, a self-isolation that accomplishes itself in and by a unification of self or a "self-integration" (cf. Jonas 2000, 39–43). Now, as is clearly apparent in the text which we have just quoted, this activity that is constitutive of individuality has a meaning only because it is exposed to an opposing force of dispersion and dissolution: this individuality is a conquest gained against the risk of falling back into continuity with external nature, which is neither more nor less than the risk of death. To say that individuality is active is to say that it must be ceaselessly restored and renewed, and this because it is permanently exposed to the eventuality of nonbeing. Thus, the distinctive difference of living organisms is a conquest over continuity with the rest of reality: it is not because a living organism is individuated that it is other than physical nature; on the contrary, it is because it is other than physical nature, on an active mode that requires ceaselessly separating itself, that a living organism is individuated. Life proceeds from a "primordial act of separation," so that it can only be conceived on the basis of a tension between being and nonbeing, which reflects the dual polarity of its relation to the world: a relation of separation, which has to be continually reestablished, and a relation of fusion, which is continually imminent. In the light of this initial analysis, it already appears clearly that according to Jonas life is conceived essentially as *survival*, as perpetuation of self by self-isolation, in other words as conservation by living organisms of their identity and thereby their very being: life is fundamentally preoccupation with self—that is, life is need.

Our third remark bears on what seems to us to be a major difficulty in this first stage of Jonas's investigation. As we have said, it is the passage by the experience that I have of my own life, an experience which distinguishes me from God the mathematician, which enables me to have access to this interiority which in the end is what characterizes the reality of living organisms. In this sense, as Jonas repeats following Canguilhem, the observer of life must be prepared by life: life can only be known by life (Jonas 1966, 92, 99). But after this passage by the experience of my own life, we still have to understand the inverse movement by which I will invest this experience in a way of knowing metabolism that will distinguish what exists as an organism. At this point, Jonas invokes an "interpolation" by which I attribute to metabolic processes seen from the outside with the sort of interiority that I have discovered in myself. The determination of the life of living organisms as "individuation by self-integration" rests, finally, on this interpolation: "It is by this interpolation of an internal identity alone that the mere morphological (and as such meaningless) *fact* of metabolic continuity is comprehended as an incessant *act*; that is, continuity is comprehended as self-continuation" (Jonas 1966, 92; see also Jonas 2000, 43). Now like all theories of projection, this solution raises the following problem: what is it, in the domain of exteriority, that will motivate my interpolation? Why will I attribute this active dimension of perpetuation of self to a plant, but not to a wave? This difficulty stems of course from the initial cleavage between interiority and exteriority. Nothing in the domain of exteriority justifies such an interpolation because, at the material level, there is nothing that distinguishes a wave from a living organism: the "interpolation" would seem to be impossible. But here is the rub: if the interpolation *were* possible, it would ipso facto become useless—because now it would have to be admitted that there *is* something in the domain of reality that motivates the interpolation . . . and it would be this something that motivates the interpolation, and not the interpolation itself, that would provide the proper definition of life. In other words, the recourse to an interpolation does not explain anything at all, because it presupposes what it was supposed to provide a basis for, that is, a distinctive characteristic of living organisms in the domain of exteriority. This difficulty springs from the split between interiority and exteriority, a split that Jonas maintains and that is the consequence of a resolutely materialist ontology.[1] Life is identified first of all in the domain of exteriority, via the concept of metabolism; because this determination is manifestly insufficient, Jonas is then obliged to appeal to the interiority of experience, but finally the articulation between this interiority of experience and the exteriority of metabolism remains totally problematic. Jonas aims to characterize life, but he first misses the mark by undershooting it—there is a lack of interiority with the concept metabolism, and then by overshooting it with the notion of interiority or "self"—an excess of interiority now leads to a lack of exteriority. It is true that the characterization of this "self" as an act reduces the gap, but this is insufficient to properly close the gap, because this act, first identified within myself, must then somehow be attributed by "interpolation" to external processes. In spite of the real advance represented by the dynamic determination of interiority, Jonas continues to conceive of action as an act performed by a self, rather than conceiving the self *as* action.

The essence of life consists of metabolism, and the latter is to be understood as the incessant act whereby a living individual perpetuates itself by renewing its matter. The difference between the form and the matter, which qualifies the form as such, is not at odds with the identity between form and matter, because the form can exceed one particular material state only by coinciding with a new material state. The transcendence of the form is only temporal: it never exceeds the domain of matter, but only a particular present state of matter. Thus, the act that is the essence of a living individual can well be defined as freedom, but Jonas emphasizes that it is a dialectical freedom because it is mediated by its opposite, because the act only detaches itself from matter by totally relying on it: organic freedom is a freedom in necessity. The force and the strength of life is the reverse side of its indigence and weakness; it is an act that proceeds from a fundamental lack, because a lack or failure of matter would also signify a negation of the form.

From this analysis of metabolism, Jonas deduces two other constitutive attributes of the essence of life. First, to the extent that living organisms ceaselessly renew their own matter, they must be in a position to obtain new matter; they are therefore primordially in relation with the external world, the inexhaustible source from which matter can be drawn. In other words, the temporal transcendence of the form with respect to its current matter implies a spatial transcendence, that is, a relation with exteriority wherefrom it can draw the wherewithal to renew itself. As Jonas sums it up, in a formulation to which we will have occasion to return, "its self-concern, active in the acquisition of new matter, is essential openness for the encounter of outer being. Thus 'world' is there from the earliest beginning, the basic setting of experience—a horizon of co-reality thrown open by the mere transcendence of want which widens the seclusion of internal identity into a correlative circumference of vital relationship" (Jonas 1966, 84). It follows immediately that because this description concerns an essence which applies to vegetable life just as well as to animal life, the transcendence which is in question refers to a simple exteriority vis-à-vis the interiority of living organisms; it could quite well be an exteriority without distance, in continuity or in contact with the living organism.

The second essential attribute of living organisms proceeds from the previous one. The relation of a living organism to exteriority cannot be completely indiscriminate; a living form requires a certain sort of matter, which means that a living organism must have the capacity to distinguish, within the world, what is adequate and appropriate to satisfy its needs. The minimal experience of a satisfaction or a frustration is the condition for a discrimination in the domain of matter to be possible, and this experience itself requires something like a subjectivity: "There is inwardness or subjectivity involved in this transcendence, imbuing all the encounters occasioned in its horizon with the quality of felt selfhood, however faint its voice. It must be there for satisfaction or frustration to make a difference" (Jonas 1966, 84). Because it proceeds from a freedom, the relation of living organisms to the world implies a subjectivity, which is not simply postulated but which Jonas presents as being *deduced* from metabolism: the necessity of matter implies a relation to the world, but the necessity of this or that *particular sort* of matter that is relevant for the form implies that this relation be a subjective one. One could therefore say that this subjectivity is a correlate of the individuation of living organisms: interiority exists only as an act, and this is why life is transitive, but there is an act only if it is oriented and selective, and this is why life is subjective. Thus, the "felt selfhood" and the opening toward exteriority are the two sides of the same coin, the two facets of a single existence which is nothing other than metabolism itself. This amounts to saying that life is necessarily consciousness, but in a sense that is not necessarily that of the perception of an object as such: it is a vital consciousness, that is, a sensitivity to that which is other than self. As Jonas writes, "Whether we call this inwardness feeling, sensitivity and response to stimulus, appetition or nisus—in some (even if infinitesimal) degree of 'awareness' it harbors the supreme concern of organism with its own being and continuation in being" (Jonas 1966, 84). The kernel of this vital consciousness is thus *concern*: a being centered on self, a being in intimate proximity with self, a being inherent to the form, because the act of this being is to lastingly sustain itself in its own being. Life as conservation of self by renewal of its own matter implies something like a concern for self, which manifests itself in minimal fashion by the discriminating and oriented nature of the response to external stimuli: the organism "knows" what suits it and what does not suit it. This vital consciousness thus has a meaning which is inseparably intentional and affective: it experiences itself through the recognition of what does or does not suit it in the world; it engenders itself passively in its affectivity by virtue of the responses that it gives to what affects it. We must therefore give Jonas credit for a conception of life that accounts for the coming forth of consciousness: in the form of metabolism, life englobes a minimal sensitivity, from which consciousness as such draws its condition of possibility. It is not so much that sensitivity is a mode of consciousness; rather, consciousness is a mode of sensitivity, which itself refers to vital concern.

The characteristics which we have just examined circumscribe the essence of life, which means that they apply just as much to plants as to animals. It therefore remains to specify these characteristics according to these two kingdoms, in other words, to account for the difference between plants and animals on the basis of metabolism. This point is decisive because, as we shall see, the way in which this difference is described reveals a fundamental decision concerning the essence of life. The difference concerns the mediate or immediate nature of the relation to the environment, which amounts to saying that the emergence of animality proceeds from the coming forth of *distance*. The metabolism of a plant is indeed characterized by its capacity to draw its subsistence from the mineral reserves of the soil with which it is always in contact, in short, to synthesize organic components directly out of inorganic matter. This is what animal metabolism is not capable of; animal metabolism requires nutrients that are already organic, which implies a free mobility. For Jonas, then, vegetable life is already a fully accomplished form of life, which is in no way inferior to animal life; one could even say that it is in vegetable life that metabolism can be perceived in its purest form, as plants continually absorb the matter that it synthesizes to perpetuate its form. Plants are thus "relieved" from the necessity of movement, because they are permanently linked to the source of their nutrition by their roots. Because of this continuity with the environment, a continuity that takes the form of contiguity, there is no distance between the living organism and the matter which nourishes it, and consequently there is no delay between the need and its satisfaction. We may nevertheless note that one cannot simply oppose animal and vegetable as the difference between a capacity and an incapacity for movement. There is a singular vegetable form of motricity (motor function) that is inherent to the fact that in spite of the spatial continuity there remains an ontological gap between the plant and its environment, a gap that is itself the expression of a difference between its form and its matter: this is the explanation for phenomena such as growth, renewal and tropism. It remains nonetheless that the advent of animal life corresponds to the advent of a radically new sort of movement. Whereas in the case of plants movement was confounded with metabolic activity as such—it is always a movement of restoration[2]—in the case of animal life, there comes forth an entirely new sort of activity (Jonas 2000, 54): an activity in the world that prolongs metabolic activity, and that certainly serves metabolism, but that is not at all confounded with it. An animal is the subject of its own movement, and is entirely carried along by it, which never seems to be the case with vegetable movement. In any case, animal life corresponds to the coming forth of a split between the organism and the environment, a split that is not only ontological but spatial: the birth of animal life is the birth of space. This coming forth is in a sense accidental; it does not seem to be intrinsically called for by the essence of life: "a particular branch of it evolves the capacity and the necessity of relating itself to an environment no longer contiguous with itself and immediately available to its metabolic needs" (Jonas 1966, 102).

Now what at first appears to be a defect with respect to vegetable life will give rise to the appearance of properties that vegetable life does not posses, simply because it has no need of them. The distance that characterizes the environment of an animal, and the mediated nature of the relation to the environment that defines animal existence, profoundly transform the nature of its metabolism. Animal metabolism demands that the distance that separates it from the matter that its form requires should be overcome. This is precisely the function of animal movement: it comes in a sense as the replacement of the contiguity which made osmotic exchange possible. But effectively overcoming distance requires a relation to that which is distant, both as being distant but also as that which must be reached, in other words, as the goal of the movement. This is why, with animal life, living sensitivity becomes genuine *perception*, an apprehension of that which is far away. On the other hand, that which is perceived at a distance can only be grasped as a *goal*, as that which must be reached, by means of *desire*. It is this desire that gives an impetus to movement and maintains its continuity, by relating it to the goal that is perceived independently of the movement itself. Thus, according to Jonas, all living organisms are characterized by need, but desire as such springs from the distance, inseparably spatial and temporal, between the need and the object which satisfies it. Desire does not denote a different *relation* to the object—there is only one such relation, which is commanded by the concern with self—but a different *status* of the object, to wit, its appearance at a distance. This new status of the object corresponds itself to a new situation of the subject, a situation which is that of a deficiency, to wit, the incapacity to synthesize organic matter. Desire is thus not something other than need, but need itself insofar as its object is spatially other, that is, at a distance. Jonas makes a careful distinction between the fact that the object is given spatially in perception, and its temporal apprehension in the form of a goal with respect to a need. He thus uses the classical distinction between perception and emotion, between cognition and pathos, in order to refer it to the dimensions of space and time. He is perfectly explicit about this: "Thus desire represents the time-aspect of the same situation of which perception represents the space-aspect. Distance in both respects is disclosed and bridged: perception presents the object 'not here but over there'; desire presents the goal 'not yet but to come': motility guided by perception and driven by desire turns *there* into *here* and *not yet* into *now*" (Jonas 1966, 101). However, we have to ask the question as to what this perceptual given-ness of the object, as distinct from the affective apprehension in desire, could actually consist of. Is the object really apprehended as an object in the world before and independently of being apprehended as a goal in desire—as though the Husserlian primacy of objectifying acts over nonobjectifying acts held sway in the animal world? In what sense are this perception and this emotion both forms of consciousness—how can the consciousness of perception, and desire, both be referred to some primeval form of consciousness? Should we not rather seek in desire itself, as being grounded directly in metabolism, the condition truly intrinsic to life itself for a primordial consciousness that will only subsequently become properly perceptual? Is it not exclusively in desire itself, as relating straight away to a goal pursued by a living organism, that a thing is primordially given to an animal?

   Jonas certainly shows, in conformity with his description of metabolism, that a living organism has to obtain from the external world the matter that is required for the conservation of its form. But does his description of metabolism really make it possible to *ground* the relation of living organisms to exteriority *as such*? In other words, does Jonas really characterize life in a mode such that the consciousness that it is, originally, will be a truly *intentional* consciousness? In this respect, there is a certain vagueness, not to say incoherency, in Jonas's formulations concerning the opening toward exteriority. He emphasizes, as an immediate consequence of metabolism as he has just characterized it, that "'world' is there from the earliest beginning, the basic setting of experience—a horizon of co-reality thrown open by the mere transcendence of want which widens the seclusion of internal identity into a correlative circumference of vital relationship" (Jonas 1966, 84). And Jonas recalls the temporal grounding of the spatial transcendence: "It is important to see that this 'spatial' self-transcendence, opening into an environment, is grounded in the fundamental transcendence of organic form relative to its matter" (Jonas 1966, 84; cf. Jonas 2000, 46, 48). Jonas affirms that a "world" (it is true that he uses quotation marks) is opened by the transcendence of want, a world that he specifies in coherent fashion as a horizon: we must understand by that a coreality, that is, the given-ness of a reality that exceeds the actual object of want, a reality that is the ground on which this object comes forth and that makes it possible to grasp the object as exterior or transcendent. Jonas does therefore recognize, at least implicitly, that a living organism could not go outside in search of the matter that it needs unless it were *originally* in relation with exteriority; he recognizes that the appropriation of this or that object is possible only in the framework of a world. Pursuit or flight, guided by appetite or fear, correspond to a vital choice, but such a choice is conceivable only if it is possible to encounter objects that are a priori neutral with respect to vital requirements, which present themselves as external objects before being qualified by need. Thus, the discriminative dimension of metabolism requires an opening to the world that must be in the first instance neutral, and that will ground the possibility of the satisfaction of a need rather than relying on it. An object can only be pursued or fled from if it emerges on the ground of a world, of a coreality; the latter cannot then be constituted in and by the pursuit or flight. But it is here that the text we have quoted presents a difficulty, because Jonas claims that this world, as a horizon of coreality, is opened by the transcendence of want or need; a little later he specifies this world as an "environment." In the light of what we have just said, this formulation is totally incoherent: the world as such cannot be opened by the transcendence of need because we have just established that this need itself, which calls for a certain mode of satisfaction, *presupposes* the transcendence of a world. As soon as the object of need is indeed what is chosen or selected by a living organism, it refers to a world that must already be given and that therefore cannot be constituted by need. One might try to retort—and this would indeed be the only way to save the coherency of the statement—that Jonas makes a distinction here between need as such, which is inherent to the temporal transcendence of the form vis-à-vis its matter, and particular, finite modes of satisfying need. Thus need, understood as a sort of requirement that is initially indeterminate, would open a world within which this or that specific need would find an object which could satisfy it. But, precisely, the concept of need does not lend itself to such a distinction; on the contrary, it is rather what obliges us to contest this sort of distinction. It is intrinsic to a need that it is determinate or qualified: a need corresponds to a definite, circumscribed lack and so it is always a need of *something* in the sense of a definite object. It is therefore impossible to distinguish, within the domain of need, between a moment of aspiration that is yet undetermined (i.e., without any specific content) on the one hand, and its specification in the form of a determinate necessity on the other: what characterizes need is that only a circumscribed object can awaken it. In other words, a need is entirely turned toward its satisfaction; it aims at nothing other than what would make it cease: it is not so much the expression of an aspiration as the sign of a want which must imperatively be satisfied. A need is always "vital" in the sense that it is indeed the very existence of the subject who experiences it that is at stake. In short, it is the same to say that a need is the expression of a want or a deficiency; that it is always assigned to a determinate object; and that what it pursues is its own satisfaction, which means its own annihilation, of which the object is finally only the means. It is intrinsically characteristic of a need that the distinction between the form (the aspiration as such) and the content, between the general and the particular, is totally inoperative: it is impossible *in principle* to discern in a need a tension or an aspiration that would exceed all finite objects so that it could never be completely satisfied. This means that a need could be only a need of nothing (in particular), and thereby become the principle that opens a world, if it ceases to be a need . . . and becomes desire. We can foresee already that recognizing the necessity of an opening toward exteriority as a precondition for a need that is always selective forces us to introduce a distinction between an aspiration without any determinate content and thus beyond any possible satisfaction on one hand, and an imperative necessity of satisfaction, of filling a want on the other—in short, a distinction between desire and need.

In truth, this conclusion follows from metabolism as it is described by Jonas. As he never stops saying, it is in the temporal transcendence of the form vis-à-vis its matter that the "spatial transcendence of self" (i.e., its opening toward exteriority) is grounded; the possible of this opening therefore refers to the precise status of this temporal transcendence. Now, metabolism is freedom in necessity, which means that the form can constitute itself and maintain itself as such only in and through its coincidence with its matter. A living organism abandons its current matter only in order to substitute for it another matter: the disparity with respect to its matter is subordinated to a coincidence; the difference is subordinated to an identity. If there is a temporal transcendence of the form with respect to its current matter, it is therefore not because a living organism is always in excess with respect to its material determination, as though no matter could ever be fully adequate for it: it is simply because the unity that a living organism realizes with its own matter is constantly undone and must therefore be continually restored. In other words, the excess of a living individuality with respect to its matter is only the reverse side of a *deficiency* in this matter with respect to its form; its (formal) transcendence is only the other side of a material restoration that is always to be reaccomplished over and over again. The transcendence of a living organism, as identified with its metabolism, is not a positive transcendence, and it does not mean that a living organism is turned toward something beyond any determinate matter: it is only the counterpart to the fleeting, fragile nature of its matter.

Now, the status of a living organism's spatial transcendence follows from that of its temporal transcendence. All that we have just recalled amounts to saying that the excess of a living metabolism cannot have any specification other than the contents of its need; that the transcendence of a living organism always corresponds to a want and therefore to the necessity of restoring a determinate content. Need can in no wise be described as an aspiration or a tendency that is as yet indeterminate, which this or that particular content would come to fulfill (but which it could only partially fulfill), and this is why need cannot be the ground for an opening on a world or a horizon that would be distinct from the objects that can subsequently come to specify it. Just as the temporal transcendence of metabolism can only sketch a future which is already *this or that* determinate future, that is, the presence of a certain organic component, so the spatial transcendence for which it provides the foundation can concern only the partial objects of need and never the ground or horizon from which these objects must nevertheless be able to detach themselves. Just as there is no veritable temporal transcendence—because a living metabolism never surpasses itself but only, so to say, catches up with itself—so there can be no veritable spatial transcendence. The constitution of a world, as distinct from the realities that a living organism can find in it, would require an authentic temporal transcendence, in other words, a temporal transcendence taut with the drive toward an indeterminate future, an excess that is not merely the reverse side of a deficiency, an aspiration that is not the consequence of a want. We are thus forced to admit that Jonas's description of the relation to exteriority that follows in the train of metabolism is branded by a fundamental inconsistency: the opening toward a world as the horizon of coreality for an object of need can in no way be grounded in metabolism. The tran-

scendence that follows from metabolism never has the scope of a world—
the exteriority that is the correlate of need is that of a circumscribed
object; it does not ground a world but presupposes it. This exteriority has
no status other than that of a mediation in the relation to self: it is
momentarily opened by the temporal disparity between matter and form—
but this opening is a false one, because this disparity is only a moment
in the frame of coincidence, a fleeting disparity that is always already
made good. This is to say that if Jonas does indeed show why living
organisms have to seek outside themselves the wherewithal to restore
their completeness, he does not show us *how* such a thing is possible,
that is, how there can be an exteriority for a living organism. This is to
say that, contrary to what it seemed at the outset, Jonas's philosophy of
life does not enable us to account for intentionality, without which consciousness can never be authentically conceived. Even if, thanks to his
theory of metabolism, Jonas reveals at the heart of living organisms a
dimension of incompleteness and therefore a principle of exteriority, he
does not succeed in grounding therein the possibility of a consciousness
that would be fundamentally a relation to otherness, a pure opening on
the world.

Nevertheless, in spite of this serious inadequacy, Jonas does indicate the
way to be followed. It is assuredly on the basis of a conception of life as
characterized by a flaw or a deficiency that we will manage to account for
its ex-static dimension, but on condition of conceiving of this flaw or
defect in such a way that it grounds the opening toward an authentic
transcendence, in other words in a much more radical way than Jonas
does. It is therefore in a dimension that exceeds that of need or want,
which will lead us to contest Jonas's determination of living organisms as
metabolism, that we will have to seek the principle of a veritable
intentionality.

As we have seen previously, movement is the primordial dimension on
which the relation to exteriority rests, or rather, movement is the actualized form of that relation. From the point of view of a phenomenology
of life, the fate of intentionality is inextricably linked with that of movement; this amounts to saying that it is rigorously impossible to conceptualize the intentionality of living consciousness without taking into
account its fundamental mobility. Consciousness is only a manifestation
in the process of advancing toward that which is manifest; a phenomenology of life, identified with the neutrality of its origins, is necessarily a
phenomenology of movement. It follows that the failure of Jonas concerning the question of the relation of a living organism to that which lies

outside or beyond it—in other words, the question of the intentionality of consciousness—must derive from a difficulty at the heart of his conception of movement. If the very possibility of a relation to anything other than the self is compromised by Jonas's theory of metabolism, it is because this theory makes it impossible to fully account for the fundamental reality of movement as such.

It is to be noted that in the chapter of his book devoted to metabolism, Jonas does not explicitly mention movement. Jonas defines metabolism as the restoration of matter by form, and from that deduces the necessity for a living organism to "turn itself to the outside," to "direct itself outwards"; however, this "essential opening for the encounter with an external being," this spatial transcendence, is at no point specified as movement. Jonas does insist on the fact that a living organism is not self-sufficient, that it must maintain a relation with that which is not itself in order to survive: a living organism is fundamentally related to an environment. But this relation does not necessarily imply motricity, in the case where everything that the organism needs is immediately accessible and not at a distance. This is exactly the situation of a plant, which exists in virtual continuity with its environment in the sense that it is capable of synthesizing its organic components out of inorganic matter. As we have seen, in the vegetable world, there is no delay between a need and the satisfaction of the need, because there is no distance between the individual and the environment which nourishes it; consequently, there is no movement worth speaking of. From this point of view, motricity appears only with animal life; corelatively, perception and emotion—in other words, a sensitivity at a distance and desire—also appear.

Now this specification of metabolism with respect to these three related terms—motricity, perception, emotion—has a corollary: the emergence of animal life would seem to be a considerable singularity, characterized by a greater precariousness. This analysis by Jonas is apparently rigorous and coherent, but it raises a serious problem, which can be formulated thus: is it possible that something as fundamental as *movement* could arise as a simple subsidiary specification of metabolism, correlated with a rather contingent feature of the situation in which the living organism finds itself? This question has two facets, one concerning the essence and the other the genesis. How is movement *possible*, from the point of view of metabolism? And how can movement, here identified with animal life, have arisen in the course of evolution? These two aspects are profoundly connected. If it should turn out that *movement* as such can be properly conceived only on the basis of a quite different construal of metabolism than that proposed by Jonas, then the strictly evolutionary approach to animal life—according to which the animal kingdom is only a special sub-branch of life characterized by metabolic precariousness—will have to be criticized and profoundly revised.

In substance, Jonas says that an animal moves in order to find what is necessary to maintain its form by renewing its material composition, that is, to go to the place where there is food or to pursue a prey. Movement is thus subordinated to a need, and replaces the osmotic exchange with the environment that characterizes plants; the difference is that there is no longer contiguity, but distance. It follows that movement is not rooted in the basic essence of living organisms as such (plants do not move), but in *distance*, which is a special situation characteristic of animals and in particular the object of their needs. Thus, for Jonas, movement is extrinsic to the essence of life: it is grounded not in life itself, but in a specific defect of being, to wit, the defect of matter due to the exposure of the organism to a hostile environment. More precisely, movement corresponds to a double defect: a defect of matter with respect to its form—this feature is characteristic of metabolism itself—and a defect in the proximity of the object that could compensate for the first defect. In short, a living organism is not mobile in itself, but on the contrary, only to the extent that it is not quite itself: movement comes to fill the ever-forming gap between itself and itself. This is why, in the point of view put forward by Jonas, the final aim of movement is to cease: movement tends toward rest. Expression of a defect of being, as for the Greeks, movement is only accomplished in the form of its own negation. From this viewpoint, movement appears to be as ontologically impossible as it is biologically neces-sary. Indeed, it is quite impossible to understand how a being which is not already movement, in its very essence, could suddenly start to move; how movement could be triggered by a need if it is not already included as a constitutive possibility in life itself. It is important to emphasize here that movement is *ontologically irreducible*. With movement, we enter into another order of reality: in classical terms, movement cannot be a mode or an attribute; it is always substantial and necessarily engages the essence of the subject. It is thus not possible to conceive of the movement of animals as something that accrues to them because of their special situa-tion, because of a need, because of something external to their essence. It is quite intrinsic to movement that it does not and cannot arise from something foreign to it; movement is not a mere contingent modality; it is not possible to enter into the sphere of movement if one is not already in it. Of course an empirical movement can start, but that is because it has always already started, because it is preceded by a form of fundamental, constitutive *mobility*, by what we should call a transcendental mobility. We may add that if movement never starts, it never stops, either; so that rest is not a negation of movement, but a constitutive moment of movement. A being that in its essence is movement can no more leave movement than it can enter it. Thus, a being can *move* itself only if it is able to move *itself*, in other words, to bring itself forward within the realm of mobility. A being can enter into movement empirically only on the condition of being characterized by a fundamental mobility: it *has* a movement only insofar as it *is* in some sense movement. It is only for nonliving entities that movement can, indeed, be merely a state, that is, a mode that does not affect their essence. Interpreting the movement of living organisms as something extrinsic to the essence of life therefore amounts to interpreting living organisms on the model of nonliving entities: it is to completely miss the phenomenological specificity of life. An essential feature of animals is that they move *themselves*, which means that they are the subject of their own movement. But this is to say that they are ontologically situated in movement, that they are on the side of mobility, that they are essentially capable of movement. To sum up, one will never understand how a living organism whose essence does not already include motricity could one day start to move in order to satisfy its needs. The conditions of being at a distance, which Jonas considers to be the cause of movement, would not cause anything at all if animals did not already exist in the sphere of movement. This is to say that—far from emanating from the *satisfaction* of a preexisting need—movement is the condition for need itself. It is not because living organisms need something situated at a distance that they start to move; on the contrary, it is because they are essentially movement that they can enter into relation with something at a distance on the mode of a need, that is, that they can actively appropriate it.

These considerations concerning movement converge here with our previous remarks concerning exteriority. The object of need toward which a living organism advances appears on a transcendental ground, and this ground can be constituted only in and by the essential mobility of living organisms. In and by this transcendental mobility, which is not yet movement toward any particular determinate object, the horizon of the world is constituted. This horizon, which is not yet specified as an object of need, is required by any object whatsoever as the form or the element of its own exteriority. We are, in a way, faced with a choice. Either living organisms are indeed capable of advancing toward distant entities in order to appropriate what they cannot synthesize—in this case, it must be admitted that the essence of living organisms envelops mobility, so that Jonas's description of metabolism is radically inadequate—or the alternative is to retain Jonas's description, but in that case one is forced to conclude that movement, although necessary to satisfy a need, is nevertheless ontologically impossible. According to Jonas, a living organism remains fundamentally a complete individual; it is substance rather than force or dynamism, and movement can have only the accidental, contingent status of that which restores completeness. The hitch is that, for the major ontological reasons we have presented earlier, if movement is *only* that, it is *not even that*: it does not exist at all. Conversely, the entry of living organisms into the sphere of movement—that is, the essential mobility required by the empirical mobility exhibited by the satisfaction of needs—means that we must undertake a profound renewal of the essence of life that Jonas referred to as metabolism. The foregoing considerations indicate already the direction that this renewal should take.

First of all, as Jonas has shown concerning animal life, living movement is a correlate of the feature that the world with which the living organism is related is situated at a distance. To this extent, conceptualizing living organisms on the basis of their constitutive mobility leads to recognizing that their lived world is characterized by an irreducible Distance. Affirming that the intrinsic nature of living movement is such that it cannot be abolished, but on the contrary is ceaselessly renewed, amounts ipso facto to recognizing that this movement never completely attains what it aims at, never comes to possess what it seeks to grasp; the object of this movement is irremediably situated at a distance. Because this Distance is manifestly irreducible, it is not spatial, which amounts to saying that this Distance is not to be confused with a simple empirically measurable length. Even in the case of plant life, proximity never abolishes vitality, which we here equate with mobility. Thus, this Distance is ontological; it may give rise to a spatial approach, but it can never be abolished. In other words, there is an *otherness* about the world of living organisms that, far from being an obstacle or a threat to life, is in reality its very condition of possibility. It follows from this first remark that the whole difficulty will be centered on the status of this Distance, which—although it can give rise to approaches and the crossing of frontiers—nevertheless remains irreducible. The life of living organisms brings us face to face with the enigma of a primordial spatiality: ontological Depth maintains a distant otherness at the very heart of an approach, precisely that distant otherness without which life would not be possible.

Next, Jonas establishes that in the sphere of animal life, the object that appears at a distance in perception is given in desire as a goal to be pursued. Desire is thus the emotion that is specific to animal life as pertaining to a future. Nevertheless, for Jonas, this desire is a sort of modified need: it is what a need becomes when its satisfaction is deferred so that the difference between need and desire is only a matter of degree. If now we revise Jonas's account by considering living organisms according to their essential mobility, in their relation to an object which is irremediably distant, we see that their fundamental "emotion," the basic form of their intrinsic subjectivity, must be characterized as desire. However, this desire is no longer a simple modification of a need. A need is something that is lacking, but that can be satisfied given the delay required to approach the object in question. Desire is quite different, because the Distance that lies between the organism and the object is such that it cannot be obliterated. Thus, instead of desire being a derivative of need, it is desire that is the primordial emotion from which need will proceed. The object of desire should not be defined as the object of need placed at a distance; on the contrary, need should be defined as that which springs from desire when the irreducible Distance takes the form of an object. Need surges forth as the need for an object that is a lure for desire, but this lure is necessary because desire is not a pure, empty aspiration. Desire tends toward its own satisfaction, and must therefore refer to objects of which it will be said that they are needed—even if none of them could sooth the aspiration or interrupt the mobility. Need is thus to Desire as the object to that Distance that it figures, that is, both reduces and conserves.

Finally, by putting forward the essential mobility of living organisms, we are led to rethink the whole relation between animal and vegetable. The question of movement engages the very possibility of animal life, that is, the surging forth of movement in the course of evolution. Now in view of what we have already established, it has become quite impossible to consider that movement "arose" and hence that animal life could be born: if movement is constitutive of the very essence of living organisms, as we have argued, then a living organism without motricity is literally inconceivable. More precisely, we have established that animal movements must be referred to an essential mobility. But precisely because it is essential, this mobility cannot have arisen as a simple empirical event at some contingent point in the course of evolution. Just as empirical movements proceed from a constitutive mobility of animals, so animal mobility itself proceeds from an essential mobility in all living organisms; this amounts to saying that mobility characterizes the essence of living organisms. This point can be put another way, from the point of view of the essence of movement: if movement does indeed belong to a specific ontological register—in other words, to an irreducible mode of being—it is impossible to separate living organisms according to the presence or absence of movement. Life is the incarnation of this mode of being, which attests to its reality, and so movement is the very substance of life. In short, one cannot infer from the apparent, empirical absence of local movement that movement is not constitutive of living organisms in their very being. But this now raises the question of vegetative life: how are we to understand the relation between plant and animal life?

We can summarize the meaning of the theory of metabolism by saying that, for Jonas, plant life remains the prime model for living organisms, so that animal life is fundamentally conceptualized on the basis of plant life. An animal seems to be a plant *plus* something—motricity, perception, emotion—because Jonas considers that an animal is, in truth, a plant *minus* something—to wit, the capacity to synthesize organic components out of inorganic material. It is true that Jonas recognizes that a "radically new sort of action" appears with animal life (1966, 116); this is mediate action—action in an external sphere. However, as the term itself indicates, this "mediate action" arises as a modification of the previously existing *immediate* action that characterizes vegetable life. All we can say is that, with animal life, the characteristics of organic life that have been demonstrated at the level of plant life "come into full light" (Jonas 2000, 49). It is hard to deny that the vegetative mode of existence constitutes the model from which the concept of metabolism has been constructed. Metabolism basically refers to the activity by which a form maintains itself as such by ceaselessly renewing its matter via a continual exchange with its external environment. And indeed, one cannot better describe the vegetative mode of being, whose individuality presents itself as a morphological unity, and whose essential activity consists of ensuring the requisite exchanges with the external environment, in words other than reconstituting its own substance by synthesizing it out of inorganic elements. The concept of freedom in necessity is eminently suitable for plant life, which can free itself from matter only by renewing it, and which thus does not so much free itself from matter as from a particular, actual set of matter.

However, if we think about it, this is not what is salient if we consider the existence of animal life, which rather manifests a freedom emancipated from necessity. Indeed, an animal manifests an activity that does not seem to be subordinated to the mere reproduction of self: an animal plays, explores, fights, rests. Thus, even if biologists can ultimately refer many of the movements of an animal to the requirements of reproduction (of the self and of the species), in truth one has rather the feeling that metabolic activity is a limited, subordinate process, a mediation in the service of a profuse activity whose meaning goes way beyond the simple aim of reconstituting the individual. To put it another way, an animal can be brought down to the level of metabolism only if it is considered at the strictly biochemical level of molecular synthesis and cellular reproduction, that is, the level that animals do share with plants, but this can be done only to the detriment of the "psychological" and ethological level, where the animal appears according to its own characteristic behavior and mode of being. Now it is clear that no mobility will ever be discovered at the level of biochemical analysis. Thus, contrary to what he claims, when Jonas puts forward the concept of metabolism, he does not describe the true *phenomenon* of life. On the contrary, he approaches life at a level that is not phenomenal, but objective (in the sense of scientific objectivity)—even if he does integrate, after the event, several elements that are borrowed from the phenomenal domain. The metabiological, philosophical subordination of the animal to the plant is in fact commandeered by an underhand subordination of the phenomenal order to the objective order, of the phenomenological to the biochemical. It is indeed at this objective level that a precise determination of vegetative life is possible.[3] And however this might be, when Jonas describes metabolism, he has in view the vegetative mode of being. The fundamental activity of this mode of being consists of the incessant reconstitution of the self, of maintaining a form that is an exception in the physical universe and that is thus always threatened by a continual renewal of matter.

We may emphasize here, to anticipate, that this choice of vegetative life is coherent with a certain idea of life as conservation, as survival. The choice of vegetative life as the matrix of all living organisms, and the characterization of life as conservation of self against the permanent threat of negation, are the two faces of the same theoretical decision that finds articulate expression in the theory of metabolism. In this perspective, it follows that the animal is a "super-plant," that is, a plant that just because of an initial inferiority—its incapacity to synthesize organic substance—has developed "faculties" (movement, perception, desire) that enable it to largely mitigate this initial defect and to conserve its individuality. Jonas emphasizes that this gain in complexity and freedom has the counterpart of an increased precariousness. To sum up, animal life is fundamentally conceptualized by reference to plant life, so that for Jonas it must be possible to reduce the qualitative gulf that separates animals and plants on the phenomenological level to a mere difference of degree. The "distance" that corresponds to the emergence of the animal mode of being is only a distension of osmotic continuity: an animal is a plant that has lost contact, and that must therefore find a way of appropriating that which is no longer in contact. Thus, Jonas considers that perception arises from a primordial sensitivity by spatial distancing of the object, that desire arises from need by temporal delay, and finally that movement arises from immobility or, more precisely, from a displacement of osmotic exchange.

Now this is precisely what we have shown to be impossible. From immobility, no movement can come forth; a vegetative form of life cannot transform itself into active domination of the world. The fact that living organisms are capable of movement therefore means that movement belongs to the very essence of life: movement arises *with* life, and never from within life. But it is important to draw all the consequences of this. Saying that movement is constitutive of living organisms as such amounts to saying that animals, so clearly characterized by their mobility, are the prototype of living organisms, the very model of living organisms. It follows that *plant life should be conceptualized with reference to animal life.* Taking movement into consideration as a condition of possibility for life itself leads to a direct inversion of Jonas's position. Animal life is not to be referred to as a specialization or complexification of plant life; on the contrary, animal life is itself the reference from which plant life is to be conceptualized—otherwise we will never gain access to the animal mode of being. An animal is not a living organism that would possess something more than a plant (on the basis of a metabolic inferiority); on the contrary, it is the plant that possesses something less than the animal, the latter representing the archetypal mode of being of living organisms. This leads us to engage in what we may call a *deprivational botany*, which is a sort of echo to Heidegger's "deprivational zoology." Just as "the ontology of life is accomplished by way of a privative Interpretation; it determines what must be the case if there can be anything like mere-aliveness [Nur-noch-leben]" (Heidegger 1962, 75), the task of the metabiology of plant life is to determine what must be, in order for something that exists only in the vegetative mode to be possible. Just as it is starting from the *Dasein* that by taking away certain features one arrives at that which is only living, so by starting from the animal one arrives, by taking away certain features, at the mode of being of the plant: it is the animal that must exist, in order for something that exists only on the vegetative mode to be possible. Animal nature thus delivers the essence of life, of which vegetable existence appears as something like a minimal modality. This inversion, which is required by considering what is required for animal movement to be possible, leads to a subordination of the biochemical level relative to the phenomenological or existential level. This is precisely what Jonas's approach did not allow.

The task that confronts us now is thus to apprehend life, taking animal life as our prototype, as a certain manner of existing characterized first and foremost by movement, and to do so in such a way that the mode of being of plants will also be described phenomenologically so that metabolism, which Jonas put to the fore, will be definitively relegated to the background. This approach leads us to reverse the signs of Jonas's description. It consists of considering plants as lacking something compared to animals, as animals *minus something*. Thus, distance is no longer a distension of osmotic continuity; it is rather a general characteristic of the relation between a living organism and its world, and thus proximity or continuity with the environment, which is specific to plants, now becomes a lack of distance. It follows that the simple, immediate satisfaction of needs, also characteristic of vegetative existence, is to be understood as a degraded form of desire: a desire lured by possession of the object that is supposed to appease it. Desire is not a need whose object happens to be at a distance; rather, need is a desire whose object happens to be in the immediate proximity. And even this proximity is a false proximity, because the relation to transcendence is constitutive of the very existence of living organisms. It follows that setting up a spatial contiguity, as is characteristic of plants, does not and cannot mean the suppression of Distance. What is to be understood here is that the primordial meaning of Distance is not spatial: space is not an a priori condition for Distance; on the contrary, space is a specific modality that derives from Distance. It is not because things are in space that they can be far away; on the contrary, it is because they *are* far away—because Distance is what characterizes their mode of being—that they can be in space. Thus, by nullifying the spatial distance that characterizes the objects of animal desire, plant life does not overcome its fundamental Distance, which indeed cannot be overcome, because it is, in a sense, interior. The distinction between animal and plant life cannot refer to the particular spatial position of their objects (at a distance or in contact), because this position is derivative with respect to a fundamental "far-awayness." Spatial distance and spatial contact are only two "geometrical" modalities of a "far-awayness" or "depth" that are, so to speak, pregeometrical and prespatial. It is precisely this far-awayness that animal existence exhibits in exemplary fashion: the spatial distance of its object reveals an ontological Distance. More precisely, the instability that characterizes animal movements, and the insatiability that is revealed by animal desire, are manifestations of the fact that underlying their relation to spatial distance, animals relate to a Distance that is ontological and therefore irreducible.

Finally, just as vegetative need is to be understood as a degraded, limited form of animal desire, so the relative immobility of plants should be understood negatively from the point of view of the movement that is constitutive of life itself. This amounts to saying that plants are not really immobile, that they are not strangers to the realm of movement; their activity is not a nonmovement but rather a lesser movement, an inchoate movement. One should not say that movement arises with animal life, but rather that movement is limited, hemmed in, hampered in vegetative life. Actually, Jonas himself does recognize that there is a form of vegetable mobility, even if it is marked by its slowness, by an absence of displacement, by continuity and irreversibility (Jonas 1968, 202). The time has come to recall that movement must not be reduced to mere local movement, which is only one modality among others of change. Change can be substantial and ontological, in which case it gives rise to a birth or a disappearance, but change can also be qualitative (alteration) or quantitative (growth). And it is doubtless because Jonas did not introduce these distinctions with sufficient care, which left him a prisoner to the spontaneous reduction of movement to mere local movement, that Jonas refrained from including movement in his general description of metabolism and reserved it to animal life alone. And indeed, vegetable activity does constitute a form of movement, but this vegetable movement expresses a relation to distance that is ontological rather than properly spatial. This is why vegetable activity does not develop in the form of displacements, at least not in displacements that carry along the living subject as a whole. In this sense, vegetative life represents a sort of minimal, purified form of vital movement; the fully spatial movement of animals is then a more fully accomplished deployment of this same vital movement. Vegetative life represents a sort of primordial discovery of exteriority, of an initiation to the world, of an entry into space: whereas animals move themselves in a world that is already available, already constituted, plants—so to speak—deploy space by occupying it, that is, by their own development. It is in this sense that the considerations of Scheler concerning vegetable life can be understood, even if the context of his discussion is quite different. In Scheler's view, "*life*, considered in its 'vegetative' *essence* as in plants . . . is an impulse which is exclusively directed *towards the outside*. The 'emotional impulse' of plants is thus 'ex-static'" (Scheler

1951, 27). What Scheler means by this is that vegetable movement is not centralized, that it does not turn back on itself, that it is exclusively deployed from the center toward the periphery.[4] Now this ex-static movement, which corresponds to vegetable growth, manifests an inchoate relation to exteriority; it is the discovery of a transcendence that is primarily ontological (growth is an aspiration to an outside, an advance toward otherness) rather than strictly spatial. Just as the continuity of vegetative life with its environment is a negation of distance, and its need a negation of desire, so the ex-static movement of plants should be understood in terms of deprivation with respect to animal movement: the latter is deployment and mastery of space, whereas plant movement is simply an entry into exteriority. Understanding that the mode of being of living organisms must be referred to the mode of being of movement—without this, the movements of animals and the primordial exteriority underlying them become definitively incomprehensible—is to understand that the only true botany is deprivational.

It follows from all this that it makes no sense to affirm that animal life "came forth." Openly basing himself on evolutionary theory, Jonas claims that "a particular branch of life" developed a capacity to enter into a dynamic relation with the environment, but this is unacceptable. Understanding that movement cannot start at some contingent point in history, that it is constitutive of life itself, amounts to recognizing that genesis refers back to essence, that the genetic order of coming forth reveals a constitutive precession. Jonas actually recognizes this himself because, although he subscribes to the Darwinian scheme, he interprets it in the opposite direction to current versions: rather than making it possible to reduce man to an animal, Jonas interprets the scheme as revealing a precession of human features at the heart of even the most elementary animal forms (Jonas 1966, 67). The hitch is that Jonas does not go the whole way, and does not fully draw the consequences of this concerning the relation between animal and vegetable life. He does, certainly, construct a theory of metabolism that is supposed to account for the possibility of animal life; to that extent, he does establish a mode of precession of the "superior" in the "inferior." But he does not take full measure of the implications of the animal mode of being and the ontological significance of movement which characterizes it, which amounts to saying that Jonas is implicitly dominated by the model of the plant. From this there follows a sort of imprecision, not to say incoherence: his theory of metabolism presupposes a primordial exteriority for which it provides no grounds, and it presupposes animal movements that cannot be explained because they have no grounding in any intrinsic mobility. Thus, by considering animal life as a mode of being to be conceived on the basis of the sort of purified metabolism exemplified by plant life, Jonas is in the end unable to account for the specificity of animal life.

Now this relative phenomenological failure reveals some presuppositions concerning both the meaning of life and the meaning of reality, and we shall conclude on this point. The activity that Jonas describes under the concept of metabolism corresponds to a theoretical formulation of a highly traditional concept of life: life is through and through a struggle for the preservation of life; it is the act of keeping itself alive. The reverse side of the existence of a living individual, of its vital activity, is its absolute submission to the pressure of need: the counterpart to its freedom is necessity, the counterpart to its force is its mean dependence. This amounts to saying that life is fundamentally survival, that life has no other goal than the preservation of living organisms, in other words of life itself. This concept of life is characterized by a logical circularity, as life is presupposed in its own definition (to live is to keep oneself alive), but this circularity is not a logical vice—it is the condition of life itself. Life is always that which presupposes itself, but in the last resort this amounts to saying that life is that which cannot have a meaning.

Now in Jonas's own account this concept of life, which underlies the theory of metabolism, comes together with an approach which addresses life from the point of view of its relation to death, with the horizon of its own destruction. Life is that which is fundamentally exposed to the risk of its abolition: it is right from the start a relation to its possible negation and so can only exist as a negation of that negation. We will here quote at length from a text that is particularly striking in this respect (and to which we will have occasion to return):

The privilege of freedom carries the burden of distress and signifies: existence in danger. Because the fundamental condition of this privilege resides in the paradoxical fact that, by an original act of separation, living substance has detached itself from the universal integration of things in the totality of nature so as to position itself in front of the world, thereby introducing, into the indifferent security of the possession of existence, a tension between 'being and not-being' [...]. Qualified at the most intimate level of its being by the threat of its negation, the being must here assert itself, and a being which asserts itself is existence in the form of a request. Thus, the living being itself, instead of being a given state, has become a possibility that must be constantly achieved, that must ceaselessly regain over its opposite which is always present, the non-being, which in the end will inevitably end up by engulfing it. (Jonas 2000, 30)[5]

Thus, in spite of his proclaimed intention to describe the phenomenon of life as such, Jonas manages only to conceive of life with reference to death: he does not grasp life in itself as an affirmation with a meaning that remains to be identified, but rather on the basis of what is not life, as a negation that does not have any meaning besides its own activity. To live is to be in a relation with one's own death; it is to counter the perpetual threat of obliteration. This initial conclusion calls for at least three remarks.

Jonas seems to take up here, in a manner that is obviously much more fully developed, a naïve (and historically overwhelming) conception of life that aligns it with survival and thus reduces it to the active satisfaction of needs. However, at the same time, his formulations seem to echo certain statements of Heidegger,[6] so much so that at times one has the impression that we are dealing with a transposition, into the domain of life in general and in the framework of a realist ontology, of certain fundamental features of the analytics of the *Dasein*. It may be this continuing dependence on Heidegger[8] that, even more than the "pragmatic" conception of life that underlies evolutionary theory, explains why the relation with death is such a pregnant theme in Jonas's approach to life. At any rate, this is the lucid suggestion of Nathalie Frogneux in her book devoted to Jonas: "Even though his aim is to 'correct' the idealistic defect in Heideggerian existentialism by grounding it in living matter, his philosophy of biology turns out to be deeply marked by existential themes (care, being for death, solitude). The question which must be asked is whether he does not concede too much to what he denounces as an aberration of contemporary idealism in order to really claim to have overcome it" (Frogneux 2001, 162).

However—and this is our second remark—precisely to the extent that Jonas places himself in the domain of living matter, the relation of living organisms to nonbeing appears to be eminently problematical as to its very possibility. Thus, the fact that living organisms manage to separate themselves from inert matter, so that they are objectively subject to the equalizing, dissolving power of the forces of inert matter, in no way implies that living organisms are exposed "in their own terms" to this threat of negation, that is, that they are themselves in relation with nonbeing as such. In other words, Jonas passes by sleight of hand from an external negation to an internal negation: he speaks as though the objective risk of destruction of living organisms, which is inherent to the laws of matter, implies that living organisms actually experience a threat, a fragility—in short, a relation to nonbeing as such. But this passage is highly problematical, to say the least: the "nonbeing" that is supposed to be the constant preoccupation of living organisms, with which their being is supposed to lie in precarious balance, does not actually have any positive content other than the existence of a physical nature; in other words, "nonbeing" as such has no content for a living organism. The negation in question is only external; it corresponds only to the tension between natural forces and a living individual, and this tension is only objective—it has a meaning only for the scientific observer but not for the living organism itself. A living organism could establish a relation with this nonbeing only if it could occupy the position of an observer and look at itself from outside—but this would be in contradiction with its essence. The tension and the objective risk of destruction are inherent to the distinction between the living organism and the world; in other words, they are inherent to the ontological closure of the organism, but from the point of view of the living organism itself, it is impossible to understand how this tension and this risk could be interiorized and actually experienced as a tension between being and nonbeing. The "nonbeing" has no content other than the existence of the world from which the living organism has separated itself by constituting itself as an individual; the negativity of external nature is only the counterpart to this first negation, which consists of this act of separation. In short, there is no negation other than the original separation on which the being of a living organism rests. But then, if "nonbeing" has no other reality than the very being of the individuated living organism, one does not see how a living organism could "waver on the edge between being and nonbeing," how nonbeing could be "an alternative contained in being itself" (Jonas 2000, 30).

Now this objection is extremely serious, because the vital dynamics of living organisms spring from this very tension. Jonas says, "Qualified at the most intimate level of its being by the threat of its negation, the being must here assert itself, and a being which asserts itself is existence in the form of a request. Thus, the living being itself, instead of being a given state, has become a possibility that must be constantly achieved" (Jonas 1966, 30). Life consists of an affirmation, the need (the request) that pushes it towards new matter, and this "affirmation" depends entirely on the fact that the threat of negation qualifies living organisms "in their most intimate nature." But in this case, the impossibility of a real relation to nonbeing radically compromises the possibility of metabolism itself: in the end, one does not see what incites living organisms to renew their matter. What is at stake here is Jonas's pretension to give a description of metabolism as an objective phenomenon; he introduces an underhand confusion between an objective, scientific point of view on one hand, and a phenomenological point of view, that of the living organism itself, on the other. In the objective domain, a relation to nonbeing is inconceivable; a "threat" can be inscribed at the heart of life only by renouncing an objective point of view. Finally, we are on the horns of a dilemma. Either we restrict ourselves to an objective approach, in the guise of a theory of metabolism—but in this case one cannot understand how a metabolism, consisting of simply satisfying needs, is possible, or else one recognizes that life is indeed a "possibility to be realized" rather than a "state," that its being is so to say entrusted to it as that which it must ceaselessly perform—but in that case it is necessary to introduce at the heart of life itself a dimension of negativity or defect which exceeds the bounds of the objective domain and therefore renders the theory of metabolism inoperant. The real question is thus the following: what is the meaning of the existence of living organisms as being capable of incessant activity, as being drawn toward its own continuation? The difficulty is that the conditions undermine that of which they are the condition, they denounce as mere appearance that which presented itself as the reality in question. Thus, Jonas limits himself to the description of a minimal vital activity, but this minimal activity can be conceived as vital only if a certain negativity is introduced at the heart of life *as its very mode of existence*. What could this mean, if not that living organisms only move and survive because nonbeing is at the heart of their being, that their very mode of existence is characterized by a fundamental defect? A living organism lives only to the extent that it is not what it is, or rather to the extent that it is what it is on the mode of a defect or a lack, on the mode of what it must everlastingly but unavailingly become. This defect is not objective; it is constitutive of the mode of being of living organisms and this is why it is irreducible. Thus, the tension between being and nonbeing can make up the fabric of life only on the condition that it forms an identity—the being of a living organism is that of a negation—which is effectively realized as a defect. There is nothing that is lacking for a living organism; nothing is missing, not because living organisms are characterized by their completeness, but on the contrary, because their whole being is situated on the mode of a defect or a lack. In short, what Jonas does not see is that a living organism can only entertain a relation with non-being, can only *have* such a relation by *being* it. This amounts to overcoming the alternative between being and nonbeing—an alternative that remains abstract because it derives from objective thought—in favor of a more profound mode of being that phenomenology has the task of elucidating. It is indeed the task of philosophy to identify the conditions of possibility that lie behind a given reality. But in the present case, we find that the conditions are incompatible with the very reality that they are supposed to make possible. By subordinating needs to this singular mode of existence that we have called "lack of self," we have overshot the mark. If living organisms exist on the mode of their own defects—that is, by not being what they are—their life cannot be reduced to the satisfaction of needs. When leaving the objective domain for the sake of an existential domain, we discover that the concept of "need" has no biological relevance. Insofar as what is lacking for a living organism is its own being (and not just a material part that is necessary for the constitution of its form)—and it is only in this sense that a living organism can be qualified by nonbeing—it is evident that its life cannot consist in the pursuit of this or that substance. To say that it exists on the mode of a defect of self amounts to saying that nothing can remedy the defect, so that life cannot consist of simply pursuing something. The whole question is then to understand on what mode this existence marked by the sign of negativity can effectively be realized, to identify what living organisms relate to in a primordial sense, to specify the positive side of the medal whose reverse side is the mode of defect. Thus, the negativity that Jonas rightly introduces into living existence can be conceptualized only on the condition of renouncing the objective approach, and hence renouncing the theory of metabolism as an activity of restoring the vital integrity, that is, of satisfying needs.

This leads us straight to our third remark. The problem comes from the notion that there is a vital integrity which requires restoration, that is, that a living organism is to be characterized as an *individual*. This is the fundamental presupposition of Jonas's description: that the reality of a living organism is that of an individual, of a self (that is to say, in fact, of a form) that constitutes itself by self-isolation from the rest of reality; when we come to think of it, vital activity is wholly at the service of this individuality that must ceaselessly be preserved and reconstituted. More radically, as we have seen, the only true individuality is that of a living organism— "only those entities are individuals whose being is their own doing" (Jonas 1968, 233)—so that being alive and being an individual are purely and simply equivalent. As soon as the being of a living organism is conceptualized as a process of separation, of segregation and thus of isolation from the rest of matter, its individuality implies doing, a continual recreation of the separation. The objective approach to living organisms as arising from a process of separation, their characterization as individuals, and the definition of their mode of being as metabolism are profoundly interconnected. But the question is: *should* living organisms be thought of as individuals? Our previous remarks concerning the specific mode of existence of living organisms obviously lead us to doubt that this is so. If a living organism exists on the mode of its own defect—that is, it is always less than itself—it cannot be thought of as an individual; on the contrary, its defect of being is ipso facto a *defect of individuality*. This does not mean that a living organism dissolves into an anonymous generality, but rather that its existence is precisely a process of individuation. A living organism is always in movement toward an individuality that always lies ahead, so that vital activity is neither more nor less than the movement of individuation. Let us be clear: a living organism is not engaged in a quest for an individuality that is both already constituted and always threatened, as is the case with Jonas's work. Rather, a living organism is engaged in producing or achieving an individuality that is always pushed further away by the very achievement, an individuality that exists as its own horizon or its own imminence.

All these considerations converge toward a single critical conclusion: in his writings about life, Jonas does not escape from an *ontology of death*, even though he himself has drawn the contours of this ontology. There are two senses in which this is so. First, Jonas addresses life in terms of its negation rather than on its own terms: the presupposition that life is the negation of death continues to underlie the concept of metabolism. Second, life is also defined as a negation of death, because it is thought of as proceeding from an "original act of separation," as being "demarcated from the universal integration of things into the totality of nature, so that it exists in opposition to the world." Thus, life is situated in the bosom of an objective nature wherein it appears as an exception. By approaching life from the point of view of that which is not life—that is, on the basis of what is "life-less"—Jonas repeats the initial gesture of the ontology of death. It is because Jonas approaches life from the viewpoint of that which is not life—that is, the viewpoint of an inert nature—that life will be defined as an opposition to its own negation: the constitutive relation of life to nonbeing results from this initial gesture of rescuing life from the clutches of inert matter. This double negation—a negation of the inert by separation from it, and an active negation of the threat of destruction that the physical world represents—exactly delineates the space of an ontology of death, which, after all, is only another name for the realist or naturalist ontology that Jonas fully accepts (Jonas 1966, 30). It is true that Jonas, fully conscious that such an ontology leads to a total impasse concerning life, subsequently sets himself to demonstrate that living organisms are ontologically irreducible, but it is by then too late. The ontological irreducibility of living organisms can be grounded only on an act—distinguishing metabolism from other similar processes—that presupposes a self, in other words, that reintroduces the dimension of a soul or a spirit. Jonas is thus inevitably led, willy-nilly, to a dualist metaphysics that is always the consequence of an ontology of death. We are lead to the conclusion that we will be able to gain access to the meaning of life only on the condition of performing an *epokhe* of death, in the twin forms of a suspension of the death to which life is exposed, and a suspension of the naturalist ontology from which this definition of life proceeds.

Notes

Translated from the French by John Stewart.

1. This is not in contradiction with the "spiritualism" that Jonas has often been criticized for; in fact, it is simply the reverse side of the same coin.

2. It should however be emphasized that plant growth can often exhibit an exuberance and a profusion that exceed the bounds of mere restoration. We shall come back to this point, which calls perhaps for a different view of the significance of plant life.

3. Even though, as Scheler in particular has shown, an expression of the primordial phenomenal order can already be found at the level of vegetative existence (cf. Scheler 1951, 28).

4. This is why there is no vegetable consciousness. Consciousness requires a reflection, a turning back to self; plants are incapable of this because they are entirely outside themselves, carried away by their own movement.

5. The term "need" would have been more precise here than the term "request."

6. Thus, concerning the individual: the only beings who are individuals are "only those entities are individuals whose being is their own doing (and thus, in a sense, their task): entities, in other words, that are delivered up to their being for their being, so that their being is committed to them, and they are committed to keeping up this being by ever renewed acts of it. Entities, therefore, which in their being are exposed to the alternative of not-being as potentially imminent, and achieve being in answer to this constant imminence" (Jonas 1968, 233). Elsewhere, life is defined as "preoccupation with self" (Jonas 1966, 93) characterized by "anxiety" (Jonas 2000, 31) and concern: "to an entity that carries on its existence by way of constant regenerative activity we impute *concern*" (Jonas 1968, 243).

7. We may recall that however severely Jonas criticizes Heidegger in *The Phenomenon of Life*, he was first of all Heidegger's pupil.

References

Frogneux, N. (2001). *Hans Jonas ou la vie dans le monde*. Bruxelles: De Boeck.

Heidegger, M. (1962). *Being and time*. Trans. John Macquarrie and Edward Robinson. Oxford: Blackwell.

Jonas, H. (1966). *The phenomenon of life*. New York: Harper & Row.

Jonas, H. (1968). Biological foundations of individuality. *International Philosophical Quarterly* 8:231–251.

Jonas, H. (2000). *Evolution et liberté*. Trans. S. Cornille and P. Ivernel. Paris: Rivages.

Scheler, M. (1951). *La situation de l'homme dans le monde*. Trans. M. Dupuy. Paris: Aubier.

4 Development through Sensorimotor Coordination

Adam Sheya and Linda B. Smith

At every moment of our lives, there is something going on, some experience. We see, hear, smell, touch, think.
—Varela, Thompson, and Rosch 1993, 59

Piaget (1952) described a pattern of infant activity that he called a secondary circular reaction. A rattle would be placed in a four-month-old infant's hands. As the infant moved the rattle, it would both come into sight and also make a noise, arousing and agitating the infant and causing more body motions, and thus causing the rattle to move into and out of sight and to make more noise. Infants at this age have very little organized control over hand and eye movement. They cannot yet reach for a rattle and if given one, they do not necessarily shake it. But if the infant accidentally moves it, and sees and hears the consequences, the infant will become captured by the activity—moving and shaking, looking and listening—and incrementally through this repeated action gaining intentional control over the shaking of the rattle. Piaget thought that this pattern of activity—an accidental action that leads to an interesting and arousing outcome and thus more activity and the re-experience of the outcome—to be foundational to development itself. Circular reactions are perception-action loops that create opportunities for learning. In the case of the rattle, the repeated activity teaches how to control one's body, which actions bring held objects into view, and how sights, sounds and actions correspond.

Edelman (1987) also pointed to the coupling of heterogeneous sensorimotor systems in the creation of cognition. Edelman's theory starts by recognizing the multimodal nature of the brain at birth; it is—from the start—a complex system made up of many heterogeneous, overlapping, interacting and densely connected subsystems. Like Piaget, Edelman proposed that development occurs through activity dependent processes.

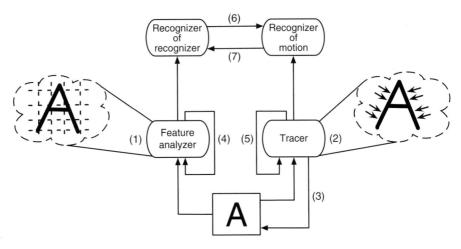

Figure 4.1
Depicts a schematic of Reeke and Edelman's (1984) network model of letter recognition. The letter A at the bottom of the figure depicts the two-dimensional input
array. This input is connected to both a feature analysis system and a tracing system.
The recurrent connection for the each of these systems represents the system's
dependence not only on input but also on its own history. The feature analysis
system is composed of feature detectors, which track the local structure of the input
array, like an oriented line segment. This system outputs to a more abstract detector
that integrates information across the local detectors capturing the global structure
of the input array. The tracing system scans the input array and detects the contour
of objects. This system, like the feature analysis system, outputs to a higher-level
network that captures shared characteristics of related input arrays. The two higher-
level networks are connected to each other, enabling the two subsystems (feature
analysis and tracing) to work together to classify letters.

Reeke and Edelman (1984) presented one demonstration of this in a
computational device that learned to recognize letters merely from interacting with them. Figure 4.1 provides a schematic illustration. This letter-
recognition device self-educates through the interaction of two subsystems
as they simultaneously process the same physical stimulus. In the feature-
analysis subsystem, line detectors are excited by corresponding patterns of
stimulation. In the tracing subsystem, information about shape is gained
through "eye-movements" as the letter is scanned. The developmental
power is in the coupling. At the same time that the feature analyzer is
analyzing features, the shape tracer is extracting a global description of
shape. The outputs of these two heterogeneous processes, at every step in
time, are mapped to each other.

There are seven mappings being accomplished simultaneously in real time. The feature analysis map (1) maps an input letter to a list of features. The tracing map (2) maps the input letter to the actions sequences of scanning. The next map—(3) from the tracing process to the physical world—determines moment by moment the input available to both subsystems. There is also the recurrent activity within each subsystem (maps 4 and 5): at any moment in time, the activity within a subsystem depends not only on the current input but also on its just preceding state. Finally there are what Edelman calls "re-entrant maps" (6 and 7); these map the activities of the two subsystems to each other. Thus, two unique subsystems take qualitatively different glosses on the perceptual information and through their re-entrant connections, by being correlated in real time, by being coupled to the same physical world, they educate each other. Reeke and Edelman's simulation successfully taught itself to recognize all varieties of A, generalizing to novel fonts and handwriting, merely from the activity of looking at As.

The thesis of the present paper is that activity-dependent multimodal experience is a core mechanism creating developmental change. This is certainly a classic idea in perceptual learning (e.g., Held and Hein 1963) but also one receiving increasing attention, in cognition and cognitive neuroscience (Barsalou et al. 2005; Martin and Chao 2001; Pulvermüller 1999; Pulvermuller et al. 2005) and in computational studies of learning (Lungarella et al. 2005; Lungarella and Sporns 2005). Here, we review behavioral evidence from human development, evidence that suggests that transformative change is driven by the sensor-motor coordinations of an active agent in a physical world.

4.1 Actions Create Coordinations

. . . constrained by a history of coupling with an appropriate world.
—Varela, Thompson, and Rosch 1993, 151

The human sensorimotor system is far more complex than the model system shown in figure 4.1. There are many more component subsystems and patterns of connectivity among them. The specific task at hand appears to organize and configure these subsystems differently, softly assembling different coordinations. In this way, different tasks create unique opportunities for change in the system. One method used by developmentalists is to give infants a novel task and then examine how experimentally induced coordination drives change in the specific task as well as how task specific

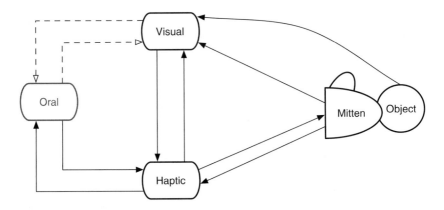

Figure 4.2
Depicts a schematic illustration of the affect of "sticky" mittens on the visual, haptic, and oral systems. The use of sticky mittens during manual exploration reorganizes the coordination of the visual and haptic systems. Although the oral system, grayed in the figure, is not directly involved in this activity, it is connected to the haptic system (infants manually and orally explore objects) and through this connection is potentially influenced by the visual-haptic reorganization.

changes generate cascading consequences in the system as a whole. These kinds of studies, termed "microgenetic studies" in the literature, are particularly powerful methods in the study of developmental process because such studies experimentally create developmental change.

In a recent and remarkably inventive demonstration of this approach, Needham, Barrett, and Peterman (2002) fit two- to five-month-old infants with Velcro®-covered "sticky" mittens. These mittens enabled the infants to grab objects merely by swiping at them, enabling them to precociously coordinate vision and reaching. Infants who were given two weeks of experiences with sticky mittens subsequently showed more sophisticated object exploration even with the mittens off. They looked at objects more and made more visually coordinated swipes at objects than did control infants who had no exploratory experiences with sticky mittens. Needham, Barrett, and Peterman (2002) found that the sticky-mitten task not only facilitated the development of reaching for objects but also visual-oral exploration. That is, infants who had experience with sticky mittens looked at objects more—even in nonreaching tasks—and also mouthed and orally explored objects in more advanced ways. Figure 4.2 provides a schematic illustration of what we take to be the profound significance of these results. Two subsystems—reaching and looking—are coordinated in the sticky-

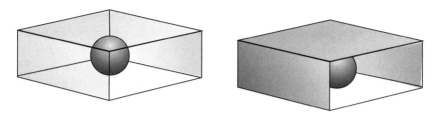

Figure 4.3
Depicts the stimuli used in experiments by Diamond (1990) and Titzer, Thelen, and Smith (2003) on transparency. The picture on the left depicts the transparent box and the picture on the right depicts the opaque box. Both boxes have openings on the right side allowing infants to retrieve contained objects.

mitten task and in so doing educate each other. But these components are also involved in other coordinations, that is, in other tasks that recruit other coalitions of subsystems. Thus, extra experience in the coordination of reaching and looking with sticky mittens ends up not being just about looking and reaching but potentially about other developments, other coordinations, generating cascading developmental consequences in other tasks in which some of the same subsystems are involved.

Another example of how tasks create change that then cascades through out the system concerns transparency. Transparent surfaces violate the usual hand-eye correlations in the world in that one can see the object but a direct line-of-sight reach is blocked. Babies (like birds) have difficulty with this violation of expectation. In one study, Diamond (1990) presented nine-month-old infants with toys hidden under boxes. The boxes were either opaque, hiding the toy, or transparent, enabling the infants to see the toy under the box. As illustrated in figure 4.3, the boxes were open on the side, so that infants, by reaching to that side, could retrieve the object. Diamond found that infants were able to reach around to the side opening given an opaque container but not a transparent one. Instead, the infants attempted to reach for the toy directly banging their hands against the surface seeming generally flummoxed as to how to proceed.

In a microgenetic study, Titzer, Thelen, and Smith (2003; Titzer 1997) gave eight-month-old infants a set of either opaque or transparent containers to play with at home. Parents were given no instructions other than to put these containers in the toy box, making them available to the infants during play. When the infants were nine months old, they were tested in Diamond's task. The babies who had played at home with opaque containers failed to retrieve objects from transparent containers, just as in the original Diamond study. However, infants who had played at home with the transparent containers sought out and rapidly found the openings and retrieved the object from the transparent boxes. Infants' at-home explorations of the transparent containers did not include the specific task of sideways retrieval of objects, although it seems likely that in their spontaneous play objects were both put into and retrieved from the openings in these containers. Titzer, Thelen, and Smith (2003) proposed that in their play—through the coordination of seeing and touching and putting objects in and out—infants learned to recognize the subtle visual cues that distinguish solid transparent surfaces from openings and had learned that surfaces with the visual properties of transparency are solid. The haptic cues from touching the transparent surfaces educated vision, and vision educated reaching and touching, enabling infants to find the openings in transparent containers.

These coordinations of touch and sight also had broader cascading consequences, as shown in a transfer test using a "visual cliff" (Gibson and Walk 1960). The "visual cliff" is a transparent but solid surface placed over a visual "drop off." Typically, eight- and nine-month-olds avoid the "visual cliff," not moving onto the transparent surface given the visual information of a vertical drop. However, babies who had experience playing with transparent containers happily crawled onto the transparent surface over the visual drop off, showing no apprehension whatsoever. The infants who had extensive play with small transparent containers were apparently both sensitive to the subtle visual cues that specify the solidity of a transparent surface and were confident of its support. Again, two subsystems—seeing and touching—are coordinated when playing with transparent containers, each system educating the other in the discovery of relevant regularities to that coupling. The changes in these component subsystems—the regularities found in one task such as play with small transparent containers—may also be transported to other tasks and other coalitions of subsystems, including those involved in evaluating surfaces for locomotion. In this way, through the coordination of multimodal subsystems in specific tasks, the system as whole—its capabilities and its potential for new learning—also change.

4.2 Actions Create Tasks

The state of activity of sensors is brought about most typically by the organism's motions. To an important extent, behavior is the regulation of perception.
—Varela 1997, 82

If tasks create coordinations, and coordinations drive developmental change, it becomes more important to understand tasks—their definition and creation. Prior to shaking the rattle, or catching a toy with the sticky mittens, infants can have no specific goal to shake or to snatch. There is no such task. Infants discover the task through their own spontaneous actions. The process of goal and task creation is profoundly important to understanding both development and the openness of human potential. Accordingly, we first review two more examples of "task creation" and then consider the deeper theoretical importance of these examples.

The first example is "infant conjugate reinforcement" (Rovee-Collier and Hayne 1987). Infants (as young as three months) are placed on their backs and their ankles are attached by a ribbon to a mobile which is suspended overhead. Each kick produces interesting sights and sounds, providing many time-locked patterns of correlations. Infants themselves discover these relations through their own movement patterns. The faster and harder they kick, the more vigorously the mobile jiggles. This is a highly engaging task for infants; they smile and laugh, and become angry when the contingency is removed. This experimental procedure, like the world, provides complex, diverse, and never exactly repeating events—yet all are perfectly time-locked with infants' own actions. It is spontaneous non-task-related movement that starts the process off by creating the opportunity for the coordination of the infant's action with the mobile's movement. It is this coordination that ultimately defines the task and thus becomes the goal.

The second example is the development of reaching, Thelen et al.'s (1993) week-by-week study of four infants transition from not-reaching to reaching for visually presented objects. Early in development, the presentation of an enticing toy aroused the infants and elicited all sorts of nonproductive actions. These actions were literally all over the place with no clear coherence in form or direction. But by acting, each baby sooner or later made contact with the toy—banging into or brushing against it or swiping it. These moments of contact selected some movements, carving out patterns that are then repeated with increasing frequency. Over weeks, the cycle repeated—arousal, action, and occasional contact. Over cycles, reaches became increasingly stable, more efficient and more effective.

However, the task of reaching is discovered by individual action, and thus, it is specific to the individual. All infants followed the general pattern, but each also had unique subtasks to solve. Some babies at first could hardly lift their arms, but sat placidly watching the world. Other babies were more high-strung and active, flailing and flapping and always moving.

These different babies had to solve very different problems in order to reach out and grasp an object. The flailer needed to become less active and to lower his hands bringing them into midline creating balance. The placid baby needed to be more active, to raise her hands, to lift them up from their usual positions on her side. What is remarkable in the developmental patterns of the children is that each found a solution by following individual action-defined developmental pathways that eventually converged to highly similar movements. Because action defines the task and because action—through the coordination of heterogeneous sensory systems—finds the solution, development is very much an individual and context-dependent matter.

If individual actions create tasks that in turn couple component systems that cause change in the system, what then is universal about the developmental process? Theorists sometimes envision development as movement through a landscape. The classic illustration of this is Waddington's (1957) epigenetic landscape, a three-dimensional surface where the branching and deepening valleys depict the increasing differentiation of structures and processes. Waddington saw the surface of the landscape as reflecting a web of changing probabilities arising from the competitive dynamics of underlying complex processes. These processes included not only multiple-gene products, but cell-to-cell interactions and the mutual influences of the environment and the organism's behavior within the environment. The main idea of the landscape was that as development proceeded, these influences worked together to constrain the possible states of the organism.

Muchisky et al. (1996) envisioned a more dynamic landscape—one in which experiences opened new possibilities, taking development in new directions, not just channeling development into preset outcomes. This more dynamic landscape is illustrated in figure 4.4. The landscape has three dimensions. The first dimension is time. The landscape progresses irreversibly from past to present. The second dimension—the surface—is a measure of the state of the developing system. Each of the lines forming the landscape represent the possible states of the system at a particular point in developmental time. The shape of the lines depicts the dynamics of the moment determined both by the history of the system up to that point in developmental time and the particulars of the moment (e.g., the state of the child as well as the social and physical context). The third dimension of the landscape represents the stability of the system at that point in time and in that context. In this view—the landscape and development itself—is self-organizing. Moment to moment, the state of the system and the task

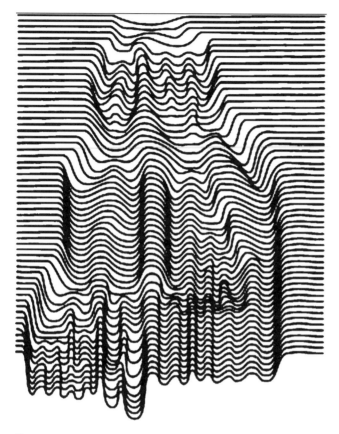

Figure 4.4
The dynamic epigenetic landscape proposed by Muchisky et al. (1996). In this land-scape, behavioral development is depicted as a series of evolving and dissolving attractors.

at hand, creates change and, moment to moment, the developmental trajectory. Because of this—because the mechanism of change is the individual's momentary task—development is open to multiple outcomes and multiple paths to the same ends. Each new coordination enables new possible assemblies of subsystems, which generate new actions, which create new tasks (opportunities for reorganization), which create new organizations. The very absence of predefined tasks and the individualistic and opportunistic nature of the tasks that cause change in the system may be the ultimate source of the adaptability and flexibility of human intelligence. Outcomes and developmental process are of course also constrained by the physics of the world and by the intrinsic dynamics of the cognitive system itself. But as a self-organizing complex system that discovers its own developmental tasks through its own action, it is dynamically open and opportunistic.

4.3 Actions Create Developmental Order

The cognitive self is its own implementation: its history and its action are of one piece.
—Varela 1997, 83

Comparative studies of other species tell us that evolution strongly selects for different patterns of motor development. For example, where species such as horses, cats, and dogs are motorically mature at birth, human infants are motorically altricial. They have very little motor control and indeed must work over the first several weeks of life to merely lift their head. Slowly, they develop enough strength and balance to roll over, to reach, to push into a sitting position (and hold it without falling over), to crawl, and to stand. Each of these achievements is slowly won, through specific interactions with the world, and is indeed individually variable (Thelen 1995; Adolph and Berger 2006). Each of these motor achievements also dramatically changes the tasks that the infant can discover, the coordinations of subsystems, and the developmental landscape as a whole. Once infants can reach for things (at three to six months of age), they can provide themselves with new multimodal experiences involving vision, haptic exploration, proprioceptive input from self-movement, and audition as they contact objects that squeak, rattle or squeal.

Ruff's (1982, 1986, 1989) landmark work on infants' manual exploration of objects presents one example of how the information in the learning environment becomes richer with motor development and experience. Ruff distinguishes several kinds of manual interactions with objects that seem to be used to acquire information (called "examining")—looking, fingering, and rotating (Ruff 1989). By seven months, and more strongly by twelve months, infants give priority to examining over mouthing and banging when faced with a novel object (Ruff 1986). Further, infants' patterns of interactions change within a session as they become more familiar with the object. Their explorations become more object-specific, such that, for example, at seven months, after an initial period of examination, infants begin to bang hard objects more than soft ones (Lockman and McHale 1989; Palmer 1989; Bourgeois et al. 2005), to finger textured objects more than smooth ones, to finger objects more in response to changes in shape and texture than to a change in weight, but to rotate an object and transfer it from hand to hand in response to weight (Bushnell 1982; Bushnell, Shaw, and Strauss 1985; Ruff 1984). These purposeful explorations seem likely to both be informed by and to inform developing visual representation.

After weeks and months of living in this new multimodal venue of sitting, looking, listening, reaching, and manipulating objects, infants' experiences—and the correlations available to them—again change radically, as infants begin to crawl and then to stand up and walk. Self-locomotion changes the nature of the visual and auditory input even more dramatically, and the evidence suggests that it also profoundly changes infants' cognitive development (Campos et al. 2000). One example concerns the A-not-B error. In this task, first used by Piaget (1954), the experimenter hides a tantalizing toy in location A. After a delay, the infant is allowed to search for the toy. On these trials, infants find the toy. After multiple hidings at A, there is the critical switch trial: the experimenter hides the object at a new location B. Infants of eight to twelve months of age reach not to where they saw the object disappear, but back to A, where they had found the object previously. This "A-not-B" error is especially compelling because it is tightly linked to a highly circumscribed developmental period; infants older than twelve months search correctly on the critical B trials.

The shift appears to be tightly tied to self-locomotion. Specifically, individual infants stop making the error when they begin to self-locomote (Horobin and Acredolo 1986). Further, when Kermoian and Campos (1988) experimentally induced early experiences in self-locomotion (by putting infants in walkers), the infants succeeded in the A-not-B task earlier, another example of cascading consequences of activity-generated developmental change. Why should experience in moving oneself about the world help one remember and discriminate the locations of objects in a hide-and-seek reaching task? Because moving oneself about—over things, by things, into things, around things—generates new experiences, new patterns of spatiotemporal relations, and it is the history of these experiences that is etched in the multimodal coordination that alters the infant's representation of objects, space, and self. In order to produce the locomotor movement, a walker must generate a synchronized ensemble of muscle contractions alternating the legs, and shifting the body's weight from one leg to the other as the feet alternate contact with the ground. Continual monitoring by the motor system of the visual system, the vestibular apparatus, and the soles of the feet enables the walker to maintain balance and make corrections for changing biomechanical demands as well as for unexpected perturbations in path, such as obstacles, uneven surfaces, and changes in direction (Thelen, Ulrich, and Wolff 1991). This complex coordination not only enables walking but alters how the infant updates spatial representations with movement (see Luo 2005 for a simulation-based study).

An action in some context creates a task that coordinates multiple sensorimotor systems, and through this coordination, the component systems and their couplings to each other are changed. The next action may form a new consortium of systems, systems that will have been shaped by their participation in previous tasks. Because action creates tasks and transformative change in the components systems, action is a strong organizer of the developmental trajectory itself. Thus, motor development has a strong effect on the ordering of development as a whole.

4.4   Actions Create Higher-Order Concepts

In brief, the term cognitive has two constitutive dimensions: first its coupling dimension, that is, a link with its environment allowing for its continuity as individual entity; second its interpretative dimension, that is, the surplus of significance a physical interaction acquires due to the perspective provided by the global action of the organism.
—Varela 1997, 81

There is a growing movement in cognitive science—much of it represented in this volume—that suggests that the body creates higher-order concepts through perception and action (see also Varela, Thompson, and Rosch 1993; Glenberg and Kaschak 2003; Clark 2004; Zwaan 2004; Gallese and Lakoff 2005; Núñez and Lakoff 2005; Yeh and Barsalou 2006). We present here one intriguing example of how sensorimotor coordinations and processes much like Piaget's circular reactions may be the developmental engine behind abstract ideas. The phenomenon concerns children's discovery of spatial classification. This kind of classification task—one in which subjects put similar things close in space and apart from dissimilar things—is ubiquitous in psychology. In doing so, subjects use space metaphorically, with nearness in space standing in for similarity. Formal theories of similarity also use space (distance) as the core metaphor defining similarity, for example, Euclidean distance in some feature space (Shepard

1987; Nosofosky 1992). In everyday life, people also put like things in spatial proximity—socks in one drawer, shirts in another, cups on the top shelf, and plates on the bottom. This habit—which allows one to locate and choose among desired objects with ease—demonstrates the functional utility of real space with respect to like things in the real world and may be the root source of the metaphor.

Between their first and third birthdays, children also begin to use space to represent similarity. Indeed, during this period they become almost compulsive spatial sorters. Confronted with an array of four identical cars and four identical dolls, for example, they physically group them—moving all the cars spatially close to each other and spatially apart from the groups of dolls even though there is no explicit task to do so. They are so reliable at doing this that many developmental psychologists use the task as a way to measure young children's knowledge of similarity (Inhelder and Piaget 1969; Starkey 1981; Nelson 1973; Mandler, Bauer, and McDonough 1991; Mandler, Fivush, and Reznick 1987; Rakison and Butterworth 1998). But, where does this behavior come from? Where does the very idea of spatial classification originate?

The developmental course suggests gradual, action-driven discovery. When nine- to ten-month-old infants are given sets of objects containing like kinds, they do not group them. However, they do pick up objects, one in each hand, and bang them together (Forman 1982). By twelve months of age, these manipulations become more systematic and children manipulate like kinds in a like manner (Sugarman 1983). For example, given four cars and four dolls, the child may systematically push each car. Around eighteen months of age, children not only manipulate objects from one category in sequence, but they also systematically manipulate in different ways objects from two different categories, for example, first pushing each car, but patting each doll. This pattern of behavior—called "sequential touching" in the literature—is compelling to adult observers and seems to be, on the part of the child, a comment on the likeness of the individual instances. From these behaviors spatial classification emerges progressively. At first, spatial groupings seem accidental to acting on like things in like ways (Gershkoff-Stowe and Namy 1995). Around twenty-four months, the sorting seems more purposeful, with all of one kind gathered to form one group and the other kind left unorganized. Ultimately, purposeful, exhaustive, and complete classification of two kinds into spatial groups emerges around thirty-six months.

Four behavioral tendencies in infancy may be enough to start the developmental progression. The first is that infants reach to objects in which they are interested. The second is that infants have a tendency to repeat just performed motor acts, and in particular to repeat reaches to nearby locations (e.g., Smith et al. 1999). Third, perceptually similar objects may be similarly enticing to infants. Fourth, infants may notice the outcomes of their own actions.

A behavioral study with twelve-, fifteen-, and eighteen-month-olds presents support for these ideas (Sheya 2005; Sheya and Smith 2010). In this task, children were presented with arrays of eight toys: five of one kind and three of another. Unlike usual studies of sequential touching or of spatial classification, the objects were fixed to a location by a spring. Fixing the locations and varying the placement of objects in those locations allowed the effect of proximity in space and similarity both to be examined. Because touches to the objects caused them to wiggle and move, the children found the task engaging, making many repeated reaches to the array.

The behavior of the children at the three age levels differed considerably, with the developmental progression being away from perseverative reaches to the same (and nearby locations) toward reaches to the same kind of thing across larger distances. This is shown in figure 4.5. Each panel shows the probability that an infant reached to a location, given that the infant first reached to the center object (marked by a large white dot in the figure 4.5a); the colors—from black to white—indicate an increasing probability that the infant next reaches to that location. The top three panels in figure 4.5b are the twelve-month-olds, the middle panels are the fifteen-month-olds, and the bottom panels are the eighteen-month-olds. The three panels for each age show reaches to three different configurations of the object array in which the locations of the members of the set of five like kinds (indicated by dark gray dots in figure 4.5a) and the members of the set of three like kinds (indicated by the white and light-gray dots in figure 4.5a) are switched. The youngest children most often reached back to the very same object and location but sometimes reached to nearby locations. The similarity of the objects mattered very little to their pattern of activity. The fifteen-month-old children were influenced somewhat by similarity; they also often reached to the same location but were more likely to reach to nearby similar objects than nearby different objects. The oldest children (bottom three panels) also often reached back to the very same object at the same location, but they were much more likely than the younger children to reach to the same kind of thing even at distant locations. In brief, sequential touching is first driven by similarity in location and progressively by similarity of

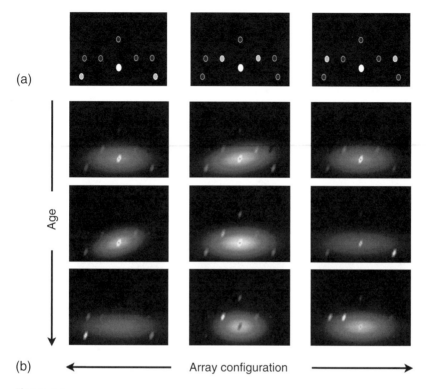

(a)

(b) ←——————— Array configuration ———————→

Figure 4.5
(a) The three panels depict the array configurations used in Sheya 2005 and serve
as the model for each column of the figure. The large center white dot in each panel
represents the location just reached to by the infants. The light-gray dots are locations that contain an object identical to the object in the center location (white
dot). The dark-gray locations contain identical objects of a different kind. (b) Each
row of panels corresponds to an age group (top panels are twelve-month-olds,
middle panels fifteen-month-olds, bottom panels eighteen-month-olds) and each
column corresponds to an object configuration. The brightness of a location indicates the probability that infants reached to that location next (lighter corresponding to higher probability and darker to lower probability). The brightness of the
distribution around the center location indicates the probability that infants reached
to a location that far from the center location next. A brighter, tighter oval would
indicate that after reaching to the center, infants next reached to locations nearby.
A dimmer, broader oval indicates that infants were more likely to next reach to
locations further away from the center.

the objects at those locations. One can think of these developmental differences in terms of the changing dynamics of a saliency map: early in development salience spreads uniformly about an activated *location* and later in development salience spreads by similarity to objects with the same *properties*.

What might drive a change in the intrinsic dynamics of such a saliency map? We think it likely that it is action itself. In the child's normal course of action, objects are not fixed to their location. An object once grasped and then let go is unlikely to be dropped at the exact same place in which it was first picked up. Thus a perseverative reach—though in normal inter-action with objects this will not occur—to very same location would typically lead to an empty hand. Thus, interaction with untethered objects in the everyday world practices object-based—not location-based—reaching. Nonetheless, the main point is this: a system whose activity is biased to both reach to similar locations and to reach to similar objects will, as a consequence of reaching and moving those things, end up with similar things near each other.

Perseverative reaching to similar things and dropping them near each other is not enough by itself to create the goal of spatial classification (although it could create the result). To create the goal, the child has to notice and like the outcome (as in the cases of shaking a rattle or jiggling a mobile with kicks). Namy, Smith, and Gershkoff-Stowe (1997) reported a result that suggests that young children do notice (and appreciate) the consequences of their own unplanned spatial groupings. The children's "training" was a fun task of putting objects into a shape sorter. As illustrated in figure 4.6, the shape sorter was a transparent container structured so that children could see the objects once they had been dropped inside. Children were given two different kinds of objects (e.g., blocks and dolls) that might be put into the container. In the experimental training condition, the opening on the top of the shape container allowed only one type of object to fit inside the hole. The children were eighteen-month-olds with perseverative tendencies to repeat the same action, and so they (quite happily) attempted to put all the objects into the container—the kinds that fit and the kinds that did not. But, of course, only one kind fit, leading to an outcome of one kind visibly near each other in the transparent container and the other kind spatially separate form these. Namy, Smith, and Gershkoff-Stowe (1997) found that children who participated in this shape-sorter task spontaneously spatially grouped even novel sets of objects in a transfer task. Children who participated in a control group in which all

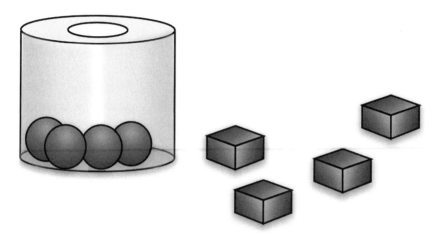

Figure 4.6
Depicts the transparent sorter used in Namy, Smith, and Gershkoff-Stowe 1997. The sorter enabled young children to spatial segregate objects of different kinds.

objects (of both kinds) fit into the shape sorter did not. It seems likely that children in the training condition noticed the product of their own actions—like objects near each other and apart from different objects—and this outcome then defined a new task.

Because action modifies the world in perceivable ways, action can create higher-order regularities—abstractions—like the metaphor between space and similarity. In 1998, Alan Kay (the inventor of programming languages and interfaces that were foundational to the Apple Macintosh) gave a visionary and now-famous lecture entitled "Doing with images makes symbols." The premise was that action and the visually perceived consequences of one's own actions create higher-order abstractions. Karmiloff-Smith (1992) similarly suggested a perception/action/re-perception loop as the foundation of representation itself. In this way, action by creating tasks that coordinate subsystems and leading to perceivable outcomes may be the engine that drives the development of cognition.

References

Adolph, K. E., and Berger, S. E. (2006). Motor development. In *Handbook of child psychology: Vol. 2, Cognition, perception, and language*, 6th edition, ed. D. Kuhn, R. S. Siegler, W. Damon, and R. M. Lerner, 161–213. Hoboken, NJ: John Wiley and Sons.

Barsalou, L. W., Pecher, D., Zeelenberg, R., Simmons, W. K., and Hamann, S. B. (2005). Multimodal simulation in conceptual processing. In *Categorization inside and outside the lab: Festschrift in honor of Douglas L. Medin*, ed. W. Ahn, R. L. Goldstone, B. C. Love, A. Markman, and P. Wolff, 249–270. Washington, DC: American Psychological Association.

Bourgeois, K. S., Khawar, A. W., Neal, S. A., and Lockman, J. J. (2005). Infant manual exploration of objects, surfaces, and their interrelations. *Infancy* 8 (3): 233–252.

Bushnell, E. W. (1982). Visual-tactual knowledge in 8-, 9½-, and 11-month-old infants. *Infant Behavior and Development* 5 (1): 63–75.

Bushnell, E. W., Shaw, L., and Strauss, D. (1985). Relationship between visual and tactual exploration by 6-month-olds. *Developmental Psychology* 21 (4): 591–600.

Campos, J. J., Anderson, D. I., Barbu-Roth, M. A., Hubbard, E. M., Hertenstein, M. J., and Witherington, D. (2000). Travel broadens the mind. *Infancy* 1 (2): 149–219.

Clark, A. (2004). Embodiment and the philosophy of mind. In *Mind and causality*, ed. A. Peruzzi, 35–51. Amsterdam: John Benjamins.

Diamond, A. (1990). Developmental time course in human infants and infant monkeys and the neural bases of inhibitory control in reaching. *Annals of the New York Academy of Sciences* 608:637–676.

Edelman, G. M. (1987). *Neural Darwinism: The theory of neuronal group selection.* New York: Basic Books.

Forman, G. E. (1982). A search for the origins of equivalence concepts through a microanalysis of block play. In *Action and thought: From sensorimotor schemes to symbolic thought*, ed. G. E. Forman, 97–134. New York: Academic Press.

Gallese, V., and Lakoff, G. (2005). The brain's concepts: The role of the sensory-motor system in conceptual knowledge. *Cognitive Neuropsychology* 22 (3): 455–479.

Gershkoff-Stowe, L., and Namy, L. L. (1995). "Sequential touching and spatial grouping: A curvilinear developmental trend." Paper presented at the Biennial Meeting of the Society for Research in Child Development, Indianapolis, IN.

Gibson, E. J., and Walk, R. D. (1960). The "visual cliff." *Scientific American* 202 (4): 64–71.

Glenberg, A. M., and Kaschak, M. P. (2003). The body's contribution to language. In *The psychology of learning and motivation: Advances in research and theory*, vol. 43, ed. B. H. Ross, 93–126. New York: Elsevier Science.

Held, R., and Hein, A. (1963). Movement-produced stimulation in the development of visually guided behavior. *Journal of Comparative and Physiological Psychology* 56 (5): 872–876.

Horobin, K., and Acredolo, L. (1986). The role of attentiveness, mobility history, and separation of hiding sites on Stage IV search behavior. *Journal of Experimental Child Psychology* 41:114–127.

Inhelder, B., and Piaget, J. (1969). *The early growth of logic in the child; classification and seriation.* New York: W. W. Norton.

Karmiloff-Smith, A. (1994). Precis of beyond modularity: A developmental perspective on cognitive science. *Behavioral and Brain Sciences* 17 (4): 693–745.

Kermoian, R., and Campos, J. J. (1988). Locomotor experience: A facilitator of spatial-cognitive development. *Child Development* 59:908–917.

Lockman, J. J., and McHale, J. P. (1989). Object manipulation in infancy: Developmental and contextual determinants. In *Action in social context: Perspectives on early development*, ed. J. J. Lockman and N. L. Hazen, 129–167. New York: Plenum Press.

Luo, J. (2005). The dynamics of permanence. Doctoral dissertation, Indiana University, 2005. *Dissertation Abstracts International* 66:369.

Lungarella, M., Pegors, T., Bulwinkle, D., and Sporns, O. (2005). *gNeuroinformatics* 3:243–262.

Lungarella, M., and Sporns, O. (2005). Information self-structuring: Key principle for learning and development. In *Proceedings of 2005 4th IEEE International Conference on Development and Learning*, 25–30.

Mandler, J. M., Bauer, P. J., and McDonough, L. (1991). Separating the sheep from the goats: Differentiating global categories. *Cognitive Psychology* 23 (2): 263–298.

Mandler, J. M., Fivush, R., and Reznick, J. S. (1987). The development of contextual categories. *Cognitive Development* 2 (4): 339–354.

Martin, A., and Chao, L. L. (2001). Semantic memory and the brain: Structure and processes. *Current Opinion in Neurobiology*, Special issue of *Cognitive Neuroscience* 11 (2): 194–201.

Muchisky, M., Gershkoff-Stowe, L., Cole, E., and Thelen, E. (1996). The epigenetic landscape revisited: A dynamic interpretation. In *Advances in infancy research*, vol. 10, ed. C. Rovee-Collier and L. P. Lipsitt, 121–159. Westport, CT: Ablex Publishing.

Namy, L. L., Smith, L. B., and Gershkoff-Stowe, L. (1997). Young children discovery of spatial classification. *Cognitive Development* 12 (2): 163–184.

Needham, A., Barrett, T., and Peterman, K. (2002). A pick me up for infants' exploratory skills: Early simulated experiences reaching for objects using 'sticky' mittens enhances young infants' object exploration skills. *Infant Behavior and Development* 25 (3): 279–295.

Nelson, K. (1973). Some evidence for the cognitive primacy of categorization and its functional basis. *Merrill-Palmer Quarterly* 19 (1): 21–39.

Nosofosky, R. M. (1992). Similarity scaling and cognitive process models. *Annual Review of Psychology* 43:25–53.

Núñez, R., and Lakoff, G. (2005). The cognitive foundations of mathematics: The role of conceptual metaphor. In *Handbook of mathematical cognition*, ed. J. I. D. Campbell, 109–124. New York: Psychology Press.

Palmer, C. F. (1989). The discriminating nature of infants' exploratory actions. *Developmental Psychology* 25 (6): 885–893.

Piaget, J. (1952). *The origins of intelligence in the children.* New York: W. W. Norton.

Piaget, J. (1954). *The construction of reality in the children.* New York: Basic Books.

Pulvermüller, F. (1999). Words in the brain's language. *Behavioral and Brain Sciences* 22 (2): 253–336.

Pulvermüller, F., Hauk, O., Nikulin, V. V., and Ilmoniemi, R. J. (2005). Functional links between motor and language systems. *European Journal of Neuroscience* 21 (3): 793–797.

Rakison, D. H., and Butterworth, G. E. (1998). Infants' attention to object structure in early categorization. *Developmental Psychology* 34 (6): 1310–1325.

Reeke, G. N., and Edelman, G. M. (1984). Selective networks and recognition automata. *Annals of the New York Academy of Sciences* 426:181–201.

Rovee-Collier, C., and Hayne, H. (1987). Reaction of infant memory: Implications for cognitive development. *Advances in Child Development and Behavior* 20:185–238.

Ruff, H. A. (1982). Role of manipulation in infants' responses to invariant properties of objects. *Developmental Psychology* 18 (5): 682–691.

Ruff, H. A. (1984). Infants' manipulative exploration of objects: Effects of age and object characteristics. *Developmental Psychology* 20 (1): 9–20.

Ruff, H. A. (1986). Components of attention during infants' manipulative exploration. *Child Development* 57 (1): 105–114.

Ruff, H. A. (1989). The infant's use of visual and haptic information in the perception and recognition of objects. *Infant Perceptual Development*, Special issue of *Canadian Journal of Psychology* 43 (2): 302–319.

Shepard, R. (1987). Toward a universal law of generalization for psychological science. *Science* 237 (4820): 1317–1323.

Sheya, A. (2005). "The origins of classification: Proximity, perseveration, and similarity." Paper presented at the biennial meeting of the Society for Research on Child Development, Atlanta, GA, April.

Sheya, A. and Smith, L. B. (2010). Changing priority maps in 12- to 18-month-olds: An emerging role for object properties. *Psychonomic Bulletin & Review* 17 (1): 22–28.

Smith, L. B., Thelen, E., Titzer, R., and McLin, D. (1999). Knowing in the context of acting: The task dynamics of the A-not-B error. *Psychological Review* 106 (2): 235–260.

Starkey, D. (1981). The origins of concept formation: Object sorting and object preference in early infancy. *Child Development* 52 (2): 489–497.

Sugarman, S. (1983). *Children's early thought: developments in classification*. New York: Cambridge University Press.

Thelen, E. (1995). Motor development: A new synthesis. *American Psychologist* 50 (2): 79–95.

Thelen, E., Corbetta, D., Kamm, K., Spencer, J. P., Schneider, K., and Zernicke, R. F. (1993). The transition to reaching: Mapping intention and intrinsic dynamics. *Child Development* 64 (4): 1058–1098.

Thelen, E., Ulrich, B. D., and Wolff, P. H. (1991). Hidden skills: A dynamic systems analysis of treadmill stepping during the first year. *Monographs of the Society for Research in Child Development* 56 (1): 1–103.

Titzer, R. C. (1997). Infants' understanding of transparency: A reinterpretation of studies using the object retrieval task and visual cliff. Doctoral dissertation, Indiana University. *Dissertation Abstracts International* 58:1570.

Titzer, R. Thelen, E., and Smith, L.B. (2003). Learning about transparency. Unpublished manuscript.

Varela, F. J. (1997). Patterns of life: Intertwining identity and cognition. *Brain and Cognition* 34 (1): 72–87.

Varela, F. J., Thompson, E., and Rosch, E. (1993). *The embodied mind: Cognitive science and human experience*. Cambridge, MA: MIT Press.

Waddington, C. H. (1957). *The strategy of the genes*. London: Allen & Unwin.

Yeh, W., and Barsalou, L. W. (2006). The situated nature of concepts. *American Journal of Psychology* 119 (3): 349–384.

Zwaan, R. A. (2004). The immersed experiencer: Toward an embodied theory of language comprehension. In *The psychology of learning and motivation: Advances in research and theory*, vol. 44, ed. B. H. Ross, 35–62. New York: Elsevier Science.

5 Enaction, Sense-Making, and Emotion

Giovanna Colombetti

There can be only an individuality that copes, relates and couples with the sur-
roundings, and inescapably provides its own world of sense.
—Weber and Varela 2002, 117

5.1 Introduction: Cartesian Anxieties

Varela, Thompson, and Rosch (1991) wrote that the enactive approach
should free cognitive science from its "Cartesian anxiety." In their characterization, this anxiety is induced by the idea that to know is to have a
mind that possesses internal detailed and complete representations of the
outside world, and that cognitive science needs accurately to reproduce
such a mind's representing powers. According to Varela, Thompson, and
Rosch, the therapy for this anxiety consists of replacing the idea that cognitive systems represent an independent world with the idea that cognitive
systems enact or bring forth their own worlds of significance.

I think that much of current emotion science suffers from a related form
of Cartesian anxiety that also needs an enactivist therapy. It is a widespread
view in emotion science that the capacity to evaluate and more generally
understand the meaning of a situation is a prerogative of cognition, understood as an abstract intellectual process; on this view, the body merely
responds to cognition's evaluations.[1] The two forms of anxiety are related,
in that both depend on the view that the body's function is to transmit
information (about the environment and the body itself) to the cognitive-
evaluative mind and then to execute motor actions, whereas the cognitive-
evaluative mind selects and elaborates sensory information and tells the
body what to do. In *The Passions of the Soul* (1988) Descartes recognized
that the emotions involve an intimate unity of mind and body (see chap.
30), yet ended up treating them as bodily stirrings that merely inform
the mind about the state of the body, and that are not in themselves

able to produce flexible and adaptive behavior. As Wheeler (2005, 47–48) notices, Descartes treats the emotions very much like bodily sensations (e.g., hunger, thirst, fatigue) whose physiological changes are not sufficient to bring about an intelligent response appropriate to the situation; the intervention of the mind is necessary for the occurrence of any response of the latter sort. Much mainstream emotion theory similarly assumes that cognitive evaluations are necessary to trigger behavioral responses appropriate to the situation. The Cartesian anxiety that characterizes much emotion science is thus one in which cognition is constantly preoccupied with monitoring, evaluating and regulating the body, and with making sure that every action is performed out of (mental) reasons, not out of (bodily) passions.

To be sure, modern emotion science has proposed accounts of emotion that are even more intellectualistic than that from Descartes. First, Descartes did endow some of the bodily changes accompanying the emotions with the capacity to produce quick-and-dirty adaptive responses (e.g., *Passions of the Soul*, chaps. 13, 38), whereas some modern emotion theories deny that bodily changes are necessary for emotion altogether. On their account, emotions are intellectual judgments and belong entirely to the cognitive-mental realm; the bodily events that may accompany them are contingent by-products. Second, some modern emotion theories assume that the bodily stirrings that accompany the emotions need to be *interpreted* by cognition in order to be experienced by the subject as a specific emotion with its own qualitative feel. Descartes posited a direct relationship between the bodily stirrings of the passions and the mind—he did not think that bodily stirrings need to be interpreted by the mind in order to bring about specific experiences. He described many different bodily processes that, once in contact with the mind, would induce specific experiences immediately, that is, without the intervention of an interpreting mind.

As I see it, much emotion science tends to disregard the *meaning-generating* role of the body and to attribute this role only to separate abstract cognitive-evaluative processes. For reasons I will explain, I think that this tendency is problematic. In particular, I think that emotion should be conceptualized as a faculty of the whole embodied and situated organism. Evaluations arise in this organism in virtue of its embodied and situated character, and the whole situated organism carries meaning *as such*—not by way of some separate abstract cognitive-evaluative faculty.

In this chapter, I will elaborate on this view by adopting two converging strategies. In the next section I will illustrate the idea of whole-organism-generated meaning by drawing on the notion of *sense-making* in the auto-poietic and adaptive system developed by Weber and Varela (2002) and Di Paolo (2005). In particular, I will interpret their notion of sense-making as *a bodily cognitive-emotional form of understanding* that belongs to all living systems, and that is present in a primordial form even in the simplest ones. In section 5.3, I will turn to modern emotion science and illustrate its tendency to overintellectualize our capacity to evaluate and understand. I will show that this overintellectualization goes hand in hand with the rejection of the idea that the nonneural body is a vehicle of meaning. I will explain why I think that this overintellectualization is problematic, and try to reconceptualize the notion of evaluation in emotion theory in a way that is consistent and continuous with the notion of sense-making presented in section 5.2. In section 5.4, I will mention issues that I think still need to be addressed in order to develop the theory of embodied meaning attempted here.

5.2   Emotion in Enaction: Autopoiesis, Adaptivity, and Sense-Making

The enactive approach and the associated concept of enaction were intro-duced by Varela, Thompson, and Rosch (1991) in order to describe and unify under one heading several related ideas. Many of these ideas were an elaboration of Maturana and Varela's (1980) theory of autopoiesis and its notion of autonomous system. Here I will focus on (one aspect of) a later development of the theory of autopoiesis, namely Weber and Varela's (2002) discussion of the origin of value in living systems, and (part of) Di Paolo's (2005) critique and elaboration of their view. What I am interested in is their notion of sense-making, which assumes that the whole organism is a vehicle of meaning. To be sure, they do not explicitly mention emotion or emotions; for example, they do not say that sense-making is emotional, or anything similar. Yet I believe that their characterization of sense-making can be naturally understood as the recognition of the constitutive emotional character of enaction (more shortly).[2]

Weber and Varela (2002) address the difficult question of the nature of teleology in living systems: is it possible to account for the purposes of individual organisms in the Newtonian mechanistic framework that domi-nates current science, including biology? Weber and Varela's solution is to make room for *natural purposes* in the living organism. This solution relies on the autopoietic nature of living systems. As Weber and Varela remind us, living systems are autopoietic in the sense that (1) they continuously regenerate the conditions of their own survival (e.g., they exchange matter with the environment, they maintain a certain temperature, and so on), and in so doing (2) they establish the boundary between themselves and the environment, and thus constitute themselves as unities.

For present purposes, it is important that Weber and Varela explicitly say that (1) and (2) are the processes whereby living systems necessarily establish a *point of view*, and moreover a *concerned* point of view that *generates meaning*. Here is how they illustrate the conceptual link between autopoiesis and this concerned meaning-generating perspective:

> The key here is to realize that because there is an individuality that finds itself produced by itself it is *ipso facto* a locus of sensation and agency, a living impulse always already in relation with its world. There cannot be an individuality which is isolated and folded into itself. There can only be an individuality that copes, relates and couples with the surroundings, and inescapably provides its own world of sense. (Weber and Varela 2002, 117)

> By defining itself and thereby creating the domains of self and world, the organism creates a perspective which changes the world from a neutral place to an *Umwelt* that always means something in relation to the organism.[3] (117–118)

This idea amounts to the recognition that *meaning* is generated within the system for the system itself—that is, it is generated and at the same time consumed by the system. Importantly, meaning is not uniquely specified by the living system in isolation from its environment. Rather, meaning is always *relational* in the sense that it depends on the specific mode of co-determination, or coupling, that each system realizes with its environment; different couplings produce different meanings.

The point of view that, on this view, emerges within the living system is the system's concern for its own autopoietic organization. The living system, by definition, aims at regenerating its viability conditions and at maintaining its identity. This view implies that to be a living system is to be, necessarily, a system concerned with its own continuation. With respect to the environment, this means that the environment is never, for the living system, a neutral world awaiting to be internally represented and evaluated in order to become meaningful. Rather, the world is directly encountered *as* meaningful by the concerned living system. The world is always the living system's own meaningful *Umwelt*.

Di Paolo (2005) has recently noted that Weber and Varela's (2002) passage from autopoiesis to sense-making is too rushed, and in particular it does not allow for the emergence of various *grades* of meaning. As he argues, the autopoietic system as characterized by Weber and Varela has only one crude concern, namely to sustain itself against the forces that would otherwise induce its disintegration. In order to account for various degrees of meaning, *adaptivity* needs to be explicitly added to the notion of a living system. Adaptivity, understood by Di Paolo as the capacity of the organism to regulate and monitor itself with respect to its viability conditions, allows for the emergence of various degrees of concern. To illustrate this idea, consider the often-mentioned example of a bacterium swimming uphill in a sugar gradient. If Di Paolo is right, the mere regeneration of the bacterium's conditions of continuation only allows for the emergence of a crude, all-or-nothing form of meaning: sugar is good, and lack of sugar is bad. If however the bacterium is conceived of as an organism able to regulate itself in relation to its conditions of viability, then the sugar gradient becomes a space of possibilities that establishes different degrees of value: concentration x of sugar is good, concentration y is better, concentration z not sufficient, and so on. The introduction of degrees of value thus makes room for a notion of organismic *preferences*.

In sum, if we take Di Paolo's (2005) arguments as a valid and useful explicitation of the adaptive nature of the living system as understood by Weber and Varela (2002), what we have is a graded notion of natural purposes in the living system.[4] The living system is by definition motivated to preserve its integrity (autopoiesis) and to satisfy its preferences (adaptivity). The explicit recognition of the adaptive, rather than merely self-maintaining, nature of the living system characterizes the system's point of view not only as concerned with its own continuation, but as able to discern gradations of value and motivated to achieve its ideal conditions of viability.

Crucially the theory of autopoiesis aims at being not only a theory of the living system, but also of *cognition*. As Thompson (2007, chap. 6) explains, in fact, for Varela any autopoietic system is a cognitive system. Varela's notion of cognition encompasses all sense-producing and self-generating systems. On this view, for a system to cognize is to produce and consume meaning in virtue of its mode of organization and coupling with the environment.

This conception of cognition is very different from the one that has characterized, and still characterizes, cognitive science and much of mainstream philosophy of mind and of cognitive science. Even most supporters of the embodied and situated approach emphasize the role of the body in cognition as that of an *interface* indispensable for the acquisition of knowledge, or, for example, as that whose structure can explain the nature of perceptual experience (e.g., Noë 2004). According to the view of cognition that emerges from the theory of the autopoietic and adaptive system, the body plays a role in cognition also thanks to its chemical and "self-regulatory" (as Thompson and Varela [2001] call it) dimension. Metabolism is necessary for the emergence of values and preferences in living systems.

Varela's notion of cognition is very similar to accounts of emotion given by scientists such as Panksepp (1998) and Damasio (1999), for example, who see emotion as playing an important role in self-regulation and adaptivity. For Damasio (1999) emotion is primarily an organismic process of self-regulation aimed at maintaining homeostasis. Emotion thus conceived also provides action-guiding values, drives and preferences. Panksepp (1998) sees emotion as a collection of meaning-generating and adaptive mechanisms underpinned by specific neural and endocrine processes; emotion allows the organism to adapt to life-challenging circumstances, is constitutive of action and organizes diverse behaviors, and modulates the activity of perceptual systems.

On this view of emotion, the account of natural purposes developed by Weber and Varela (2002) and Di Paolo (2005) as a theory of bodily sense-making is as much a theory of emotion as it is a theory of cognition. In these works, the theory of autopoiesis becomes, more explicitly than in other texts, a theory of the origin of meaning in living systems. At this level of description, to cognize and to make sense in virtue of one's autopoietic and adaptive nature are one and the same process. This process can also be seen as emotional, in that it provides values and induces actions accordingly (motivation), and in that these values and actions are self-regulating and adaptive organismic processes.

What about the *emotions* of mainstream emotion theory (e.g., fear, happiness, anger, and so on)? Mainstream emotion theory typically sees emotion as a psychological faculty constituted by various individual emotions that are more or less violent experiences and/or bodily stirrings, and that are distinct from nonemotional phenomena. In this section, emotion has been characterized rather as the capacity that we share with other living systems to make sense of our environment in virtue of our being self-organizing and adaptive organisms. This is a broader conception of emotion, according to which fear, anger, happiness, guilt, anguish, and so on are only *some* of the many ways in which sense-making manifests itself in experience and in the body. To endorse the view that even the simplest organisms have values and preferences does not imply, of course, that all living systems have fear, anger, happiness, and the like (not to mention complex and/or idiosyncratic human emotions). The issue at stake is not how far down in the realm of the living systems we are happy to go until we decide to stop attributing emotions to organisms; the issue is, rather, what it is about living systems that makes the emergence of meaning possible. The theory of autopoiesis illustrated here places the conditions of possibility of meaning in the processes of self-generation and adaptivity that define living organisms and that, in the simplest ones, constitute a primordial form of bodily cognitive-emotional understanding. A corollary of this view is that the traditional distinction between emotional and nonemotional episodes falters. It remains of course possible and often useful to distinguish various forms of sense-making, but in the account defended here there is no room for emotionless cognition.

5.3   Enaction in Emotion: Enacting Appraisals

As part of its endeavor to dispel Cartesian anxieties, the enactive approach should underscore the continuity between the bacterium's sense-making, and what it means for me to understand the several meanings of my *Umwelt* and to regulate my behavior accordingly. This involves resisting the temptation to explain the way we humans make sense of our world by endowing our minds with abstract evaluative and meaning-generating powers. In this section, I will show that this attitude is alive and thriving in emotion science. I will then say why I think this attitude is problematic, and I will replace it with an integrated view that is consistent and continuous with the theory of embodied meaning in the autopoietic and adaptive system delineated previously.

   In the area of emotion theory known as appraisal theory, my capacity to evaluate events in my environment and to regulate my behavior accordingly is explained with reference to the process of *appraisal*. Appraisal is usually characterized as a cognitive process, and as separate from bodily *arousal*.[5] Typically, appraisal is the process that evaluates and understands the environment, and that ultimately brings about specific emotions (e.g., to appraise something as dangerous brings about fear, to appraise something as offensive brings about anger). Bodily arousal is typically an effect of appraisal that does not exert any causal power on it—it is a *by-product* of appraisal. Appraisal theories vary according to whether they consider arousal a *necessary* component of emotion, or merely a *contingent* concomitant. We will see that, even in the former case, arousal tends to play no role in differentiating among emotions, and thus in qualifying a subject's emotional state.

   Arnold (1960) introduced the notion of appraisal to overcome the difficulties of the most influential theories of emotion of her time. These difficulties concerned the role of the body in emotion and feeling, and the relationship between stimulus-detection and emotional response. According to James, an emotion was a bodily event and the experience of that emotion—the feeling—the perception of that bodily event; "*the bodily changes follow directly the* PERCEPTION *of the exciting fact, and . . . our feeling of the same changes as they occur* IS *the emotion*" (1884, 189–199). James famously insisted that "a purely disembodied human emotion is a nonentity" (194); if you imagine an emotion without its bodily symptoms, you will be left with "some cold-blooded and dispassionate judicial sentence, confined entirely to the intellectual realm" (194). James also believed that the body is richly differentiated and that there is an "immense number of parts modified in each emotion" (192); in his view, the muscles, the heart, and the circulatory system all contribute to the generation of different emotional feelings. Other influential emotion theories were activation theories (such as Duffy 1941) and behavioristic theories (such as Skinner 1953). The former identified emotion with activation or "energy" in the organism, and different emotions with different degrees of such energy. Behaviorism, on its part, saw emotions primarily as dispositions to behave in a certain way.

Arnold (1960) complained that none of these theories paid sufficient attention to how emotions are *elicited*. They were thus unable to explain why, for example, the same situation can induce different emotions in different individuals. What all these theories lacked, she remarked, was an account of how individuals *interpret* their environment. According to Arnold, emotions were first of all *personal* responses to the environment and had to involve a process of subjective evaluation—appraisal, as she called it.

In the heydays of cognitivism, the notion of appraisal underwent a process of reification and appraisal became a box in the mind. For Lazarus (1966) appraisal was (and still is) a cognitive process that is *necessary and sufficient* for emotion. Lazarus's account of the relationship between appraisal and emotion is paradigmatic of the "disembodied stance" that characterizes his and other cognitive theories of emotion (see Colombetti and Thompson 2008). In his view, bodily arousal follows cognitive appraisals and is not necessary for emotion. The appraisal process does everything alone—it appraises the environment, it causes bodily changes accordingly, it reappraises the environment and the subject's possibility to deal with it, it causes other bodily changes, and so on. Appraisal is here abstract and disembodied, in the sense that it is conceptually, causally, and phenomenologically distinct from bodily arousal.

This disembodied conception of the evaluative faculty goes hand in hand with what I have called *corporeal impersonalism* (Colombetti 2007), or the assumption that one's nonneural body does not contribute to subjective, personal understanding—in short, is not a vehicle of meaning. Corporeal impersonalism is evident in Lazarus's conception of bodily arousal as unnecessary for emotion and understanding, but it is found also in theories according to which bodily arousal *is necessary* for emotion. According to Schachter and Singer (1962), for instance, bodily arousal and cognitive appraisals are both necessary for emotion. In their view, however, bodily arousal is not emotion-specific; it is "a general pattern of excitation of the sympathetic nervous system" (379) that only contributes to the *intensity* of emotion. Crucially, bodily arousal needs to be *interpreted* in order for a specific emotion—for example, fear, anger, happiness, and so on—to arise (according to related subsequent "causal attribution theories," arousal needs to be *attributed to a specific cause*). In other words, bodily arousal plays a role in the differentiation of emotion only through the mediation and interpretation of appraisal, typically conceptualized as separate from bodily arousal. This view is characterized by corporeal impersonalism, because in order for the subject to experience her bodily arousal as a specific emotion experience, the mediation of a nonbodily interpretive capacity is required. Without such mediating interpretation, bodily arousal is nonspecific, unintelligible and meaningless to the subject.

Corporeal impersonalism also comes out in Schachter and Singer's claim that when one knows the causes of one's bodily arousal, no need to interpret it arises ("Given a state of physiological arousal for which an individual has a completely appropriate explanation, no evaluative needs will arise and the individual is unlikely to label his feelings in terms of the alternative cognitions available"; Schachter and Singer 1962, 398).[6] Because for Schachter and Singer arousal and appraisal are both necessary for emotion and emotion experience, it follows that when one knows the causes of one's bodily arousal, no emotion and emotion experience arise.

To be sure, the experiments that Schachter and Singer carried out to provide evidence for their theory have been criticized several times. Their theory of emotion however still influences contemporary conceptions of emotion. At present most emotion scientists believe that only some emotions have distinctive bodily signatures, and that cognitive appraisals provide further differentiation (for a sophisticated version of this view, see, e.g., Cacioppo et al. 2000). This compromise still presupposes corporeal impersonalism, because it implies that some aspects of emotion and of meaning in emotion experience do not come from the body.[7]

What exactly is wrong with these views? There are two senses in which, I think, corporeal impersonalism and the disembodied stance are problematic. First, they are *phenomenologically* implausible, in that they do not do justice to many instances of lived human experience. Second, they are *structurally* implausible, in the sense that they presuppose a brain/body dichotomy that is nothing more than the materialistic version of Cartesian mind-body dualism—namely, a brain-body dualism that, like Descartes' mind-body dualism, fails to elaborate on the implications of the rich interconnectivity of the brain, the body and the environment. In what follows I shall illustrate these two forms of implausibility and try to offer a reconceptualization of appraisal that is consistent and continuous with the theory of embodied meaning in the autopoietic and adaptive system presented in the previous section.

Appraisal theorists themselves acknowledge that it is not clear what appraisal is (e.g., Roseman and Smith 2001). It is unclear, for example, whether it refers to a conscious process, an implicit one, or both. This ambiguity leaves room for interpretations of Schachter and Singer's (1962) theory that fail to do justice to human lived experience. Consider their view that bodily arousal is uniform, and that emotions are differentiated by the intervention of the cognitive appraisal that evaluates the situation and interprets arousal accordingly. Now, it seems highly unlikely that affective specificity always depends on one's capacity to interpret, or find the cause for, one's bodily arousal. One often finds oneself in a state of bodily arousal for which one has no explanation, yet this state of arousal does not feel emotionally neutral. I often wake up groggy, depressed, or energetic without knowing why. Sometimes I know right away that that my state is due to cyclic hormonal fluctuations, yet my emotion does not dissolve because I have found that my arousal has no "emotional cause" (I wish it did!). Other times I do attribute the cause of my emotional states to some emotional source—for example, last night's fight with my housemate. In these cases, it is often my bodily arousal, already felt as a specific emotion, that guides my interpretation and reminds me of the cause of my emotion—not vice versa as Schachter and Singer's view seems to imply.

There are also studies that have shown that uninterpreted arousal (arousal for which subjects do not have an explanation) is not meaningless or experienced as emotionally neutral. It actually seems that unexplained arousal tends to be experienced as a negatively toned affective state (Marshall and Zimbardo 1979; Maslach 1979). Interesting cases reported by Damasio (2003, 67–79) suggest that specific behaviors and experiences can be induced by direct manipulation of bodily arousal. In one case, a woman started to show facial expressions of sadness, and then to cry and sob, as soon as an electrode stimulated a specific part of her brainstem. Once the electrode contact was removed, the sobbing stopped together with the feeling of sadness, and the subject reported that she did not know why she had felt so awful. In another case, following brain surgery a patient would suddenly burst into crying or laughter without apparent cause. Sometimes these bursts took place in quick succession, leaving the patient "barely time enough to take a breath and say that he was not in control, that neither laughter nor crying were really meant as such, that no thoughts in his mind justified this strange behavior" (Damasio 2003, 78).

As we saw, Schachter and Singer also claimed that when one knows that the source of one's bodily arousal is not emotional, no necessity for interpreting it ensues and bodily arousal is thus not accompanied by any emotion experience. This idea also looks implausible when confronted with lived human experience. Knowing that my euphoria at the party is caused by alcohol, for example, does not reduce it; knowing that my exhilaration is due to physical exercise does not eliminate it; and so on. Here too there are studies that cast doubt on Schachter and Singer's claim. Frijda (1986) observed that subjects knowingly receiving adrenaline can still experience emotion (such as anxiety), especially if they are predisposed to it. Reisenzein (1983, 249–250) mentioned several studies showing that subjects who clearly knew the source of their arousal reported genuine emotions. Also, attempts to make subjects believe in the wrong cause of their arousal (so-called misattribution manipulation studies) can fail for subjects particularly prone to certain emotions—see Reisenzein 1983 for further references.

The view according to which arousal is a mere by-product of appraisal (as in Lazarus) is also, I think, phenomenologically implausible. It seems to me that appraisal is experientially integrated with arousal, in the sense that I appraise the meaning of a situation *through* my being embodied and situated in it, and through the specific state of my body. In other words, bodily arousal seems to me to be part of the experience of appraisal. Mainstream emotion theory typically conceives of emotion experience as the feeling of one's body being aroused, and of appraisals as feelingless processes. Yet there are feelings of appraisal, and such feelings are part of emotion experience. Consider my anxiety during a job interview. I am sweating, my hands shake, and I am short of breath. Yet I am not reflectively paying attention to my bodily arousal, because I am focusing on the interviewers' questions. There is a sense, however, in which the interview-situation is evaluated and experienced as anxiety-provoking *through* the state of my body. Not only do I notice the shortness of my breath and my fingers shaking while I speak, but the interviewers' questions are, so to speak, "felt in my heartbeat." The whole experience (including the experience of the room in which the interview is taking place, of the interviewers' attitude, of my own demeanor, and so on) includes a sense of my bodily arousal, is "colored"—for lack of a better term—in a certain way through my arousal.

What is this sense of bodily arousal through which I live the experience of the interview? The notion of *the lived body* is useful here. In philosophical phenomenology, the lived body refers to the prereflective bodily self-consciousness that constitutes perceptual experiences (see Thompson and Zahavi 2007 for a clear illustration of this complex notion). The lived body is the backdrop against which my perceptual experiences take place. For example, while typing on this computer I experience the whiteness of the virtual sheets, the smoothness of the keys, the hardness of the chair, and so on, and at the same time I am aware of my body as that through which these experiences are made possible. In the case of an emotion experience like my anxiety during the interview, I am also similarly aware of my bodily arousal as that through which I am living the situation as anxiety-provoking. As far as I know, the notion of the lived body appears mainly in accounts of perceptual experience. Yet it need not be restricted to perceptual experience. Patočka (1998), for example, emphasizes the striving and affective character of the lived body, and he talks of experiences of our environment as "physiognomic impressions" (see also Thompson and Zahavi 2007 for a related discussion of Husserl's *affectivity*).

The other sense in which corporeal impersonalism and the disembodied stance are implausible has to do with how the brain and the nonneural body relate to each other. We have seen that the psychological mechanism of appraisal is typically conceived of as separate from arousal. Arousal, on its part, is typically a set of events in the nonneural body. Because appraisal is separate from arousal thus conceived, it follows that appraisal must depend on the brain, or on some part of it.

From the point of view of the organism, however, the separation of appraisal and arousal is fuzzy. As Lewis (2005) points out, for example, systems for appraisal largely overlap with systems for arousal (and with other traditional constituents of emotion such as feelings, action, and attention). His analysis of the subpersonal processes that lie beneath appraisal and emotion, including arousal, reveals a distributed network of self-organizing and mutually influencing brain and bodily processes, each of which subsumes various functions. The amygdala, for example, plays a dual role in appraisal and arousal; the anterior cingulate cortex is involved in planning, attentional orientation, and emotion experience; bodily arousal (autonomic and endocrine activity) maintains the organism's homeostatic equilibrium, contributes to emotion experience, enhances attention, and prepares for action. Lewis (2005) in particular points out that there are phenomena of *emotional interpretation* during which systems subsuming appraisal and emotion, including arousal, become deeply integrated via reciprocally constraining processes of positive and negative feedback (self-amplification and self-stabilization).

Lewis's account is many ways analogous to Freeman's (2000) model of sensorimotor integration, in which appraisal and arousal are also structurally integrated within the whole embodied organism.[8] Freeman points out that sensorimotor integration is continuously modulated by the amygdala—a part of the brain traditionally considered important for arousal. The amygdala contributes to deciding what is relevant for the organism and how the organism should act. Freeman characterizes this process not as a hierarchical one of evaluation and control of the organism on the part of the amygdala, but as a self-organizing process in which perception, action, and the amygdala modulate one another in the service of the organism's viability.

On the resulting view, it is hard to see why only some systems should be those in charge of evaluating and understanding, whereas others should be merely reacting and deprived of any meaning-generating role. In the integrated model that emerges from Lewis's and Freeman's discussion, it is the whole situated organism that subsumes the capacity to make sense of the environment and to act in it. Bodily arousal is here *constitutive* of the process of interpreting a situation (understanding) traditionally conceived of as the function of a disembodied, or merely brainy, appraisal.

In sum, in this section I have argued that to conceptualize appraisal as a cognitive process separate from arousal implies a disembodied view of appraisal that is both phenomenologically and structurally implausible. Appraisal should be conceived of as experientially corporeal and as structurally embodied, consistently and coherently with the theory of embodied meaning in the autopoietic and adaptive organism presented earlier. From the enactive standpoint defended here, bodily arousal is not merely a response to the subject's evaluation of the situation in which he or she is embedded. It is rather the whole situated organism that subsumes the subject's capacity to make sense of his or her world.

5.4   Looking Ahead: Coexisting Bodily Appraisals, Irrationality, and Neurochemical harmonization

I would now like to emphasize that the view sketched here allows for different ways to generate meaning within the same organism. In particular, one thing that distinguishes the bacterium's sense-making from mine is that I have available different sources of bodily meaning. Following Jonas (1966), Di Paolo puts this idea in terms of the emergence of "new forms of life" as organisms increase in complexity:

This new form of life is not contrary or indifferent to metabolism. Made possible by the latter, it will mostly be at its service, but it may also be independent of it to the extent that the adaptivity of metabolism does not dictate a unique way of doing what is necessary for its continuation. Within this independence, the new form of life will be able to generate, via a process of adaptive closure analogous to metabolism, its own set of values, thus making the process irrevocable and resulting in the *coexistence of different identities in a same organism*. (2005, 446; emphasis in original)

It is thus possible to find clashing bodily appraisals within the same organism. A case in point is the one of behaviors traditionally deemed "irrational." Irrational behaviors by definition are not in accordance with our judgments—as when John experiences fear and jumps away as he sees a spider, despite the fact that he judges it as innocuous (an instance of irrational fear), or as when Mary lights up her cigarette while judging that it is bad for her health and that she should quit smoking (a case of akratic action, or of weakness of the will). How does the present view account for the deemed irrationality of these behaviors? This is a difficult question, and a complete answer would require a well-developed theory of rationality, concepts, and responsibility. I would like to point out, however, that the present view can accommodate these scenarios as instances of coexisting meanings or bodily appraisals in the same organism. Importantly, many of the behaviors that are traditionally deemed irrational (e.g., irrational fears and addictions) are not unintelligible and do have scientific explanations, such as evolutionary and neurophysiological ones. These explanations often reveal a striking bodily intelligence, and to deem those bodily happenings irrational would mean to overlook some of the organism's "reasons." Churchland (1998) points out that, from the point of view of the organism, it is unlikely that there is a principled distinction between voluntary and involuntary actions, or between being in control and being out of control. She notices that some desires or fears can be very powerful, and that we have more self-control in some circumstances rather than others; hormonal changes, for example, make certain patterns of behavior highly likely. There are neurochemical explanations of phenomena of lack of volition, such as alien hand syndrome, obesity or Tourette syndrome. In many cases, chemical intervention and behavioral therapy can affect these phenomena and reestablish control. The resulting view is one in which "rationality" amounts to a range of optimal values for the relevant chemical and neural parameters. As Churchland puts it, when values fall within the optimal range, the agent's behavior is in his or her control; when they fall within the suboptimal range, the agent is unable to control his or her behavior. In between, there are many gray areas.

From this perspective, John's and Mary's irrational actions are instances of lack of control (that is, failed or incomplete harmonization of different bodily judgments), yet actions that obey their own intelligible rules. Importantly, it is possible to bring clashing appraisals into harmony, with the help of chemistry and/or through practice. At present we do not know exactly how to define the optimal range of integration, and as Churchland points out, there is not going to be one universal specification, because in-control individuals are likely to have different temperaments and different cognitive strategies. This point is analogous to Di Paolo's remark reported earlier that there are many ways to preserve metabolism. Further work on this question would need to discuss more specifically how neurochemical harmonization is realized. Also, the view developed in this chapter cries for an account of how human judgments and values (such as social values) relate to organismic values and sense-making. In this chapter, I have claimed that as enactivist theorists, we should resist the temptation to separate the appraising mind from the appraised and/or merely reacting body; also, I have argued that appraisal is phenomenologically and structurally embodied. Yet I have not said anything about how to move from a theory of organismic sense-making toward human evaluations and social values.

My last considerations regard the notion of *valence*, which is mentioned by both Weber and Varela (2002) and Varela and Depraz (2005). I think that acknowledging the coexistence of different forms of sense-making and bodily meaning in complex organisms has important implications for this notion. The notion of valence is used in emotion science to refer to the positive and negative character of emotions and/or their aspects, such as feelings, behavior, appraisal, and so on (Colombetti 2005). Weber and Varela mention valence to refer to initial forms of meaning-generation in the autopoietic system: "Stimuli from outside enter the sphere or relevance of such a unit only by their existential meaning for the keeping of the process of self-establishment. They acquire a valence which is dual at its basis: attraction or rejection, approach or escape" (2002, 117). In a similar vein, Varela and Depraz also conceive of valence as a basic organismic disposition, "a tension that takes several forms: like-dislike, attraction-rejection, pleasure-displeasure" (2005, 70).

I think that whereas this duality is useful to describe the behavior of simple organisms, it is constraining when it comes to describe the variety of experiences, behaviors, appraisals, and so on of complex organisms. The main problem with the notion of valence is that it is typically characterized as a dimension whose poles are mutually exclusive, which logically rules out the possibility of conflicts and mixtures. Yet our life is dominated by mixtures and ambivalences (for arguments, see Colombetti 2005)—something that depends on the coexistence of different values and meaning-generating processes in complex organisms. The question is whether it is possible to enrich the current notion of valence (perhaps by replacing it with a notion of "multidimensional valence," as some emotion theorists including Varela and Depraz [2005] suggest), or whether this notion should rather be abandoned. A story of how to move from a theory of organismic sense-making toward human judgments and social values might prove useful to provide a theoretical framework within which it is possible to decide on this issue, and perhaps to characterize the idea of a "multi-dimensional valence" in more detail.

I hope that the suggestions of this chapter can provide the impetus for further work on enaction and emotion. The work on sense-making illustrated here, together with other works in phenomenology and enactive cognitive science, are unpacking the many ways in which the body makes up the mind. At the same time, emotion is becoming increasingly important in the study of mind and cognition. Several philosophers argue that emotion can be rational, and psychologists and neuroscientists agree that emotion is centrally involved in cognitive processes such as decision-making, memory, and attention. It is thus time to develop a view of agency in which emotion—including its bodily, experiential and behavioral aspects—is not a secondary and circumscribed phenomenon. In its endeavor to provide a new paradigm for cognitive science, the enactive approach should dispel the Cartesian anxiety induced by the idea that the mind's task is to hold the reins of the body via ongoing cognitive-evaluative processes. To acknowledge that emotion and the body are constitutive of the capacity to understand and act adaptively is, I believe, a crucial step in this direction.

Notes

1. By "body" I mean here specifically the *nonneural* body. Yet note that in the psychology of emotion, there is not much discussion of the neural processes that might subsume the capacity to evaluate either. Cognitive evaluations are thus very much "mental" in Descartes' sense, although of course all emotion scientists would claim that cognitive evaluations are embodied in the brain or in some part of it.

2. In their discussion of the place of emotion in enaction, Varela and Depraz announce that "emotions cannot be seen as a mere 'coloration' of the cognitive agent, understood as a formal and un-affected self, but are immanent and inextricable from every mental act" (2005, 61). They also say that their analysis aligns perfectly with the phenomenological analysis of the relationship of emotion and movement offered by Sheets-Johnstone (1999). These papers do not mention autopoiesis or sense-making, but their views are consistent with the one that I will defend here. This consistency makes me hope that I am not misinterpreting the original intentions of Varela and colleagues.

3. The term *Umwelt* was used by von Uexküll (1921) to refer to the features of an animal's environment that are salient for the animal itself. The *Umwelt* is the environment experienced by the animal, that is, the lived or phenomenal environment.

4. It is interesting to recall that Maturana and Varela (1980) had explicitly banned purposes from the autopoietic system. Thompson (2007, chap. 6) illustrates some of the reasons (including his own exchanges with Varela) for the shift of perspective that eventually led to the notion of natural purpose in Weber and Varela (2002).

5. When psychologists of emotion talk of bodily arousal, they usually refer to visceral and musculoskeletal changes. This is the notion of arousal with which I am concerned here. Neuroscientists on their part characterize certain brain areas (such as the amygdala, the anterior cingulate cortex, the insula, and others) as importantly involved in emotional arousal. My arguments also apply to neuroscientific theories that neatly distinguish between brain areas specifically involved in cognitive appraisal, and brain areas specifically involved in arousal.

6. This claim refers specifically to some of the results of Schachter and Singer's (1962) controversial experiments. They found that subjects who had been injected with adrenaline and who had been adequately informed about the physiological effects of the injection, did not label their bodily arousal as an emotion.

7. An appraisal theorist at this point might want to defend herself by saying that she does not hold a view of cognition as some ethereal Cartesian mental substance, and that of course appraisal depends on the brain (see note 1). The problem with appraisal theory, however, is precisely that it relies on an unclear notion of cognition. At a closer look, the view that cognition, *and not the body*, specifies which

emotion one is having, is mysterious. How can cognition determine a specific emotional feeling? How can a cognitive appraisal, whose relation to the brain and the body is left unaccounted for, induce a specific experience? What does it mean, ultimately, to claim that cognition distinguishes among emotions and specifies which emotion one is having?

8. For a discussion of Lewis's and Freeman's models in the context of the enactive approach and in relation to phenomenological accounts of protention and affectivity, see Thompson 2007 (chap. 11).

References

Arnold, M. B. (1960). *Emotion and personality*. New York: Columbia University Press.

Cacioppo, J. T., Berntson, G. G., Larsen, J. T., Poehlmann, K. M., and Ito, T. A. (2000). The psychophysiology of emotion. In *Handbook of emotion*, 2nd edition, ed. M. Lewis and J. M. Haviland-Jones, 173–191. New York: Guildford Edition.

Churchland, P. S. (1998). Feeling reasons. In *On the contrary: Critical essays*, ed. P. M. Churchland and P. S. Churchland, 231–254. Cambridge, MA: MIT Press.

Colombetti, G. (2005). Appraising valence. *Journal of Consciousness Studies* 12 (8–10): 103–126.

Colombetti, G. (2007). Enactive appraisal. *Phenomenology and the Cognitive Sciences* 6:527–546.

Colombetti, G., and Thompson, E. (2008). The feeling body: Toward an enactive approach to emotion. In *Developmental perspectives on embodiment and consciousness*, ed. W. F. Overton, U. Müller, and J. Newman, 45–68. New York: Lawrence Erlbaum.

Damasio, A. R. (1999). *The feeling of what happens: Body, emotion and the making of consciousness*. London: Vintage.

Damasio, A. R. (2003). *Looking for Spinoza: Joy, sorrow and the feeling brain*. Orlando, FL: Harcourt.

Descartes, R. (1988). The passions of the soul. In *Selected philosophical writings of René Descartes*, ed. J. Cottingham, R. Stoothoff, and D. Murdoch, 218–238. Cambridge: Cambridge University Press.

Di Paolo, E. A. (2005). Autopoiesis, adaptivity, teleology, agency. *Phenomenology and the Cognitive Sciences* 4:429–452.

Duffy, E. (1941). An explanation of "emotional" phenomena without the use of the concept "emotion." *Journal of General Psychology* 25:283–293.

Freeman, W. J. (2000). Emotion is essential to all intentional behaviors. In *Emotion, development, and self-organization: Dynamic systems approaches to emotional develop-*

ment, ed. M. D. Lewis and I. Granic, 209–235. Cambridge: Cambridge University Press.

Frijda, N. H. (1986). *The emotions.* Cambridge: Cambridge University Press.

James, W. (1884). What is an emotion? *Mind* 9:188–205.

Jonas, H. (1966). *The phenomenon of life.* New York: Harper and Row.

Lazarus, R. S. (1966). *Psychological stress and the coping process.* New York: McGraw Hill.

Lewis, M. D. (2005). Bridging emotion theory and neurobiology through dynamic systems modeling. *Behavioral and Brain Sciences* 28 (2): 169–194.

Marshall, G., and Zimbardo, P. G. (1979). Affective consequences of inadequately explained physiological arousal. *Journal of Personality and Social Psychology* 37:970–988.

Maslach, C. (1979). Negative emotional biasing of unexplained arousal. *Journal of Personality and Social* Psychology 37:953–969.

Maturana, H. R., and Varela, F. J. (1980). *Autopoiesis and cognition: The Realization of the living. Boston studies in the philosophy of science,* vol. 42. Dordrecht: D. Reidel.

Noë, A. (2004). *Action in perception.* Cambridge, MA: MIT Press.

Panksepp, J. (1998). *Affective neuroscience.* Oxford: Oxford University Press.

Pato ka, J. (1998). *Body, community, language, world.* Chicago: Open Court.

Reisenzein, R. (1983). The Schachter theory of emotion: Two decades later. *Psychological Bulletin* 94:239–264.

Roseman, I. J., and Smith, C. A. (2001). Appraisal theory: Overview, assumptions, varieties, controversies. In *Appraisal processes in emotion,* ed. K. R. Scherer, A. Schorr, and T. Johnstone, 3–19. Oxford: Oxford University Press.

Schachter, S., and Singer, J. E. (1962). Cognitive, social, and physiological determinants of emotional state. *Psychological Review* 69:379–399.

Sheets-Johnstone, M. (1999). Emotion and movement: A beginning empirical-phenomenological analysis of their relationship. *Journal of Consciousness Studies* 6 (11–12): 259–277.

Skinner, B. F. (1953). *Science and human behavior.* New York: Free Press.

Thompson, E. (2007). *Mind in life: Biology, phenomenology, and the sciences of mind.* Cambridge, MA: Harvard University Press.

Thompson, E., and Varela, F. J. (2001). Radical embodiment: Neural dynamics and consciousness. *Trends in Cognitive Sciences* 5:418–425.

Thompson, E., and Zahavi, D. (2007). Philosophical issues: Continental phenomenology. In *The Cambridge handbook of consciousness*, ed. P. D. Zelazo, M. Moscovitch, and E. Thompson, 67–88. Cambridge: Cambridge University Press.

Varela, F. J., and Depraz, N. (2005). At the source of time: Valence and the constitutional dynamics of affect. *Journal of Consciousness Studies* 12 (8–10): 61–81.

Varela, F. J., Thompson, E., and Rosch, E. (1991). *The embodied mind: Cognitive science and human experience*. Cambridge, MA: MIT Press.

von Uexküll, J. (1921). *Umwelt und Innenwelt der Tiere*. Berlin: Springer.

Weber, A., and Varela, F. J. (2002). Life after Kant: Natural purposes and the autopoietic foundations of biological individuality. *Phenomenology and the* Cognitive Sciences 1:97–125.

Wheeler, M. (2005). *Reconstructing the cognitive world: The next step*. Cambridge, MA: MIT Press.

6 Thinking in Movement: Further Analyses and Validations

Maxine Sheets-Johnstone

I

I would like to begin by citing a statement Piaget made in conjunction with one of his documented observations of an infant, specifically a mouth gesture made by his sixteen-month-old daughter Lucienne as she was trying to open a matchbox. The statement highlights in a dramatic way both the phenomenon of thinking in movement and the all-too-common oversight of thinking in movement. To lead up to the statement and put it in its proper context, I need to say something first about our spatial perceptions and cognitions as infants and cite some supporting literature.

Infant spatial perceptions and cognitions are intimately tied to movement and are constituted from the ground up by infants themselves—without a manual and without instruction from anyone. Their spatial intelligence is clearly if at times implicitly evident in descriptive accounts of their developing spatial awarenesses. Psychologists describe the fascination of infants and young children with *insideness*, for example, that is, with being *in* or *inside*, or with *putting inside*. Piaget, for instance, documents the fact that his daughter Lucienne watches her hand closely as she repeatedly opens and closes it (see Piaget 1968, 90, 96). He does not mention *insideness* or *insides* in relation to the movement pattern, but clearly, in watching her hand alternately closing and opening, Lucienne alternately hides and discloses *insides*. Infant psychologist T. G. R. Bower, in the context of corroborating observations made by Piaget of his children, writes that "Piaget's son was surely typical in finding the relation 'inside' fascinating." Bower adds, "One of my own daughters spent the best part of one night placing small objects in my hand, closing my hand on them, moving my hand to a new location, and then opening it up to see if the object were still there. This kept her happy and busy till nearly 4 a.m." (Bower 1974, 238).

As with *insides*, putting one thing inside another has an attraction for infants and small children. Although the attraction is explained in terms of learning the rule that two objects can be in the same place provided one is inside the other (see Bower 1982, 240–241, for a discussion of this rule), such an explanation falls short of its mission: it says nothing of the *natural penchant* of infants and young children to put one thing inside another and nothing of their elemental fascination with *insideness* to begin with. Piaget's descriptive account of his sixteen-month-old daughter trying to open a matchbox testifies dramatically to the oversight. Lucienne, Piaget says, looks "very attentively" at the slit into which she slides her finger to open the matchbox, then "opens and closes [her] mouth several times, at first weakly, then wider and wider!" (Piaget 1968, 294; my translation). To judge from his punctuation, Piaget is astonished by the young child's corporeally rooted spatial intention and understanding. He does not, however, interpret his observation along the lines of thinking in movement and a developing tactile-kinesthetic body; an experientially resonant thinking body does not enter into his theory of the development of human intelligence. On the contrary, he explains Lucienne's lingual movement as a *faute de mieux*: "Lacking the power to think in words or clear visual images [Lucienne] uses, as 'signifier' or symbol, a simple motor indication" (Piaget 1968, 294).

The oversight in Piaget's explanation is readily apparent: the basic tactile-kinetic analogy between Lucienne's mouth gesture and manual gesture is far too powerful to be reduced to "a simple motor indication" (see Sheets-Johnstone 1990, 238). The term "motor" is in fact an insult to Lucienne's innate kinetic ingenuity, her capacity *to think in movement*. Lucienne is not a machine nor are her movements mechanistic; she is an animate being whose movements are meaningful. The *kinetic* analogy she spontaneously draws between opening a matchbox and opening her mouth testifies to the meaningfulness of her movements. No one, after all, has taught her or told her to open her mouth as she opens the matchbox. Moreover the kinetic exactness of her analogy is itself striking: Lucienne does not raise her shoulders or put her right foot on her left knee as she opens the matchbox. On the contrary, she makes a gesture that is kinetically consonant with her intention to open the matchbox.

In addition to overlooking the aptness of Lucienne's kinetic analogy and the fact of the analogy itself, Piaget's explanation suffers from an adultist bias; that is, from a typical adult point of view, movement is regarded a prelinguistic phenomenon—something that merely chronologically precedes language—when in actuality language is and should be regarded *post-kinetic* (Sheets-Johnstone 1999). Language-learning indeed develops on the basis of an infant's first learning its body and learning to move itself. The same adultist bias is apparent in studies of language acquisition that explain specific word acquisitions as a function of motor programs and rules. An excellent example in fact concerns the prepositional primacy of the word *in* as both locative state and locative act; '*in*' has been shown to be the first spatial concept understood by an infant/child as signifying perceptually a certain locational relationship—as "the match is in the matchbox"—and as signifying behaviorally a certain locational act or acts—as "I put the match in the matchbox" (Clark 1973, 1979; Cook 1978; see also Grieve, Hoogenraad, and Murray 1977). What requires recognition in this context is similar to what requires recognition with respect to Lucienne's mouth gesture, namely, a recognition of movement as the generative source of spatial concepts, in this instance, the concept of *in*. If children as early as one-and-a-half years have a conceptual mastery of *in* as locative state and locative act, then surely their life experiences must be taken into account; that is, their conceptual mastery is less plausibly explained by rules and motor programs as per research accounts (e.g., Huttenlocher, Smiley, and Ratner 1983, 211), than by the fact that their experiences of *in, insides, being inside,* and *putting inside* have been reiterated many times over every day of their lives in such acts as sucking, eating, defecating, urinating, being held in the arms of others, being put in a crib, grasping something in their hand, putting a foot in a shoe, an arm in a sleeve, a thumb in a mouth, and so on.

II

Research studies of infant understandings of *in, insideness,* and so on, are in fact of particular interest for what they say and do not say about kinesthesia and thinking in movement. Careful reflection on these studies from an experiential perspective shows that we put the world together in a spatial sense through movement and do so from the very beginning of our lives. Spatial concepts are born in kinesthesia and in our correlative capacity to think in movement. Accordingly, the constitution of space begins not with adult thoughts about space but in infant experience. A consideration of perceptions and cognitions of what we call *near* and *far* will further exemplify this claim.

The concept of "distance" is commonly taken for granted and is in turn far less researched by infant/child psychologists than other spatial concepts such as open and closed, inside and outside, appearing and disappearing, and under and over. Yet both the perception and conception of *near* and *far* are integral dimensions of our everyday lives: we reach for things that are reachable; we walk to something not quite within reach; we drive or fly to a place that we cannot reach on foot or bicycle; and so on. Even brief reflection on such everyday facts of life readily points to the certainty that *near* and *far* are basically facts of *bodily* life: they are rooted in bodily experience, specifically experiences of one's tactile-kinesthetic body. A summary phenomenologically informed sketch will suffice to show the soundness of the corporeal linkage and the perceptual and conceptual lines of its development.

Studies of infants watching objects appear and disappear show that in the beginning what occupies an infant's attention is solely what is present. They show that an infant later keeps track of objects appearing and disappearing, which means they are cognitively aware of movement and change. Studies of infants show too that in the beginning, infants put whatever is present at hand—grasped objects as well as their own thumbs and fingers—into their mouths. They show furthermore that infants make inchoate reaching movements toward objects they see, movements that over time become refined into coordinated movements toward things within reach. Moreover they show that infants point and often make a sound of some kind when they want something that is out of reach. All such studies take for granted *the tactile-kinesthetic body* that is the center of an infant's world, the primary sensory base on which it experiences and explores the world and on which its thinking in movement is grounded. Not only does movement itself attract attention, but moving to touch or to withdraw from something originate in felt kinetic motivations and contribute to an infant's developing spatial knowledge of itself in face of a surrounding world. *Near* and *far* are thus tethered to the tactile-kinesthetic body. They are tied to the "zero-point" of all possible orientations; that is, as phenomenological philosopher Edmund Husserl points out, everything anyone might experience is "'there'—with the exception of . . . the Body, which is always 'here'" (Husserl 1989, 166)—or as he later observes, "I do not have the possibility of distancing myself from my Body" (167).

The zero-point or "hereness" of an infant is, one might say, a concentrated zero-point or "hereness"; a limited range and repertoire of movement restrict a freely changing hereness. In effect, what is near is *something present and immediately touchable, something present that an infant can move toward and touch or draw away from*; what is far is *something present that is beyond its range of movement or movement possibilities, hence beyond touch*. The perception of something as near or far and the concept of near and far are thus originally nonlinguistic tactile-kinesthetic perceptions and concepts. *Visual* percepts and concepts of near and far develop on the basis of these original nonlinguistic tactile-kinesthetic perceptions and concepts.[1] The original tactile-kinesthetic meanings of *near* and *far* are indeed the basis on which not only later visual percepts and concepts develop but the basis on which more complex tactile-kinesthetic meanings arise. In other words, original meanings are kinesthetically as well as objectively elaborated in the course of development. For example, tactile-kinesthetic experiences of near and far come to be fleshed out along the lines of ease, fatigue, or effort—along the lines of a specific felt flow of movement, its strains and tensions or lack thereof in the pursuit of some goal. They come to be objectively elaborated when distance becomes a measured or measurable quantity, a specific space to be traversed in a physicomathematical sense—so many doors to pass on the way to a meeting, so many blocks to the store, so many miles to the airport, and so on. The objective sense of near and far has its roots in an objective body, a body no longer exclusively experienced as the "zero-point" of orientation but as an item in the prevailing landscape, a body that, passing a certain number of doors, walking a set number of blocks, or driving a set number of miles, is experienced as an object *in* space and as moving *in* space.

III

Experiencing one's body as an object *in* space, one commonly experiences not movement, that is, not a *kinetic dynamics*, but oneself as an *object in motion* (Sheets-Johnstone 1979, 1999). The kinetic dynamics of self-movement are swallowed up in the objectification of both body and space; that is, body and space are objectified in ways that turn attention away from if not nullify the kinetic dynamics of movement. The kinetic dynamics, however, remain the sine qua non of the objectification. In other words, experiences of a kinetic dynamics precede in both a chronological and logical sense the experience of oneself as an object in motion. Indeed, the possibility of the latter experience rests on and could not arise without the former experiences. When we learn our bodies and learn to move ourselves, we do so not analytically as objects in motion or objects in space, but dynamically as animate forms. Studies of infant development implicitly document this fact in their descriptions of movements such as reaching, turning over, sitting, standing, and so on (see Thelen and Smith 1994; Bower 1979, 1982). In short, the experience of ourselves as objects in motion, objects in space, is possible only on the basis of our having learned our bodies and learned to move ourselves, and these early learnings are anchored in a fundamental kinetic dynamics that is the backbone of our thinking in movement and the basis of our everyday capacities to move effectively and efficiently in the world.

An important conceptual aspect of the distinction between experiencing the kinetic dynamics of self-movement—what famed Russian neurophysiologist Alexander Luria terms "kinesthetic or kinetic melodies"—and experiencing oneself as an object in motion turns precisely on the common adult concept of space as a container. The moment one speaks of being "in space," one has objectified it by conceiving it a container filled with objects, a populated repository whose population also includes oneself. As indicated earlier, however, descriptive studies of infancy show that an infant's world stretches out in the beginning only to whatever is present. An infant does not have a concept of space as a container of objects—chairs, cribs, blankets, and so on—any more than it has a concept of its body as a container of organs, nerves, and muscles. Its elemental, nonlinguistic concept of space is rooted in its immediate experience of itself and the world about it. The spatial vista or expanse that it perceives consists simply in whatever lies *beyond its felt hereness*. That is, whatever might be spatially present or *there*—bureaus, chairs, pillows, blankets, stuffed animals, and so on—is neither perceived nor conceived as being *in* space, but is simply *there*. What is near and what is far are thus in the beginning markers of a spatially open distance between a felt bodily *hereness* and a *thereness* of some kind, markers in a tactile-kinesthetic sense of an expanse that neither contains objects nor is itself contained within, or by, a larger universal or worldly space—even the space of a room or a house.

An infant's fascination with *insides* and with putting one thing *inside* another, and a child's later understanding of the preposition *in* as both a locative state and locative act, testify to this same elemental tactile-kinesthetic spatiality. Here too, an adult bias easily deflects us, precipitating us precisely toward container interpretations of infant perceptions and conceptions of space rather than toward a recognition of an elemental spatiality. Clearly, an infant has a sense of its mouth, for example, as the locus of pleasant and unpleasant tactile and gustatory experiences, as the locus of tactile explorations of whatever it grasps, and as the center of movement in the form of a tongue. Though its lips close in on its thumb and whatever other items it puts in its mouth, however, it does not have a sense of its mouth as a container. Similarly, though in opening and closing its hand, it makes an inside appear and disappear, it does not make and unmake a container. A container notion of space emerges only later, on the basis of its tactile-kinesthetic experiences. When it puts one thing inside another, it is building on its primary tactile-kinesthetic spatiality. Putting one thing inside another is indeed akin to putting food or a thumb in a mouth. Analogical thinking is thus again evident. Just as there is a tactile-kinesthetic analogy between opening one's mouth coincident with opening a matchbox, so there is a tactile-kinesthetic/tactile-kinetic analogy between putting one's thumb in one's mouth or one's arm in a sleeve and putting one thing inside another. Tactile-kinesthetic analogical thinking is an elemental mode of thinking.

The adult concept of *in* operative in the notion of containment, like the adult concept of "being *in* space," is foreign to this mode of thinking because it is basically a visually forged concept that is foreign to a tactile-kinesthetic/tactile-kinetic spatiality. Only as an original tactile-kinesthetically charged expanse becomes perceived as a container—a becoming undoubtedly helped along by language, which emphasizes early on the *naming* of containers such as cups, bottles, rooms, houses, cars, and so on—does a young child begin to perceive and conceive her/himself as being *in* space and to perceive and conceive the world of objects about her/him as being *in* space.

When a container notion of space takes over entirely, thinking in movement loses its lived, dynamic character and becomes no more than a mode of measurement, which, while certainly of everyday practical value, has little or no kinetic value: Can I put all this stuff in the suitcase? How near is the store? How far did I kick the ball? When the practical overruns experiences of a kinetic dynamics, tactile-kinesthetic feelings of movement can fade so far into the background that the kinetic melodies of movement are lost, and with them, experiences of the spatial qualities that make any movement the movement it is. Spatial qualities—a rounded, curved space, as in wending one's way on a downhill slope in skiing, or an angular, jagged space, as in dodging this way and that in a game of tag—are qualities that movement itself creates. The distinctive spatial qualities movement creates are integral to the distinctions infants make in learning to move themselves and that we all made in learning to move ourselves. For example, through their attentiveness to the spatiality of their movement (see Bower 1971, 1982; Bloom 1993; Bruner 1990), infants continually shape their movement spatially to the intentional urgings that prompt them to move. In a very real sense, they play with movement, discovering kinetic awarenesses and possibilities in the course of moving. Over time, they hone their movement to better effect—changing their orientation, for example, or the range of their movement. Their focus of attention is not on themselves as objects in motion, but on the spatiality of movement itself, what it affords and does not afford with respect to touching things that are near, grasping them, pulling them toward themselves, crawling toward those that are distant, pointing toward them, and so on. This experiential space, or better this *tactile-kinesthetic spatiality*, has nothing to do with measured or measurable distances but is an experiential dimension of movement itself. Space in this experiential sense is precisely *not* a container in which movement takes place but a dynamic tactile-kinesthetically charged created space.

Multiple psychological studies of infants attest to a tactile-kinesthetic-based spatiality, and thereby show that meaning and thinking are basically linked to movement. The studies attest to an infant's attentiveness to movement over shape (Bower 1971), for example, and to its grasp of if/then relationships (Bloom 1993; Stern 1985). Consider, for example, simply the fact that if you close your eyes, it gets dark (Stern 1985, 80). We experience just such an if/then relationship from the very beginnings of life. Moreover, as infant psychologist Jerome Bruner shows on the basis of a broad range of empirical research, infants are focally attentive to agent and action, to what Bruner terms "agentivity." Agentivity, I might add, has a distinct resonance with "I cans," Husserl's term for both kinetic and cognitive accomplishments, as in I can throw, I can calculate, I can spin a top, I can judge, and so on. Finally, we might note that infants visually discriminate differently shaped pacifiers on the basis of their tactile-kinesthetic experiences of the pacifiers: they discriminate a rounded pacifier with a single nipple from a knobby or multiple-nippled one (Meltzoff and Borton 1979).

All the previously mentioned studies of infants attest to the fact that a tactile-kinesthetic spatiality is there from the beginning, that it is a foundational dimension of our thinking in movement, and that thinking in movement is our original—and abiding—mode of thinking. Though we cannot remember our experiences as infants, we were all nevertheless infants. We built our knowledge of movement and of the world on the basis of having learned our bodies and learned to move ourselves. We accomplished such learning by thinking in movement. An adult bias precludes recognition of that capacity. When we describe or explain how we come to conceive space and build our knowledge of space from the viewpoint of an adult, we commonly take for granted knowledge gleaned from the perspective of an infant, in part because as adults we commonly take movement itself for granted, in part because, as adults, we are already experienced in the ways of the world and take "the world" for granted. As adults, we nevertheless have the possibility of experiencing fundamental aspects of space, that is, fundamental aspects of what we already know as "space" simply by paying attention to our experience of movement. However untrained we might be in such an endeavor, by paying close attention, we have the possibility of experiencing a diversity of spatial qualities, including ones thus far unmentioned—for example, a resistant space as we walk into a strong wind or shove a heavy box across a floor; an angular space when we feel ourselves cutting sharp corners; a yielding space in the course of running across an open meadow; a circular space in molding our arms to pick up a large bowl. Whatever the spatial quality, we experience it kinesthetically.

If we ask specifically what corporeal-kinetic knowledge we glean as maturing infants, we readily see that, in the beginning, movement is not a pregiven program of proficiencies and capacities, but something we must actively learn—precisely by moving ourselves.[2] Kinesthesia—the experience of self-movement—is the ground on which we do so. In reaching and kicking, we discover particular kinetic possibilities of our bodies and correlative spatiotemporal-energic dynamics in the process. In each instance, our movement has a particular flow, the dynamics of which are kinesthetically felt. When we learn to turn over, we experience a spatiotemporal dynamics quite different from reaching and kicking, a kinesthetically felt *coordination dynamics* (Kelso 1995) that grounds our capacity ultimately to turn over any time we wish. When we learn to walk, we learn a complex and challenging coordination dynamics that is, again, kinesthetically felt. Indeed, kinesthesia is an ever-present modality whether one is an infant or an adult. We cannot in fact close off kinesthesia in the way we can readily close our eyes and turn away from the visual, close our mouths, pinch our nose, clamp our hands over our ears, and similarly turn away from other sensory modalities.

While negligibly treated in physiology and psychology textbooks, kinesthesia is central to animate life, a fact dramatically illustrated both by the loss of the modality (Gallagher and Cole 1995; Cole 1995) and by its neuro-embryology: kinesthesia and tactility are the first sensory systems to develop. In brief, kinesthesia is the gateway to those coordination dynamics that make the world familiar to us and allow us to know what to expect (Sheets-Johnstone 1999, 2003). Luria implicitly indicates as much when, in describing "the working brain," he speaks of kinesthetic as well as kinetic melodies and of "integral kinaesthetic structures" (1973, 176). His insights into "complex sequential movement" show that a close study of kinesthesia is essential reading for those studying animate movement.

In sum, we build our perceptions and conceptions of space originally in the process of moving ourselves, in tactile-kinesthetic experiences that in fact go back to prenatal life where the movement that takes a thumb to a mouth originates (Furuhjelm, Ingelman-Sundberg, and Wirsén 1966). When we learn our bodies and learn to move ourselves, we are kinesthetically attuned to a kinetic dynamics—to kinesthetic melodies—and our concepts of space are grounded in that dynamics. On the basis of our original learnings, we develop more complex notions of space, later coming to perceive and conceive ourselves as spatially bounded bodies and objects in motion. Our early experiences are the foundation of this transition to objectification. We might in fact say that our capacity to think in movement takes a turn for the worse when we come to objectify ourselves, and this because, in objectifying ourselves, we easily lose touch with our first-person moving bodies. We may no longer appreciate how thinking in movement informs our lives, from adeptly climbing over rocks and stepping over stones on a hiking trail to playing the violin or performing abdominal surgery. We may forget that thinking in movement precedes thinking in words. To remain true to the truths of experience, we must obviously go back to experience. We might thereby be led to question, if not forego, received wisdom concerning language and not only remind ourselves of our beginnings, but delve deeply into the foundations of our cognitive skills that are the basis of our knowledge of ourselves and the world.

IV

Thinking in movement is in fact the bedrock of our intelligence in more than an ontogenetic sense: it is not only an empirically evident ontogenetical fact, but an empirically evident phylogenetic fact (see Sheets-Johnstone 1999, 507–516). That is, thinking in movement is part of our evolutionary as well as developmental history. It is furthermore attested to by an older neuroscience that, unlike studies in present-day neuroscience, was not tethered to *the brain* in either functional or structural ways that failed to appreciate its living significance. Let me first spell out several basic evolutionary facts of life that attest incontrovertibly to thinking in movement, and then turn very briefly to an older neuroscientific fact that does so.

It is apposite to turn attention first to movement and language in the broader context of evolution, and correlatively to thinking in movement and thinking in words. Verbal language did not descend out of the blue. Like tool-making, counting, and so on, it evolved in the course of human evolution and has roots in nonhuman animal life (Sheets-Johnstone 1990). An awareness of oneself as a sound-maker, for example, is integral to the invention of a verbal language and an awareness of oneself as a sound-maker is hardly limited to humans. The invention of a verbal language is in fact grounded in the capacity to think in movement with respect both to an awareness of oneself as a sound-maker and to generated meanings. In particular, linguistic research into primordial language has shown that in its beginnings, language did not *name* things but specified a *motional-relational* complex of some kind, precisely as when one presses one's lips together to make the sound "m": in articulating the sound "m," a particular spatial relationship is kinetically produced (Foster 1978). Analyses of the symbolic structure of primordial language show that the sound "m" referred to spatial meanings embodied in producing the sound "m": to crushing (as in pounding stones), to pressing together (as one body to another), to resting on (as in leaning against). Such studies show in a quite fundamental sense not only that meaning is linked to movement, but that thinking is linked to movement. That is, our most fundamental concepts come from the body, from a kinetic *bodily logos* or intelligence (Sheets-Johnstone 1990). Clearly, from the viewpoint of the origin and evolution of verbal languages, humans did not think basically in words but in movement.

Further evolutionary examples of thinking in movement cast a broader net, one that encompasses nonhuman animals and makes certain evolutionary relationships apparent. All animals eat, for example, and multiple species of animals—including the human ones of long ago—secure their food by hunting. The practice of hunting is an evolutionary staple and, as will be evident, it has basic commonalities with sport.

Consider first how predatory animals are able to detect suitable prey out of a milling mass of animals. Whatever their species, predatory animals are engaged in a kinetic drama, forging it out of the very sinew and stride of their being. Predatory animals think in movement. Group-hunting predators are attentive to and understand straight off certain behaviors of others as certain states of affairs—for example, "that animal is vulnerable"—or as certain actions or possibilities of action—for example, "my colleague over there is now going to rush the herd from the side instead of straight on, and I will balance her efforts by changing the direction of my rush also." Cooperation in this sense is grounded in being attentive and in noticing. Without a quintessential awareness of the direction, rhythm, and flow of individual and mass movements by prey and fellow predator alike, there could be no concerted action toward picking out a suitable prey

(Sheets-Johnstone 1986). Hunting lionesses notice and understand move-ment—kinetic comportments—as lines of force and correlatively, as poten-tial increases or decreases in vulnerability. Moreover they understand these comportments straightaway. A hunting lioness does not wonder: "What did *that* mean?" when its prey changes direction or its colleague increases speed. There is an immediacy of meaning that bespeaks a ready and sharp kinetic intelligence not to be confounded either with stimulus-response models of behavior or with an intelligence devoid of thought, that is, a mere sensorimotor intelligence. Their hunting behavior, like the hunting behavior of any animal, is not run off by a motor program, not least because it is not a "behavior" in the common stereotyped sense of "behav-ior" in the first place. A hunt is not and cannot be a specific and repeatable sequence of actions, both because the world is not the same from one day to the next or possibly even from moment to moment with respect to terrain or weather, for example, and because the movement of living crea-tures is not the same from one day to the next or even from moment to moment. In essential ways, it is unpredictable. Indeed, a hunt takes place in a constantly unfolding kinetic present that has no set and "motor" program.

The cooperative hunting of lionesses is a paradigm of this unfolding kinetic present, this kinetic drama, and the thinking in movement that undergirds it (Sheets-Johnstone 1986). Viewed as the kinetic drama it is, cooperative hunting flows forth kinetically in intrinsically linked happen-ings that are anchored in a continuously unfolding present toward an undetermined future. Because the situation is dynamic, evolving in an immediate moment-to-moment now, what needs to be done in the way of a successful hunt is continuously being redefined by the qualitative sum of all individual movements and maneuvers. In finer kinetic terms, to cooperate in hunting is to experience shifting spatial relations, to feel and see moving lines of force, to see and feel vulnerabilities, and simultane-ously to see, in both an individual and global sense, what needs to be done.

Spelled out in this way, an analogy is readily evident between coopera-tion in hunting and cooperation in team sports. (I might add parentheti-cally that with respect to lines of force and vulnerabilities, there is also an analogy between hunting and the game of chess. Indeed, thinking in movement undergirds many different kinds of games as well as sports.)

Looking more closely still at the phenomenon of cooperative hunting, we find a deeper aspect of the capacity to think in movement that under-girds the very possibility of cooperating. To cooperate, after all, is neces-sarily to be an individual among other individuals; it is to have and to be part of an interanimate world. To cooperate is thus a social phenomenon, an elemental reciprocal being-with-others that anchors the very possibility of being perceptually attuned to, and of kinetically tuning, a particular global situation toward a common good. This coming together toward a mutually chosen end might be described in Sartrean terms as one's being for others as one is for oneself, a choosing for the good of others and at the same time a choosing for one's own good. Balancing and choosing in this way are not abstract reflective maneuvers but actively lived-through structures in the form of judgments, discriminations, and movements, whether in the context of a hunt or of a team sport. They are palpable forms of intelligence that are grounded in the having of and being part of an interanimate world. It is precisely this sensed communality that paleo-anthropologist Richard Leakey pointed toward when he wrote of the importance of "intentional clues" among social carnivores (Leakey and Lewin 1977, 155). These clues have barely been acknowledged much less seriously taken up and analyzed. They may indeed lie beyond the reach of full human understanding except in the sense that, like their nonhuman kinfolk, humans too understand each other on the basis of intentional clues. Team sports are a paradigm of these social understandings no less than is hunting; that is, knowledge of both one's teammates and one's opponents in a team sport is akin to knowledge of one's fellow creatures and prey in cooperative hunting.

Finally, we might note that in both individual and cooperative hunting, as in both individual and team sports, a strategic motivation is seminal to the enterprise. When a lioness waits in ambush for a prey in order to take it by surprise, for example, or when any creature stalks another with the same visible intent, a judgment-mediated choice of movement and an anticipation of its effect are articulated in the flesh. If I creep up slowly and silently, for example, the other will be unaware of me and unable to escape. In essence, the strategy articulates an if/then relationship: if I do such and such, then I can catch the other off guard. Just such if/then relationships undergird strategies in both individual and team sports as in individual and cooperative hunting. Anticipation is at the core of these strategies. In nonabstract, existential terms, anticipation means that an animal has a general, but not imprecise knowledge about the way in which creatures in its environment move and react and may be expected to move and react. More specifically, it means knowledge of one's fellow creatures as moving lines of force and of oneself as a moving line of force. To bring these lines of force into coincidence with one another is in fact the very essence of the hunt, its raison d'être, and it obviously requires thinking.

To anticipate a future in terms of *moving lines of force* is to think concretely in kinetic terms and in so doing to wield a concrete power of intelligence. This concretely realized power is as apparent in team sports—and in chess—as it is in hunting. To think in movement toward a future moment is in all such instances to have a sense of the power of movement, and in potential as well as actual terms, that is, as possible or present lines of force that can meet, and in such a way that one line can cancel out the other.

V

I would like to conclude with a sequence of thoughts of earlier neurophysiologists who, in studying the brain, called central attention to its real-life significance, a significance largely ignored or missing in present-day neuroscientific studies of the brain, so much so that we might aptly term it a brain *deficit*.

In 1966, neurophysiologist H. L. Teuber wrote, "[We] always start at the sensory end and try to come out at the motor side. I very much agree with the late [Ernst] von Holst when he suggests that we start at the other end and work our why (sic) back toward sensation. . . . It requires some different way of looking" (Teuber 1966, 440–441). It is not present-day neuroscientists but present-day dynamic systems theorists who in large measure start at the other end, and this because they recognize that life and living creatures are dynamic phenomena, and that movement is the natural starting place to approach an understanding of them.

In 1974, neurophysiologist E. V. Evarts wrote that "understanding of the human nervous system, even its most complex intellectual functions, may be enriched if the operation of the brain is analyzed in terms of its motor output rather than in terms of its sensory input" (Evarts 1974, 1398). Evarts's work parallels that of Roger Sperry, the renowned neurophysiologist who, ironically, is more renown for his experimental work on brain commissurotomies than for his extended research and deep understandings of the living function of the brain. Early in his career, in 1939, Sperry wrote, "An objective psychologist, hoping to get at the physiological side of behavior, is apt to plunge immediately into neurology trying to correlate brain activity with modes of experience. The result in many cases only accentuates the gap between the total experience as studied by the psychologist and neural activity as analyzed by the neurologist. But the experience of the organism is integrated, organized, and has its meaning in terms of coordinated movement" (Sperry 1939, 295). Luria's mid-twentieth-century research findings and conclusions regarding complex sequential activity and the working brain accord with Sperry's observation (Luria 1966, 1973, 1979, 1980). As for present-day research, it is again dynamic systems theorists who are in tune with Sperry's elemental understanding. J. A. Scott Kelso's writings on *coordination dynamics* are particularly cogent and well known (1995). Indeed, they are in perfect accord with Sperry's later observation that the brain is an organ of and for movement: "To the neurologist, regarding the brain from an objective, analytical standpoint, it is readily apparent that the sole product of brain function is motor coordination" (1952, 297).

What I have said here of thinking in movement with respect to infant spatial perceptions and cognitions and with respect to the evolutionary significance of thinking in movement adds strong support to the observations of these scientists. I hope it serves as an impetus for others to pursue studies along the same lines.

Notes

The original version of this essay was presented at the University of Copenhagen (June 9, 2006) at the invitation of Professor Reinhard Stelter, Head of the Department of Human and Social Sciences. I am grateful to Dr. Stelter not only for his invitation, but for his keen and abiding interest in movement and his innovative work as a psychologist in this domain. I should note too that "Thinking in Movement" is the title of chapter 12 of *The Primacy of Movement* (Sheets-Johnstone 1999) and of an earlier article (Sheets-Johnstone 1981). This present essay offers precisely further analyses and validations of thinking in movement.

1. They do so in a way similar to the way in which the perception and conception of visually drawn straight lines derive from the perception and conception of tactilely felt straight edges (see Sheets-Johnstone 1990, chap. 1).

2. Dynamic systems theorist J. A. Scott Kelso's concept of "intrinsic dynamics," which infant/child psychologists Esther Thelen and Linda Smith utilize in their analyses of the development of movement proficiencies and capacities, is significant in this respect. The concept is furthermore akin to what I have termed "primal animation." See Kelso 1995, Thelen and Smith 1994, and Sheets-Johnstone 1999.

References

Bloom, L. (1993). *The transition from infancy to language: Acquiring the power of expression*. New York: Cambridge University Press.

Bower, T. G. R. (1971). The object in the world of the infant. *Scientific American* 225 (4): 30–38.

Bower, T. G. R. (1974). *Development in infancy*. San Francisco: W. H. Freeman.

Bower, T. G. R. (1979). *Human development*. San Francisco: W. H. Freeman.

Bower, T. G. R. (1982). *Development in infancy*. 2nd edition. San Francisco: W. H. Freeman.

Bruner, J. (1990). *Acts of meaning*. Cambridge, MA: Harvard University Press.

Clark, E. V. (1973). Non-linguistic strategies and the acquisition of word meanings. *Cognition* 2:161–182.

Clark, E. V. (1979). Building a vocabulary: Words for objects, actions and relations. In *Language acquisition*, ed. P. Fletcher and M. Garman, 149–160. Cambridge: Cambridge University Press.

Cole, J. D. (1995). *Pride and a daily marathon*. Cambridge, MA: MIT Press.

Cook, N. (1978). On and under revisited again. In *Papers and reports on child language development*, vol. 15, 38–45. Stanford, CA: Stanford University Press.

Evarts, E. V. (1974). Brain mechanisms in motor control. *Life Sciences* 15 (8): 1393–1399.

Foster, Mary LeCron. (1978). The symbolic structure of primordial language. In *Human Evolution: Biosocial Perspectives*, ed. S. L. Washburn and E. R. McCown, 77–121. Menlo Park, CA: Benjamin/Cummings.

Furuhjelm, M., Ingelman-Sundberg, A., and Wirsén, C. (1966). *A child is born*. New York: Delacorte Press/Seymour Lawrence.

Gallagher, S., and Cole, J. (1995). Body image and body schema in a deafferented subject. *Journal of Mind and Behavior* 16 (4): 369–390.

Grieve, R., Hoogenraad, R., and Murray, D. (1977). On the young child's use of lexis and syntax in understanding locative instructions. *Cognition* 5:235–250.

Husserl, E. (1989). *Ideas pertaining to a pure phenomenology and to a phenomenological philosophy*, Second Book (Ideas II), trans. R. Rojcewicz and A. Schuwer. Dordrecht: Kluwer Academic.

Huttenlocher, J., Smiley, P., and Ratner, H. H. (1983). What do word meanings reveal about conceptual development? In *Concept development and the development of word meaning*, ed. T. B. Seiler and W. Wannenmacher, 210–233. Berlin: Springer-Verlag,

Kelso, J. A. Scott. (1995). *Dynamic patterns*. Cambridge, MA: Bradford Books/MIT Press.

Leakey, Richard, and Lewin, R. (1977). *Origins: What new discoveries reveal about the emergence of our species and its possible future*. New York: E. P. Dutton.

Luria, A. R. (1966). *Human brain and psychological processes*, trans. Basil Haigh. New York: Harper & Row.

Luria, A. R. (1973). *The working brain*, trans. Basil Haigh. Harmondsworth, Middlesex, England: Penguin Books.

Luria, A. R. (1979). *The making of mind*, ed. M. Cole and S. Cole. Cambridge: Harvard University Press.

Luria, A. R. (1980). *Higher cortical functions in man*, trans. Basil Haigh. 2nd edition. New York: Basic Books.

Meltzoff, Andrew N., and Borton, R. W. (1979). Intermodal matching by human neonates. *Nature* 282 (5737): 403–404.

Piaget, J. (1968). *La naissance de l'intelligence chez l'enfant*. 6th edition. Neuchatel, Switzerland: Delachaux et Niestlé.

Sheets-Johnstone, M. (1979). On movement and objects in motion: The phenomenology of the visible in dance. *Journal of Aesthetic Education* 13 (2): 33–46.

Sheets-Johnstone, M. (1981). Thinking in movement. *Journal of Aesthetics and Art Criticism* 39 (4): 399–407.

Sheets-Johnstone, Maxine. (1986). Hunting and the evolution of human intelligence: An alternative view. *Midwest Quarterly* 28 (1): 9–35.

Sheets-Johnstone, M. (1990). *The roots of thinking*. Philadelphia: Temple University Press.

Sheets-Johnstone, M. (1999). *The primacy of movement*. Amsterdam and Philadelphia: John Benjamins.

Sheets-Johnstone. M. (2003). Kinesthetic memory. *Theoria et historia scientiarum* 7 (1) (special issue on Embodiment and Awareness, ed. S. Gallagher and N. Depraz): 69–92.

Sperry, R. (1939). Action current study in movement coordination. *Journal of General Psychology* 20:295–313.

Sperry, R. (1952). Neurology and the mind-brain problem. *American Scientist* 40:291–312.

Stern, D. (1985). *The interpersonal world of the infant*. New York: Basic Books.

Teuber, H.-L. (1966). Preface to A. R. Luria's *Human brain and psychological processes*, trans. Basil Haigh, vii–xi. New York: Harper and Row.

Thelen, E., and Smith, L. B. (1994). *A dynamic systems approach to the development of cognition and action*. Cambridge, MA: Bradford Books/MIT Press.

7 Kinesthesia and the Construction of Perceptual Objects

Olivier Gapenne

7.1 Introduction

Inspired by the constructivist project of Piaget as presented in *Construction du réel chez l'enfant* (1937),[1] the aim of this chapter is to study the micro- and ontogenetic processes involved in the phenomenological constitution of space and perceived objects in humans. We shall not attempt to revisit the totality of Piaget's project, but rather reexamine the initial structural and functional conditions with a view to reformulating the process of the construction of spatialized objects of perception. Our goal is to lend support to a radical constructivist thesis that holds, first, that the point of departure for an experience of the world is the lived body, and second, that the constitution of percceived objects is both constrained and made possible by the repertoire of actions available to the subject.

More precisely, the thesis we wish to put forward seeks to ground the process[2] of enaction—that is, "the enactment of a world and a mind on the basis of a history of the variety of actions that a being in the world performs"—in the integrative and morphogenetic role of kinesthesia. To this end, we start with a discussion of proprioception, emphasizing its role in providing a matrix for the constitution of bodily phenomenology. Then we introduce the concept of *kinesthetic function*, according to which the mechanisms underlying the constitution of the lived body and the bodily schema are not limited solely to the modality of proprioception, and consider the role of this kinesthetic function in the constitution of the way that distant objects appear to a subject. We shall argue that this microgenesis rests on two primary, fundamental mechanisms: the constitution of the exteriority/tangibility of the object, and the constitution of its appearance as a spatial form. The evidence for these mechanisms comes from the literature on the early development of perception, in animals as well as human infants and fetus, and from the domain known as "sensory substitution," where it is possible to study the constitution of perception in adult human subjects.

Before entering into the heart of the subject, we wish to briefly recall the general hypothesis underlying this text: to wit, that conscious experience and knowledge are the result of a process of construction or constitution (Stewart 2001). This implies that neither the capacity to know and to experience in an organized fashion—in short, to perceive—nor the objects of perception are pregiven; they require a genesis. This is an epistemology of constitution, which radically renews the status of objectivity. In particular, we hold that the actions of a lived body[3] constitute both a constraint and a condition of possibility for the ontogenesis of perception and for learning. This epistemology, at least in its present state of development, does not claim to solve the question of qualia and consciousness as such. It does however claim, radically, that the properties of lived experience of the world and of self (and their relation) are defined by the properties of the system of actions available to the subject, or, more precisely, by the properties of the *coupling* (which can include prosthetic devices or instruments) between agent and environment which organizes the relation between "world" and "self." This leads to the idea that the causality of experience cannot be reduced to a purely internal construction, whether this be active or passive (Lenay 2006). On the basis of a large body of philosophical and scientific work, which we cannot even summarize here, we take as sufficiently established the thesis that action is absolutely necessary for the constitution and structuring of phenomenological experience.

The point we wish to focus on in this chapter, and which in our view has not been sufficiently investigated, is the importance of prereflexive tacit knowledge *about* the actions performed by an agent. Our hypothesis is that such *knowledge of action* is quite essential for the ontogenesis of perception to take place, and this whatever the perceptual modality in question. In this respect, it is relevant to mention the contribution of Gibson, who has proposed two complementary concepts that are extremely fruitful in the quest for a formalization of perceptual learning. These are the concepts of *proprioceptive function*[4] and *co-perception*.[5] Briefly, the concept of kinesthetic function posits that the sensory flows associated with movement of the subject and/or the environment intervene both in the regulation of postural tonus, and in bodily experience. The concept of co-perception goes further and posits that, if these flows intervene in the constitution of an *ecological self*, they simultaneously specify "the world." These two complementary notions promise a framework that will make it possible to deepen our conceptualization of the constitution of experience in terms of *invariants, sensorimotor schemas,* or, in a more recent reformulation, *laws of sensorimotor contingency.*

To conclude this introduction, we draw our reader's attention to the fact that the phenomena we propose to study and to interpret here pose two major methodological difficulties that we will deal with as best we may. The first is that access to the very first stages of phenomenological experience (which occur during fetal life) can be inferred only indirectly from studies of the activity of human infants and animals. We consider that human infants possess at birth, and probably before, a form of conscious experience that has been diversely identified as consciousness in act (Piaget 1974), prereflexive consciousness (Husserl 1950), primary consciousness (Edelman 1992), mental awareness (Shanon 1990), ecological self (Neisser 1991), or direct consciousness (Vermersch 2000). Piaget (1974) proposed two criteria for validating this "consciousness in act": (1) the behavioral manifestation of the fact that the subject takes into account properties of the world in a differentiated and articulated manner; (2) the incapacity of the subject to name linguistically what he knows how to do. Furthermore, as we shall see, this primary consciousness in the course of constitution possesses forms that seem to be much more sophisticated than was suggested by the early work of Piaget referred to in this introduction; this does not facilitate the task of examining the initial conditions for the constitution of perception. However, as has been suggested by Stern (1985), by combining and cross-checking multiple sources of information—experimental and clinical data from the psychology of development and psychoanalysis, including the empathetic shared experience of parenthood—it is possible to form a reasonable empirical basis for this enquiry. Moreover, it is important to recall that the difficulties involved in exploring early phenomenological experience are not magically dissipated when we reach the adult stage; the difficulties in studying first-person lived experience remain considerable, and are the object of important contemporary reflections in the context of the global project of the paradigm of enaction (Varela and Shear 1999). The second problem is that a positive demonstration of the constitutive role of action remains fundamentally problematical, because the control condition (absence of action) can only be satisfied exceptionally, locally, and even then with great difficulty. Except when it is dead, the body is never really static. Thus, constructivist hypotheses concerning the role of movement in the genesis of perception can rarely be tested directly.

7.2   Proprioception and Bodily Phenomenology

With reference to Piaget's speculation concerning the construction of perception in a world without objects, where the action schemes function
initially for and in themselves (Piaget 1937, 11–12), we propose to recall
briefly how the proprioceptive system provides a grounding for this sort
of possible experience of the body for itself.

Proprioception, in the literal sense of the term, defines a system of
coupling which intervenes in the perception of bodily movement (kinesthesis) and bodily position (statesthetesis). Like every system of coupling,
it is not restricted to a set of sensory organs (neuromuscular spindles,
neurotendinous organs, or articulatory sensors) with their specific modes
of transduction (Matthews 1972). The proprioceptive system also involves
cortical and subcortical neuronal networks (in particular the sensorimotor
cortex, the premotor cortex, the left parietal cortex, and the bilateral
cingulate cortex, as well as the supplementary motor area; Romaiguère
et al. 2003); effector organs (muscles, and in particular the antagonistic
set of muscles, which include contractile and sensitive structures); and
environmental constraints (gravity, friction). Without entering into the
details of this coupling, we mention a few main points: (1) each movement is associated with a specific reafferent sensory flow that constitutes
a veritable signature; (2) microneurographic studies (Vallbo and Hagbarth
1968) have shown that each movement (or posture) is associated with a
specific reafferent sensory flow that is sensitive to the acceleration, the
speed, the direction, and the duration of the movement (Roll, Bergenheim,
and Ribot-Ciscar 2000); and (3) this system is constantly activated by the
configuration and the deformations of the static[6] and dynamic body. With
respect to the constructivist thesis, this proprioceptive coupling could give
rise to the constitution of reliable invariants related to the body, by mobilizing the body itself. From this point of view, proprioception can be
considered as the first of all sensory modalities, making it possible to
calibrate the others, and thus playing the role of an overall matrix (Roll
2003). The fact that the proprioceptive system is sensitive only to oriented
deformations of the body confers on it a unique status that is not shared
by other systems that are also involved in a general sensitivity to movement and position. There are at least three such systems: the vestibular
system, graviception, and the tactile system. These other systems, unlike
the proprioceptive system, can and do generate sensory flows independently of the active or passive deformation of the body. It is true that
even the proprioceptive system can be activated passively, in which case

it would be "exafferent" (i.e., unrelated to the activity of the subject), and this might seem to contradict our general hypothesis on the role of kinesthesia in the constitution of the perception of objects. However, several arguments limit the portent of this objection: (1) in natural conditions, the passive production of a gesture is quite exceptional, and fortunately so, as the capacity of the subject to judge "whether I acted or not" is a criterion of viability; (2) in situations where the "passive" displacement of a limb occurs, it is not at all clear that the subject is *phenomenologically* passive; (3) even in completely nonecological cases of direct passive stimulation of the receptor organs, either in the surgical context of extension of the tendons or experimentally by vibratory stimuli, it is reasonable to suppose the functional traces that are activated were only constituted in the first place through action; (4) finally, the recourse to passive movements for the study of proprioceptive function is largely a matter of experimental convenience, and in fact comparison of the measured signals shows that they are generally distinct in the passive versus active condition (Jami 1992). Thus, overall, it is fair to conclude that the proprioceptive system is unique in the fact of being stimulated *only* by actions of the subject. This singularity reinforces the foundational role of the proprioceptive system as a matrix for the emergence of a stabilized bodily experience that can be called the "bodily schema." Neuropsychological studies have long since shown that when the proprioceptive system is perturbed, bodily phenomenology is also profoundly affected (Schilder 1950). More recently, experimental studies in which the proprioceptive coupling is artificially activated confirm that this coupling is the basis not only for bodily consciousness, but also for consciousness of gesture (Goodwin, McCloskey, and Matthews 1972; Roll and Ghilodes 1995). We may recall here the studies on induced illusions concerning the movement and position of anterior and posterior limbs, the perceived position of the arm during the phase of adaptation to wearing a prism, or to the feelings of a phantom limb (Jones 1988). These studies are spectacular manifestations of the fact that there can be a discrepancy between bodily experience and the organic body: the body can be perceived where it is not, and even when it no longer exists. Moreover, it is important to note that these illusory experiences can themselves evolve over time. If we bear in mind the many situations that can give rise to the illusory perception of objects, it appears that the constitution of bodily experience is not different from the constitution of the experience of objects, in the sense that illusions can be constituted in both cases. The fact that bodily experience can manifest such plasticity invites us to make a clear distinction between the notions of lived body and bodily schema on the one hand, and the biological/organic/mechanical body on the other.

Be this as it may, the important point with which we shall conclude this section is the fact that this specific phenomenology of the body, which largely involves the proprioceptive system, is not habitually in the focus of consciousness; the latter is generally turned toward the distal appearance of the external world. It is only on rather special occasions (pain, the practice of sport or dance, certain forms of meditation) that bodily consciousness as such comes to the fore. This frequent "absence" from the field of consciousness does not however lead us to minimize or even to obliterate the constitutive role of the lived body in the genesis of the appearance of objects at a distance; quite the contrary! We shall return later to this difficult point.

7.3   Kinesthetic Function and Enactive Dynamics

Movement inscribes the subject in a temporal unity, which has repercussions on a multitude of modes of coupling. The unity of action is in fact a vector of integration by way of redundancy, by way of the complementarity of multisensorial reafferents. We adopt here an externalist, peripheral approach to perception. It is true that the existence of efferent copies, or corollary discharges, raises the possibility of an internalist determination of perceptual experience. However, it is quite possible to view the emergence of efferent copies as a secondary consolidation, enabling the nervous system to better stabilize its function of establishing a mode of coupling. Besides, Roll (1994) indicates that if an efferent copy can have the status of a representation of the motor command, and a function of updating sensory maps, it cannot represent the parameters of movement as actually performed. There is a distinction to be made between a gesture, and the spatial and bodily effects of that gesture. In any case, as Petit (2002) points out, this does not change anything fundamental concerning the phenomenological question of the constitution of appearances.

The integration concerning the moto-proprioceptive loop takes place very early in fetal life; but the integration also concerns prenatal sensorimotor loops involving other sensory flows (graviceptor, tactile, visual, auditive, and even olfactive). A flow may be defined as the continuous variation of an energy (e.g., mechanical, photonic, chemical) at the interface with a sensory organ (e.g., retina, cochlea). This variation is necessary to avoid the phenomena of saturation and adaptation; it can be due to changes in the position and/or orientation of the sensory organs, or to variations in the energy flow itself. The important thing for the subject is to be able to dissociate these sources of variation. In fact, the organism has permanently at its disposal a series of signals concerning the successive deformations of its body in space; this constitutes what is called the "deep sensitivity." Exteroceptive flows will be associated, or rather integrated,[7] with this deep sensitivity. Exteroceptive flows are classically described as "reafferent" when they are linked to the activity of the subject, and "exafferent" when they are independent of this activity. We shall not retain this distinction here as such; because the subject is *always* in movement, *all* flows would have to be classified as "reafferent." This in no way diminishes the vital importance for the subject of being able to constitute the dissociation between sources of variation, *within* this single class of "reafferent" flows. It is the coordination of these two types of flow (extero versus proprioceptive) that constitutes the kinesthetic function. The possibility of detecting temporal coincidences between these two flows constitutes the bases for learning regularities within sensorimotor loops. It is to be noted that the kinesthetic function mobilizes sensory organs with low spatial resolution and high temporal resolution (peripheral visual tract, spinothalamic tactile tract, etc.). This point is important, because it emphasizes the sensitivity of this system to the temporal contiguity of events, and to repetition of these co-occurrences. Many examples, in both experimental research and clinical studies, demonstrate the importance of mastering these flows for establishing posture, in particular verticalization (Bullinger 1998). It is on the basis of this organization that a veritable instrumentation of the body can be set up, which augurs the progressive disappearance of consciousness of the lived body, to be replaced by a consciousness of the environment. By "instrumentation," we mean both accommodation and appropriation.

This active exploration of the relation to the world, which conditions the meaning that the subject will be able to attribute to it, obviously requires a base of reference; in the event, a stable tonico-postural organization. To introduce this question, we may mention the penetrating propositions of certain specialists in psychomotor development, in particular those from the French-speaking scientific community (Grenier 1981; André-Thomas and Ajuriaguerra 1948; Wallon 1949). These authors consider that tonic and muscular activity is not only an area for the expression of the psyche, but more profoundly as a constraint and a condition of possibility for the very emergence of a psyche. In a similar vein, neuropediatric studies (Amiel-Tison and Grenier 1985) and studies of psychomotricity (Robert-Ouvray 1997) consider the pathological dimension of this construction, and shed further light on the functional relations that link motricity with psychical development. The fundamental hypothesis that emerges from all this work is that motor integration is accompanied by an expansion of subjective experience concerning the human and physical environment; moreover, more than a simple consequence of motor integration, this expansion is a veritable conquest related to the active engagement of the infant. These studies[8] have been particularly attentive to questions of muscular tone and bodily mechanics that bring into play an antagonism between folding (the skeleton) and straightening up (the muscles). The "motor" body comprises three fundamental architectural elements, that is, the bones, the articulations, and the orifices, which define a bodily geometry in terms of axes, spheres and orifices. We may add that the "organic" body composed of hollow organs (heart, intestines, etc.) is articulated with the "motor" body by means of membranes known as "fascias" (Robert-Ouvray 1997). We cannot here enter into the biomechanical details of these initial motor schemas. To sum up briefly, we note simply that these schemas minimally involve pairs of antagonistic muscles (for example, the brachial biceps and the long triceps, in the case of arm movement). The contraction of the agonist muscle provokes a rotational conflict; the latter activates in turn a tension that ensures the movement.[9] The central element is obviously the tension between local and global structure; the physiological counterpart to this is tone, which is the only free variable. The trunk is the site where the whole set of local motor schemes are coordinated. From this point of view, the neonatal tonic regime is of prime importance, as it is the site of a central tonic antagonism between the hypertonicity of the limbs and a hypotonicity of the vertebral axis. The first months of life are notably devoted to the conquest and mastery of an inversion of this tonic regime, which is necessary to allow the emergence of symmetrical postures (dynamic stabilization of the vertebral axis) and asymmetrical postures (crossing the median axis starting from lateralized postures of the Asymmetric Tonic Neck Reflex type, posture known as the fencer). The main variables involved in the regulation of muscular tone are: the level of vigilance, bringing into play motosensory loops, and tonic dialogs.[10] The neonatal behavior known as "*liberated* motricity"[11] demonstrated by Grenier (1981) is a prime example of this mobilization of multiple factors in the constitution of the bodily axis. Many empirical studies have shown the role of the kinesthetic function in the constitution of the head-trunk axis, which opens unprecedented exploratory possibilities for head movements (Bullinger 1977), manual gestures (Grenier 1981), or again oculo-motor movements (Mellier et al. 1990); in each case, this constitutes new opportunities for perceptual constitution. Certain authors (e.g., Robert-Ouvray 1997) suggest that, on the basis of implicit kinesthetic knowledge, the infant attains an experience of a bodily and psychic axis that organizes and orients her relations with the environment; and that being able to dissociate "reafferences" and "exafferences" (but see note 8), she attains an early psychic apprehension of the back-and-forth relation between that which is experienced as internal and as external.

7.4 Exteriority and Form of the Perceived Object: A Developmental Approach

7.4.1 Exteriority/Tangibility

As recalled by Metzger (1974), in a critical text on the theoretical postures that consider that exteriority is a creative act or the production of a subject, this question has a long history of philosophical and scientific debate. Meztger (1974) cites the example of Shopenhauer, who in 1818 asked the question as to "how it happens that objects are seen where they are, instead of at the place of the physiological processes in the retina or in the cortex." Starting from this position, an entire research tradition, notably following Helmholtz, will attempt to elaborate an internalist theory invoking unconscious processes that manage to "put at a distance" the objects as seen by the "mind's eye." We shall not even enter into a presentation and discussion of this "internalist" approach, but rather pass directly to an alternative approach, which concerns us more directly. As we shall see shortly, the question is anything but simple even when considered from the point of view of the enaction of distal perception. This explains, indeed, why the question of the fusional—or, conversely, differentiated—nature of the experienced relation of the subject to his environment remains one of the most hotly debated issues in the realm of early phenomenology. By "fusional," we mean the hypothesis that the initial psychological events, in general, would give rise to an experience on the part of the subject, without being perceived thematically as "external phenomena." At this point, we need to introduce an additional, finer distinction between two aspects of the question: perceiving an object as *distinct* from self, and perceiving it as being *at a distance*.

Rochat (1995) recalls that early or "initial" experience has often been conceived as being adualist and confused, whereas this is not the case for Piaget (1937). According to the latter, phenomenological appearing certainly "adheres" to the subject, but takes the form of organized bidimensional "pictures"; depth, and hence perception of the object as being at a distance, would result from a specific construction involving visuotactile relations. Piaget (1937) thus implies that the infant is unable to distinguish sensory variations due to his or her own activity, from variations produced by an event in the world. The reason that Piaget gives for this is that the schemes available to the infant apply to objects that are not of a kind to perturb the coupling of the infant with himself. The object to be perceived does not exist as such, it is simply assimilated to the ongoing activity of the infant, which would tend to show "how much this primitive universe remains phenomenal, how far it is from immediately constituting a world of [resistant and lasting] substances" (Piaget 1937, 16).

Concerning this last point, several results in the current literature seem to put Piaget's hypotheses into question. Rochat and Hespos (1997) have shown, in controlled experiments, that from the moment of birth an infant presents differentiated behaviors depending on whether he or she is exposed to an external stimulus (for example, the finger of the experimenter), or whether the infant stimulates himself with his or her own finger (situation of *double touch*), even though the zone of peri-oral stimulation is the same in each case. In the case of external stimulation, the infant orients and moves his mouth toward the finger (rooting and/or Babkin behavior); in the case of self-stimulation, it is the finger that moves toward the mouth. This difference confirms other observations—in particular, those of Butterworth and Hopkins (1988)—and shows that newborn infants are able to dissociate the origin of certain stimulations. The results of this experimental study are also in agreement with the clinical observations of Stern (1985) concerning a pair of Siamese twins aged three months and three weeks. Stern noted that each infant resisted when an attempt was made her own finger from the mouth of her sister, but that this resistance was not observed when the infant was sucking the finger of the other twin. In addition, in the second case, the infants make a stretching movement of the head toward the finger, which they do not do when sucking their own finger. These observations indicate that the infants have the capacity to distinguish sucking their own finger from sucking the finger of their twin. In other words, these data demonstrate a capacity to differentiate between "self" and "world," an early form of self-consciousness that doubtless involves the kinesthetic function. However, although these studies do seem to show that infants are able to discriminate, the demonstration is only partial, because there is no indication of a capacity to discriminate between reafference and exafference *within* an exteroceptive flow, which was after all Piaget's main concern.

Another set of studies, devoted to the kinesthetic function (classically termed "proprioceptive function") of vision and to its effects on posture, has brought additional light to this difficult question. The effect of light on the regulation of tone can be measured in many contexts (Paulus, Straube, and Brandt 1984). However, here we shall concentrate on the postural adjustments induced by movement of the visual field in stationary subjects. In the situation known as the *moving room*, initially proposed by Lishman and Lee (1973), adult and children subjects make substantial postural adjustments (which may go so far as falling over) when they are exposed to a sagittal movement of the room. It has been shown, repeatedly, that these adjustments occur in the direction of the optical flow, whether this be straight or curved. Thus, for example, an anteroposterior movement of the flow produces a backward movement of the body, and similarly for forward movements. These postural adjustments by the subject are never immediate;[12] it seems that they are determined, in part at least, by the perception of an illusory displacement of the lived body classically known as "vection." This phenomenon has also been demonstrated in infants (Butterworth and Hicks 1977) and newborn humans (Jouen and Gapenne 1995; Jouen et al. 2000). According to Butterworth (1995), this shows that infants clearly differentiate between a change in their own point of view, and a change in the state of the world. More precisely, what is at issue for the infant confronted with a change (transformation or displacement) in the perceived visual flow is to distinguish between the case where this change is due to a *change of place* related to his own (real or illusory) movement (in which case the change is reversible), and the case where it is due to an alteration in the flow itself, a *change of state* unrelated to the subject's own movement (and therefore potentially irreversible). Given that the infant makes a postural adjustment when he or she is really displaced relative to a stationary visual field, the fact that the infant makes the same postural adjustment when he or she is in fact stationary but is exposed to a moving visual flow tends to show that the infant interprets the change in the optic flow as resulting from his or her own movement. These results thus indicate that at birth the newborn infant already has a kinesthetic function sufficiently developed for him or her to experience the exteriority of certain sources of stimulation. The conclusion is that the initial constitution of the lived body is the result of mechanisms that must already be at work during fetal life.

The idea that proprioception plays the role of a referential matrix for the constitution of bodily phenomenology is coherent only if it is interpreted in terms of embryological precedence, and the fact that the proprioceptive flow is the only one that is not potentially ambiguous concerning the source of variation as being related (or unrelated) to the subject's own activity. The data currently available concerning fetal motility and sensory capacities leave no doubt that such an early constitution of a kinesthetic function differentiating internal versus external sources of variation is indeed possible (de Vries, Hopkins, and van Geijn 1993). Every movement of the fetus in the embryo is indeed the cause of a multisensory feedback, which is a priori sufficient for constituting the kinesthetic function. Furthermore, the kinesthetic function can be employed—and extended—very soon after birth in the context of an instrumentation of the coupling between subject and world. The work of von Hofsten (1982) and Grenier (1981) in the context of so-called liberated motricity concerning the production of reaching gestures by newborn infants indicates that such gestures are certainly present at birth, even if they are very imprecise. This would seem to show that beyond simply experiencing exteriority, newborn infants possess an apprehension of depth and therefore of the *distal* nature of certain sources of stimulation.

All this leads us to distinguish two aspects: (1) the perceptual experience of the subject as an internal event, and (2) the perceived object (not the external object itself) of which the subject has experience. In the classical computational theory of mind, these two aspects are confounded, but this is problematical. From the externalist point of view of enaction, they should be distinguished. The point is that the object as perceived by the subject (not only the object itself) is out there in the world, and not in the head, whereas the perceptual experience that the subject has of the object is internal or, rather, personal (in the sense that this experience belongs to the subject). It follows from this that perception is essentially *relational*, and that this relation simultaneously co-determines both the subject and the object. If one accepts the idea that the object of perception is indeed out there in the world, and that the perceptual experience that the subject has of the object results from the relation between the subject and the object, one understands that the properties of the coupling that both constrain and make possible the dynamics of this relation are indeed the basis for both the perceptual experience and the perceived form.

7.4.2   Sketch/Form

We now turn to the question of the morphological constitution of the object perceived as being at a distance, concentrating on the role of proprioception in this process. By contrast with objects which can be handled and which give rise directly to a tactile-kinesthetic experience of the object, the particularity of the distal perception of forms is that it must be constituted without encountering resistance, without any obstruction of the action. Thus, from the point of view of enaction, what is at issue in the distal perception of objects is the auto-constitution of a "quasi resistance" via control of the exploratory activity. Classically, the behaviors (in particular oculomotor behaviors) of exploration and centering on discontinuities, which were proposed by Piaget (1961) and which have been well described by Haith (1980) in the newborn infant, are supposed to optimize the amount of information concerning the object and to maximize the cortical activation. Here, we propose rather to consider that these strategies correspond to a reading of contours, and that the perception of the form results from a gestural experience that is intrinsically relational. More profoundly, we consider that the constitution of the appearance results from a dynamics that has two complementary aspects: the first is that of the auto-constituted "quasi resistance" associated with the proprioceptive guidance of the exploratory activity; the second is the inscription of the exteroceptive flow in the kinesthetic field. We shall return to this hypothesis in the section concerning perceptual supplementation, where it is possible to address it more precisely and more directly. From a philosophical point of view, the renewed formulation of the relations between motricity and perception proposed by Barbaras (2002, 686–687) seems to be compatible with this hypothesis. On the other hand, our hypothesis is contrary to the proposal of Metzger (1974), according to which the purpose of movement is to enable a synthetic operation on elements that are individually and successively stored in memory.

Putting it another way, we consider that proprioception—which we take to be implicit knowledge concerning gestures and movement—both guides the action and grounds a spatial knowledge of the object (its form and its apparent rigidity).

An abundance of empirical data indicates that newborn infants, and even fetuses, have the capacity to perceive and to recognize shapes; the capacity to perceive dynamic invariants is thus a very early activity. It is however often interpreted as a capacity to extract invariants from an afferent (or reafferent) sensory flow without any reference to moto-proprioceptive coupling—and this in spite of the well-known work of Held and Hein (1963; see also Hein and Held 1967), which clearly shows the calibrating role of proprioception. Kittens raised in the dark, and deprived of the opportunity to move themselves around during the periods when they are exposed to light, exhibit massive deficiencies in their visuomotor behavior (significant alterations in adjustments while conducting visual placements): they not only stumble against obstacles but give a start when they do so, just like blind kittens who have never been exposed to light at all. This contrasts with the control group of kittens, who received a virtually identical visual exposure, but whose visual experience *did* result from their own motor activity; these kittens showed no impairment of their visuomotor activity. The important point of this experiment is, of course, that the purely afferent visual exposure of the kittens in the experimental group was insufficient to allow the constitution of a structured perception, as illustrated by their incapacity to perform complex behaviors such as extending a paw toward a surface on which they can put their weight. Human infants are capable of similar behavior. Held and Hein pursued their study by equipping the kittens with a hood so that they could see in front of them but not their own paws or body, thus showing that it was not immobility as such that affected the genesis of perceptual activity, but rather the impossibility of establishing a relation between the visual flow and the proprioceptive flow.

This major result has been further explored in a more carefully controlled series of studies by Buisseret, Gary-Bobo, and Imbert (1978) and by Buisseret, Gary-Bobo, and Milleret (1988). The aim of these studies, which we shall present in some detail in view of their fundamental importance, was to demonstrate the role of proprioception in the genesis of the sensitivity of cortical neurons to orientation. The experimental procedure is always essentially the same. Kittens were raised entirely in the dark during six weeks after birth, exposed to light during six hours, and then returned to the dark for twelve hours prior to testing. The neurophysiological examination consisted of extracellular recordings in visual area 17. The cellular activity was classified in three categories according to the level of selectivity of the cells to the orientation of a visual stimulus: nil (the cellular activity is similar whether the stimulus is a circular spot or an oriented bar); moderate (the range of orientations giving an increased activity is greater than 70 degrees); and high (the range of activating orientations is less than 70 degrees). According to the experimental conditions, the animals were subjected to various surgical operations prior to their exposure to light, and the regime of exposure to light was also varied. The results show:

1. The selectivity of cortical cells to orientation is not constituted if the animals are not exposed to light.

2. By contrast, following six hours of exposure to light with complete freedom of movement, the cortical selectivity is practically equivalent to that of control animals raised in normal lighting conditions since birth and depends on the properties of the visual signal; in an environment consisting of regular vertical black and white stripes, the sensitivity of the cells is essentially focused on that vertical orientation.

3. If the animals are deprived of movement, except for ocular movements, during the phase of exposure to light, the sensitivity to orientation is still largely constituted (70 percent of the cells are selective); however, a complete absence of movement, including ocular movements (either by total section of the oculomotor muscles, or by bilateral section of the intracranial oculomotor nerves) prevents the constitution of selectivity to orientation.

4. If the blockage of oculomotor movements is incomplete, so that certain axes of rotation are retained, the cortical neurons show some selectivity; when four of the six muscles are sectioned, the selectivity is focused on the orientation orthogonal to the plane of the available ocular movements.

5. Animals exposed to light during six hours, with complete freedom of movement, do not constitute a sensitivity to orientation if the ophthalmic branch of the trigeminal nerves involved in the transmission of the proprioceptive signal to the subcortical structures is sectioned.

6. An animal deprived of proprioceptive reafferences at the level of one eye (which remains completely mobile), and having the other eye occluded with proprioception reduced to a single plane of rotation, constitutes a sensitivity to orientation orthogonal to the plane of rotation of the occluded eye.

These results are further strengthened by the demonstration of so-called visual cortical neurons whose activity is modulated by proprioceptive stimuli. It is thus undeniable that there are neuro-anatomical links between proprioceptive afferences (or reafferences) and the so-called visual primary cortex. Moreover, and quite remarkably, the majority of cortical cells modulated by a proprioceptive stimulus from a given muscle develop a selectivity that is orthogonal to the plane of activity of that muscle. A cell in the so-called[13] visual cortex is thus doubly modulated, visually and proprioceptively, and in a congruent fashion. Altogether, these results demonstrate rather conclusively that proprioceptive signals (and not just the fact of action) play an essential role in the constitution of the sensitivity of the nervous system to distal signals. More precisely, these studies show that the sensitivity to a morphological property of distant objects results from a psychobiological construction on the basis of a certain coupling.

In humans, at a more strictly perceptual level, clinical studies indicate that distal perceptual experience is affected by congenital oculomotor disturbances such as nystagmus, themselves associated with alterations in the proprioception of extra-ocular muscles (Donaldson 2000). Experimentally, the old studies by Riggs, Armington, and Ratliff (1954) showed that there is an increase in the visual size of a point, related to an increase in the amplitude of the micronystagmus during prolonged ocular fixation. More indirectly, the studies of Lackner and Levine (1979) showed, in the adult human, that the activation of proprioception by applying a vibration to the biceps or triceps can affect the perceived position of a luminous target: the target (which is attached to a finger) appears to undergo an illusory movement in concert with the illusory movement of the arm. In a similar fashion, Roll, Velay, and Roll (1991) have demonstrated systematic errors in manual pointing at visual targets following the application of vibrations to certain muscles,[15] which produces an apparent displacement of the target. In this same study, the authors were able to show that the bilateral stimulation of the external oculomotor muscles produces the illusion that the visual target moves closer. Recent results obtained by de Vignemont, Ehrsson, and Haggard (2005) demonstrate similar phenomena in the tactile modality.

7.5 Perceptual Supplementation: A Paradigm Case

In the field of study concerning the mechanisms underlying the genesis and the organization of perception in humans, the basic situation of sensory substitution[14] proposed by Bach-y-Rita (1972) offers a relevant opportunity to test the hypotheses put forward previously. In general, the so-called sensory substitution systems transform the stimuli belonging to one sensory modality (for example, signals that activate the retina) into stimuli of a different sensory modality (for example, tactile stimuli). Such systems classically consist of three distinct elements: (1) a sensor, which captures a certain form of energy (light, sound, mechanical or other); (2) a transducer, which converts the initial energy into signals that can be interpreted by a natural system of coupling; and (3) a set of stimulators in the new sensory modality, which can be suitably activated by output from the transducer. Thus, these systems convert signals that are not initially accessible by means of a double transduction: that effected by the artificial sensor, and that which produces an activation of a natural sensor. Beyond simply providing a prosthetic transduction, the interest of these systems is that, under certain suitable conditions, they can provide the user with unprecedented perceptual experiences.

As an example, the TVSS (tactile vision substitution system) converts an image captured by a video-camera into a "tactile image" (Bach-y-Rita 1972). In the standard version, the tactile image is produced by a matrix of 400 stimulators (20 lines and 20 columns of solenoids that are 1 millimeter in diameter). The matrix is placed on the back (the very first version), on the chest, or on the brow. Equipped with a TVSS, the subjects (either blind persons, or blindfolded sighted persons) are almost immediately able to detect simple targets and to approach them. They are rapidly capable of discriminating vertical versus horizontal lines, and to indicate the direction that a mobile target is moving in. However, the recognition of geometrical shapes, even very simple ones, requires a longer period of learning (50 trials to achieve a 100 percent success rate). The condition for learning of this new perceptual capacity to occur is that the subject must be able to manipulate the artificial sensor, in this case the video camera. The requisite learning is even longer when the task is to recognize familiar objects in unusual orientations. This last task requires a dozen hours of practice to obtain a recognition latency of five seconds or less. All the research carried out in this context clearly shows the necessity of movement, of an active engagement of the user, for the constitution of a prosthetic perception of objects identified as being distinct from the prosthesis itself. Indeed, a key observation is that the emergence of the capacity for the active recognition of shapes is accompanied by an exteriorization, a projection of the percepts into a distal space. At the beginning, the user feels only shifting tactile stimulations, which are located on the skin. However, as the user engages in the learning process, consciousness of the stimulations fades away (just as we are not normally conscious of light-induced stimulation of the retina), and is replaced by the perception of stable objects at a distance, "out there" in the space in front of the subject. The blind (or blindfolded) person thus experiences properties such as parallax, shadows, or the interposition of objects, but in a quite new perceptual modality.

At a functional level, these prosthetic devices, and especially the conditions that are necessary for their appropriation, make it possible to claim that cognition and perception can no longer be considered simply as the result of information processing of sensory input from the outside. Here, the empirical proof is direct: there is no perception without action.

Perception results from the dynamic loop linking motor commands and multimodal reafferent signals. The work of Bach-y-Rita and his colleagues represents a first step. Subsequent studies have deliberately simplified the initial device in order to deepen the analysis from both philosophical and scientific points of view (Lenay, Canu, and Villon 1997; Hanneton et al. 1999; Sribunruangrit et al. 2004; Tyler et al. 2002; Jansonn 1998). In the next section, we shall focus on these later studies and their distinctive contributions. The essential point on which we shall insist is that although action is a necessary condition for the perception of objects, it is not alone sufficient: kinesthetic knowledge concerning the exploratory activity is indispensable. Before going further in our discussion of the perception of distal objects, we note here that access to a prosthetic sensory flow can contribute to establishing body tone and to the constitution of a novel bodily experience (Bullinger and Mellier 1988; Tyler, Danilov, and Bach-y-Rita 2004). These studies thus show that a prosthetic sensory flow can contribute to the kinesthetic function as we have previously defined it.

7.5.1 Exteriority/Tangibility

The passage from the experience of proximal sensations (on the skin) to an experience of the perception of distal objects was described in the very first research with the TVSS; however, this passage has until now received very little more attention. Indeed, the question of the distality of the perceived object did not even arise as such, because the instructions given to the subjects explicitly stated that the shapes to be perceived were those of objects that the experimenter himself presented as being "out there." Thus, the tactile stimuli could be attributed only to external sources. This does not mean that the subject could simply short-circuit the displacement of his perceptual experience, from the surface of the skin to "out there" in space; merely intellectual knowledge that there is an external object is no guarantee that the object will be actually *experienced* as being "out there." We may note here that the phenomenon is general: grasping a tool always opens up a novel perceptual space, and the displacement from proximal interaction with the tool to distal interaction with objects in the new "world" is always an issue. The classical example is the blind person's cane: the interaction is perceived not in the palm of the hand that grasps the cane, but at the end of the instrument, there where the subject is acting and interacting with the environment.

The first and until recently almost the only study concerning the interpretation of such perceptual experience in terms of a distal object was carried out by Epstein et al. (1986). The experimental situation was a "forced-choice" situation in which subjects had to choose between several scenarios; the scenario according to which the received signals resulted from the subject's own activity, and that they referred to a distal object, was only one among many. The main result of this fascinating study was that the "distal" scenario was *not* generally favored by the subjects. In other words, when the subjects are not informed in advance about the working of the system, and they are not told that they have to perceive a shape "out there," they do not spontaneously interpret their experience with the device as resulting from a relation with an external distant object that is the source of the stimulation. A new experimental study, and a reanalysis of the experiment of Epstein et al., has led Auvray et al. (2005)[16] to refine the earlier result, and to propose a succession of stages toward "immersion"; the attribution of distality is an important step in this process. The stages are the following:

• Contact: this implies learning the sensorimotor regularities that must be mastered in order to stabilize and maintain perceptual contact with the stimulus.
• Distal attribution (this is the phenomenon that interests us here): it corresponds to understanding the origin of the sensations as resulting from an encounter with an object situated in the perceptual space opened up by the device.
• Mastery of the distal space: this corresponds to learning about variations in the point of view, and establishing distal reference points that make it possible to achieve egocentric localization of objects and events.
• Distal localization: this is defined as the impression of being "in" the perceptual space, and implies an automatized mastery of the sensorimotor coupling so as to consolidate the experience of "being there where one acts".
• Distal experience: the constitution of this stage requires sharing the perceptual experience with other persons, which allows constitution of the meaning, the emotions, and the shared values that characterize this particular experience.

With reference to these stages, it is very clear that in the experiment of Epstein et al. (1986), the subjects reach stage 1, that of "contact," where they express their consciousness of a relation between their actions and reafferent sensation; however, under the conditions of this experiment, they were not able spontaneously to go further. This stage allows the constitution of the experience of a subject/object distinction. Auvray et al. (2005) found the same result, but went on to show that if the subjects are given the opportunity to *manipulate* the object (a luminescent ball), or if they can manipulate an obstacle (a sheet of paper) which can be interposed between the source and the sensory device, that greatly favors the constitution of a distality of the object.

How can this result be interpreted with respect to the role of the kinesthetic function in the constitution of distal exteriority? In this particular experimental situation, the subject can actively manipulate the totality of the subject/object relation (camera and ball), and can interrupt this relation at will. These manipulations provide a basis for making a distinction, within the flow of sensations, between sensations that are related to the subject's own movements (and thus to the proprioceptive flow), which can be called *reafferences*; and sensations related to independent variations of the environment, called *exafferences*. However, this distinction alone cannot give access to distality unless the subject has the possibility of three-dimensional actions sufficient to establish a triangulation (Lenay, Canu, and Villon 1997). We see here that the knowledge of one's own action that is necessary for the constitution of the perception of a distal object is not limited to knowing whether one is acting (simple agency), but requires in addition a knowledge of one's own *gesture*.

Philipona, O'Regan, and Nadal (2003), far from any phenomenological considerations, have taken up this problem in a highly formal way: they propose an algorithm, based on inputs and outputs, that is able to deduce the geometry and the dimensions of external space without any a priori knowledge. Their calculating device (a poly-articulated robot) has two types of input signal: proprioceptive signals, whose variation is precisely calibrated to movements of the robot, and exteroceptive signals, resulting from activation of a sensor by an external source. Finally, there are effectors (motors), controlled by the algorithm, which produce movements of the robot limbs. First, the algorithm learns to distinguish statistically these two types of signal (proprioceptive versus exteroceptive) according to their relation with its own movements. Next, the algorithm learns to discriminate, within the class of exteroceptive signals, between those which are produced when the robot is in movement (reafference) and those which occur when the robot is static (exafference). These latter two types of signal are used to generate two vectors: one related to the exafferences and called "representation of the state of the environment"; the other related to the reafferences and called "representation of the exteroceptive body." Finally, based on an analysis of reversibility (called "compensability" in the article), and in particular on the constraints on the motor commands that are necessary for reversibility to be achieved, the calculation can deduce from the *recapture* of a previous multisensor signal that the latter emanates from an external source to which it is possible to attribute rigidity. We may note again, as earlier, that reversibility gives possible access to depth perception only if a triangulation is possible. We may also note that, from the point of view of an external observer, "reversibility" is possible only if the configuration of sensors situated on various arms of the robot is itself kept "rigid" in three dimensions by appropriate constraints on the movements generated by the algorithm. According to the authors, who insist on their sensorimotor approach, it is at this moment "that body and environment are immersed in a single entity that we call space" (Philipona, O'Regan, and Nadal 2003, 2033). This work has the great interest of proposing a mathematical formulation of the distinctions that an organism can—and must—make in order to perceive itself as distinct from its environment, and to constitute certain aspects of this environment as the position of fixed reference points. It does, however, have a serious limitation stemming from the fact that the model considers the relation between proprioception and exteroceptive reafferences merely as a possible intersection. In our view, as we shall discuss later, the constitution of phenomenological appearances is greatly concerned by an *articulation* between proprioception and exteroception, and not merely by a more or less fortuitous intersection of a proprioception and an exteroception that are presupposed to be distinct.

As we have indicated previously, these experimental situations involving human subjects do not generally induce an attitude where the subject may be lead to *doubt* the existence of an external space already constituted. What the subject has to constitute concerns the features of a particular object (distance, shape, orientation, size), but not the existence of space itself. In other words, when the subject receives a tactile stimulation, there is no reason to doubt that the origin of this stimulation is an object situated somewhere "out there" at a certain distance from the subject. Even so, these situations (and also the experiments with the Tactos device, which we shall discuss in the next section) have a particular feature, which is that the object to be perceived does not manifest its presence directly by producing a resistance (as is the case with touch). The "quasi resistance," and thus the tangibility of the object, must be self-engendered with reference to the kinesthesia that is dynamically mobilized in the movements and their control.

7.5.2 Sketch/Form

In order to further investigate the fundamental issues in perceptual cognition that are involved, the experiments we shall now present have renewed Bach-y-Rita's original study by deliberately simplifying the sensory input to its simplest possible expression—that is, a single point of tactile stimulation, which is either active (x) or inactive (o) (Hanneton et al. 1999; Lenay, Canu, and Villon 1997). To this end, we have developed an experimental platform, "Tactos," which enables the haptic reading of a digital graphic form. The principle is simple. The subject moves a stylus on a graphic tablet, which controls the movement of a cursor in the digital space (just as a mouse moves a cursor on the screen). This cursor constitutes the surface of a "sensory captor" (which can have various shapes and configurations of subfields). When this receptor field of this sensory surface crosses a black pixel in the digital space, it triggers the activation of a tactile stimulation by an electronic Braille cell. Thus, when the receptor field is reduced to the strict minimum (one pixel), the tactile stimulation has no other function than to indicate the presence of an object in the digital environment. In this deliberately minimalist setup, the perception of an object as a whole requires an active exploration of the object; the generation of appropriate patterns of exploration is what we call a "strategy." In this technical context, it is useful to distinguish two spaces of action, one "bodily" space (the stylus on the graphic tablet), and one "digital" (the cursor on the screen).

In many experiments, the perceptual task we have chosen is the identification of simple two-dimensional forms—broken lines and curves—which are of course not seen by the blindfolded subjects. Under these conditions, the sensory input is reduced to a temporal sequence: "ooooo-oxxooooxxoxxxxxx" and so on. It is thus immediately evident that there is no conceivable "information processing" of the input signal that could convert it into the perception of a two-dimensional line or curve. In other words, we have quite deliberately employed an experimental setup that illustrates, paradigmatically, the thesis of "active perception"; that is, there is no perception in the absence of actions on the part of the subject. The question arises as to whether the sensory input has not been impoverished to such an extent that perception is impossible even if the subject *can* act, but the answer to this question is that the subjects do indeed succeed in perceiving two-dimensional forms, and are able to demonstrate their perception by drawing the figures as they have perceived them. A major advantage of this experimental setup is that forces an externalization of the actions of the subjects so that it is possible to record, analyze, and model them, in the form of a trace of the successive positions of the tip of the pen (Stewart and Gapenne 2004). These trajectories, together with the drawings by the subjects of the figures as perceived, constitute a rich set of empirical data.

The important point we wish to insist on yet again is that action is clearly a necessary condition for perception to be possible, but in itself is insufficient for the constitution of an object, even with the resource of the tactile feedback. In this situation, access to the proprioceptive flow is also a necessary condition for the recognition of a form. This role is all the more essential when the system of coupling is minimal. As we have already indicated, in this case only a knowledge of the gesture performed can lead to a recognition of the form. In this particular case, one effective "exploratory strategy" consists of deliberately and rather rapidly scanning back and cross the form in a direction orthogonal to the contour, and to advance more gradually tangentially along the form. At this level, the nature of the all-or-nothing sensory feedback (acoustic, tactile, or optical) has no differential effect on the recognition of the forms (Gapenne et al. 2005). Enriching the coupling—for example, by increasing the size and number of receptor fields,[17] allows the emergence of novel exploratory strategies—for example, continuously following the contour without an excessive risk of "losing" contact (Gapenne et al. 2001). Two important points may be noted here: (1) the parallelism is in a sense a sort of "scanning movement already carried out" (a sort of encapsulation of a tactile micronystagmus), which facilitates the relevant control of the current movement; and (2) this facilitation of the control of the exploratory trajectory in the virtual digital space has an immediate effect on the gestural experience in the bodily space.

The point we want to make is that the perception of a virtual digital object, which in itself provides no resistance,[18] is made possible by deploying an exploratory strategy; the closer the morphological proximity between the exploratory trajectory and the form to be perceived, the easier the recognition of the form. In other words, the production of a trajectory that continuously follows the form is a highly effective strategy for recognizing the form under the conditions of coupling described earlier. This point emerges clearly from all the studies we have done. Consequently, in these studies of perceptual supplementation, the conditions of sensorimotor coupling allow for the autoconstitution of a *kinetic* "quasi resistance" of the virtual object—here, a two-dimensional geometrical form—which is necessary for its recognition.[19] The expression according to which recognizing a form consists of recognizing the gesture of producing that form— "reading *is* writing"—applies in full force here. Nevertheless, we have also shown that when the conditions of the coupling do not allow the emergence of direct continuous following of the contour, the deployment of a strategy of orthogonal microscanning across the contour can suffice to enable recognition of the form. This is not unlike the oculomotor scanning observed by Haith (1980) in neonatal infants, and it is also reminiscent of the oculomotor scanning necessary for the constitution of visual sensitivity to orientation in kittens described previously. In other words, the exact form of the movement need not be immediately, literally identical to the form itself for effective perception of the form to occur. In fact, if the "microscanning" movements are "smoothed out" by averaging over an appropriate sliding time window, the *overall* movement does closely follow the form to be perceived. These rapid oscillations are not themselves part of the actual perception; they serve functionally to robustly maintain contact with the form while advancing regularly along the contour. Our interpretation here is contrary to that of Metzger (1974); citing the work of Stratton (1902) on patterns of oculomotor exploration, Metzger considers the discrepancy between the form of the movements and the form to be perceived to refute the constructivist approach to the constitution of perception that we ourselves are proposing here. Metzger even goes so far as to consider that perception can occur only during the episodic *pauses* between ocular movements, on the grounds that the subjects do not appear to perceive anything at all during the saccadic phases themselves. He considers "the true meaning of action in perception" to consist of a continuous exploratory activity, a variation in the point of view, aimed at maximizing the amount of information contributed by the sensors. This leads him to formulate a complementary hypothesis, according to which the duration of the pauses between movements increases when the complexity of the sensor increases (i.e., there is more information to be processed). It seems to us, however, that Metzger has not properly grasped the full implications of a non-representationalist conception of perception, which have been clearly spelled out by O'Regan (1992). Our interpretation of the possible increase in the duration of the pauses is not so much related to an increase in the amount of information obtained per unit time; the pauses serve rather to (re)constitute a "scanning movement already carried out," as we have already suggested previously. In other words, an increase in the resolution of the sensor improves the precision of the autoconstituted "quasi resistance" of the object, because it increases the gain of the control on the exploratory trajectory. Our own complementary hypothesis would be to say that a sensor with a weak resolution is not necessarily incompatible with perception, on condition that the repertoire of available actions allows the deployment of an appropriate strategy. In this case, the appropriate strategy involves the "microscan" oscillations; these movements can be generated by the subject, or they could also result from an automatic mechanism (somewhat like the ocular micronystagmus, which could be rather easily implemented algorithmically in the case of action in a digital environment). This helps to understand why and how the quality of perception is a function of the domain of variation of the point of action. In this sort of situation, the sensory feedbacks do not serve to specify the shape to be perceived as such, but rather, to constrain and to guide the sensorimotor coupling and to favor the emergence of motosensory and gestural invariances.[20] Thus, the movements of the subject give rise to kinesthetic reafferences, which come to specify the gesture itself; the prosthetic sensory flow provided by the Tactos interface characterizes the gesture and constrains it; the overall circular dynamics of this process constitutes the fact of being an agent.

In the few studies that have attempted to radically address the constitution of perception in a minimalist perspective, such as those described earlier, the question of kinesthesia and more precisely the question of the relation between kinesthesia and other sensory flows has been insufficiently thematized. This is very clear in the case of correlational or associational approaches, which have frequently been developed in robotics (Maillard et al. 2005; Suzuki, Floreano, and Di Paolo 2005). However, inspired by the tradition of Husserlian phenomenology, there are some attempts to go further. We may mention the hypothesis concerning the "physionomical" character of perceptual experience, according to which such experience is actually the expression of its own process of constitution. Thus, an expressive dynamics would be present in every figurative unity that is perceived as such (Werner 1934, cited in Rosenthal 2004). In the same vein, we may recall the concept of *praktognosie* evoked by Merleau-Ponty (1945, 164).[21] More technically, in the context of an explicit project of "naturalizing phenomenology," the role of kinesthesia has been assimilated into that of a gluing operator of successive sketches (Petitot 2004). This work is quite explicitly presented as a possible *mathesis* of the role of kinesthesia initially proposed by Husserl in *Ding und Raum* (1907) (Husserl 1989). Petitot forcibly argues that if Husserl had had available certain mathematical formalisms, notably in the domain of differential geometry, he would himself have been able to express his phenomenology in mathematical terms. This point of view, although quite legitimate, is of course highly debatable. It is also important to note that the very conception of the role of kinesthesis evolved considerably over the course of his life's work (see Havelange, chapter 12, this volume). Lavigne (Husserl 1989, 462) gives a useful note on the history of this concept, and the meaning that Husserl attributes to it in this work. This operation of gluing takes place in a kinesthetic space, which is itself the space of the temporal synthesis of images. Initially, the kinesthesia are supposed to play a non-motivated role of control over the field, and contribute to the display of external objects without being themselves displayed. It is suggested that subsequently typical kinesthetic trajectories, falling into natural categories, are constituted; these trajectories associate, now in a motivated fashion, images and kinesthesia. In a certain sense, this proposition corresponds to the constitution of perceptual strategies as we have described previously. However, taking up again our own hypothesis concerning the role of kinesthesia in perception, we are tempted to reverse Petitot's proposition, and to suggest that it is the kinesthesia which are the true ground for intentionality; the sensations/images play the role of controlling the deployment of the kinesthesia. It seems to us that this is fundamentally more compatible with the perspective of enaction. However, this reversal has consequences that go beyond the question of the constraints that guide the exploratory dynamics. What is at stake is the question as to whether the quality of spatial extension is an immediate given, intrinsic to sensations as they are primitively displayed. Common sense, dominated by the example of vision and retinal images, considers of course that this is the case. On the one hand, if one accepts the proposition of Petitot (2004), the operation of gluing (which already presupposes that a certain spatiality is given) can without difficulty be applied recursively in a fractal fashion. The alternative is to consider that the minimal phenomenological extension of the sensations themselves is brought about by kinesthetic continuity. In other words, either one considers that the spatiality of appearances is given, locally, and that the role of the kinesthesia is to achieve a globalization of the overall appearance, or, alternatively, one considers that phenomenological appearance has any spatiality at all only because of its inscription in the movement of the body. It will be clear that we favor this second possibility, and this leads us to propose the opening of a formal enterprise aimed at defining an operator not of gluing, but of *stretching*, where the spatial extension of that which appears is directly linked to the extension of the body. In other words, we propose here that perceived spatiality or distal extension results from a spatial deployment associated with movements of the living body. This proposition is coherent with the results of Buisseret, Gary-Bobo, and Imbert (1978) and Buisseret, Gary-Bobo, and Milleret (1988), which suggest that the constitution of the sensitivity of the biological system to variations in physical signals is structured by the possibilities of spatial deployment of the system itself.

7.6   Conclusion

In this chapter, we have attempted to shed some light on two of the most fundamental mechanisms[22] in the constitution of phenomenological experience: the constitution of distality, and that of morphological appearance. We have adopted the conceptual framework of *genetic* constructivism (Visetti 2004), and we have applied ourselves to show how the constitution of distal experience is inscribed in bodily experience. By following the path from Piaget to Varela, we have grounded the coming forth of perceptual experience in the capacity for action; the (sensory) effects of action in turn feed back to guide subsequent actions, thus forming a spiral which structures the ongoing process. From this perspective, we have emphasized the constitutive role of kinesthesia, concerning both the experience of the lived body and that of distal objects. In this respect, our propositions echo the work of Hanna and Thompson (2003) and Thompson (2005) concerning the "mind-body-body problem" and an *animalistic* approach in which the body, living and the seat of lived experience, is considered as the site of a morphogenetic autonomy. More globally, we hope that our proposition will contribute to pursuing an exploration of the links that, on one hand, articulate the living and the phenomenological, as suggested by the work of Varela, which has been clearly synthesized by Rudrauf et al. (2003), and on the other hand, to illuminate their respective constructions.

Acknowledgments

I particularly wish to thank Véronique Havelange, Charles Lenay, Victor Rosenthal, Katia Rovira, John Stewart, and Yves Marie Visetti for their comments and/or the inspiration I have found in their work.

Notes

1. This work is probably one of the first (if not *the* first) scientific formulation of the constructivist thesis concerning the macro- and microgenetic constitution of the conscious experience of the external world in human infants. The dimension of microgenesis has been studied in greater depth by recent work of the Geneva school (Inhelder and Cellérier 1992).

2. We put the usefulness of the concept of possibility, and not merely that of actuality, for an inquiry into the bodily constitution of experience as enaction. We consider how the possibilities of action that may (or may not) be available to the subject help to shape the meaning attributed to perceived objects and to the

situation occupied by the subject within her environment. This view is supported by reference to empirical evidence provided by recent and current research on the perceptual estimation of distances and the effects brought about by the use of a tool on the organization of our perceived immediate space (Declerck and Gapenne 2009).

3. "Lived body" is a translation of the German *Leib*, which designates the living body as the seat of phenomenological experience, as contrasted with *Körper*, which designates the body as a physical object.

4. This term, proposed by Gibson, has given rise to much confusion, due to the fact that "proprioception" is often used to designate a specific perceptive system. In what follows, we shall therefore employ the term "kinesthetic function."

5. From our point of view, the concept of "co-perception" is theoretically close to the concepts of "enaction" (Varela, Thompson, and Rosch 1991) and "transductive relation" (Simondon 2005): the point being that the subject on one hand, and the "world" (be it natural, human, and/or technical) on the other, are "brought forth" or arise *conjointly* in the course of action (or more precisely, in the dynamic relation between agent and environment). Nevertheless—and this is the central point of this chapter—the conceptualization of the mechanisms at work has been the object of rather diverse propositions, which we propose to examine and to discuss.

6. The physiological tremor is one of the dynamic forms of the quasi immobility that does occur.

7. The choice of the term employed to designate this articulation or coordination of flows is very delicate, particularly in the context of possible modeling. We shall return at greater length to this point at the end of this chapter.

8. These studies, many of which were carried out some time ago, were often interpreted by a scheme of causal explanation in terms of *maturation*. This type of explanatory scheme is currently largely discredited (cf. the numerous studies of Thelen and Smith on perceptual motor development, e.g., Thelen 1988 and Thelen and Smith 1994), but the empirical findings remain valid and illuminating.

9. The movement is deployed in the three spatial planes at the level of each articulation: flexion/extension (sagittal plane), internal/external rotation (horizontal plane), and adduction/abduction (frontal plane).

10. This notion of "tonic dialogs" describes the postural co-adjustments produced by an adult and an infant in situations of direct contact—for example, when the infant is being carried (Pinol-Douriez 1984). We take advantage of this note to indicate that in order to illuminate more fully the constitution of the perceptual and cognitive activities that concern us here, it will be imperative to introduce the social dimension.

11. The term "liberated motricity" designates the behaviors of a newborn infant, which consist of gestures aimed at touching objects presented within reach, and the

production of communicational behavior. These behaviors require a momentary inversion of the tonic regime; their emergence depends on massaging the neck muscles, an alert state of attention, and eye-to-eye contact.

12. Although any movement of the visual field obviously has a perceptive effect, it does not necessarily produce this type of proprioceptive effect. Special experimental conditions are required, inducing a succession of phenomenological stages: initially a perception of the movement of the field, followed by the perception of self-movement relative to a stationary field (the illusion of vection).

13. We insist rather heavily on the so-called visual cortex because many studies have shown that certain occipital cortical zones can be exclusively dedicated to tactile flows (Wanet-Defalque et al. 1988).

14. The results obtained in this study clearly illustrate the notion of a "propriocep-tive chain," as the apparent visual displacement of the target can be produced by vibrations in the muscles of the ankle, neck, or eyes.

15. The term "sensory substitution," initially proposed by Bach-y-Rita, appears to us inappropriate not only in the framework of an enactive approach, but also and above all in view of the results obtained by Bach-y-Rita and his colleagues themselves. In short, it is not a purely *sensory* substitution, because the subject must *act* so as to set up a sensori*motor* dynamic, and it is not a sensory *substitution*, because the new perceptual modality that arises is not identical to normal ocular vision. For a fuller discussion, see Lenay et al. (2003). This has led us to propose the term "perceptual supplementation."

16. In this experiment, the stimulus is acoustic (Vibe device) and not tactile as in the experiment of Epstein. However, as we shall mention shortly, when the supplementation devices are (deliberately) minimal, this difference in the biological sensory organ does not affect the results.

17. For example, a set of sixteen adjacent receptor fields, $2 \times 2 = 4$ pixels each, organized in a 4×4 matrix so as to cover 64 pixels overall.

18. As we have already noted, this situation is very similar to that of distal visual perception, where the autoconstitution of the resistance of the distal object/form results from the oculomotor exploration, which is guided/constrained with respect to morphological singularities. Both situations are, indeed, quite different from the case of force-feedback (e.g., with a Phantom device) where guidance and constraint of the exploratory gestures is directly physical.

19. In a certain sense, this is a sort of transposition of the notion of "rigid transfor-mation" proposed by Philipona et al. (2003), which likewise integrates the contribu-tion of proprioception in the constitution of the perceived rigidity.

20. In fact, rather than "invariances," what is at issue is rather the progressive con-stitution of a *prospective* control, which dynamically organizes the longer-term

unfolding of the exploratory trajectory. The study of the genesis of these exploratory movements, be they manual or oculomotor, is highly revealing from this point of view, and shows that the achievement of this control is constituted in the course of the activity itself (von Hofsten 1993).

21. The mechanisms involved can be explicitly conceptualized as "cycles of operation," which define integrated sequences of behaviors.

References

Amiel-Tison, C., and Grenier, A. (1985). *La surveillance neurologique du nourrisson au cours de la première année de la vie*. Paris: Masson.

Auvray, M., Hanneton, S., Lenay, C., and O'Regan, J. K. (2005). There is something out there: distal attribution in sensory substitution, twenty years later. *Journal of Integrative Neuroscience* 4:505–521.

Bach-y-Rita, P. (1972). *Brain mechanisms in sensory substitution*. New York: Academic Press.

Barbaras, R. (2002). Le vivant comme fondement originaire de l'intentionnalité perceptive. In *Naturaliser la phénomenologie*, ed. J. Petitot, F. J. Varéla, B. Pachoud, and J. M. Roy, 681–696. Paris: CNRS Editions.

Buisseret, P., Gary-Bobo, E., and Imbert, P. (1978). Ocular motility and recovery of orientational properties of visual cortical neurons in dark-reared kittens. *Nature* 272:816–817.

Buisseret, P., Gary-Bobo, E., and Milleret, C. (1988). Development of the kitten visual cortex depends on the relationship between the plane of eye movements and visual inputs. *Experimental Brain Research* 72:883–948.

Bullinger, A. (1977). Orientation de la tête du nouveau-né en présence d'un stimulus visuel. *L'Année Psychologique* 2:357–364.

Bullinger, A. (1998). La genèse de l'axe corporel, quelques repères. *Enfance* 1:27–35.

Bullinger, A., and Mellier, D. (1988). Influence de la cécité congénitale sur les conduites sensori-motrices chez l'enfant. *European Bulletin of Cognitive Psychology* 8:191–203.

Butterworth, G. (1995). An ecological perspective on the origins of self. In *The body and the self*, ed. J. L. Bermudez, A. Marcel, and N. Eilan, 87–105. Cambridge, MA: Bradford Books/MIT Press.

Butterworth, G., and Hicks, L. (1977). Visual proprioception and postural stability in infancy: a developmental study. *Perception* 6:255–262.

Butterworth, G., and Hopkins, B. (1988). Hand-mouth coordination in the newborn baby. *British Journal of Developmental Psychology* 6:303–314.

Declerck, G., and Gapenne, O. (2009). Actuality and possibility: On the complementarity of two registers in the bodily constitution of experience. *Phenomenology and the Cognitive Sciences* 8:285–305.

de Vignemont, F., Ehrsson, H. H., and Haggard, P. (2005). Bodily illusions modulate tactile perception. *Current Biology* 15:1286–1290.

de Vries, J. I. P., Hopkins, B., and van Geijn, H. P. (1993). La construction prénatale du développement postnatal. In *Les comportements du bébé: Expression de son savoir?*, ed. V. Pouthas and F. Jouen, 13–32. Liège: Mardaga.

Donaldson, I. M. L. (2000). The functions of the proprioceptors of the eye muscles. Philosophical Transactions of the Royal Society B. *Biological Sciences* 1404: 1685–1754.

Edelman, G. M. (1992). *Bright air, brilliant fire: On the matter of mind*. New York: Basic Books.

Epstein, W., Hugues, B., Schneider, S., and Bach y Rita, P. (1986). Is there anything out there? A study of distal attribution in response to vibrotactile stimulation. *Perception* 15: 275–284.

Gapenne, O., Lenay, C., Stewart, J., Bériot, H., and Meidine, D. (2001). Prosthetic device and 2D form perception: the role of increasing degrees of parallelism. In *Proceedings of the Conference on Assistive Technology for Vision and Hearing Impairement (CVHI'2001)*, 113–118. Italy: Castelvecchio Pascoli.

Gapenne, O., Rovira, K., and Lenay, C. Stewart, J., and Auvray, M. (2005). Is form perception necessary tied to specific sensory feedback? Paper presented at the 13th International Conference on Perception and Action (ICPA), July 5–10, Monterey, CA.

Goodwin, G. M., McCloskey, D. I., and Matthews, P. B. C. (1972). The contribution of muscle afferents to kinaesthesia shown by vibration induced illusions of movement and by the effects of paralysing joint afferents. *Brain* 95:705–748.

Grenier, A. (1981). La "motricité libérée" par fixation manuelle de la nuque au cours des premières semaines de vie. *Archives Francaises de Pediatrie* 38:557–561.

Haith, M. M. (1980). *Rules that babies look by. The organization of newborn activity*. Hillsdale, NJ: Lawrence Erlbaum.

Hanna, R., and Thompson, E. (2003). The mind-body-body problem. *Theoria et Historia Scientiarum* 7:24–44.

Hanneton, S., Gapenne, O., Genouëlle, C., Lenay, C., and Marque, C. (1999). Dynamics of shape recognition through a minimal visuo-tactile sensory substitution interface. Paper presented at the Third International Conference on Cognitive and Neural Systems, May 26–29, Boston.

Hein, A., and Held, R. (1967). Dissociation of the visual placing response into elicited and guided components. *Science* 158:390–392.

Held, R., and Hein, A. (1963). Movement produced stimulation in the development of visually guided behavior. *Journal of Comparative and Physiological Psychology* 56:872–876.

Husserl, E. (1950). *Idées directrices pour une phénomenologie*. Paris: Gallimard.

Husserl, E. (1989). *Chose et Espace. Leçons de 1907*. Trans. J.-F. Lavigne. Paris: PUF.

Inhelder, B., and Cellérier, G. (1992). *Le cheminement des découvertes de l'enfant*. Lausanne: Delachaux et Niestlé.

Jami, L. (1992). Golgi tendons organs in mammalian skeletal muscle: Functional properties and central actions. *Physiological Reviews* 70:623–666.

Jansonn, G. (1998). Haptic perception of outline 2D shape: The contributions via the skin, the joints and the muscles. In *Advances in perception-action coupling*, ed. B. Bril, A. Ledebt, G. Dietrich, and A. Roby-Brami, 25–30. Paris: Editions EDK.

Jones, L. A. (1988). Motor illusions: What do they reveal about proprioception? *Psychological Bulletin* 103:72–86.

Jouen, F., and Gapenne, O. (1995). Interaction between vestibular and visual System in the neonate. In *The self in early infancy: Theory and research*, Advances in Psychology 112, ed. P. Rochat, 277–301. Amsterdam: Elsevier Science Publishers.

Jouen, F., Lepecq, J. C., Gapenne, O., and Bertenthal, B. I. (2000). Optic flow sensitivity in neonates. *Infant Behavior and Development* 23:271–284.

Lackner, J. R., and Levine, M. S. (1979). Changes in apparent body orientation and sensory localization induced by vibration of postural muscles: Vibratory myesthetic illusions. *Aviation, Space, and Environmental Medicine* 50:346–354.

Lenay, C. (2006). Enaction, externalisme et suppléance perceptive. *Intellectica* 43:27–52.

Lenay, C., Canu, S., and Villon, P. (1997). Technology and perception: the contribution of sensory substitution systems. In *Second International Conference on Cognitive Technology*, 44–53. Aizu, Japan, and Los Alamitos: IEEE.

Lenay, C., Gapenne, O., Hanneton, S., Marque, C., and Genouëlle, C. (2003). Sensory substitution: Limits and perspectives. In *Touch for knowing*, ed. Y. Hatwell, A. Streri, and E. Gentaz, 275–292. Amsterdam: John Benjamins.

Lishman, J. R., and Lee, D. N. (1973). The autonomy of visual kinaesthesis. *Perception* 2:287–294.

Maillard, M., Gapenne, O., Hafemeister, L., and Gaussier, P. (2005). Perception as a dynamical sensorimotor attraction basin. *Lecture Notes in Computer Science* 3630:37–46.

Matthews, P. B. C. (1972). *Mammalian muscle receptors and their central action.* London: E. Arnold Publishers Ltd.

Mellier, D., Dupont, V., Rovira, K., and Fessard, C. (1990). Analysis of newborn preterm motility according to active tonic regulation: assessment of visual pursuit activity. Paper presented at the IVth European Conference on Developmental Psychology, August 27–31, Stirling, UK.

Merleau-Ponty, M. (1945). *Phénoménologie de la perception.* Paris: Gallimard.

Metzger, W. (1974). Can the subject create his world? In *Perception. Essays in Honor of James J. Gibson,* ed. R. B. MacLeod and H. L. Pick, 57–71. Ithaca, NY, and London: Cornell University Press.

Neisser, U. (1991). Two perceptually given aspects of the self and their development. *Developmental Review* 11:197–209.

O'Regan, J. K. (1992). Solving the "real" mysteries of visual perception: The world as an outside memory. *Canadian Journal of Psychology* 46:461–488.

Paulus, M., Straube, A., and Brandt, T. (1984). Visual stabilization of posture: Physiological stimulus characteristics and clinical aspects. *Brain* 107:1143–1164.

Petit, J. L. (2002). La constitution par le mouvement: Husserl à la lumière des données neurobiologique récentes. In *Naturaliser la phenomenology,* ed. J. Petitot, F. J. Varéla, B. Pachoud, and J. M. Roy, 283–311. Paris: CNRS Editions.

Petitot, J. (2004). Géométrie et vision dans *Ding und Raum* de Husserl. *Intellectica* 39:139–167.

Philipona, D., O'Regan, K., and Nadal, J. P. (2003). Is there something out there? Inferring space from sensorimotor dependencies. *Neural Computation* 15:2029–2049.

Piaget, J. (1937). *La construction du réel chez l'enfant.* Neuchâtel et Paris: Delachaux et Niestlé.

Piaget, J. (1961). *Les mécanismes perceptifs.* Paris: PUF.

Piaget, J. (1974). *La prise de conscience.* Paris: PUF.

Pinol-Douriez, M. (1984). *Bébé agi—Bébé actif. L'émergence du symbole dans l'économie interactionnelle.* Paris: PUF.

Riggs, L. A., Armington, J. C., and Ratliff, F. (1954). Motion of the retinal image during fixation. *Journal of the Optical Society of America* 44:315–321.

Robert-Ouvray, S. (1997). Intégration motrice et développement psychique. Une théorie de la psychomotricité. 2nd rev. edition. Paris: Desclée de Brouwer.

Rochat, P. (1995). Early objectification of the self. In *The self in early infancy: Theory and research*, Advances in Psychology 112, ed. P. Rochat, 53–72. Amsterdam: Elsevier Science Publishers.

Rochat, P., and Hespos, S. J. (1997). Differential rooting response by neonates: Evidence for an early sense of self. *Early Development & Parenting* 6:105–112.

Roll, J.-P. (1994). Sensibilités cutanées et musculaires. In *Traité de psychologie expérimentale*, vol. 1, ed. M. Richelle, J. Requin, and M. Robert, 483–542. Paris: PUF.

Roll, J.-P. (2003). Physiologie de la kinesthèse. La proprioception: sixième sens ou sens premier? *Intellectica* 36/37:49–66.

Roll, J.-P., and Ghilodes, J.-C. (1995). Proprioceptive sensory codes subserving movement trajectories: human hand vibration-induced drawing illusions. *Canadian Journal of Physiology and Pharmacology* 73:295–304.

Roll, J.-P., Bergenheim, M., and Ribot-Ciscar, E. (2000). Proprioceptive population coding of 2D limb movements in humans (Part II). Muscle spindle feedback during "drawing like movements." *Experimental Brain Research* 134:311–321.

Roll, R., Velay, J.-L., and Roll, J.-P. (1991). Eye and neck proprioceptive messages contribute to the spatial coding of retinal input in visually oriented activities. *Experimental Brain Research* 85:423–431.

Romaiguère, P., Anton, J. L., Roth, M., Casini, L., and Roll, J.-P. (2003). Kinaesthetic activates both motor and parietal cortical areas in humans: a parametric fMRI study. *Cognitive Brain Research* 16:74–83.

Rosenthal, V. (2004). Formes, sens et développement: quelques aperçus de la microgenèse. Texto! revue électronique. http://www.revue-texto.net/Inedits/Rosenthal/Rosenthal_Formes.html.

Rudrauf, D., Lutz, A., Cosmelli, D., Lachaux, J. P., and Le Van Quyen, M. (2003). From autopoiesis to neurophenomenology: Francisco Varela's exploration of the biophysics of being. *Biological Research* 36:27–65.

Shanon, B. (1990). Consciousness. *Journal of Mind and Behavior* 11:137–152.

Schilder, P. (1950). *L'image du corps*. Paris: Gallimard.

Simondon, G. (2005). *L'individuation à la lumière des notions de formes et d'information*. Grenoble: Millon.

Sribunruangrit, N., Marque, C., Lenay, C., Gapenne, O., and Vanhoutte, C. (2004). Speed-accuracy trade off during performance of a tracking task without visual feedback. *IEEE Transactions on Neural Systems and Rehabilitation Engineering* 12:131–139.

Stern, D. (1985). *The interpersonal world of the infant*. New York: Basic Books.

Stewart, J. (2001). Radical constructivism in biology and cognitive science. *Foundations of Science* 6:99–124.

Stewart, J., and Gapenne, O. (2004). Reciprocal modelling of active perception of 2-D forms in a simple tactile-vision substitution system. *Minds and Machines* 14 (3): 309–330.

Stratton, G. M. (1902). Eye movements and aesthetics of visual form. *Philosophische Studien* 20: 336–359.

Suzuki, M., Floreano, D., and Di Paolo, E. A. (2005). The contribution of active body movement to visual development in evolutionary robots. *Neural Networks* 18: 657–666.

Thelen, E. (1988). Dynamical approaches to the development of behavior. In *Dynamic patterns in complex systems*, ed. J. A. S. Kelso, A. J. Mandell, and M. F. Schlesinger, 348–369. Singapore: World Scientific.

Thelen, E., and Smith, L. B. (1994). *A dynamic systems approach to the development of cognition and action*. Cambridge, MA: MIT Press.

Thomas, André, and de Ajuriaguerra, J. (1948). *L'axe corporel, musculature et innervation. Etude anatomique, physiologique et pathologique*. Paris: Masson et Cie.

Thompson, E. (2005). Sensorimotor subjectivity and the enactive approach to experience. *Phenomenology and the Cognitive Sciences* 4:407–427.

Tyler, M. E., Danilov, Y. P., and Bach-y-Rita, P. (2004). Asymmetry of head and body interactions during posture control in patients with bilateral vestibular dysfunction. In *Proceedings of the 34th International Meeting of the Society for Neuroscience*. October 23–28. San Diego.

Tyler, M. E., Haase, S. J., Kaczmarek, K. A., and Bach-y-Rita, P. (2002). Development of an electrotactile glove for display of graphics for the blind: Preliminary results. In *Proceedings of the 2nd Joint Conference IEEE Engineering in Medecine and Biology Society and Biomedical Engineering Society*, 2439–2440, October 24–27. Houston, TX.

Vallbo, A. B., and Hagbarth, K. E. (1968). Activity from skin mechanoreceptors recorded percutaneously in awake human subjects. *Experimental Neurology* 21: 270–289.

Varela, F. J. and Shear, J. (1999). *The view from within: First-person approaches to the study of consciousness*. Thorverton, Exeter, UK, and Bowling Green: Imprint Academic.

Varela, F. J., Thompson, E., and Rosch, E. (1991). *The embodied mind: Cognitive science and human experience*. Cambridge, MA: MIT Press.

Vermersch, P. (2000). Conscience directe et conscience réfléchie. *Intellectica* 31:269–311.

Visetti, Y. M. (2004). Constructivismes, émergences: Une analyse sémantique et thématique. *Intellectica* 39:229–259.

von Hofsten, C. (1993). Prospective control: A basic aspect of action development. *Human Development* 36:253–270.

Wallon, H. (1949). *Les origines du caractère chez l'enfant.* Paris: PUF.

Wanet-Defalque, M.-C., Veraart, C., de Voder, A. G., Metz, R., Michel, C., Dooms, G., and Goffinet, A. M. (1988). High metabolic activity in the visual cortex of early blind human subjects. *Brain Research* 446:369–376.

Werner, H. (1934). L'unité des sens. *Journal de Psychologie Normale et Pathologique* 31:190–205.

8 Directive Minds: How Dynamics Shapes Cognition

Andreas K. Engel

The future progress of cognitive science looks set to involve ever-increasing efforts to anchor research to the real world poles of sensing and acting. Thus anchored, time, world and body emerge as significant players in the cognitive arena. How could we ever have forgotten them?
—Clark 1995, 101

In the cognitive sciences, we currently witness a "pragmatic turn"[1] away from the traditional representation-centered framework toward a paradigm that focuses on understanding the intimate relation between cognition and action. Such an "action-oriented" paradigm has earliest and most explicitly been developed in robotics, and has only recently begun to have a notable impact on cognitive psychology and neurobiology. The basic concept is that cognition should not be understood as a capacity of deriving world-models, which then might provide a "database" for thinking, planning, and problem solving. Rather, it is emphasized that cognitive processes are not only closely intertwined with action but that cognition can actually best be understood as "enactive," as a form of practice itself. Cognition, on this account, is grounded in a prerational understanding of the world that is based on sensorimotor acquisition of real-life situations.

The goal of this chapter is to explore possible implications of such a "pragmatic turn" for cognitive neuroscience. In addition to reviewing major conceptual components of this new framework, I will discuss neurobiological evidence supporting this notion. Specifically, I will relate this new view to recent findings on the dynamics of signal flow in the nervous system and on encoding dimensions of neural activity patterns. As I will argue, new vistas on the "meaning," the functional roles, and the presumed "representational" nature of neural processes are likely to emerge from this confrontation.

8.1 Criticizing Orthodoxy: Problems with Representationalism

Numerous authors have criticized the "orthodox" stance of cognitive science (e.g., Winograd and Flores 1986; Varela, Thompson, and Rosch 1991; Dreyfus 1992; Kurthen 1994; Clark 1997; Engel and König 1998; O'Regan and Noë 2001; Noë 2004), and hence I confine myself to some short critical remarks. In a nutshell, the following core assumptions characterize the classical cognitivist view:

• Cognition is understood as computation over mental (or neural) representations.
• The subject of cognition is not engaged in the world, but conceived as a detached "neutral" observer.
• Intentionality is explained by the representational nature of mental states.
• The processing architecture of cognitive systems is conceived as being largely modular and context-invariant.
• Computations are thought to occur in a substrate-neutral manner.
• Explanatory strategies typically reference to inner states of individual cognitive systems.

These assumptions, which go back to the work of Fodor (1979), Newell and Simon (1972), and other protagonists of the representational theory of mind (RTM), seem to be present, albeit with different accentuation, in all versions and schools of cognitivist theorizing.

A key question in the debate is whether the representational account adequately describes the nature of cognition, and the relation between cognitive system and world. As stated earlier, the RTM implies (1) realism: perceptually relevant distinctions are "fixed" and observer-independent; (2) a separation of cognitive system and world: the subject is conceived as detached observer, who is not "engaged in" the world; and (3) passiveness of the cognitive system, which behaves in a merely receptive way, just "re"-acts, and takes copies of prespecified information. Many authors have argued that, along all these lines, the orthodox stance misconstrues the relation between cognitive system and world, and that it actually fails to appreciate the very nature of cognitive processes (Winograd and Flores 1986; Varela, Thompson, and Rosch 1991; Dreyfus 1992; Kurthen 1994; Clark 1997).

Long before the emergence of research on "active sensing," philosophers have emphasized the active nature of perception and the intimate relation between cognition and action. The American pragmatist John

Dewey stated: "Upon analysis, we find that we begin not with a sensory stimulus, but with a sensorimotor coordination . . . and that in a certain sense it is the movement which is primary, and the sensation which is secondary, the movement of the body, head and eye muscles determining the quality of what is experienced. In other words, the real beginning is with the act of seeing; it is looking, and not a sensation of light" (1896, 358–359).[2] With striking convergence, the same thought can be found more than forty years later in the writings of French phenomenologist Merleau-Ponty, who concluded that

the organism cannot properly be compared to a keyboard on which the external stimuli would play. . . . Since all the movements of the organism are always conditioned by external influences, one can, if one wishes, readily treat behaviour as an effect of the milieu. But in the same way, since all the stimulations which the organism receives have in turn been possible only by its preceding movements which have culminated in exposing the receptor organ to external influences, one could also say that behavior is the first cause of all stimulations. Thus the form of the excitant is created by the organism itself. (1962, 13)

Perception, according to these authors, is a constructive process whose operations are highly selective. Perceptual acts define, first of all, relevant distinctions in the field of sensory experience, and this occurs by virtue of the cognitive system's neural and bodily organization, as well as "top-down" factors (Engel, Fries, and Singer 2001), such as previous learning, emotion, expectation, or attention. Cognition, on this account, is not neutral with respect to action, but arises from sensorimotor couplings by which the cognitive agent engages in the world (Varela, Thompson, and Rosch 1991; O'Regan and Noë 2001). Eventually, this overturns the central notions of RTM: the purpose of cognitive processing is the guidance of action, not the formation of mental representations.

8.2 The Concept of a Pragmatic Turn

The "pragmatic" stance can be seen as a direct antagonist of the cognitivist framework, implicating a point-by-point opposing view regarding each of the assumptions that have been mentioned thus far:

• Cognition is understood as capacity of "enacting" a world.
• The subject of cognition is an agent immersed in the world (as suggested by the phenomenological concept of "being-in-the-world").
• System states acquire meaning by their relevance in the context of action.

• The architecture of cognitive systems is conceived as being highly dynamic, context-sensitive, and captured best by holistic approaches.
• The functioning of cognitive systems is thought to be inseparable from its substrate or incarnation ("embodiment").
• Explanations make reference to agent-environment or agent-agent-inter-actions ("situatedness").

Clearly, it's time for a turn, and the central credo of the proponents of the new paradigm could be phrased as "cognition is action" (Varela, Thompson, and Rosch 1991; Kurthen 1994).[3] That said, the adherents of this motto are facing challenges that may be even more severe than the ones discussed for the cognitivist legacy mentioned earlier; obviously, the pragmatic credo needs both explication and elaboration. It needs to be spelled out what the implications of this view possibly are, and whether it has the potential to inspire a new style of thinking, or—even more importantly—new styles of designing and performing experiments. In what follows, I will try to contribute a few modest ideas to this emerging field of debate.

The pragmatic turn, as envisaged here, is rooted in European and American philosophical movements of the late nineteenth and early twentieth centuries. Tracing these roots would require a detailed analysis that is far beyond the scope of this chapter, and only few remarks will be made to highlight some of the important links. On the one hand, American pragmatism has been influential, with John Dewey (1859–1952) and George Herbert Mead (1863–1931) as two leading protagonists. Dewey's early sensorimotor approach to perception has been cited already (Dewey 1896), and many aspects developed in later writings such as his "event ontology" and his genetic analysis of mind as emerging from cooperative activity (Dewey 1925) are highly relevant in this context. Along a similar vein, Mead's theory of the emergence of mind and self from the interaction of organic individuals in a social matrix (1934) and his analysis of perception and the constitution of reality as a field of situations through the "act" (1938) bear high relevance to pragmatic cognitive science and deserve further exploitation.

On the other hand, there are clear and explicit links to the European phenomenological-hermeneutic tradition, notably, to the early writings of Martin Heidegger (1889–1976) and the writings of Maurice Merleau-Ponty (1908–1961). Essentially, all motifs of the pragmatic turn can be traced back to these two philosophers, as noted by proponents of this new view (Dreyfus 1992; Varela, Thompson, and Rosch 1991; Kurthen 1994, 2007; Clark 1997; Noë 2004). As cited already, Merleau-Ponty strongly advocates an anti-representationalist view, emphasizing that the structures of the perceptual world are inseparable from the cognitive agent (Merleau-Ponty 1962, 1963) and that therefore "world-making" rather than "world-mirroring" lies at the heart of cognition. Heidegger develops his concept of "being-in-the-world" ("In-der-Welt-Sein," adopted by Merlau-Ponty using the expression of "être-au-monde") to overcome the Cartesian split between subject and world and to ground intentionality (Heidegger 1986, 1989). From this new way of seeing the relation between subject and world, characterized by mutual intertwinement, a direct path leads to a redefinition of the cognitive system as "extended mind," including both the cognitive agent and its environmental niche (Varela, Thompson, and Rosch 1991; Kurthen 1994, 2007; Clark 1997). The relation to the world can be only one rooting in practice, in acting, and practice, in turn, is mediated through the body. Thus, both Merleau-Ponty and Heidegger develop a view on cognition as grounded in concrete sensorimotor activity, in a prerational practical understanding of the world (Heidegger 1986, 1989; Merleau-Ponty 1962, 1963). From these premises, two concepts unfold that are of key importance to pragmatic cognitive science: the concept of "situation" (or "situatedness") and the concept of "embodiment."

According to Heidegger and Merleau-Ponty, what we encounter as cognitive agents are never "bare" objects or arrays of contingent features, but rather meaningful situations, that is, contexts we have already structured by prior activity and in which objects are defined as a function of our needs and concerns. Even for the newborn, the world is not a heap of coincident features, as its own needs in concert with the social context define what the world should look like. In his phenomenological analysis of situatedness, Heidegger coins the term *Bewandtnisganzheit* (Heidegger 1989), denoting a "referential nexus" across all components of the situation that is thus characterized by a holistic structure, and a merging or "intertwinement" of cognitive system and world. As part of the pragmatic view advocated here, these considerations suggest that the cognitivist ontology of "neutral features" should be replaced by a holistic ontological framework. Following Merleau-Ponty, the world does not have a prespecified structure that exists prior to and independent of any cognitive activity. Rather, the world is an a priori unlabeled "field of experience" in which cognition (as embodied action) draws relevant distinctions. If indeed the world is organized in "referential wholes" that cannot be decomposed into neutral objects, then the concept of "situation" should figure as the more basic ontological category.

Clark (1997) has discussed a number of consequences arising from this view. "Situatedness," in his view, implies that cognition does not build upon universal, context-invariant models of the world, but is subject to constraints of the local spatiotemporal environment, which need to be coped with in a highly context-dependent manner. This leads Clark to a notion of "minimal representationalism" that posits "action-oriented representations." This denotes the idea that internal states simultaneously describe aspects of the world and "prescribe" possible actions—a view that to him provides a compromise between the cognitivist and the pragmatic framework. Furthermore, Clark uses the concepts of situatedness and embeddedness to counteract the individualist stance of cognitivism. These notions imply a fundamental coupling through ongoing interaction between cognitive agent and environment. Therefore, the latter should be viewed not only as a task domain, but also as a resource that "scaffolds" cognitive acts. Slightly radicalizing this insight, one might then say that, in fact, the cognitive system comprises the brain, the body, and the environmental niche (Kurthen 1994, 2007). As Clark phrases it, "in the light of all this, it may . . . be wise to consider the intelligent system as a spatio-temporally extended process not limited by the tenuous envelope of skin and skull. . . . Cognitive science . . . can no longer afford the individualistic, isolationist biases that characterized its early decades" (1997, 221).

Compared to Clark (1995, 1997), other eminent proponents of the pragmatic turn, such as Varela, O'Regan, Noë, and Kurthen argue for a much more radical rejection of the cognitivist view (Varela, Thompson, and Rosch 1991; O'Regan and Noë 2001; Kurthen 1994, 2007). Drawing on the phenomenological tradition, Varela, Thompson, and Rosch have explored the implications of defining "cognition as embodied action" (1991, 172). As they emphasize, cognition should be considered from the viewpoint of action. Cognition is not detached contemplation, but a set of processes that determine possible actions. Perception, accordingly, must be understood as a process of defining relevant boundaries, not of grasping preexisting features, and "perceiving a world" means distinguishing possibilities for action. The criterion for success of cognitive operations is no longer a "veridical representation" of environmental features, but viable action in a certain situation. In a nutshell, cognition, as Varela, Thompson, and Rosch put it, can be understood as the capacity of "enacting" a world:

The overall concern of the enactive approach to perception is not to determine how some perceiver-independent world is to be recovered; it is, rather, to determine the common principles or lawful linkages between sensory and motor systems that explain how action can be perceptually guided in a perceiver-dependent world.

Consequently, cognition is no longer seen as problem solving on the basis of representations; instead, cognition in its most encompassing sense consists in the enactment or bringing forth of a world by a viable history of structural coupling. (1991, 173, 205)

Exploiting Heideggerian thinking, Kurthen (1994, 2007) has developed a "hermeneutical theory of cognition." The term "hermeneutic," in his account, is not referring to the hermeneutic nature of the scientific method, but rather to the idea that cognition itself is construed as a hermeneutical faculty. In his framework, "intentionality is not generated by representation, but . . . by primarily non-representational concrete activity of the cognitive system within its environmental niche" (2007). Kurthen stresses several important ideas: he suggests that only through the embodied nature of the cognitive system can internal states acquire meaning (or significance); however, as he also points out, the "embodied action" approach alone does not yet solve the problems of the orthodoxy, because what is actually needed is an account of teleology. According to Kurthen, embodiment can only be a mediator, a "vehicle" of teleology. What needs to be considered is subsystems of the organism that support motivational and emotional states. "Under this conative view the functional subsystems of the organisms are to be rearranged. While most 'embodiment approaches' . . . stress the role of the sensorimotor system in embodied cognition, this system turns out to be of only secondary relevance from a teleological point of view. . . . Needs, desires and other conative states that fuel our actions are rooted in different parts of the organism: in the endocrine system, the autonomous nervous system and its target organs . . . as well as their regulatory centers in the brain stem" (2007, 140).

The notion that cognition can only by understood by taking into account the organization and function of the body is also a key ingredient of the sensorimotor contingency theory (SCT) put forward by O'Regan and Noë (2001). According to the SCT, the agent's sensorimotor contingencies—that is, the rules governing sensory changes produced by various motor actions—are constitutive for cognitive processes. "Seeing," according to the SCT, is not having something on the retina, is not having a detailed internal "representation"; rather, seeing corresponds to knowing you are currently engaged in a visual manipulations, to exploratory activity, mediated by knowledge of sensorimotor contingencies. The brain enables us to see, but the neural activity does not in itself constitute the seeing; rather, the brain supports vision by enabling exercise and mastery of sensorimotor contingencies. I believe that the SCT potentially has interesting implications regarding the significance of internal states and neural activity patterns. I will elaborate on this issue in the next section.

8.3   Action-Oriented View on Neural Processing

If we decide to go for a pragmatic turn in cognitive science, our view of the brain and its function seem to be changing profoundly. The conceptual premises of the pragmatic stance can be mapped to the neuroscientific level of description, and thus lead us to redefining at least some of the neurobiologist's explananda. What neuroscience, then, has to explain is not how brains act as world-mirroring devices, but how they can serve as "vehicles of world-making" that support, based on individual learning history, the construction of the experienced world and the guidance of action.

The following premises might become part of a framework for "pragmatic neuroscience":

• Primary concern of the experimenter is not the relation of neural activity patterns to stimuli, but to the action at hand and the situation the subject under study is currently engaged in.
• The function of neural circuits has to be studied making reference to the view that cognition is a highly active, selective, and constructive process.
• Sensory processing must be considered in a holistic perspective, and as being subject to strong top-down influences that constantly create predictions about forthcoming sensory events and eventually reflect constraints from current action.
• The function of neurons and neural modules must not be considered in isolation, but with proper reference to other subsystems and the actions of the whole cognitive system.
• The investigation of the intrinsic dynamics of the brain becomes increasingly important, because interactions within and across neural assemblies are constitutive for the operations of the cognitive system.
• Because the representational view is largely abandoned, a new view on the functional roles of neural states needs to be developed; rather than "encoding" information about pregiven objects or events in the world, neural states support the capacity of structuring situations through action.

There is ample neurobiological evidence to suggest a fundamental role of action and of sensorimotor activity in perception and cognitive processing. In the following, I will briefly highlight some key findings that match the premises phrased thus far and thus seem to support a pragmatic stance for cognitive neuroscience.

Key evidence supporting the pragmatic view is provided by findings on the role of exploratory activity and sensorimotor interactions for neural development and plasticity. It has been known for a long time that developmental processes in the nervous system are activity-dependent. For instance, development of neural circuits in the visual system and acquisition of visuomotor skills critically depend on sensorimotor interactions and active exploration of the environment (Held 1965; Majewska and Sur 2006). Even in the adult brain, there is considerable plasticity of cortical maps—for instance, in the somatosensory and motor system—that has been shown to depend on action context and, interestingly, also on attention (Blake, Byl, and Merzenich 2002; Münte, Altenmüller, and Jäncke 2002). Similar evidence is available for the human brain, as in highly trained musicians who often show functional and structural changes in their sensorimotor system resulting from action-dependent plasticity (Münte, Altenmüller, and Jäncke 2002). One conclusion from these studies is that appropriate action, allowing exercise of relevant sensorimotor contingencies, is necessary throughout life to stabilize the functional architecture in the respective circuits.

Another important line of evidence concerns research on the function and neural mechanisms of "corollary discharge" or "reafference" signals, which are necessary for an organism to distinguish self-generated sensory changes from those not related to own action (Desmurget and Grafton 2000; Crapse and Sommer 2008). In technical contexts, the same principle is often referred to as a "forward model." Supporting the SCT, this research shows that predictions about the sensory outcome of movement are critical for the basic interpretation of sensory inputs. The importance of reafference has been shown in the context of eye movements and grasping or reaching movements. Interestingly, similar principles of predicting sensory inputs seem to play a key role also in more complex cognitive processes like language comprehension (Pickering and Garrod 2006) or predictions about the actions of other subjects in social context (Wilson and Knoblich 2005). A point of key interest is that in all these cases, activity of motor planning regions seems involved in generating the prediction about sensory events, possibly by modulating neural signals in sensory regions (Wilson and Knoblich 2005; Christensen et al. 2007). Malfunction of such modulatory signals and associated disturbance of forward models have been implicated in the pathogenesis of psychiatric disorders such as schizophrenia (Frith, Blakemore, and Wolpert 2000).

If guidance of action is a dominant function of the brain, one would predict that neuronal response profiles in sensory or association regions should strongly depend on action context. Indeed, there is clear evidence for such an action-relatedness. For instance, activation of visual neurons changes profoundly if unrestrained, self-induced eye movements are permitted, as compared to passive viewing of stimuli under controlled fixation (Gallant, Connor, and VanEssen 1998). Furthermore, properties of parietal and premotor neurons strongly depend on action context (Graziano and Gross 1998). In premotor cortex, the spatial profile of multimodal receptive fields depends on body and limb position (Graziano, Hu, and Gross 1997). Tactile and visual receptive fields of premotor neurons are in dynamic register and seem "anchored" to body parts even if these are moving, suggesting that such polymodal neurons support predictions about expected changes in sensory input. Given the abundance of sensorimotor "gain" modulation of neural responses (Salinas and Sejnowski 2001), it seems likely that neural "representations" are always, to considerable degree, action-related or action-modulated (Clark 1997).

In the present context, another highly intriguing finding is that motor and premotor systems are also active during "virtual actions" (Jeannerod 2001), like, for instance, "mental rotation" of objects (Richter et al. 2000). Conversely, "virtual action" apparently can have a profound influence on experienced sensory structure. This is beautifully demonstrated by a study of Bisiach and Luzzatti (1978) in two patients suffering from unilateral neglect due to damage in the right parietal cortex. The term "neglect" denotes a profound inability to access sensory information in peripersonal space contralateral to the lesion. Interestingly, in these patients neglect was also found under conditions of visual imagery: when asked to imagine known spatial settings, the patients could report only the right half of the respective scene; even more striking, when now the same patient imagined turning by 180 degrees, she could suddenly access, in her imagination, the parts of the scene on the formerly neglected side. These observations on the relation between neglect and imagined action suggests a fundamental role of action planning centers in modulation of complex cognitive processes.

From the observations discussed thus far, one may conclude that the functional significance of neural states or activity patterns needs to be redefined, because a representational account ultimately fails to provide a satisfying view. As we have discussed already, neural patterns do not carry "images" of the external world. What these patterns support are not abstract structural descriptions of objects and scenes but, rather, kinds of know-how about sets of possible actions that produce viable segmentations of the scene. Neural activity patterns, on this account, support the organisms capacity of structuring situational contexts; they "prescribe" possible actions, rather than "describing" states of the outside world. In fact, their functional role in the guidance of action is what determines the "meaning" of internal states. Clark summarizes: "the brain should not be seen as primarily a locus of inner descriptions of external states of affairs; rather, it should be seen as a locus of inner structures that act as operators upon the world via their role in determining actions" (1997, 47).

The need to redefine the functional role of internal states has apparently been acknowledged by forerunners of the pragmatic turn who, in different versions, made attempts to soften up the connotations of the term "representation" by introducing additional qualifiers. To denote the action-relatedness of internal states and to emphasize that objects and events of the current situation are specified with respect to the cognitive agent, concepts like "deictic representation," "deictic codes," "indexical representation," "control-oriented representation," or "action-oriented representation" have been introduced (e.g., Clark 1995, 1997). Though all this is helpful, I think that these indecisive attempts to undermine the usage of the notion of "representation" can be moulded more radically—eventually, I suggest, the smarter move is to drop the term "representation" altogether and to replace it by an expression that does not carry about so much of the cognitivist burden.

This is why I will use, in the remainder of the chapter, the expression "directive" rather than "representation" for characterizing the functioning of dynamic patterns of interactions in a cognitive system. Introducing this term as part of the pragmatic framework, it is important to stress that directives are not simply internal states of the brain. They are, of course, supported by neural activity patterns, but they correspond to states of the cognitive system in its entirety. As I see it, such action-oriented patterns will always include certain aspects of bodily dynamics, such as certain biophysical properties of the skeletomuscular system. Actually, they might best be described as *patterns of dynamic interactions extending through the entire cognitive system*. This is why "directive" is *not* just a different term for "action-oriented representation." The latter is "in the head"; the former denotes the dynamics of the "extended mind."

What, then, is the relation of directives to actions and objects on the one hand, and to neural states on the other? In my view, directives are immediately related to action selection. Activating directives directly controls the respective action. More generally, directives correspond to dispositions for meaningful actions; as such, they correspond to ways of "knowing how" rather than "knowing that." Object concepts, then, correspond to sets of related directives; on this account, knowing what a glass or a tree is does not mean possessing internal descriptions of such objects, but to master sets of sensorimotor skills, paths of possible action that can be taken to explore or utilize the respective object. Objects are not "targeted by" directives but are rather constituted by these, because in fact an object is defined by the set of possible actions that can be performed on it. We do not first perceive a chair by setting up an abstract geometric description, and then compute its suitability for sitting; rather, perceiving a chair *is* to detect the opportunity of sitting. The concept of an object corresponds to "nothing but" the set of possible actions relating to this object; there is no context-neutral "description" above and beyond the directives.

The relation between directives and their neural underpinnings can be phrased as follows: directives correspond to functional roles of neural states; conversely, neural activity patterns support and partially implement directives as their functional roles. Thus, directives provide a network of functional roles, defined by current action, that are supported by (filled by) dynamic patterns in neural activity. It is important to note that neural activity patterns are not directives themselves, but only those "traces" accessible to neurophysiological experimentation. The "neural vehicles" of directives, of course, are highly complex, involving cell populations distributed across numerous brain regions. With all likelihood, this requires dynamic interactions between sets of neurons in different sensory modalities as well as with neurons in premotor and prefrontal cortical regions, the limbic system, and the basal ganglia.

8.4 Exploiting Neural Dynamics

If directives, as suggested earlier, are carried by complex neural patterns, it becomes crucial to investigate the dynamic interactions in highly distributed neuronal populations. Generally speaking, the implementation of directives will require highly specific and flexible interactions in the brain, involving not only sensory regions, but specific coupling to motor signals, as well as to activity in limbic and memory regions. To allow the selective integration of sensory and motor signals during an act such as visually guided grasping, a dynamic "binding principle" is required to coordinate the local processes that are all part of the "neural vehicle" of the grasp directive. In the following, I will briefly discuss a mechanism that can do the job—neural synchrony.

Originally, the notion that synchrony might be important for dynamic integration of neural signals had been proposed in the context of perceptual processing and scene segmentation (von der Malsburg 1981; Engel et al. 1992; Singer and Gray 1995). More than two decades ago, this temporal correlation hypothesis (TCH) was already motivated by the insight that perception, like most other cognitive functions, is based on highly parallel information processing involving large neural assemblies spread out across numerous brain areas. One of the key predictions of the TCH in its original version (von der Malsburg 1981) was that neurons that support perception of a sensory object might fire their action potentials in temporal synchrony. However, no such synchronization should occur between cells whose firing relates to different objects (figure 8.1). According to the TCH, synchronization of spatially separate neurons is a key principle of brain function, as it allows the formation of functionally coherent activity patterns supporting particular cognitive functions. In the example illustrated in figure 8.1, locally specific desynchronization of visual cortical neurons would enable the process of figure-ground segregation in the center of the gaze.

Interestingly, physiological studies in the visual system of cats and monkeys have demonstrated that neuronal synchronization indeed depends on the stimulus configuration. It was found that spatially separate cells show strong synchronization only if they respond to the same visual object. However, if responding to two independent stimuli, the cells fire in a less correlated manner or even without any fixed temporal relationship (Gray et al. 1989; Kreiter and Singer 1996). In the pragmatic framework discussed here, this experimental observation would not be interpreted as indicating a switch in the buildup of "object representations," but as resulting from the effect that the neuronal populations in visual cortex eventually support different directives, that is, different patterns of action, depending on the outcome of the segmentation process.[4]

Work of the past two decades suggests that correlated activity of neurons is quite ubiquitous in the nervous system and occurs on multiple time scales (for review, see Engel et al. 1992; Engel, Fries, and Singer 2001; Singer and Gray 1995). As observed in many animal studies and confirmed in human EEG and MEG experiments, synchrony is often associated with oscillatory activity, that is, rhythmic recurrence of neuronal discharges. It has been argued that, at least over larger distances, such oscillations may be critical in setting up neuronal communication (Engel, Fries, and Singer 2001; Fries 2005). The available studies demonstrate that specific changes in neural synchrony, leading to dynamic reconfiguration of communication in neural populations, are associated with a wide variety of cognitive processes, such as perceptual integration, attention, memory formation,

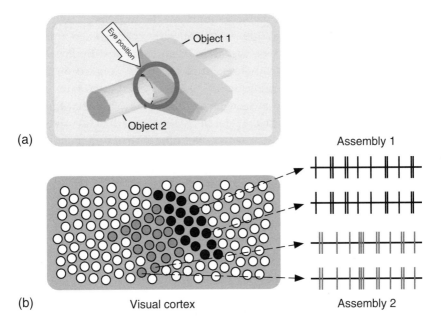

Figure 8.1
Establishment of coherent neural assemblies by temporal correlations. (a) Visual
scene comprising two objects. The circle demarcates the current direction of gaze at
a particular region of the scene. (b) The TCH posits that segmentation of the scene
is associated with the buildup of two assemblies of cells in visual cortex. The cells
that make up each assembly are coherently active. In contrast, the signals of cells
that are part of different assemblies are desynchronized (right). In this model, synchrony is supposed to occur with millisecond precision.
© Andreas K. Engel

and even awareness (Engel and Singer 2001; Engel, Fries, and Singer 2001;
Herrmann, Munk, and Engel 2004).

A critical prediction of the TCH is that neural synchrony that is observed
locally in sensory areas can be modulated, in fact, strongly by large-scale
dynamics of the cognitive system (Engel, Fries, and Singer 2001; Varela
et al. 2001; Herrmann, Munk, and Engel 2004). In the case of perceptual
integration, factors like expectation, attention or previous knowledge
about the objects encountered are often crucial for the outcome of the
segmentation process. The TCH accounts for this by assuming that temporally coordinated signals from other regions of the network can have
a strong impact on assembly formation in sensory regions by modulating
the local neural dynamics in a top-down manner (Engel, Fries, and Singer
2001). This seems to agree well with predictions that derive from the

pragmatic stance. If feature-specific desynchronization of neurons indeed supports buildup and selection of directives for action, then temporal patterning in sensory populations should strongly be shaped by the action context and, possibly, by direct interactions with assemblies involved in action-planning. Although, at this point, experimental evidence is still sparse, some studies seem to support the idea that neural synchrony may be related to generation of actions.

Recent studies on neural mechanisms of attention provide first hints that the modulatory effects on the timing in sensory assemblies in fact arise from premotor and prefrontal regions. Strong evidence for an attentional modulation of neural synchrony is provided by experiments in behaving macaque monkeys. Steinmetz et al. (2000) investigated cross-modal attentional shifts in monkeys that had to direct attention to either visual or tactile stimuli that were presented simultaneously. Neuronal activity was recorded in the secondary somatosensory cortex. As the study shows, synchrony in this area depended strongly on the monkey's attention, being most prominent in the condition where the animal attentively worked on the tactile task. In the visual system, strong attentional effects on temporal response patterning were observed in monkey V4 (Fries et al. 2001). In this study, two stimuli were presented simultaneously on a screen, one inside the receptive fields of the recorded neurons and the other nearby. The animals had to detect subtle changes in one or the other stimulus. If attention was shifted toward the target location, there was a marked increase in local synchronization. More recently, this finding has been confirmed by Taylor et al. (2005) using a demanding visual task where monkeys had to track changes in an object's shape over time. In humans, several EEG and MEG studies also suggest a clear relation between attention and modulation of neural synchrony in the auditory (Tiitinen et al. 1993; Debener et al. 2003), the visual (Tallon-Baudry et al. 1997; Kranczioch et al. 2006; Siegel et al. 2008), and the tactile system (Bauer et al. 2006).

Interestingly, a number of attention studies suggest that the modulatory bias may, indeed, arise from regions involved in action planning. In a recent study using the so-called attentional blink paradigm (figure 8.2), we have obtained evidence that a network of premotor, parietal, and limbic regions modulates the dynamics of visual processing (Kranczioch et al. 2005). Along similar lines, in recent MEG experiments on visual attention we could show that premotor regions like the frontal eye field are very likely involved in top-down modulation of the timing in sensory assemblies (Siegel et al. 2008). Together with behavioral data showing that

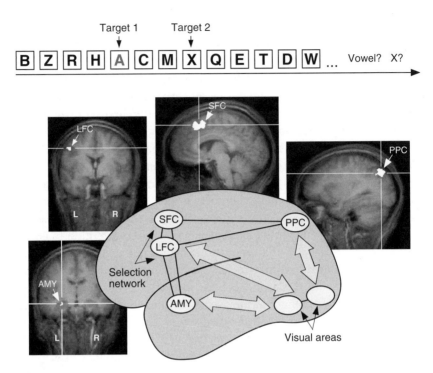

Figure 8.2

Frontoparietal selection networks involved in the attentional blink. *Top panel*: During a typical "attentional blink" experiment, subjects have to attentively process two targets that appear in a stream of distractor stimuli and to respond by button-presses after the end of the stimulus sequence. In the version used by Kranczioch et al. (2005), subjects were asked if a green letter (defined to be target 1) had been a consonant or a vowel; in addition, they had to indicate whether a black X (target 2) had been perceived somewhere after target 1. If the two targets appear in close temporal succession, the X often goes unnoticed (the "attentional blink"). *Bottom panel*: Results obtained with fMRI indicate that, in this task, a frontoparietal selection network may be involved in controlling the access of signals to awareness. This network seems to include a region in posterior parietal cortex (PPC), regions in superior and lateral frontal cortex (SFC, LFC), as well as the amygdala (AMY). Big arrows symbolize top-down interactions between the selection network and sensory areas.

© Andreas K. Engel

movement preparation can lead to attentional shifts and to changes in the acquisition of object-related information (Craighero et al. 1999; Eimer and van Velzen 2006; Fagioli, Hommel, and Schubotz 2007), these findings support what sometimes is called a "premotor theory of attention": the idea that selection of sensory information should be modulated and focused by constraints arising from current action planning and execution. If so, this would suggest that attention may be "nothing but" a bias in sensory processing that is introduced by the selection of particular directives in the context of current or imminent action.

If synchrony in sensory regions supports the buildup of directives, one would also predict that temporal patterns that transiently emerge in certain regions must be "read out" through interaction with other brain regions such as frontal cortex or the basal ganglia and thus increase in impact in the generation of a specific action. In this way, synchronized neural assemblies could support particular directives, thus adopting a specific functional role in the respective action context. Indeed, there is some evidence to suggest that synchrony may provide a dynamic binding principle for structuring and selecting sensorimotor couplings. Synchronization between sensory and motor assemblies has been investigated in a number of studies in cats, monkeys, and humans during execution of tasks requiring sensorimotor coordination (Murthy and Fetz 1996; Roelfsema et al. 1997; Aoki et al. 2001). The results of these studies clearly show that synchrony between sensory and motor assemblies occurs specifically during task epochs requiring the linkage of perception and movement. The specificity of such interactions might allow, for instance, the selective channeling of sensory information to different motor programs that are concurrently planned or executed. Interestingly, the studies on awake cats (Roelfsema et al. 1997) provide evidence that dynamic interactions between motor regions and parietal cortex already occur before the appearance of the task-relevant stimulus, probably reflecting the animal's state of expectancy.

In this context, experiments in awake monkeys are of particular interest that specifically have addressed the relation between neural synchrony and selection of a motor act (Riehle et al. 1997). Riehle et al. showed that in a delayed reaching task (figure 8.3), synchrony occurred particularly at those times when the monkey was expecting a "Go" signal to appear on the screen. Interestingly, in those trials in which the "Go" signal appeared after prolonged periods of expectation, the number of significantly synchronized events increased over the delay period (figure 8.3), and spike synchrony became more precise as the "Go" cue approached. This indicates that, during selection of the reach directive, there is a relationship between

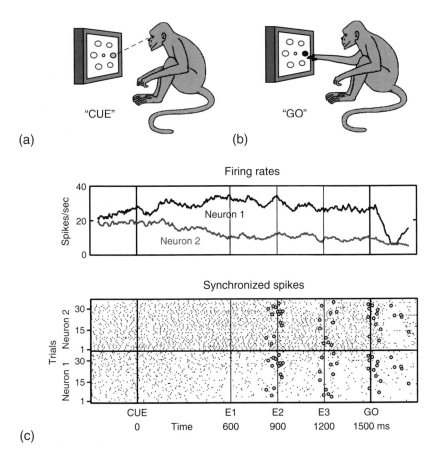

Figure 8.3

Synchrony expresses predictions about sensory events in primary motor cortex. The figure illustrates an experiment performed by Riehle et al. (1997) in which monkeys were trained on a delayed-pointing task. (a) During each trial, a first stimulus was given as a spatial "Cue" indicating the target position of the requested hand movement. (b) A second stimulus in the same location served as a "Go" signal instructing the animal to make the required movement. (c) Randomized across trials, the interval between "Cue" and "Go" corresponded to either 600, 900, 1200, or 1500 ms. The panels in (c) show data from trials where the "Go" signal appeared after 1500 ms. *Top panel*: For most recorded neurons, the firing rates did not modulate with the monkeys expectancy or the "Go" signal. *Bottom panel*: However, analysis of spike synchronization revealed that correlated firing increases significantly above chance level during time points (E2, E3) where the monkey expects the "Go" stimulus to occur and, finally, shortly before and during the moment when the second stimulus is given. Synchronized spikes are indicated by circles in the bottom panel.

Modified from Engel, Fries, and Singer 2001

growing stimulus expectancy and the synchronization in the motor
network. Although highly surprising from the viewpoint of classical representationalism, an action-oriented view clearly predicts that traces of
expectancy should appear in motor regions, even if the expectation—
prima facie—concerns a perceptual event. It is tempting to speculate that
these dynamic patterns actually implement procedural knowledge of sensorimotor contingencies as required by the SCT.

8.5 Epilogue

In this chapter, I have—trying to build on recent developments in the
field—introduced two concepts that might be useful in the discussion
on how to create a *better* science of the mind. The first is the concept
of a pragmatic turn, which denotes more of an agenda than a paradigm
already in place. As should have become clear, the punch line is to
eventually transform the whole theory of cognition into a theory of
action. Notably, this is not a behaviorist move, as the dynamics of the
cognitive system is in the very heart of the enterprise, and clear reference is made to "states in" the cognitive system. I have tried to show
that an action-oriented framework is not only conceptually viable, but
in fact is already supported by much experimental evidence. Numerous
findings in neuroscience either overtly demonstrate the action-relatedness
of cognitive processing, or can be reinterpreted more elegantly in this
new framework. In particular, research in the young field of neural
dynamics seems to support central intuitions of the pragmatic turn,
providing an avenue toward understanding how coordinated action can
emerge from the highly distributed architecture of a cognitive system.
The second notion I have introduced is that of a "directive," which I
nominate as a conceptual antagonist to the cognitivist notion of "representation." Future work will tell if my hypotheses on "directives" can
be consolidated into a robust theory of intrinsic dynamics of cognitive
systems.

In an earlier section of this chapter, I outlined how key assumptions
may be changing in a "pragmatic neuroscience." As I have mentioned,
a key question is whether these conceptual shifts may eventually lead us
to a different style of experimentation, to different settings and paradigms,
to new "laboratory habits." I think they will, and actually many harbin-
gers have arrived and have begun taking effect. More and more researchers
in the field implicitly seem to set up their own prescriptions for a pragmatic cognitive science and are starting to use natural stimuli, complex

sensorimotor paradigms, massively parallel recording techniques, and—most important—less restrained subjects. The fans of the pragmatic turn should be the first to realize that the return of the active cognizer to the lab is, above all, a matter of practice, rather than of theory.

Acknowledgments

This work has been supported by grants from the European Commission (IST-027268 "Perception on Purpose"; NEST-043457 "Mindbridge") and the Volkswagen Foundation (project "Representation").

Notes

1. The term "pragmatic" is used here to make reference to action-oriented viewpoints such those developed by the founders of philosophical pragmatism, William James, Charles Sanders Peirce, and John Dewey. Grossly simplifying, pragmatism entails, for instance, that an ideology or proposition is true if it works satisfactorily, that the meaning of a proposition is to be found in the practical consequences of accepting it, and that unpractical ideas are to be rejected. However, using the term "pragmatic turn," I am *not* meaning to suggest a return to exactly the positions put forward by these authors.

2. Note the striking resemblance between the notion of "sensorimotor coordination" used by Dewey and the concept of "sensorimotor contingencies" introduced by O'Regan and Noë (2001).

3. The concept of "action" contrasts with that of "behavior" and also with that of "movement." Evidently, there are many instances of action that do not involve any (overt) movement. Mental calculation would provide such a case. The description of "acts" or "actions" typically makes references to goals that often the agent has adopted on the basis of an overall practical assessment of his options and opportunities. "Behavior," in contrast, can be described and explained (at least according to certain psychological schools) without making reference to mental events or to internal psychological processes. Clearly, therefore, the pragmatic turn cannot not lead back to "behaviorism."

4. In the studies mentioned, the effects were observed under anesthesia (Gray et al. 1989) and in the awake, albeit passively stimulated animal (Kreiter and Singer 1996). This does not, in principle, contradict my interpretation. The findings seem to suggest that, even if the stimuli are not task-relevant, there is a disposition of the cortical network to synchronize in a stimulus-specific way *because certain rules relevant for the generation of directives have been inscribed by learning into the network*. Of course, the effects should be stronger if the scene segmentation is directly task-relevant.

References

Aoki, F., Fetz, E. E., Shupe, L., Lettich, E., and Ojemann, G. A. (2001). Changes in power and coherence of brain activity in human sensorimotor cortex during performance of visuomotor tasks. *BioSystems* 63:89–99.

Bauer, M., Oostenveld, R., Peeters, M., and Fries, P. (2006). Tactile spatial attention enhances gamma-band activity in somatosensory cortex and reduces low-frequency activity in parieto-occipital areas. *Journal of Neuroscience* 26:490–501.

Bisiach, E., and Luzzatti, C. (1978). Unilateral neglect of representational space. *Cortex* 14:129–133.

Blake, D. T., Byl, N. N., and Merzenich, M. M. (2002). Representation of the hand in the cerebral cortex. *Behavioural Brain Research* 135:179–184.

Christensen, M. S., Lundbye-Jensen, J., Geertsen, S. S., Petersen, T. H., Paulson, O. B., and Nielsen, J. B. (2007). Premotor cortex modulates somatosensory cortex during voluntary movement without proprioceptive feedback. *Nature Neuroscience* 10:417–419.

Clark, A. (1995). Moving minds: situating content in the service of real-time success. In *AI, connectionism, and philosophical psychology: Philosophical perspectives,* vol. 9, ed. J. E. Tomberlin, 89–104. Atascadero, CA: Ridgeview Pub. Co.

Clark, A. (1997). *Being there: Putting brain, body, and world together again.* Cambridge, MA: MIT Press.

Craighero, L., Fadiga, L., Rizzolatti, G., and Umilta, C. (1999). Action for perception: A motor-visual attentional effect. *Journal of Experimental Psychology. Human Perception and Performance* 25:1673–1692.

Crapse, T. B., and Sommer, M. A. (2008). Corollary discharge across the animal kingdom. *Nature Reviews Neuroscience* 9:587–600.

Debener, S., Herrmann, C. S., Kranczioch, C., Gembris, D., and Engel, A. K. (2003). Top-down attentional processing enhances auditory evoked gamma band activity. *Neuroreport* 14:683–686.

Desmurget, M., and Grafton, S. (2000). Forward modelling allows feedback control for fast reaching movements. *Trends in Cognitive Sciences* 4:423–431.

Dewey, J. (1896). The reflex arc concept in psychology. *Psychological Review* 3:357–370.

Dewey, J. (1925). *Experience and nature.* Chicago: Open Court.

Dreyfus, H. L. (1992). *What computers still can't do.* Cambridge, MA: MIT Press.

Eimer, M., and van Velzen, J. (2006). Covert manual response preparation triggers attentional modulations of visual but not auditory processing. *Clinical Neurophysiology* 117:1063–1074.

Engel, A. K., and König, P. (1998). Paradigm shifts in the neurobiology of perception. In *Intelligence and artificial intelligence: An interdisciplinary debate*, ed. U. Ratsch, M. M. Richter, and I.-O. Stamatescu, 178–192. Berlin: Springer.

Engel, A. K., and Singer, W. (2001). Temporal binding and the neural correlates of sensory awareness. *Trends in Cognitive Sciences* 5:16–25.

Engel, A. K., Fries, P., and Singer, W. (2001). Dynamic predictions: Oscillations and synchrony in top-down processing. *Nature Reviews Neuroscience* 2:704–716.

Engel, A. K., König, P., Kreiter, A. K., Schillen, T. B., and Singer, W. (1992). Temporal coding in the visual cortex: new vistas on integration in the nervous system. *Trends in Neurosciences* 15:218–226.

Fagioli, S., Hommel, B., and Schubotz, R. I. (2007). Intentional control of attention: Action planning primes action-related stimulus dimensions. *Psychological Research* 71:22–29.

Fodor, J. A. (1979). *Representations: Essays on the foundations of cognitive science.* Cambridge, MA: MIT Press.

Fries, P., Reynolds, J. H., Rorie, A. E., and Desimone, R. (2001). Modulation of oscillatory neuronal synchronization by selective visual attention. *Science* 291:1560–1563.

Fries, P. (2005). A mechanism for cognitive dynamics: Neuronal communication through neuronal coherence. *Trends in Cognitive Sciences* 9:474–480.

Frith, C. D., Blakemore, S.-J., and Wolpert, D. M. (2000). Explaining the symptoms of schizophrenia: Abnormalities in the awareness of action. *Brain Research: Brain Research Reviews* 31:357–363.

Gallant, J. L., Connor, C. E., and VanEssen, D. C. (1998). Neural activity in areas V1, V2 and V4 during free viewing of natural scenes compared to controlled viewing. *Neuroreport* 9:85–89.

Graziano, M. S. A., Hu, X. T., and Gross, C. G. (1997). Visuospatial properties of ventral premotor cortex. *Journal of Neurophysiology* 77:2268–2292.

Graziano, M. S. A., and Gross, C. G. (1998). Spatial maps for the control of movement. *Current Opinion in Neurobiology* 8:195–201.

Gray, C. M., König, P., Engel, A. K., and Singer, W. (1989). Oscillatory responses in cat visual cortex exhibit inter-columnar synchronization which reflects global stimulus properties. *Nature* 338:334–337.

Heidegger, M. (1986). *Sein und Zeit.* Tübingen: Niemeyer.

Heidegger, M. (1989). *Die Grundprobleme der Phänomenologie*. Frankfurt: Klostermann.

Held, R. (1965). Plasticity in sensory-motor systems. *Scientific American* 11 (65): 84–94.

Herrmann, C. S., Munk, M. H. J., and Engel, A. K. (2004). Cognitive functions of gamma-band activity: Memory match and utilization. *Trends in Cognitive Sciences* 8:347–355.

Jeannerod, M. (2001). Neural simulation of action: A unifying mechanism for motor cognition. *NeuroImage* 14:S103–S109.

Kranczioch, C., Debener, S., Schwarzbach, J., Goebel, R., and Engel, A. K. (2005). Neural correlates of conscious perception in the attentional blink. *NeuroImage* 24:704–714.

Kranczioch, C., Debener, S., Herrmann, C. S., and Engel, A. K. (2006). EEG gamma-band activity in rapid serial visual presentation. *Experimental Brain Research* 169:246–254.

Kreiter, A. K., and Singer, W. (1996). Stimulus-dependent synchronization of neuronal responses in the visual cortex of awake macaque monkey. *Journal of Neuroscience* 16:2381–2396.

Kurthen, M. (1994). *Hermeneutische Kognitionswissenschaft*. Bonn: Djre Verlag.

Kurthen, M. (2007). From mind to action: The return of the body in cognitive science. In *The body as interface: Dialogues between the disciplines,* ed. S. Sielke and E. Schäfer-Wünsche, 129–143. Heidelberg: Winter Verlag.

Majewska, A. K., and Sur, M. (2006). Plasticity and specificity of cortical processing networks. *Trends in Neurosciences* 29:323–329.

Mead, G. H. (1934). *Mind, self and society*. Chicago: University of Chicago Press.

Mead, G. H. (1938). *The philosophy of the act*. Chicago: University of Chicago Press.

Merleau-Ponty, M. (1962). *Structure of behavior*. Boston: Beacon Press.

Merleau-Ponty, M. (1963). *Phenomenology of perception*. New York: Humanities Press.

Münte, T. F., Altenmüller, E., and Jäncke, L. (2002). The musician's brain as a model of neuroplasticity. *Nature Reviews Neuroscience* 3:473–478.

Murthy, V. N., and Fetz, E. E. (1996). Oscillatory activity in sensorimotor cortex of awake monkeys: Synchronization of local field potentials and relation to behavior. *Journal of Neurophysiology* 76:3949–3967.

Newell, A., and Simon, H. A. (1972). *Human problem solving*. Englewood Cliffs, NJ: Prentice-Hall.

Noë, A. (2004). *Action in perception*. Cambridge, MA: MIT Press.

O'Regan, J. K., and Noë, A. (2001). The sensorimotor account of vision and visual consciousness. *Behavioral and Brain Sciences* 24:939–1031.

Pickering, M. J., and Garrod, S. (2006). Do people use language production to make predictions during comprehension? *Trends in Cognitive Sciences* 11:105–110.

Richter, W., Somorjai, R., Summers, R., Jarmasz, M., Menon, R. S., Gati, J. S., et al. (2000). Motor area activity during mental rotation studied by time-resolved single-trial fMRI. *Journal of Cognitive Neuroscience* 12:310–320.

Riehle, A., Grün, S., Diesmann, M., and Aertsen, A. (1997). Spike synchronization and rate modulation differentially involved in motor cortical function. *Science* 278:1950–1953.

Roelfsema, P. R., Engel, A. K., König, P., and Singer, W. (1997). Visuomotor integration is associated with zero time-lag synchronization among cortical areas. *Nature* 385:157–161.

Salinas, E., and Sejnowski, T. J. (2001). Gain modulation in the central nervous system: Where behaviour, neurophysiology, and computation meet. *Neuroscientist* 7:430–440.

Siegel, M., Donner, T. H., Oostenveld, R., Fries, P., and Engel, A. K. (2008). Neuronal synchronization along the dorsal visual pathway reflects the focus of spatial attention. *Neuron* 60:709–719.

Singer, W., and Gray, C. M. (1995). Visual feature integration and the temporal correlation hypothesis. *Annual Review of Neuroscience* 18:555–586.

Steinmetz, P. N., Roy, A., Fitzgerald, J., Hsiao, S. S., Johnson, K. O., and Niebur, E. (2000). Attention modulates synchronized neuronal firing in primate somatosensory cortex. *Nature* 404:187–190.

Tallon-Baudry, C., Bertrand, O., Delpuech, C., and Pernier, J. (1997). Oscillatory gamma-band (30–70 Hz) activity induced by a visual search task in humans. *Journal of Neuroscience* 17:722–734.

Taylor, K., Mandon, S., Freiwald, W. A., and Kreiter, A. K. (2005). Coherent oscillatory activity in monkey V4 predicts successful allocation of attention. *Cerebral Cortex* 15:1424–1437.

Tiitinen, H., Sinkkonen, J., Reinikainen, K., Alho, K., Lavikainen, J., and Naatanen, R. (1993). Selective attention enhances the auditory 40-Hz transient response in humans. *Nature* 364:59–60.

Varela, F. J., Thompson, E., and Rosch, E. (1991). *The embodied mind: Cognitive science and human experience*. Cambridge, MA: MIT Press.

Varela, F., Lachaux, J.-P., Rodriguez, E., and Martinerie, J. (2001). The brainweb: Phase synchronization and large-scale integration. *Nature Reviews Neuroscience* 2:229–239.

von der Malsburg, C. (1981). *The correlation theory of brain function.* Internal Report 81/2. Göttingen: Max Planck Institute for Biophysical Chemistry. Reprinted in *Models of neural networks II*, ed. E. Domany, J. L. van Hemmen, and K. Schulten, 95–119. Berlin: Springer 1994.

Wilson, M., and Knoblich, G. (2005). The case for motor involvement in perceiving conspecifics. *Psychological Bulletin* 131:460–473.

Winograd, T., and Flores, F. (1986). *Understanding computers and cognition.* Norwood, NJ: Ablex Publishing Corp.

9 Neurodynamics and Phenomenology in Mutual Enlightenment: The Example of the Epileptic Aura

Michel Le Van Quyen

One thing is clear: the specific nature of the mutual constraints is far from a simple empirical correspondence or a categorical isomorphism. Three ingredients have turned out to play an equally important role: (1) the neurobiological basis, (2) the formal descriptive tools mostly derived from nonlinear dynamics, and (3) the nature of lived temporal experience studied under reduction. What needs to be examined carefully is the way in which these three ingredients are braided together in a constitutive manner. What we find is much more than a juxtaposition of items. It is an active link, where effects of constraint and modification can circulate effectively, modifying both partners in a fruitful complementary way.
—Varela 1999a

9.1 Introduction: Neurophenomenology as a Methodology

One of the main outstanding problems in the cognitive sciences is to understand how ongoing conscious experience is related to its biological and physical roots. The recent development of large-scale brain imaging techniques such as electroencephalography (EEG) or functional magnetic resonance imaging progress made in the mathematical analysis of neuronal signals (cf. Engel, Fries, and Singer 2001; Varela, Thompson, and Rosch 2001; Le Van Quyen 2003), which allow the study of the living human brain at work, have provided an essential experimental framework for research into consciousness. Nevertheless, in spite of many theoretical propositions (Dennett 1991; Tononi and Edelman 1998; Baars 2003; Crick and Koch 2003) as well as encouraging experimental results on the neural correlates of consciousness (Logothetis and Schall 1989; Rodriguez et al. 1999; Lutz et al. 2002), the scientific community is still grappling with what is known as the "explanatory gap" (Levine 1983): the *relationships* between an individual's neurophysiological processes and his subjective experience remain obscure. Computationalist, functionalist or neuroreductionist approaches generally lead to a paradoxical eliminativism, that is, the elimination of consciousness during the very process of explanation of our subjective experience (Rudrauf et al. 2003). Clearly, no evidence about the *relation* between the objective and subjective realms can be provided if the initial explanandum itself (that which has to be explained) has been banished as a valid object of study. A shift in this theoretical tradition came when the embodied/enactive approach to the brain was introduced (Varela, Thompson, and Rosch 1991). A crucial issue of this new paradigm is that "the mind cannot be separated from the *entire* organism. We tend to think that the mind is in the brain, in the head, but the fact is that the environment also includes the rest of the organism; the brain is intimately connected to all of the muscles, the skeletal system, the guts, and the immune system, the hormonal balances and so on and so on. It makes the whole thing into an extremely tight unity. In other words, the organism as a meshwork of entirely co-determining elements makes it so that our minds are, literally, inseparable—not only from the external environment, but also from what Claude Bernard already called the *milieu intérieur*, the fact that we have not only a brain but an entire body" (Varela 1999b). A direct consequence is that the proper object of cognitive science is neither mind per se nor matter per se but instead living subjects that are bearers of irreducible phenomenological properties and biological properties alike (Petitot et al. 1999; Rudrauf et al. 2003). Following this enactive paradigm, Francisco Varela formulated in his late work a particular methodology called "neurophenomenology" directly using the essential complementarity of neurobiological and firsthand phenomenological descriptions (Varela 1996). As experimentally explored in a small but growing literature (Lutz et al. 2002; Jack and Roepstorff 2003; Gallagher and Brøsted Sørensen 2006), neurophenomenology takes the step of incorporating in neurosciences so-called first-person methods—techniques that subjects can use to increase the threshold of their awareness and thereby provide more refined first-person models of their experiences. Furthermore, at the heart of this strategy, the central aim is to create experimental situations that produce so-called mutual constraints (or mutual enlightenments) between first-person phenomenological data and third-person neuroscientific data (Varela 1996; Lutz and Thompson 2003). In these experimental situations, the subject is actively involved in generating stable experiential categories and describing them; the neuroscientist can be guided by these first-person data in the analysis and interpretation of brain processes; reciprocally, the identification of new neuroscientific data may lead to a refinement of the corresponding first-person descriptions. Based on this new neurophenomenological circulation, we review here some of the ongoing work of our research group concerning epilepsy. In particular, special attention is here paid to interdependence of neurodynamic and phenodynamic structures associated with the beginning of an epileptic seizure, the so-called aura.

9.2 The Epileptic Aura

Epilepsy is a brain disorder characterized by spontaneous, repeated seizures (see Engel 1989 for a history and summary of this literature). During seizures, neurons fire in massive, synchronized bursts. Many epileptic attacks leave people unconscious—sometimes looking "frozen in place," sitting or standing for minutes, but without consciousness. Nevertheless epileptics very often have specific "aura" experiences at the beginning of a seizure (figure 9.1a). The epileptic aura is that portion of the seizure which occurs before consciousness is lost and for which memory is retained afterwards (Gloor 1990). In the case of simple partial seizures, the aura itself may be the entire extent of the epileptic episode; in others there is a transition to a full-blown seizure (Commission on Classification and Terminology of the International League Against Epilepsy 1981). During the aura, the subjects rapport a variety of experiential events (Silberman et al. 1994): for example, memories may invade the subject's experience and cause a *déjà-vu illusion*, an experience in which a person has the intense conviction of having been through exactly what is happening now in the past. In other cases, the patient may experience *forced thinking*, in which a sudden thought imposes itself on one's awareness with such force that it gives the impression of certainty and, occasionally, even of clairvoyance. In an extreme case of forced thinking, the paroxysmal experience can affect visual and auditory modalities in the form of *hallucinations*, in which the patient may see a particular familiar scene or fact, or hear a voice or music (Gloor 1990). The patient is usually aware of the illusionary nature of his experience. In the same context, the subject suddenly has the vivid impression of observing him- or herself as wholly or partially different from normal. This *depersonalization* experience is always accompanied by strangeness and anguish. In this context, most of the epileptic experiences are associated with emotional components. For example, feeling of fear is the commonest affective symptom associated with epileptic discharges from mesial temporal origin. Special emotional auras consist of an attack of anguish and terror that suddenly takes over the consciousness with such intensity that the subject has the impression she or he is losing control of the situation, which will have a terrible end, perhaps madness or even death. In other emotional auras, the experience consists of a sudden state of *joy* with no apparent cause, and it takes over the consciousness passively for a few short moments, filling it with awe and strangeness. The prime example of this experience is that of Prince Mychkine in Dostoyevsky's *The Idiot*: "He was thinking . . . there was a moment or two in his epileptic condition . . . when suddenly amid the sadness, spiritual darkness, and depression, his brain seemed to catch fire at brief moments . . . all his agitation, all his doubts and worries seemed composed in a twinkling, culminating in a great calm, full of serene and harmonious joy and hope, full of understanding and knowledge of the final cause." Dostoyevsky was known to be epileptic and so it seems reasonable to assume that he was describing his own experience.

9.3 Collecting Phenomenological Data of the Aura Experience

First-person reports of the aura in epilepsy have always been recognized as essential components of its clinical picture. Nevertheless, the level of detail of the patient descriptions used in the medical circle for describing seizures provide only weak and incomplete information about subjective experiences (Johanson et al. 2003). There are several reasons of this traditional tendency to neglect the subjective dimension in medical diagnoses: first, the clinical approach tends to believe that, ultimately, the only good level of description of subjectivity relies on the description of brain processes. Consciousness becomes an epiphenomon of the neuronal machinery that, operating behind our back, creates illusions at the level of consciousness and possible distortions in the contents of consciousness during the seizure. This results in the belief that first-person reports cannot help to identify the origins of a mental illness. Second, the clinical view isolates the individual patient and considers a mental illness separated from the interconnections with his or her body/environment. A third reason is the difficulty that the patients confront in reporting their own experiences (Le Van Quyen and Petitmengin 2002; Johanson et al. 2003). Indeed, the verbal repertoire and the level of insight displayed by the subjects sometimes fail to meet the needs of an adequate introspective exploration. This is especially true for the epileptic experience, because it affects the very condition of experience and its reportability. In particular, the perception of warning signals often triggers an emotional reaction of stress and panic, which in turn hampers the perception of warning signals. Furthermore, the patient may experience warning signals but doesn't remember them because of postictal amnesia. All this does not encourage the awareness of epileptic signals or the will to describe them. Furthermore, these difficulties have prompted the medical circle to dismiss verbal reports as useful indicators of epileptic states, and have led it to rely instead on purely behavioral measures, such as video monitoring and button press if a seizure occurs.

Clearly, complementary methodological approaches must be taken into consideration to translate introspective reports into scientifically useful characterizations (Hurlburt and Heavey 2001). In particular, special attention must be paid to specific and stable, experiential categories taking place during the aura. In this respect, rigorous methods have been developed, in the lineage of Husserl's psycho-phenomenology, for collecting precise descriptions of subjective experience. These "first-person" methods suppose a departure from the naive belief that becoming conscious of one's lived experience is immediate and easy. A large part of our cognitive processes is preconscious, prereflective—that is, it unfolds below the threshold of consciousness. This explains the paucity of initial verbal self-reports on any subjective experience. But it is possible to gain access to this prereflective experience thanks to very specific "interior gestures" (as the "phenomenological reduction") that may be trained (Depraz , Varela, and Vermersch 2002), and/or prompted in the context of an interview, thanks to specific techniques (Petitmengin 2006). In our own work, in order to help the patients to become aware of their ictal experience and to describe it, we use specific interview techniques that guide them toward the concrete evocation of a particular experience from the past. This process of explicitation unfolds in three stages (Petitmengin, Baulac, and Navarro 2006). First, we choose a particular seizure from the past for which the patient retains a memory. If the patient sometimes feels warning sensations, we choose a seizure in which these sensations were especially vivid; if the patient does not experience warning sensations, we choose a recent seizure or one that she or he remembers. Then we have to identify the right moment to begin the description. In the case of warning sensations, we choose a temporal marker shortly before the start of these sensations, and begin the description there. Second, we guide the patient toward a concrete evocation of this particular preictal experience, by helping him or her to rediscover, in a precise manner, the visual, kinesthetic, auditory and olfactory context of the experience, until the patient feels that she or he is "reliving" it. Third, when the evocation is sufficiently stabilized, we help the patient to turn his or her attention toward the internal process, which may have been preconscious or "prereflected," until then. By use of a specific form of questioning, the patient is guided through an exploration of various registers of her or his subjective experience: visual, kinesthetic, auditory, and olfactory sensations; emotions; and internal dialog. Clearly, this process of explicitation requires a sustained and intimate effort from the patient. The establishment of a mutual relationship of truth, while providing the patient with the possibility of becoming an active co-researcher, is therefore the cornerstone of the interview.

9.4 Phenodynamic Structures of the Epileptic Aura

We have analyzed a group of patients with drug-resistant partial epilepsy with subjective symptoms preceding their seizures. They were selected from patients examined at the Epilepsy Unit of La Pitié-Salpêtrière Hospital in Paris. The interviews were done in hospital in a specialized video telemetry unit where EEG and video were recorded at the same time. The level of detail of the patient descriptions varied depending on the time since the seizure. Descriptions taken within twenty-four hours were more detailed, as were descriptions from those who had more practice in reporting their experiences. Here the main aim is to obtain, through descriptions of the target experience, an account of that which is invariant (or stable) as a feature of the experience, regardless of whether it is one or another subject that undergoes it. Our main observations allowed us to recognize that, despite a great variety of clinical manifestations (see section 9.2), epileptic auras have in common several invariant features that we called: (1) thought interference, (2) forced attention and (3) self-awareness:

1. *Thought interference* In a usual first-person perspective, the stream of consciousness is a sense of *consciousness as a temporal flow*. William James, in his famous chapter on "The Stream of Thought" (James [1890] 1981, chapter IX), provides a detailed description of the structure of this flow. This flow oscillates between "static" moments of explicit cognitive-emotional activity and vaguely articulated tendencies of transitions into new directions ("fringes of consciousness"; see Varela 1999a). Even though the stream may be sometimes saccadic, the stream of consciousness remains uninterrupted as the same flow. In particular, in a given temporal moment of the stream, its constituent contents (e.g., thoughts, images, sensations) are co-conscious, that is, united in an experiential whole. In contrast, during an epileptic aura, the patient experiences thoughts or ideas that suddenly pop up in the mind as if from nowhere and break into the main line of thinking or interfere with it. One patient described this feeling by saying: "These are sudden projections of images from the past, flash backs that impose themselves on me, that jump on me. They are for me the signs that a seizure is just coming." Thought interference often becomes intensi-

fied in frequency during the aura, ending up as thought pressure, where the patient is overwhelmed by new thoughts going in different directions. In association, the patients often report a fundamental change in the experience of time, such as a sense of time rushing ahead, time slowing down, standing still or time losing its continuity and becoming fragmented. These experiences of thought interferences show significant similarities with the observations reported by Penfield by electrical stimulation of the temporal lobe in epileptic patients during surgical procedures He observed that local stimulations at the level of an epileptogenic zone can reproduce epileptic experiences (Penfield 1959). Furthermore, the patients are somewhat aware of their environment, yet totally caught by the vividness of the emotional experiences induced by the electrical stimulation of the temporal lobe. Penfield's conclusion was that these patients were simultaneously experiencing "two separate streams of consciousness" (Penfield 1968). Interestingly, a very similar concept dates back to Hughlings-Jackson, who called the symptoms of the "dreamy state" a "double consciousness" (Taylor 1958). In this state, patients were vaguely aware of ongoing events (one consciousness), but were preoccupied with the intrusion of an "all-knowing" or "familiar" feeling (a second consciousness).

2. *Forced attention*   As mentioned before, attention is very strongly affected during the aura experience. The scope of attention becomes narrow and the focus of attention is directed inward, away from external stimuli. Some patients called this phenomenon "forced attention," because it included the narrowing of the focus of attention and the absence of the voluntary control of the direction of attention. Although largely underrecognized, forced attention to interfering thoughts seems to characterize the early stage of the seizure and appears to be a fairly common element in the subjective experience of the seizure. For example, some patients reported being totally absorbed in a compelling seizure-induced experiential phenomenon. When asked why they did not reply to the examiners questions during the episode, these patients usually reply that they "were there" but indicate their complete absorption in the experience.

3. *Self-awareness*   In strong relationship with the phenomenon of forced attention, patients often experience a phenomenological distance between their experiences and the sense of self. In usual cognition, the sense of self and experience is one and the same thing; they are completely fused. During the aura, there is a constant self-monitoring in which the patient excessively takes himself as an object of reflection. This is also associated with turning away from the external world and may prevent the patient from a natural, smooth engagement in the interactions with the world. In this phenomenological distance, the self is observing its own mental

contents and activities and this state may intensify into a sense of having a double of a split self. The patient says that he sometimes feels as if he was "outside" himself as a sort of a double, watching or observing him and others (One patient described this feeling by saying that "my self/my ego moves out of me."). Clearly related with this phenomenological distance, the epileptic aura is also often associated with spatialization of experience where thoughts are experienced in *a spatialized way*, for example localized to a particular part of the head or body (e.g., "My thoughts are pressing on the skull from the inside") or being described in spatial terms (e.g., "One thought in front of the other," "Thoughts are encapsulated"). This raises a qualitative difference with usual consciousness in which a thought does not seem to be experienced as a "thing" with specific location and spatial characteristics; its introspective contents are transparent or immediately given in a nonspatial way (i.e., the contents are not like physical objects lending themselves to a description in spatial terms).

9.5 Neurodynamics Structures of the Epileptic Aura

The epileptic changes associated with the aura can also be addressed by third-person neuroscientific data. Focal epileptic seizures originate in specific parts of the cortex and either remain confined to those areas or spread to other parts of the brain. The epileptic aura is related to the initial local activation of a cortical zone in which the seizures start. This view has been supported by so-called EEG-video monitorings in which brain EEG signals and video of the patient were recorded at the same time. The combined information clearly correlates the initial clinical signs of the seizure with the sudden appearance of a specific EEG pattern out of the ongoing background brain activity (Engel 1989; see figure 9.1b). In particular, during the phase of presurgical evaluation of subjects with pharmacoresistant epilepsy, invasive EEG recording from intracranial electrodes was often required to determine the exact extension of the epileptic zone. In contrast to scalp EEGs, intracranial recordings provide a high signal-to-noise ratio and a good spatial precision, down to millimeter spatial resolution. At the start of an epileptic seizure, these intracranial recordings clearly demonstrate that high-frequency oscillations, especially in the gamma frequency range of 40–120 Hz (Fisher et al. 1992), occur at the site of seizure origin. Very high-frequency oscillations (100–500 Hz) were also found in intracerebral recordings of the epileptic focus near the time of the onset of the seizure (Traub et al. 2001; Jirsch et al. 2006). Taken together, local high-frequency oscillations are correlated with the aura experience and reflect

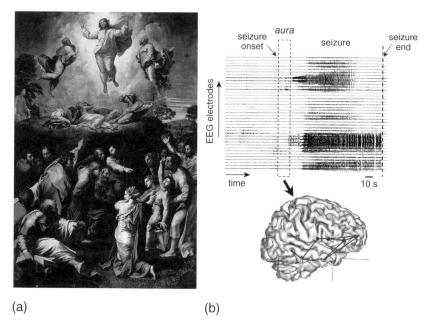

Figure 9.1

(a) The aura experience: Raphael's last painting, called *Transfiguration of Christ* (from the Vatican Museum of Art), depicts the healing of the boy with an epileptic seizure (lower part). It is based on the passage in the Bible: "Teacher, I brought my son to you, because he has an evil spirit in him and cannot talk. Whenever the spirit attacks him, it throws him to the ground, and he foams at the mouth, grits his teeth and becomes stiff all over" (Mark 9:17–18). The painting can be seen as a representation of an epileptic aura in which the patient experiences a transcendent religious event. (b) EEG recordings correlated with the aura. *Top panel*: An example of intracranial EEG recording. The seizure onset is here characterized by the sudden appearance of an ictal discharge out of the ongoing background activity. The epileptic aura is correlated to the initial local activation of a cortical zone in which the seizures start. *Bottom panel*: Transient synchronization of gamma oscillations (frequency band from 40–120Hz) during an epileptic aura (lines indicate statistical significant synchronization; circles indicate intracranial electrodes). This synchronous pattern is here projected on a three-dimensional MRI reconstruction of the patient's brain. We can observe that these phase-locked patterns of brain activity appear spatially widespread, transiently linking different cortical regions. These synchronizations may break into the main line of global normal activities of the brain.

the pathological synchronization of distributed neuronal ensembles around the epileptogenic zone (see figure 9.1b for an example).

Spatiotemporal synchronized patterns are ubiquitous in the normal brain dynamics brain at the large scale (Le Van Quyen 2003). As suggested by several recent observations, much of the nervous system can be viewed as a massively parallel distributed system of highly specialized neuronal processes transiently bounded through a kind of temporal resonance. Gamma neuronal oscillations are thought to provide a temporal structure relative to which the activities of individual neurons are organized in a millisecond timescale across distributed neural networks (Singer and Gray 1995; Chrobak and Buzsaki 1996; Rodriguez et al. 1999; Varela, Thompson, and Rosch 2001). In each moment of time, one singular, specific coalition of neuronal activities becomes dominant and incorporates or discards into its components multiple neuronal activities distributed over both cortical and subcortical regions (Le Van Quyen 2003). These dominant coalitions are dynamically unstable and would therefore be continually "forming, growing, or disappearing" (Crick and Koch 2003). Furthermore, these transient neural assemblies mediate the coordination of sensory and motor surfaces, and sensorimotor coupling with the environment constrains and modulates this neural dynamics. Tononi and Edelman termed this process the "dynamic core," in order to emphasize both its integration and its constantly changing activity patterns (1998).

Following this new neurodynamical framework, several authors have proposed that the transient emergence of dissociable elements in the flow of conscious experiences can be related with the flow of metastable patterns in the subject's neural activity. For example, Tononi and Edelman stress that consciousness is not a thing, but a process, and therefore should be explained in terms of neural processes and global interactions, and not in terms of specific brain areas or local activities. More specifically, they postulate that phenomenal awareness emerges when a certain threshold of neuronal synchronization, especially in the high-frequency gamma range, that has been overcome (for a certain amount of time) by a coalition of neuronal activities, enabling it to become conscious (Tononi and Edelman 1998; Crick and Koch 2003). In the same way, the global workspace theory (Baars 2002) suggests that conscious experience emerges from a nervous system in which multiple processing modules compete for access to a broadcasting capability; the winning process can disseminate its information globally throughout the brain. Following the same idea, the occurrence of experiential phenomena during the aura has been explained in terms of a critical mass of neuronal synchronization in the gamma frequency range (see, for example, Herrmann and Demiralp 2005). The arguments are as follows: if the neuronal synchronizations are suddenly increased in the epileptic zone—for example, due to epileptogenic neuro-chemical disturbances in the brain—this activity is able to reach a level that is normally driven by a specific context for perception and action. As a consequence, these synchronizations may trigger a dominant neuronal assembly that incorporates or discards into its components multiple neuronal activities distributed over other cortical regions. If large enough, these synchronizations may break into the main line of global normal activities and can automatically popup in the patient's consciousness. For example, the patient get the feeling to perceive familiar scenes (faces or voices), because such increased gamma activity is normally only then present, when the sensory input receives feedbacks through its correspon-dence to the memory content. If the feeling of familiarity occurs in isola-tion, it is often inappropriately attached to the present, creating the illusion that the present is like the reenactment of a past situation or event of déjà vu.

Clearly, in this neurobiological explanation of the aura experience, the issue of *how* to relate such patterns to *experience* as a first-person phenom-enon has been left untouched. In particular, several epistemic questions arise: how many different phenomenal states does synchronized gamma neuronal oscillations correlate with? Are gamma oscillations a necessary condition for an aura experience? or a part of the more general condition of wakefulness? Can gamma oscillation appear without an experiential content? These questions have not yet received anything near a satisfac-tory answer from the neuroscientific community. Clearly, the gap between phenomenology and neurobiology is here still very large. What is the right way to conceptualize this relation, and what is the best way to approach it methodologically? In line with the neurophenomenological approach, we believe that mental properties are neither identical to nor logically supervenient on physical properties, yet remain causally related to physical properties.[1] Therefore, a possible strategy to gain some insights about the relations between first-person phenomenological data and neuroscientific data is to create experimental situations in which they reciprocally guide and constrain each other.

9.6 Constructing Neural and Phenomenal State Spaces

The purpose of this section is to discuss a possible formalism based on a state space approach that may give a potentially fruitful way of moving productively from one domain to the other. Although still in its infancy, a theoretical framework to afford this issue has been proposed by the physical-mathematical framework of nonlinear dynamics (Nicolis and Prigogine 1977; Schreiber 1999; Le Van Quyen 2003). In a nutshell, the traditional starting point of all these descriptions consists in conceptualizing the dynamics geometrically, in terms of positions, regions, and trajectories in the space of possible states called a *state space*. The global state of any complex system composed of n independent variables can be geometrically represented by a single point in an abstract n-dimensional state space. This mathematical representation permits a multidimensional view of all the dynamic variables needed to specify the instantaneous state of the system. A sequence of such states followed in time defines a trajectory, also known as the system flow. The shape of the flow is determined by the system's intrinsic dynamics—the force that push the system state in one direction or another, depending on where the current state is located. They can be thought of as constituting a kind of landscape over which the behavior of the system moves. An "attractor" is a trajectory in phase space to which the system will converge from any set of initial conditions. The global shape of dynamical landscape is determined by the so-called order parameters. For autonomous dynamical systems, these global parameters are solely created by the intrinsic interactions among the individual parts of the system. They in turn govern the behavior of the individual parts. The dynamics of these order parameters (by definition, this dynamics is slower than that of the system) characterize how the dynamical landscape is formed and evolves in time.

In a general way, nonlinear dynamics has a natural appeal for neurophenomenology, since it provides an explicit view of neuro- or phenodynamic structures as trajectories in a state space. Further, these descriptions make explicit generic structures of the dynamics, that is, characteristics that are observed independently of the particular variation of the context or the components of the system under consideration. The key feature is here given by the intrinsic dynamical landscape that brings the flow into particular trajectories, depending on where the current state is located. Importantly, dynamic system theory can help us to describe order parameters of dynamics, characterizing how its intrinsic dynamics is constituted and unfolds in time, possibly around some instabilities.

How constructing these neuronal and phenomenal state spaces? Concerning neurosciences, the application of phase-space techniques have prompted an intensive search for low-dimensional deterministic phenom-

ena in brain activities. Prominent among such studies is the research of
W. Freeman on mass action in the nervous system using macro-potential
in awake animals (1975). In spite of some technical difficulties that arise
in the estimation or interpretation of phase space for neuronal signals,
this approach remains simple and has profoundly modified the manner
in which brain processes are viewed and described (Skarda and Freeman
1987; Elbert et al. 1994; McKenna et al. 1994; Le Van Quyen 2003). As a
good example of such a state space approach, color perception has been
described by three-dimensional vectors in a state space where each dimension corresponds to activity rates in one of the three classes of photo-
receptors present in the retina (Churchland 1989). Concerning a state
space of phenomenal states, there are several methodological problems
(Cleeremans and Haynes 1999); a first problem lies in the definition of a
minimal set of subjective variables spanning the main dimensions of an
individual experience. Clearly, an agreement upon the variables defining
the phenomenal state could be a matter of debate. Second, another
problem is the exact determination of the point of time at which a phenomenal experience occurs. In any case, it seems to be impossible to reach
here the same temporal resolution as can be reached in the neuronal
domain, because of the subjective fusion of experiences occurring within
a time window of several tens of milliseconds. Nevertheless, in some controlled situations, several phenomenal variables can be correlated with
operationalized measures in order to be empirically accessible through
these measures. For example, Hobson (2001) has introduced a three-
dimensional state space for the classification of mental states during
sleep and wakefulness.

In the specific case of the epileptic aura, let us briefly sketch the road
of our current state space strategy. As described in section 9.4, three
invariant phenomenological dimensions of the aura experiences can be
distinguished: the level of *arousal* (primary consciousness, from alert
wakefulness to sleep), *selective attention* (focal awareness, clearly defined
experiences within the current center of attention), and *self-awareness*
(consciousness of being in a specific mental state, thoughts about subjective experience). Although exploring inner experience is often not trivially
easy for epileptic patients, these phenomenological variables can be operationally defined in a clinical environment with several days of training
and in the mediation of a skilled questioner (see Petitmengin et al. 2006
for details). Furthermore, in order to be able to capture the dynamics of
experience itself, we used a *measure* of these dimensions. In our current
work, the patients were requested to draw by hand a curve representing

the temporal progression of a given dimension. At a first coarse level, we found that a simple drawing gives a good one-to-one monotonic correspondence between the dynamics of the subjective experiences under investigation and a quantitative variables. The co-variations of the three curves give rise to trajectories in a three-dimensional phenomenal state space. Following this rudimentary phenodynamic approach, we recently used this experimental protocol to investigate one patient with a visual aura (figure 9.2). The descriptions produced by the subject showed some interesting features about the time course of the aura experiences: before the seizure, the patient's level of arousal was almost constantly high, while the levels of focal attention and self-awareness show greater variability, depending on the environmental stimuli. As soon as the seizure begins, the patient's attention was strongly absorbed inwards in a strong self-monitoring and the patient experienced an increase in the level of self-awareness and a decrease in the attention to the surrounding visual world. Furthermore, on the basis of the co-variations of these three dimensions, it was possible to sketch rough generic phenodynamic structures of the transition to the aura in a three-dimensional phenomenal state space (figure 9.2a). In this transition, we observed that the trajectories along the different dimensions appear to become trapped in a basin of attraction in such a way it limits "wandering" on the state space, so "giving directions" to cognitive processes. The flows appear to be strongly contracting, leading to the convergence of trajectories from any particular state. In parallel, we described the corresponding neural domain by analyzing the EEG signals recorded at the same time. We used here three state variables (figure 9.2b): the amount of synchronized delta, alpha, and gamma oscillations. A similar state space approach has been proposed in a recent study showing that global brain states can be mapped into a low-dimensional space based on the degree of local frequency-dependent synchronization (Gervasoni et al. 2004). On the basis of this neuronal state space, it was possible to disentangle the neurodynamic structures of the transition to seizures. During the normal state, because of an intrinsic instability of this dynamics, no stable regions exist in this space, but rather ongoing sequences of transient visits of specific attracting places in a complex pattern of motion. During the transition to seizure, the most frequent trajectories are surprisingly simple in the neural phase space, showing, on average, a tendency to follow a flow converging to an attracting region correlated with the aura (figure 9.2b). As outlined in section 9.5, gamma oscillatory activity is the main electrical signature of this dynamical state.

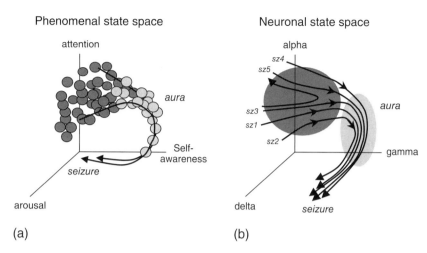

Figure 9.2

State space approach: As an example, phenomenal states (a) and simultaneous neuronal state (b) are characterized by points and trajectories in three-dimensional state spaces. For the phenomenal space, we chose three fundamental dimensions of the aura experiences: the level of *arousal, selective attention,* and *self-awareness*. In this space, it is possible to sketch generic phenodynamic structures of the transition to the seizure. In particular, a large basin of attraction drives the trajectories into a specific state where the dynamics is trapped in a flow to the seizure. In the neural domain, the amount of synchronized delta, alpha, and gamma oscillations have been used to distinguish different neuronal states. The depicted trajectories are estimated from five seizures (here denoted as "sz1" to "sz5") of a particular patient. One can observe that the topological structures of the flows in one space are preserved in the other space, suggesting a homeomorphic relationship between neuro- and phenodynamical structures.

9.7   Homeomorphisms between Neurodynamic and Phenodynamic structures

As illustrated previously, a parallel recording of phenomenal and neurophysiological trajectories could be established using a state space approach, and it should be possible to establish a relationship between the two phenomena by comparing the dynamics of those measures. From our first observations, it seems clear that the point-to-point linear time correlation is insufficient here. Rather, similarities between neurodynamical and phenodynamical structures exist between their *dynamical trends*. Indeed, we observed that during the transition to seizure, if there is a continuous transition between phenomenal states, then there is also a continuous transition between the corresponding neural states, and vice versa. Translated into mathematical terms, this means that there is a *homeomorphic* relationship between the phenomenal and neuronal domain in this situation. More precisely, a homeomorphism is a continuous one-to-one transformation between two sets of states, with a likewise continuous inverse transformation. This implies that topological structures of the flows of trajectories in one space are preserved in the other space. It is important here to stress that these relations are much more than simple passages, but display effective links that may guide and enrich both domains (Thompson and Varela 2001). Under this view, these bridges may be exploited to better explore the changes in the internal structure of the epileptic patterns that co-varied with specific experiences. In particular, some patients may be able to abort their own epileptic seizures by cognitive countermeasures (i.e., concentrating on a specific thought pattern or rubbing the body part involved in the aura). This approach is illustrated by the classic example reported by Efron (1957). His patient had complex partial seizures with a long olfactory aura. A strong olfactory stimulus, such as perfume, could abort her seizures. This stimulus was placed on a bracelet and, a few months later, the sight of the patient's bracelet was substituted for the strong smell. Finally, a cognitive, non-pharmacological control of epilepsy was possible: just thinking about the bracelet was effective in aborting seizure. This study marked the beginning of our understanding of how a "downward" (global-to-local) causation (Thompson and Varela 2001) could be systematically used to alter and inhibit the development of an ongoing seizure. A recent study has shown that detailed self-observation aimed at identifying warning signals and the development of proper countermeasures achieved a significant reduction of seizures and can contribute to improving long-standing intractable epilepsies (Schmid-Schönbein 1998). Again, this cognitive control of epilepsy using the reciprocal causation between a human experience and the brain functioning require further careful conceptual and empirical investigation.

9.8 Conclusion

The aim of the present study was to start developing a new approach to the systematic description of the neuro- and phenodynamical structures of epileptic patients in connection with seizures. We believe that epileptic seizures may represent a privileged window into the complex relationship between consciousness and its neural correlates. Nevertheless, a precise first-person methodology appears here crucial to describe these experiences in a rigorous way. Furthermore, the efficiency of this approach needs a continuous circulation between the field of phenomena revealed by the patient's experience and the correlated field of phenomena established by the neurodynamics. We proposed that this circulation can be based on a state space strategy, revealing homeomorphisms linking the topologies of phenomenal and neuronal states. These homeomorphic relationships between neurodynamical and phenodynamical structures are reminiscent of Müller's psychophysical isomorphism (1896; see also Cleeremans and Haynes 1999). Nevertheless, in strong contrast to the psychophysical proposals, our position is that the relationships between phenomenology and experimental neuroscience are more than passive passages, but display an active circulation that may extend both domains and may lead to a productive co-determination. For example, progress in neurosciences will motivate a more finely detailed phenomenological description developed under the regime of phenomenological description, and a more detailed phenomenology will contribute to better define an empirical research program. Furthermore, this co-determination may lead to new kinds of therapy for epileptic patients.

Acknowledgments

We thank Dr. A. Lutz (United States), Dr. C. Petitmengin (France), and Dr. J. P. Lachaux (France) for reading the manuscript and for helpful comments.

Note

1. That A and B are "causally" related means that "A is linked to B by a law." This doesn't mean at all that A is reducible to B, or B to A. And this link is symmetrical (if A is linked to B, B is linked to A).

References

Baars, B. J. (2002). The conscious access hypothesis: Origins and recent evidence. *Trends in Cognitive Sciences* 6:47–52.

Baars, B. J. (2003). How brain reveals mind: Neural studies support the fundamental role of conscious experience. *Journal of Consciousness Studies* 10 (9–10): 100–114.

Chrobak, J. J., and Buzsaki, G. (1996). High-frequency oscillations in the output networks of the hippocampal-entorhinal axis of the freely behaving rat. *Journal of Neuroscience* 16:3056–3066.

Churchland, P. (1989). *A neurocomputational perspective*. Cambridge, MA: MIT Press.

Cleeremans, A., and Haynes, J.-D. (1999). Correlating consciousness: A view from empirical science. *Revue Internationale de Philosophie* 3:387–420.

Commission on Classification and Terminology of the International League Against Epilepsy. (1981). Proposal for revised clinical and electroencephalographic classification of epileptic seizures. *Epilepsia* 22:489–501.

Crick, F., and Koch, C. (2003). A framework for consciousness. *Nature Neuroscience* 6:119–126.

Dennett, D. (1991). *Consciousness explained*. Boston: Little, Brown.

Depraz, N., Varela, F., and Vermersch, P., eds. (2002). *On becoming aware: Steps to a phenomenological pragmatics*. Amsterdam: Benjamins.

Efron, R. (1957). The conditioned inhibition of uncinate fits. *Brain* 80:251–261.

Elbert, T., Ray, W. J., Kowalik, A. J., Skinner, J. E., Graf, K. F., and Birbaumer, N. (1994). Chaos and physiology: Deterministic chaos in excitable cell assemblies. *Physiological Reviews* 74:1–47.

Engel, A. K., Fries, P., and Singer, W. (2001). Dynamic predictions: Oscillations and synchrony in top-down processing. *Nature Reviews Neuroscience* 2:704–716.

Engel, J. (1989). *Seizure and epilepsy: Contemporary neurology series*. Philadelphia: F.A. Davis Company.

Fisher, R. S., Webber, W. R., Leeser, R. P., Arroyo, S., and Uematsu, S. (1992). High-frequency EEG activity at the start of seizures. *Journal of Clinical Neurophysiology* 9:441–448.

Freeman, W. J. (1975). *Mass action in the nervous system*. New York: Academic Press.

Gallagher, S., and Brøsted Sørensen, J. (2006). Experimenting with phenomenology. *Consciousness and Cognition* 15 (1): 119–134.

Gervasoni, D., Lin, S. C., Ribeiro, S., Soares, E. S., Pantoja, J., and Nicolelis, M. A. (2004). Global forebrain dynamics predict rat behavioral states and their transitions. *Journal of Neuroscience* 24:11137–11147.

Gloor, P. (1990). Experiential phenomena of temporal lobe epilepsy. *Brain* 113:1673–1694.

Herrmann, C. S., and Demiralp, T. (2005). Human EEG gamma oscillations in neuropsychiatric disorders. *Clinical Neurophysiology* 116:2719–2733.

Hobson, J. A. (2001). *The dream drugstore: Chemically altered states of consciousness.* Cambridge, MA: MIT Press.

Hurlburt, R. T., and Heavey, C. L. (2001). Telling what we know: Describing inner experience. *Trends in Cognitive Sciences* 5:400–403.

Jack, A., and Roepstorff, A. (2003). Trusting the subject (volume 1). *Journal of Consciousness Studies* 10:9–10.

James, W. [1890] (1981). *The principles of psychology.* Cambridge, MA: Harvard University Press.

Jirsch, J. D., Urrestarazu, E., LeVan, P., Olivier, A., Dubeau, F., and Gotman, J. (2006). High-frequency oscillations during human focal seizures. *Brain* 129: 1593–1608.

Johanson, M., Revonsuo, A., Chaplin, J., and Wedlund, J. E. (2003). Level and content of consciousness in connection with partial epileptic seizures. *Epilepsy & Behavior* 4:283–288.

Le Van Quyen, M., and Petitmengin, C. (2002). Neuronal dynamics and conscious experience: An example of reciprocal causation before epileptic seizures. *Phenomenology and the Cognitive Sciences* 1:169–180.

Le Van Quyen, M. (2003). Disentangling the dynamic core: A research program for a neurodynamics at the large-scale. *Biological Research* 36:67–88.

Levine, J. (1983). Materialism and qualia: the explanatory gap. *Pacific Philosophical Quarterly* 64:354–361.

Logothetis, N., and Schall, J. (1989). Neuronal correlates of subjective visual perception. *Science* 245:761–763.

Lutz, A., Lachaux, J. P., Martinerie, J., and Varela, F. J. (2002). Guiding the study of brain dynamics by using first-person data: Synchrony patterns correlate with ongoing conscious states during a simple visual task. *Proceedings of the National Academy of Sciences of the United States of America* 99:1586–1591.

Lutz, A., and Thompson, E. (2003). Neurophenomenology: Integrating subjective experience and brain dynamics in the neuroscience of consciousness. *Journal of Consciousness Studies* 10:31–52.

McKenna, T. M., McMullen, T. A., and Shlesinger, M. F. (1994). The brain as a dynamic physical system. *Neuroscience* 60:587–605.

Müller, G. E. (1896). Zur Psychophysik der Gesichtempfindungen. *Zeitschrift für Psychologie mit Zeitschrift für Angewandte Psychologie* 10:1–82.

Nicolis, G., and Prigogine, G. (1977). *Self-organization in nonequilibrium systems.* New York: Wiley.

Penfield, W. (1959). The interpretive cortex: The stream of consciousness in the human brain can be electrically reactivated. *Science* 129:1719–1725.

Penfield, W. (1968). *The cerebral cortex of man.* New York: Hafner.

Petitmengin, C. (2006). Describing one's subjective experience in the second person: an interview method for the science and phenomenology of consciousness. *Phenomenology and the Cognitive Sciences* 5:229–269.

Petitmengin, C., Baulac, M., and Navarro, V. (2006). Seizure anticipation: Are neurophenomenological approaches able to detect preictal symptoms? *Epilepsy & Behavior* 9:298–306.

Petitot, J., Varela, F., Pachoud, B., and Roy, J.-M., eds. (1999). *Naturalizing phenomenology: Issues in contemporary phenomenology and cognitive science.* Stanford, CA: Stanford University Press.

Rodriguez, E., George, N., Lachaux, J. P., Martinerie, J., Renault, B., and Varela, F. J. (1999). Perception's shadow: Long-distance synchronization of human brain activity. *Nature* 397:430–433.

Rudrauf, D., Lutz, A., Cosmelli, D., Lachaux, J. P., and Le Van Quyen, M. (2003). From autopoiesis to neurophenomenology: Francisco Varela's exploration of the biophysics of being. *Biological Research* 36:27–66.

Schmid-Schönbein, C. (1998). Improvement of seizure control by psychological methods in patients with intractable epilepsies. *Seizure* 7:261–270.

Schreiber, T. (1999). Interdisciplinary application of nonlinear time series methods. *Physics Reports* 308:1–40.

Singer, W., and Gray, C. M. (1995). Visual feature integration and the temporal correlation hypothesis. *Annual Review of Neuroscience* 18:555–586.

Silberman, E. K., Sussman, N., Skillings, G., and Callan, M. (1994). Aura phenomena and psychopathology: A pilot investigation. *Epilepsia* 5:778–784.

Skarda, C. A., and Freeman, W. J. (1987). How brains make chaos in order to make sense of the word. *Behavioral and Brain Sciences* 10:161–195.

Taylor, J., ed. (1958). *The selected writings of John Hughlings Jackson.* New York: Basic Books.

Thompson, E., and Varela, F. (2001). Radical embodiment: neuronal dynamics and consciousness. *Trends in Cognitive Sciences* 5:418–425.

Tononi, G., and Edelman, G. M. (1998). Consciousness and complexity. *Science* 28:1846–1851.

Traub, R., Whittington, M. A., Buhl, E. H., LeBeau, F., Bibbig, A., Boyd, S., et al. (2001). A possible role for gap junctions in generation of very fast EEG oscillations preceding the onset of, and perhaps initiating, seizures. *Epilepsia* 42:153–170.

Varela, F. (1996). Neurophenomenology: A methodological remedy for the hard problem. *Journal of Consciousness Studies* 3:330–335.

Varela, F. (1999a). The specious present: A neurophenomenology of time consciousness. In *Naturalizing phenomenology*, ed. J. Petitot, F. J. Varela, B. Pachoud, and J.-M. Roy, 266–314. Stanford, CA: Stanford University Press.

Varela, F. J. (1999b). Steps to a science of Interbeing: Unfolding the Dharma implicit in modern cognitive science. In *The psychology of awakening: Buddhism, science and our day to day lives*, ed. S. Bachelor, G. Claxton, and G. Watson, 71–89. New York: Rider/Random House.

Varela, F., Lachaux, J. P., Rodriguez, E., and Martinerie, J. (2001). The brainweb: Phase synchronization and large-scale integration. *Nature Reviews Neuroscience* 2:229–239.

Varela, F., Thompson, E., and Rosch, E. (1991). *The embodied mind*. Cambridge, MA: MIT Press.

10 Language and Enaction

Didier Bottineau

Linguistic behavior is orienting behavior; it orients the orientee within his cognitive domain to interactions that are independent of the nature of the orienting interactions themselves.
—Maturana and Varela 1980, 30

How can I tell what I think until I hear myself speak?
—C. S. Peirce

10.1 Toward an Enactive Outlook on Language

Describing language in the light of the enactive paradigm is a most challenging issue: language is to be reconsidered in terms of sensorimotor interactions with an environment in which both the individual and the environment are modified, in which not one,but several individuals are involved—an experience that is, all in one, that of the speaker and hearer at the instant of uttering or thinking; that of the child developing into an adult through social intercourse; that of the tribe turning to a full-fledged civilization; and that of the linguist interfering with his object of scrutiny by linguistic means. As a selection has to be made, this chapter will primarily focus on the immediate experience of languaging, and secondarily broach more general subjects like acquisition and evolution.

The proposals of the enactive paradigm (Maturana and Varela 1987) bring about a whole range of novel views that upset firmly established dichotomies: the subject and the object, the innate and the acquired, the interior and the exterior, the physical and the mental (Stewart 1996). This model destabilizes what Foucault (1966) called the epistemological basis of our knowledge, and challenges traditional scientific protocols.

In a recent book, Keller contends, in a purely Whorfian way, that the lexicon in use plays a major role in shaping a culture's thinking and provides ready-made conceptual frames out of which any discourse is to be assembled, restricting intellectual creativity to recombining preestablished stereotypes (2006). Keller's view can be interpreted as an application to language of Varela's view of experience: once the subject/object dichotomy is revoked, the traditional distinction between individual experience of an external object and scientific "objective" scrutiny of an "objective" object is made redundant or at least questioned. The cliché has it that linguistic science is the only discipline to study its own object, language, using it as an instrument in the form of lexically marked concepts and discursively expressed descriptions and theories. But *talking* about language *using* language will inevitably *alter* the language, to the extent of making many words redundant, among which the words *language* and *word* themselves. Either linguists have *faith* in the existence of abstract entities such as *words, sentences, morphemes, nouns, verbs, subjects, objects, phonemes, structures, syntax, meaning,* their *evolution,* the *transmission of information,* the *acquisition of a language by an infant, representation, expression, communication,* and so on, and make a consistent use of them; or they reject them, with two possibilities: coining ever more abstract concepts, or looking back on experience to restore a phenomenological contract between the empirical basis and the theory. In a subversive fashion, the enactive questioning will consist in suggesting that all of those concepts correspond to no pregiven reality but are enacted by the linguist experiencing the linguistic environment he is studying and, above all, such as his own perception has reorganized it: is the NP/VP pair actually experienced, does it have any consistency other than on paper? A supposedly descriptive grammar is a self-ignorant formalism, and a deliberate formalism should be clear about the nature of the experience it enacts. For the same reason, it seems hazardous to postulate the existence of a conceptual architecture that gets revealed by linguistic forms in the process of communicative externalization, unless the individual and collective history and experience of the communicative process play a central role in the formation of the model[1]. Linguistic models are based on an astonishingly poor samples of data with regard to the actual complexity of the multimodal processes experienced by speakers, and the enactive outlook aims at including this diversity in the modeling process.

The linguist is not the only one to enact metalinguistic experiences. Children are known to anticipate morphological systems by analogy (Slobin 1996): *to bring, brang, brung.* Some French learners of the English language produce such utterances as *he can played football*: their past experience in romance languages invites them to enact a universally inflected infinitive, making the perception of the uninflected verb stem unacceptable in their system of anticipations, which causes them to override the evidence by superimposing a "rule." And in the absence of any available inflection in the English system, they will simply retrieve the homophony linking the infinitive and the past participle in French: *jouer/joué*; hence the English infinitive will sound like *played*. This cannot be explained in simple terms of analogy or overgeneralization. In so doing, the erring beginner is actually enacting an experience of the infinitive that is motivated by previously formed anticipations leading to decision and action upon passive perception; coming up with a personal pattern is so much easier than sorting out the perceptual chaos.

As for the speaking community, the way it enacts its own language is monitored by the standards set by the academic authorities and vulgarized by the schooling system: a language is an ensemble of morphological features (a lexicon, an inflectional system, morphosyntactic patterns) governed by explicit rules; one may learn and obey them and/or create new ones characterizing rebellious communities rejecting the authority of parents and institutions symbolized by the norms. For example, French *verlan* (from *l'envers* "reverse" reverted into *vers-l'en* > *verlan*) consists in coining new words by (1) inverting the order of syllables, (2) deleting the nucleus and coda of the final syllable (apocope), and (3) opening the vowel in the new final syllable: *femme* > **mefa* > *meuf*. Teenagers are outraged when their parents violate their own symbolic authoritative status by using such words or even worse, coining new ones as I did (for "priest," *curé* > **récu* > *reuc*). As soon as a *verlan* word is firmly established and perceived as a standard, it may be reinverted to renew the rebellious shift: *Arabe* > **Beara* > *Beur* > *Reubeu* (with epenthetic *e*). In some cases, the young reinvent words that had long existed in previous generations and fallen out of use, which they will never acknowledge.

In the introduction to his recent *Grammaire du Gallo*, whose title refers to a romance regional language spoken in the eastern half of French Brittany, Patrik Dreano (2006) declares that his initial goal was merely to collect instances of how he and the natives of his region actually spoke, on the basis of recordings of spontaneous conversations and storytelling by native subjects of varying generations, dialects, and origins. However as the corpus developed, he became aware of an emerging general consistency and diversity in the data, which made him turn the initial project into an extensively documented comprehensive grammar including the lexicon, phonology, morphology, syntax, and expressivity; scavenging through the data resulted in enacting the language, that is, turning the dim awareness of the *parler* into the proud identity of an actual *langue* by producing a grammar, a seminal representation that inevitably sets itself as a reference, and therefore a standard. From a sociolinguistic viewpoint, a *langue* may be considered as a heterogeneous, multidialectal *parler* that has turned into a unified, consistent system through the selective and organizational decisions required by an academic description, which leads to institutional prescription and the emergence of a consensus mustering all social classes and domains of activity; a *langue* emerges as an autopoietic dynamic system (Maturana 1980) in the process of detecting and ruling its own collectively constructed experience. It is not an individual entity or self-organized system (Oudeyer 2006) endowed with a transmissible genetic identity, but it does form a structured dynamic phenomenon involving a boundary or "membrane"—the general coherence of lexical and morphosyntactic patterns, the phonological and prosodic system as homogenized human behaviors—that delimitates what is recognizable as belonging to the system (sounds, words, correctly formed sentences) or not. Dreano's introduction is remarkable in that it autobiographically summarizes the enactive metalinguistic experience that he went through in a personal and historical shortcut, along with the growing awareness that by publishing the book, he was actually spreading the word throughout the potential community; and indeed Gallo rural native readers are surprised when, leafing through the book, they realize that their own *parler* does comprise as many consistent and expressive features as French, all the more so, as they would normally not have regarded Gallo as a language.[2]

10.2   The Act of Speech, the Interlocutors, and the Linguist

Modeling language in the light of the enactive paradigm entails some methodological choices that highly constrain the heuristic approach. First, one must eliminate all theoretical prejudice regarding the general categories: the traditional objects of linguistics (*langage, langues, parole,* grammar, etc.) cannot be taken as scientific objects of scrutiny as long as they have not been redefined in terms of dynamic sensorimotor experience (McNeill 2005): language, like any form of living cognition, is embodied (in the sense of Erard 1998, Wilson 2002, and Ziemke 2003). Strikingly enough, the very notion of *experiencing language* is commonly found among literary writers or critics, (especially of poetry and drama), pathologists, and psychoanalysts, but much less so among linguists (Gardiner [1932] 1951). Second, this requires an empirical selection of how language is actually experienced by speakers in real life: the act of speech in all its forms, *languaging*. This heuristic funneling will not restrict the domain to the empirical data, but all abstract general concepts will be rooted in the dynamics of living. And third, the linguist must hold fast to her own position: languaging is an interactional process. When he thinks he observes his object, he is effectively interacting with the linguistic environment, that is, (1) playing the role of the interpreter of the linguistic data and (2) *languaging* a discourse about it using his own lexicon and grammar. So this section is about how the immediate experience of languaging—the act of speech— may be enacted by the linguist.

At least three basic types of languagings may be experienced (an inventory that is not to be found in the introductory section of manuals and treatises): *introverted languaging*, experienced in the form of verbalized mental discourse; *extraverted vocal languaging*, or speaking; and *extraverted manual languaging*, or writing and signing. Other marginal communicative forms of manual languaging, which will not be described here, involve various sensorimotor experiences such as whistling,[3] beating drums, and sculpting smoke clouds, all of which have possibilities and constraints of their own.[4] Foot languaging does not seem to ever have emerged,[5] but one may imagine it as potentially experienceable in the form of tap dancing. The preceding typology will be used because it is convenient, but it is inaccurate for two reasons:

1. Languaging, like any experience, is multimodal, and cannot be reduced to any one of the media involved. In vocal languaging, the voice is experienced as the prevailing feature, the one playing the major role in the elaboration of meaning. But this does not preclude the role of head, body, and hand gestures, and spatial positioning and eye contact, known as the kinetic nonverbal modalities of conversation.[6]

2. Those categories must be mapped against the interactional pattern involved. Intraverted languaging is executed by a single languager. Extraverted vocal and sign languaging is simultaneously experienced and concerted by at least two languagers mustering in the same perceptual environment in space and time, which can be artificially expanded by technological means (Bruner's *amplifiers*; see Bruner 1983), both spatially (telephone, etc.) and temporally in the case of recordings. And finally, graphic manual languaging involves a stabilized alteration of the material environment, a piece of writing, that can bridge a spatial and temporal gap between the writing and the reading, no matter whether the latter is carried out by the same person or by a different one.

The preceding elements are of course trivial and are commonly overlooked. Yet they show how heterogeneous the languaging experience is, how difficult it is to construct a unified theory of language out of this diversity. Most models happen to be constructed out of an extremely narrow, if not adulterated, selection of empirical features. When speech is said to *express one's thoughts*, the stress is laid on the communicative role of voicing or writing, but nothing is said about why intraverted speech requires languaging too and how it reflexively *impresses* individual thinking.

10.2.1 Acoustic Languaging

Vocal utterance is a process in which a "speaker" embarks upon affecting the atmospheric environment by somatic means: the air's molecules are made to vibrate following oscillatory patterns that can be controlled by articulators including the vocal chords, the tongue, the different parts of the oral tract, and, occasionally, the nasal cavity. This eventful action is perceived by all human beings present: (1) by the hearer(s), whether they are the addressees or not (Coursil 2000), who will match the auditory inputs with all relevant other experiences items acquired through perception (the speaker's general appearance and attitude, the situation, the psychological contexts, the cultural references and knowledge, whether shared or not); (2) by the speaker him- or herself, who happens to detect his or her own activity both directly and indirectly: by the tactile proprioception of his or her muscular activity, and by the auditory perception of his or her own acoustic output. In short, if the speaker causes the hearer to construe meaning, the speaker will also cause him- or herself to follow the same procedure, so that voicing amounts to a physical process of semantic mental co-alignment. "Communication" should not be modeled as a one-way arrow as in Bühler's ([1934] 1990) and Jakobson's empirically selective models, but rather as a retroacting radial propagation that will constantly affect the consciences in presence and be reprofiled in real time according to transitory effects and actions: a binary structural loop in which two living bodies' cognitive experiences are alternatively controlled and synchronized through somatic interference with the shared medium.

In other words, linguistic cognition involves cortical, muscular, and environmental dynamic events shared by individual beings in a continuous experiential shell forming a *social body*. In this process, vocal interplays synchronizing mental dynamics amount to forming *complex transitional synapses between conscious selves at the intercortical level using acoustic signals as transmitters across the atmospheric medium* (Bottineau and Roulland 2007), with a dramatically enhanced level of complexity: whereas the "physics" of the chemical synapses is simple (one given chemical transmitter with a stable structure), that of the vocal synapse is infinitely versatile (lexical, morphosyntactic, prosodic variation); whereas the semantics of the former is simple (a binary 0/1 alternative between firing or no firing), that of the latter is infinitely open.

This synaptic coordination of mental dynamics by linguistic verbal processes causes both individual and collective consciousness (experience, knowledge, culture, concerted actions, *civilization*) to emerge and gives cognitive-biological substance to the notion of social body, whose spatial boundaries and temporal extension and continuity will vary with the profile of the communicative pattern (number of participants, technological amplifications, synchronization of the alternations or recordings). A large-scale social body (in time and space) such as a linguistic, ethnic, religious, cultural, tribal social body may be enacted as a continuous entity precipitated—in the chemical sense—by discontinuous speech acts experienced by each individual member joining in the incorporative, emerging process.

10.2.2   Optical Languaging

If one is to define a piece of writing rigorously, including the way in which it is experienced by the writer and the reader (including the chapter-writing linguist), a text is a light-reflecting (or emitting) surface whose visible profile has been altered by manmade gestures (from carving to dictating through writing and typing) in a way that can be perceived visually and converted into a *reading*, that is, a simulation of what actual voicing might have been had the human participant shared the same medium in space and time.[7] Whereas talking affects the medium the time that the voicing lasts, writing affects the environment more durably by introducing a permanent alteration and makes it possible to extend, amplify, and multiply synaptic connections between consciences over spaces and times spanning extensions far beyond the reach of human voice and even individual life: if talking is basically local, writing is universal, although both can be amplified (Bruner 1983) in space (telephone, television, radio, the Internet) and time (oral and written recordings and multiple copies).

Writing systems correlate varying aspects of recorded experience with the act of reading: letter and syllabic systems associate the visual bottom-up input with a vocal prediction of the acoustic counterpart, as in the reformed syllabic alphabet of present-day Korean, a vocal and cultural writing that causes the reader to enact human vocal output in the first place, and, from there, the semantic counterpart in general experience;

ideogram systems (Chinese keys and first-generation Egyptian hieroglyph-
ics) associate the optical unit with the experience of the "object" and not
that of any human vocal output: the writing system is targeted at the
nonvocal part of physical experience. Some hybrid systems combine the
two approaches like Japanese ("kanji" ideograms for lexical units and com-
pounds vs. hiragana syllabic characters for grammatical morphemes, with
kanji allowing for contrasted historical readings anchored in the Chinese
and Japanese vocal traditions known as *kun* and *on* interpretations); lexical
reference to natural experience is paired with the optical marking of the
natural sensing, the sensory side of the enactive interface, and grammatical
combination is associated with the graphic marking of vocal, cultural
output (the motor, controlled side of the enactive interface). For English- or
French-reading learners of written Chinese and Japanese, the challenge is
to explore those undocumented, exotic enactive interfaces. Some writing
systems based on letters are *linear*, like the roman alphabet, and tend to
blur the borders between syllables; other nonlinear systems focus on the
syllable, either phonetically (hiragana) or semantically (Chinese); some
systems assemble syllable around vowels by peripheral nonlinear extensions (Mongolian) and some linear letter-based systems underline syllables
by masking their central component, the vowel (Arabic). So to model a
writing system is both to decipher the nature of the vocal or nonvocal
experiences the writing gesture is connected with and to understand how
the very format of the gesture (in terms of linearity and fragmentation) is
reciprocally intertwined with its meaning.

As a result, reading is never exclusively linear, even in linear systems,
and involves the mapping of visual perception with a system of predictions
(involving lexical selections, grammatical order, etc.) acquired through
experience and training. Moreover, the reader experiences meaning to
emanate not from a physically present biological agent (the speaker), but
from a stabilized material object, the piece of writing, left by some remote
and dimly envisaged agent, the writer. Meaning acquires material autonomy, the word becomes a kind a fetish, nonhuman sources may be envisaged (with far-reaching consequences for religions, especially if based on
partially cryptic writing systems concealing the vowels and calling for
interpretation), and humans are willing to fight over objective notions and
truths crystallized by the written word, forgetting that the original word
is no more than a mind-guiding piece of voicing. Stabilized pieces of
writing lead to the formation of versatile social bodies with spatial boundaries that materially fluctuate in time with personal connections with the
support, but that are enacted by the community as stabilized assemblies

known as *readership*. Barring oversimplification, writing is essentially *public* and speaking *private*, and both can be extended by technological artifacts and social rituals (public meetings).

Interestingly enough, the English lexicon reminds the reader of the sensorimotor experience of writing in the very morphological structure of the corresponding words. In the verb *write*, of Germanic origin, the onset /r/ is spelled *wr-*, a consonant cluster that has long been identified as an *ideograph* connected with the notion of a circular movement of torsion, as in *wrist, wring, wrath, wriggle, wrestle, wrought, wreck, wreak,* and maybe *work* and *word*.[8] And in the onset of the stressed stem of *scripture*, the consonant cluster *scr-*, of romance origin, is connected with a phonosymbolical imitation of the scratching sound of the writing as in *screech, scratch, scrub, scrawl, Scrooge, scrum, scribble,* etc. (some of them of Germanic origin); those words are morphologically categorized into a selected and relevant sensorimotor class of experience, and writing is mainly categorized as a type of movement and marginally as a movement-caused sound. The two enactive traditions were introduced by two of the ethnic and cultural contributors of lexicon in English (the Romans, the Saxons) and hybridized, randomly or coherently, by their mixing offspring. Semitic languages are known to display feature matrices of consonant clusters motivated by the common multimodal experience associated to the voicing and the notion (Bohas 2006). Whether a neural theory substantiates these correspondances is another debate (Feldman and Narayanan 2004; Gallese and Lakoff 2005).

10.2.3   Reflexive Languaging

Inner discursive, linguistic thinking is a serious challenge. It is essentially *intimate* languaging (as opposed to *private* and *public*), in that it is not meant to transitively affect any identified target other than one's own self, reflexively. It consists in interpreting one's own verbal production and actively become aware of some construed, enacted representation—in the dramatic sense, not in the diplomatic one—that could not be achieved through any other means than languaging. The difficulty is that the function of transitive speech, externalizing one's preestablished thoughts, is in blatant contradiction with that of reflexive speech, making up one's ideas by verbal means; this paradox is best summed up by the following quotation: "Language is the formative organ of thought. Intellectual activity, entirely mental, entirely internal, and to some extent passing without trace, becomes through sound, externalized in speech and perceptible to the senses. Thought and language are therefore one and inseparable from each other" (von Humboldt ([1836] 1988, 54). Do Austin's (1962) and Searle's (1969) classifications of speech acts apply to introverted speech? It would seem that they do not, as they are based on a communicative conception of discourse requiring a clear-cut distinction between an addresser and an addressee, even in the case of soliloquy.

As regards action, the experience of languaging can be located between two extreme situations. One is when the thinker speaks with himself, that is, fully voices the whole utterance, causing himself to recapture it through proprioception and audition and interpret it. The other is when the speaker totally refrains from any single detectable motor action during the process of mental wording and contents himself with an intimate experience of what the utterance would sound like if it were actually voiced, which includes word and sentence stress, tone units, melodic patterns, and so on. And in between, the commonest of all, is the case when a speaker unwittingly "motors" some barely detectable movements of the lips, jaws, tongue, and other members ordinarily involved in private, vocal (multimodal) languaging. Admitting this simple experiential insight into the empirical basis of languaging has far-reaching consequences.

First, it implies that in all cases, intimate thinking is a sensorimotor experience in its own right, no matter how and how much the private sensorimotor interferences with the perceivable environment are inhibited. Recent neural imaging has revealed unexpected connections between perceptual and motor areas even in cases when vocal production is not involved, and recent studies in infants have shown these connections to be active long before the articulatory system is operational: regardless of whether one does or even can speak, the processing of acoustic signals in linguistic terms is correlated with the controlling of the muscles that will produce them. Should this be interpreted as a hint of the inborn character of the coupling? An alternative hypothesis is that in its experience of adult languaging the infant jointly sees and hears adults speaking and develops relevant sensorimotor matchings acquired through perception, and that these pave the way for future production without requiring immediate practice at the time of their emergence. Vygotsky (1962) hypothesized (against Piaget 1972) that the child's egocentric speech, far from vanishing with development, would functionally and structurally split between specialized internal discourse and external speech. This illustrates the difference between a direct feedback effect and an enactive structural loop, in which a relevant system of anticipated decision and action is synthesized out of a selective and reorganized set of empirical data that may not involve the execution of the action in question.

Second, it entails that in the languaging experience in all its forms, even the innermost intimate pondering, the elaboration of meaning can never be envisaged out of the realm of bodily action: "linguistic cognition" coincides with the sensorimotor experience of the voicing and hearing of the speech act, and strictly confining this structural coupling within the motor-tight intracortical neural compartment turns out to be virtually impossible—let the reader just try to look as if he or she were not reading these lines while still doing it and he or she will feel the impossibility of not "somatizing" somehow the innermost neural dynamics of languaging. Languaging is embodied. This calls for more explanation.

At any time in the history of human thinking about language, spanning from Presocratics and Cratyle to present-day models and including other traditions (Arabian, Indian, Chinese), there has always been what may be loosely called an *enactive bias:*[9] yes, the lexicon and the morpho-syntax do somehow derive from pragmatic experience and reflect sensations phonosymbolically or organize one's mental categories according to experienced entities (the Sapir-Whorf hypothesis: Sapir 1951; Whorf 1956), actions (Langacker 1987) and encounters or confrontations involving force dynamics (Talmy 2000), all of which are recorded in lexical forms, cognitive patterns underlying semantic representations (Pottier 1992), abstract grammatical processes (Guillaume 1964), elocutive or interlocutive configurations (Givon 1994; Coursil 2000; Douay 2000), lexical distributions (Whorf 1956), and culturally formed phrases and metaphors (Lakoff and Johnson 1999). The idea here is not to deny that somehow language (as general know-how) and languaging (as a singular doing) reflect bodily experience of the world by the subject, or to suggest that all this is not commonplace. It is to suggest that embodiment *stricto sensu* is not the binary, mental, symbolical copy of experience, and that metaphors do little to illustrate embodied languaging—they underline how the mind acknowledges the body's personal life in a kind of dialog: metaphors underline how general knowledge is formed through action (cf. the role of practical or sensorimotor intelligence in children's cognitive development according to Piaget 1972), but they do not show how language in general, even if not metaphorical, is a "cognogenetic experience." By definition, languaging is embodied in that experiencing the sensorimotor coupling of voicing and hearing is instrumental in the construction of thinking at every level of the experience—intimate, private or public, and this is what the enactive paradigm has to bring in beyond the traditional embodiment described by the symbolic cognitivist paradigm.

10.3 Meaning

Languaging (the act of speech) is understood here as an intimate, private, or public sensorimotor process, *la parole*, enabling all participants to construct some form of mental event or scene. This section is about the kind of meaning achieved through languaging, an enactive experience that could not be achieved by any other means. Before turning to the respective roles of lexicon, morphology, syntax, and prosody, a first approach to meaning is required.

10.3.1 Languaging as an Alternative Medium

In private languaging, an addresser causes an addressee to come up with an original piece of experience. Not that the "idea" should be new or original—*Buses are always late, aren't they?*—most of our daily production is cliché. A speaker will make a hearer become aware of something (real or not), that is, enact a piece of sensorimotor experience through languaging, either because he or she has seen from the hearer's attitude that the "real fact" has not been taken into account and does not bring about the expected intellectual, emotional, or pragmatic reaction (Sperber and Wilson 1995), or because the speaker computes that introducing this piece of experience might serve his or her purposes, directly or indirectly (seducing someone else), and so on. Speaking does not *refer* to the world; it *causes an experience* that happens to coincide or not with the narrow situation or the larger reality such as it is enacted, and has to be mapped against the environmental medium, including the psychological environment.

As long as the hearing or reading of the sentence lasts, the interpreter's awareness, will, and action, in one word, dynamic experience, is entirely concentrated on plotting out (neither *computing* nor *representing*) the sensorimotor enaction gradually emerging from the lexical inputs as they are matched with one another, following a constructional procedure specified by the morphosyntactic input. The reader of these lines has probably become unaware of the table he or she is sitting at, if any, unless it is too low, causing an experience of discomfort that may override the reading. In one word, speaking is an alternative cultural medium that can override the natural medium and be utilized to control enactive experiencing instead of letting the physical world "decide" on what should be lived by humans. By "polluting the atmosphere" with acoustic waves, the emitter will make all receiving souls present focus on experiencing the forefronted acoustic interference at the expense of the backgrounded unperturbed medium, including the table.

Example 1   In a famous comic strip for children, *Rupert*, the layout falls into two parts: above are four pictures representing an adventure, like the teddy bear catching a kite, accompanied by a small caption in the simple present tense, *he catches the kite*; and below is an autonomous paragraph narrating the story. The caption is not in the continuous present *he is catching the kite*, because it does not refer to or describe the picture standing for actual experience; it causes the young reader to experience the catching of the kite by interfering with the text as a parallel and alternative experience to interfering with the natural environment symbolized by the picture. The caption is the verbal alternative in the presence of the picture, and the narrative below is the verbal alternative in its absence, as the layout compels the reader to lose sight of the figurative drawings. The child is thus gradually taught to disconnect the verbal process from the nonverbal one and learn how to enact worlds through alternating media. Other strategies will teach the distinction between fictional worlds and downright lie.

Example 2   Black humor is the dark side of the farce. In this statement, several polysemic units (*Black*), references (*Dark Side*: Star Wars, Pink Floyd), substitutions (*force/farce*) cause the interpreter to enact a semantic chain reaction, a kind of mental fireworks (one *cracks* a joke) in which diverging trains of thought are explored simultaneously, echoing and feeding one another in proliferating structural loops, implying irreconcilable evaluations of the speaker's attitude ranging from genius to delirium through playful but serious subversion, until all hell breaks loose. If there were no sensorimotor "fuse" to interrupt the runaway plottings, any good joke might trigger sensorimotor crises comparable to epilepsy. At some point, the victim bursts out laughing: an exhausting, air- and energy-consuming spastic periodic emotion generating tremendous tactile and auditory signals that will momentarily suspend all interpretation, all conversation, all verbal thinking—just try to think anything while you laugh, just try *even to remember to try*. Laughing is a periodic spasm overriding runaway sensorimotor experiences including the plotting of a joke and physical tickling. Alternative vocal spasms, characterized by other frequencies and the absence of periodicity, namely the cries of physical and emotional pleasure or pain, play analogous roles in attempting to master similarly dangerous, exceedingly intense nonverbal events. The very existence of a sensorimotor antidote for runaway verbal plotting underlines the coexistence of rivaling media: a laugh, a body-made respiratory and vocal spasm, will disconnect the verbal medium by mere physical exhaustion and bring about a gradual restoration of the natural medium before social verbal interplay can be restored.

10.3.2 Defining the Import of the Languaging Medium

The verbal event affects the producer (intimate languaging) and/or the "consumer(s)" (private and public languagings). In the latter case, the producer may be causing the "consumer" to enact an intended experience following the relevant ritual lexical and morphosyntactic coupling. And as the sentence makes the consumer become aware of a world that has not (or could not) be captured through experience, this world is intrinsically an original one and need not be structurally different from the experience that might be enacted through direct interference with the natural, non-verbal medium. If one centers languaging on communication, one need not hypothesize that linguistic meaning is any different from natural meaning in direct experience.

Very different is the case of intimate languaging. If I see and hear my dog barking, I will recognize both the being and the action and have no difficulty in identifying the class—this is a dog, my dog, whose name I know, and what he is doing is to bark, a loud cry they do when happy, angry, afraid, and so on. All this can be executed without any linguistic help, and I do not need to name the dog and the barking to identify them as such. However, something in this experience remains unsatisfactory—the barking annoys or frightens me, I do not detect its origin, I cannot anticipate its end, and I do not see what I have to do, whether I should start investigating into its cause—an intruder in the garden?—or incite the dog to put an end to it. In a nutshell, *enaction is stalled and action is paralyzed, and comes to a standstill*: I have failed to enact the natural medium. In reaction and with the positive purpose of restarting the experiencing dynamics, I launch the alternative enactive process, languaging: *Why on earth is the idiot barking?* In so doing, I actively take hold of the enactive problem of the cause (*why*) and the displeasure (*on earth*) involving the identities that I have recognized and enacted in this perspective (*the idiot*: because he is annoying me) that which have to be mentioned not because wording them is required for identification, but because they are involved in the enactive stalling and may be verbally enacted in the perspective of the problem they have raised: a structural loop. This might seem to relate with the pulsional basis of phonation (Fónagy 1983) and the Thwarting Theory of the origin of language (Salzen 2006), except that this model is not exclusively centered on the producer and gives the interpreter's reception a major role (Coursil 2000). In talking,

I make myself focus on and become fully aware of what really matters, the anxiety, excluding all other pending matters, and I start acting upon myself by verbal means in order to proceed toward the determination of the relevant decision to be made and course of action to be undertaken; if consciousness is devoted to action in the world rather than computation (Bruner 1990; Shanon 1993), languaging is used to launch or relaunch action in the face of an enactive stalling or obstacle in natural experience, which includes the social encounter with other selves. Private and public languaging will trigger or concert actions including other selves, while intimate languaging will install personal experience. Action is here taken in the sense of general sensorimotor living and cognitive experience; it includes physical doings as well as intellectual learning, sensations, emotions, judgments, and the like.

10.3.3 How Languaging Catalyzes Action

A word like *dog* is a reiterated vocal action over the manifold experiences of the animal (both direct or indirect) in an individual's life and in social context from the infancy into adulthood. Using the word an additional time will serve as a behavioral trigger connecting the immediate experience with the long-running encyclopedic knowledge about it, acquired through all previous "verbal encounters" and forming a general network of hierarchized features known as notion or prototype (depending on the semantic theory considered: Culioli [1981] 1990); the word dynamically re-presents (re-stages) an historical excerpts of individual experience organized into a category (involving perceptual properties, human actions, cultural values, emotions, etc.) that can be mapped against the immediate situation causing a problem: I have seen dogs bark in a whole range of situations, so maybe the solution for this one is to be found among those. To speak is to command vocally the connection between the immediate and recorded experiences by reproducing the controllable sensorimotor experience, the word, used as a token or common denominator (rather than *symbol*): the lexicon has to be reconstructed from a phenomenological point of view, and is connotational rather than denotational (Maturana 1978; Kravchenko 2004).

The deliberate experience of voicing and hearing of the word, either intimately or privately, is the key to unzipping the encyclopaedic file required for installing enaction through further verbal and nonverbal action. The sensorimotor action of voicing is used as a corporal levy catalyzing that of recollecting an extensive network that could not activate itself alone: literally, *languaging amplifies intelligence* and enables a shift from a network of local spatial-temporal correlations to an enormous lif-escape trespassing the boundaries of immediate experience. *In so doing, languaging is instrumental in constituting reflexive consciousness:* it consists in a general course of actions enabling to match immediate, *actual experience* against the encyclopedic knowledge of sensations and actions retained from previously recorded *virtual experience.* Language makes it possible to convert what is experienced in the here and now into an occurrence of something more general. It is not simply that "this dog" is compared with "other dogs" but that "my experience of this dog" is set against "my previous experiences of this or other dogs." Thus, merely voicing the token *dog* will mechanically induce the distance-taking effect (*Verfremdungseffekt* in the Brechtian sense) and cause the voicer to put immediate and distant livings in perspective—"ceiving" discrete instances of one's living self both as a background (virtual experience) and salience (actual experience); "*déjà vu*" entails "I remember now that I was there."[10] The reflexive self is the one that emerges through languaging out of this contrast between the reflecting and reflected consciousnesses. The continuous entity represent-ing the constant linking of two occurrences of analogous experience is separated from the varying behaviors and events (situations) in which it is perceived to be engaged: comparing the stretching cat and the meowing cat will sort out the unvarying parts of the cat and the varying attitudes. As Bickerton (1990) pointed out, no language in the world has simple words mixing entities and attitudes. By definition, languaging, a vocal comparator of experiences, will stage the difference between the continu-ous and the variable, paving the way for lexical categorization (nouns, verbs) and syntactic distributions (nominals, predicates).

The goal of lexical semantics is to define the nature of what is remi-nisced by lexical units and how those programs are formed in personal experience. That of morphology is to define the nature of the connective procedures forming the resulting network. That of syntax is to model the ritualized temporal sequence of vocally marked intellective operations fol-lowed in a given language in this assembling process. That of prosody is to couple the mechanistic dimension of the preceding items with the personal choices about any of them at any moment in the general psycho-logical context. This involves the syntactic steering and the emotional coloring of the vocal motoring (whether private or intimate).

10.4   The Lexicon

The word has been defined as a vocal rite commanding an extended and ever-growing network of heterogeneous, hierarchized recorded experiences in a hybrid architecture that can be mapped against immediate experience to retrieve relevant decisions and plans, and, on occasion, to make them evolve or add new ones. By definition, the word *cat* does not point to the animal that I may or may not be encountering when using the word (except if the prosody clearly directs the syllable to the cat);[11] it revives the network of knowledge acquired in my past experience of cats. This is why determiners and deictics are required to establish the link (if any) between this ensemble and ongoing experience (*a cat, the cat, this cat*), and why it is possible to envisage a cat freely with no connection with the situation, as I am doing in these lines. A lexical unit is *concrete* when it tokenizes a recurring set of experiences that can easily be retrieved by perceptual means without using the word, like a *cat*. It is *abstract* if the collection of events it tokenizes is not perceptually federated by a center that could be retrieved directly, like *society*; words may refer to notions that cannot be treated as entities or events, but to sensations, emotions, and abstract categories born out of highly heterogeneous experiences with no material core. This is due to the fact that the network of experiences out of which the notion is born is not only personal, but also collective and constructivistic in its genesis: the notions of *cat* and *probity* do not stem from *my* experience, but from that of all the persons who used the word publicly enough to have a say in the kind of situation recorded in the word's usage.[12] As a result, this collection is atemporal, in that the personal history of the personal encounters with the thing is blurred, to be replaced by a hierarchy of relevant features organized in terms of frequency, reciprocal links and contextual necessary conditions to be activated (as in Rastier's interpretive semantics; see Rastier 2009).[13] This collection may turn out to be inconsistent, or even contradictory, paving the way for polysemy,[14] but the very principle of the word is that the vocal token is used as an operator of reminiscence to federate disconnected sets of experiences, originating the nominalistic illusion that any word does revolve around a firm conceptual core.

Metaphors, for example, are usually associative and based on analogy (*a bluebottle*), but they may also appear as downright misnomers (French *bouse* "cow dung," for a car) by which the interpreter is forced to redefine his favorite possession in the terms imposed by the speaker (which can only be done in unequivocal situations requiring a demonstrative or a possessive rather than an indefinite article: **une bouse > cette bouse, ta bouse*). Such distortions, if reiterated, are recorded by all speakers in their individual experience, so that the deviant uses of the word are inscribed in the notional network along with the "undistorted" features: transgression is included in the standard. For this reason, it is impossible to draw a general semantic theory on the basis of a simple subject-world relation: what is at stake is a *world-based subject-subject relation* and, ever since the very "beginning," the lexicon has been determined by the conditions and intentions motivating its use—so that the individual-centered theories of conceptual metaphor (CMT) and blending (BT) (Grady, Oakley, and Coulson 1999) in which individual representational operations overrule social intercourse are highly suspicious.

The way in which the various languagings of the fluctuating lexical units in a given language can be taken as an empirical basis for raising the conventional enactive questioning: how does one describe the sensorimotor experience of the motoring, that is, the acoustic disturbance as it is enacted by the coupling of the vocal output with the tactile and auditory input? And by correlating this description with the interpretive effect experienced by the competent and intuitive linguist in the process of languaging the object of his own study, what can one infer about the architecture of the network[15] of recorded experience that is controlled by the vocal key? Does one really isolate cultural prototypes, or is the format of the "prototyping" universal? Typological diversity strongly suggests that this is not the case and the enormous body of data made available by typological description makes it possible to undertake a systematic modeling of the accurate profile of the structural loops characterizing what nonvocal experience is tokenized by what vocal experience, and how the profile of the latter and the architecture of the former foster each other in the long-term process of personal experience and language formation (rather than acquisition).

The analysis of the properties of the lexical word, both formal and semantic, play a major role in orienting the question about its origin, or, more accurately, the word-forming process in human experience. Current models state that language was originally imitative (Merlin Donald [2001]: human actions mimicking the properties of the object), deictic (Corballis [2003]: silent gestures pointing to objects or animals), emotional (expressions of frustration, effort, pleasure, pain, disgust, fear, anger, etc.). All we can do is guess; there is no theoretical reason why one should decide that one approach is more relevant than any other in the first place. Any repeatable vocal action that happens to correlate with mimicking, pointing, or reacting is a potential candidate for tokenizing: if a caveman walks on a snake, gets bitten and yells, the event may be remembered in any relevant form ranging from the imitation of the yell to that of the hissing animal slithering away. In *Tlön, Uqbar, Orbis Tertius*, Borges [1940] 1956 fancied a language coined by idealist philosophers in which no stable word referred to objects like the moon—any relevant description of sensation and emotion had to be coined in the spur of the moment, making the word an unpredictable, fluctuating *haiku*. Second, there is no reason either why there should have been an equation between words and things in the first place: if the yell tokenizes the whole event, it is neither a noun nor a verb, but a sentence, that is, a single syllable connected with a whole event involving both actors and action. Only later does the yell get specialized in referring to one of the event's components: the biting or the shouting, the man or the snake; in Wolof, *niao* is not the meowing of the cat, but the animal itself, tokenized by the imitation of one of its most striking audible attitudes: a *symbol* in the etymological sense. The syntax of some languages like Inuktitut and Mayan is suggestive that the sentence is not actually composed by assembling free lexical units, but, on the contrary, that specialized lexical cores tend to emerge out of complex clusters decomposing entire scenes or events into fragmentary subparts. In much the same way, bilabial syllables uttered by infants are associated with breastfeeding, the milk, the mother, and only later does *mum* become associated with one feature of the network, the mother herself, while other vocal candidates are proposed by the surrounding adults for the other elements; a vocal token may get increasingly attached to one of the features of the global scene that originally motivated it.

10.5   Syntax

Linguistic typology identifies word orders in which the prototypical sentence is asserted in a given language: the verb is initial in Irish, medial in English, and final in Basque. Most languages have a prototypical pattern ordering lexical units (excluding pronouns): SVO, SOV, VSO, and so on. This raises the question of the relevance and universality of the categories used for the description, and it falls short of elucidating how syntactic categories marked by morphemes and/or location are experienced by the languager, formed in the experience of languaging, and what role they play in assembling meaning.

Syntax is an algorithm collectively and culturally formed through personal experience in the course of individual experience and collective history of language forming, learning, using, and teaching. This algorithm is an ordered sequence of actions: grammatical relations are to be reconstructed in real time in the process of interpreting sentences (Valin 1981). According to a variety of traditions, the *agenda* (literally, "the actions to execute") of the prototypical English sentence schedules a nominal section known as the subject or NP and a verbal section known as the predicate or VP.

Together, they constitute the *orthosyntactic agenda*, the core of the syntactic program, the general network of the languaging unit. This pattern is doubly versatile and can vary in two ways, globally and locally. Globally, it may be complemented by optional expansions before, between, and after the two steps of the orthosyntactic agenda; the *parasyntactic addenda*, that is, adverbial phrases. And locally, each step of the agenda is to be executed by a versatile local network whose expansion ranges from the lexical singleton to the entire clause: the subject is realized either by a pronoun, or an NP, or a nonfinite clause, or a finite clause introduced by a complementizer. In the same way, the predicate is either saturated by an intransitive verb, or expanded by a transitive verb, a whole range of complements, and so on. The parasyntactic addenda are ruled by the same global versatility at the local scale: an adverbial clause is saturated by an adverb or expanded by a prepositional phrase, a nonfinite or a finite clause introduced by a conjunction. If expanded and complex enough, the execution of the subject in the orthosyntactic agenda may incorporate an internal parasyntactic addendum in the form of a relative clause or be suspended by an insertion; the same incorporative or suspensive diversions may be improvised within a parasyntactic addendum (e.g., a relative clause within a finite temporal adverbial clause). The interpreter of the utterance is trained in the practice of tracing the syntactic route in real time just as the speaker is trained to profile it, so that dialog can effectively alternate individual roles in semantic orienting, with metasyntactic prosody anticipating directional decisions for both speech and interpretation (for an enactive analysis of prosody, see Auchlin et al. 2004).

Example In Basque (*Euskara*), an ergative and agglutinative non-Indo-European language spoken in the Basque country (the western tip of the Spanish and French Pyrenees), the prototypical sentence begins with nominal and adverbial arguments and ends with the verb. For each argument, the *lexical phrase* falls into two sections, a notional phrase receiving all notional elements (adverb, noun, adjective, demonstrative) suffixed by a functional phrase receiving all grammatical specifications (case markers, determiners, number); the functional phrase is attached to the last lexical element present (the noun, the adjective or the demonstrative): *[((oso)) andre (polit)]-a* "[((very)) woman (pretty)]-the."

Adverbials are obtained by suffixing notional phrases with one or several spatial or relational case markers forming "simple" cases (the inessive, the allative, the ablative, the genitives, the instrumental, and so on: *etxera* "to

the house") and complex cases (the prolative, the comitative, the destina-
tive, and so on): *etxerakoan* "in the of to house" > "while going home."
Nominal arguments of the verb receive a simple case marked by no or one
suffix: the absolute (A, -Ø), the ergative (E, -*k*) and the dative (D, -*i*). It
can be demonstrated that this specific morphological trio is in fact a grammatical distributor of gestaltian positions coupling notional phrases with
functional roles, namely a *base* (the obligatory and unmarked absolutive),
a *dynamic peak of instability* (the optional ergative, marked like a kind of
genitive in relation to the absolutive base) and a *trough of stabilization* (the
dative, similarly optional and marked). This results in four argumental
configurations (A, EA, DA and EDA) in which the unmarked absolutive is
enacted as a site, a patient, a cause or a trajector depending on whether it
is isolated or accompanied by the dominating ergative, the dominated
dative or both: *emaztea*^{A} "the wife" (isolated base); *senarrak*^{E} *emaztea*^{A} "the
husband, the wife" (agent, patient); *emaztea*^{A}, *senarrari*^{D} "the wife, to the
husband" (cause, experiencer); *senarrak*^{E} *lorea*^{A} *emazteari*^{D} "the husband,
the flower, to the wife" (source, trajector, target). In this system, valency
converges on the uninflected absolutive NP, with the optional and inflected
ergative and dative NPs connected with the former like genitival or adjectival adnominals: (E-*k*) > A (Ø) < (D-*i*), that is, [(peak) > base < (trough)] or
[(+) > 0 < (–)].

As regards the VP, the final finite form incorporates a series of bound
pronouns retrieving the previously coupled notional/functional NPs, thus
echoing by multiple agreement the nominal, absolutive-centered argument structure. This agglutinative conjugation either revolves around the
lexical verb stem (*daramakiot* "it-bring-to him-I" > "I bring it to him") or
accretes into an autonomous final auxiliary (devoid of any lexical root),
while the verb stem receives aspectual suffixes: *eramango diot* "bring-geni-
tive it-to him-I" > "I'll bring it to him." In this system, (1) verbal valence,
incorporated in the form of the bound pronouns by multiple agreement,
tends to adjust to the initial nominal configuration (even if some minor
verbal categories do tend to export their own requirements), and (2) placing
the same notional argument in two distinct functional roles is prohibited
as in **senarrak*^{E} *senarra*^{A} the husband, the husband (agent, patient), so that
reflexive double agreement is strictly banned, albeit morphologically pre-
dictable and interpretable (Bottineau and Roulland 2007). The complete
sentence comes out as follows:

Senarrak	emazteari	lorea	emango	dio
Husband-the-E	wife-the-D	flower-the	give-of	it-her-(he)

"The husband will give the flower to his wife."

The interpretation of the system is the following (Bottineau 2005a, 2005b): sentencing in Basque consists in producing separately an analysis and a synthesis of the "scene": a *dramatis personae* or *cast* (with the husband starring the source, the flower the trajector, the wife the goal) in which notional actors (the husband, the flower, the wife) are analytically coupled with functional roles (the peak, the base, the trough). This results in the formation of one to three arguments: three, in this example. In the verb phrase, the plot consists in recombining them (the agglutinative multiple argument *dio*) in the context of the time, mode and dialogical specifications (marked by other affixes: *zion* in the past, *lioke* in the conditional) around the verb stem (if it is free, *daramakiot*) or in an emancipated "auxiliary" (if the verb stem receives aspectual parameters, *emango*).

This seemingly mechanistic algorithm is to be relativized by the ortho-syntactic, parasyntactic, and metasyntactic couplings; not all arguments need be explicitly stated, some may be fore-fronted or back-grounded for specific motives, the verb may "disagree" with the nominal argument structure (passive intransitivization, antipassives, allocutive inclusion), all of which generates the same amount of local and global versatility as in English. This piece of algorithm operates both locally, in each part of the clause, and globally, over the whole sentencing process. This could be analyzed in terms of Robert's fractal grammar, possibly an emerging formalization of structural loops.

Each language is characterized by a dynamic versatile orienting algorithm of the kind exemplified earlier; those syntactic models illustrate the way in which languaging, according to Maturana 1978, is the reciprocal coordination of actions between orienters and orientees, with both functions constructively carried out by both participants.

10.6   Forming Lexical and Grammatical Semantics

10.6.1   Forming Notions and Relations: An Authentic Example
The following excerpt was actually uttered by a mother playing with her two-year-old daughter at a French skiing resort:

Regarde! C'est de la neige. Regarde! C'est blanc, c'est froid, ça colle, on peut en ramasser et en faire une boule, et la jeter sur papa, tiens, regarde, poum! [Look! This is snow. Look! It's white, it's cold, it sticks, you can pick some an make a ball, and throw it at Daddy, look, splash!] And they all burst out laughing.

A traditional vision of the meaning of *est* in "c'est blanc" and so on is that the verb *refers* to a continuous state, a transitional or permanent property, or attaches a unit to an ensemble. But what is overlooked is the general architecture of this piece of collective experience in which the playing and the languaging are intermingled. Before this passage is given, the child is not supposed to have even begun to detect the snow, let alone identify it as such, let alone remember its "noun." In the aftermath of the utterances, the child has been given the opportunity, all in one, to experience the snow in all its sensorimotor dimensions (the color, the tactile effects, and what one can actually do with it on account of those properties), and each of these elements has been matched with a vocal sensorimotor event in the form of the very words *snow, white, cold, sticks, pick, throw*: the child has been presented (in Brentano [1874] 1944's sense) with the cultural properties of the snow such as the word, a reproducible external memory, records them.[16] The simultaneous creation of the semantic and lexical fields are part and parcel of the same bundle of experiences in which no theoretical reason should justify that one draw a clear-cut distinction between the verbal and the nonverbal. Semantic features and phonological ones are both sensorimotor predictions formed in the course of long-running experience and training; the articulatory and auditory features should be placed among the semantic features of the notion rather than separated because they are of the same nature—a position that is reminiscent of *phonology as a human behavior* (Diver 1979).

This is also true of the abstract verb *be*, whose connective value is experienced whenever the child is confronted with this kind of situation, and of the demonstrative *this*, which is associated with a deictic windowing of the child's attention oriented by the mother's bodily movements. The child needs no previous knowledge that *ce* is deictic, nor does he even have any inborn cognitive "deictic functional slot" to be filled (*parametered*) by a language-specific marker.

In the present day, nobody could decisively demonstrate that postulating an inborn universal grammar is a downright error, but it certainly is an extremely costly, implausible, and unnecessary hypothesis in an historical scientific context in which the exploration of nonvocal and vocal couplings (even before birth) is only beginning, paving the way for modeling how cognition is embodied in experience.

10.6.2   The Network-Forming Value of Grammatical Operators: Some Examples

In Basque, each notional phrase like *etxe* "house" is suffixed by a functional phrase like -*a* "a/the." The orthosyntactic pattern, at every level, consists of identifying one or several notions and then incorporating them in the forming network by means of a relation marked by the one or several postpositions involved in the process. -*a* validates the correlation between the notional network tokenized by the vocal experience of the word and nonvocal experience of the situational reality; *etxe* applies to both the memory of experiences past and to the newly added present experience (including, precisely, memory as a present experience). This is not symbolical, it does not mean that there is an iconic correspondence linking the "represented" abstract house with an identifiable one, but that the same network of heterogeneous features is co-activated by the vocal experience of the voiced word and the nonvocal experience of "reality"; -*a* enacts a convergence, the present merger of experiences retrieved from different moments in personal history. When -*a* is absent, immediate experience is excluded from the converging process, which only mobilizes recorded history.

In Guillaumean terms, this is called *représentation* and *actualisation*, a binary model with a strong enactive bias. The core value of Basque -*a* is the convergence of experiences acquired in the past and in the immediate present concerning the set of features tokenized by the immediately preceding notional unit (or set): (1) *etxe* restores the network (by intelligence amplification), (2) -*a* restores the converging process. This is how the intimate, private or public orientee is made to "network" meaning and obtain a semantic event—something experienced as real happens to be a house, or, more precisely, in the opposite order; the previously experienced set of events vocally and conventionally tokenized as *etxe* happens to zero in on some fragment of immediate experience, -*a*. -*a* may seem to point to an external reality (referential semantics), but what with the definition of experience, medium, and enaction, it should be clear that what -*a* stages cannot be the binary pointing of an object by a subject, but a merging, unifying process.

As regards the role of -*a* in the orthosyntactic algorithm, analysis/synthesis in Basque, the "determiner" provides the answer for the problem raised by the notion: "*etxe*, house. (Yes, I know what this is, so what, here and now? Yes, house here and now, -*a*.) Some authors anchor syntactic patterns in narrative procedures and semantic ordering in cognitive constructional processes carried out by the speaker (Guillaume 1964; Adamczewski and Delmas 1982; Cotte et al. 1993; Rousseau 2005); others investigate the hypothesis that they may fossilize or sediment ritual dialogic patterns involving alternating turns of speech at different phrasing scales in the sentencing process (Givon 1994; Douay 2000; Bottineau and

Roulland 2007). Although Langacker's (1987) cognitive semantics is not primarily devoted to morphemes as the markers of orienting procedures, there do emerge occasional analyses which unmistakably involve this kind of approach.[17]

In the case of Basque, the question/answer ritual—which normally spans two sentences spoken successively by two interlocutors, not one—seems to have been embedded in at least three increasingly concentrated levels in the orthosyntactic algorithm:

1. At the global level of the clause, in the form of the analysis/synthesis pattern discriminating the argumental cast and the verbal plot: x is E, y is A, z is D, > (implicit intermediary question: so that, knowing each actor's respective roles, how do I plot their encounter in my experience?) > answer for the purported question: verb + all specifications.

2. At the local level of each argument, the notional phrase, by summoning an amplified network of recorded experiences forming a notional network, raises the question of how the latter relates with other networks (summoned by other notional phrases) and immediate experience (both vocal and nonvocal), which is the same thing (as notional networks are summoned by words). The answer to this question is provided by the functional phrases (postpositions) comprising case markers (connections linking phrases with other phrases: the ergative with the absolutive, the inessive and instrumental with the verb, etc.), and determiners and quantifiers (connections linking recorded networks with the environment of immediate experience at large).

3. In-between, on each side of the clause (NPs and VP, in the analytical and synthetic phases), the lexical cast (nouns, verb) is interconnected by the grammatical network (postpositions, bound pronouns and temporal, modal, and allocutive markers).

All this is far too complex for illustration, but the principle remains that at every stage, the binary algorithms are federated by an intermediary implicit question raised for the orientee by the first segment and answered by the second, which amounts to saying that the algorithm, as a general rule and whatever its position, composition, and range, sediments and embeds the dialogic experience of asserting, questioning, and answering, making the ritual of each languaging act the prediction of the experienced narrative structure of the social intercourse. In this respect, Basque appears to be narratively iconic in that the [statement-(question)-answer] procedure experienced in the alternating [speaker1-(speaker2)-speaker1] dialogic sequence is recorded in the grammatical pairs staging the alternations [orienter-(orientee)-orienter] in the same order at the global, intermediary, and local levels (clause, phases, and phrases).

In contrast, the French and Breton languages forefront the determiner *la maison, an ti*: in both cases, the answer concerning how the notion is to be interconnected with the general assembly is provided even before this question is actually raised by the lexical specification of the notion. Basque anticipates the need for an answer; Breton and French anticipate the question itself in the act of predetermining the answer, which is an example of how a structural loop originates predictive decisions in the phrase and sentence planning of interpretation. This holds true for prepositions, auxiliaries, and conjunctions at the scale NPs, VPs, and clauses, all of which are forefronted in Breton and French, back-fronted in Basque.

The orthosyntactic algorithm sediments the dialogic experience (incorporates in it the languaging experience at all its levels by the structural looping)—what O. Fischer calls "diagrammatic iconicity (Fischer and Nänny 2001)."[18] But the algorithms are language-specific; one of the factors of variation is the range of the prediction (the answer or the question preceding it), and the dialogic pattern may not be universally definable in the terms of questions and answers (a track unexplored as of now). The network-forming value of a grammatical morpheme cannot be understood outside the frame of the orthosyntactic algorithm defined as a languaging rite sedimenting the dialogic experience.

10.6.3 Submorphology
The operational value of a lexical or grammatical marker is not supposed to be found in the phonological features making up the phonemes involved in the syllable(s): *dog* tokens a set of experiences, but there is no obvious analogical connection between the non-vocal ones (the barking, the drooling, the fretting, and so on) and the vocal one (the wording). In binary terms, the arbitrary word is not phosymbolic in that the sensorimotor experience of the linguistic unit is not akin to that of the nonvocally experienced "thing"; in unitary terms, the vocal features forming the linguistic experience incorporated in the general network are not akin to the other features originated by direct interaction with the phenomenon. All that federates the network is repeated co-occurrence.

In the same way, a grammatical morpheme is not supposed to be *suggestive* of the operation to be carried out, *reminiscent* only, just as there is no resemblance between Proust's tea and madeleines and the *Piazza San Marco*. And yet! Onomatopoeia is based on an imitation of nonvocal experience by vocal action, in some cases implying multimodal synesthesia. In many languages,[19] the lexicon is at least partially underlain by internal, submorphological consistency (phonesthemes, ideophones, *racines*, *matrices*, *étymons*) that may at its own level be either "arbitrary" (fully contingent, like *sp* for centrifugation in English) or, in some cases, possibly motivated (like *st* for immobilization in English), at least in a very remote past, and psychologically relevant (Bergen 2004). Lexical classifiers in Bantu languages are similarly organized in a consistent way (Reid, Otheguy, and Stern 2002).

The semantic effects of this property of the lexicon have long been recognized (Wallis [1653] 1969). A reasonable hypothesis in this domain is that for the efficiency of the languaging performance, it is profitable to elaborate a limited number of submorphemes that are used as experiential classifiers of lexical networks, and even more so if one happens to come up with a combination of phonemes whose sensorimotor experience coincides with that of the nonvocal features of the assembly: suggestion is more powerful than reminiscence, and cultural convergence around this fact will make imitations easier to convene upon than random couplings (which neutralizes the traditional opposition between natural motivation and social convention). So if imitation is by no means necessary in diachronic lexical emergence, it is a useful catalyzer for the individual as well as the community; this fits well with the data, as although human language is widely documented to be unmotivated, there tends to emerge locally remarkably organized subsystems—islands of order in oceans of chaos—which are strongly suggestive of an underlying ordering principle.

The same holds true for grammatical morphology. The word *be* is by no means vocally suggestive of its combinatory role in the orthosyntactic train. But in English, there exists a finite paradigm of morphemes including *the, this, that, there, then, thus, though*, all of which begin with *th-*, and all of which signal the retrieval of something immediately available from memory, whose category is differentiated by the rest of the operator (*there*: a locus, *then*: a moment, *the* + N: a notion, *this* and *that*: situated nonvocal experiences that may be specified by a notion, etc.). The submorpheme *th-* manifestly alternates with *wh-* signaling the unavailability of any relevant preestablished knowledge in working memory and in the field specified (*who, which, what, where, when, why*). On top of the submorphological pair, some operators do alternate as wholes (*where/there, when/then, which/this, what/that*), revealing other semantically relevant phonological minimal pairs (*i/a, s/t, r/n*) that happen to have long and massively been evidenced in similar functions in altogether unrelated linguistic types

(Atlantic, Bantu, Altaic, Semitic, Caucasian languages) and across diverse grammatical categories (Robert 2003).

While some pairs appear to be purely un- or demotivated (how should *th-* be suggestive of memory?) in the current synchrony at least, others are easy to connect with their operational value: *i*, a sensorimotor experience of conjunction and contact, is frequently used as an operator for the same relation between semantic phases in the algorithm (examples are by the thousands in natural languages). *a*, enacting vocal disjunction and distance in aperture, is apt to operate the same kind of semantic connection. *s* for (sibilant fricative) continuity, *t* for late (plosive) interruption (as in Toussaint's 1983 model), *k* for precocious interruption, *r* (apical or velar) for forceful launching (*passage en force*), *n* for (nasal) by-passing (of the oral tract) as in negation in Indo-European languages (but also Japanese). In a theoretical frame known as cognematics (Bottineau 2003, 2008), I have proposed a model according to which, within the formal morphophonological constraints of voicing (syllable structure, phonemic compatibilities) such as they have evolved to the present day (cf. the great vowel shift in English), there does exist, in grammatical morphology, a strong subterranean trend or force dynamics presiding over a quest for relevance in phonological selection and placing in the formation of morphemes; cognematics appears to be at least highly compatible with motor theories of the origins and current workings of language (Studdert-Kennedy and Goldstein 2003; Allott 1995; Lieberman 1991).

Morphosemantic connections are not necessary: (1) not all morphemes need be componential, and (2) not all phonemes need have been selected for such a relevance. A strongly catalyzing factor is when a limited number of markers form a finite paradigm in which they can echo one another both vocally and semantically, forming a kind of virtual, discontinuous poem in which family resemblances are easy to detect, contrary to what happens in the larger lexicon—except in local semantic-lexical fields, precisely because they are federated by the same principle. In short, the very idea that in local subsystems the sensorimotor patterns of voicing may be directly utilized to ensure semantic connections is not to be censored for the sake of safeguarding the orthodoxy of randomness. This appears as an extremely deep case of embodied cognition in which the sensorimotor action controlling the rhetorically distinguished voicing and meaning actually fully coincide in one single process, entirely revoking binary symbolism. The process is not a ruling principle for all lexical and grammatical units, far from it; it is only a potential principle that will emerge only when viable, that is, productive and efficient, or at least relatively more so in relation to existing strategies.

10.7   Perspectives

This chapter has not discussed some crucial topics. The enactive bias to
be observed in ancient and modern linguistic thought has been merely
alluded to, but not explored. One should itemize the various features
making up the enactive paradigm (autopoiesis, allopoiesis, action, structural loops, sensorimotor experience, the medium, embodiment, life,
cognition, anticipation and decision, individuation processes, membrane,
self, boundary, and the revocation of binary thinking and wording: innate/
acquired, interiority/exteriority, subject/object, stable/dynamic, perma-
nent/transitional, symbolism, etc.), assess whether they do form a self-
sustaining paradigm in which all components are organically attached
and mutually necessary, or whether they form a consistent but relatively
loose collection of concepts with no real gravitational centers as some
critics suggest. This is essential for the linguist (and any discipline indeed)
as the qualitative variation of the "enactive bias" in models can be explored
in terms of which component of the enactive model is retained, in isolation or in collaboration with others, and incorporated in a preexisting
frame that may be compatible or not, depending on whether one operates with a loose or strict construction of the enactive paradigm. The
perfect example is embodiment and force dynamics in symbolic models,
probably the most obvious topic regarding the linguistic/enaction
connection.

Other related questions are the acceptability of some of these concepts
in a field studying a living behavior rather than the being itself. Indeed,
the living is the action, and the loop is looped: the enactive approach will
inevitably reform the "object" and the "subject" of scientific enquiry into
a medium including the discourse. A reader relying on symbolical orthodoxy may have judged some terms metaphorical, which amounts to rejecting the structural loop mutually affecting the language and the languaging,
the reduction of binarism. If the notion of individuating autopoietic viable
development is accepted for social bodies, it is applicable to the emergence
of dialects, literary genres, conversational rites, stylistic conventions, gram-
matographies, linguistic theories, and formalisms.

As regards the question of the origin of language, everybody feels concerned with the topic and has something to say on the matter—the social
link par excellence, the "sport" turning the growing individual into a full-
fledged cultural person. The question, of course, is ill-worded, and some
misunderstandings are to be removed. Language is not an object; it cannot
be acquired. The forming of personal languaging is part and parcel of the
forming of the person, just as walking, jumping, or flying. In the same

way, but at a different scale, the forming of a community's social languaging is part and parcel of the cultural forming of the tribe. Through continuous structural looping, a whole range of heterogeneous actions with
diverging functions gradually accrete, in a self-individuating autopoietic
emergence, into what we presently enact as a unified function. Why should
language have *one* origin, or be based on a single primitive perceptual or
agentive channel, such as vision in Givon 1994, or connections between
biological and cognitive evolution (Leroi-Gourhan 1964), or tool-manipu-
lating and language-sequencing (Greenfield 1991)? Why should not the
bow-wow theory and all the others coexist separately in their own experiential domains, or be linked in a looser connection that falls short of
deserving the name *language* such as we enact it today? Why should not
iconographic engravings have emerged from prehistoric painting separately from the articulated shouts, to merge later into what one now calls
writing? Why should not the various social functions (expressions of
thwarting, threat, seduction, order, emotions, religious spelling, etc.) have
emerged through unrelated channels, vocal or not, to precipitate later into
a unified system? The prevailing controversy opposing mono- and polyge-
netic views might well turn out to be irrelevant: for it to be valid, language
has to be unified in the first place, no matter whether it "appears" in one
or several places, simultaneously or in succession.

And is language a unified phenomenon by any other means than the
very word that crystallizes the cluster of individual, social, instantaneous,
eternal, human experiences? Is it a property of the being—a competence
emanating from biological evolution—or of the species organizing itself
into co-allied assemblies (Dessalles 2000)? Does the question not arise from
the very word? How many languages do not have any such word, and is
the question universally relevant in human thinking? Language looks
like the Amazon rather than the Nile—to find the origin, seek the sources.

Language is clearly a question of vocal action tokenizing experiential
events and actions in real life. When the ape comes across the leopard, it
does not respond by a specific, recording- and reminiscence-triggering yell
that may be later reproduced in the absence of the predator but in the
presence of the conspecifics; the human being does. This amounts to a 0/1
opposition in which an insignificant change in behavior, yelling or not
yelling at important times, will change the species' destiny forever: either
the animal does not create vocal tokens for the diversity of experience, or
it does, and this slight change may either result from evolutionary continuity, or stem from a purely accidental change in habits that turned out to
provide good results.

It is very likely that language has never been simple; it may have suddenly emerged in a kind of critical change when some individuals embarked upon a new behavioral pattern, the vocal accompaniment of experience, with some individuals performing it efficiently (in terms of selection for mating for example, and then transmitting the habit to the offspring), others not. It may also have gradually shifted from the voicings of one's emotions and feelings (pain, fear, desire, anger) to that of the external realities causing them (predators, food, mates) in a kind of hypallactic shift. One cannot know how long it took to eliminate the individuals who did not participate in the change, but one may hypothesize that for one given individual, the change was not gradual: either one did not vocalize, and used zero words, or one did, and tokenized as many experiences as appeared relevant in real life.

If it was so, the sheer number and diversity of voicings raised the question of syntax right at the start: how did two tokens relate with one another, how did the receivers tackle joint occurrences? As for the cognitive capacities required for the efficiency of vocal tokenizing, especially in terms of memory and centralizing the diversity of heterogeneous experiences under one label, either the brain was somehow ready for the change, or it got trained to become competent in this task, stimulated by the recurring occurrences of the task, just as one is not born with big muscles but acquires them through training; if all the offspring undergoes the same process, it becomes "natural," that is, inevitably attached to the developing process of each individual, no matter whether this translates into some form of biochemical genetic encoding. Parrots can imitate the human voice with a vocal organ that is entirely different, but do not speak. Some primates do have the required auditory capacities to develop phonological aptitudes, but do not do so even if immersed in a human community for a long time (Karmiloff and Karmiloff-Smith 2001). Language is not an individual behavior transcending the species; the form of language we know characterizes our species and is *imposed by social life* in the course of individual development at a time when the individual is not yet a full-fledged person: growth breathes and feeds on a chatty world. Chomsky's 1965 hypothesis of a universal grammar is as unnecessary as it is arbitrary, and Pinker's 1994 individual-centered suggestion of a language instinct, whether or not formalized by a UG and materialized by an "organ," requires that the person be fully autonomous and undergoing a social experience-tight development in the first place to acquire the knowhow as an external activity, opting to do so rather than stay on the sidelines.

Language is, all in one, an enactive all-selves-encompassing way of organizing knowledge and controlling action through direct intervention in the world.[20] Languaging alters the environment and accretes the selves into a cultural body that self-defines itself as one of the living species— mankind. The symbolical denial of this unity stems from the failure to acknowledge that a signifier is not exclusively physical, just as a concept is not purely mental, and that none of them control the other in a one-way relation. Notions, or social-cultural enactive knowledge, is information gained through reciprocal and collective perception-action in the environment.

Language is the school of human life and individuation; it enables the species to survive socially, thanks to the concerted production of food and artifacts, *out of its ecological niche*, or *make the entire accessible universe an ecological niche of its own*, spread over the planet and beyond; it is even to be feared, to overwhelm other species within the expanded niche and destabilize the henceforth fragile balance of biodiversity as is currently witnessed, with an increasingly dramatic number of living species *and human languages* collapsing even before we have become aware that they exist. How language is turning into the instrument of universal survival and doom might be worth investigation.

Notes

1. Talmy's project (2000) is to study the linguistic representation of conceptual structures. In theory, sentences prompt listeners to construct mental representations, but communication appears extremely late (vol. 2, chap. 6, 337–369) and in strictly pragmatic terms; despite the symbolic connection between the two levels, the dynamic procedure is not made explicit.

2. For example, the Basque and Breton languages had not developed the technical vocabulary of new technologies until academic authorities decided that their lexicons had to fill the gaps that appeared when the languages were mapped with Spanish, French, and English. Over the past few years were published a manual of teaching methods in mathematics in the Breton language, along with a *Geriadur ar Fizik* (An Noalleg 2006), an impressive collection of scientific and technological terminology, have recently been published. Lexicons are *potentially* universal, but they *actually* cover the areas their community has substantially experienced.

3. For a sample of conversation in Sochiapam Chinantec (Mexico), see http://www .sil.org/mexico/chinanteca/sochiapam/13i-Conversacion-cso.htm.

4. The pitch variation of African talking drums makes it possible to imitate the languages' tones and convey some relatively complex messages, including the "drum names" of the sender and the addressee.

5. Toyi-toyi, a southern African dance used in demonstrations during the apartheid period, is occasionally called "foot language," but its "semantics" is limited to the expression of the hostility of a social group in the face of the enemy, like the Maori *haka* war dance.

6. Joly in Cotte et al. 1993, 46.

7. What one reads is fully understood if and only if the relevant intonation and rhythm guide the mental voicing. Otherwise, itemizing a list of disconnected words is semantically unproductive.

8. This is not to say that the structure of the word is iconically and phonosymbolically motivated by the sensorimotor properties of the phonemes and/or graphemes: the spelling *wr-* is no less arbitrary than the whole word *write*. Simply put, English has a strong tendency to retain a whole gamut of such arbitrary consonant clusters, nonetheless specifying the semantic field to which the lexical belongs. These fields happen to reflect the way in which the "object" or "action" is experienced through sensorimotor dynamics.

9. The most striking example is, no doubt, Lakoff and Johnson's title *Philosophy in the Flesh: The Embodied Mind and Its Challenge to Western Thought* (1999), a book in which Varela, Thompson, and Rosch's *The Embodied Mind* (1993) is not mentioned.

10. Basque has an extraordinary way of displaying this dynamics in morphology. "I was" is said *nintzen*. *Zen* is "was" in the third person singular. *Ni* is the first person pronoun "I," and *-n* is the marker of the past, but also the genitive (possesser, as in *aitaren kapela* "Daddy's hat") and the inessive (location in a frame or background as in *etxean* "at home"). So the whole cluster is to be interpreted as *nin + zen* (*t* is epenthetic), that is, *ni-n*, "the past version of me" (taken as a background against which the present instance of the speaking I stands in the here and now) "was" (in the third person). If the subject pronoun is given explicitly, *ni nintzen*, as in French "moi j'étais," "I" is envisaged both as a present reflecting self (*ni*) and as a past reflected instance (*nin*), and in *nintzen*, the past is marked twice: once for the event (*zen*) and once for the occurrence of the self experiencing it (*ni-n*). Verbal paradigms consistently evidence this kind of analysis.

11. Cf. this anecdote: I once saw a two-year-old boy kill a bird accidentally. Trying to bring it round, the boy desperately called it, saying "Oiseau! Oiseau!" using the noun as a proper name.

12. I myself remember reading dozens of occurrences of the word *probité* in Jules Verne's novels when I was a teenager; in my experience of this word in French, this

quality is attached to the kind of character described by this author in the cultural context of the late nineteenth century, and the word would sound irrelevant to characterize contemporary individuals presenting analogous virtues.

13. Cf. Bickerton 1991: the ape does have a "representation" of the leopard, but the relevant features are grounded in perception and are strictly idiosyncratic, formed in the "personal" history of the animal's encounters with the predator. A notion is much more than a collection of features allowing recognition; it is a socially and historically elaborated prediction of possible actions and events in association with a given entity, and, most important of all, the notion is a substitute for individual experience, in that it provides a knowledge that need not have been experienced individually to be acquired. Language is the school of the species' life.

14. Hence the aporia in Plato's *Menon*: if the existence of a word for *virtue* is no guarantee for the consistency of the collectively assembled network of experiences it records, the quest for the Idea may be bound to fail.

15. Guillaume considered that lexicons of different languages differed not only by the way in which they organized personal experience into cultural notions shaping varying and unmappable "mindscapes," but by the very nature of the semantic experience they commanded.

16. This "instrumental" function of the word matches that of technological tools in general: "La représentation humaine se présente ainsi comme un processus qui, par la médiation d'une mémoire technique, *rend présents* pour des sujets toujours-déjà sociaux un monde non originaire et un passé non vécu" (Havelange, Lenay, and Stewart 2003).

17. "We can now attempt to characterize the meaning of the definite article: *use of the definite article with type description T in a nominal implies that (1) the designated instance t_i of T is unique and maximal in relation to current space; (2) S has mental contact with t_i; and (3) either H has mental contact with t or the nominal alone is sufficient to establish it.* The basic import of "the" is that the speaker and the hearer, just by using the nominal it grounds, establish mental contact with the same instance t_i; at that point coordination of reference has been achieved" (Langacker 1987).

18. Imagic iconicity is grounded in the mapping of the visual perception of objects or events against words; diagrammatic iconicity, more abstract, parallels syntactic patterns with chains of events. In our approach, the sequence in question is not that of the event described, but that of the alternated roles in the linguistic interplay.

19. Italian: Dogana 2002; French: Toussaint 1983; English: Philps 2003, Bottineau 2008; Semitic languages: Tobin 1997, Bohas 2006.

20. This connects with Bruner's three successive modes of representations in the child's cognitive development, as the "iconic" and "enactive" ones (in his terminol-

ogy—sensory vs. motor amplifications), once reunited into a structural loop, originate the "symbolic" one (intellectual amplification); cf. also Peirce's ([1984] 1998) three categories of signs: the icon, the index, and the symbol, corresponding to Bruner's (1983) modes of representation: the third class should be derived from the association of the first two.

References

Adamczewski, H., and Delmas, C. (1982). *Grammaire linguistique de l'Anglais*. Paris: Colin.

Allott, R. (1995). Syntax and the motor theory of language. In *Syntactic iconicity and linguistic freezes*, ed. M. E. Landsberg, 307–329. Berlin: Mouton de Gruyter.

An Noalleg, Y.-B. (2006). *Dictionnaire de la physique, Breton-Français, Français-Breton*. Plomelin, France: Preder.

Auchlin, A., Filliettaz, L., Grobet, A. and Simon, A. C. (2004). (En)action, expérienciation du discours et prosodie. *Cahiers de linguistique française* 26:217–249.

Austin, J. L. (1962). *How to do things with words*. Oxford: Clarendon Press.

Bergen, B. K. (2004). The psychological reality of phonæsthemes. *Language* 80 (2), 290–311.

Bickerton, D. (1990). *Language and species*. Chicago: The University of Chicago Press.

Bohas, G. (2006). The organization of the lexicon in Arabic and other semitic languages. In *Perspectives on Arabic Linguistics XVI, Papers from the Sixteenth Annual Symposium on Arabic Linguistics, Cambridge, March, 2002*, ed. S. Boudelaa, 1–37. Amsterdam: John Benjamins.

Borges, J. L. [1940] (1956). Ficciones. *Obras Completas*. Buenos Aires: Emecé editores.

Bottineau, D. (2003). Les cognèmes de l'anglais et autres langues. In *Parcours énonciatifs et parcours interprétatifs, Théories et applications, Actes du Colloque de Tromsø organisé par le Département de Français de l'Université, 26–28 octobre 2000*, ed. A. Ouattara, 185–201. Gap, France: Ophrys.

Bottineau, D. (2005a). Prédication et interaction cognitive en basque. In *Les constituants prédicatifs et la diversité des langues, Mémoires de la Société de Linguistique*, vol. 11, ed. J. François and I. Behr, 97–132. Louvain: Peeters.

Bottineau, D. (2005b). Périphrases verbales et genèse de la prédication en langue anglaise. In *Les périphrases verbales, Lingvisticæ Investigationes Supplementa*, ed. N. Le Querler and H. Bat-Zeev Shyldkrot, vol. 25, 475–495. Amsterdam: John Benjamins.

Bottineau, D. (2008). The submorphemic conjecture in English: Towards a distributed model of the cognitive dynamics of submorphemes. *Lexis 2*. Toulouse. http://screcherche.univ-lyon3.fr/lexis/spip.php?article90.

Bottineau, D., and Roulland, D. (2007). Le problème de la réflexivité en basque. In *L'énoncé réfléchi*, ed. A. Rousseau, D. Bottineau, and D. Roulland, 205–228. Rennes, France: Presses Universitaires de Rennes.

Brentano, F. [1874] (1944). *Psychologie vom Empirischen Standpunkt*. Trans. M. de Gandillac. Vienna: Aubier.

Bruner, J. (1983). *Child's talk: Learning to use language*. New York: Norton.

Bruner, J. (1990). *Acts of meaning*. Cambridge, MA: Harvard University Press.

Bühler, K. [1934] (1990). *Theory of language: The representational function of language*, trans. Donald Fraser Goodwin. Foundations of Semiotics 25. Amsterdam: John Benjamins.

Chomsky, N. (1965). *Aspects of the theory of syntax*. Cambridge, MA: MIT Press.

Corballis, M. (2003). *From hand to mouth: The gestural origins of language*. Princeton: Princeton University Press.

Cotte, P., Joly, A., O'Kelly, D., Gilbert, E., Delmas, C., Girard, G., Guéron, J. (1993). *Les théories de la grammaire anglaise en France*. Paris: Hachette.

Coursil, J. (2000). *La fonction muette du langage*. Ibis Rouge Éditions. Guadeloupe: Presses Universitaires Creoles.

Culioli, A. [1981] (1990). Sur le concept de notion. *BULAG no. 8*. Reprinted in *Pour une linguistique de l'énonciation, t.1: Opérations et représentations*. Gap, France: Ophrys.

Dessalles, J.-L. (2000). *Aux origines du langage—Une histoire naturelle de la parole*. Paris: Hermès.

Diver, W. (1979). Phonology as human behavior. In *Psycholinguistic research: Implications and applications*, ed. D. Aaronson and R. Rieber, 161–182. Hillsdale, NY: Lawrence Erlbaum.

Dogana, F. (2002). *Le parole dell'incanto. Esplorazioni dell'iconismo linguistico*. Milan: Franco Angeli.

Donald, M. (2001). *A mind so rare: The evolution of human consciousness*. New York: W. W. Norton.

Douay, C. (2000). *Eléments pour une théorie de l'interlocution, Un autre regard sur la grammaire anglaise*. Rennes, France: Presses Universitaires de Rennes.

Dreano, P. (2005). *Grammaire du Gallo*. Ploudalmézeau: Label LN.

Erard, Y. (1998). De l'énonciation à l'enaction. L'inscription corporelle de la langue. In *Cahiers de l'Institut de Linguistique et des Sciences du Langage, n° 11, Mélanges offerts en hommage à Mortéza Mahmoudian*, vols. 1 and 2. Lausanne: Lausanne University.

Feldman, J., and Narayanan, S. (2004). Embodied meaning in a neural theory of language. *Brain and Language* 89:385–392.

Fischer, O., and Nänny, M., eds. (2001). *The motivated sign: Iconicity in language and literature 2*, 249–276. Amsterdam: John Benjamins.

Fónagy, I. (1983). *La vive voix, essaie de psycho-phonétique*. Paris: Payot.

Foucault, M. (1966). *Les mots et les choses, Archéologie des sciences humaines, Gallimard*. Paris: NRF.

Gallese, V., and Lakoff, G. (2005). The brain's concepts: the role of the sensory-motor system in conceptual knowledge. *Cognitive Neuropsychology* 22 (3/4): 455–479.

Gardiner, A. H. [1932] (1951). *The theory of speech and language*. Oxford: Clarendon Press.

Givon, T. (1994). On the co-evolution of language, cognition and neurology. Paper presented at the 10th meeting of Language Origins Society, Berkeley.

Grady, J. E., Oakley, T., and Coulson, S. (1999). Blending and metaphor. In *Metaphor in cognitive linguistics*, ed. G. Steen and R. Gibbs, 101–124. Amsterdam: John Benjamins.

Greenfield, P. M. (1991). Language, tools and brain: The ontogeny and phylogeny of hierarchically organized sequential behavior. *Behavioral and Brain Sciences* 14:531–595.

Guillaume, G. (1964). *Langage et science du langage*. Paris and Quebec: Nizet/P. U. Laval.

Havelange, V., Lenay, C., and Stewart, J. (2003). Les représentations: Mémoire externe et objets techniques. *Intellectica* 35:115–131.

Jakobson, R. (1963). *Essais de linguistique générale. Tome I: les fondations du langage*. Paris: Editions de Minuit.

Karmiloff, K., and Karmiloff-Smith, A. (2001). *Pathways to language: From fetus to adolescent*. Cambridge, MA: Harvard University Press.

Keller, P.-H. (2006). *Le dialogue du corps et de l'esprit*. Paris: Odile Jacob.

Kravchenko, A. V. (2004). Essential properties of language from the point of view of autopoiesis. http://cogprints.org/4008/01/PropertiesOfLanguage.pdf.

Lakoff, G., and Johnson, M. (1999). Philosophy in the flesh: The embodied mind and its challenge to western thought. New York: Basic Books.

Langacker, R. W. (1987). *Foundations of cognitive grammar*. Stanford, CA: Stanford University Press.

Leroi-Gourhan, A. (1964). *Le geste et la parole. I. Technique et langage. II. La mémoire et les rythmes*. Paris: Albin Michel.

Lieberman, P. (1991). *Uniquely human: The evolution of speech, thought, and selfless behavior*. Cambridge, MA: Harvard University Press.

Maturana, H. (1978). Biology of language: The epistemology of reality. In *Psychology and biology of language and thought: Essays in honor of Eric Lenneberg*, ed. G. Miller and E. Lenneberg, 27–64. New York: Academic Press.

Maturana, H. (1980). Man and society. In *Autopoiesis, communication, and society: The theory of autopoietic system in the social sciences*, ed. F. Benseler, P. Hejl, and W. Köck, 11–32. Frankfurt: Campus Verlag.

Maturana, H. R., and Varela, F. J. (1980). *Autopoiesis and cognition: The realization of the living*. Dordrecht: Reidel.

Maturana, H., and Varela, F. J. (1987). *The tree of knowledge*. Boston: Shambhala.

McNeill, D. (2005). *Gesture and thought*. Chicago: University of Chicago Press.

Oudeyer, P.-Y. (2006). *Self-organization in the evolution of speech*. Oxford: Oxford University Press.

Peirce, C. S. [1894] 1998. What is a sign?. In *The essential Peirce: Selected philosophical writings, vol 2. (1893–1913)*. Bloomington: Indiana University Press.

Philps, D. (2003). S- incrémentiel et régénération submorphémique en anglais. *Bulletin de la Société de Linguistique de Paris* 98 (1):163–196.

Piaget, J. (1972). *Le langage et la pensée chez l'enfant*. Neuchâtel: Delachaux et Niestlé.

Pinker, S. (1994). *The language instinct: How the mind creates language*. New York: Harper Collins.

Pottier, B. (1992). *Sémantique générale*. Paris: Presses Universitaires de France.

Rastier, F. (2009). *Sémantique interprétative*. 3rd edition. Paris: Presses universitaires de France, coll. "Formes sémiotiques."

Reid, W., Otheguy, R., and Stern, N., eds. (2002). *Signal, meaning, and message: Perspectives on sign-based linguistics*. Amsterdam: John Benjamins.

Robert, S., ed. (2003). *Perspectives synchroniques sur la grammaticalisation*. Louvain: Peeters.

Rousseau, A. (2005). La notion de 'schème cognitif' en typologie des langues. In *Linguistique typologique*, ed. G. Lazard and C. Moyse-Faurie. 249–260. Villeneuve d'Ascq, France: Presses Universitaires du Septentrion.

Salzen, E. A. (2006). From calls to words: How ethology can bridge the divide. *Marges linguistiques* 11:160–166. http://www.marges-linguistiques.com.

Sapir, E. (1951). *Selected writings of Edward Sapir in language, culture, and personality.* Ed. D.G. Mandelbaum. Berkeley: University of California Press.

Searle, J. R. (1969). *Speech acts: An essay in the philosophy of language.* Cambridge: Cambridge University Press.

Shanon, B. (1993). *The representational and the presentational: An essay on cognition and the study of mind.* London: Harvester-Wheatsheaf.

Slobin, D. (1996). From thought and language to thinking and speaking. In *Rethinking linguistic relativity*, ed. J. J. Gumperz and S. C. Levinson, 70–96. Cambridge: Cambridge University Press.

Sperber, D., and Wilson, D. (1995). *Relevance: Communication and cognition.* 2nd edition. Oxford and Cambridge, MA: Blackwell.

Stewart, J. (1996). Cognition = Life: Implications for higher-level cognition. *Behavioural Processes* 35:311–326.

Studdert-Kennedy, M., and Goldstein, L. (2003). Launching language: The gestural origin of discrete infinity. In *Language evolution*, ed. M. H. Christiansen and S. Kirby, 235–254. Oxford: Oxford University Press.

Talmy, L. (2000). *Toward a cognitive semantics, volumes I and II.* Cambridge, MA: MIT Press.

Tobin, Y. (1997). *Phonology as human behavior: Theoretical implications and clinical applications.* Durham, NC: Duke University Press.

Toussaint, M. (1983). *Contre l'arbitraire du signe.* Paris: Didier.

Valin, R. (1981). *Perspectives psychomécaniques sur la syntaxe.* Quebec: Les Presses de l'Université Laval.

Varela, F., Thompson, E., and Rosch, E. (1993). *The embodied mind: Cognitive science and human experience.* Cambridge, MA: MIT Press.

von Humboldt, W. [1836] (1988). *On language: The diversity of human language-structure and its influence on the mental development of mankind.* Cambridge: Cambridge University Press.

Vygotsky, L. S. (1962). *Thought and language.* Trans. E. Hanfmann and G. Vakar. Cambridge, MA: MIT Press.

Wallis, J. [1653] (1969). *Grammatica linguæ anglicanæ*. Ed. R. C. Alston. Reprint 142. Menston, UK: Scolar Press.

Whorf, B. (1956). *Language, thought, and reality: Selected writings of Benjamin Lee Whorf*. Ed. J. B. Carroll. Cambridge, MA: MIT Press.

Wilson, M. (2002). Six views of embodied cognition. *Psychonomic Bulletin and Review* 9 (4): 625–636.

Ziemke, T. 2003. What's that thing called embodiment? In *Proceedings of the 25th Annual Meeting of the Cognitive Science Society*, 1305–1310. Hillsdale, NY: Lawrence Erlbaum.

11 Enacting Infinity: Bringing Transfinite Cardinals into Being

Rafael E. Núñez

Following on his work with Humberto Maturana on the nature of living systems (Maturana and Varela 1987), Francisco Varela proposed, in the late 1980s, a view for understanding the nature of cognition that he called "enaction" (Varela 1989). Essential to this view of the mind—and contrary to most mainstream cognitive science of the time—was the inherent historical coupling between observer and environment, the primacy of common sense in the emergence of cognition, and the dismissal of mental representation as a fundamental concept for explaining how cognition works. As he put it, "the greatest ability of living cognition . . . consists in being able to pose . . . the relevant issues that need to be addressed at each moment. These issues and concerns are not pregiven but are enacted from a background of action, where what counts as relevant is contextually determined by our common sense" (Varela, Thompson, and Rosch 1991, 145). An important case study that helped Varela support his arguments was vision and color perception. With extreme clarity, he showed the implications of the fact that there is simply no one-to-one correspondence between perceived color and locally reflected light, and that therefore there is no ultimate preexisting "real" color "out there" in a pregiven world but only chromatic experiences that observers bring forth—enact—as forms of sense-making based on the biological coupled history of organism and medium. The study of visual systems—a very important area of Varela's work— and of color perception, in particular, turned out to be a perfect arena for addressing issues concerning physical objective reality (e.g., light flux at various wavelengths), subjective perceptual experience, and the nonprimacy of a pregiven external world as a point of departure for explaining cognition. The study of visual systems and color perception thus turned out to be crucial for Varela's formulation of enaction as a view that went beyond the traditional and limiting objective-subjective dichotomy.

Enaction, in the form of genuine embodied cognition, was Varela's middle-way proposal.

But, what happens with the enaction paradigm when addressing an area of cognition that, by definition, lacks an empirically observable physical reality? That is, what happens when there are no actual physical "light flux and various wavelengths" to be measured? When there is no pregiven world to be mentally *re*-presented? What happens with this paradigm when dealing with rigorous and precise cognitive entities that are entirely *imaginary*? What happens then with enaction as that middle way between extreme solipsism and mind-independent realism, if the very physical reality is, by definition, absent? In this chapter, I want to argue that such a case is provided by one of the most abstract and precise conceptual systems the human being has ever created: mathematics. In particular, I will argue that mathematical infinity, as a form of cognition that by definition is not directly available to experience due to the finite nature of living systems, is an excellent candidate for fully exploring the power of enaction as a paradigm for cognitive science. I'll focus on a particular form of *actual infinity*—infinity as a complete entity—namely, the transfinite cardinal numbers as they were conceived by one of the most imaginative and controversial characters in the history of mathematics, the nineteenth-century mathematician Georg Cantor (1845–1918). As we will see, Cantor created a very precise and sophisticated hierarchy of infinities that opened up entire new fields in mathematics, giving shape to, among others, modern set theory. Many celebrated counterintuitive and paradoxical results follow from his work. An important part of my arguments comes from discussions that Francisco Varela and I had on this topic while I was living in Paris in the late 1990s, and from *Where Mathematics Comes From*—a book on the cognitive science of mathematics that Berkeley linguist George Lakoff and I were writing at that time (Lakoff and Núñez 2000). I'll eventually show that human everyday cognitive mechanisms, such as conceptual metaphor and blending—known to be major players in generating human imagination and abstraction—extend common sense in specific ways that bring mathematical infinity to being. The human mind enacts the infinite.

11.1 Why Mathematics? Why Infinity?

Mathematics is a very peculiar form of conceptual system in which the entities constituting the subject matter are imaginary—not perceived through the senses, yet incredibly precise and amazingly stable. In this sense, mathematics distinguishes itself from other bodies of knowledge and human cognitive activity in that it is highly idealized and fundamentally abstract. No purely empirical methods of observation can be directly applied to mathematical entities. Think, for instance, of the simplest entity in the Euclidean plane—the point. As characterized by Euclid, the point has only location but no extension! How could we possibly test a conjecture about Euclidean points by carrying out an experiment with *real* physical points if they don't have extension? This, and other properties of mathematics, such as precision, universality, and consistency for any given subject matter give shape to its peculiar character, as well as to the unique manner in which knowledge is gathered. Unlike science, in which knowledge is gained largely via careful empirical testing of hypotheses, in mathematics knowledge is gathered and sanctioned via proving theorems, and by carefully concocting axioms and formal definitions. A profound consequence of proof-oriented deductive ways of gathering knowledge is that once a theorem is proved, it stays proved forever! This highly peculiar practice of knowledge gathering sustains the extraordinary stable conceptual system that we call mathematics. Any account of the nature of mathematics, philosophical, cognitive, or other, must take into account these properties. And this includes one of the most peculiar and fruitful concept in mathematics: the infinite.

If mathematics is abstract, infinity is a fortiori quintessentially abstract. Besides, infinity—full of paradoxes and controversies—is one of the most intriguing concepts in which the human mind has ever engaged. It is an elusive and counterintuitive idea that has managed to raise fundamental issues in domains as diverse and profound as theology, physics, and philosophy, and it has even played a foundational role in defining the precise and consistent field of mathematics. In this chapter, we will pay special attention to the notion of actual infinity, that is, infinity seen as a "completed," "realized" entity. This powerful notion has become so rich and fruitful in mathematics that if we decided to eliminate it, most of mathematics as we know it would simply disappear, from projective geometry, to infinitesimal calculus, to set theory, to point-set topology. In a nutshell, actual infinity constitutes the ultimate challenge to views of cognition that take—as enaction does— common sense and everyday aspects of cognition as primary: how do we grasp the infinite if, after all, our bodies are finite, and so are our experiences and everything we interact with? How does an elusive and paradoxical idea such as the infinite structure an objective and precise field such as mathematics? What cognitive mechanisms make it possible?

These, of course, are neither simple nor new questions. Some of them have been already approached in the fields of philosophy and formal logic. These disciplines, however, developed quite independently of the natural sciences, and of the necessity of looking at how human reasoning, imagination, and conceptual development work. As a result, when dealing with the nature and structure of mathematical concepts, they fail to consider important constraints imposed by findings in the contemporary scientific study of the human mind, the human language, and their biological underpinnings. In philosophy and logic, the study of the nature and the foundation of mathematical entities is often reduced to discussions over axioms and formal proofs, which, needless to say, are far from how human reasoning and conceptual structures work. What we really need to do in order to answer the previously mentioned questions is to take into account how the human mind actually works, and to provide cognitively plausible answers that eventually could be tested through empirical investigation.

11.2 Infinities, Potential and Actual

Since the time of the great Greek philosophers, the infinite has been handled with extreme care. Many considered the infinite as an undefined entity with no order—chaotic, unstructured. As a result, the infinite was seen as an entity to be avoided in proper reasoning. Aristotle (384–322 BC) made the distinction between *potential* and *actual* infinity, that is, infinity as something that can only potentially exist, and infinity as an actual completed entity. Ever since, this distinction has been followed, resulting in the acceptance of infinity as an idea that only evokes potentiality and by questioning, or simply rejecting, the idea of infinity as a completed achieved entity (see Maor 1991; Núñez 2005). This is the view of the infinite that dominated most of the debate in the Western world until the Renaissance.

Potential infinity is characterized by a process that is iterated again and again endlessly. For instance, this is what occurs when we think of an unending sequence of regular polygons with increasingly more sides (keeping the distance from the center to any of the vertices constant). The first polygon is a triangle, which is followed by a square, then a pentagon, a hexagon, and so on. Each polygon in the sequence has a successor and therefore there is the potential of extending the sequence again and again without end (figure 11.1). At any given stage, the process is formed by a finite number of iterations, but as a whole it doesn't have an end and therefore does not have a final resultant state.

Figure 11.1

An instantiation of potential infinity: the sequence of regular polygons with n sides (starting with $n = 3$). This is an unending sequence, with no polygon characterizing a final resultant state.

What is really interesting in mathematics, however, is not potential infinity but *actual* infinity, which, as we have said, characterizes an infinite process as a *realized* thing. In this case, even though the process is *in*-finite (no end), it is conceived as being "completed" and as having a *final resultant state*. Going back to the example of the sequence of regular polygons, we can see that after each iteration the number of sides grows by 1, the sides become increasingly smaller, and the distance r from the center to the vertices remain constant. As we go on and on with the process the perimeter and the area of the polygon become closer and closer in value to $2\pi r$ and to πr^2, respectively, which correspond to the values of the perimeter and the area of a circle. What actual infinity does is to impose an "end" *at infinity* where the entire infinite sequence does have a final resultant state, namely, a circle conceived as a regular polygon with an infinite number of sides (see figure 11.2). This circle has the prototypical properties circles have (i.e., area, perimeter, a center equidistant to all points on the circle, π being the ratio between the perimeter and the diameter, and so on) but conceptually it *is* a polygon.

So what makes actual infinity so rich and fruitful in mathematics? The answer is the final resultant state it provides. At the same time, however, it is also this same feature that has made the idea of actual infinity extremely controversial, because it has often led to indetermination or contradictions—the worst evil in mathematics. A classic example is what happens when we "divide" by zero. Normally when we divide, say, a positive number k by some other positive number (the denominator), the result becomes increasingly bigger as we make the denominator smaller and smaller. This may lead us to think that when the denominator is so small that it "is actually" zero, then the result is as big as it can be: infinite. In symbols, we obtain the "equation" $k/0 = \infty$, where k is our constant, the number we are dividing. The problem is that accepting this result would also mean accepting that $(0 \cdot \infty) = k$, that is, the multiplication of zero times infinity could be equal to *any* number. This, of course,

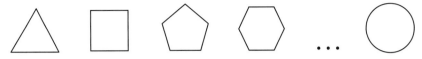

Figure 11.2
An instantiation of actual infinity: the sequence of regular polygons with n sides (starting with $n = 3$). The sequence is endless, yet it is conceived as being completed. The final resultant state is a specific entity: a circle conceived as a polygon with infinitely many sides of infinitely small magnitude.

doesn't make any sense, leaving the left side of our "equation" as a nondeterminate entity. Because of cases like this one, many brilliant mathematicians, such as Galileo (1564–1642), Gauss (1777–1855), Cauchy (1789–1857), Weierstrass (1815–1897), and Poincaré (1854–1912), energetically rejected actual infinity. Up to the nineteenth century, there was a well-established consensus among mathematicians that actual infinity could, at best, provide some intuitive ideas—when dealing with limits, for example—but that no consistent and rigorous mathematics could possibly come out of infinity as actually realized. Georg Cantor, following some preliminary work by Bolzano (1781–1848) and Dedekind (1831–1916) radically challenged this view, seeing in actual infinity a genuine mathematical entity. His work was highly controversial and produced many counterintuitive results, and for most of his professional life Cantor had to struggle against heavy criticism (for an in-depth analysis of Cantor's work and intellectual path, see Ferreirós 1999 and Dauben 1983, 1990). His highly disputed view of actual infinity, however, generated extraordinary new mathematics.

11.3 Georg Cantor and His Transfinite Cardinal Numbers

Europe witnessed one of the most productive periods in the history of mathematics during the nineteenth century. Exciting new fields were created, from non-Euclidean geometries to the so-called arithmetization of analysis. It is in this *zeitgeist* that Cantor created his transfinite numbers, dispelling well-established views that abolished the use of actual infinities in mathematics. Nowadays, Cantor is best known for the creation of a mathematical system in which numbers of infinite magnitude define very precise hierarchies of infinities with a precise arithmetic, giving mathematical meaning to the idea that infinities can have different magnitudes, some being "greater" than others.

A starting question for Cantor was how to determine the number of elements in a set (which he called *Menge*, aggregate). This, of course, is a trivial problem when dealing with finite sets, but when dealing with sets containing infinitely many elements (e.g., the natural numbers 1, 2, 3 . . .), this is literally an impossible task. How do you count *all* the elements if there are infinitely many of them? Cantor shifted his attention to a fundamental property of finite sets. When comparing the relative size of finite sets, not only we can count their elements, but we can also set up pairs by matching their elements. Indeed, when two finite sets have the same number of elements, a one-to-one correspondence between them can be established. And conversely, when a one-to-one correspondence between two finite sets can be established, they have the same number of elements. So he brought this idea of one-to-one correspondence into the realm of the infinite, and asked questions such as: are there more natural numbers than even numbers? A similar question had already been asked in the first half of the seventeenth century by Galileo, who observed that despite the fact that the squares of natural numbers are contained in the collection of these numbers, they can be matched, one by one, ad infinitum. So, he asked, how could it be that a smaller collection contained in a bigger one could have its elements matched one-to-one with those of the larger collection? Facing this paradoxical situation, Galileo concluded that attributes such as "greater than," "smaller than," or "equal to" simply shouldn't be used to compare collections with infinitely many elements.

In the nineteenth century, Cantor could get around the "paradox" by building on the previous highly creative (though not well-recognized) work by Bernard Bolzano and by Richard Dedekind. These two mathematicians were the first to see the possibility of matching the elements of an infinite set with one of its subsets as an *essential* property of infinite sets rather than as a paradoxical situation. Their work allowed Cantor to propose an answer to the question of the relative "size" of the sets of natural and even numbers. Cantor declared that "whenever two sets—finite or infinite—can be matched by a one-to-one correspondence, they have the same number of elements" (Maor 1991, 57). Because a one-to-one correspondence between natural and even numbers can be established (figure 11.3), he concluded that there are "just as many" infinitely even numbers as there are infinitely natural numbers, despite the fact that even numbers are contained in the natural numbers.

But could other (more complicated) sets of infinitely many numbers be put in one-to-one correspondence with the natural numbers? For example, when natural numbers and even numbers are ordered according

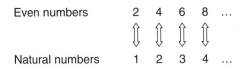

Even numbers   2   4   6   8   ...

Natural numbers   1   2   3   4   ...

Figure 11.3
A mapping establishing the one-to-one correspondence between the sets of even and natural numbers.

to magnitude, each of them has a definite successor. So what would happen if the analysis is done with a set that doesn't have this property, say, the *rational* numbers? Rational numbers are *dense*; that is, between any two rational numbers, we can always find another rational number, and therefore they don't have successors. The set of rational numbers seems to have infinitely many more elements than the naturals, because not only we can find infinitely many rationals greater or smaller than a given number, but also we can find infinitely many rationals between any two rationals. So the question is: are there more rational numbers than natural numbers?

Checking where there is a one-to-one correspondence between the rationals and the naturals requires that both sets have their elements somewhat organized "one by one." In the case of even and natural numbers, that organization was provided by order of magnitude. But because rationals are dense, they can't be ordered by magnitude. Cantor found a way of displaying *all* rationals, one by one, in a smart *infinite array*, which displayed all possible fractions (figure 11.4). In such an array, fractions with numerator 1 appear in the first row, fractions with numerator 2 in the second row, and so on. And similarly, fractions with denominator 1 appear in the first column, fractions with denominator 2 in the second column, and so on. In 1874, using this array, Cantor was able to show—against his own intuition!—that it was possible to establish a one-to-one correspondence between the rationals and the naturals. The correspondence is established by assigning the natural number 1 to the first fraction in the array, the number 2 to the second fraction, and so on, ad infinitum (figure 11.4).

Cantor declared that when such a one-to-one correspondence is established between two infinite sets, they have the same *power* (*Mächtigkeit*) or cardinal number. He named the power of the set of natural numbers, $\aleph_0$, the smallest transfinite number (denoted with the first letter of the Hebrew alphabet, aleph). Nowadays we call infinite sets that can be put in a one-to-one correspondence with the natural numbers (i.e., with cardinality $\aleph_0$) *denumerable* or *countable*.

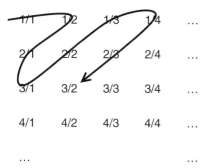

Figure 11.4
Georg Cantor's infinite array of rational numbers, conceived for the proof of their denumerability. Each fraction covered by the arrow can be mapped to a unique natural number, thus establishing a one-to-one correspondence between the rational numbers and the naturals.

The obvious next question was: are all infinite sets countable? Cantor found, toward the end of 1873, that the answer was no. He was able to prove that the real numbers cannot be put into one-to-one correspondence with the natural numbers, and that therefore the set of real numbers is not denumerable. Cantor provided, a little later, a simpler proof known today as the famous proof by diagonalization. The proof works by the principle of reductio ad absurdum. He assumed that a correspondence between the natural numbers and the real numbers between zero and one *was* possible, and by reaching a contradiction in the reasoning, he established the falsity of its original assumption. The one-to-one correspondence between reals and naturals then is not possible. This is what he did. Because every real number has a unique nonterminating decimal representation, he wrote down the correspondence as follows:

1. $\rightarrow 0.a_{11}a_{12}a_{13} \ldots$
2. $\rightarrow 0.a_{21}a_{22}a_{33} \ldots$
3. $\rightarrow 0.a_{31}a_{32}a_{33} \ldots$
... $\rightarrow$ . . . . . .

The proof requires all real numbers in the list to be written as nonterminating decimals. For example, the number 0.3 should be written as 0.2999. . . . The list, according to the original assumption, includes *all* real numbers between 0 and 1. Cantor then showed that it was possible to construct a real number that wasn't included in the list, a number of the form $0.b_1b_2b_3 \ldots$ where the first digit b_1 of this number is different from a_{11} (the first digit of the first number in the list), the second digit

b_2 of the new number is different from a_{22} (the second digit of the second number in the list), and so on. As a result, the new number $0.b_1b_2b_3$ . . . , which is greater than 0 but smaller than 1, is necessarily different from any of the numbers in the list in at least one digit. Indeed, the digit b_k (the kth digit of the new number) is always different from the digit a_{kk} given by the diagonal (the kth digit of the kth number of the list). This leads to a contradiction, as the original list was supposed to include *all* real numbers between 0 and 1. Therefore the assumed one-to-one correspondence between the naturals and the reals in the interval (0, 1) cannot be established. Because the set of natural numbers is a subset of the set of the reals, the set of real numbers constitutes a nondenumerable set that has a power higher than the naturals. Its cardinality is a transfinite number greater than $\aleph_0$, which Cantor, thinking of the power of the continuum, called c.

Cantor's investigation of transfinite numbers went well beyond $\aleph_0$ and c. Other than the work with transfinite ordinal numbers, he showed that there is an infinite and very precise hierarchy of transfinite cardinal numbers and added many more counterintuitive and controversial results to his long list of achievements (see Dauben 1983 and Sondheimer and Rogerson 1981). Cantor thus developed a rich and precise arithmetic for transfinite cardinals, where unorthodox equations hold:

$\aleph_0 + \aleph_0 = \aleph_0$;

$\aleph_0 + k = k + \aleph_0 = \aleph_0$, for any natural number k;

$\aleph_0 \cdot \aleph_0 = \aleph_0$;

$\aleph_0 \cdot k = k \cdot \aleph_0 = \aleph_0$, for any natural number k;

$(\aleph_0)^k = \aleph_0$, for any natural number k

Cantor's transfinite arithmetic consolidated an extraordinary improvement in the study of the infinite, leaving behind, once and for all, the old days when the symbol ∞ denoted vagueness and ambiguity. With Cantor's work, infinite numbers acquired a precise meaning constituting the cornerstone of extremely creative and ingenious new mathematics. Realizing how deep and rich Cantor's work was, David Hilbert, one of the greatest figures of modern mathematics, wrote, "No one shall drive us out of the paradise which Cantor has created for us" (Hilbert [1925] 1964, 141).

But how did Cantor create this "paradise"? What cognitive mechanisms—if any—made them possible? How does the human mind enact these entities, which not being real in any physical sense, have the highest level of precision and stability so essential to mathematics? These are the questions that we'll be addressing in the following sections.

11.4   Enacting Actual Infinity: Metaphor, Blending, Aspect, and Common Sense

We now turn to everyday common sense, keeping in mind that our goal is to understand the cognitive nature of actual infinity and the conceptual organization underlying transfinite cardinals. In particular, we will look at three main mechanisms of everyday cognitive activity: *conceptual metaphor* (Lakoff and Johnson 1980; Lakoff and Núñez 2000), *conceptual blend* (Fauconnier and Turner 2002), and *aspect* (Comrie 1976). These everyday bodily grounded mechanisms of human cognition provide some of the most important building blocks for understanding how the embodied mind (Johnson 1987; Varela, Thompson, and Rosch 1991) enacts imaginary entities bringing the infinite to being.

11.4.1   Conceptual Metaphor

Consider the following two everyday linguistic expressions: "The summer lies *ahead* of us" and "The big game is now *behind* us." Literally, these expressions don't make any sense. "The summer" is not something that can physically be "ahead" of us in any measurable or observable way, and a "game" is not something that can be physically "behind" us. Human everyday language displays hundreds of thousands of these expressions, whose meaning is not literal—in any real physical sense—but *metaphorical*. These expressions are linguistic manifestations of human everyday common sense and make human imagination possible by conveying precise meanings beyond physical reality. A branch of cognitive science—cognitive linguistics—has studied this phenomenon in detail and has shown that the semantics of these hundreds of thousands metaphorical linguistic expressions can be modeled by a number of *conceptual metaphors* (Lakoff and Johnson 1980; Lakoff 1993). These conceptual metaphors, which are inference-preserving cross-domain mappings, are cognitive mechanisms that allow us to project the inferential structure from a *source domain*, which usually is grounded in some form of basic bodily experience, into another one—the *target domain*—that is usually more abstract. A crucial component of what is modeled is *inferential organization*, the network of inferences that is generated via the mappings. By now conceptual metaphor is a well-studied cognitive mechanism. A substantial body of research has investigated how it works in many domains of human thought and reasoning, through various theoretical and empirical methods, from cross-cultural and cross-linguistic studies to experiments in psycholinguistics and cognitive neuroscience, to computer modeling (for an overview, see Gibbs 2008).

In the previous examples, although the expressions use completely different words (i.e., the former refers to a location *ahead of us*, and the latter to a location *behind us*), they are both linguistic manifestations of a single general conceptual metaphor, namely, TIME EVENTS ARE THINGS IN UNIDIMENSIONAL SPACE. As in any conceptual metaphor, the inferential structure of target domain concepts (time, in this case) is created via a precise mapping drawn from the source domain (unidimensional space, in this case), which can be studied in detail. For instance, in what concerns time expressions, cognitive linguists have identified two main forms of this general conceptual metaphor, namely, TIME PASSING IS MOTION OF AN OBJECT (which models the inferential organization of expressions such as *Winter is coming*) and TIME PASSING IS MOTION OVER A LANDSCAPE (which models the inferential organization of expressions such as *we are approaching the end of the month*) (Lakoff 1993).[1] The former mapping has a fixed canonical observer by whom times are seen as entities moving with respect to the observer, while the latter has times as fixed objects where the observer moves respect to events in time. These two forms share some fundamental features: both map (preserving transitivity) spatial locations in front of ego with temporal events in the future, co-locations with ego with events in the present, and locations behind ego (also preserving transitivity) with events in the past. Spatial construals of time are, of course, much more complex, but this is basically all what we need to know here (for details, see Lakoff 1993 and Núñez 1999; for cross-linguistic and gestural studies, Núñez and Sweetser 2006). For the purposes of this chapter, there are two very important points to keep in mind:

1. *Truth* and "reality," when imaginary entities are concerned, are always relative to the inferential organization of the mappings involved in the underlying conceptual metaphors. For instance, "last summer" can be conceptualized as being *behind us* as long as we operate with the general conceptual metaphor TIME EVENTS ARE THINGS IN UNIDIMENSIONAL SPACE as mentioned earlier, which determines a specific bodily orientation respect to metaphorically conceived events in time, namely, the future as being "in front" of us, and the past as being "behind" us. In collaboration with Eve Sweetser, I have shown, however, that the details of that mapping are not universal (Núñez and Sweetser 2006). Through ethnographic field work, as well as cross-linguistic gestural and lexical analysis of the Aymara language of the Andes highlands, we provided the first well-documented case violating the postulated universality of the metaphorical orientation future-in-front-of ego and past-behind-ego. In Aymara, for instance, "last summer" is conceptualized as being *in front* of ego, not behind ego, and

"next year" not as being in front of ego, but *behind* ego. The point is that there is no ultimate truth regarding these imaginative structures. In this case, there is no ultimate truth about where is the definitive (metaphorical) location of the future (or the past). Truth will depend on the details of the mappings of the underlying conceptual metaphor. As we will see, this will turn out to be of paramount importance when mathematical concepts are concerned: their ultimate truth is not hidden in the structure of the universe, but it will be relative to the underlying human conceptual mappings (e.g., metaphors) that enacted them.

2. The abstract conceptual systems we develop are possible *because* we are biological beings with specific morphological and anatomical features. In this sense, human abstraction is *embodied* in nature. It is because we are living creatures with a salient and unambiguous front and a back that we can build on these properties (and the related bodily experiences) that we can bring forth stable and solid concepts such as "the future in front of us." This wouldn't be possible if we had the body of, say, a jellyfish. Moreover, abstract conceptual systems are not "simply" socially constructed, as a matter of convention. Biological properties and specificities of human bodily grounded experience impose very strong constraints on what concepts can be generated. Although social conventions usually have a huge number of degrees of freedom, many human abstract concepts don't. For example, the color pattern of the euro bills was socially constructed via convention (and so were the design patterns they have). But virtually any color ordering would have done the job. Metaphorical construals of time, on the contrary, are, as far as we know, based *only* on a spatial source domain. And this is an empirical observation, not an arbitrary or speculative statement: there is simply no known language or culture on earth where time is construed in terms of thermic or chromatic source domains. Moreover, not just any spatial domain does the job. Spatial construals of time are, as far as we know, always based on some form of unidimensional space. Human abstraction is thus not merely "socially constructed." It is constructed through strong nonarbitrary biological and cognitive constraints that play an essential role in constituting what human abstraction is. Human cognition is thus embodied, shaped by species-specific nonarbitrary constraints. Again, this property will turn out to be very important when mathematical concepts are concerned.

11.4.2 Conceptual Blending
This is another important type of conceptual mapping studied in cognitive linguistics. Although research in this area is younger than in conceptual

metaphor, the study of conceptual blending has advanced substantially (Fauconnier and Turner 2002). Unlike conceptual metaphor, the mappings are not unidirectional (from source to target domain), but they establish correspondences between entities in different *input spaces* and project (often partially and selectively) the properties to a third space, the *blended space*. This new imaginary space gains emergent entities and potential inferences that weren't available in the original input spaces alone. An example may illustrate how conceptual blending works.

Consider a situation in which a male college student, Mike, is babysitting, taking care of a five-year-old boy. At some point he says to the kid, "If I were your mother, I wouldn't allow you to eat so many sweets." Young children are remarkably good at understanding expressions like this one, even though the sentence doesn't make any sense in any concrete literal way. In fact, there is no possible physical real world in which that sentence makes literal sense: mothers are females and Mike is a male, so he cannot be a mother himself; the kid already has a mother, and therefore nobody else can actually *be* his mother; and so on. So how come expressions like this one are effortlessly meaningful in everyday conversations? Conceptual blending theory explains the meaning of such expressions (called *counterfactuals* in this case) as emerging in the blended space. The space builds up on the correspondences between two input spaces: the "mother" input space that has built-in properties such as (A) "mothers are females," (B) "mothers are older than their children," (C) "mothers take care of their children," and so on. On the other hand, there is the "Mike-the-baby-sitter" input space whose instantiation is provided by the actual male college student, Mike. This input space also has built-in properties: (a) "Mike is a male," (b) "babysitters are older than the kids they are in charge of," (c) "babysitters take care of the kids they are in charge of," and so on. The blended space then, is formed by the projections of correspondences between the two elements: B-b (the relationship "being older than the kid"), C-c (the action of "taking care of the children"), and so on. But—and this is crucial—as a result of the clashing provided by the lack of direct correspondence A-a (female vs. male gender), the blended space has only a selected partial gender projection, namely, Mike's gender. The new emergent purely imaginary entity in the blended space then is "A male 'mother' named Mike who is older than the kid and takes care of him."

The study of conceptual blending is, of course, more complicated and goes beyond counterfactuals. For the purposes of this chapter, what matters is to understand how, in everyday discourse, selected inferential properties of input spaces are combined in specific ways to generate new emergent meaning, which, originally, wasn't available in the input spaces themselves. As we will see, this will turn out to be essential in the emergence of actual infinity.

11.4.3 Aspect

In cognitive semantics, aspectual systems characterize the structure of event concepts. The study of aspect allows us to understand, for instance, the cognitive structure of iterative actions (e.g., "breathing," "tapping") and continuous actions (e.g., "moving") as they are manifested through language in everyday situations. Aspect can tell us about the structure of actions that have inherent beginning and ending points (e.g., "jumping"), actions that have starting points only (e.g., "leaving"), and actions that have ending points only (e.g., "arriving"). When actions have ending points, they also have *resultant states*. For example, "arriving" (whose aspectual structure has an ending point) in *I arrive at the airport*, implies that once the action is finished, I am located *at* the airport. When actions don't have ending points, they don't have resultant states. Many dimensions of the structure of events can be studied through aspect.

An important distinction is the one between *perfective aspect* and *imperfective aspect*. The former has inherent completion; the latter does not. For example, the prototypical structure of "jumping" has inherent completion, namely, when the subject performing the action touches the ground or some other surface that puts and end to the action. We say then that "jumping" has perfective aspect. "Flying," on the contrary, does not have inherent completion. The prototypical action of "flying" in itself does not define any specific end, and does not involve touching the ground. When the agent performing the action, however, touches the ground, the very act of touching puts an end to the action of flying but does not belong to "flying" itself. We say that "flying" has imperfective aspect.

The point of bringing the study of aspect here is to show that this everyday cognitive schema has a word to say about the nature of potential infinity: it has imperfective aspect. Indeed, potential infinity involves processes that explicitly *lack end points*, and therefore have no completion, and no final resultant state. Potential infinity then, via imperfective aspect, can be characterized in terms of everyday cognitive phenomena. But, what about actual infinity?

11.5 BMI: The Basic Mapping of Infinity

Actual infinity is, essentially, what most of mathematics is about. And it is what we really care about in this chapter. Here is where a particular conceptual mapping, the *Basic Mapping of Infinity* (or BMI), comes in. The BMI is a general conceptual mapping, which occurs inside and outside of mathematics, but it is in the precise and rigorous field of mathematics that it can be best appreciated (for details, see Lakoff and Núñez 2000). Lakoff and I have hypothesized that the BMI is a single human everyday conceptual mechanism underlying all kinds of mathematical actual infinities, from infinite sums and infinite sets, to points at infinity in projective geometry, to infinitesimal numbers and limits. When seen as a conceptual blend, the BMI has two input spaces that involve iterative processes. One is a space involving *Completed Iterative Processes* (with perfective aspect), that is, processes defined in the finite realm. The other input space involves *Endless Iterative Processes* (with imperfective aspect), which, as we saw in the previous section, characterizes processes involved in potential infinity. In the blended space, what we have is the emergent inferential structure required to characterize processes involved in actual infinity (see figure 11.5).

Very much like in the case of the gender clash in our earlier counterfactual example, the correspondence between the two input spaces involves all the elements with the exception of one: in this case the very last one, the single element that distinguishes in a fundamental way a finite process from a potentially infinite process. This provides a major conflict, a clash between a characterization of a process as explicitly *having an end* and a *final resultant state*, and one as explicitly characterizing the process as *being endless* and with *no final resultant state*. These conflicts often lead to paralysis, where no blended space is formed at all, leaving the original input spaces as they were with their own local inferential structure. This, I believe, is what occurred to Galileo: After observing that natural numbers and a subcollection of them—their squares—could be put in one-to-one correspondence(!), he was not able to reach any conclusions. Such an extra step would have required *completing* an *endless* process.[2] Rather than paralysis, a conceptual blend of this sort handles the conflict in a creative way, providing fundamentally new inferential structure in the blended space.

Several interesting things occur in the BMI. First, from the Completed Iterative Process Input (with perfective aspect) the fact that the process *must have an end* and *a final resultant state* is profiled and projected to the blended space, overruling the clause that the *process must be finite*. Second,

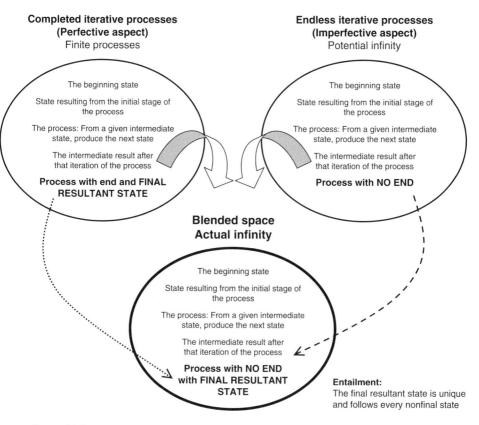

Figure 11.5
The Basic Mapping of Infinity (BMI) as a conceptual blend.

from the Endless Iterative Process Input (with imperfective aspect), the fact that the process *has no end* is profiled and projected into the blended space, overruling the clause that the processes *does not have a final resultant state*. Finally, as a result, the blended space has new emergent inferential structure, which provides *an endless process* with *an end* and *a final resultant state*.

Lakoff and I have pointed out that a crucial entailment of the BMI is that the final resultant state is *unique* and *follows every nonfinal state* (Lakoff and Núñez 2000). The uniqueness is inherited from the input space of completed processes, where for any completed process, the final resultant state is unique. The fact that the final resultant state is indeed *final* means that there is no earlier final state. That is, there is no distinct previous state within the process that both follows the completion stage of the process yet precedes the final state of the process. Similarly, there is no later final state of the process. That is, there is no other state of the process that both results from the completion of the process and follows the final state of the process.

We can illustrate how the BMI works by going back to the example involving the sequence of regular polygons (figure 11.2). In order to get from the BMI as a general cognitive mechanism to special cases of actual infinity, we need to *parameterize* the mapping. That is, we must characterize precisely what are the elements under consideration in the iterative process. In our example, the first input space (located on the left in figure 11.5) provides a finite process with perfective aspect. The process is a specific sequence of regular polygons in which the distance from the center to any of the vertices is kept constant. The process starts with a triangle, followed by a square, then a pentagon, and so on, all the way to a polygon with a finite number of sides—say, 58 sides. At each stage, we have specific values for the perimeter and area of each polygon in the sequence, which get closer to $2\pi r$, and πr^2, respectively (where r is the distance from the center to the vertices). The perimeter and the area of the final resultant state in this first input space (i.e., polygon with 58 sides) have the closest values to $2\pi r$, and πr^2, respectively. The second input space (located on the right in figure 11.5), involves the sequence shown in figure 11.1, that is, an endless sequence of regular polygons (which has imperfective aspect). At each stage, we obtain specific values for the perimeter and area of each polygon in the sequence, which get *endlessly* closer to $2\pi r$, and πr^2, respectively. The distance from the center to any of the vertices is always constant, namely, r. The second input space has no final resultant state. All the corresponding elements from the two inputs are thus projected to the blended space, which gives us the sequence of regular polygons with a triangle, a square, a pentagon, and so on. But the blended space has new emergent structure. The clash between the final resultant state of a finite sequence of polygons (i.e., a polygon of 58 sides) and the endless nature of the sequence is handled by the blend to enact an endless sequence of regular polygons with a final resultant state (with infinitely many sides). At this final resultant state, no difference in terms of perimeter, area, and distance from center to vertices can be detected between the "final" polygon obtained via the BMI and a circle. For the circle the values of the perimeter, the area, and the radius are precisely $2\pi r$, πr^2, and r, respectively. Therefore, when parameterized in this manner, the final resultant state is conceived as an actual unique polygon-circle: a very peculiar kind of polygon with an infinite number of sides, a distance from center to vertices equal to r, a perimeter equal to $2\pi r$, and an area equal to πr^2. The BMI guarantees both that no polygon in the process comes after the polygon-circle, and that this figure—the final resultant state—is unique.

11.6 Enacting Transfinite Cardinal Numbers

We now have the basic elements for addressing our original question: how did everyday commonsensical cognitive mechanisms such as metaphor, blending, and aspect make Cantor's brilliant work possible? Let us start with Cantor's basic conceptual metaphor.

11.6.1 Cantor's Metaphor: Making "Pairability" Mean "Same Number As"
The analysis of Cantor's original texts reveals that in order to characterize his notion of power (*Mächtigkeit*)—cardinal number—for infinite sets (*Mengen*, aggregates), Cantor makes use of a very important conceptual metaphor: SAME NUMBER AS IS PAIRABILITY (Cantor 1955; see Lakoff and Núñez 2000 and Núñez 2005, for details). This metaphor for establishing *equivalence* allows him to layout the foundations for his conceptual apparatus. It provides a precise metaphorical meaning to the comparison of number of elements of infinite sets.

Our common sense treats ideas such as "same number as" and "more than" with a very precise "logic," which emerges from everyday experience dealing with *finite* collections. Their inferential organization can be characterized as follows:

1. *Same Number As:* A (finite) collection A has the same number of elements as (a finite) collection B if, for every member of A, you can take away a corresponding member of B and not have any members of B left over.
2. *More Than:* A (finite) collection B has more elements than (a finite) collection A if, for every member of A, you can take away a member of B and still have members left in B. If collection A happens to be contained in B, the subcollection of elements *left over* after the matching is equal to the subcollection of elements in B that are not in A.

This is simply common sense, but it can be described as rigorously as we want. There is nothing uncontroversial about it, to the point that we totally take these ideas for granted. More than half a century ago, the Swiss psychologist Jean Piaget described in detail how six- and seven-year-old children spontaneously start mastering these fundamental notions (Piaget 1952). So, if we operate with these everyday notions and extend the *leftover* idea to infinite cases, we get an unambiguous answer to the question: are there more natural numbers than even numbers? We can match the elements of both sets as shown in figure 11.6 and observe that the odd numbers are *left over*. Based on the commonsensical notion of "more than" just described, the collection of even numbers is contained in the collection of natural numbers, and therefore what is *left over* after the matching corresponds to the subcollection of elements in the natural numbers that are not in the collection of even numbers—the odd numbers. In this sense, concluding that there are *more* natural numbers than even numbers is straightforward.

But because the two sets can be put in a one-to-one correspondence, they are also *pairable* (figure 11.3). Pairability and "same number as," however, are two very different ideas. For finite collections, they do have the same extension (i.e., they cover the same cases, giving the same results). But cognitively, they are not the same. Their inferential structures differ in important ways. In his investigations into the properties of infinite sets, Cantor used the concept of *pairability* (equivalence) in place of our everyday concept of *same number as*. In doing so, and by implicitly dropping the commonsensical "leftover" idea, he established a conceptual metaphor, in which one concept (same number as) was conceptualized in terms of another one (pairability). The mapping of this simple but crucial conceptual metaphor is shown in figure 11.7.

It is essential to see that the nature of this new conception of number is intrinsically metaphorical. When infinite collections are concerned, operating with pairability, in itself, doesn't give you rich entailments. As we said earlier, this is what happened to Galileo two centuries before Cantor. Galileo did establish a one-to-one correspondence between the natural numbers with their squares, but he wasn't able to reach any conclusions. In order to be able to extend the notion of cardinality from finite sets (which we can literally count) to infinite sets we do need to actively

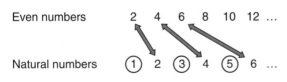

Figure 11.6
A mapping between the even numbers and the naturals based on the everyday notion of "same as" and "more than." We can pair elements of the two collections and have the odd numbers left over (shown with a circle). The entailment is that there are more natural numbers than even numbers.

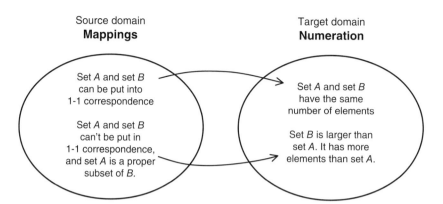

Figure 11.7

SAME NUMBER AS IS PAIRABILITY. Georg Cantor's simple but ingenious conceptual metaphor, which is at the core of transfinite numbers and modern set theory.

ignore the "left over" clause embedded in the ordinary notion of "more than." It is only at that point that we can operate with the metaphorical extension to conceive cardinality for infinite sets.

The metaphorical nature of Cantor's notion of "how many" is rarely recognized in the mathematical community. In reference to Cantor's work, we often see in texts and articles statements like "there are just as many even numbers as there are counting numbers, just as many squares as counting numbers, and just as many integers (positive and negative) as counting numbers" (Maor 1991, 57). But according to a cognitive account of our ordinary notion of "as many as," Cantor proved no such things. What Cantor did was to prove that those infinite sets were *pairable*. And this, of course, assumes—via the BMI—that you can pair *all* of the natural numbers with their corresponding even integers. Fitting a rather Platonic view of mathematics, the mathematical literature often portrays these truths as being mind-independent, and as saying something about the ultimate reality of infinity in itself. From the point of view of enaction, however, it is only when operating with Cantor's metaphor that we can claim that he "proved" that there are, metaphorically, "just as many" even numbers as natural numbers or integers.

Recognizing that these truths are enacted entailments from a human conceptual metaphor doesn't lessen Cantor's brilliant results. Cantor's ingenious metaphorical extension of the concept of pairability to infinite sets constitutes an extraordinary conceptual achievement in mathematics. What he did in the process was create a new technical mathematical concept—pairability (equivalence)—and with it, new mathematics. This new mathematics couldn't have been invented with just our everyday ordinary notions of "same number as" and "more than." It needed that crucial metaphorical extension. But Cantor also intended pairability to be a *literal generalization* of the very idea of number. Because of his philosophical orientation, he took his *extension* of our ordinary notion of "same number as" from finite to infinite sets to be transcendentally real (for historical details, see Dauben 1983 and Ferreirós 1999). There, Cantor was mistaken. From a cognitive perspective, it is a metaphorical rather than literal extension of our very precise commonsensical notion of pairability.

11.6.2   The BMI and the Denumerability of the Rational Numbers

Earlier we saw how Cantor proved the denumerability of a dense set—the rational numbers—by establishing a one-to-one correspondence between the natural numbers and the rationals. It is a very simple, elegant, and powerful proof that makes implicit use of conceptual metaphor and blending. In Cantor's infinite array of fractions (figure 11.4), for instance, the BMI is implicitly evoked in several crucial steps. It is used in each row and column of the array, for assuring that *all* fractions are included. The BMI is thus used in the first row for assuring that a*ll* fractions with numerator one are included in a *completed* collection, without missing a single one. Then, the BMI is used to assure that *all* fractions with numerator two are *actually* included, and so on. In the same way, the BMI provides completion to each column of the array to assure that *all* fractions with corresponding denominators one, two, three, and so on, are actually included in this infinite array. Finally, the BMI is used in conceptualizing the endless arrow covering a *completed* path. The arrow covers every single fraction in the array assuring, via the BMI, the possibility of the one-to-one correspondence between *all* rationals and naturals. The multiples uses of the BMI in this infinite array along with Cantor's SAME NUMBER AS IS PAIRABILITY metaphor validate the diagram as a proof that the natural numbers and the rational numbers have the same cardinality (power), that is, that they can be put into one-to-one correspondence.

11.6.3   The BMI in Cantor's "Diagonal" Proof

The proof of the nondenumerability of real numbers is perhaps one of Cantor's most famous ones. It is as creative as it is powerful. And this proof, which works by reductio ad absurdum, also makes implicit use of various special cases of the BMI. First, the BMI is used to characterize infinite decimals. Each line has the form $0.a_{j1}a_{j2}a_{j3}$ . . . , where j is a natural number denoting the number of the line. The BMI guarantees that each of these unending lines can be conceived as being infinite, yet complete. In fact, the proof even imposes that fractions with terminating decimals (e.g., 0.6) must be expressed as nonterminating decimals (i.e., 0.5999 . . .). The BMI assures that the latter ones are simply "different names" for the former ones. Second, there is the use of the BMI for the set of *all* natural numbers. Each row corresponds to a natural number, thus establishing the conditions for testing the assumed denumerability of the real numbers between 0 and 1. Third, the proof assumes that *all* real numbers between 0 and 1 are included in the list. The BMI guarantees that there is a contradiction if a number is constructed that is not included in the originally assumed *completed* list. The constructed infinite decimal $0.b_1b_2b_3$. . . is precisely such a number, and the BMI makes it complete. Fourth, there is the sequence along the diagonal formed by the digits of the form a_{jk}, where $j = k$, which again must include *all* such digits on the diagonal. The fact that all real numbers must be written as nonterminating decimals guarantees that a digit a_{jk} where $j = k$ (on the diagonal) is not a part of an endless sequence of zeros (i.e., an endless sequence of zeroes for digits a_{jk} where $j < k$, which would be the case of a fraction such as 0.6000 . . .). This is another implicit use of the BMI. Finally, the process of constructing the new number $0.b_1b_2b_3$ . . . through the replacement of each digit a_{jk} (with $j = k$ on the diagonal) with another digit also requires the BMI. The replacement process is unending, but must cover the *entire* diagonal, and must create the new real number—not included in the original list—expressed as a complete nonterminating decimal. The BMI makes this possible.

11.7 Discussion

Mathematics, and mathematical infinity in particular, offers a wonderful case study for exploring the depth and richness of enaction as a paradigm in cognitive science. Mathematical entities are not *real* in any physical sense and infinity is not empirically observable in any direct form. Therefore, by their very nature, these conceptual entities provide an abstract realm of cognition where—as we saw in the opening quote, the "issues and concerns are not pre-given but are enacted from a background of action" (Varela, Thompson, and Rosch 1991, 145). When dealing with mathematical infinities there is no possible *re*-presentation, no preexisting ontology. Mathematics is indeed a product of human imagination, yet it is precise, stable, and "objective," in the sense that for those in the mathematical community who properly play the imaginary "game," specific truths and entailments follow (called theorems). Enaction, as a paradigm in cognitive science, can study in detail how such a highly sophisticated and precise human imaginary conceptual system is brought forth out of everyday action, ordinary cognitive mechanisms, social demands, and common sense. Our analysis showed that contrary to the beliefs of many mathematicians and philosophers, the nature of potential and actual infinity can be understood and characterized, not in terms of transcendental (or platonic) truths or meaningless symbols in formal logic, but in terms of human *ideas* and human cognitive mechanisms. In particular, we saw that Georg Cantor's transfinite cardinal numbers were made possible by the recruitment of three forms of everyday human cognitive mechanisms: (1) aspectual systems (with perfective and imperfective structures, initial and resultant states, and so on), (2) conceptual metaphors (e.g., SAME NUMBER AS IS PAIRABILITY), and (3) conceptual blending (such as the multiple implicit uses of the BMI—the Basic Mapping of Infinity—in Cantor's proofs). These mechanisms are not mathematical in themselves, nor are they the outcome of some kind of mathematical or infinity-specialized "module" in the brain. They are human-embodied cognitive mechanisms, realized and constrained by the peculiarities of human bodies and brains, that—when combined in specific ways—allow for the enaction of extraordinary concepts. The transfinite cardinal numbers are such a result: a masterful combination of conceptual metaphor and conceptual blending realized by the very creative mind of Georg Cantor.

But we ought not to think that the creative ideas involved in Cantor's work are merely imaginary sophisticated social conventions. These ideas are bodily grounded and *not arbitrary*. As such, they are deeply constrained by the peculiarities of human morphology, neuroanatomy, and other species-specific biological phenomena (Varela, Thompson, and Rosch 1991; Thelen and Smith 1994; Núñez and Freeman 1999). Abundant literature in conceptual metaphor and blending tells us that source and target domains, input spaces, mappings, and projections are realized and constrained by bodily grounded experience such as thermic experience, visual perception, and spatial experience (Johnson 1987). In the case of transfinite numbers, these constraints are provided by container-schemas for understanding (finite) collections and their hierarchies, species-specific quantity-discrimination mechanisms, visual and kinesthetic experience involved in size comparison and the matching of elements, correlates between motor control and aspect, and so on (for details, see Lakoff and Núñez 2000, chap. 2). The strong biological constraints operating on these mechanisms provide very specific inferential organizations, which—unlike the color of dollar bills or the typeface used in traffic signs—are far from being mere "social conventions." Transfinite cardinal numbers are the result of highly biologically constrained enaction.

Finally, transfinite cardinals provide just one example of a very rich and interesting case of actual infinity. But it is only one case. Lakoff and I showed that there are many other instantiations of actual infinity in mathematics realized via the BMI, such as points at infinity in projective and inversive geometry, infinite sets, limits, transfinite ordinals, infinitesimals, least-upper bounds, and many others (Lakoff and Núñez 2000). These mathematical actual infinities belong to completely different fields within mathematics, and, in mathematics proper, have their existence guaranteed by very specifically concocted axioms in their respective fields. In set theory, for instance, one can make use of infinite sets simply because there is a specific axiom, the *axiom of infinity*, that grants their existence. The existence of other mathematical actual infinities in other fields is guaranteed by similar axioms. But there is no such thing as a "unifying axiom of actual infinity." How can we study what is in common to all forms of actual infinity? Axioms don't provide the answer. The BMI, which in its generic form is part of human common sense and lies outside of mathematics, provides a naturalistic and unified account of the nature of these various instantiations of actual infinity. It explains with a single mechanism cases of actual infinity occurring in different nonrelated mathematical fields. Whereas in mathematics actual infinities are characterized by different sets of axioms in different fields, cognitively, they can be characterized by a single cognitive mechanism: the BMI. Moreover, unlike formal axioms and platonic statements, the BMI provides a cognitively plausible explanation of the nature of actual infinity that is constrained by what is known in the scientific study of human cognition, human conceptual structures, human language, and the peculiarities of the human body and brain. Mathematical axioms don't have to comply any constraints of this kind, because they operate only within mathematics itself. Axioms, therefore, can't provide explanations of the nature of transfinite cardinals, actual infinities, or, for that matter, of mathematical concepts in general. What allows us to study the human nature of actual infinity is the detailed investigation of human cognition and imagination, and the primacy of biological organization, action, social demands, and common sense. Enaction provides such a paradigm, allowing us to understand how via metaphor, blend, and aspect the human mind brings actual infinity—and transfinite cardinals—into being.

Notes

1. For a more recent taxonomy based on linguistic data, as well as on gestural and psychological experimental evidence, see Núñez and Sweetser 2006.

2. As we will see later, an important component contributing to his paralysis was, of course, that at that time he wasn't able to operate with the conceptual metaphor SAME NUMBER AS IS PAIRABILITY, which is a conceptual metaphor introduced by Georg Cantor two centuries later.

References

Cantor, G. [1915] (1955). *Contributions to the founding of the theory of transfinite numbers*. New York: Dover.

Comrie, B. (1976). *Aspect: An introduction to the study of verbal aspect and related problems*. Cambridge Textbooks in Linguistics. New York: Cambridge University Press.

Dauben, J. W. (1983). Georg Cantor and the origins of transfinite set theory. *Scientific American* (June): 122–154.

Dauben, J. W. (1990). *Georg Cantor: His mathematics and philosophy of the infinite*. Princeton, NJ: Princeton University Press.

Fauconnier, G., and Turner, M. (2002). *The way we think: Conceptual blending and the mind's hidden complexities*. New York: Basic Books.

Ferreirós, J. (1999). *Labyrinth of thought: A history of set theory and its role in modern mathematics*. Boston: Birkhäuser.

Gibbs, R., ed. (2008). *The Cambridge handbook of metaphor and thought*. Cambridge, UK: Cambridge University Press.

Hilbert, D. [1925] (1964). On the infinite. In *Philosophy of mathematics*, ed. P. Benacerraf and H. Putnam, 134–151. Englewood Cliffs, NJ: Prentice-Hall.

Johnson, M. (1987). *The body in the mind: The bodily basis of meaning, imagination and reason*. Chicago: University of Chicago Press.

Lakoff, G. (1993). The contemporary theory of metaphor. In *Metaphor and thought*, 2nd edition, ed. A. Ortony, 202–251. Cambridge: Cambridge University Press.

Lakoff, G., and Johnson, M. (1980). *Metaphors we live by*. Chicago: University of Chicago Press.

Lakoff, G., and Núñez, R. (2000). *Where mathematics comes from: How the embodied mind brings mathematics into being*. New York: Basic Books.

Maturana, H., and Varela, F. (1987). *The tree of knowledge: The biological roots of human understanding*. Boston: New Science Library.

Maor, E. (1991). *To infinity and beyond: A cultural history of the infinite*. Princeton, NJ: Princeton University Press.

Núñez, R. (1999). Could the future taste purple? Reclaiming mind, body, and cognition. In *Reclaiming cognition*, ed. R. Núñez and W. Freeman, 41–60. Thorverton, UK: Imprint Academic.

Núñez, R. (2005). Creating mathematical infinities: Metaphor, blending, and the beauty of transfinite cardinals. *Journal of Pragmatics* 37:1717–1741.

Núñez, R., and Freeman, W., eds. (1999). *Reclaiming cognition: The primacy of action, intention, and emotion*. Thorverton, UK: Imprint Academic.

Núñez, R., and Sweetser, E. (2006). With the future behind them: Convergent evidence of Aymara language and gesture in the crosslinguistic comparison of spatial construals of time. *Cognitive Science* 30:401–450.

Piaget, J. (1952). *The child's conception of number*. New York: W. W. Norton.

Sondheimer, E., and Rogerson, A. (1981). *Numbers and infinity. A historical account of mathematical concepts*. Cambridge: Cambridge University Press.

Thelen, E., and Smith, L. (1994). *A dynamic systems approach to the development of cognition and action*. Cambridge, MA: MIT Press.

Varela, F. (1989). *Connaître les sciences cognitives: Tendencies et perspectives*. Paris: Seuil.

Varela, F., Thompson, E., and Rosch, E. (1991). *The embodied mind: Cognitive science and human experience*. Cambridge, MA: MIT Press.

12 The Ontological Constitution of Cognition and the Epistemological Constitution of Cognitive Science: Phenomenology, Enaction, and Technology

Véronique Havelange

12.1 Introduction

In the elaboration of an alternative paradigm in cognitive science, the question of constitution requires particular attention in order to avoid reducing enaction merely to the level of sensorimotor processes. There are two aspects to this question of constitution: the ontological constitution of cognition (the question of the nature and the genesis of mind), which we shall denote by OCC, and the epistemological constitution of cognitive science (the theoretical activity by which scientists forge the categories and concepts of cognitive science), hereafter ECCS.

In classical cognitive science (the computational theory of mind), and also in reformist versions (connectionism, self-organization), these two aspects of constitution are insufficiently differentiated and articulated. Briefly: in the first, ECCS is conflated with OCC and hence collapses; in the second, OCC is conflated with ECCS and hence eluded. The theories of autopoiesis and enaction radically renew the following questions of constitution.

On the one hand, by grounding the mind in the living body, which is itself considered from the viewpoint of its genesis, the theory of autopoiesis thematizes the ontological constitution of cognition. Maturana (1988) also explicitly raises the question of observation. However, when the object of observation is a living organism, Maturana has recourse to an analogical fiction to give a "voice" to the organism: the pilot in the submarine does not perceive the storm, the reefs, and so on, but only the meter readings and the levers to pull; similarly, bacteria do not perceive "objects" as such, but only as sensory inputs that guide their actions. It is not for nothing that Maturana categorically refuses to envisage any relation between the theory of autopoiesis and phenomenology.

On the other hand, the Varelian theory of enaction brings phenomenology into play; taking into account the phenomenality of the mode of appearance of objects of perception, it profoundly modifies the question of the epistemological constitution of cognitive science. However, the question of the articulation between enaction and autopoiesis—and hence the question of ontological constitution—is not entirely clear.[1]

In this text, I propose to review the major analyses of Husserlian phenomenology, and to show how this renews the questions of OCC, ECCS, and their relation. On this basis, I shall propose a new view of the possible relations between phenomenology and cognitive science, quite different from the "naturalization of phenomenology" (Petitot et al. 1999). This proposition is based on two guiding principles:

1. Taking into account the "double and mutual presupposition between science and the pregivenness of the world," to employ the terms used by Husserl (1925, §45), and the resultant hermeneutical circularity between phenomenology and cognitive science. The *hermeneutical* dimension of the *method* of phenomenological reduction indeed implies a circular relation between the *static method* (which thematizes the constitution of the *objects* of perception and other intentional acts), and the *genetic method* (which thematizes the *genesis* of aperceptual acts themselves, that is, the genesis of consciousness). This is the key question of *reflexive phenomenology*, which was first raised by Fink, and which Husserl later took up on his own account.

2. Taking into account in a principled way the question of technical artifacts as thematized in Husserl's writings, which will lead me to present and to discuss the thesis that technical artifacts play a constitutive role in cognition.

Finally, I shall take the work of the Perceptual Supplementation Group at the Technological University of Compiègne as a metonym, to show how taking into account these two themes can renew the relation between phenomenology and contemporary cognitive science—a relation quite different from a "naturalization" of phenomenology, quite different also from any sort of psychophysical parallelism, but where phenomenology and cognitive science are clearly differentiated while providing sources of mutual stimulation for each other.

12.2 Husserlian Phenomenology

A remarkable feature of Husserl's thought is that it never ceased to evolve during the course of his long working life; we shall attempt to summarize this evolution, and to draw its consequences. The crucial feature is the shifting relation between the *static* method and the *genetic* method. There remains right to the end a tension between static and genetic constitution, because Husserl considered that the limits to the sovereign constitutive power of the transcendental *ego* were only provisional. Nevertheless, Husserl opened the way to a radical questioning of the fracture between the empirical and the transcendental: time, the living body, the Other, worldly objects, and culture are not merely constitut*ed*, they are irreducibly constitut*ive* of the subjective, intersubjective and sociohistorical life of intentional consciousness. There is thus a transcendental *genesis* of intentional consciousness, which certainly does not eliminate the more traditional static constitution by the transcendental *ego*, but which is in turn irreducible, so that static constitution and genetic constitution enter into a *circular* relationship.

Finally, to close these preliminary remarks, we may note that Husserlian phenomenology arose in a scientific context dominated by positivism. Against "psychologism" and "historicism," which naïvely trace a mere "factual genesis," Husserl constantly reaffirms the necessity of a phenomenological critique, which always has precedence *in principle* because it alone is able to identify, *before* any empirical enquiry, the *constitution* of different regions of knowledge which are the precondition for empirical enquiry to be possible. This critique alone is able to ensure the grounding of objectivity, and hence to escape relativism and skepticism. The phenomenological "reductions" (see the following discussion) are first and foremost a means of neutralizing mere psychological genesis, and indeed any merely factual genesis. This helps to explain why, in Husserl's work, there is such a tension between static and genetic constitution.

12.2.1 Husserl's Concept of Intentionality

Phenomenology leads to a recategorization of consciousness. The basic method is that of *phenomenological reduction* or *Epokhè*. This consists of "putting into parentheses" the naïve thesis of the existence of the external world—of neutralizing belief in the existence (or indeed the nonexistence) of objects in the world. This is methodologically necessary in order to focus attention on the *mode of appearance* of objects, and hence to define the a priori conditions for them to appear. It is important not to confuse the phenomenological reduction with a restriction or limitation, and certainly not with reductionism as it may (legitimately) be practiced in the context of scientific enquiry.

The phenomenological reduction leads to the discovery of the *intentional* structure of consciousness. While firmly maintaining the Kantian insistence on the transcendental a priori conditions of possibility of the phenomenon, Husserl redefines consciousness in terms of intentional acts. Consciousness consists of dynamic *acts* whereby [the subject] *aims at* [something]. Phenomenology thus introduces a double shift from the main classical approaches to the question of knowledge:

• On the one hand, contrary to Descartes, for whom both consciousness and its objects are substances (*res cogitans* and *res extensa*), phenomenology does not seek to account for the object that appears, but to describe the *way in which* the object appears. This process of appearing supposes that there is an a priori correlation between consciousness and its objects: experience—and hence knowledge—only exists *for* [a subject of consciousness]; conversely, consciousness is always consciousness *of* [something].

• On the other hand, contrary now to Kant, for whom the a priori categories of understanding (space, time and the Aristotelian categories) are purely formal, phenomenology seeks to grasp the conditions of *lived experience*. For Husserl, the very categories of understanding are a matter of intuition. This idea, though related to the transcendental tradition, renews it radically: the notion of lived experience (*Erlebnis*), which is the center of gravity of phenomenology, implies that consciousness and knowledge are not possible without a grounding in embodiment.

Thus, the first stage of phenomenology (Husserl [1913] 1982) redefines epistemological constitution as *the intentional constitution of objects*, and seeks to elucidate the rules of this process. This constitution is certainly always dynamic, because it takes into account the temporality of lived experience as an intentional act. However, it is "static" in the sense that it is transversal, that it is concerned with objects of experience that are merely transcendent ("worldly" objects, or "external" objects, to use a non-Husserlian vocabulary). This *static* phenomenological enquiry is initially supposed to be situated at a more fundamental level than scientific research, and to provide the latter with its concepts.

It is this primacy of static constitution that will be shaken by taking into account the living body and intersubjectivity, and by considering the facticity of worldly objects in relation to temporality. In the next two sections, we shall examine how these two aspects ruin the project of a sovereign constitution of its objects by a transcendental subjectivity. This will result in recognizing the impossibility of an absolute constitution.

12.2.2   The Living Body, Mediator of Perception and of Intersubjectivity

12.2.2.1   The Living Body and Perception   Husserl makes an important distinction between two aspects of the body. On the one hand, there is the *Körper*, the objective body considered as a physical object. On the other hand, there is the *Leib*, the body as it exists in first-person experience. These aspects are distinct, and yet quite inseparable: neither can exist without the other. The essential difference between a living body (*Leib*) and any other body is that it can be apprehended *either* as a physical entity (*Körper*), a spatial object among other objects, *or* as one's own flesh (*eigen Leib*), the seat of the ego-body (*Ichleib*). These considerations concerning the nature of the body will be crucial when we address the question of perception.

A striking feature of Husserlian phenomenology is the paradigmatic status that it accords to the everyday perception of worldly objects.[2] By so doing, Husserl sets himself the challenge of responding to two problems, and escaping from the symmetrical risks that are associated with them. How does a spatial object *constitute itself* in immanence (the risk being of remaining at the level of the worldly object as such)? And how, after having performed the reduction, can I discover an intentional act such that it gives me the object *out there*, and not solely in the immanence of my consciousness (the risk of solipsism)? These questions are particularly examined in *Ding und Raum* (Husserl [1907] 1997).

The first result of the phenomenological reduction is to reveal that perception is an absolute given. Husserl emphasizes that, by contrast with external perception in the natural attitude, perception after the reduction is

not only consciousness whose essential character is to be consciousness of the immediate presence of the object, but it is also characterized, as a consciousness which is an absolute source of donation, as something which effectively possesses the object in its "flesh-and-blood presence," possesses it in such a way that doubt and incredulity are excluded. (Husserl [1907] 1997, §8)

What are the implications of this analysis, not only in its results, but from the point of view of the presuppositions that underlie it? For Husserl, the donation of a spatial object, which is an exemplary case of perception, is a donation by "sketches" (*Abschattungen*); it is a fundamental structure of perception that an object is only given to me in one of its aspects at a time, but nevertheless I am able to identify it completely. The donation of a spatial object thus involves a temporal dimension. Moreover, strictly speaking, there is only perception of a spatial object when its three-dimensional nature is taken into account. As soon as Husserl thematizes this idea, he confers an essential role to kinesthetic sensations. However, this role is marked by a profound ambiguity. Husserl introduces the notion of kinesthesia as a condition of possibility for the exposition of spatial objects, a condition which however exposes nothing by itself. Then, he gives kinesthetic sensation its full meaning in relation to the notion of own-body (*eigen Leib*). But immediately afterward, Husserl removes the lived-body from his analysis to focus on the physico-objectivizing function of the constitution of the spatial object, all the while continuing to refer constantly to the "kinesthetic sensations." Husserl thus seems to consider that one can envisage kinesthetic sensations either in the perspective of their "integration" by "subjectivizing apprehension" into the lived-body, or, optionally, from the point of view of their "physico-objectivizing function" in the three-dimensional constitution of spatial objects. This amounts to supposing that one can make use of the lived-body, without however actually taking it into consideration.

This is a major inconsistency, because in all rigor there is no such option. Once the dimension of the lived-body is introduced, one can no longer make abstraction of it, on pain of contradiction. The consequence of this contradiction is that Husserl ceaselessly oscillates between invoking kinesthetic sensation in the perspective of static constitution and in that of genetic constitution, without any effective criterion for demarcating between these two perspectives: it is always the same "kinesthetic" sensations that are invoked, sometimes in one direction, sometimes in the other. There is an incessant ambiguity here: we do not know whether we are in the natural attitude or the phenomenological attitude. Is kinesthesia merely an objective motivating circumstance, or is it a constitutive dimension of embodied intentionality?

Of course, Husserl himself did not rest content with this uncomfortable inconsistency. In his late manuscripts, he no longer defines the *Leib* as an *ego*, but as an originary Self that passively affects itself. As such, the Self is an unobservable a priori, the pre-objective structure of possibility of spatiality and temporality (Depraz 1994).

This implies that sensorimotricity, kinesthesia, and proprioception pertain to the level of originary passivity.

12.2.2.2 The Lived-Body and Intersubjectivity There are several stages in the evolution of Husserl's thought on the question of intersubjectivity; we shall simplify drastically by indicating his initial position, the problems with it, and the modified conclusions to which he was drawn.

Initial Period (1905–1910)   Husserl's initial attempt to account for the constitution of "the Other" is based on the distinction between the lived-body (*Leib*) and the objective body (*Körper*). I start by apprehending the Other as external, as a *Körper*; however, because I myself have an intimate experience of the intrication between *Leib* and *Körper*, I can imagine that because the Other is a *Körper*, he is also a *Leib*. While perceiving the Other's objective body, I invest it with the qualities and powers of my own lived-body, by a process of analogy (*Analogisierung*) that pertains to empathy (*Einfülhung*). Husserl calls this specific type of aperception an *appresentation*, and later adds the dimension of imaginative transfer (*Übertragung*). This analysis is an expression of an egological approach that Husserl will later call the "Cartesian way" of phenomenology: it rests on the premise that the *ego* benefits from an immediate, primordial aperception of itself. If this is accepted, then it follows that "the Other" can only be found secondarily, in a mediate mode by analogy.

However, this premise engenders a major *aporia*. The problem lies in the very possibility for the *ego* to experience within himself the distinction, and the intrication, between *Leib* and *Körper*. How can I understand that my own lived-body is *also* an objective body among others, unless it be that it appears so to others? In order to have such an experience, I must *already* possess the viewpoint of objectivity, that is, the viewpoint of the Other who constitutes me as an objective body. At this stage, the analysis of the constitution of the Other engenders a vicious circle. This has two unfortunate consequences. On the one hand, the Other is only apprehended after the fashion of the *ego*, as a pure *alter ego*, rather than in his concrete alterity as a subject in his own right; conversely, the role of the Other in the constitution of the *ego* itself is not taken into account. This puts into question the purely egological nature of the primordial sphere, and introduces a thematization of the irreducible *passivity*[3] of the lived-body.

Later Writings (1920–1927)   In "the way of psychology," which he develops from the 1920s onwards, Husserl himself calls this "Cartesian" scheme into question. In Husserl ([1923/1924] 1956/1959), he recognizes the vicious circle in which the initial analysis of the constitution of the Other was trapped, with the inherent risk that the Other will be apprehended only as an ideality, as a result of my perceptive syntheses. On the contrary, it is necessary to apprehend the Other as a psychic subject who really exists for himself:

[The] Other does he not live his own life, can he not practice the transcendental reduction just as well as I can, can he not discover himself as absolute subjectivity and apprehend *me* as *his* 'alter ego', just as well as I apprehend him in my own life? Just as I exist for myself, just as I am not merely an intentional event in the life of the Other, so conversely the Other naturally exists for himself and is not a simple event in my life of consciousness. (Husserl [1923/1924] 1956/1959, *II*, 36th lecture)

To this end, Husserl complexifies the postulate of a pure *ego* with its attendant risk of solipsism. The imbrication of the intentional operations that characterizes the analysis of subjectivity makes it possible to introduce the subjectivity of the Other into the method, and makes possible a quite new type of reduction, an *intersubjective reduction*. This profoundly modifies the field of phenomenology: instead of limiting the analysis to the lived experience of a singular *ego*, transcendental phenomenology now has pure intersubjectivity as its complete theme. Now, because the Other is initially apprehended as an object given in exteriority, this requires taking into account empirical signs (*Indikationen*) of its existence—facial expressions, mimics, and bodily and linguistic expressions. A phenomenological psychology, giving a rightful place to facticity as well as to the transcendental, must therefore intervene to complete transcendental phenomenology in the analysis of the living body and intersubjectivity. By contrast with the Cartesian way, the reduction that is performed in the "way of psychology" no longer takes anything away from the existence, from the psychic life of other subjects.

Phenomenological psychology (Husserl [1925] 1962) goes even further. The thesis that the complete theme of phenomenology is not the experience of a singular *ego*, but rather pure intersubjectivity, gives rise to the thematization of a relation of *mutual presupposition*, of *explicit imbrication* (*Ineinander*) between transcendental phenomenology and phenomenological psychology. Phenomenology indeed has the task of accounting for prescientific experience of the world, by a transcendental doctrine of intentionality, but it must also account for this intentional structure of experience at the level of scientific knowledge. This implies that there is simultaneously an a priori necessity at the level of science, which redoubles the first dimension from the inside. This "problem of the transcendental" leads Husserl to consider that there is a "double and mutual presupposition between science and the pre-givenness of the world" (Husserl [1925] 1962, §45). The result is that phenomenological psychology is not just a simple introduction to transcendental phenomenology, or a mere parallel to it (a shift in attitude ensuring their mutual interconvertibility). Taking empirical signs into account in the constitution of transcendental intersubjectivity implies a profound blurring of the traditional demarcation between the empirical and the transcendental. Transcendental phenomenology provides the foundations for phenomenological psychology, but in return, the empirical signs in the latter domain participate in the elaboration of transcendental intersubjectivity as such. It is precisely this that will lead Husserl, later, to develop a phenomenology of expression and communication.

12.2.3 Cultural Objects and Technical Artifacts, Constitutive of Sociality

In order to instantiate and to develop the "double and mutual presupposition between science and the pre-givenness of the world" envisaged by Husserl, a key aspect is to radically rethink the status of technical objects and systems. One way into this question is to consider the question of temporality, which plays a major role in phenomenology. Briefly, Husserl ([1905–1917] 1991) makes an important distinction between "primary retention" and "secondary retention." The concept of *primary retention* emphasizes that the intentional consciousness is primitively a passive flow with an irreducible duration. Husserl employs the example of a temporal object, a melody, to illustrate the fact that the lived present is always composed of a "retention"—the memory of the immediate past—and a "protention," the anticipation of that which is just to come. "Secondary retention" is quite different; it is derivative with respect to primary retention and consists of the faithful reproduction of a prior perception of object; it is thus akin to "memories" in the usual sense of the word, the conscious and deliberate evocation of past experiences.

In a penetrating critique, Stiegler (1998, chap. 4) has analyzed the problems posed by this initial Husserlian conception of temporality. Because Husserl postulates—even if only in principle—the infinity of retention, he maintains a strict demarcation between *retention* on the one hand, and *imagination* or "consciousness of images" on the other. According to Stiegler, to the contrary, the retention is finite. Hence, in order to last, retention must be externalized in worldly objects such as portraits, pictures, books, monuments, and so on. Stiegler therefore proposes to extend the Husserlian scheme to include an external "tertiary retention," which grounds a "technological genesis of intentionality" (1998).

In fact in *Ideen II*, Husserl ([1912–1928] 1980) himself makes a similar move that does indeed open up a thematization of the questions of society and history. We have already seen that the question of the "shared world" as it appears in experience is no longer framed in terms of intersubjectivity based on empathy; Husserl now invokes the living body and cultural objects (the tools and instruments of daily life, institutions, works of art, scientific knowledge, and so on) that are *pregiven* for the individual consciousness. These entities are "worldly," but at the same time "mind-laden" ("*begeistete*" *Objekten*); they signify a unity of consciousness, the psyche, and objects, and the fusion of these elements constitutes objectivities of a higher order than those apprehended by the natural attitude.

As such, the lived-body and the "mind-laden objects" are pregiven; they are "found" already-there in worldly experience: a passive synthesis is deployed on this basis. Thus, although it was initially conceived as a deployment of the program of static constitution traced out in 1913 in *Ideen I*, it turns out that *Ideen II* plays a key role in initiating the program of genetic constitution.[4] We will mention just two important consequences of this:

a. By the detour of a "phenomenology of culture," Husserl reverses the analyses carried out in the natural attitude, and thus redefines the subject as directing himself immediately toward that which is "mindful" in the Other and in cultural objects, and not toward them as physical bodies or things. This is why the lived-body is always already laden with meaning by bodily expression and the communicative intent which is rooted in them: it is insofar as it is addressed (*Anrede*) to an Other and received from him (*Aufnehmen der Rede*) that a discourse or an expression constitute the "social bond." This leads to a radical change in the status of empathy, which no longer derives from grasping the Other by analogy on the basis of an apprehension of his objective body; rather, empathy has as its "substrate of immediate meaning" the bodily and linguistic expressions of the Other. I thus grasp the communicative intention of the Other with respect to me; in turn, the empathetic consciousness that I have of this intent engenders in me the motivation for a corresponding intent. The bodily and linguistic expressions not only enable me to intuitively understand the experience of the Other by "putting myself in his place" and to predict his behaviors (with a certain margin of indeterminability); these expressions also engender a succession of mutual intents and actions between me and the Other. Husserl characterizes the links in this succession not as natural causality, but as *motivation*, the "structural fundamental law of the life of the mind" (Husserl [1912–1928] 1980, §56). Similarly, the "mind-laden objects"—tools, furniture, liturgical objects, weapons, and so on—are not only objects that are empirically constitut*ed*: in their role as pregiven elements of worldly experience that are the basis for the deployment of passive syntheses, they are originally constitutive of the passive constitution of the social subject and the social bond. These cultural objects—books are a prime example—therefore provide the grounding not only for intersubjectivity, but for an original sociality. Thematizing the double facticity—bodily and cultural—of the genesis of the subject and sociality, this perspective further signifies that *the categories that are forged by the phenomenologist, and that underlie the constitution of the sciences of mind, do not develop in a separate site below the surface of social life: they develop in the course of social life itself.* Husserl himself sketches the notion of a *mutual constitution between phenomenology and the sciences of mind:* the discrimination of different types of person, of different styles of being and acting as types, presupposes a general aperception of human beings or persons as defined by an essence, but these types cannot be determined from the outside, independently of a lived experience of the course of social life. Husserl thus revokes radically—if implicitly—the transcendental idealism that *Ideen II* was initially supposed to deploy following *Ideen I.*

b. In *The Origin of Geometry,* Husserl ([1938/1939] 1954) emphasizes that transcendental subjectivity is historical, and shows that it goes beyond the bounds of lived experience and phenomena. In order to thematize this chaotic, unordered genesis, Husserl considers the historicity of the *logos* on the mode of a teleology: reason is revealed to itself as the conscious awareness of an infinite task, and the conversion of philosophy into phenomenology is the ultimate stage of this differentiation. This process of externalization in the *Lebenswelt* (the world of social life), which implies that reason displays itself in technical artifacts and in writing, is indispensable for the constitution of the ideal truth of geometrical objects and theorems (Derrida 1978). One may ask whether there is not a contradiction between the teleology of reason, and its externalization in the techniques of measurement and graphical notation. Rather than seeing here an insuperable *aporia,* as many commentators have proposed, it seems to us more judicious to emphasize that, by the notion of a "concrete *a priori* of historicity" and the question in return (*Rückfrage*) toward the *Lebenswelt,* Husserl sets up a relation of hermeneutical circularity between the thematization of technical facticity, and the transcendental genesis of intentionality.

Husserl thus considers that it is by an externalization of reason in the techniques of writing, and by the structure of a hermeneutical circularity—in constant movement—between technical facticity and the concrete a priori of historicity, that it is possible to account not only for the constitution of scientific idealities as such, but also for the recomprehension and transmission of their meaning, and hence for the traditional character of science.

This analysis explodes the idea that the being-together of humans in society is nothing more than intersubjectivity. Sociality cannot be thought of as a simple generalization, an extrapolation of intersubjectivity; it implies and requires a third element that makes possible face-to-face meeting as such (Benoist 2001). I propose that this "third element" that makes possible the institution of the symbolic dimension is to be found in the "mind-laden objects," the cultural objects that must be rethought, as Husserl indicates in *The Origin of Geometry*, not only as constitut*ed*, but also as constitut*ive* of socialization and history. However, it is only to the extent that they are *articulated* with the primordial self-affection of the *Urhylè*—with a living, embodied Self that is primordial self-affection, an indeterminate drive to intentionality that is never completely achieved— that these "third elements" (which in themselves are only inert and non-experienced residues) can become actualized, that their meaning can be reactivated and transmitted as such. It is on this condition that they ground the formation of the transcendental *We* and historicity. Husserl, evoking with respect to writing a "graphic body," a "spiritual embodiment" (*geistige Leiblighkeit*), emphasizes this point in *The Origin of Geometry* and in many other places.

Thus, although he never freed himself entirely from transcendental idealism, Husserl opened the way to a thematization of technical artifacts as not only constitut*ed*, but as constitut*ive* of (inter-)subjectivization and socialization.

12.2.4 Summary: The Contribution of Husserlian Phenomenology

What can we say, in conclusion, concerning the relation between static phenomenology and genetic phenomenology? We have seen that the project of an absolute constitution by a sovereign transcendental *ego* is impossible. But in the end, this very impossibility requires and makes possible a genetic constitution that upsets the primacy, the principled precedence of phenomenology over the sciences. The genetic constitution that is elaborated in the framework of the "way of psychology" and the "way of the life-world (*Lebenswelt*)" requires taking into account the constitutivity of the living body, of worldly objects and historical traces in their facticity. The frontier between "phenomenological psychology" and psychology, between "phenomenological sociology" and sociology, is thus not impermeable. What emerges is a figure of hermeneutical back-and-forth between static constitution and genetic constitution. When this is enriched by an explicit consideration of the role of technical artifacts, there are a number of ontological and epistemological consequences for the sciences of mind (*Geisteswissenschaften*)—in particular, sociology and psychology.

The ontological consequences may be briefly summarized as follows:

a. There is a relation of circular determination between social structures and human action. The social structures condition the very possibility of most forms of human action; at the same time, these social structures have no other origin than the human actions that they themselves have made possible. In this respect, it is also to be noted that social structures have a dual character: they both *institute* real possibilities for action, hence the importance of social *institutions*. At the same time, and inseparably, they *constrain* the actions that can be performed.

b. Technical artifacts, technology, and technological systems present the same institutional/constraining duality as social structures in general. The thematization of technical artifacts by phenomenology confers on the relational nature of the social a dimension that is not only linguistic, but also *material*; this importance of material artifacts has long been under-estimated, if not entirely ignored, by traditional social science.

c. A system of technical artifacts functions as a *collective memory* that is always already-there for members of a given society, but that is not a part of their own experience before they themselves (re)appropriate it. This appropriation is performed by individuals, but the technical system is always already-social; thus, the system mediates a process of individuation which is inseparably psychic and collective. This articulation between the individual and the social is a key element in the formation of the social bond.

d. The actions that are made possible by a technical system do not derive logically from preexisting intentions; rather, they take the form of a stream of actions that are essentially prereflexive. These actions do presuppose a certain form of knowledge and capacity, but this knowledge is practical and does not (necessarily) have to be formulated by the actor in proposi-tional terms.

e. Such actions are open to reflexive control, but this control should be regarded as partial and plastic. In fact, the motivation is not always con-scious for the actor, and the structural conditions of his action are often unknown to him. The rationalization of his course of actions should thus be regarded as opening up the possibility of significant developments in the actor's understanding of himself and the social world.

The thematization of technical artifacts also has a number of epistemologi-cal consequences, which may be briefly summarized as follows.

a. This new perspective makes it possible to go beyond the long, drawn-out opposition between "holism"—the insistence that society is more and something other than the sum of its parts, even in interaction, but with a corresponding difficulty of analyzing what happens at the level of individuals—and "individualism," which puts the emphasis on individuals and their local interactions, but which misses the very notion of society as a whole. Thematizing the role of technical artifacts—which are, of course, in the last resort, produced by individual actions—clearly identifies a level that is more and other than the resultant dynamics of individual actions, and at the same time, leaves room for the study of the processes of individuation which occur as individuals (re)appropriate technical artifacts designed and produced by absent Others, including past generations. This perspective orients sociological research toward social *processes,* toward society as it is continually "in the making," rather than reifying society as a static fait accompli.

b. Because the social sciences study an entity (society) that is *already* interpreted by the human actors themselves, and where the meanings elaborated by these actors enter into the actual production of their social world, there is at work a *double hermeneutics* (Giddens 1984) specific to the human sciences, which has no counterpart in the natural sciences. As a complexifying extension, this means that the interpretations produced by social scientists can perfectly well be (re)appropriated by the actors themselves. There is thus a continual slippage concerning the concepts elaborated by social scientists, which can become inherent characteristics of the behavior they study.

c. This gives a peculiar twist to the problem of the nondesired effects of action (as illustrated by the case of "self-fulfilling prophecies"). There is a peculiar indetermination to the epistemology of the social sciences, which is thus quite different from the indeterminacy of quantum physics.

d. There is a sociological problem concerning the *appropriation* and the *use* of technical systems. The "goals" that are followed emerge from a social process that is distributed among many actors, and that no single individual can totally master. Experience shows clearly that technical devices and systems systematically outrun the preconceived goals of the engineers and industrialists who first designed them.

12.3   Implications for Enaction

In this section, I shall examine some implications of this new perspective for cognitive science and technology. I shall take, as a metonymical example, the work of the Perceptual Supplementation Group at the University of Compiègne.

12.3.1 Cognitive Psychology and Perceptual Supplementation

Many commentators have remarked that the "phenomenological psychology" of Husserl has an uncertain status between transcendental phenomenology on one hand, and psychology considered as an empirical science on the other. We shall here propose the thesis that this "phenomenological psychology" is neither more nor less than psychology reconsidered in the perspective of enactive cognitive science. Here, cognition is no longer considered as a linear input/output sequence (as was the case in classical cognitivism), but rather in terms of a dynamic sensorimotor loop by taking into account the fact that the actions themselves produce feedback effects on subsequent sensations. Action is thus no longer a simple output; it becomes actually constitutive of perception. What is perceived and recognized in perception are the invariants of the sensorimotor loops, which are inseparable from the actions of the subject.

This reversal of perspective is particularly well illustrated when the action is mediated by a technical device; the intervention of such a device makes manifest what can otherwise easily be ignored. This is clearly shown by a classical series of experiments by Bach-y-Rita (1972), involving a "Tactile Visual Sensory Substitution" device (TVSS) aimed at procuring visual-type perceptions for blind subjects. The device is the following: the output of a video camera is transformed electronically into a pattern of tactile stimulation by a 20×20 matrix of elements placed on the skin. In the control situation, learning takes place passively: the experimenter puts various objects with simple shapes in front of the camera; the subject tries to recognize them. The results are disappointing: after several weeks of training, the subjects manage, with difficulty, to recognize a few simple forms. By contrast, in the experiment itself, learning (and perception) is active: the subjects are able to orient the camera from left to right, up and down, and to zoom in and out. The results are dramatic: in these conditions, learning is vastly more rapid and effective—the subjects can, for example, recognize faces. Moreover, there is a fascinating corollary: the subjects no longer feel shapes on their skin, but rather perceive *objects* that are situated "out there" in space. In other words, the constitution of distal perception requires an engagement of the subject in action. Experiments of "perceptual supplementation" using a graphic tablet and the TACTOS software for the perception of two-dimensional forms lead to similar conclusions (Lenay and Sebbah 2001; Lenay, Stewart, and Gapenne 2003). This primacy of action means that one really perceives only what results from one's own actions. Far from being a passive reception of input stimuli followed by computational information processing and leading to internal representations of external objects, perception is inseparable from the activity of the subject and the regularities in the sensorimotor loops that are thereby constructed. It can be concluded that *perception,* far from being a representation or a correspondence relation with an independently constituted object, is fundamentally *action,* and as such, *perception is the conjoint bringing forth of the "subject" and the "object"* (Havelange, Lenay, and Stewart 2002). This process of enaction, which characterizes living organisms in general, is rendered particularly manifest by employing simple technical devices, as the constitutive sensorimotor dynamics mediated by such devices are externalized in a form that makes them particularly easy to observe.

What are the implications of this approach? We shall examine them thematically, and then methodologically (Havelange 2005).

Thematically, this research shows that a new technical device—be it a means of action, an instrument of measure, or a device for mediating the transmission of linguistic signs—becomes really effective only when it is so intimately *integrated by use* into the dynamics of the perception-action loop that it *disappears from consciousness* and becomes in effect an extension of the lived-body; this is the case with the TVSS and the TACTOS systems, as indeed with everyday tools.

The methodological aspect of this approach follows directly from these considerations. The *modes of appropriation* of a technical device potentially form a *concrete attestation,* a *practical operator* of the phenomenological reduction and phenomenological constitution. As such, they open the way to an experimental cognitive psychology *articulated* with a phenomenological approach. There are two stages in this research.

1. The first stage consists of inviting the subjects to give an explicit, analytical description of their actions as mediated by the technical device. This description makes it possible to grasp the constitution of the spatial object, disconnected from any reference to an "object" that is already constituted. In a way, making this sort of explicit description plays the role of a phenomenological reduction, because it suspends the "natural attitude" where attention is focused on the object "out there." Let us recall that in normal, accomplished use, the technical device is not thematized as such; it becomes "transparent" and disappears from consciousness. The important point is that when the subjects give an explicit account of their own actions, the technical device that formats these actions comes back into consciousness—and concomitantly, the object "out there" disappears. Phenomenological analysis thus reveals that there is an incompatibility,

something like a Gestalt "switch," between the routine performance of the perceptual actions on one hand, and on the other an explicit analytical description of the actions. This mutual exclusion between the two attitudes means that there is no unconditional object "in itself"; yet there is a relation between these two attitudes, because mutual exclusion itself is not an absence of relation. It is important to note that the difference in attitude is *not* that between a first-person and third-person point of view, because the same first-person subject can shift from one attitude to the other. The difference is internal to the first-person point of view; it does not concern the course of action, but the point of focal attention *during* the course of action. *Either*, during perception in the act, I am present to the object, my attention is directed to the object "out there" (in phenomenological terms, the object appears in the natural attitude), *or*, during explicit analytical description of the action, I am attentive to the actions through which the object is constituted (in phenomenological terms, the mode of appearance of that which appears, which is accessible via the reduction)—but in this case, the "object out there" disappears from my field of experience.

2. The second stage in the psychology of perceptual supplementation consists of using the analytical descriptions of their actions by the subjects, to formulate a mathematical model of the sensorimotor dynamics that generate these actions. Now, to the extent that these models are a reformulation and reinscription of the analytical descriptions of the actions mediated by the TACTOS device, the question arises as to the status and the validity of these models. If the scientific objective is to account for the perceptual activity as it occurs when the subjects act spontaneously, "without thinking about it," can these models claim to achieve this goal? Rather than considering them to be an objectivized "sign" or "clue" that "runs parallel" to the phenomenological description, it seems better to consider these models as a *new inscription*, a *new device*, which forms a compromise between what the subjects did spontaneously in the natural attitude and their own analytical descriptions of their activity. The models, far from being neutral, are constrained by the particular requirements of scientific explanation,[5] but in the end, they are themselves devices that contribute to the mediation of the action. It is thus not surprising that, just like the TVSS and TACTOS, a period of learning is necessary for them to be appropriated and integrated into the lived-body. In the present experimental setting, the subjects are at first uneasy about the model. But as they practice integrating the model into their routine instrumental action, the time comes when they *forget* the model; a bodily *habitus* is installed, so that the subjects can again "act without thinking." It is at this

moment, but at this moment only, that the "object out there" makes its reappearance.[6]

This approach has three consequences. First, it emphasizes that what is at stake in instrumental perceptual action is the *appropriation of the technical devices that mediate the action.* The lived-body and its passive, preobjective activity are fundamental to perception. As Merleau-Ponty (1962) has pointed out, a technical device becomes constitutive only to the extent that it is appropriated by an original lived-body that is a capacity for engagement in the world; it is to the extent that it is grasped and integrated into the lived-body that a technical device can become an extension of the body, and hence reconfigure perceptual modalities and open up new fields of possible experience. This is why *learning, anchored in the lived-body,* is a central dimension of perception.

The second consequence of this approach is to make it both possible and necessary to differentiate between the concepts of "motricity" and "action." Between the two poles of *motricity* as a primordial form of intentionality, and *action* as the result-laden impulsion whereby a human agent engages the world and operates the synthesis of self that constitutes him as a subject (Salanskis 2000), the *use* of technical devices appears in the first instance as an intermediary moment wherein it is possible to establish a manner of *doing* characterized by habits and inherited gestures that are not thematized as such. However, this relation to technical devices and systems is not necessarily fixed or definitive. On the contrary, the frontier between *use* and *action* is constantly moving. It is indeed quite possible for the focus of attention to shift and to settle on the technical device itself, accompanied by a reflexive thematization of its role in the constitution of perception, but it is important to see that such a thematization itself requires a *new* material inscription (in the example given previously, the formulation of mathematical models), and the appropriation of these *new* technical devices will in turn engender—and constrain—new fields of experience.

Finally—and this point follows from the two preceding ones—this analysis sheds new light on the problem of "naturalization" in cognitive science. It should be quite clear that what is envisaged here is in no way a "naturalization of phenomenology." Rather, the psychology of perceptual supplementation proposes a dynamic relation of hermeneutical circularity—itself constantly shifting—between the natural attitude, phenomenological description, and scientific enquiry. As Husserl emphasized in his late writings, phenomenological reduction is a methodological moment that, based on a concrete a priori (in this context, that of the lived-body), both *presupposes* the natural attitude of the *Lebenswelt*, and ceaselessly brings us back to it—which calls for new reductions, so that overall there is constantly renewed movement. Scientific activity is truly meaningful only if it recognizes itself as a specific moment in this overall movement.

12.3.2 Emotional Motivation and Social Bond in the Appropriation of Perceptual Devices

In this perspective, we shall evoke an aspect of the research on perceptual supplementation that has recently been explored by Charles Lenay (2004). A serious limitation of the original TVSS device, and its successors, is that they have never really been taken up by the blind community (whether the blindness is congenital or accidental in later life); an obvious reason for this is that these devices do not convey any significant emotional or affective values. Lenay has suggested that this lack of emotional investment in the perceptual supplementation devices results from the fact that their appropriation occurs in a strictly individual fashion. It is therefore important to reject the ego-centered approach of Husserl's initial analysis of intersubjectivity that we have presented, and criticized, in section 12.2.2.2. On the contrary; the Other can be recognized not by analogy on the basis of his objective body, but by his own perceptual activity and capacity to act. The question of the mutual constitution of two subjectivities has been studied experimentally with a variant of the TACTOS interface. Here, two subjects each move in a common space. The conjoint dynamics of the two perceptual trajectories gives rise to an oscillation between synchronization and desynchronization, a *metasynchronization* that is the delicate and subtle point where the two trajectories attract each other without fusion; this is when the perceptual co-constitution of the subjects occurs. Described from a first-person perspective, the metasynchronization means that "insofar as he escapes me, I perceive the Other as a constitutive subject; insofar as I can grasp him, he is spatialized; the perception of this duality is the perception of a point of view that is different from mine" (Lenay 2004).The interest of this approach is that it establishes an articulation between, on the one hand, the co-constitution of two (or several) subjects via their prosthetic action (these subjects thereby form a community of shared practice), and on the other hand the emergence of a social symbolism. The spatial articulation of the different points of view makes it possible to recognize certain stabilized behaviors as having the value of *signs* or *symbols* of belonging to a community. The condition for the co-constitution of this shared objectivity is that the different partners should engage in a *common* environment where their lived-bodies, and the images of their objective bodies, can interact. The condition of possibility for these co-ordinations is then defined as the capacity of each subject to understand the point of view of the other subjects—which implies a spatial localization of the point of view of the Other: "It is only on this condition that the Other is present, that his gestures are meaningful to me, that I have the feeling that we share the same world, the same problems and the same goals for a collaborative activity" (Lenay 2004). This is very close to the conceptual framework deployed by Husserl in the third section of *Ideen II*, where social subjects and social action are instituted by the perception of the expressions and the actions of others as being immediately meaning-laden; these actions are typically mediated by cultural objects or "mind-laden objects." This concept, which was taken up by Schutz (1967) implies that it is possible to put myself in someone else's place, to understand their intentions by practical engagement in the relation with them; this is possible because they—and I myself—are *immediately*, right from the start, social beings.

When the perceptual supplementation device is appropriated not in individual isolation, but straight away in a collective way, the device no longer stigmatizes the blind person in the eyes of others, but rather becomes an integral part of his lived-body that is immediately and directly a social body. It thus becomes, in the same way as my spectacles (for example), "something that can be interpreted just like other features of my face, that I recognize and accept in a vocabulary that we share sufficiently" (Lenay 2004). The constitutive status of technical mediation in the formation of the social bond can henceforward be thematized; a technical device becomes "transparent" to the very extent that it contributes to the constitution of a common world.

The problem of our society of hyper-reproducible mass media is, according to Lenay, not so much the uniformization as such; rather, it is the "parallelism" of the perceptual activities that it induces. It is the absence of spatializing interactions that prevents the constitution of a reciprocity in points of view. What is at stake in the (re)production of technical devices is the fact that, when they place us in the situation of having identical possibilities of action-perception with respect to the environment, they condemn us to isolation, because they deprive us of the possibility of constituting points of view that are spatially differentiated from each other. In these conditions, perceptual crossing is no longer possible, and so there is no longer the possibility of constituting either (inter)subjectivity or objectivity. As Lenay emphasizes, depending on the functional relationships they institute, technical devices can either lead to the formation of communities with a history, or else reduce the users to anonymity and to the isolation of parallelism.

The question of the critical reappropriation of technical devices is thus posed at the very level of scientific research and technological invention considered as social activities. The double hermeneutics that characterizes cognitive science places scientists and engineers squarely in front of their social responsibilities.

12.4 Conclusions and Perspectives

What conclusions can be gathered from the ground we have covered? I shall summarize the main results, first from the point of view of a philosophical elaboration of the concept of technical artifacts and, conjointly, of social being; then concerning the renewed relation between phenomenology and cognitive science that this elaboration makes possible; and finally from the viewpoint of the constitution of cognitive psychology and sociology.

In the first place, the major achievement of the work we have studied is to rescue technical artifacts from their classical status of being merely empirically constituted instrumental means, and to raise them to a fully philosophical plane. This is the common feature that, in spite of all their differences, marks the approaches of Husserl, Derrida, and Stiegler, as well as the Perceptual Supplementation Group. This work establishes a decisive distinction between the empirical notion of *technical artifact* and the philosophical notion of *technicity*. The latter can be variously identified as the concrete a priori conditioning the constitution and historical transmission of idealities (Husserl [1938/1939] 1954); as a quasi-transcendental structure, neither sensible nor intelligible, that makes all material inscriptions possible and that authorizes different forms of supplementarity and differentiation (Derrida 1978); or as an a-transcendental structure that enables the inheritance of that which is historically always already-there, and that enables also an anticipation of the future (Stiegler 1998). This distinction between *technical artifacts* and *technicity* turns out to be crucial in order to avoid apprehending technical artifacts in a positivist manner, and by contrast to confer on technicity the conceptual status of a mediation that the dominant traditional metaphysics denies to it. In this perspective, technicity emerges as the indispensable element for conceiving of genesis and individuation as dimensions of being in constant differentiation.

Conjointly, this work makes it possible to raise *social being* to the status of a philosophical concept. Thus, social being can no longer be conceived as a simple generalization or extrapolation of intersubjectivity. As we have already noted, sociality implies a third element which *creates the possibility* for face-to-face relations and the institution of a symbolic realm (Benoist 2001). This "third element" is to be found in the "mind-laden objects," the technical and cultural objects which are to be thought of as *constitutive* of socialization and history. However, it is only insofar as they are articulated with a *passive bodily Self, which is primordial self-affection and indeterminate drive to intentionality,* that these third elements can be more than inert and nonexperienced residues, that they can be actualized, and that their meaning can be reactivated and transmitted as such.

The second result is that this distinction between technical artifacts and technicity opens the way to thematizing a renewed relation of *reciprocal presupposition*, of *hermeneutical circularity in constant movement*, between phenomenology on one hand and cognitive science on the other. This requires a double thematization of constitution in enactive cognitive science: an *epistemological* constitution of the mode of appearance of objects via the method of phenomenological reduction, and an *ontological* constitution in terms of the construction (*Bildung*, formation) of the types of aperceptual acts performed by cognitive subjects. This approach is quite different from the project of "naturalizing phenomenology," where phenomenology is reduced to the role of an "inspired precursor," which can be discarded once its translation into an adequate *mathesis* is achieved (Petitot 1999). What we envisage here is establishing a *nonreductionist, nonnaturalizing* relation between phenomenology and science. This involves a double requirement: on one hand keeping constantly open the problem of the methods and goals of phenomenology; on the other, ceaselessly posing the question of the preconditions for the constitution of scientific knowledge. On this condition, but only on this condition, a relation of hermeneutical circularity between these two fields of research can emerge in a constant movement of mutual critique and renewal.

Finally, this phenomenological enquiry has also exerted a fruitful influence on the sciences of mind (*Geisteswissenschaften*). It is through the impulsion of phenomenology that contemporary cognitive psychology and sociology deepen our understanding of the constitutive role of the lived-body and mind-laden technical objects in conjointly bringing forth human beings and their *Lebenswelt*. Human techniques, in their specificity, must be referred to a technicity that engages not only a thematization of technical objects and devices, but also a thematization of embodiment and the diverse modes of appropriation and actual use by human agents. In this way, a renewed form of cognitive psychology and sociology bring their attention to bear on the technical devices which are at the heart of the processes of subjectivation and socialization. In return, the constitution of these disciplines themselves turns out to be grounded in a double hermeneutics, wherein the specifically anthropological dimension of technicity can be discerned.

Notes

1. The term "autopoiesis" is absent from the index of *The Embodied Mind* (Varela, Thompson, and Rosch 1991). This question of a "hiatus" between ontological and epistemological constitution—here, between autopoiesis and enaction—is related to the reflexive character of cognitive science. This question also arises in other texts in this book, and is briefly addressed in the introduction.

2. This contrasts, notably, with the primacy that Kant accorded to Newtonian physics.

3. Passivity, in Husserl's work, is not to be understood as opposed to activity, but solely to conscious, deliberate activity.

4. It is probably because it corresponds to a transmutation of Husserl's initial program that the elaboration of *Ideen II* was extended over many years (1912–1928).

5. Husserl ([1935/1937] 1970), and later Merleau-Ponty ([1945] 1962), have insisted on the fact that scientific experience is one among many forms of lived experiences, with its own highly specific constraints.

6. This is the process that Stewart and Gapenne (2004) have called "reciprocal modelling." It is blatantly clear that here, scientific observation and modeling interfere with what is observed. These authors argue that this is acceptable, assuming of course that the "co-construction" of the model and the observed behavior converges to a stable, coherent solution.

References

Bach-y-Rita, P. (1972). *Brain mechanisms in sensory substitution*. New York: Academic Press.

Benoist, J. (2001). Intersubjectivité et socialité: la phénoménologie et la question du tiers. In *Phénoménologie et sociologie*, ed. J. Benoist and B. Karsenti, 19–42. Paris: P.U.F.

Depraz, N. (1994). Le phénomène de l'affection dans les manuscrits tardifs sur la temporalité (1929–1935) de Husserl. *Alter* 2:63–86.

Derrida, J. (1978). *Edmund Husserl's* Origin of Geometry. Stony Brook, NY: Nicolas Hays.

Giddens, A. (1984). *The constitution of society*. Oxford: Polity Press, and Cambridge, MA: Blackwell.

Havelange, V., Lenay, C., and Stewart, J. (2002). Les représentations: mémoire externe et objets techniques. *Intellectica* 35:115–129.

Havelange, V. (2005). De l'outil à la médiation constitutive: pour une réévaluation phénoménologique, biologique et anthropologique de la technique. In *Suppléances perceptives et interfaces*, vol. 1, ed. O. Gapenne and P. Gaussier, 8–45. http://www.univ-rouen.fr/Arobase/v8/havelange.pdf.

Husserl, E. [1905–1917] (1991). *Vorlesungen zur Phänomenologie des inneres Zeitbewusstseins [On the phenomenology of the consciousness of internal time]*. Husserl Collected Works, vol. 4, trans. J. B. Brough. Dordrecht: Kluwer.

Husserl, E. [1907] (1997). *Ding und Raum [Thing and space]: Lectures of 1907*. Husserl Collected Works, vol. 7, trans. R. Rojcewicz. Dordrecht: Kluwer.

Husserl, E. [1913] (1982). *Ideen I, Ideas pertaining to a pure phenomenology and to a phenomenological philosophy, First book: General introduction to a pure phenomenology*. Husserl Collected Works, vol. 2, trans. F. Kersten. Dordrecht: Kluwer.

Husserl, E. [1912–1928] (1980). *Ideen II, Ideas pertaining to a pure phenomenology and to a phenomenological philosophy, Second book: Studies in the phenomenology of constitution*. Husserl Collected Works, vol. 3, trans. R. Rojcewicz and A. Schuwer. Dordrecht: Kluwer.

Husserl, E. [1923/1924] (1956/1959). *Erste Philosophie I, II [First philosophy]*, *Husserliana VII–VIII*. Ed. K. Boehm. The Hague: Martinus Nijhoff.

Husserl, E. [1925] (1962). *Phänomenologische Psychologie [Phenomenological psychology]*, *Husserliana IX*. Ed. W. Biemel. The Hague: Martinus Nijhoff.

Husserl, E. [1935/1937] (1970). *Krisis: The crisis of European sciences and transcendental phenomenology*, trans. D. Carr. Evanston: Northwestern University Press.

Husserl, E. [1938/1939] (1954). Die Frage nach dem Ursprung der Geometrie als intentional-historisches Problem [The origin of geometry]. *Revue Internationale de Philosophie I*, ed. E. Fink, 203–225. Reprinted in *Husserliana VI*, ed. W. Biemel, 365–386. The Hague: Martinus Nijhoff.

Lenay, C. (2004). Croisements perceptifs et spatialisation des points de vue: prothèses et communautés techniques. In *La lutte pour l'organisation du sensible: Comment repenser l'esthétique?*, ed. B. Stiegler and G. Collins. Normandy: Colloque de Cerisy-la-Salle.

Lenay, C., and Sebbah, F. (2001). La constitution de la perception spatiale. Approches phénoménologique et expérimentale. *Intellectica* 32:45–85.

Lenay, C., Stewart, J., and Gapenne, O. (2003). Espace d'action, technique et geste perceptif. In *Le geste technique: Réflexions méthodologiques et anthropologiques*, ed. B. Bril and V. Roux, 215–230. TIP, Revue d'Anthropologie des connaissances. Paris: Erès.

Maturana, H. R. (1988). Ontology of observing: The biological foundations of self consciousness and the physical domain of existence. In *Proceedings of the Conference on Texts in Cybernetic Theory*. Felton, CA: American Society for Cybernetics.

Merleau-Ponty, M. [1945] (1962). *Phenomenology of perception*. London: Routledge.

Petitot, J. (1999). Morphological eidetics of perception. In *Naturalizing phenomenology: Issues in contemporary phenomenology and cognitive science*, ed. J. Petitot, F. Varela, B. Pachoud, and J.-M. Roy, 427–484. Stanford, CA: Stanford University Press.

Petitot, J., Varela, F., Pachoud, B., and Roy, J.-M., eds. (1999). *Naturalizing phenomenology: Issues in contemporary phenomenology and cognitive science*. Stanford, CA: Stanford University Press.

Salanskis, J.-M. (2000). *Modèles et pensées de l'action*. Paris: L'Harmattan.

Schutz, A. (1967). *The phenomenology of the social world*, trans. G.Walsh and F. Lehnert. Evanston, IL: Northwestern University Press.

Stewart, J., and Gapenne, O. (2004). Reciprocal modelling of active perception of 2-D forms in a simple tactile-vision substitution system. *Minds and Machines* 14:309–330.

Stiegler, B. (1998). *Technics and time, 1—The fault of Epimetheus*, trans. R. Beardsworth and G. Collins. Stanford, CA: Stanford University Press.

Varela, F., Thompson, E., and Rosch, E. (1991). *The embodied mind*. Cambridge, MA: MIT Press.

13   Embodiment or Envatment?: Reflections on the Bodily Basis of Consciousness

Diego Cosmelli and Evan Thompson

Suppose that a team of neurosurgeons and bioengineers were able to remove your brain from your body, suspend it in a life-sustaining vat of liquid nutrients, and connect its neurons and nerve terminals by wires to a supercomputer that would stimulate it with electrical impulses exactly like those it normally receives when embodied. According to this brain-in-a-vat thought experiment, your envatted brain and your embodied brain would have subjectively indistinguishable mental lives. For all you know—so one argument goes—you could be such a brain in a vat right now.[1]

Daniel Dennett calls this sort of philosophical thought experiment an "intuition pump" (1995). An intuition pump is designed to elicit certain intuitive convictions, but is not itself a proper argument: "Intuition pumps are fine if they're used correctly, but they can also be misused. They're not arguments, they're stories. Instead of having a conclusion, they pump an intuition. They get you to say 'Aha! Oh, I get it!'" (Dennett 1995, 182).

Philosophers have used the brain-in-a-vat story mainly to raise the problem of radical skepticism and to elicit various intuitions about meaning and knowledge (Putnam 1981). The basic intuition the story tries to pump is that the envatted brain, though fully conscious, has systematically false beliefs about the world, including itself. Some philosophers reject this intuition. They propose that the envatted brain's beliefs are really about its artificial environment or that it has no real beliefs at all. According to these proposals, the mental lives of the two brains do not match, despite their being subjectively indistinguishable.

Dennett (1978) tells a classic variant of the brain-in-a-vat story, one in which he sees his own envatted brain and knows that it remotely controls his own body, but still cannot experience himself as located where his brain is located. Here the thought experiment serves to raise questions about the locus of the self in the physical world.

Underlying these varied uses and rival assessments lies a fundamental, shared intuition—that a suitably working human brain is not only necessary, but also sufficient all on its own for the instantiation or realization of our subjective mental life. Given our knowledge that the physical processes crucial for human mentality occur in the human brain, it seems imaginable that these processes could occur in the absence of the rest of the body, as long as the right causal supports were provided, and that such disembodiment would make no difference to our subjective experience. This idea is the deeper "Aha! Oh, I get it!" intuition the brain-in-a-vat story pumps.

As Dennett notes, philosophers often fail to set up their intuition pumps properly by failing to think carefully about the requirements and implications of their imagined scenarios. Brain-in-a-vat stories typify this shortcoming. Philosophers help themselves to this scenario and the basic intuition that it is supposed to pump without thinking about what the scenario actually demands of our imagination when we try to spell out the story in sufficient detail. In this way, they make substantive empirical assumptions about the biological requirements for consciousness that may well be false, and they ignore the difficult conceptual problem of how to distinguish within those biological requirements between what contributes only causally to the production of subjective experience and what constitutes or instantiates or realizes subjective experience.

We propose to take Dennett's advice to heart and think carefully about the details of this thought experiment. Given our knowledge of the brain, what do we need to specify in order to imagine properly a brain in a vat? In addressing this question, we intend to put the brain-in-a-vat thought experiment to a new use, namely, to address the biology of consciousness and to develop some new considerations in support of the enactive approach in cognitive science (Thompson 2007).

13.1 The Argument in a Nutshell

When theorists invoke the notion of a brain in a vat, they invariably take a unidirectional control perspective and view the brain as a kind of reflexive machine whose activity is externally controllable. Yet numerous neurobiological considerations count against this viewpoint and indicate that the brain needs to be seen as a complex and self-organizing dynamical system that is tightly coupled to the body at multiple levels. The following points in particular deserve mention:

• Brain activity is largely generated endogenously and spontaneously.

• Brain activity requires massive resources and regulatory processes from the rest of the body.

• Brain activity plays crucial roles in life-regulation processes of the entire organism and these processes necessitate the maintenance of viable sensorimotor coupling with the world.

• Thus the neurally enlivened organism meets the world on its own, endogeneously generated sensorimotor terms.

Given these points, we propose the following null hypothesis for the brain-in-a-vat thought experiment: Any truly functional "vat" would need to be a surrogate body subject to control by the brain. By "body" we mean a self-regulating system comprising its own internal, homeodynamic processes and capable of sensorimotor coupling with the outside world. In short, the so-called vat would be no vat at all, but rather some kind of autonomous embodied agent.

This supposition has an important implication. It implies that our default assumption should be that the biological requirements for subjective experience are not particular brain regions or areas as such, but rather some crucial set of integrated neural-somatic systems capable of autonomous functioning. This assumption is one of the core working assumptions of the enactive approach (Thompson 2007).

13.2   Enactive versus Neurocentric Views of Consciousness

Before looking at the supporting evidence for the previous argument, we need to introduce some important concepts and distinctions. We can begin with the following enactive proposal about the brain basis of consciousness: "We conjecture that consciousness depends crucially on the manner in which brain dynamics are embedded in the somatic and environmental context of the animal's life, and therefore that there may be no such thing as a minimal internal neural correlate whose intrinsic properties are sufficient to produce conscious experience" (Thompson and Varela 2001, 425). According to this proposal, the processes crucial for consciousness are not confined to the brain, but include the body embedded in the environment. For example, somatic life-regulation processes contribute to affect and sense of self (Damasio 1999), and dynamic sensorimotor activity contributes to the qualitative content of perceptual experience (Hurley and Noë 2003).

Ned Block (2005a) has recently argued that this sort of proposal fails to distinguish clearly between causation and constitution, that is, between what causally contributes to consciousness and what neurobiologically constitutes consciousness. In the orthodox view, although conscious experience causally depends on the body and environment, it is directly determined by brain activity.[2] This view can be given either a neuroscientific or philosophical formulation. According to the neuroscience version, some specific neural system or set of neural processes is the minimal biological substrate for conscious experience. According to the philosophy version, some specific set of neural processes is the minimal sufficient condition or minimal supervenience base or minimal realizing system for conscious experience.

A proper statement of this orthodox view, however, requires some refinements. We need to distinguish between the *core neural realization* and the *total neural realization* of consciousness or a given conscious state (Block 2005b; Chalmers 2000). In general, the core realization of a property or a capacity suffices for that property or capacity only when placed in the context of a larger system that constitutes the total realization (Shoemaker 1981; Wilson 2001). Block proposes that "the core NCC [neural correlate of consciousness] is the *part* of the total NCC that distinguishes one conscious state from another—the rest of the total NCC being considered as the enabling conditions for the conscious experience" (Block 2005b, 47).

Yet even this formulation remains incomplete. In general, the total realization of a property or a capacity suffices for that property or capacity only given the appropriate *background conditions* (Wilson 2001). So the total neural realization suffices for consciousness only given certain background conditions, which in the normal case include nonneural parts of the body and the environment.

We can now give a fuller statement of the orthodox and neurocentric view of consciousness. Given the appropriate background conditions (e.g., in the body and the environment), the total neural realizer suffices for consciousness all by itself; the core neural realizer suffices to determine a given conscious state (as specified by its content) and thus to distinguish one conscious state from another.

When we spell out the neurocentric view in this way, we bring to light a number of important problems that have been largely ignored by philosophical discussions that rely on the causal-versus-constitutive distinction for the brain basis of consciousness. Here is a list of these problems:

• In the case at hand, it is not clear how to draw the causal/constitutive distinction. What are the criteria for determining what is causal and what is constitutive in the neurobiology of consciousness?

• The same question can be raised about the notions of core realization, total realization, and background conditions. What are the criteria for drawing these distinctions and applying them to the neurobiology of consciousness?

• A given core realizer and/or constitutive supervenience base are usually identified by appealing to what plays the most salient causal role with regard to the instantiation of some property. In the case of the brain basis of consciousness, however, what plays the most salient causal role in any given case is far from clear (see the next point).

• The question "What plays the most salient causal role?" typically cannot be answered for complex (nonlinear) systems, such as the brain, by pointing to the behavior of individual elements independent of the context of all the other state variables of the system (Cosmelli, Lachaux, and Thompson 2007; Wagner 1999). In dense nonlinear systems in which all state variables interact with each other, any change in an individual variable becomes inseparable from the state of the entire system. In such cases, the distinction between regular causes (regularities in the system's behavior) and singular causes (unique nonrepeatable events that change the system's behavior) becomes meaningless (Wagner 1999), and there is arguably no core realizer for a given property or behavior less than the system itself.

• Finally, causal salience is an interest-relative and context-sensitive notion. Therefore, we seem to have no independent grip on constitution or realization (as metaphysical notions) apart from particular explanatory contexts.

These considerations suggest the following thoughts. At present, we have no clear way to draw the line between what is constitutive and what is causal in the biology of consciousness. To draw this line, we would need to have a far more developed understanding of the brain as a complex system and how its activity as a complex system is related to the body and environment. In the absence of this knowledge, we cannot assume that the brain suffices to realize consciousness all on its own apart from the body, or that particular neural systems suffice to realize one or another conscious state independent of the rest of the brain and the body.

How, then, might we proceed in the face of these problems? One way would be to ask what we could remove on the bodily side from a normal embodied brain while still preserving consciousness. Indeed, the brain-in-a-vat thought experiment proceeds exactly this way, by assuming that we could remove the body entirely, as long as everything else in the brain were held constant. In this way, the body can be shown to be inessential for the realization of consciousness, that is, as merely causally supportive or enabling, but not constitutive. Yet what if it were not possible to hold everything in the brain constant in the absence of the body? If certain brain processes simply could not be realized in the absence of the body, and these brain processes included those crucial for consciousness, then we would have reason to believe that the body is not merely causally enabling for consciousness, but also constitutive. The argument of this paper is that the brain-in-vat thought experiment, when spelled out with the requisite detail, suggests precisely this result.

13.3   A Close Look at the Brain in a Vat

We now need to examine in some detail the supporting evidence for this argument. In particular, we need to consider: (1) the demands of keeping the brain alive and up and running, (2) the spontaneous and endogenous activity of the brain in relation to the body, and (3) what it takes to mimic precisely the stimulation the nervous system normally receives from the environment.

13.3.1   Keeping the Brain Up and Running

Before getting to the point where we can stimulate the envatted brain or nervous system in a way that duplicates the stimulation it normally receives from the body and environment, we need to keep it alive and functioning. This already is no mean feat.

First, we need some protective apparatus for the brain. This apparatus serves to replace the skull (and spine, if we choose to keep the spinal cord). To ensure the brain's flotation, the protective device must be filled with a liquid analogous to the cerebrospinal fluid (CSF). This liquid needs to be able to remove waste products of neuronal metabolism and therefore needs to be continually recycled (Brown et al. 2004; Davson and Segal 1971; Segal 1993). One way to achieve such recycling would be to couple the protective fluid to the second thing we need—a circulatory system.

Almost everyone has experienced the intense dizziness that accompanies standing up fast and the resultant cognitive impairment. The unimpeded supply of blood to every part of the brain is critical for its functioning and by no means a trivial physiological accomplishment. To envat the brain, we must provide an adequate blood supply (or alternatively, a fluid with similar biochemical properties). For this task, we could probably choose to keep the vascular system in place as a delivery structure. Alternatively, in the true spirit of the thought experiment, we can imagine replacing the entire cerebral vasculature with some synthetic device that shows similar properties of selective permeability and local and systemic responsiveness to the ongoing demands of the brain-to-be-maintained. Such local and systemic responsiveness is absolutely crucial. Without it, there would be no way to compensate for even minimal departures from homeostasis due to neuronal activity, with fatal consequences for our experiment.

As early as 1890, Roy and Sherrington proposed that there should exist "an automatic mechanism by which the blood supply of any part of the cerebral tissue is varied in accordance with the activity of the chemical changes which underlie the functional activation of that part" (1890, 105). The coupling of blood flow and neuronal activity is a well established and basic physiological fact known as functional hyperemia (Hyder, Shulman, and Rothman 1999; Raichle and Stone 1971; Shulman, Hyder, and Rothman 2002). Indeed, many of the results informing contemporary hypotheses about the relation between brain and mind come from measurements of neuronal activity (fMRI, PET) that rely on different aspects of this coupling (Logothetis and Pfeuffer 2004). Although the actual mechanisms underlying this tight coupling are not fully understood, it appears that a variety of processes participate in the regulation of local blood flow, including direct neuronal release of vasoactive metabolic factors (such as H^+, K^+, lactate, adenosine, glutamate-induced neuronal production of nitric oxide, and several neurotransmitters; see Kandel, Schwartz, and Jessell 2000; Krimer et al. 1998; Paspalas and Papadopoulos 1998; Yang et al. 2000), astrocyte-mediated K^+ siphoning from active synaptic regions to the local microvasculature, and Ca^{2+} dependent release of vasoactive molecules through the astrocyte perivascular end-feet (Anderson and Nedergaard 2003; Zonta et al. 2003). Our sustaining system must therefore be capable of responding locally to these (and probably other) factors in a highly specific and efficient way in order to sustain the local needs arising from ongoing neuronal activity. It is not difficult to see that any such synthetic apparatus would probably be as sophisticated as an actual vascular system in both its structural features and functional capacities.

Suppose we have succeeded in setting up such an immensely complex system. It would then be necessary to move the fluid through the delivery structure. Here some kind of pump is needed, as well as some minimal and highly selective recycling system for replenishing the fluid's necessary components, including oxygen, glucose, and the numerous soluble ions, proteins, and other biomolecules that account for the fluid's osmotic, nutrient, and regulatory properties.

This pump and recycling system needs to be responsive to the brain's actual demands. To achieve this goal, some level of the brain's activity needs to be coupled to the functioning of the circulatory system. Such coupling would ensure the local availability of the soluble factors provided by the circulatory system and would keep the concentration of the circulating molecules and ions within a physiological range despite continuous demands from the neuronal tissue.[3]

To meet these needs, the brain normally relies on a series of mechanisms involving multiple regulatory loops (in addition to those controlling the mechanical circulation of the blood). For example, the main neuroendocrine regulatory loop responsible for the control and allocation of glucose—probably one the most important parameters for brain function (Kandel, Schwartz, and Jessell 2000; Peters et al. 2002; Peters et al. 2004)—is the limbic-hypothalamic-pituitary-adrenal (LHPA) axis. Under normal conditions, the brain controls the allocation of glucose through at least two mechanisms. On the one hand, a tight coupling exists between neuronal activity and glucose uptake from the blood through the astrocyte end-feet glucose transporter GLUT1. This local and rapid on-demand mechanism depends on synaptic glutamate release and an adequate electrochemical sodium gradient across the astrocytic membrane, and therefore already represents an important level of coupling between energy availability and ion balance. On the other hand, the brain can regulate the level of glucose in the blood through the LHPA system, whereby it controls the release from adrenal cortex of cortisol (which acts as a feedback signal to control the activity of the LHPA system through corticosteroid brain receptors) and adrenalin release from the adrenal medulla (through sympathetic innervations). The release of these hormones—along with the inhibition of insulin release from the pancreas and suppression of muscular and adipose tissue glucose uptake—results in the rise of glucose concentration in the blood in a manner that directly depends on the actual workings of the brain (and probably the body). The multiplicity and complexity of analogous regulatory loops involving organs outside the brain, including such factors critical to neuronal function as electrolyte balance (Hebert, Brown, and Harris 1997; Simard and Nedergaard 2004; Yano, Brown, and Chattopadhyay 2004) and water homeostasis (Amiry-Moghaddam and Ottersen 2003; Grubb, Raichle, and Eichling 1977), can be seen by reviewing any standard physiology textbook.

Let us summarize the discussion up to this point. However simplified the life-sustaining system we produce for a brain in a vat, this system must involve at least the capacity to keep up with the energetic, ionic, osmotic, and recycling needs of the brain. It will therefore include some kind of circulatory system, plus the necessary pumps, oxygenating devices, and additional subsystems for ensuring the maintenance of physiological levels in the circulating fluid. These points are obvious. The following point, however, is not so obvious: what the brain requires at any given instant depends on its own ongoing, moment-to-moment activity. Therefore, the life-sustaining system must not only be supportive of this activity, but also locally and systemically receptive and responsive to it at any given instant, independent of any external evaluation of the brain's needs. Consequently, to keep the brain alive and functioning, this responsive system will most likely need to be energetically open, and self-maintaining in a highly selective manner. In other words, it will need to have some kind of autonomy. This system is starting to look less like a vat and more like a body.

13.3.2   Life, Homeodynamics, and the Body-Coupled Brain

In trying to fill in some of the design specifications for a system capable of keeping an envatted brain up and running, we began by taking an external and unidirectional control perspective. From this perspective, the issue is how to control the brain from outside so that it remains alive and functioning. Yet once we take into account the brain's endogenous workings, it becomes obvious that our life-sustaining system must be intimately coupled to the nervous system's labile activity at almost every level of this system's construction and operation. This fundamental requirement necessitates a radical shift in how we think about our vat. Whatever life-sustaining system we construct, the functioning of its every part, as well as its overall coordinated activity, must be kept within a certain range by the nervous system itself in order for the brain to work properly. Hence the external and unidirectional control perspective is not generally valid. Instead, our life-sustaining system and the brain need to be seen as reciprocally coupled and mutually regulating systems.

The tight coupling between brain and body lies at the heart of the maintenance of organismic unity (Damasio 1999; Shewmon 2001; Swanson 2002). On the one hand, the nervous system tightly couples to the functioning of the body through numerous regulatory loops; on the other hand, the body's proper functioning ensures the brain's persistence as a functional subsystem. The nervous system's basic role is to ensure the maintenance of a homeodynamic regime. The nervous system evolved to coordinate movement—probably one of the most challenging threats to homeostasis—by systematically coupling motor and sensory surfaces while providing a stable, internal biochemical milieu (Swanson 2000, 2002). In constructing our vat, we need to keep in mind this crucial fact of neurally mediated organismic integration, because it provides the basic reference point for understanding the significance of neuronal activation overall. According to a number of authors, it also provides the basic underpinnings for subjectivity or the phenomenal sense of self (Craig 2002; Damasio 1998, 1999; Panksepp 1998a, b; Parvizi and Damasio 2001; Saper 2002).

From da Vinci's pithed frog to current studies on the tight relationship between damage to midbrain structures and comatose or persistent vegetative states, the importance of the nervous system for keeping the organism alive, awake, and behaving adaptively has been amply demonstrated (Blessing 1997). Yet specific proposals about how consciousness is related to bodily life-regulation have only recently appeared (Damasio 1999; Panksepp 1998a, b; Parvizi and Damasio 2001). According to these proposals, the physiological constitution of a stable yet dynamic "core self" acts as an essential organizing principle for consciousness and derives from the nervous system's capacity to monitor and ensure the body's integrity. If our envatted brain is to have a subjective sense of self comparable to that of an embodied brain, then we need somehow to preserve this core self for the brain in a vat. To appreciate the complexity of this requirement, it is worth mentioning a few details from these proposals about the neural constitution of the core self.

According to Damasio (1998, 1999), the nervous system provides a stable ongoing map of the body by continually tracing the state of the body through a series of core neural structures. This neural map constitutes a "proto-self" that provides a reference point for cognitive and conscious capacities, thereby anchoring these capacities in a fundamental life-preservation cycle (Parvizi and Damasio 2001). The relevant core neural structures comprise several levels of the neuraxis, including brainstem nuclei of bodily regulation, hypothalamus and basal forebrain, and insular and somatosensory cortices, including medial parietal areas. In this framework, interoception provides the organism with continuous updated information about the internal state of the entire body, not just the viscera (Craig 2002, 2003; Saper 2002). Signals converging onto core neural structures (mainly at the level of the brainstem) from proprioceptive, vestibular, visceral, and other internal sources, combined with corresponding efferent regulatory processes that keep these parameters within a tight domain of possible values, establish internal dynamical regularities that ensure the organism's viability through changing internal and external conditions. To support "mental processes and behaviors conducive to further homeosatic regulation" (Parvizi and Damasio 2001, 151), global bodily signals need to be integrated with the state of activation of the cortex. This integration occurs through brainstem nuclei providing a complex network of modulatory effects on cortical activity,[4] while rostral structures (such as the amygdala, cingulate gyrus, insula, and prefrontal cortex) provide descending influences on these brain-stem structures.

The importance of the basic self-preserving and self-monitoring organization of the nervous system within the body is likewise a central theme in Panksepp's work on affective neuroscience (1998a, b). According to Panksepp, a specific region in the midbrain, the periaqueductal gray (PAG), qualifies as a massive convergence zone where emotional and attentional circuits coming from rostral regions in the forebrain interact not only with sensory and vestibular signals converging from the adjacent colliculi and deep tectal areas, but also with motor maps present in the deep layers of the superior colliculi (SC) as well as motor signals from the mesencephalic locomotor region (Panksepp 1998b). Panksepp proposes that primary consciousness is more closely linked to internal motor processes than exteroceptive sensory processes. The primal motor map in the SC maintains more stable motor coordinates than do the corresponding sensory maps and thus provides a secure self-referential set of internal motor coordinates upon which various sensory and higher perceptual processes can operate (Panksepp 1998b). PAG constitutes the core of the visceral-hypothalamic-limbic axis responsible for the primitive self-centered emotional and motivational systems that interact with the cognitively oriented core of the somatic-thalamic-neocortical axis. Thus, in Panksepp's view, PAG serves as the substrate for a primal affective and sensorimotor sense of self.

Although Damasio and Panksepp differ on various specifics, they converge on certain fundamental points. First, life-regulation processes involving neural mappings of the body constitute a core self that grounds both neural activity overall and neural activity relevant to consciousness in particular. Second, primary consciousness includes an invariant basal awareness that remains constant across changing sensory contents. Third, this basal awareness is structured by an affective sense of phenomenal selfhood and thus constitutes a minimal form of subjectivity. Finally, primary consciousness or subjectivity needs to be seen as a large-scale feature of the homeodynamic life-regulation processes effected by the nervous system.

One more type of evidence for the notion of a vigilant and homeodynamically dedicated brain bears mention here. This evidence comes from functional magnetic resonance imaging (fMRI) studies. By analyzing a series of studies showing systematic task-independent decrease in activation in certain brain areas, Gusnard and Raichle (2001) uncovered a set of cortical regions that appear to be continuously active during the resting state and whose activity decreases only upon goal-directed behavior. These cortical regions fall into four main groups: (i) posterior medial cortices, including medial parietal regions (these regions form part of the proto-self for Damasio); (ii) inferior lateral parietal cortices that also show significant activation when recovering from anesthesia; (iii) ventral medial prefrontal areas, which interestingly receive convergence of internal bodily information and external sensory information through the orbital regions, and have strong connections to limbic structures, amygdala, ventral striatum, hypothalamus, PAG, and other brainstem nuclei; and (iv) dorsal medial prefrontal cortex, which is also active during self-directed behavior, such as monitoring one's own mental state (Gusnard and Raichle 2001). These results are consistent with the hypothesis that the brain, during resting conditions, is in a state of active bodily self-monitoring.

Furthermore, Raichle discusses another relevant issue in this context from a cost-analysis perspective (Raichle 2006; Raichle and Mintun 2006). Given that the brain needs no more than 1 percent of its total "energy budget" to deal with environmental demands, maintaining endogenous activity within viable limits is probably the most relevant task for the brain. In our view, this point suggests that self-sustaining ongoing activity, which is crucially coupled to the functioning of the body, holds the highest level in the control of brain functioning.

Let us return once again to our brain in a vat. If the previously mentioned proposals and hypotheses are sound, and if we were able to set up a life-sustaining system that also enabled the brain to maintain these self-related homeodynamic regimes, then we would have reason to believe that some kind of phenomenal subjectivity had been realized or instantiated by the envatted brain. This instantiation of subjectivity would depend on the integrity of the regulatory loops both within the brain and between the brain and its supporting vat-system, for these loops are what ensure the existence of the self-sustaining domain of physiological activity crucial for subjectivity.

From a neurocentric and unidirectional control perspective, it would seem that the brain is the superordinate controller of these regulatory loops. But this perspective is one-sided. It overlooks basic physiology, which tells us that the brain's functioning is also subordinate to the maintenance of bodily homeostasis. As we have seen, the nervous system's activity is inextricably coupled to the body and subordinate to the integrity of regulatory processes that extend throughout the body. Thus brain and body are simultaneously both subordinate and superordinate in relation to each other. Put another way, neither one is intrinsically subordinate or superordinate; rather, they are reciprocally coupled and mutually regulating.

The point we wish to stress now is that this sort of dense reciprocal coupling between neuronal and extraneuronal systems must be in place in order for our envatted brain to instantiate or realize the neural processes crucial for phenomenal selfhood or subjectivity. Hence the total realization base for the subjectivity of the envatted brain corresponds to the system constituted by the coupling of these neuronal and extraneuronal subsystems. In other words, the total realizer sufficing for subjectivity is the brain-plus-vat and not the brain alone.

What about the core realizer for subjectivity? Is it purely neural? It is difficult to say. If we could turn subjectivity on and off by affecting neuronal activation alone while leaving everything extraneuronal unchanged, then we would most likely conclude we had found the core neural realizer for subjectivity. Of course, unless our brain in a vat could somehow report its states to us, we would have no way of knowing whether we were turning subjectivity on and off. Philosophers are familiar with this sort of problem; it is a variant on the problem of other minds. It is not this problem, however, we wish to emphasize, but rather the following one. Given the dense reciprocal coupling between neuronal and extraneuronal systems, there can be no neural change without a cascade of changes in many extraneuronal parameters. Turning subjectivity on and off would entail systematic alteration of these extraneuronal parameters just as much as systematic alteration of the neuronal ones. As we have seen, any change in neuronal activation implies a departure from homeostasis that demands immediate physiological compensation and this compensation must itself be regulated by the nervous system. To use dynamical systems language, neuronal and extraneuronal state variables are so densely coupled as to be nonseparable. From this perspective, the core realizer for subjectivity looks to be nothing less than some crucial set of densely coupled neuronal and extraneuronal processes. If this is right, then there may be no such thing as a purely neural core realizer for subjectivity.

13.3.3 Mimicking Environmental Stimulation

We still need to consider what it would take to produce specific conscious states, distinguished by their sensory contents, in the envatted brain. Here the minimal requirement is to deliver stimulation to the neuronal terminals that duplicates or matches precisely the stimulation the brain normally receives from the environment.

The first point to be stressed is that such stimulation would have to be delivered without disrupting the life-sustaining system already established. This point is crucial. Adequate stimulating devices need to be constructed so that they can be integrated seamlessly into the vat. The complexity of such devices cannot be underestimated. Imagine an artificial device capable of stimulating every fiber of the optic nerve in perfect correlation with the light pattern of the scene to be recreated, guaranteeing all the dynamic receptive field relations found originally among retinal cells, maintaining perfect synchrony with the exploratory motor efference of the brain as it scans through the virtual image, and updating its activity so as to match precisely the sensory reafference.

Our artificial stimulating devices must therefore meet two basic requirements. On the one hand, the stimulation delivered to the neuronal terminals must mimic that obtained by the embodied nervous system. On the other hand, the devices must not disrupt the overall homeodynamic domain of activity crucial for life-regulation and subjectivity. These requirements suggest that our artificial stimulating devices must themselves be subject to tight regulation from the nervous system through artificial sensorimotor loops.

It is worth considering in this connection some examples of the important role that peripheral, nonneuronal processes play in the generation of neural activity. Consider first the development of spinal reflex circuits (Schouenborg 2003, 2004). Here it is crucial that the sensorimotor circuit be finely matched to the periphery for functional adequacy. Sensory feedback from spontaneous muscle twitches (occurring during sleep and analogous to human fetal movements) is critical for adapting the connections in spinal reflex modules to body anatomy (Petersson et al. 2003) and for determining the somatotopic functional organization of the somatosensory cortex (Khazipov et al. 2004). As Schouenborg remarks, "It is not the afferent input per se that is important . . . but rather the sensory feedback resulting from activity in the sensorimotor system" (2004, 694).

Convergent work on the development of the auditory cortex also points to the crucial role of peripheral structures in adapted neural activity. Mrsic-Flogel and collaborators used a "virtual acoustic space" to enable infant ferrets to hear through virtual ears of mature animals. Their results showed how changes in spatial coding during development of the auditory cortex seemed to be entirely due to changes in peripheral nonneuronal sensory structures (Mrsic-Flogel et al. 2001; Mrsic-Flogel, Schnupp, and King 2003;

see also Grubb and Thompson 2004). This finding reinforces the point that the choice of which peripheral structures to use to stimulate the envatted brain is not trivial.

Recent work on a realistic model of the neuromuscular system responsible for feeding behavior in the mollusk *Aplysia* also reveals the importance of the tight coupling between central neuronal systems and peripheral nonneuronal ones (Brezina, Orekhova, and Weiss 2000, 2003a, b; Brezina, Horn, and Weiss 2005). Among other things, this work addressed the following question: given that central (neural) motor commands show stochastic behavior, whereas the periphery (the complex network of muscle and modulatory neurotransmitters and neuropeptides) presents a slow, history-dependent dynamics, to what extent is the peripheral system under the control of the nervous system? Brezina and collaborators show that the periphery works to a certain extent in a semi-autonomous manner (Brezina, Horn, and Weiss 2005). The nervous system does not control the peripheral musculature in a hierarchical master/slave fashion; rather, optimal performance emerges only from the collective behavior of the interacting neuromuscular system (central and peripheral) in a given environment. These authors suggest that the peripheral network is responsible for part of the predictive and control functions of the neuronal tissue. In their words: "In vertebrates as well as invertebrates, the structural and dynamical complexity of the periphery can be as large as that of the central nervous system, so that, seen more abstractly, *the computational capability of the periphery rivals that of the nervous system that is attempting to control it*" (Brezina, Horn, and Weiss 2005, 1523; our emphasis).

Similar co-dependence of functional outcome can be observed at the level of neuronal networks themselves. Network activity is determined both by the intrinsic properties of the network and the modulatory environment, mainly through the modulation of synaptic behavior (Marder 1998; Marder and Thirumalai 2002). Therefore, together with neuronal firing, complex modulatory interactions between central neuronal cells and peripheral nonneuronal elements determine the nervous system's response.

These examples are intended to stress the immense complexity of the neural and extraneural interactions that ultimately determine brain activity in the living organism. The list of functional systems dependent on brain-body coupling to provide the organism with coherent perception of the world also includes the entire interoceptive, autonomic system (Craig 2002, 2003; Saper, 2002), vestibular-autonomic regulation (Balaban and

Porter 1998; Yates and Miller, 1998), balance and somatic graviception
relying on hydrostatic properties of blood pressure and inertial mass of
abdominal viscera (Mittelstaedt 1996, 1997; Vaitl et al. 2002), as well interaction between the senses occurring at both central and peripheral levels
(Howard 1997).

Let us return to our brain in a vat. The foregoing kinds of complex
dependencies of neural activity on peripheral, extraneural systems must
somehow be established for our envatted brain in order to mimic precisely
peripheral stimulation as well as the way the embodied brain responds to
such stimulation. Given the computational complexity involved, it is hard
to imagine how to accomplish this feat simply by stimulating the neuronal
terminals with electrical impulses generated by a supercomputer (Dennett
1991). Rather, it seems that we must equip the brain with real sensorimotor
systems. Furthermore, as we suggested earlier, the brain must be able regulate these peripheral systems. Thus, at any given moment, the state of the
peripheral systems will depend on the brain's endogenous dynamics,
which always shapes the sensory inflow (Engel, Fries, and Singer 2001;
Varela et al. 2001); the state of the central systems will depend on how the
peripheral systems are operating and what they have provided. Once all
these structural and dynamical features are added to our already self-
maintaining and energetically open vat, however, our so-called envatted
brain looks a lot less like a brain in a vat and much more like an autonomous sensorimotor agent.

13.4 An Evo-Devo Digression

Before we present the results of our reflections on the brain-in-vat thought
experiment, it is worth reminding ourselves of some basic facts about the
evolutionary and developmental biology of the nervous system.

From an evolutionary perspective, brain and body are co-evolved structures that match one another's properties through a history of adaptive
phylogenetic changes in different species (Aboitiz 1990, 1996; Chiel and
Beer 1997; Funes and Pollack 1998). This fact already suggests that considering the brain as some kind of internal director of the organism uniquely
responsible for its cognitive capacities is not the only possible theoretical
stance. From a naturalistic standpoint, there is a strict correlation between
cognitive capacities and consciousness, on the one hand, and neuronally-
animated-bodies-in-the-world, on the other hand, whereas there is no
evidence of freely wandering nervous systems displaying cognitive capacities, even in liquid media. One might naturally hypothesize, therefore, that
cognitive capacities as well as consciousness have tightly coupled brain-

body systems as their core biological realizers, and not simply the brain alone.

Consider also the ontogeny of the individual organism. It is well known that the development of neural tissue depends on a complex pattern of interaction between proneural and nonneural tissues in the developing embryo. This interaction happens through selectively inhibiting and promoting the expression of a complex network of soluble and cell-associated molecules, such as growth factors, transcription factors, and membrane proteins (Glavic et al. 2004; Weinstein and Hemmati-Brivanlou 1999). Dorsal ectoderm, for instance, which is the origin of the entire central nervous system, differentiates into neural tissue in response to signaling from (nonneural) dorsal mesodermal tissue (the Spemann's organizer in amphibians or the node in amniotes, such as the chick or the mouse) (De Robertis and Kuroda 2004; LaBonne and Bronner-Fraser 1999). Neural crest cells, which are the precursors of the peripheral nervous system, also give rise to bone tissue and smooth muscle, among other nonneural tissues (LaBonne and Bronner-Fraser 1999). Furthermore, peripheral factors, such as the sexual hormones testosterone and estrogen, as well as the hormone adipocyte-derived leptin, play a critical role in determining patterns of synaptogenesis and axon guidance, and therefore deeply influence the development of the nervous system (Lathe 2001; Morris, Jordan, and Breedlove 2004; Simerly 2005).

Thus, from a developmental perspective, it is not as if a commanding nervous system wraps itself with a body. Rather, it would be better to say that the body constructs a nervous system within itself. Clearly, the brain plays an undeniable role in enabling cognitive functions, as neuropsychological patients poignantly attest. Nevertheless, the brain is first and foremost responsible for the organism's integrity while also being entirely dependent on that integrity. As we have seen, the brain plays this role by establishing and maintaining the internal regulatory processes and sensorimotor regularities that make up the homeodynamic domain that is the living body. As Piaget (1971) noted, this self-regulating domain shapes all cognitive processes and provides the ground state upon which any neural process, including those crucial for consciousness and subjectivity, can operate.

13.5 A Null Hypothesis for the Brain-in-a-Vat Thought Experiment: A Body in a World

The philosopher's brain-in-a-vat thought experiment abstracts away from the ontogeny and evolution of adaptive brain-body-environment interactions, and thus begins with a brain that already has a set of capacities or behavioral possibilities that transcend its actual structure. In other words, the thought experiment abstracts away from historical constraints on the biological realization of mind. Although some philosophers would argue that such historical constraints are relevant to whether a given biological structure at a given time instantiates or realizes a particular perceptual or cognitive state, almost all philosophers would argue that such constraints are irrelevant to the metaphysical question of whether a given biological structure at a given time instantiates or realizes subjectivity and consciousness.

We will not dispute this point. Rather, we wish to make a different observation. When we take into consideration the functional and structural interdependence of brain and body that evolutionary, developmental, physiological, and behavioral evidence suggest, then the philosopher's naïve view of the brain in a vat simply will not do. The body is not just some kind of container, replaceable by a vat, that supports a commanding brain. The body is an active partner in the immensely complex and wide biological computations that the organism as a whole engages in while encountering an unpredictable world and maintaining its identity through time (Chiel and Beer 1997; Kutas and Federmeier 1998; Thompson and Varela 2001). Hence any "vat" capable of coupling with the brain in the requisite way must be able to duplicate these complex bodily processes.

We therefore propose the following null hypothesis for the brain-in-a-vat thought experiment: any vat capable of performing the necessary functions will have to be a surrogate body that both regulates and is regulated by the nervous system. In other words, the vat will have to exhibit a level of complexity at least as high as that of a living body with respect to bodily systems of life-regulation and sensorimotor coupling. Thus the entire system (vat plus brain) must satisfy these two basic requirements: (1) it must be energetically open and able to actively regulate the flow of matter and energy through it so as to control its own external boundary conditions (life-regulation), and (2) it must be capable of actively regulating its own sensorimotor interactions with the outside world (sensorimotor agency). In short, the entire system must amount to a biologically autonomous, sensorimotor agent.[5] The null hypothesis is thus that a brain in a vat would in fact have to be a body in the world.

Given this null hypothesis, we can also advance the following more general hypothesis, the rejection of which entails the rejection of the enactive position:

The total realizer for consciousness (including subjectivity or phenomenal selfhood and specific states of phenomenal consciousness) is not the brain or some neural subsystem, but rather a whole living system, understood as an autonomous system made up of some crucial set of densely coupled neuronal and extraneuronal subsystems.

13.6 Putting Life Back into Consciousness

In conclusion, let us highlight two implications of our discussion that are relevant to the widely acknowledged explanatory gap between consciousness and the brain. First, given that consciousness is so clearly subordinate to the organism's homeodynamic integrity, it may be more productive for research to proceed on the assumption that consciousness is a function of life-regulation processes involving dense couplings between neuronal and extraneuronal systems, rather than a function of neural systems alone (Thompson and Varela 2001). Second, mere neural correlates of consciousness will always leave an explanatory gap unless we know what role these neural correlates play in the context of the organism's life-regulation and sensorimotor engagement with the world. The enactive approach aims to put life back into consciousness by building on these two points.

Notes

1. Searle thinks you really are a brain in a vat right now: "The vat is the skull and the 'messages' coming in are coming in by way of impacts on the nervous system" (1983, 230).

2. We are here setting aside the hard problem of what metaphysically constitutes consciousness.

3. Although the brain represents only approximately 2 percent of the total body mass, it is responsible for 20 percent of the energy from oxygen consumption in the body.

4. These include not only global arousal levels, but also the facilitation of selective patterns of regional synchronization within the general desynchronized cortical activity.

5. For the notion of biological autonomy, see Ruiz-Mirazo and Moreno 2004; Thompson 2007; and Varela 1979.

References

Aboitiz, F. (1990). Behavior, body types and the irreversibility of evolution. *Acta Biotheoretica* 38:91–101.

Aboitiz, F. (1996). Does bigger mean better? Evolutionary determinants of brain size and structure. *Brain, Behavior and Evolution* 47:225–245.

Amiry-Moghaddam, M., and Ottersen, O. P. (2003). The molecular basis of water transport in the brain. *Nature Reviews Neuroscience* 4:991–1001.

Anderson, C. M., and Nedergaard, M. (2003). Astrocyte-mediated control of cerebral microcirculation. *Trends in Neurosciences* 26:340–344.

Balaban, C. D., and Porter, J. D. (1998). Neuroanatomic substrates for vestibulo-autonomic interactions. *Journal of Vestibular Research* 8:7–16.

Blessing, W. W. (1997). Inadequate frameworks for understanding bodily homeostasis. *Trends in Neurosciences* 20:235–239.

Block, N. (2005a). Review of Alva Noë, *Action in Perception*. *Journal of Philosophy* 102:259–272.

Block, N. (2005b). Two neural correlates of consciousness. *Trends in Cognitive Sciences* 9:46–52.

Brezina, V., Orekhova, I. V., and Weiss, K. R. (2000). The neuromuscular transform: The dynamic, nonlinear link between motor neuron firing patterns and muscle contraction in rhythmic behaviors. *Journal of Neurophysiology* 83:207–231.

Brezina, V., Orekhova, I. V., and Weiss, K. R. (2003a). Neuromuscular modulation in Aplysia. I. Dynamic model. *Journal of Neurophysiology* 90:2592–2612.

Brezina, V., Orekhova, I. V., and Weiss, K. R. (2003b). Neuromuscular modulation in Aplysia. II. Modulation of the neuromuscular transform in behavior. *Journal of Neurophysiology* 90:2613–2628.

Brezina, V., Horn, C. C., and Weiss, K. R. (2005). Modeling neuromuscular modulation in Aplysia. III. Interaction of central motor commands and peripheral modulatory state for optimal behavior. *Journal of Neurophysiology* 93:1523–1556.

Brown, P. D., Davies, S. L., Speake, T., and Millar, I. D. (2004). Molecular mechanisms of cerebrospinal fluid production. *Neuroscience* 129:957–970.

Chalmers, D. J. (2000). What is a neural correlate of consciousness? In *Neural correlates of consciousness*, ed. T. Metzinger, 18–39. Cambridge, MA: MIT Press.

Chiel, H. J., and Beer, R. D. (1997). The brain has a body: Adaptive behavior emerges from interactions of nervous system, body and environment. *Trends in Neurosciences* 20:553–557.

Cosmelli, D., Lachaux, J.-P., and Thompson, E. (2007). Neurodynamical approaches to consciousness. In *The Cambridge handbook of consciousness*, ed. P. D. Zelazo, M. Moscovitch, and E. Thompson, 731–772. New York: Cambridge University Press.

Craig, A. D. (2002). How do you feel? Interoception: The sense of the physiological condition of the body. *Nature Reviews Neuroscience* 3:655–666.

Craig, A. D. (2003). Interoception: The sense of the physiological condition of the body. *Current Opinion in Neurobiology* 13:500–505.

Damasio, A. R. (1999). *The feeling of what happens: Body and emotion in the making of consciousness*. New York: Harcourt, Inc.

Damasio, A. R. (1998). Investigating the biology of consciousness. *Philosophical Transactions of the Royal Society of London B Biological Sciences* 353:1879–1882.

Davson, H., and Segal, M. B. (1971). Secretion and drainage of the cerebrospinal fluid. *Acta Neurologica Latinoamericana* 1 (Suppl. 1): 99–118.

De Robertis, E. M., and Kuroda, H. (2004). Dorsal-ventral patterning and neural induction in Xenopus embryos. *Annual Review of Cell and Developmental Biology* 20:285–308.

Dennett, D. C. (1978). Where am I? In *Brainstorms*, ed. D. C. Dennett, 310–323. Cambridge, MA: MIT Press/Bradford Books.

Dennett, D. C. (1991). *Consciousness explained*. Boston: Little Brown.

Dennett, D. C. (1995). Intuition pumps. In *The third culture*, ed. J. Brockman, 182–197. New York: Simon and Schuster.

Engel, A. K., Fries, P., and Singer, W. (2001). Dynamic predictions: Oscillations and synchrony in top-down processing. *Nature Reviews Neuroscience* 2:704–716.

Funes, P., and Pollack, J. (1998). Evolutionary body building: Adaptive physical designs for robots. *Artificial Life* 4:337–357.

Glavic, A., Silva, F., Aybar, M. J., Bastidas, F., and Mayor, R. (2004). Interplay between Notch signaling and the homeoprotein Xiro1 is required for neural crest induction in Xenopus embryos. *Development* 131:347–359.

Grubb, M. S., and Thompson, I. D. (2004). The influence of early experience on the development of sensory systems. *Current Opinion in Neurobiology* 14: 503–512.

Grubb, R. L., Raichle, M. E., and Eichling, J. O. (1977). Peripheral sympathetic regulation of brain water permeability. *Acta Neurologica Scandinavica* 64:490–491.

Gusnard, D. A., and Raichle, M. E. (2001). Searching for a baseline: Functional imaging and the resting human brain. *Nature Reviews Neuroscience* 2:685–694.

Hebert, S. C., Brown, E. M., and Harris, H. W. (1997). Role of the Ca(2+)-sensing receptor in divalent mineral ion homeostasis. *Journal of Experimental Biology* 200:295–302.

Howard, I. P. (1997). Interactions within and between the spatial senses. *Journal of Vestibular Research* 7:311–345.

Hurley, S. L., and Noë, A. (2003). Neural plasticity and consciousness. *Biology and Philosophy* 18:131–168.

Hyder, F., Shulman, R. G., and Rothman, D. L. (1999). Regulation of cerebral oxygen delivery. *Advances in Experimental Medicine and Biology* 471:99–110.

Kandel, E. R., Schwartz, J. H., and Jessell, T. M. (2000). *Principles of neural science.* New York: McGraw-Hill.

Khazipov, R., Sirota, A., Leinekugel, X., Holmes, G. L., Ben-Ari, Y., and Buzsaki, G. (2004). Early motor activity drives spindle bursts in the developing somatosensory cortex. *Nature* 432:758–761.

Krimer, L. S., Muly, E. C., III, Williams, G. V., and Goldman-Rakic, P. S. (1998). Dopaminergic regulation of cerebral cortical microcirculation. *Nature Neuroscience* 1:286–289.

Kutas, M., and Federmeier, K. D. (1998). Minding the body. *Psychophysiology* 35:135–150.

LaBonne, C., and Bronner-Fraser, M. (1999). Molecular mechanisms of neural crest formation. *Annual Review of Cell and Developmental Biology* 15:81–112.

Lathe, R. (2001). Hormones and the hippocampus. *Journal of Endocrinology* 169: 205–231.

Logothetis, N. K., and Pfeuffer, J. (2004). On the nature of the BOLD fMRI contrast mechanism. *Magnetic Resonance Imaging* 22:1517–1531.

Marder, E. (1998). From biophysics to models of network function. *Annual Review of Neuroscience* 21:25–45.

Marder, E., and Thirumalai, V. (2002). Cellular, synaptic and network effects of neuromodulation. *Neural Networks* 15:479–493.

Mittelstaedt, H. (1996). Somatic graviception. *Biological Psychology* 42:53–74.

Mittelstaedt, H. (1997). Interaction of eye-, head-, and trunk-bound information in spatial perception and control. *Journal of Vestibular Research* 7:283–302.

Morris, J. A., Jordan, C. L., and Breedlove, S. M. (2004). Sexual differentiation of the vertebrate nervous system. *Nature Neuroscience* 7:1034–1039.

Mrsic-Flogel, T. D., Schnupp, J. W., and King, A. J. (2003). Acoustic factors govern developmental sharpening of spatial tuning in the auditory cortex. *Nature Neuroscience* 6:981–988.

Mrsic-Flogel, T. D., King, A. J., Jenison, R. L., and Schnupp, J. W. (2001). Listening through different ears alters spatial response fields in ferret primary auditory cortex. *Journal of Neurophysiology* 86:1043–1046.

Panksepp, J. (1998a). *Affective neuroscience: The foundations of human and animal emotions*. Oxford: Oxford University Press.

Panksepp, J. (1998b). The periconscious substrates of consciousness: Affective states and the evolutionary origins of self. *Journal of Consciousness Studies* 5:566–582.

Parvizi, J., and Damasio, A. R. (2001). Consciousness and the brainstem. *Cognition* 79:135–160.

Paspalas, C. D., and Papadopoulos, G. C. (1998). Ultrastructural evidence for combined action of noradrenaline and vasoactive intestinal polypeptide upon neurons, astrocytes, and blood vessels of the rat cerebral cortex. *Brain Research Bulletin* 45:247–259.

Peters, A., Schweiger, U., Fruhwald-Schultes, B., Born, J., and Fehm, H. L. (2002). The neuroendocrine control of glucose allocation. *Experimental and Clinical Endocrinology and Diabetes* 110:199–211.

Peters, A., Schweiger, U., Pellerin, L., Hubold, C., Oltmanns, K. M., Conrad, M., et al. (2004). The selfish brain: Competition for energy resources. *Neuroscience and Biobehavioral Reviews* 28:143–180.

Petersson, P., Waldenstrom, A., Fahraeus, C., and Schouenborg, J. (2003). Spontaneous muscle twitches during sleep guide spinal self-organization. *Nature* 424: 72–75.

Piaget, J. (1971). *Biology and knowledge: An essay on the relations between organic regulations and cognitive processes*. Chicago: University of Chicago Press.

Putnam, H. (1981). *Reason, truth and history*. Cambridge: Cambridge University Press.

Raichle, M. E. (2006). The brain's dark energy. *Science* 314:1249–1250.

Raichle, M. E., and Stone, H. L. (1971). Cerebral blood flow autoregulation and graded hypercapnia. *European Neurology* 6:1–5.

Raichle, M. E., and Mintun, M. A. (2006). Brain work and brain imaging. *Annual Review of Neuroscience* 29:449–476.

Roy, C. S., and Sherrington, C. S. (1890). On the regulation of the blood supply of the rat brain. *Journal of Physiology* 11:85–108.

Ruiz-Mirazo, K., and Moreno, A. (2004). Basic autonomy as a fundamental step in the synthesis of life. *Artificial Life* 10:235–259.

Saper, C. B. (2002). The central autonomic nervous system: conscious visceral perception and autonomic pattern generation. *Annual Review of Neuroscience* 25: 433–469.

Schouenborg, J. (2003). Somatosensory imprinting in spinal reflex modules. *Journal of Rehabilitation Medicine*. Suppl. 41:73–80.

Schouenborg, J. (2004). Learning in sensorimotor circuits. *Current Opinion in Neurobiology* 14:693–697.

Searle, J. R. (1983). *Intentionality: An essay in the philosophy of mind*. Cambridge: Cambridge University Press.

Segal, M. B. (1993). Extracellular and cerebrospinal fluids. *Journal of Inherited Metabolic Disease* 16:617–638.

Shewmon, A. D. (2001). The brain and somatic integration: insights into the standard biological rationale for equating "brain death" with death. *Journal of Medicine and Philosophy* 26:457–478.

Shoemaker, S. (1981). Some varieties of functionalism. *Philosophical Topics* 12: 93–119.

Shulman, R. G., Hyder, F., and Rothman, D. L. (2002). Biophysical basis of brain activity: implications for neuroimaging. *Quarterly Reviews of Biophysics* 35:287–325.

Simard, M., and Nedergaard, M. (2004). The neurobiology of glia in the context of water and ion homeostasis. *Neuroscience* 129:877–896.

Simerly, R. B. (2005). Wired on hormones: Endocrine regulation of hypothalamic development. *Current Opinion in Neurobiology* 15:81–85.

Swanson, L. W. (2000). Cerebral hemisphere regulation of motivated behavior. *Brain Research* 886:113–164.

Swanson, L. W. (2002). *Brain architecture: Understanding the basic plan*. Oxford: Oxford University Press.

Thompson, E. (2007). *Mind in life: Biology, phenomenology, and the sciences of mind*. Cambridge, MA: Harvard University Press.

Thompson, E., and Varela, F. J. (2001). Radical embodiment: Neural dynamics and consciousness. *Trends in Cognitive Sciences* 5:418–425.

Vaitl, D., Mittelstaedt, H., Saborowski, R., Stark, R., and Baisch, F. (2002). Shifts in blood volume alter the perception of posture: Further evidence for somatic graviception. *International Journal of Psychophysiology* 44:1–11.

Varela, F. J. (1979). *Principles of biological autonomy.* New York: Elsevier North Holland.

Varela, F. J., Lachaux, J.-P., Rodriguez, E., and Martinerie, J. (2001). The brainweb: Phase synchronization and large-scale integration. *Nature Reviews Neuroscience* 2:229–239.

Wagner, A. (1999). Causality in complex systems. *Biology and Philosophy* 14: 83–101.

Weinstein, D. C., and Hemmati-Brivanlou, A. (1999). Neural induction. *Annual Review of Cell and Developmental Biology* 15:411–433.

Wilson, R. A. (2001). Two views of realization. *Philosophical Studies* 104:1–31.

Yang, G., Huard, J. M., Beitz, A. J., Ross, M. E., and Iadecola, C. (2000). Stellate neurons mediate functional hyperemia in the cerebellar molecular layer. *Journal of Neuroscience* 20:6968–6973.

Yano, S., Brown, E. M., and Chattopadhyay, N. (2004). Calcium-sensing receptor in the brain. *Cell Calcium* 35:257–264.

Yates, B. J., and Miller, A. D. (1998). Physiological evidence that the vestibular system participates in autonomic and respiratory control. *Journal of Vestibular Research* 8:17–25.

Zonta, M., Angulo, M. C., Gobbo, S., Rosengarten, B., Hossmann, K. A., Pozzan, T., et al. (2003). Neuron-to-astrocyte signaling is central to the dynamic control of brain microcirculation. *Nature Neuroscience* 6:43–50.

14 Toward a Phenomenological Psychology of the Conscious

Benny Shanon

In this text, I outline a new framework for the psychological study of the conscious.[1] Essentially, the greater part of contemporary psychology and cognitive science is concerned with the unconscious. Specifically, the view dominating the field today is that the bulk of workings of the mind take place in a province that is not amenable to consciousness. This holds true of all major paradigms in cognitive science: the classical paradigm of symbolic processing (to be referred to here as the representational-computational view of mind, or RCVM, and occasionally referred to as cognitivism or representationalism), the alternative paradigm of connectionism, as well as models entertained in social psychology and in the neurosciences. By all these approaches, both the structures underlying cognitive activity and the processes that produce cognitive performance pertain to a covert level to which the cognitive agent is, in general, not privy. This has been labeled as the "cognitive" unconscious (Kihlstrom 1987), a notion that joins the more famous psychodynamical unconscious (be it Freudian or Jungian) as well as the Chomskian notion of "knowledge of language," which, in effect, is not known to the speakers who are said to possess it (Chomsky 1972). All told, it can be said that in essence, the psychology of the greater part of the twentieth century is a psychology of the unconscious.[2] This essay comes with a call for a radical paradigm change for the twenty-first century, one shifting the core of psychology to the realm of the conscious.[3] It should be noted that the following presentation outlines the development of my thinking and research, which in many respects has been carried out independently and not within any established paradigm. By no means is this purported to be an exhaustive historical survey of the study of consciousness as such, or a review or discussion of the contemporary state of the art in the field.

14.1   From the Critique of RCVM to the Phenomenology of Experience

In my monograph *The Representational and the Presentational* (Shanon 1993a), I have presented a comprehensive critique of the notion of internal mental representation and of the psychological theories founded on it. The critique was based both on a systematic empirical examination of practically all domains of human cognitive activity (language, memory, perception and action, thought processes and reasoning, learning and cognitive development) and on a conceptual-philosophical analysis. In a nutshell, my main conclusion is that underlying mental representations as they are standardly defined in the cognitive literature cannot serve as the basis for the workings of the mind. If anything, representational-like (note the adjectival, not nominal, term) patterns are the product of cognitive activity, not its substrate or source. This is coupled with the following key assessments:

a. The basic capabilities of the human cognitive system are not symbol manipulation and information processing, but rather being and acting in the world.
b. The locus of cognitive activity is not exclusively internal and mental, but rather external, taking place in the interface where organism and world meet.

This nonrepresentational view is in line with other, independent, nonorthodox lines of thought: the seminal critiques of computationalism by Dreyfus (1992), Searle (1980), and Winograd and Flores (1986); the ecological psychology of James Gibson and his followers (see Gibson 1966, 1979; Turvey and Shaw 1979; Turvey et al. 1981; as well as Michaels and Carello 1981); Vygotsky (1978) and his followers in the Soviet school of activity theory (see Wertsch 1985a, b); Maturana and Varela and the school of autopoiesis (Maturana 1978; Maturana and Varela 1980, 1987; Varela, Thompson, and Rosch 1991); as well as the earlier philosophical works of Merleau-Ponty (1962) and Wittgenstein (1953). For further reference, the reader is referred to the anthology by Still and Costall (1991); for a review of the various possible alternatives to representationalism, the reader is referred to Shanon 1990a.

Let me put things in a broader perspective. Intellectually, the postulation of mental representations in the late 1960s gave birth to a major paradigm shift in psychology. It introduced a new level of analysis, one whose conceptual foundations were from within psychology proper. Chomsky (1959) and Fodor (1968, 1975) pointed out that human cognitive behavior involves a recourse to a mental level of knowledge and of meaning that cannot be reduced to the physical, biological, or behavioral. This came in contrast to the earlier perspectives adopted by both behaviorism and the brain sciences (as well as later by the nonrepresentational paradigm of connectionism), which set themselves to explain the psychological by means of concepts and theoretical frameworks taken from the family of the sciences at large. With its proclaiming an autonomous psychology, the cognitive revolution heralded a break with reductionistic explanation. The basic insight here is that material or ontological reductionism does not entail explanatory or methodological reductionism: even in terms of its material constitution, the mind is realized in the brain without there being any autonomous psychic entities, understanding the regularities of the mind need not be achieved by means of a conceptual machinery drawn from either physics or biology (see Fodor 1975; Pylyshyn 1984).

Personally, I endorse the cognitive criticism of the reduction of psychology to the natural sciences, and agree that the basic terms of psychological theory should be psychological, not biological. The problem is, however, that my critique of RCVM has led me to believe representational models to be fundamentally unwarranted. The ensuing implications are radical. A priori, three levels are discerned: (1) the high level of the psychological, which is directly manifest in experience and behavior, (2) the fundamental, low level of brain, and (3) the intermediary level of mental representations. Levels (1) and (2) are part and parcel of the fabric of the world,[4] whereas level (3) is theoretically postulated (hence, not actual). RCVM proposed to account for (1) in terms of (3)—this was supposed to offer an explanation that is reductive (in the sense that it involves going down a level) yet maintains a psychology that is autonomous (in that it is not founded on the natural sciences). I, and others, have argued that RCVM does not fulfill its promises, and therefore cannot accept (3). Brain scientists, on the other hand, advocate the reduction of psychology to biology; in other words, to account for (1) in terms of (2). Myself, I cannot accept the representational option, because I think it is unwarranted, nor can I adopt the biological orientation, because I opt for a psychology that is genuinely psychological. If both (2) and (3) are dismissed, then one is left with level (1). This implies that no reduction is involved, and that psychological explanation remains on the manifest level of experience. Substantively, this is tantamount to saying that level of psychological study and analysis is the phenomenological. As argued at length in Shanon 1993a, this directs cognitive research and theory from covert, underlying internal mentality to the directly experienced level of consciousness.

The foregoing comments were, in the main, methodological. Let us now turn to substance, to the topic of consciousness. As far as RCVM is concerned, the primary arena of cognitive life (the domain in which the cognitive ball game takes place, so to speak) is the underlying, covert level of the unconscious. Furthermore, this being the case, it might even be that consciousness as such is devoid of function, or is perhaps merely an epiphenomenon—a dispensable luxury, akin to the frosting on a cake (for such an opinion, see Rey 1983). By contrast, my view is that consciousness is the hallmark of psychology and that essentially, the domain of the psychological is constituted by the realm of the conscious. As explained in Shanon 1993a, the key determinant of this realm is meaning, or rather—meaningfulness. Unlike underlying semantic representations and computational operations, neural networks or brain processes, being-and-acting in the world—which, by my alternative view, constitutes the basic feature of human cognition—is intrinsically laden with meaningfulness (see also Heidegger [1927] 1962, and the famous "Chinese Room" argument in Searle 1980). In Shanon 1990a, I have referred to this characteristic as intrinsic intensionality (with "s"). My view is in the spirit of Merleau-Ponty's (1962) notion of the livelihood of cognitive expression and performance. In modern cognitive psychology, the one paradigm founded on a notion exhibiting such a characteristic is that line of ecological psychology centering on the notion of affordance (see works cited previously). Kindred notions include the Vygotsky psychological unit (Vygotsky 1986) and, in another sense and in a totally different field, the Jungian archetypes (Jung 1964).

In sum, methodologically the critique of RCVM and the embracing of a psychology that is sui generis psychological confine us to the manifest phenomenological level. Substantially, my alternative view of mind entails a conversion between the psychological and the conscious. Together, the methodological and substantial considerations direct to a psychology that is, by and large, a phenomenological investigation of consciousness. In the following sections I outline several frameworks for such an endeavor. I should note that the following presentation is not meant to offer a complete review of the paradigms of investigation in question; for such full accounts, the reader is referred to works cited in these sections as well as a forthcoming monograph.

Before I proceed, I find it in place to comment on my use of the term "phenomenology" (and its derivative "phenomenological"). Obviously, the copyright on this term is due to Husserl, a philosopher (see Kockelman 1994). His aim was to develop a philosophy of essences in which considerations of epistemology are kept in abeyance. This approach was meant to provide for a study of the mental without being bogged down by onto-logical and metaphysical considerations. In contemporary psychology and (nonphilosophical) cognitive science, however, the use of the term "phe-nomenology" is rather different. Actually, in practically all cases, psycholo-gists use the term without even being at all cognizant of the Husserlian tradition. De facto, what is meant is an analysis of the psychological data as such, without the consideration of the underlying mechanisms that assumedly correspond to it, be they psychological, computational, or neu-ronal. The original philosophical use and the current psychological one both share a common feature, namely, the disregard of issues and/or domains or levels of analysis that are commonly taken to be pertinent; both are grounded in the belief that such disregard is essential for the conduct of the science of mind. But the issues, domains, and levels con-sidered and not considered in the two cases are very different, and conse-quently, the nature of "phenomenological research" in the two disciplines is distinctly different. My own use of the term here is strictly in line with that pursued in psychology and the (nonphilosophical) cognitive sciences (see also Spiegelberg 1975).

14.2 Thought Sequences and the Function of Conscious Mentation

Personally, I arrived to the study of consciousness even before, and inde-pendently of, my theoretical critique of RCVM. This was about twenty-five years ago, when the study of consciousness was frowned upon by practi-cally all cognitive psychologists as not being amenable to, or worthy of, serious scientific investigation. Trained in linguistics, I entertained an interest in a domain that would be akin to language but pertained to psy-chology, not to the domain of verbal discourse. With this, I got involved with what I called *thought sequences*, trains of verbal-like expressions that spontaneously pass through people's minds.

We all have such sequences daily. By way of example, I cite sequence (1), which is longer and richer than the ordinary. It was furnished by an informant residing in Jerusalem; a day earlier, the thinker had tried to remember a friend's name and could not. That same day, friends from Haifa[5] came to visit and someone said: "You've got it cold in Jerusalem." The sequence starts with a recollection of that utterance:

(1) 1. You've got it cold in Jerusalem
     2. And in Haifa? and in Tel Aviv?
     3. In Tel Aviv—Gabi

4. "Tip of the tongue" is an interesting phenomenon
5. This is "TOTT" (reminded of the abbreviation for the phenomenon's name)
6. No, "TOT"
7. "TOP"
8. The concept of "iceberg" and its "top"
9. Freud: the conscious is like the top part and the unconscious consists of the bottom part
10. How wise Freud was

I have collected a large corpus of such thought sequences and set myself to determine the regularities they manifest (Shanon 1989a). Obviously, the only way to obtain such data is via introspective reports. Although introspection was highly respected in the first years of modern scientific psychology, notably with the Würzburg school, soon it has gone into disrepute (for historical reviews, see Crovitz 1970; Humphrey 1963; Mandler and Mandler 1964; Shanon 1984). Admittedly, the method involved problems and pitfalls. My work is based on a re-evaluation of this method and concrete proposals for how to accommodate for the problems in question (see Shanon 1984). Since then, along independent lines, introspective methods—nowadays referred to as first-person methodologies—have gained renewed acceptance in the cognitive sciences. Among these is the paradigm of neurophenomenology advocated by Laughlin, McManus, and d'Aquili 1992 and further developed by Varela and his associates (Varela 1996; Lutz and Thompson 2003; for programmatic presentations of the use of such methods in contemporary consciousness research, the reader is referred to the anthology by Varela and Shear (1999).

Approaching the corpus of thought sequences, my perspective is analogous to that of the grammarian, and unlike that of the psychoanalyst: my interest was not in the contents of thought sequences and their import to the particular individual entertaining them, but rather in the structural and dynamical relationships that may hold between consecutive expressions in a sequence. Structurally, I have found, these coupling relationships may be grounded not only in semantics (as associations are) but also in sensory-like facets of articulation, as well as in logical, formal, and syntactical ones. Thus, in example (1), the coupling between expressions 2 and 3 is associative; that between 1 and 2 pertains to a semantic set; those linking 5, 6, and 7 have to do with phonological or graphemic form; and that between 8 and 9 involved a pictorial-like rendering of content. Together, the entire spectrum of these structural relationships may be viewed as a Mendeleev-like table of the basic operations of the mind (see Shanon 1989a). Dynamically, the progression of thought sequences sheds light on the question: What makes thoughts run? The analysis of the upcoming example (2) hinges on one aspect of this question (see Shanon 1988).

Although the occurrence of thought sequences is mundane, careful analysis reveals that in their totality, they constitute a domain that, like natural language, is multifarious, rich, and complex. Moreover, examined abstractly and mapped onto a formal conceptual framework, this domain reveals patterns that are far from being trivial or intuitive. This is not the place to present, not even in summary form, the main phenomena or my theory thereof. Here I shall confine myself to discussing the import of these sequences for the study of consciousness. Why do thought sequences take place at all? If, as assumed by most cognitive scientists, the bulk of thought processes pertains to the province of the unconscious, then, in principle, such sequences should not at all be. Or rather, one should expect sequences to begin with questions, or puzzles, and terminate with solutions, decisions, or perhaps dismissals and dissolutions. This cognitive state of affairs would be analogous to that of a master of an estate interested in his property being well maintained and the requisite services provided to his full content, but not at all wishing to be bothered by how all this is carried out and executed. The master will be aware of things that have to be taken care of and cognizant, on the one hand, of his commands and demands, and, on the other hand, with the tasks having been accomplished, or perhaps not. An empirical examination of a large corpus of thought sequences reveals that this suggested state of affairs is not the case—most sequences do not begin with the types just indicated and many go on even after solutions or answers have been found. Thus, standard functionalist terms do not account for the very existence of thought sequences. Over the years, it dawned upon me that the answer as to why such sequences occur in the first place ipso facto provides an answer to the more general, and more fundamental, question as to what is the functional benefit of consciousness, or rather, to the question as to why on occasion we are conscious of our thoughts. I have presented a full discussion of my view on this issue in Shanon 1998a; here, due to limitations of space, I shall focus on two paradigmatic cases only.

My procedure was to check my corpus of thought sequences for patterns that could not have occurred had mentation taken place without its being consciously experienced. Sequence (2) is an example of the first such case; this sequence was triggered when the informant saw a girl calling an agitated dog by the name of "Doni"; thereafter this individual went on thinking:

(2) 1. It is really frisky.
    2. She should have called it "Shedoni" [in Hebrew, diminutive for devil].
    3. Or for short, "shed" [in Hebrew, devil].
    4. That has a meaning in English too, "shed."

The move of interest is that between the last two expressions in the sequence. This move is based on a commonality of phonological form, a commonality which from a semantic point of view is meaningless. Specifically, the Hebrew word for "devil" happens to be homophonic to the (totally unrelated) English word "shed." This commonality is, of course, purely accidental, yet without it the sequence could not have progressed in the manner it did. The significance of this progression is the fact that it came as a surprise even to the thinker who entertained it. It was unplanned and unexpected, and with it the topic of mentation changed— it moved from the consideration of a dog to that of the word "shed" in English. With this it could have continued to ruminations on trees shedding leaves, or perhaps people crying.

The significance of sequences of this sort is that in them cognitive agents come to think of contents they had not intended or planned to consider. This is achieved through mentation momentarily proceeding not along a semantic path, but rather in a manner involving the medium of expression. In example (2), the medium pertains to linguistic phonology; in others it pertains to linguistic graphology or to perceptual-like expressions in all sensory modalities. Focusing on language, we note that usually the medium of articulation is semantically irrelevant. In cases such as that discussed here, it becomes relevant through what may be regarded as a local coupling and decoupling of medium and content. Normally, medium and content are tied together—each word pairs a specific phonological form with a specific meaning. Decoupling lends the medium local independence from content whereby the content is disregarded and the medium becomes autonomous. The decoupling is, of course, only momentary, as verbal expressions consisting only of medium are meaningless. Locally, however, the decoupling is of great import. When the medium is again coupled with content, the cognizer may find him/herself entertaining new contents, ones that he or she had not envisioned at all. Were thought conducted without a medium and governed only by considerations of content, one could think only of what one intends to, and would be confined to one's already established repertory of knowledge and belief. The articulation of thought in a specific medium and the introduction of aspects that are irrelevant from the perspective of content can introduce new elements that, in turn, may lead one's train of thought in new directions. In sum, the articulation in a particular medium presents the possibility for the generation of novelty. And what brings this articulation about is thought being phenomenologically experienced; that is, consciousness.[6]

Medium effects need not be confined to the domain of language. Similar progressions and interplay between medium and content are also encountered in mental imagery (Shanon 1989b). Moreover, patterns of this genre seem to play a crucial role in artistic creation. I have found this in classical music, jazz improvisation, animated film, poetry as well as talmudistic and kabbalistic scholastic reasoning (see Shanon 1990b).

Thought sequence (3) is an example of the second case marking the functional significance of being conscious of one's mentation. I myself entertained it years ago when about to go to Paris and reside at the Cité Universitaire, a university residence. The sequence consists of an imaginary conversation I conducted in my head with S., a friend who had once resided at that residence:

(3) 1. They gave me a room at the Cité Universitaire
    2. Do you know whether they provide sheets there?
    3. Oh, I can ask S. whether they provide sheets at the C.U.

What is remarkable about this sequence is that it presents an action that is first executed in the mind and only afterward followed by a decision to perform it in the real world. Specifically, in the sequence I first enact in my mind a conversation in which I pose a question to S.; only having done this does it occur to me that it would indeed be a good idea to contact S. and ask her that question. Thus, virtual acting in the mind preceded the decision to act in the world. Indeed, it was the very acting in the mind that brought forth the latter decision. I refer to this kind of action-like mentation as *enactment* (Shanon 1987, 1988).[7]

Enactment is interesting because it provides a setting in which thought expressions are not ideas that one entertains, but rather actions that one performs. In sequence (3), these actions are of the type one normally engages in when conversing with other people. The phenomenon may be viewed as the cognitive analog of the linguistic performative. Traditionally, language was regarded as the expression of ideas one entertains in one's mind. This view was criticized by Wittgenstein (1953, 1958), who suggested that, rather than being the expression of ideas, meaning is often manifested in the use of language in the world. Following this basic insight, Austin (1962) suggested that language enables people "to do things with words." In saying this, Austin was arguing against the traditional view according to which people only "say things with words." Austin claimed that verbal utterances serve not just for saying or expressing what is on one's mind, but actually to perform acts in the real world. For instance, when uttered by a priest or a rabbi, the expression "I hereby pronounce you husband and wife" is not a description of a state of affairs in the world but rather a creation of one—with the making of the verbal pronouncement a new relationship in the real world is established. Austin called such usages of language "performatives"; these are to be contrasted with the seemingly more standard use of language, the "constative." However, theoretically speaking, all verbal usages may be regarded as performative, with the constative being one specific kind of act that speakers may do with the words they utter. Subsequently, the performative view of language has been further developed and expanded by Searle in his theory of speech acts (1969). What I would like to propose here is that the phenomenon of enactment as encountered in the context of thought sequences presents us with a performative use of thought. Usually, thoughts are regarded as a vehicle for the entertainment of ideas in one's mind. In enactment, however, one does not entertain ideas in one's mind; rather, one acts. Just as in the case of publicly articulated words, one may do things with words rather than convey ideas through them, so in the case of internally articulated verbal-like speech, one may do things with thoughts rather than entertain contents through them.

At first glance, the pattern exhibited by enactment may seem paradoxical. Shouldn't the entertaining of ideas, along with the reflection and decision associated with it, precede action? Indeed, in the standard views of cognition, all action is the product of prior mental processing. The phenomenon of enactment suggests that this view is wrong. Apparently, enactment occurs because action is not dependent on prior mental computation. Rather, action in the manner normally undertaken in the world seems to be the basic and most primary human capability. The role of consciousness is to enable us to carry out our cognitive work in the most natural way: to think not by means of computational operations but rather in a manner akin to what we seem to do best, namely, act in the world. Thus, consciousness is of functional importance, because it is ingrained in the very workings of mind. With this, the study of thought sequences and their import to consciousness found a link with my critique of RCVM and the alternative view of mind that I endorse.

In example (3), enactment was manifested in simulated, virtual verbal discourse. In other examples, it is manifested in virtual handling of objects or in virtual navigation through space. It appears that eons before the invention of computer technology, nature created virtual reality in the internal realm of personal subjectivity. Indeed, this is the second functional advantage of consciousness to be highlighted here: the provision of a domain in which simulated, virtual action can be conducted—an inner theater, so to speak. This is most beneficial, for there are many situations in which actual action in the real world is not feasible (as in the case of the conversation in (3), for S. is not present at the time), or is risky, dangerous, frightening, and the like. Acting in the simulated, virtual domain can also serve one to prepare oneself to later actual activities (as, for instance, before an important interview), rehearse and gauge alternative courses of action, and so forth. For similar ideas in the domains of reasoning and memory, the reader is referred to the theory of mental models of Johnson-Laird (1983); for another theory characterizing consciousness as an internal theater and a work space, see Baars 1988, 1997.

Taken together, the two cases (there are others; see Shanon 1989c, 1993b) we have discussed attest to a common feature, namely, concreteness. The first case presented mentation based on the nonabstract (hence concrete), sensory-like (hence not semantic) facets of mentation. The second case presented cognitive activity akin to actual action in the external world. For it to attain concreteness of either kind, mentation has to be experienced or felt; this is achieved by virtue of its being conscious. In other words, consciousness is functionally beneficial, because it affords cognition with concreteness. It shall be noted that such concreteness is achieved in neither RCVM nor connectionism, both of which involve abstract modeling.

14.3   The Typological Study of Subjective Experience and Its Extensions

As indicated, my original interest in thought sequences did not concern consciousness per se, but was rooted in my appraisal that these sequences constitute a natural, and sufficiently rich, psychological domain that affords systematic analysis and may reveal new and interesting cognitive regularities. My first engagement with consciousness proper proceeded along another line of inquiry. In the late 1980s, I examined the—by then not very extensive—literature on consciousness and realized that different investigators—mostly psychologists and philosophers—employed the term "consciousness" in different ways and associated different senses with it. This implied that when speaking of "consciousness," different investigators actually had different referents in mind, and investigating consciousness, they were addressing phenomena that were not necessarily the same.

Inspecting this matter further, it occurred to me that the variation encountered in the literature is not just a symptom of differences in the intellectual interests and theoretical orientations of different investigators. Rather, it reflects something real, something pertaining to the domain of inquiry itself. Specifically, consciousness is a multifaceted phenomenon, and there is not one, but several types of consciousness. Guided by this basic assessment, I further noted that the different notions of consciousness, and the different types of consciousness to which they are associated, may be grouped into a small number of main clusters. In Shanon 1990c, I distinguish three such clusters, which define three types of consciousness. Because these types are related to each other in an orderly hierarchical fashion, they may also be regarded as constituting three levels of consciousness. As shall be described later, my theoretical conceptualization subsequently developed and underwent revision. However, it seems to me that the exposition shall be simpler and easier to follow with the introduction of the pertinent distinctions as pertaining to types of consciousness. Later in this discussion, more abstract analyses will be introduced and with them, the conceptualization of the distinctions will be modified. The general picture drawn will be extended as well.

The three types of consciousness I distinguish are *sensed being* or *sentience*, *mental awareness*, and *meta-mentation*. In Shanon 1990c, I refer to these as Con_1 (for consciousness), Con_2, and Con_3, respectively; here, for stylistic reasons, instead of Con, I use the label Cons.

Sensed being is the most rudimentary type, and correspondingly, it defines the most basic feature of consciousness. It consists of the quality that distinguishes a sentient living organism from an inanimate or a dead one. In essence, this is the elemental quality of sentience. The basic state of $Cons_1$ lacks definite structure and no specific contents are associated with it. For this reason, it is very difficult (perhaps impossible) to define $Cons_1$ positively (that is, not by way of contrast) and hardly anything substantial can be said about it.

As presently conceptualized, mental awareness, or $Cons_2$, consists in human beings having subjective experiences that are distinct and differentiated. It is manifested in the totality of our articulated mental life and it comprises all those internal events of which we are aware, and which have well-defined content and well-formed structure. Included in it are thought sequences, mental images, dreams and daydreams and, for some people, also musical ideations. Locke's classical (and apparently, the oldest in the modern Western literature) definition of consciousness as being "the perception of what passes in a man's own mind" (Locke [1690] 1964) is a fitting characterization of this state. Modern studies that focus primarily on this type of consciousness include Mandler 1975, Jaynes 1976, Pope and Singer 1978, as well as chapter 3 of Dennett 1991; this also corresponds to what Velmans calls "inner consciousness" (2000).

An evaluative comment is in place here. When one comes to think about it, the very fact that we experience states and events that are within the province of our own individual minds is remarkable. Ordinarily, things seen are perceived with the eyes, things heard are perceived with the ears, verbal discourse is conducted by means of mouth and ear, objects are manipulated with the hands, spatial navigation is achieved with the feet. But, as manifested by $Cons_2$, and as pointed out by Locke, we also see (or as-if see, etc.), hear, talk and act, internally, in a virtual manner, without involving our sensory organs or bodies at all. This state of affairs is banal, but, in fact, isn't it astonishing?

The third type, Con_3, consists of meta-mentation. It pertains to the mind's ability to take its own productions as objects for further inspection and/or reflection. Not only is it the case that human beings can be aware of their mentations, but also these mentations may themselves become the objects of thought and other cognitive activities. $Cons_3$ has various manifestations: meta-observation, reflection, monitoring, and control (see also Shanon 1988). Often, the term "self-consciousness" is employed, but to my mind this risks confusion, for meta-mentation is distinct from con-sciousness of the self; more on this will be said shortly when selfhood is discussed. Further, it shall be noted that for some investigators reflection and self-awareness are the criterial features of consciousness. Hence, for them only $Cons_3$ is taken to be "consciousness." As made explicit through-out this discussion, my position is categorically different—one may not be aware of one's being conscious, but this does not imply that one is not conscious.

Significantly, meta-observations of one's inner mentations are them-selves instances of mentation. Thus, once articulated in the mind, meta-thoughts may become thoughts *tout court*. This amounts to $Cons_3$ turning into $Cons_2$. By way of example, consider the following constructed scheme of a thought sequence:

(4) 1. This woman's behavior is enigmatic
    2. This [my] observation is interesting, perhaps insightful
    3. Insight is a wonderful cognitive feat

The first expression in this sequence is an ordinary thought on the normal level of $Cons_2$. Expression (2) consists of a meta-thought that relates to this thought, and hence it is one level up, that is, $Cons_3$. Expression (3) is a continuation of the thought entertained in (2) and thus it runs on the same track, so to speak. But as far as its type is concerned, (3) is not a meta-thought; rather, it is a regular thought concerning a content encountered in (2). Yet, there is no shift down from (3) and (2)—the two are entertained on the same channel (see Shanon 1987). Thus, we have gone up a level (from (1) to (2)), and without stepping down we found ourselves (in (3)) being again on ground level. This, I reckon, demonstrates that conscious mentation exhibits a topology defying a simple Euclidian-like characterization. More appropriate, it seems, is a picture like that of a Möbius strip or the ascending yet closed forms that serve as the basis for many of Escher's paintings (e.g., the climbing of a staircase that, despite its direction upward, brings one back to the ground floor).

The three types of consciousness are not just three types. As detailed in Shanon 1990c, they are interrelated in an orderly fashion and together they comprise a coherent and compact well-integrated system. Therefore, as noted, these three types can be regarded as the three levels of one unified whole. In particular, the three levels mark an ordered progression, hierarchical structure, and a closure, and the relations between them exhibit parallelism and internal logic.

Though conceptually and structurally distinct, in the actuality of their dynamics, the three levels of consciousness are in flux and they vacillate between themselves. The foregoing example of the relationship between $Cons_2$ and $Cons_3$ is a clear attestation of this. As shown in example (4), meta-mentation does not stay as such for long, but reverts into an ordinary line of mentation. The converse pattern is also common, whereby the observing self interferes with the flow of thought and without the thinker deciding about it, thoughts turn into meta-thoughts. The state of affairs at hand is reminiscent, I find, to that encountered with the chemical phenomenon of resonance, whereby a molecule of a given atomic composition is associated with several alternating structural (isometric) configurations. In effect, the actual state of affairs consists of a dynamic hybrid between the vacillating configurations. Likewise, the types/levels we have surveyed do not present themselves in a fixed, static fashion. Rather, they change and blend into each other so that consciousness dynamically alternates between them.

Originally, I defined the three types in conjunction with what is the core of the phenomenon of consciousness—namely, internal subjective experience—and I regarded them as types of consciousness. However, by and large, my erstwhile characterization of these types, along with what has been said about them so far, pertains to one specific facet, or region, of the system of consciousness: to wit, having internal subjective experiences. Although internal, subjective experience is the most central facet of the system of consciousness; it is not the only one. The other facets or regions are Self, World, and Temporality. These correspond to personal identity, the coupling of cognition and the world, and the temporal aspects of experience, respectively. What I have previously referred to as $Cons_1$, $Cons_2$ and $Cons_3$ are, in fact, the three types, or levels, of the core facet of subjective internal experience, and thus, more accurately they should be called SIE_1, SIE_2, and SIE_3, respectively. As far as substance is concerned, practically all that has been said thus far, remains true.

Given the foregoing picture, the following question naturally comes to mind: Are there any other types or levels of consciousness? This question has intrigued me for a long time. In Shanon 1990c, I have answered it in the negative, arguing that reflection of reflection (or metacognition further layers up) is still reflection (or metacognition). With the study of the phenomenology of nonordinary states of mind, I have encountered additional types of consciousness, of which I had not been previously aware. To this topic I turn in the next section of this essay.

As my conceptualization of consciousness developed, it occurred to me that each type or level may be viewed as corresponding to a key structural feature, with this feature manifesting itself in all the facets of the system. The feature corresponding to $Cons_1$ defines the basic, undifferentiated state of the system, the one corresponding to $Cons_2$ constitutes the mind's having differentiated, articulated expressions or states, and that corresponding to $Cons_3$ pertains to its reflective nature. Significantly, viewed in this fashion, the same distinctions apply to all facets of the system of consciousness. Thus, consider the Self. $Self_1$ marks the basic, rudimentary quality of autonomous living existence. $Self_2$ defines the well-formed differentiation between self and world and with it, the distinct qualities of one's being a particular individual cognitive agent. $Self_3$ distinguishes the special quality of one's being aware of one's selfhood and being able to reflect upon it.[8] Temporality exhibits analogous patterns. $Temp_1$ is constituted by the basic quality of temporality. As avowed by St. Augustine and many following him, this quality defies definition. $Temp_2$ is manifested in one's having distinct temporal experiences as they exhibit particular specifications (i.e., now or 4:10 p.m.), extension (5 minutes long) and relations (i.e., before and after, a moment ago). $Temp_3$ comes about in the acknowledgment of the patterns of $Temp_2$ and in one's being able to relate to them, state them, and reflect upon them.

The foregoing characterization suggests still another way by which $Cons_1$, $Cons_2$, $Cons_3$ may be conceived—as basic capabilities, or specifications in a technical-instrumental sense, that the system of consciousness affords. Let me clarify what I mean by an analogy with a compound, sophisticated audiovisual system. Examining (as a potential buyer might) such a system one would inquire what the system affords. The spectrum of possibilities may include: audio and visual information (either one or both) with the former being transmitted either in mono or in stereo and the latter screened in black and white or in color. The visual components may include a TV monitor, a VCR and/or a DVD player. The amplifier may have various parameters, programming may be included, and computer facilities and remote control may be added. All in all, the set of all affordances defines what the system at hand can do. Likewise with the system of consciousness with the three hierarchically ordered features I have noted: the fundamental quality of consciousness ($Cons_1$), the having of well-defined, well-formed states and experiences ($Cons_2$), and being able to take these differentiated states and experiences as the objects for further mentation and reflection ($Cons_3$).

As the same key features manifest themselves in all facets of the system, the same types or levels are encountered in all facets or regions of consciousness.[9] Viewed more abstractly, then, the typology of consciousness is generated by the tripartite scheme applied across several facets or regions. All told, adopting a more abstract view, consciousness is to be regarded as a multifactorial system that spans (in the sense employed in algebra) different states of profiles. The latter are defined by the n-tuple of indices i (so far 1, 2, and 3) specifying the level corresponding to each facet or region of consciousness. In their totality, these profiles constitute the various possible states of conscious experience. This further marks the internal structure of the system of consciousness and attests to its being one coherent and integrated unified whole. Indeed, it appears that consciousness is both one and many. On the one hand, there are several different prototypical types of consciousness that are phenomenologically distinct. On the other hand, these different types are all the manifestations of a unitary cognitive whole, one exhibiting coherence and compact internal structure. Thus, the phenomenon to which we refer as human consciousness actually consists of the dynamic interplay between various psychological manifestations, which together are the different faces of one multidimensional coin, so to speak.

The characterization in terms of basic features, specifications, or capabilities has the advantage that, unlike that in terms of types or levels, it offers flexibility. The flexibility is twofold. First, unlike types or levels which are discreet, states or profiles need not be all-or-none. However, on all its faces, patterns of consciousness portray more variations than captured by the three indices 1, 2, and 3. Thus, between the undifferentiated primitive quality of sentience and the full-fledged domain of articulated internal experiences a whole spectrum of experiences may be encountered. These exhibit different degrees of differentiation, well-definedness, well-formedness, and articulation. The three types or levels mark three key points—three prototypes, in this spectrum—but they do not exhaust it. Hence, one can envision states corresponding to indices whose numerical value is not an integer. Second, the conceptualization in terms of features and the states/profiles they span/generate allows for independent variation in the different facets/regions of the system. In other words, one facet may take one value, whereas another level may take another. Were the levels fixed, one should have expected strict co-variation of the values in all facets.

The foregoing sketch of the typological study of consciousness presents not only a new conceptualization of consciousness but also a novel outlook for psychological theory and for psychology as a science. As I see it, the aim of the scientific psychological enterprise is to chart the entire spectrum of the phenomenology of experience and to formulate lawful regularities in it. A psychological theory of consciousness would define the parameters of the system of consciousness, the structural relations between these parameters, the various values these may receive, the dynamics of their change in time, their dependence on context and various contingent factors, as well as their development in the course of ontogenesis. Further manifestations of this spectrum are considered in the next section.

14.4 Ayahuasca and Nonordinary States of Mind

A major turn in my work on consciousness happened unplanned. It concerns the study of nonordinary states of mind (the common term is altered or alternate states of consciousness, but I am not very content with it; see note 15). I came to this serendipically, in the course of traveling in the Amazonian region of South America. There I encountered Ayahuasca, a powerful plant-made psychoactive brew. For millennia, this brew has been central in the indigenous tribal cultures of the entire region, serving as the basis for their religious beliefs and practices, mythologies and cosmologies, and major societal rituals and acts, as well as their medicinal lore. Practically all Amazonian shamanism involves the use of this potion. Ayahuasca is especially famous for its induction of vivid, fantastic visions that usually depict things that have nothing to do with one's regular life and prior knowledge and that exhibit beauty surpassing anything imaginable (for remarkable artistic depictions of Ayahuasca visions, see Luna and Amaringo 1991). Following my first experiences with the brew, and delving into the anthropological literature, I was startled to find out that the kinds of things I had seen in my visions were of the same semantic categories as those reported to be seen by the indigenous Amerindians. They included big cats (notably, jaguars and pumas), reptiles (especially, serpents), birds, human beings, mythological and phantasmagorical creatures, landscapes, enchanted cities, fabulous palaces, and objects of art and magic. This kindled my puzzlement: how come I, a person with a totally different personal and sociocultural background, saw items of similar kinds? Truly, I was perplexed.

I decided to probe further into the matter—not as an academic researcher but as an explorer and apprentice. I returned to Brazil, Peru, Colombia, and Ecuador and partook of the brew many times, doing this in various geographical locales and sociocultural settings.[10] Only after having amassed sufficient firsthand experience, I began to interview people and collect data on the phenomenon. Thus, I have questioned hundreds of individuals in different places, following various traditions of use, and having different levels of expertise with Ayahuasca. Eventually, with a large corpus at my disposal, I subjected the data to categorization and analysis, both structural and dynamical. I shall note that this is the largest corpus of experiential data ever collected on Ayahuasca and their treatment is the first cognitive psychological (as distinct from clinical or neuropsychological) ever; to this date, it is still the most comprehensive investigation of the special state of mind induced by the brew. This research presents a systematic charting of the phenomenology of the Ayahuasca experience and attempts to account for it from a cognitive-psychological point of view, philosophical ramifications are examined as well; see my monograph *The Antipodes of the Mind* (Shanon 2002a) as well as in a series of more focalized papers (Shanon 1998b, 2001, 2002b, 2003a, b). The phenomenological domain at hand encompasses affective effects, nonordinary perceptions in all sensory modalities, ideations, modifications in the sense of self and reality, altered temporality, nonordinary mentations and ideations, spiritual and religious effects, as well as patterns of overt behavior (i.e., singing). Further, examined in its totality, this domain reveals systematic patterns exhibiting internal cognitive regularity and well-orderliness. All in all, it unravels what may be regarded (as the writer Aldous Huxley proposed following his firsthand experimentation with mescaline; see Huxley 1971) as the heretofore hidden territories of the mind (hence his term "Antipodes," which I have adopted in the title of my own book). Inspecting these, one is drawn to the conclusion that the human cognitive system, including the system of consciousness, is amazing to the utmost, and radically different from the way in which it is normally conceived by cognitive psychologists and other academic researchers.

This is not the place to review, not even schematically, this extraordinary, multifarious phenomenological domain. Here I shall highlight only four selected topics, presenting some findings of my research that I find significant with respect to the study of mind and consciousness in general. The first concerns the interpersonal commonalities in the experiences that different individuals have with Ayahuasca. First and foremost, these are manifested in the visions. Although what each individual sees each time he or she partakes of the brew is different, and although the experiences of different individuals participating in the same session differ as well, inspecting visions reported by a large number of individuals, I have indeed found remarkable recurrent patterns, with some semantic categories being especially prevalent, seen by different individuals in different places and in different contexts. Intellectually these findings are most intriguing (see also Shanon 2003a). Striking interpersonal similarities are also encountered in the ideations entertained under the influence of Ayahuasca (Shanon 1998b). Alternative ways to account for them are discussed at length in Shanon 2002a.

The second topic to be considered here relates to the foregoing analysis of the typology of consciousness. As said at the end of the previous section, with Ayahuasca I have discovered two new types (levels/features) that are to be added to those constituting the tripartite system I had endorsed for many years. The first of these, to be referred to as *Cons4*, consists of mentations that one directly experiences (as is the case with the mentations comprised under Cons2) but which (unlike the ordinary mentations of $Cons_2$) are not experienced as being generated by one's own mind and seem to come from an independent, external source or to have a separate existence of their own.[11] The paradigmatic, and often spectacular, manifestations of this are the visions experienced with Ayahuasca. These are often so vivid and so otherworldly that people feel that they cannot be but glimpses of actual other realities. Ideations, notably spiritual and metaphysical, are another manifestation of $Cons_4$. Remarkably, philosophical ideas are frequently entertained by people with no prior background in philosophy (or no advanced education at all) (Shanon 1998b). Traditional users of Ayahuasca also attribute the impressive singing that the brew induces in some persons as "received" (as contrasted with composed or created) from external sources.

Extending the system even further, the type $Cons_5$ will be noted. Like $Cons_1$, it consists of a pristine, undifferentiated state without any specific, articulated mental contents, yet in contradistinction to $Cons_1$, but like $Cons_4$, it is experienced as not pertaining to one's own individual self. Reports of this type are abound in the mystical traditions of cultures all over the world, as well as in the contemporary literature of transpersonal psychology (see Assaglioli 1973; Tart 1992). They have been referred to as nirvana, samadhi, mystical union (Merkur 1989, 1999), cosmic consciousness (Bucke [1901] 1991; Smith and Tart 1998), pure consciousness (Forman 1990), and superconsciousness (Grof 1975, 1998). Paradigmatic analyses of these are found in James ([1902] 1929), Underhill (1955), and Stace (1961). Even though experienced as not individualistic or internal, as attested by the reports of many Ayahuasca drinkers, $Cons_5$ is conceived as involving "coming back home" and/or "the source or fountain of everything."

Just as the original, ordinary three types of consciousness are interrelated, so are the two types encountered with Ayahuasca. This is so both with respect to the relationship the two have with one another and as far as the relationship with the ordinary types is concerned. As already indicated, $Cons_4$ corresponds to $Cons_2$ in that both consist of distinct, differentiated, and articulated mental material. $Cons_5$ corresponds to $Cons_1$ in that both consist of elemental undifferentiated experiential states. Both $Cons_4$ and $Cons_5$ share the feature of being experienced as independent of the individual cognitive agent at hand. As such, these two contrast with both $Cons_2$ and $Cons_1$ (respectively, note the reversal in order) which are ingrained in individuated cognitive agency. Finally, on the one hand, $Cons_5$ is both experienced and conceived as being the ultimate, most advanced, state of consciousness, and as such as being farthest from the primitive $Cons_1$, which is also shared by animals and infants. On the other hand, in its being pristine and undifferentiated, $Cons_5$ is also the closest to $Cons_1$. Thus, the five-layered system marks a curious closure. In sum, the new types of consciousness discovered with Ayahuasca integrate coherently into the original tripartite system constructed on the basis of the inspection of ordinary consciousness.[12]

Turning, as we have done earlier, to the analysis in terms of features or specifications, $Cons_4$ and $Cons_5$ each presents a specific feat that human consciousness affords. The feature corresponding to $Cons_4$ is externality or otherness. Consciousness affords human beings with not only having their own personal subjective world within the confines of their own minds (recall that this has been a focal topic in the section on thought sequences), it also allows for externalization, whereby one's own mentations and the products of one's own mind are experienced as being external, having an independent existence of their own, and/or being the manifestation of another agent or source. Theoretically, this feature is especially interesting for it introduces a distinction between two cognitive characteristics that normally go hand in hand together and are usually regarded as synonymous. Both are the manifestations of what James ([1890] 1950), in his classical analysis of the stream of thought, singled out as the first property of consciousness, namely, its pertaining to a single, determined person. One might say that the mental locus of mental contents/activity is the mind of an individual person. Normally (and as also implied in the Jamesian account) this is understood as implying that: (1) the person in question is the only one privy to the mentations at hand, and (2) this person is the generator of the said mentations. The former stipulation is tantamount to saying that the individual is the owner of mentation, the latter that he or she is its author. $Cons_4$ shows that phenomenologically, these two characterizations can be divorced and thus, that psychologically they are distinct (see Shanon 2003c). Similar observations were made in the context of psychopathology (Graham and Stephens 1994), and in fact, we all experience such a state of affairs with dreams.

The feature corresponding to $Cons_5$ is having pristine, undifferentiated experiences, typically experienced as superior states of mind colored by especially positive affect and meaningful spiritual sentiments (see James [1902] 1929; Stace 1961). It further marks an intrinsic, built-in characteristic feature of the human mind, namely, to have the potentiality for religiosity and spirituality. This is, of course, a statement far from being trivial, and it deserves ample, serious discussion; this, however, extends beyond the scope of the present essay.

Pursuing the featural analysis, we note that the features associated with $Cons_4$ and $Cons_5$ and encountered in subjective internal mentation also manifest themselves in all facets/regions of the system of consciousness.[13] Thus, consider selfhood. $Self_4$ consists of one's feeling that one's personal identity changes. This results in the experience of personal transformation or metamorphosis. The transformations most commonly encountered with Ayahuasca are those into a jaguar, a serpent, or a bird. In the traditional Amerindian context, the transformation into a jaguar was regarded as the paramount, demonstrative achievement that one is a veritable *ayahuasquero* (i.e., an Ayahuasca shaman) (see Reichel-Dolmatoff 1975). $Self_5$ consists in one losing the sense of individual selfhood and being immersed in a higher unity. In traditional Hindu terminology, this happens when the Atman transcends into the Brahman (see Deutsch 1969). Similarly,

Temp$_4$ is encountered when one experiences oneself being in times other than the actual one. Immersion in scenarios pertaining to ancient civilizations are common examples. With Temp$_5$, temporality is not only modified, but transcended. With this, people feel that they reach the realm of the eternal and are freed from the dominion of time (see Shanon 2001).

I shall not go into the details of these nonordinary experiences. Important for our discussion here is the appreciation that the extending of the types and regions of consciousness naturally coheres into the structure of the system of consciousness developed in conjunction with ordinary states of mind. In other words, unusual though they are, the phenomena of nonordinary states of mind are not haphazard. Rather, they reveal the inherent logic of the system underlying the already familiar, ordinary manifestations of consciousness. With this, the coherence and internal structure of the psychological system of consciousness are further highlighted.

The third topic I shall consider has to do with parameters and their values. Along with other nonordinary states of consciousness, the Ayahuasca state of mind presents patterns that highlight parameters of the system of consciousness that otherwise are undetected or unappreciated. Apart from its intrinsic phenomenological interest, which will be presented shortly, this topic provides an instructive illustration of the import of the study of nonordinary states of consciousness for the study of consciousness at large. By way of clarifying this, let me use an analogy with eyeglasses. People who wear glasses all the time take the glasses for granted and are oblivious to their features. However, when the specifications of the lenses are altered, this is no longer the case. For instance, if the lenses are to be tinted, the coloring of all one sees would be modified and with this, the existence of the eyeglasses, their specifications and their contribution to one's vision would become apparent. Likewise with consciousness, only more so. Eyeglasses can be taken off, but consciousness is always with us, or rather—everything we experience is always grounded in consciousness. It is here that the fundamental cognitive-psychological importance of the study of nonordinary states of mind is manifest. In these states, the values assigned to the parameters of the system of consciousness are modified and consequently, the parameters, which normally are unheeded, become apparent. By the theoretical perspective endorsed here, the goal of the cognitive psychological study of consciousness is precisely this: identify the set of parameters of the system of consciousness, determine the values that they may take, define the manner these may change and formulate the constraints to which their variation is subject.

Returning to the phenomenology of consciousness proper, the parameters revealed by Ayahuasca are those of meaningfulness, aesthetic value, and sanctity as well as that responsible for the sense of realness (see Shanon 2003c). It is very typical for powerful psychoactive agents to make the world appear as invested with extra (usually deep and at times enchanting or enchanted) meaning, exhibiting remarkable beauty (often, as reality turned into an artistic composition), and manifesting a dimension of the holy; often, they are also deemed to be "more real than real." Firsthand descriptions of these effects are to be found in Huxley 1971, Watts 1962, and throughout Shanon 2002a; for discussions thereof, the reader is referred to Masters and Houston 1966, Ludwig 1969, Tart 1969, White 1972, Grof 1975, and Tart 1975, as well as the various contributions in Metzner 1968.

Moreover, phenomenological patterns encountered with Ayahuasca indicate that properties commonly assumed to be paradigmatic of consciousness are actually contingent, potentially variable, values along parameters. Examples is the sense of realness that in nonordinary states of consciousness may be experienced as either heightened or lowered, and the feeling of connectedness or separation relative to the external world. Of similar nature are the symptoms of depersonalization and derealization encountered in psychopathology (Nemiah 1989).

The fourth and last topic I shall mention here (but, again, there are so many others) brings us back to the visions. As already indicated, and as detailed in Shanon 2002a, these vividly present what are experienced to be (as if) real entities and states of affairs. Usually, the contents of these visions resembles nothing one knows or is familiar with from the context of one's ordinary life, and often they are more beautiful and fabulous than anything one would have ever imagined. Consequently, practically all users of Ayahuasca—indigenous and traditional as well as contemporary and "civilized" alike—take the visions to depict nonordinary realities that actually exist in other places, times and/or dimensions. I am one of the very few who do not share this view. But if they are not real, where do the visions come from? In Shanon 2002a, I propose that they are the products of an unusual short-term and creative, artistic-like, power that Ayahuasca bestows. I view this nonordinary feat as manifesting inherent qualities of the human cognitive system—poetic sense, metaphoricity, fictionality, and the propensity for art and fantasy. But regardless of the specific account given to them, Ayahuasca visions attest that the human mind, and human consciousness, are radically different, and by far more wondrous, than practically all cognitive scientists contend.

14.5 Broader Ramifications

The phenomenological part of this discussion is complete. We now turn to the consideration of some broader ramifications. These concern the intellectual-psychological challenge that consciousness presents, the methodology for the psychological study of consciousness, and the nature of psychology as a science.

Let me begin with the intellectual challenge of the psychological study of consciousness. In the last decade it has become increasingly popular for both cognitive psychologists and other scholars interested in consciousness to highlight the relationship of consciousness and the brain and to regard this as the most important topic of inquiry in consciousness studies. The topic is so much in vogue that it has (following Chalmers 1995a, b) even received its own catchy label—the hard problem.[14] It concerns the relationship between brain and consciousness: "How or (in another phrasing, why) does the brain produce subjective experience?" Evidently, this is a modern variant of the old mind-body (or mind-brain) problem. Most neuroscientists nowadays engaged with consciousness maintain that this is the principal question in the domain, with some of them even claiming that they have solved the problem or are close to doing so (see Crick 1995; Crick and Koch 2003; Koch 2004). In contrast, there are others, usually philosophers, who maintain that this is to remain a mystery defying our current conceptual frameworks or even human intelligence forever (Nagel 1974; McGinn 1991).

There is no question that the hard problem does indeed present a tremendous intellectual challenge. Although not denying this, here I would like to underscore intellectual challenges of consciousness that lie elsewhere. First, it should be appreciated that the hard problem is not a psychological one, and as such, it is not one that should be expected to be ever solved, or even elucidated, by psychologists.[15] Given that this much-acclaimed problem has to do with the relationship between two realms of reality, and correspondingly, two levels of scientific discourse (the biological and the mental), it may be characterized as vertical. Further, as far as psychology is concerned, it is external: it involves the relationship between the psychological level and another level that is not psychological (in this case, the biological). But if the hard problem is outside the realm of psychology, and if psychologists are not expected to advance our understanding of the puzzle it presents, does this mean that from a psychological point of view that consciousness is not puzzling, not intellectually challenging? In other words, is consciousness mysterious only because we cannot fathom how the brain generates it? I categorically reject this conclusion. Besides the specific substantive and methodological ideas presented here, the main message of this essay is that consciousness, and psychology at large, is interesting and intellectually challenging in its own right. Moreover, psychological phenomenology presents patterns that are quite unexpected and some of them defy commonly held conceptualizations of the order of things.

Following is a summary list of the various kinds of intellectual challenges, perhaps even puzzles, that consciousness presents. All of them are horizontal (i.e., pertaining to one level of reality or discourse, not the relationship between such levels) and internal (in the sense of pertaining to phenomena within a level) psychological; in one way or another, these have been alluded to throughout the foregoing discussion:

1. *Fundamental conceptual problems*   The key features of consciousness defy analytic definition. These include sentience, the essence of experiencing, selfhood and the intrinsic feel of a subject, the psychological sense of realness, and time. Note that all are associated with the level labeled here $Cons_1$ as it manifests itself across the various regions of consciousness. It seems to me that like space and time, matter and energy, these features have to be accepted as such and rather than being the topic of definitional analysis be taken as themselves defining the foundations of any framework for the further study of the domain of consciousness.

2. *Non-Euclidian patterns*   Throughout the foregoing phenomenological survey I have highlighted patterns that defy ordered hierarchies and what may be conceived as Euclidian-like geometry. Included in these are the dynamic fluctuation between levels of thought, the coupling and decoupling between aspects of articulation, and the phenomenon of self-consciousness.

3. *Nonapparent distinctions*   Nonordinary states of mind reveal that features normally taken to be synonymous or to go hand in hand together need not be such. An example is the noted dissociation between the ownership of mental material and the experienced generation thereof. Another case is the dissociation between the time of perception and that associated with the percepts at hand. Normally, the temporal location of the perceiver and that of the object of his or her perception are identical. If I am looking at a tree in front of me, then it goes without saying that the tree and I are co-temporal, both being temporally located in the same moment. In a state of mind such as that induced by Ayahuasca, people often experience themselves watching scenarios taking place at other times; paradigmatic cases

are visions in which one feels one is privy to seeing scenes of past civilizations.[16]

4. *Parameters and values*   There are phenomenological patterns indicating that commonly assumed paradigmatic properties of consciousness are actually context-dependent and subject to modification and variation. As such, they are not to be conceived as fixed properties or defining characteristics (as in the classical analysis in chapter 9 of James [1890] 1950), but rather as potential, changeable values along parameters. Likewise, there are phenomenological patterns that bring to the fore otherwise unappreciated parameters. Examples of the former are the sense of realness that in nonordinary states of consciousness may be experienced as either heightened (as with Ayahuasca) or lowered (as in extreme fatigue or with alcohol), and the higher meaningfulness conferred to things (which is common with all psychedelics). The latter are manifested by the nonordinary states in which aesthetic value and sanctity are accentuated. By the view advocated here, these correspond to built-in structural parameters of the system of consciousness that are not apparent under ordinary conditions. This implies that cognitive theory should incorporate considerations involving aesthetics and the holy.[17] Conventional cognitive theories do not include parameters of these kinds.[18]

5. *Extraordinary feats of consciousness*   These include substance-induced visions, metamorphosis of identity, unusual mental lucidity and insight, altered temporality as well as remarkable manifest performances (e.g., playing of musical instruments and singing). In traditional cultures as well as by most laypersons today, effects of these sorts are regarded as paranormal. As argued at length in Shanon 2002a, I do not subscribe to such a view, but instead approach them as manifestations of heightened cognitive functioning and of enhanced creativity.

6. *The ineffable*   Finally, there are facets of the phenomenology of consciousness that defy both verbal description and logical conceptualization. The prime examples of these have been noted by mystics throughout the ages. Indeed, in the mystical literature the limitation of logic to cope with these states has been explicitly noted and actually viewed as an intrinsic, and even valued, determinant of the states at hand (see Deutsch 1969, Wolfson 1994, and de Cusa 1960, for Hinduism, Judaism, and Christianity, respectively, as well as the philosophical analysis by Scharfstein 1993).

Taken together, the very existence of phenomenological patterns of these kinds indicates that consciousness has facets that are far from being ordinary or expected. These are all interesting, all intellectually challenging, and all pertain to the psychological domain proper. The recognition of these promotes my call for a psychology of the conscious. As I see it, psychology (and cognitive psychology in particular) should be concerned not with underlying, covert structures and processes—be they ones that pertain to the brain or ones that pertain to hypothetical mental organs—but rather, with the phenomenology of experience, both external and internal.

As argued at the beginning of this essay, within the phenomenological framework advocated here, not only the empirical phenomena of interest are there on the surface, so is the theoretical apparata employed for their understanding. The dismissal of RCVM implies that the models normally employed in cognitive science today are of no avail. Moreover, remaining on the manifest surface we no longer have recourse to process models formulated by way of specifying the underlying mechanics of mind. But then, what kind of research can we conduct? What kind of theories can we have? What kind of explanation can our alternative psychology offer?

I have to confess that when first confronted with this eventuality I was seriously distressed. If the picture of mind for which I was arguing entailed the relinquishment of procedural, mechanistic explanation, didn't it amount to a bankrupt psychology as a theoretical science? Not necessarily so. Though dominant in the natural sciences, modeling by means of the specification of covert structures and mechanism need not be the only type of scientific explanation. The aim of science—any science—is to discover lawful regularities in a given domain of reality, to create a conceptual scheme to characterize them, and to develop a theoretical framework so as to attain a comprehension of the domain at hand. As I see it, this is precisely what investigations of the kind presented here are committed to.[19]

Grosso modo, all three lines of research described earlier, adopt the same basic methodological procedure, namely, the collection of large corpora of empirical data and the systematic characterization thereof. As it proceeds, the analysis gets to be more and more abstract, and with this, lawful regularities along with nontrivial theoretical principles and generalizations are discovered. Further, it is hoped that the generalizations compose into an integral system so as to form a theory lending fruitful comprehension of the domain of interest. With this, the goal of the scientific endeavor is achieved.

What I am proposing here is a project of a general theory of human consciousness. The epithet general comes by way of accentuating that the theory is to encompass all states of human consciousness. These are regarded as constituting the set of possible variations of one unified system, spanned by the various concatenations of values associated with a given structural matrix. Rather than fixing any particular set of values, the general theory of consciousness will define the pertinent dimensions and parameters of the system, the range of values they may take, and the dynamics governing the changes of these values in different contexts and in the course of time.[20] Furthermore, supplementing the systematic formulation of all that is potentially possible, the project advocated here will also specify constraints defining what variations are not actualized and offering theoretical reasoning for why this is the case. In my studies of both thought sequences and the phenomenology of the Ayahuasca experiences I have presented nontrivial examples of such negative cases.[21]

Interestingly, the view presented here is very much in line with one marshaled long ago by one of the first modern thinkers of psychology, Franz Brentano. In his *Descriptive Psychology*, Brentano (1995) distinguished between two kinds of psychology—genetic and descriptive. The former is concerned with underlying physiological structures and processes, the latter (called also psychognosy) focuses only on the phenomenological level of experience. Brentano is adamant that psychology proper should deal only with the latter. Further, he characterizes psychognosy as "pure psychology" and claims that only it, not physiological psychology, is an exact science.

In this conjunction, and before closing, let me recount an episode that I have personally witnessed some thirty years ago. The context was the founding meeting of the American Society for the Philosophy of Psychology, held at MIT in the fall of 1975. The invited keynote speaker was the polymath neuroscientist Jerry Lettvin. Lettvin looked at his audience, all psychologists and philosophers, and in more or less the following words said,

I am looking forward to a time, one day in the future, when no one of you all will be needed. At that future time, we shall know everything that is to be known about the brain, and we shall not need you psychologists any longer. I do not know when this will happen, but I am certain one day it will. Today, however, we brain scientists crucially need you. Embarking upon projects such as the brain substrates of memory or the physiology of perception, it is essential for one to have an educated understanding of what memory or perception are. It just makes no sense to launch the biological investigation with psychological conceptualizations that by and large are those of the man in the street. It is in this respect that you psychologists are essential to us. It is only with the initial charting of the terrain and the knowledge that you provide, that meaningful brain investigation can proceed.

I propose to push Lettvin's question further. It seems to me that the key question is what will be the situation in that utopian future when all that is to be known about the brain will actually be at our disposal. Will psychology be needed then? It seems to me that this is *the* key question that every student of mind should pose to himself or herself. My own stance is antithetical to Lettvin's. I strongly believe that complete knowledge of brain cannot come in lieu of psychological research. In fact, to my mind, the veritable psychological questions are precisely those that will remain even when the great progress in the neurosciences is achieved. These questions are the very ones that should be at the focus of psychological research today. They concern that intrinsic, irreducible level of the psychological whose defining characteristics are consciousness and meaning. Surely, all psychological achievements have neural correlates and they cannot be accomplished without the brain and the nervous system. Yet, to my mind, comprehending them should involve a theoretical framework which is genuinely psychological. I hope that in this essay I have succeeded in showing that the psychological domain is rich in phenomena and interesting in its own right, and that a genuinely psychological cognitive science is both intellectually challenging and worthwhile to pursue.

Acknowledgments

I thank Gabriel Bukobza, Zvi Carmeli, Adam Cohen, and Gabriel Levin for their helpful comments on earlier draft of the text, and Ido Amihai and Eran Laish for their help in the preparation of the manuscript.

Notes

1. This text is based on a lecture given at the Oléron Enaction Summer School held in July 2006. The lecture, in turn, surveyed research conducted during a period of about two decades before then. In other words, the ideas presented in this text were conceived independently and prior to the development of the paradigm of enaction to which this book is devoted. For this reason, the key term *enaction* is not employed here, but rather the term *enactment*, which I coined independently in an article published in 1987 in the *Journal of Mental Imagery* (Shanon 1987). Further developments of the theoretical framework presented here were subsequently published in Shanon 2008. A full development of the theory in question is a topic of a monograph in preparation.

2. In the early days of modern academic psychology, the situation was different. The Würzburg school employed introspection as the key method of cognitive

research, and William James and Titchener were most sympathetic to it. However, mainstream psychology has subsequently repudiated this orientation.

3. All this is said from the perspective of modern academic western psychological research. Of course, in Asia there have been long and venerable traditions of the study of mind. Both Hinduism and Buddhism have cultivated empirical, experiential methods for the study of consciousness as well as theoretical analyses thereof, unparalled in the West. For a discussion establishing a dialog between the two traditions, see Wallace 2000.

4. Following William James ([1890] 1950, 1912), I maintain that experience is a real ingredient of the nature of things, not because of any metaphysical reason but for the empirical fact that it is directly sensed and known by all.

5. Tel Aviv, Jerusalem, and Haifa are three large cities (and the only large cities) in Israel.

6. Usually in the psychological literature, thought patterns of this kind are associated with nonrational, perhaps primitive, mentation as encountered either in what psychoanalysts call primary processes or in psychopathology. In fact, the only well-studied such case is that of "sound associations," which are taken to be a typical symptom of schizophrenia (Arietti 1974).

7. I coined the term "enactment" about twenty years ago to refer to mental activity that is akin to the performative in linguistic pragmatics, thus marking the fact that mentation is not sheerly semantic. Because this has been developed independently of, and prior to, the enaction paradigm of Varela and his associates, I do not discuss the latter. The two notions are in syntony, in that they both highlight the role of action and being-in-the-world in cognition and both are grounded in a nonrepresentational perspective. The paradigm of enaction has broader epistemological, philosophical, and general scientific ramifications than my own cognitive-psychological work. A discussion of these is beyond the scope of this essay, which focuses on consciousness research.

8. In passing, let me make a comment of clarification with regard to the notion of self-consciousness. In the literature, as well as in common parlance, this notion is regarded as a kind, perhaps especially important, of consciousness. In the conceptualization presented here, the pertinent notion are those of Con_3, the third level of consciousness that cuts across the entire system, and $Self_3$, this third level as manifested in the specific region of the self. It seems to me that keeping these two senses distinct is important.

9. Hence, the tendency to regard $Cons_i$ as three types of consciousness, is, in fact, natural.

10. It is important to note that traditionally, Ayahuasca was never taken alone or for recreational purpose. It was always embedded in rigorous, well-structured

rituals administered by a person especially trained for this function, the ayahuas-quero. Typically, the rituals were either religious ceremonies or healing sessions (the distinction between the two is not clear-cut). In all contexts of use, music plays a major role. Although the rituals vary in different geographical places and with different ethnic and religious groups, the brew itself is essentially the same in all.

11. It should be emphasized that I am not making any metaphysical, ontological, or mystical claims. In a strict empirical fashion, I am defining the different types of experience encountered in human psychological phenomenology and am attempt-ing to conceptualize them theoretically. It is an empirical, phenomenological obser-vation that in some situations, human beings experience their perceptions and mentations as not being theirs. The literature on Ayahuasca, including texts written by Western academic and semi-academic authors, is rife with sensational claims that I myself find utterly unwarranted.

12. The similarity between the lowest and highest levels in the system is reminiscent of patterns detailed throughout the work of Wilber (see Wilber 1990).

13. Admittedly, the phrasing is somewhat odd here. As I, the cognitive psychologist, see it the experience is internal, but as far as the subjective feel of the experience is concerned, it is deemed to be external.

14. The term is not innocuous, for one may object to the very distinction between "easy" and "hard" problems of consciousness. In fact, it seem to me that this distinc-tion presupposes a general view of cognition and mind that I do not subscribe to. With this, my position is similar to that of Lowe (1995). The issues at hand are important, but they extend beyond the scope of this discussion.

15. Perhaps biologists would not solve it either, but for different reasons.

16. Most people who have had these experiences interpret them as involving para-normal time travel. I do not.

17. In fact, the same applies to the brain as well. D'Aquili and Newberg (1999) have proposed that religiosity (and, in particular, the belief in God) is ingrained in the very structure of the human brain.

18. These parameters may, in fact, be added to the set of non–purely cognitive factors discussed at the outset of this essay.

19. In developing the perspective advocated here I was also influenced by Chom-skian generative linguistics. There regularities of language are accounted within a rigorous, formal system without this being taken to be an actual processing model (see Fodor, Bever, and Garrett 1975). I am not a Chomskian, and by no means is Chomsky a phenomenologist, but in terms of how theory construction and scien-tific explanation are concerned, there are, I think, fundamental similarities between his paradigm and mine.

20. Consciousness being dynamical is of its very nature. States of consciousness are always changing, and the entire system is in constant flux. It is because consciousness is in perpetual alternation that I am not comfortable with the term "altered/alternate states of consciousness" as designating special nonordinary states and I refrain from using it.

21. This consideration of what is not the case follows the seminal insights of Chomsky (1965) when setting down the goals of syntactical theory, namely, both to give full analytic accounts of all the grammatical sentences in a language and to explain why other sentences are not grammatical.

References

Arietti, S. (1974). *Interpretation of schizophrenia.* New York: Basic Books.

Assaglioli, R. (1973). *The act of will.* New York: Viking Press.

Austin, J. (1962). *How to do things with words.* Oxford: Clarendon Press.

Baars, B. (1988). *A cognitive theory of consciousness.* Cambridge: Cambridge University Press.

Baars, B. (1997). *In the theater of consciousness.* Oxford: Oxford University Press.

Brentano, F. (1995). *Descriptive psychology.* London: Routledge.

Bucke, R. [1901] (1991). *Cosmic consciousness.* New York: Penguin Books.

Chalmers, D. (1995a). Facing up to the problem of consciousness. *Journal of Consciousness Studies* 2:200–219.

Chalmers, D. (1995b). The puzzle of conscious experience. *Scientific American* 273:62–68.

Chomsky, N. (1959). A review of B. F. Skinner's *Verbal behavior. Language* 35:69–80.

Chomsky, N. (1965). *Aspects of the theory of syntax.* Cambridge, MA: MIT Press.

Chomsky, N. (1972). *Language and mind.* Revised edition. New York: Harcourt Brace Jovanovich.

Crick, F. (1995). *The astonishing hypothesis: The scientific search for the soul.* New York: Simon and Schuster.

Crick, F., and Koch, C. (2003). A framework for consciousness. *Nature Neuroscience* 6:119–126.

Crovitz, H. P. (1970). *Galton's walk.* New York: Harper and Row.

d'Aquili, E., and Newberg, A. (1999). *The mystical mind: Probing the biology of religious experience.* Minneapolis, MN: Fortress Press.

de Cusa, N. (1960). *The vision of god*. New York: Frederick Ungar Publishing.

Dennett, D. (1991). *Consciousness explained*. Boston: Little, Brown & Co.

Deutsch, E. (1969). *Advaita vedanta: A philosophical reconstruction*. Honolulu, HI: East-West Center Press.

Dreyfus, H. (1992). *What computers can't do: A critique of artificial reason*. 2nd revised edition. New York: Harper and Row.

Fodor, J. (1968). *Psychological explanation: An introduction to the philosophy of psychology*. London: Random House.

Fodor, J. (1975). *The language of thought*. New York: Crowell.

Fodor, J., Bever, T., and Garrett, M. (1975). *The psychology of language: An introduction to psycholinguistics and generative grammar*. New York: McGraw Hill.

Forman, R., ed. (1990). *The problem of pure consciousness: Mysticism and philosophy*. Oxford: Oxford University Press.

Gibson, J. J. (1966). *The senses considered as a perceptual system*. Boston: Houghton Mifflin.

Gibson, J. J. (1979). *The ecological approach to visual perception*. Boston: Houghton Mifflin.

Graham, G., and Stephens, L. (1994). *Philosophical psychopathology*. Cambridge, MA: MIT Press.

Grof, S. (1975). *Realms of the human unconscious: Observations from LSD research*. New York: Viking Press.

Grof, S. (1998). *The cosmic game: Exploration of the frontiers of human consciousness*. Albany: State University of New York Press.

Heidegger, M. [1927] (1962). *Being and time*. New York: Harper and Row.

Humphrey, G. (1963). *Thinking, and introduction to its experimental psychology*. New York: Wiley.

Huxley, A. (1971). *The doors of perception and heaven and hell*. Harmondsworth: Penguin Books.

James, W. [1890] (1950). *The principles of psychology*. New York: Holt, Rinehart and Winston.

James, W. [1902] (1929). *Varieties of religious experience*. New York: Modern Library.

James, W. (1912). *Essays in radical empiricism*. New York: Longmans, Green & Co.

Jaynes, J. (1976). *The origin of consciousness in the breakdown of the bicameral mind*. Boston: Houghton Mifflin.

Johnson-Laird, P. (1983). *Mental models.* Cambridge, MA: Harvard University Press.

Jung, C. (1964). *Man and his symbols.* London: Aldus.

Kihlstrom, J. F. (1987). The cognitive unconscious. *Science* 237:1445–1452.

Koch, C. (2004). *The quest for consciousness: A neurobiological approach.* Colorado: Ben Roberts.

Kockelman, J. (1994). *Edmund Husserl's phenomenology.* West Lafayette, IN: Purdue University Press.

Laughlin, C. D., McManus, J., and d'Aquili, E. G. (1992). *Brain, symbol, and experience: Toward a neurophenomenology of human consciousness.* New York: Columbia University Press.

Locke, J. [1690] (1964). *An essay concerning human understanding.* London: Collins Sons & Co.

Lowe, E. (1995). There are no easy problems of consciousness. *Journal of Consciousness Studies* 2:266–271.

Ludwig, A. (1969). Altered states of consciousness. In *Altered states of consciousness,* ed. C. Tart, 9–22. New York: Wiley.

Luna, L., and Amaringo, P. (1991). *Ayahuasca visions: The religious iconography of a Peruvian shaman.* Berkeley: North Atlantic Books.

Lutz, A., and Thompson, E. (2003). Neurophenomenology: Integrating subjective experience and brain dynamics in the neuroscience of consciousness. *Journal of Consciousness Studies* 10 (10–11): 31–52.

Mandler, G. (1975). Consciousness: Respectable, useful and probably necessary. In *Information processing and cognition: The Loyola symposium,* ed. R. Solso, 229–254. Hillsdale, NJ: Lawrence Erlbaum Associates.

Mandler, J. M., and Mandler, G. (1964). *Thinking: From association to gestalt.* New York: Wiley.

Masters, R., and Houston, J. (1966). *The varieties of psychedelic experience.* New York: Holt, Rinehart and Winston.

Maturana, H. (1978). Biology of language: The epistemology of reality. In *Psychology and biology of language and thought,* ed. G. Miller and E. Lennberg, 27–63. New York: Academic Press.

Maturana, H., and Varela, F. (1980). *Autopoiesis and cognition.* Dordrecht: D. Reidel.

Maturana, H., and Varela, F. (1987). *The tree of knowledge: The biological roots of human understanding.* New York: Shambhala.

McGinn, C. (1991). *The problem of consciousness: Essays towards a resolution*. Oxford: Basil Blackwell.

Merkur, D. (1989). Unitive experiences and the state of trance. In *Mystical union and monotheistic faith: An ecumenical dialogue*, ed. M. Idel and B. McGinn, 125–153. New York: Macmillan.

Merkur, D. (1999). *Mystical moments and unitive thinking*. Albany: State University of New York.

Merleau-Ponty, M. (1962). *Phenomenology of perception*. London: Routledge and Kegan Paul.

Metzner, R., ed. (1968). *The ecstatic adventure*. New York: Macmillan.

Michaels, C., and Carello, C. (1981). *Direct perception*. Englewood Cliffs, NJ: Prentice Hall.

Nagel, T. (1974). What is it like to be a bat? *Philosophical Review* 83: 435–450.

Nemiah, J. (1989). Dissociative disorders (hysterical neuroses, dissociative type). In *Comprehensive textbook of psychiatry,* 5th edition, ed. H. Kaplan and B. Sadock, 1028–1044. Baltimore, MD: Williams & Wilkins.

Pope, K. S. and Singer, J. L. (1978). Regulation of the stream of consciousness. In *Consciousness and self-regulation*, vol. 2, ed. R. J. Davidson and G. E. Schwartz, 101–137. Chichester: Wiley.

Pylyshyn, Z. W. (1984). *Computation and cognition*. Cambridge, MA: MIT Press.

Reichel-Dolmatoff, G. (1975). *The shaman and the jaguar: A study of narcotic drugs among the Indians in Colombia*. Philadelphia: Temple University Press.

Rey, G. (1983). A reason for doubting the existence of consciousness. In *Consciousness and self regulation*, ed. R. J. Davison, G. E. Schwartz, and D. Shapiro, 1–36. New York: Plenum Press.

Scharfstein, B. (1993). *Ineffability*. New York: State University of New York Press.

Searle, J. R. (1969). *Speech acts: An essay in the philosophy of language*. Cambridge: Cambridge University Press.

Searle, J. R. (1980). Minds, brains and programs. *Behavioral and Brain Sciences* 3:417–457.

Shanon, B. (1984). The case for introspection. *Cognition and Brain Theory* 7:167–180.

Shanon, B. (1987). Enactment and Gedanken experiments. *Journal of Mental Imagery* 11:142–144.

Shanon, B. (1988). Channels of thought. *Discourse Processes* 11:221–242.

Shanon, B. (1989a). Thought sequences. *European Journal of Cognitive Psychology* 1:129–159.

Shanon, B. (1989b). *Mental images—a phenomenological investigation.* Working Paper no. 28. Jerusalem: The Goldie Rotman Center for Cognitive Science in Education.

Shanon, B. (1989c). Why do we (sometimes) think in words? In *Lines of thought: Reflections in the psychology of thinking,* vol. 1, ed. K. Gilhooly, M. Keane, R. Logie, and G. Erdos, 5–14. New York: Wiley.

Shanon, B. (1990a). Nonrepresentational frameworks for psychology: A typology. *European Journal of Cognitive Psychology* 2:1–22.

Shanon, B. (1990b). Novelty in thinking. In *Substance: A Review of Theory and Literary Criticism* 62/63:48–54.

Shanon, B. (1990c). Consciousness. *Journal of Mind and Behavior* 11:137–152.

Shanon, B. (1993a). *The representational and the presentational: An essay on cognition and the study of mind.* London: Harvester-Wheatsheaf.

Shanon, B. (1993b). Why are we (at least sometimes) conscious of our thoughts? *Pragmatics & Cognition* 1:25–49.

Shanon, B. (1998a). What is the function of consciousness? *Journal of Consciousness Studies* 5:295–308.

Shanon, B. (1998b). Ideas and reflections associated with Ayahuasca visions. *Bulletin of the Multidisciplinary Association for Psychedelic Studies* 8:18–21.

Shanon, B. (2001). Altered temporality. *Journal of Consciousness Studies* 8:35–58.

Shanon, B. (2002a). *The antipodes of the mind: Charting the phenomenology of the ayahuasca experience.* Oxford and New York: Oxford University Press.

Shanon, B. (2002b). Ayahuasca visualizations: A structural typology. *Journal of Consciousness Studies* 9:3–30.

Shanon, B. (2003a). The contents of Ayahuasca visions. *Mana: Estudos de Antropologia Social* 9:109–152.

Shanon, B. (2003b). Hallucinations. *Journal of Consciousness Studies* 10 (2): 3–31.

Shanon, B. (2003c). Altered states and the study of consciousness—The case of Ayahuasca. *Journal of Mind and Behavior* 24:125–154.

Shanon, B. (2008). A psychological theory of consciousness. *Journal of Consciousness Studies* 15:5–47.

Smith, A., and Tart, C. (1998). Cosmic consciousness experience and psychedelic experiences: A first person comparison. *Journal of Consciousness Studies* 1:97–107.

Spiegelberg, H. (1975). *Doing phenomenology: Essays on and in phenomenology*. Hague: Martinus Nijhoff.

Stace, W. (1961). *Mysticism and philosophy*. London: Macmillan.

Still, A., and Costall, A., eds. (1991). *Against cognitivism: Alternative foundations for cognitive psychology*. Hemel Hempstead, UK: Harvester Wheatsheaf.

Tart, C. (1969). *Altered states of consciousness: A book of readings*. New York: Wiley.

Tart, C. (1975). *States of consciousness*. New York: E. P. Dutton.

Tart, C., ed. (1992). *Transpersonal psychologies: Perspectives on the mind from seven great spiritual traditions*. San Francisco: Harper.

Turvey, M., Shaw, R., Reed, E., and Mace, W. (1981). Ecological laws of perceiving and acting: In reply to Fodor and Pylyshyn. *Cognition* 3:237–304.

Turvey, M. T., and Shaw, R. (1979). The primacy of perceiving: An ecological reformulation of perception for understanding memory. In *Perspectives on memory research: Essays in honor of Uppsala University 500th Anniversary*, ed. L. G. Nillson, 167–222. Hillsdale, NJ: Lawrence Erlbaum.

Underhill, E. (1955). *Mysticism: A study in the nature and development of man's spiritual consciousness*. New York: Meridian.

Varela, F. J. (1996). Neurophenomenology. *Journal of Consciousness Studies* 3 (4): 330–349.

Varela, F., and Shear, J., eds. (1999). *The view from within: First-person approaches to the study of consciousness*. Thorverton, Exeter, UK, and Bowling Green: Imprint Academic.

Varela, F., Thompson, J., and Rosch, E. (1991). *The embodied mind*. Cambridge, MA: MIT Press.

Velmans, M. (2000). *Understanding consciousness*. London: Routledge.

Vygotsky, L. (1978). *Mind in society*. Cambridge, MA: Harvard University Press.

Vygotsky, L. (1986). *Thought and language*. Cambridge, MA: MIT Press.

Wallace, A. B. (2000). *The taboo of subjectivity: Towards a new science of consciousness*. New York: Oxford University Press.

Watts, A. (1962). *The joyous cosmology: Adventures in the chemistry of consciousness*. New York: Pantheon Books.

Wertsch, J. V. (1985a). *Culture, communication and cognition: Vygotskian perspectives*. Cambridge: Cambridge University Press.

Wertsch, J. V. (1985b). *Vygotsky and the social formation of mind.* Cambridge, MA: Harvard University Press.

White, J. (1972). The search for ecstasy. In *The highest state of consciousness,* ed. J. White, 6–13. New York: Anchor Books.

Wilber, K. (1990). *Eye to eye: The quest for the new paradigm.* Expanded edition. Boston: Shambhala.

Winograd, T., and Flores, C. (1986). *Understanding computers and cognition: A new foundation for design.* Norwood, NJ: Albex.

Wittgenstein, L. (1953). *Philosophical investigations.* Oxford: Blackwell.

Wittgenstein, L. (1958). *The blue and brown books.* Oxford: Blackwell.

Wolfson, E. R. (1994). *Through a speculum that shines: Vision and imagination in medieval Jewish mysticism.* Princeton, NJ: Princeton University Press.

15 Enaction, Imagination, and Insight

Edwin Hutchins

15.1 Introduction

Distributed cognition is a framework for exploring the cognitive implications of the commonsense observation that in systems characterized by multiple levels of interacting elements, different properties may emerge at different levels of organization. Thus, a colony of social insects has different properties than any individual insect in the colony (Seeley and Levien 1987; Turner 2000; Holldobler and Wilson 2009). At the level of organisms, bodies have different properties than organs, which have different properties than cells. In the realm of cognition, a neural circuit has different properties than any of the neurons in the circuit. The same can be said of a brain area with respect to the neural circuits that compose it, or of an entire brain with respect to the areas that interact within the brain. This is also true of the body/brain system with respect to either brain or body, and the world/body/brain system with respect to any of its parts. A system composed of a person in interaction with a cognitive artifact has different cognitive properties than those of the person alone (Bruner, Olver, and Greenfield 1966; Cole and Griffin 1980; Norman 1994; Hutchins 1995a, b; Clark 2001, 2008). A group of persons may have cognitive properties that are different from those of any person in the group (Halbwachs 1925; Roberts 1964; Hutchins 1995a; Surowiecki 2004; Sunstein 2006). This layering of scales of integration finds expression in the boundaries among traditional scientific disciplines. More recently developed interdisciplines, of which cognitive science is but one example, search not only for regularities and explanations within levels, but also for patterns in the regularities across levels. The cognitive accomplishments of all human groups depend on the simultaneous operation of cognitive processes on all of these levels from neuron to social group. The big questions in contemporary cognitive science concern the ways that humans, understood as biological creatures, can produce culturally meaningful outcomes.

A central claim of the distributed cognition framework is that the proper unit of analysis for cognition should not be set a priori, but should be responsive to the nature of the phenomena under study. For some sorts of phenomena, the skin or skull of an individual is exactly the correct boundary. For some phenomena, the whole person is just too big and including the whole organism would involve too many interactions. For other phenomena, setting the boundary of the unit of analysis at the skin will cut lines of interaction in ways that leave key aspects of the phenomena unexplained or unexplainable. Most work in distributed cognition to date has focused on systems that are larger than an individual (Hutchins 1995a, b, 2000, 2005, 2006). In these systems, high-level cognitive functions such as memory, planning, decision making, reasoning, error detection and correction, computation, learning, and so on can be identified and analyzed in the culturally organized activities of groups of people in interaction with one another and with technology. Moving the boundaries of the unit of analysis out beyond the skin of the individual human is one important strategy for the distributed cognition approach. It allows us to see how it can be that many of the cognitive accomplishments that have routinely been attributed to individual brains are in fact the accomplishments of cognitive systems that transcend the boundaries of individual bodies. This strategy worked well because the language that classical cognitive science had used to describe internal cognitive processes turned out to be perfectly suited to describing external cognitive processes. Of course, this was no accident. The language of classical cognitive science arose from a distillation of folk observations about external cognitive processes and was given metaphorical extension to the unobservable internal processes (Gentner and Grudin 1985; Hutchins 1995a, chap. 9).

Distributed cognition as applied to socio-cultural systems suggested an answer to the question of how low-level processes create high-level cognition. The idea is that high-level cognition is produced by the culturally orchestrated application of low-level cognitive processes to cultural materials, that is, elements of language, sign systems, and inscriptions of all sorts (Vygotsky 1986; Norman 1994; Hutchins 1995a; Clark 2001).

A simple example of this idea taken from the world of ship navigation is provided by the so-called three-minute rule, which navigators use to compute ship's speed from elapsed time and distance traveled. This instance of high-level cognition computes the value of an abstraction, speed, which is a relationship between distance and time that can be sensed, but cannot be measured directly or expressed with precision by the organic human body. The three-minute rule depends on a serendipitous interaction between two systems of distance units and a system of time units. A nautical mile is very nearly 2000 yards, and an hour is exactly 60 minutes. This means that three minutes is one-twentieth of an hour and 100 yards is one twentieth part of a nautical mile. Thus, the number of hundreds of yards traveled by an object in three minutes equals the speed of the object in nautical miles per hour.[1] This convenient fact is put into practice in navigation in the following way. Two successive positions of a ship are plotted on a three-minute interval. Suppose the distance between them is 1500 yards. The navigator computes ship's speed to be 15 knots by doing the following: "The distance between the fix positions on the chart is spanned with the dividers and transferred to the yard scale. There, with one tip of the divider on 0, the other falls on the scale at a tick mark labeled 1500. The representation in which the answer is obvious is simply one in which the navigator looks at the yard-scale label and ignores the two trailing zeros" (Hutchins 1995a, 151–152). In this analysis, high-level cognitive functions were seen to be realized in the transformation and propagation of representational states. The span between the fix positions on the chart is a representational state that is transformed into a span on the dividers. This representational state is then transformed into a span on the yard scale. Finally, the span on the yard scale is transformed into the answer by reading the label on the designated tick mark in a particular way. Notice that, even though they are obviously involved, in this account, little is said about the use of the eyes, and nothing at all is said about the use of the hands or other parts of the body. In the next section, I will try to show what can be gained by examining the role of the body more closely.

15.2 Embodied and Enacted Cognition

Over the past two decades, cognitive science has been shifting from a concept of cognition as a logical process to one of cognition as a biological phenomenon. As more is learned about the biology of human cognition, the language of classical cognitive science, which described external cognition so well, appears increasingly irrelevant to internal cognitive processes. As Clark puts it,

Perception itself is often tangled up with the possibilities for action and is continuously influenced by cognitive, contextual, and motor factors. It need not yield a rich, detailed, and action-neutral inner model awaiting the services of "central cognition" so as to deduce appropriate actions. In fact, these old distinctions (between perception, cognition, and action) may sometimes obscure, rather than illuminate, the true flow of events. In a certain sense, the brain is revealed not as (primarily) an engine of reason or quiet deliberation, but as an organ of *environmentally situated control*. (Clark 2001, 95; emphasis in the original)

Embodiment and enaction are names for two approaches that strive for a new understanding of the nature of human cognition by taking seriously the fact that humans are biological creatures. Neither approach is yet well defined, but both provide some useful analytic tools for understanding real-world cognition.

Embodiment is the premise that the particular bodies we have influence how we think. The rapidly growing literature in embodiment is summarized in Wilson 2002, Gibbs 2006, and Spivey 2007. I lack the space needed to sort out the many strands of this literature. Let us simply note here that according to the embodied perspective, cognition is situated in the interaction of body and world, dynamic bodily processes such as motor activity can be part of reasoning processes, and offline cognition is body-based too. Finally, embodiment assumes that cognition evolved for action, and because of this, perception and action are not separate systems, but are inextricably linked to each other and to cognition. This last idea is a near relative to the core idea of enaction.

Enaction is the idea that organisms create their own experience through their actions. Organisms are not passive receivers of input from the environment, but are actors in the environment such that what they experience is shaped by how they act. Many important ideas follow from this premise. Maturana and Varela (1987) introduced the notion of "structural coupling" between an organism and its environment. This describes the relations between action and experience as they are shaped by the biological endowment of the creature. Applying the enaction concept to perception, Noë (2004) says that perception is something we *do*, not something that happens to us. Thus in considering the way that perception is tangled up with the possibilities of action, O'Regan and Noë (2001) introduced the idea of sensorimotor contingencies. In the activity of probing the world, we learn the structure of relationships between action and perception (thus the title of Noë's recent book, *Action in Perception* (Noë 2004). These relationships capture the ways that sensory experience is contingent upon actions. Each sensory mode has a different and characteristic field of sensorimotor contingencies.

One of the key insights of the embodied cognition framework is that bodily action does not simply express previously formed mental concepts;

bodily practices including gesture are part of the activity in which concepts are formed (McNeill 2005; Alač and Hutchins 2004; Gibbs 2006, chap. 4). That is, concepts are created and manipulated in culturally organized practices of moving and experiencing the body. For example, Natasha Myers (2008) described biochemists reasoning about molecular structure by using their bodies to imagine stresses among the parts of a complex molecule. James Watson (1968) reported that he and Francis Crick spent hours cutting out stiff cardboard models of nucleotide pairs and then discovered the double helix of DNA by fitting the pieces of cardboard together. This discovery, like so many (perhaps most) others in science was enacted in the bodily practices of scientists. Similarly, gesture can no longer be seen simply as an externalization of already formed internal structures. Ethnographic and experimental studies of gesture are converging on a view of gesture as the enactment of concepts (Núñez and Sweetser 2006; Goldin-Meadow 2006). This is true even for very abstract concepts. For example, studies of mathematicians conceptualizing abstract concepts such as infinity show that these too are created by bodily practices. (Núñez 2005; Lakoff and Núñez 2000).

Let us now reconsider the three-minute rule with these general principles in mind. This will show that an embodied analysis of the three-minute rule creates explanatory possibilities that simply have no place in the disembodied analysis presented earlier.

The navigator's first step is to see and apply the dividers to the span of space between the position fixes (figure 15.1). This is a visual activity, but also a motor activity. Techniques for the manual manipulation of the dividers require precise hand-eye coordination. As a consequence of decades of experience, skilled navigators acquire finely tuned habits of action and perception. These include sticking the point of one arm of the divider into the previous fix triangle on the chart, adjusting the spread of the dividers while keeping the point planted, and locating the next fix triangle first visually, and then with the other arm of the dividers. What makes one fix triangle the "previous fix" and the other one the "next fix"? Or, even more basically, what makes a particular set of lines on the chart a fix triangle? The answer to these questions brings us to some fundamental issues concerning interactions with cultural worlds. Many people seem to assume that the status of external representations qua representations is unproblematic. But what makes a material pattern into a representation, and further, what makes it into the particular representation it is? The answer in both cases is enactment. To apprehend a material pattern as a representation of something is to engage in specific culturally shaped

Figure 15.1
Using the dividers to span the distance between successive position fixes.

perceptual processes.[2] Regardless of whether the pattern is a sound (apprehended as a word) or a pattern of lines on a chart (apprehended as a
position fix), this most powerful of cognitive processes cannot be accomplished any other way.

This fact is expressed differently in different approaches. Goodwin
(1994) describes a process by which discursive practices (plotting lines of
position, for example) are applied to a domain of scrutiny (a region on a
navigation chart) to produce phenomenal objects of interest (a position
fix, for example). The label "discursive practices" suggests a narrow a class
of perceptual processes that can be so applied. I prefer to say that the
enactment of cultural practices in interaction with culturally organized
worlds produces the phenomenal objects of interest. In the tradition of
phenomenology, the experienced set of phenomenal objects of interest
would be referred to as an "own world" (*monde propre*). It is important to
notice here that the own world does not consist of isolated objects, but of
a system of enacted understandings. The fix is seen as a representation
of the position of the ship only when the chart is seen as a representation
of the space in which the ship is located. The cultural practices that enact
these understandings may become over-learned and operate outside the
consciousness of the person engaging in them.

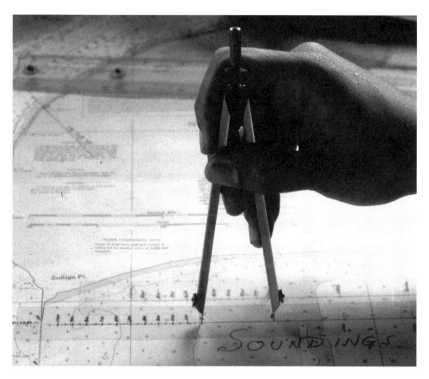

Figure 15.2
Transferring the spanned distance to the scale where the span may be read as either
a distance or a speed depending on the way the spanned space is embedded in the
navigator's activity.

The navigator's activity at any given moment is embedded in the knowledge of many other moments. The visual appearance of the current span
may be compared to other spans that have been plotted. The manual feel
of the current span may be compared to other spans or to the largest or
smallest distance that can be comfortably spanned with this set of dividers.
Once the distance traveled has been spanned with the dividers, a different
set of manual skills is required to move the span to the scale (figure 15.2).
The navigator must now raise the dividers and move them without changing the span. He must then stick one arm into zero point of the scale,
bringing the other arm down to the scale without changing the span.[3]

The activity at any given moment is not only shaped by the memory
of past activities, but is also shaped by the anticipation of what is to come.
The navigator's grip on the dividers and the position of his body while
spanning the distance on the chart are configured in ways that anticipate

moving the span to the yard scale. Thus, experience is not only multi-modal, but is also multitemporal or temporally extended in the sense that it is shaped both by memories of the past (on a variety of time scales ranging from milliseconds to years) and by anticipation of the future (over a similar set of time scales).

The activity of using the chart and plotting tools with the three-minute rule involves multimodal experiences in which visual and motor processes must be precisely coordinated. That fact is obvious, but is it relevant? Isn't it safe to disregard these movements of eye and hand as mere implementation details? I believe that we do so at our peril. These embodied multimodal experiences are entry points for other kinds of knowledge about the navigation situation. Bodily experience in the form of unusual muscular tension, for example, can be a proxy for important concepts such as the realization that an atypical distance is being spanned. This implies that sensorimotor contingencies are also learned when the perception of the world is mediated by tools. Chart distances apprehended via the hands and dividers are characterized by a different set of contingencies than distances apprehended visually.

Havelange, Lenay, and Stewart (2003) make an important claim about the difference between human enacted experience and the experience of other animals. In humans, the apparatus by which structural coupling is achieved may include various kinds of technologies.

"We have seen that the own-world of animals is constitutively shaped by the particularities of their means of structural coupling. It is the same for human beings with the enormous difference that the means of structural coupling of humans includes their technical inventions" (Havelange, Lenay, and Stewart (2003, 126; translation by the author). These technologies range from the basic human cognitive technology of language—words are, after all, conceptual tools—to charts and computers and all of the other cognitive artifacts with which humans think. The relevance of this to our current discussion is that a tool—in this case, the divider—is part of the system that produces the particular set of relations between action and experience that characterize the structural coupling of the navigator to his world.

Recent work in embodied cognition suggests that interactions among modes in multimodal representations may be more complex than previously thought. For example, Smith (2005) shows that the perceived shape of an object is affected by actions taken on that object. Motor processes have also been shown to affect spatial attention (Engel, this volume, chapter 8; Gibbs 2006, 61). Thus, we should expect that embodied, multi-modal experiences are integrated such that the content of various modes affect one another. Although the sensorimotor contingencies of perceptual modes are distinct from one another, as long as an activity unfolds as expected, the contents of the modes should be congruent with one another. That is, what the navigator sees should agree with what the navigator feels in his hands as he manipulates the tools. The interactions among the contents of various modes of experience will be an important part of the argument to follow.

Once the divider is placed on the distance scale, the navigator uses the pointer of the divider arm to direct his attention to the region of the scale under the pointer. Through this perceptual practice, the divider pointer is used to highlight (Goodwin 1994) a position on a distance scale. The complex cultural skills of scale reading and interpolation produce a number that expresses the value of the location indicated on the distance scale. The scale is perceived in a particular way by embedding that perception in action. What is then seen on the scale is a complex mix of perception, action, and imagination. The cultural practice of speaking or subvocalizing the number expresses the value of the location indicated on the distance scale, and in coordination with the visual and motor experience of the pointer on the scale forms a stable representation of the distance. The congruence of the contents of the many modes of experience lends stability to the enactment of the measured distance.

Notice that what is seen is not simply what is visible. What is seen is something that is there only by virtue of the activity of seeing being conducted in a particular way. That is, what is seen is what is enacted. Even more fundamentally, seeing a line, a set of crossing marks, and the numbers aligned with the marks as a scale of any sort is itself already an instance of enacted seeing. Ingold's (2000) claim that perception is properly understood as a cultural skill fits well with the enaction perspective. The role of enactment of meaning becomes even more evident in the moment when the "distance" scale is *seen* as a "speed" scale, and the distance spanned by the compass/dividers is read as a speed. It is the same scale and similar practices of interpolation are applied to it. But the practice of reading the span on the scale as a speed rather than as a distance is a different practice; a practice that *sees* something different in the very same visual array. In the opening moments of this activity, the span of the dividers is a distance, but the property of being a distance is created by nothing other than the cultural practices of the navigator. As the navigator moves the span toward the yard scale, the span becomes a speed, but again only because that is how the navigator enacts it in that moment. If perception were a passive process, then this same visual array should give rise to the same experience in both moments of perception. But the fact is that reading the span of the dividers on the scale as a speed is a different experience from reading the span of the dividers on the scale as a distance. In this way, cultural practices orchestrate the coordination of low-level perceptual and motor processes with cultural materials to produce particular higher-level cognitive processes. Which higher-level process is produced depends on learned cultural practices as much as it does on the properties of the culturally organized material setting. Under just the right conditions, an enculturated person can place an extent of space on a scale and can read the span there as either a distance or a speed.

Among the points I hoped to demonstrate here are the following: humans make material patterns into representations by enacting their meanings. A phenomenal object of interest in navigation—in this case, the speed of the ship—is enacted in the engagement of the culturally organized world through the cultural practices that constitute the navigator's professional competence. Because the role of the number produced by reading the scale in the navigator's "own world" is the speed of the ship, we can call it an enacted representation of ship's speed. When a triangle of lines on a chart is "seen as" a position fix, or when the chart itself is "seen as" a depiction of the space in which the ship is located, we can also refer to these as enacted representations. These enacted representations involve the simultaneous engagement of perception, action, and imagination. Enacted representations are dynamic, integrating memory for the immediate past, experience of the present, and anticipation of the future. They are multimodal, in the sense that they may involve the simultaneous coordination of any or all of the senses and any modes of action. They are saturated with affect. They are, of course, dependent on the particularities of the sensorimotor apparatus of the organism. The contents of enacted representations are complex multimodal wholes (worlds) rather than isolated objects. Objects are seen (grasped) to be what they are by virtue of the ways they may be engaged by the acting subject.

The emerging picture of the brain as an organ of environmentally situated control is both compelling and problematic. Clark summarized the problem as follows: "What in general is the relation between the strategies used to solve basic problems of perception and action and those used to solve more abstract or higher level problems?" (Clark 2001, 135)

Combining the basic embodiment premise that low-level action and perception are inextricably linked (Clark 2001; Noë 2004) with the idea from Havelange, Lenay, and Stewart (2003) that technologically mediated interaction is part of the process of forming enacted representations, opens a new space of possibilities for understanding how high-level cognitive processes can arise in enactment. This paper is an admittedly speculative attempt to sketch out a map of that space of possibilities. If the embodiment premise and the enaction framework are correct, then cognitive processes should be visible in the fine details of the engagement of a whole person with a whole culturally organized world. Whether such an analysis is possible, and if it is possible whether it will help us understand human cognition is at present unknown. In the following sections, I will attempt to perform such an analysis and I hope to show that it does indeed contribute something new to our understanding of the relations between low- and high-level cognition.

15.3   An "Aha!" Insight Seen through the Lens of Enaction

Until recently, ship navigation was performed on paper charts using manual plotting tools (Hutchins 1995a). The data on which this analysis is based were originally collected in the early 1980s on the bridge of a U.S. Navy ship when these practices were still common. In order to fix the position of a ship, navigators measure the bearing from the ship to at least three landmarks. When plotted on a chart, the bearing of a landmark from the ship becomes a line of position (LOP); that is, it is a line on which the ship must be located. Plotting an LOP involves setting the measured bearing on a protractor scale on a plotting tool (called the "hoey") and then placing the hoey on the chart so that the protractor arm passes through the depiction of the landmark on the chart and the base of the protractor scale is aligned with the directional frame of the chart. Once the plotting tool is correctly placed, the navigator uses a pencil to draw a line on the chart along the edge of the protractor arm in the vicinity of the projected position of the ship. Two intersecting lines of position determine, or "fix," the position of the ship. Navigators usually try to plot three lines of position, because the intersection of three LOPs forms a triangle. A small fix triangle indicates that the position fixing information is good. A large triangle indicates problems somewhere in the chain of representations that lead to the fix triangle. In general, the navigator's confidence in a fix is inversely proportional to the size of the fix triangle.

I happened to be on the bridge of a large ship, video-recording navigation activities, when, while entering a narrow navigation channel, the ship suffered the failure of its main gyrocompass. Upon losing the gyrocompass, the navigation crew could no longer simply read the true bearing of a given landmark and plot that bearing. Rather, they were then required to compute the true bearing by adding the corrected magnetic ship's heading to the relative bearing of the landmark (bearing of the landmark with respect to ship's heading). The magnetic compass is subject to two kinds of errors: deviation and variation. The local magnetic environment of the compass can induce small errors, called deviation, that are a function of the interaction between the compass, the ship, and the earth's magnetic field. Deviation errors vary with magnetic heading, are empirically determined, and are posted on a card near the magnetic compass. Magnetic variation is the extent to which the direction of the earth's magnetic field diverges from true north in the local area. The correct equation is: true bearing of the landmark equals compass heading plus deviation plus magnetic variation plus the relative bearing of the landmark (TB = C + D + V + RB). The loss of the gyrocompass disrupted the ability of the crew to plot accurate positions for the ship. The crew explored various computational variations of TB = C + V + RB while plotting thirty-eight lines of position. Then they discovered[4] that a key term, deviation (D), was missing from their computations. After reconfiguring their work to include the deviation term, the team gradually regained the functional ability to plot accurate positions.

How can the discovery that this term was missing be explained? The discovery appeared as an "Aha!" insight. In some sense, the "Aha!" insight that this analysis seeks to explain happened just when we would expect it to appear. It happened when the increasing size of the fix triangles led the plotter to explore explanations for the decreasing quality of the fixes. However, neither the navigator's obvious frustration nor the fact that he was looking for something that would improve the fixes can explain the insight. The analysis presented here seeks to reveal the nature of the process by which the plotter examined the fixes and how that process led to the insight that the deviation term was missing. Taken in the context of the computations that the crew was doing, this discovery was, like most creative insights, mysterious. There was nothing in the pattern of computational efforts leading up to the discovery that indicated that the navigators were nearing this development. The processes that underlie the "Aha!" insight remain invisible to a computational perspective in part because that perspective represents everything in a single monomodal (or even amodal) system.[5] A careful examination of the way a navigator used his body to engage the tools in the setting, however, helps to demystify the discovery process, and to explain why and how it happened when it did. The insight was achieved in, and emerged out of, the navigator's bodily engagement with the setting through enacted representations.

Here is a very brief account of the course of events. Lines of position had been plotted to each of three landmarks, but the fix triangle that was produced was unacceptably large. That the triangle was unacceptably large is clear in a comment from the plotter to one of his coworkers. He said, "I keep getting these monstrous frigging god-damned triangles and I'm trying to figure out which one is fucking off!" This also illustrates the emotional character of the experience of these triangles for the plotter. Such a large triangle was clear evidence of the presence of an error somewhere in the process that created the fix. The LOPs were then checked, and at least one possible source of error was tested with respect to each one. These checks did not reveal the source of the problem with the position fix. The plotter then used the plotting tools and the chart to explore changes to LOPs that might improve the position fix. It should be noted that reasoning about the relationships among imagined LOPs is a common practice among navigators (Hutchins 2006). Let's examine this exploration in more detail.

Table 15.1 contains two columns. In the left column are descriptions of the observable actions. In the right column are descriptions of the enactment of the phenomenal objects of interest that can be expected to accompany the observed behavior, given the understanding that enactment is dynamic, multimodal, temporally extended, and affectively colored activity that integrates perception, action, and imagination. I recommend that the reader first read down the left column consulting the accompanying figures to get a sense of the course of action undertaken by the plotter. Once the course of action is clear, the reader will be able to judge the aptness of the descriptions of the enactment. I take the descriptions of the observed activities to be unproblematic. They are based on good quality video with multiple audio streams and informed by an extensive body of background ethnographic information (see Hutchins 1995a). Some of the descriptions of enactment are also straightforward. Some follow directly from the observed activity and others can be inferred and justified by the background ethnography. There are, however, some aspects of the enactment that are clearly speculative. I have marked these in the table with the phrase, "Let us *speculate*."

Table 15.1
Observed actions and the hypothesized enactment of phenomenal objects of interest

Observed activity	Enactment of phenomenal objects
The plotter aligned the hoey arm approximately for one landmark, and placed his right index finger on the location of the landmark forming a pivot. He then moved the base of the hoey left, rotating the arm slightly clockwise with respect to the previously plotted LOP for that landmark. This rotation brought the provisional LOP into the interior of the previously plotted triangle, thus reducing the size of the triangle formed with the other two LOPs.	This manipulation of the hoey on the surface of the chart integrates motor, visual, proprioceptive, and tactile experience in an enacted representation of a new LOP. Performed in the culturally meaningful space of the chart, this enacts complex conceptual content. Not just a tentative new LOP, but a clockwise rotation, a shift of the LOP to the west-southwest, a smaller triangle, and an improved fix. Examining the placement of the tool on the chart adds stable visual elements to the enacted representation. And these are only the aspects that are demonstrably relevant to the current activity. The navigator must have also experienced the friction of the hoey on the chart surface, the mass distribution of the hoey, and the transparency of the plastic in the hoey arm. These are present in the sensorimotor contingencies of tool manipulation. The tentative nature of this act marks this exploratory manipulation as an example of the class of actions that Murphy (2004) has called "action in the subjunctive mood." These are "as-if" actions or "may it be thus" actions. These actions produce ephemeral experience of potential, but not yet realized states of affairs or processes. The fact that these activities are enacted in the subjunctive mood, marked as projecting or anticipating a possible future, is very important. Let us *speculate* that this projection keeps the enacted, embodied anticipation of clockwise rotation active during the following seconds of activity.
Observed activity	Enactment of phenomenal objects
He then quickly shifted the hoey on the surface of the chart and aligned it approximately with the second landmark, placing his left thumb on the hoey arm near the landmark to serve as a pivot. He also adjusted this LOP slightly clockwise by pulling his right hand and the hoey arm slightly toward his body (figure 15.3).	In these first two moves, the plotter used his body and the tools (chart and hoey) to imagine LOPs that, if they could somehow be created in the future, would make the fix triangle smaller.

Table 15.1
(continued)

Observed activity	Enactment of phenomenal objects
The plotter spoke (self-regulatory speech) the remembered bearing to the third landmark, "one two zero" degrees, while the hoey was still lying on the chart.	Self-regulatory speech enacts the bearing in the verbal modality to form a more stable guide to action. Skilled navigators experience bearing numbers as bodily sensations with respect to a cardinal direction frame. The enactment of the spoken bearing is also embodied in these sensations, and this would have been part of the active context for the next action.
The plotter then picked up the hoey in his left hand and used his right thumb to move the arm counterclockwise in the direction of the 120-degree scale position.	Let us *speculate* that the plotter attends visually to the scale values on the protractor in the context of "felt" directions, and the still active enactment of a seen fix triangle and the multimodal anticipation of the small clockwise rotations of LOPs.
The plotter made a sharp intake of breath, stopped pushing the hoey arm with his thumb, quickly lowered the hoey held in the left hand to the chart surface, lowered the right hand, which was holding a pencil, to the chart surface beside the hoey, and looked up away from the hoey and chart. All of this happened in less than a second.	This is a clear abandonment of the activity of setting the hoey arm to a scale position, which would have been the first step in plotting the third LOP. Let us *speculate* that the elements of the enacted representations have now combined such that the anticipated multimodal experience of small clockwise rotation is superimposed on the visual experience of the protractor scale (figure 15.4). This combination would produce as an emergent property the concept that adding a small number (small clockwise rotation on the scale) to the bearing for LOP3 will reduce the size of the fix triangle.

Table 15.1
(continued)

Observed activity	Enactment of phenomenal objects
The plotter said to himself, "I know what he's doing!" He tapped the eraser end of his pencil on the chart three times. He then took three actions in quick succession: (1) He turned away from the chart and moved toward the helm station saying, "Let me try . . . Let me try . . . Let me try with my new ones . . ." He consulted the deviation table posted near the magnetic compass at the helm station. (2) The plotter then came back to the chart table, saying, "say three, say three (accompanied these words with beat gestures), add three to everything." (3) Upon hearing the plotter say this, the bearing timer asked, "Add three? Because we're shooting relative?" The plotter responded, "Um, no. On a southwest heading add three." The plotter then re-plotted the three LOPs, adding 3 degrees to each. This produced the desired small fix triangle.	This action sequence contains more self-regulatory speech. Three new concepts have been integrated in this moment. They correspond, in order to the three observed action elements. They are as follows: (1) That the small number that would improve the LOP is deviation. The deviation table is posted at the helm station. (2) That all three LOPs will be improved by adding to them a small number. He says "add three to everything." (3) That deviation, 3 degrees, is the small number that has been missing from the calculations up to this point. This is clear from the plotter's statement linking the ship's heading to the need to add 3 degrees to the LOPs. These three concepts form a synergistic cognitive ecosystem in which each of them makes the others stronger.

Figure 15.3
The positioning of the body of the plotter while adjusting the second LOP slightly clockwise. The left thumb acts as a pivot while the right hand slides the hoey arm slightly toward the plotter's body.

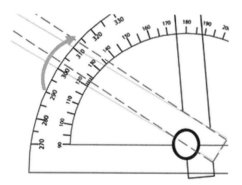

Figure 15.4
The superimposition of imagined clockwise rotation (motor anticipation) onto the visual experience of the hoey degree scale. Light-gray solid lines represent the position of the hoey arm when aligned with the 120-degree mark. Dashed lines represent the imagined location of the hoey arm if it were rotated slightly clockwise. The image of a number slightly larger than 120 is an emergent property of this interaction between contents of visual experience and motor anticipation.

There are two speculations here, both of which concern the process of sensorimotor integration. The first is that the enactments of the LOPs produced by the plotter are temporally extended such that anticipatory elements formed early in the process can affect elements that are formed later in the process. The second speculation is that the representations enacted by the plotter are multimodal and that the contents of the various modes may interact with one another. There is ample evidence for the presence of processes that support both of these speculations. First, prediction and anticipation are core functions of animal perception/action systems (Churchland, Ramachandran, and Sejnowski 1994; Noë 2004) and the temporal dynamics of many sorts of action are characterized by both feedforward and feedback effects (Spivey 2007). In fact, the perception of a match between anticipated and current experience even appears to play an important role in an organism's sense that activity belongs to the self (Gibbs 2006). It is therefore plausible that anticipated elements of an enacted representation could interact with elements of subsequent enactments. Second, not only do the contents of various perceptual modes interact with one another, but these interactions have also been linked to success in insight tasks. Spivey (2007, 266–268) describes Glucksberg's (1964) replication of Duncker's (1945) famous candle problem. The problem is to mount a candle on a wall using only the candle, a book of matches, and a cardboard box full of thumb tacks. (The solution is to use the tacks to affix the box to the wall, and use the box as a shelf for the candle.) Glucksberg recorded what the participants did with the actual objects as they attempted to solve the problem. Those who successfully solved the problem tended to touch the box more than those who did not. For those that did solve it, Spivey observes, "Moreover, right before that 'Aha!' moment, the object that these participants had most recently touched was always the box—*and in most cases that touch had been adventitious and nonpurposeful.* It is almost as if the participant's hands suspected that the box would be useful, in and of itself, before the participant himself knew!" (Spivey 2007, 268; emphasis in the original).

This suggests that the embodied processes of interacting with the material objects may have included the imagination of manipulations of the box that could be useful in solving the problem. More recently, Goldin-Meadow (2006) has shown that children explaining their incorrect answers to arithmetic problems sometimes produce gestures that do not entirely match the contents of their spoken words. In particular, the "gesture-speech mismatches" sometimes highlight with gesture aspects of the correct solution that the student is not yet capable of describing in words. This condition is shown to be an indicator of a readiness to learn the correct solution procedure. Again, reasoning processes playing out in the actions of the hands may hold content that can lead to insights.

The fact that low-level processes can acquire conceptual content when they are deployed in interaction with cultural technology (Hutchins 2005; Havelange, Lenay, and Stewart 2003) suggests that the mechanisms that govern the integration of sensorimotor representations could also shape the integration of conceptual representations. A truly difficult set of questions remain. What principles govern the integration of enacted representations? Do the processes that control the integration of perceptual content also control the integration of conceptual content? Why does cross-modal or cross-temporal integration not destroy representations? These difficult questions need empirical investigation. Ultimately, the answers to these questions will determine the plausibility of the speculations set forth in this chapter.

In the fix plotting example, the "Aha!" insight is that the deviation term is missing. The enactment approach gives us a way to see how this insight could emerge from the embodied, multimodal, temporally extended enactment of provisional LOPs that will reduce the size of the fix triangles. The descriptions of the enacted representations I offer earlier are simply what would be expected given the observable behavior of the plotter. No speculation is required to produce the elements from which the solution emerges. The observed enactment of the provisional LOPs includes the experience and anticipation of clockwise rotation of the LOPs. The visual experience of the protractor scale is a necessary component of the activity the navigator is engaged in.[6] The most controversial claim here is that a visual/motor memory of an activity performed in the subjunctive mood a few seconds in the past could somehow combine with current visual/motor perception to produce visual/motor anticipation of activity projected to take place a few seconds in the future. To put that claim in concrete terms: memory for trying out a rotation of the hoey arm on the chart combines with seeing the hoey arm on the scale in a way that anticipates rotating the hoey arm on the scale. I believe that the enactment approach predicts the integration of the particular elements described above in enacted representations. If this does indeed occur, then this instance of "Aha!" insight is no longer mysterious.

In a traditional cognitive explanation of creative insight, one would postulate the entire discovery process in terms of interactions among unobservable internal mental representations. What makes such accounts mysterious is that such internal representations are isolated from the body and world by theoretical fiat. They may be responsive to body/ world relations or react to body/world relations, but they are not part of body/world relations. By construing the engagement of the body with culturally meaningful materials in the working environment as a form of thinking, we can directly observe much of the setup for the insightful discovery.

15.4   Enaction and Cultural Practices

The processes described thus far can be characterized in terms of some general implications of the embodied enacted view of cognition. In certain culturally constructed settings, bodily motion acquires meaning by virtue of its relation to the spatial structure of things. Goodwin calls this phenomenon "environmentally coupled gesture." In some circumstances, the body itself becomes a cognitive artifact, upon which meaningful environmentally coupled gestures can be performed (Enfield 2006; Hutchins 2006). In such settings, motion in space acquires conceptual meaning and reasoning can be performed by moving the body. Material patterns can be enacted as representations in the interaction of person and culturally organized settings. Courses of action then become trains of thought. For example, when working on the chart, movement away from the body is conceptually northward, toward the body is south, and clockwise rotation is increasing measure of degrees. When actions are performed by experts in these domains, the integration of bodily sensations with directional frames produces embodied reasoning. Navigators sometimes speak of their reasoning skills in as "thinking like a compass." I believe this could be better described as "enacting compass directions in bodily sensations." The enactments of external representations habitually performed by practitioners who live and work in complex culturally constituted settings are multimodal. It must be assumed that these enacted multimodal representations are involved in the construction of memories for past events, the experience of the present, and the anticipation of the future. Complex enacted multimodal representations are likely to be more stable than single-mode representations (Gibbs 2006, 150). One way to accomplish this multimodal integration is to embed the representations in durable material media—what I have elsewhere called "material anchors for conceptual blends" (Hutchins 2005).

Another way to do this is to enact the representations in bodily processes. These bodily processes become "somatic anchors for conceptual
blends." Stabilization of complex conceptual representations by either
means facilitates their manipulation. Finally, culturally embedded embodied thinking and acting benefit from adaptive possibilities created by
both the variability in interactions with material representations and
the variability inherent in social interaction. We know least about this
aspect of these systems.

15.5   Discussion

From the perspective of a formal representation of the task, the means
by which the tools are manipulated by the body appear as mere implementation details. When seen through the lenses of the related stances
of embodiment and enactment, these real-world problem-solving activities take on a completely different appearance. The traditional "action-
neutral" descriptions of mental representations seem almost comically
impoverished alongside the richness of the moment-by-moment engagement of an experienced body with a culturally constituted world. The
dramatic difference in the richness of these descriptions matters. Attempts
to explain complex cognitive accomplishments using models that incorporate only a tiny subset of the available resources invariably lead to
distortions.

The ways that cultural practices adapt to the vicissitudes of situated
action are a source of variability in performance, but are often considered
to be formally irrelevant to the accomplishment of the task. However, this
variability in "task irrelevant" dimensions may be a resource for adaptive
processes when routine activity is disrupted.

Multimodality is a fundamental property of lived experience, and the
relations among the contents of various modes appears to have cognitive
consequences. Goldin-Meadow (2006) proposes a single dimension of
variation in the relations between gesture and speech. The contents of
these two modes (of course, each, by itself, is richly multimodal) can carry
roughly the same information and be matching, or they can carry different
information and be mismatched. However, the space of possible relations
is larger that this. The contents of gesture and speech can match or mismatch in several ways. Let us call the match condition a case in which
the contents of the modes are congruent. The condition that Goldin-
Meadow calls "mismatch" could better be described as complementary.

The contents differ, but they differ in ways that can combine to make a single coherent concept. The contents of gesture and speech could also be contradictory, or they could be incongruent in the sense that they are simply irrelevant to each other. Congruence among the contents of modes appears to lend stability to the enacted representations of which they are a part. Complementarity among the contents of modes may give rise to emergent phenomena, as was the case with the "Aha!" insight described in section 15.3 (see also Hutchins and Johnson 2009). Contradictory contents are sometimes produced deliberately in sarcasm. Truly incongruent contents probably occur, but it will be difficult to know how frequently this happens. Incongruent contents will most likely go unnoticed, or, if noticed, will be dismissed as noise.

The enaction perspective reminds us that perception is something we do, not something that happens to us. And this is never truer than when a person perceives some aspect of the physical world to be a symbol or a representation of any kind. Everyone agrees that perceiving patterns as meaningful is a human ability. But as long as perception was conceived as something that happened to us, it was possible to ignore the activity in the world that makes the construction of meaning possible. And although the enaction of cultural meanings is something that our bodies and brains *do* in the world, it is not something that our bodies or brains do by themselves. The skills that enact the apprehension of patterns as representations are learned cultural skills.

Putting things together this way reveals new analytic possibilities for understanding interactions of whole persons with the material and social worlds in which they are embedded. Learned cultural practices of perception and action applied to relevant domains of scrutiny enact the phenomenal objects of interest that define activity systems. High-level cognitive processes result when culturally orchestrated low-level processes are applied to culturally organized worlds of action.

Every mundane act of perception shares something fundamental with creative insight; the fact that what is available to the senses and what is experienced can be quite different. Reading the same scale for distance or speed in the use of the three-minute rule is a simple example. Similarly, a navigator can read the 120-degree mark on the protractor scale as a stable target on which one can position the hoey arm. Or the same navigator might read the same mark as a referent with respect to which a small clockwise rotation produces a new target, a slightly larger number on the scale, that fits better the anticipated course of action. In reading the mark this way, he suddenly sees what had been hidden. "Aha! Add three to everything." What makes ordinary acts of perception ordinary is only that the cultural practices of enacting them are over-learned and the outcomes follow as anticipated. Creative acts of perception can occur when emergent relations arise in the enaction of integrated, multimodal, temporally extended, embodied representations.

Acknowledgments

The Santa Fe Institute's program on Robustness in Social Systems provided funding for the work reported here. Erica Jen served as grant monitor. Alisa Durán transcribed the data and helped me focus the analysis on the problem of insight. Figure 15.3 was drawn from a video frame by Whitney Friedman. I am grateful to Andy Clark, Kensy Cooperrider, Deborah Forster, Charles Goodwin, Rafael Núñez, and John Stewart for valuable comments on an earlier version of this chapter.

Notes

1. Virtually all ship navigators know this rule and can use it, but few know why it works.

2. For my purposes, a practice will be labeled cultural if it exists in a cognitive ecology such that it is constrained by or coordinated with the practices of other persons.

3. Notice that the two tasks, adjusting the span, followed by maintaining the span while moving it, put conflicting demands on the tool. It must be mutable one moment, and immutable the next. This problem is solved for dividers by an adjustable friction lock. In fact, friction locks are common, and it is likely that wherever a friction lock is present, embodied knowledge is at work.

4. Other verbs that might be placed here include "noticed" and "remembered." Each implies something about the nature of the process. "Notice" highlights the aspect of happenstance. "Remember" highlights the fact that this is something that all navigators already know. "Discover" emphasizes the fact that they were searching for something that would improve the quality of the fixes when they became aware that D was missing. Including the previously missing D term did improve the fixes and thus ended their search.

5. In Hutchins 1995a, I provide a disembodied analysis of this event that fails to explain how the discovery of the missing term was made.

6. Of course, we cannot conclude anything about the quality of that visual experience from the available data.

References

Alač, M., and Hutchins, E. (2004). I see what you are saying: Action as cognition in fMRI brain mapping practice. *Journal of Cognition and Culture* 4(3): 629–661.

Bruner, J., Olver, R., and Greenfield, P., eds. (1966). *Studies in cognitive growth: A collaboration at the Center for Cognitive Studies.* New York: John Wiley and Sons.

Churchland, P. S., Ramachandran, V. S., and Sejnowski, T. J. (1994). A critique of pure vision. In *Large-scale neuronal theories of the brain*, ed. C. Koch and J. Davis, 23–60. Cambridge, MA: MIT Press.

Clark, A. (2001). *Mindware: An introduction to the philosophy of cognitive science.* Oxford: Oxford University Press.

Clark, A. (2008). *Supersizing the mind: Embodiment, action, and cognitive extension.* Oxford: Oxford University Press.

Cole, M., and Griffin, M. (1980). Cultural amplifiers reconsidered. In *The social foundations of language and thought: Essays in honor of Jerome Bruner*, ed. D. Olson, 343–364. New York: Norton.

Duncker, K. (1945). On problem solving. *Psychological Monographs* 58 (5): 1–270.

Enfield, N. (2006). Social consequences of common ground. In *Roots of human sociality: Culture, cognition and interaction*, ed. N. J. Enfield and S. C. Levinson, 399–430. Oxford: Berg Publishers.

Gentner, D., and Grudin, J. (1985). The evolution of mental metaphors in psychology: A 90-year retrospective. *American Psychologist* 40 (2): 181–192.

Gibbs, R. (2006). *Embodiment in cognitive science.* New York: Cambridge University Press.

Glucksberg, S. (1964). Functional fixedness: Problem solution as a function of observing responses. *Psychonomic Science* 1:117–118.

Goldin-Meadow, S. (2006). Meeting other minds through gesture: How children use their hands to reinvent language and distribute cognition. In *Roots of human sociality: Culture, cognition and interaction*, ed. N. J. Enfield and S. C. Levinson, 353–373. Oxford: Berg Publishers.

Goodwin, C. (1994). Professional vision. *American Anthropologist* 96 (3): 606–633.

Halbwachs, M. (1925). *Les cadres sociaux de la memoire.* Paris: Albin Michel.

Havelange, V., Lenay, C., and Stewart, J. (2003). Les représentations: mémoire externe et objets techniques. *Intellectica* 35:115–131.

Holldobler, B., and Wilson, E. O. (2009). *The superorganism: The beauty, elegance, and strangeness of insect societies*. New York: Norton.

Hutchins, E. (1995a). *Cognition in the wild*. Cambridge, MA: MIT Press.

Hutchins, E. (1995b). How a cockpit remembers its speeds. *Cognitive Science* 19:265–288.

Hutchins, E. (2000). The cognitive consequences of patterns of information flow. *Intellectica* 1 (30): 53–74.

Hutchins, E. (2005). Material anchors for conceptual blends. *Journal of Pragmatics* 37:1555–1577.

Hutchins, E. (2006). The distributed cognition perspective on human interaction. In *Roots of human sociality: Culture, cognition and interaction*, ed. N. J. Enfield and S. C. Levinson, 375–398. Oxford: Berg Publishers.

Hutchins, E., and Johnson, C. (2009). Modeling the emergence of language as an embodied collective cognitive activity. *Topics in Cognitive Science* 1: 523–546.

Ingold, T. (2000). *The perception of the environment: Essays in livelihood, dwelling, and skill*. Oxon, UK: Routledge.

Lakoff, G., and Núñez, R. (2000). *Where mathematics comes from: How the embodied mind brings mathematics into being*. New York: Basic Books.

Maturana, H., and Varela, F. (1987). *The tree of knowledge: The biological roots of human understanding*. Boston: Shambhala.

McNeill, D. (2005). *Gesture and thought*. Chicago: University of Chicago Press.

Murphy, K. (2004). Imagination as joint activity: The case of architectural interaction. *Mind, Culture, and Activity* 11 (4): 267–278.

Myers, N. (2008). Molecular embodiments and the body-work of modeling in protein crystallography. *Social Studies of Science* 38 (2): 163–199.

Noë. A. (2004). *Action in perception*. Cambridge, MA: MIT Press.

Norman, D. (1994). *Things that make us smart: Defending human attributes in the age of the machine*. Boston: Addison-Wesley.

Núñez, R. (2005). Creating mathematical infinities: The beauty of transfinite cardinals. *Journal of Pragmatics* 37:1717–1741.

Núñez, R., and Sweetser, E. (2006). With the future behind them: Convergent evidence from Aymara language and gesture in the crosslinguistic comparison of spatial construals of time. *Cognitive Science* 30:401–450.

O'Regan, J. K., and Noë, A. (2001). A sensorimotor approach to vision and visual consciousness. *Behavioral and Brain Sciences* 224 (5): 939–973.

Roberts, J. (1964). The self-management of cultures. In *Explorations in cultural anthropology: Essays in honor of George Peter Murdock*, ed. W. Goodenough, 433–454. New York: McGraw-Hill.

Seeley, T., and Levien, R. (1987). A colony of mind: the beehive as thinking machine. *Sciences* 27 (4): 38–43.

Smith, L. (2005). Action alters shape categories. *Cognitive Science* 29 (4): 665–679.

Spivey, M. (2007). *The continuity of mind*. Oxford: Oxford University Press.

Sunstein, C. (2006). *Infotopia: How many minds produce knowledge*. Oxford: Oxford University Press.

Surowiecki, J. (2004). *The wisdom of crowds*. New York: Doubleday.

Turner, J. S. (2000). *The extended organism: The physiology of animal-built structures*. Cambridge, MA: Harvard University Press.

Vygotsky, L. S. (1986). *Thought and language*. Cambridge, MA: MIT Press.

Watson, J. (1968). *The double helix: A personal account of the discovery of the structure of DNA*. New York: Simon and Schuster.

Wilson, M. (2002). Six views of embodied cognition. *Psychonomic Bulletin & Review* 9 (4): 625–636.

Contributors

Renaud Barbaras Université Paris-1 Panthéon-Sorbonne, France

Didier Bottineau CNRS, Université Paris 10, France

Giovanna Colombetti University of Exeter, Devon, United Kingdom

Diego Cosmelli Universidad Católica de Chile, Chile

Hanne De Jaegher University of Sussex, Brighton, United Kingdom

Ezequiel A. Di Paolo University of the Basque Country, San Sebastián, Spain, and University of Sussex, Brighton, United Kingdom

Andreas K. Engel University Medical Center, Hamburg-Eppendorf, Germany

Olivier Gapenne Université de Technologie de Compiègne, France

Véronique Havelange Université de Technologie de Compiègne, France

Edwin Hutchins University of California, San Diego

Michel Le Van Quyen Pitié-Salpêtrière Hospital, Paris, France

Rafael E. Núñez University of California, San Diego

Marieke Rohde University of Sussex, Brighton, United Kingdom

Benny Shanon The Hebrew University, Israel

Maxine Sheets-Johnstone University of Chicago

Adam Sheya Indiana University

Linda B. Smith Indiana University

John Stewart Université de Technologie de Compiègne, France

Evan Thompson University of Toronto, Canada

Index

Von Uexküll, J., 4, 5
Vygotsky, 9, 77, 276, 388, 390, 426

Waddington, C. H., 7, 130,
Weber, Andreas, 39, 46, 51, 145–150,
 159
Weierstrass, Karl, 312
Wittgenstein, Ludwig, 388, 395
World, vii–xiii, 3, 12, 24–28, 33, 38–39,
 42–45, 53, 61, 71, 73, 77, 89–107,
 111–117, 120, 127, 129–135,
 138–139, 145, 148, 157, 167–177,
 183–186, 188–189, 192–194, 200,
 219–229, 251, 258, 277–284,
 297–298, 307–308, 336–339,
 342–348, 352, 354, 361, 363, 375,
 377–379, 388–390, 395–397, 401,
 405–409, 425–435, 444–446
 animal, 4, 5, 10
 human, 4, 5, 18, 19, 69
 physical, 125, 320
Writing, 22–27, 205, 271–275, 296,
 345–346

Zahavi, Dan, 156
"Zero-point" (Husserl), 168, 169